ISUZU
AMIGO/PICK-UPS/RODEO/TROOPER
1981-96 REPAIR MANUAL

CHILTON'S ™

President	Dean F. Morgantini, S.A.E.
Vice President–Finance	Barry L. Beck
Vice President–Sales	Glenn D. Potere
Executive Editor	Kevin M. G. Maher, A.S.E.
Manager–Consumer	Richard Schwartz, A.S.E.
Manager–Professional	George B. Heinrich III, A.S.E., S.A.E.
Manager–Marine/Recreation	James R. Marotta, A.S.E., S.T.S.
Manager–Production	Ben Greisler, S.A.E.
Production Assistant	Melinda Possinger
Project Managers	Will Kessler, A.S.E., S.A.E., Todd W. Stidham, A.S.E., Ron Webb
Schematics Editor	Christopher G. Ritchie, A.S.E.

CHILTON™ Automotive Books
PUBLISHED BY W. G. NICHOLS, INC.

Manufactured in USA
© 1999 W. G. Nichols
1020 Andrew Drive
West Chester, PA 19380
ISBN 0-8019-9134-X
Library of Congress Catalog Card No. 99-070682
1234567890 8765432109

Contents

Contents

7 DRIVE TRAIN

8 SUSPENSION AND STEERING

9 BRAKES

10 BODY AND TRIM

GLOSSARY

MASTER INDEX

See last page for information on additional titles

SAFETY NOTICE

Proper service and repair procedures are vital to the safe, reliable operation of all motor vehicles, as well as the personal safety of those performing repairs. This manual outlines procedures for servicing and repairing vehicles using safe, effective methods. The procedures contain many NOTES, CAUTIONS and WARNINGS which should be followed, along with standard procedures to eliminate the possibility of personal injury or improper service which could damage the vehicle or compromise its safety.

It is important to note that repair procedures and techniques, tools and parts for servicing motor vehicles, as well as the skill and experience of the individual performing the work vary widely. It is not possible to anticipate all of the conceivable ways or conditions under which vehicles may be serviced, or to provide cautions as to all possible hazards that may result. Standard and accepted safety precautions and equipment should be used when handling toxic or flammable fluids, and safety goggles or other protection should be used during cutting, grinding, chiseling, prying, or any other process that can cause material removal or projectiles.

Some procedures require the use of tools specially designed for a specific purpose. Before substituting another tool or procedure, you must be completely satisfied that neither your personal safety, nor the performance of the vehicle will be endangered.

Although information in this manual is based on industry sources and is complete as possible at the time of publication, the possibility exists that some car manufacturers made later changes which could not be included here. While striving for total accuracy, NP/Chilton cannot assume responsibility for any errors, changes or omissions that may occur in the compilation of this data.

PART NUMBERS

Part numbers listed in this reference are not recommendations by Chilton for any product brand name. They are references that can be used with interchange manuals and aftermarket supplier catalogs to locate each brand supplier's discrete part number.

SPECIAL TOOLS

Special tools are recommended by the vehicle manufacturer to perform their specific job. Use has been kept to a minimum, but where absolutely necessary, they are referred to in the text by the part number of the tool manufacturer. These tools can be purchased, under the appropriate part number, from your local dealer or regional distributor, or an equivalent tool can be purchased locally from a tool supplier or parts outlet. Before substituting any tool for the one recommended, read the SAFETY NOTICE at the top of this page.

ACKNOWLEDGMENTS

W. G. Nichols expresses appreciation to American Isuzu Motors Inc. for their generous assistance.

1
GENERAL INFORMATION AND MAINTENANCE

HOW TO USE THIS BOOK

This Chilton's Total Car Care manual for Isuzu trucks is intended to help you learn more about the inner workings of your vehicle while saving you money on its upkeep and operation.

The beginning of the book will likely be referred to the most, since that is where you will find information for maintenance and tune-up. The other sections deal with the more complex systems of your vehicle. Systems (from engine through brakes) are covered to the extent that the average do-it-yourselfer can attempt. This book will not explain such things as rebuilding a differential because the expertise required and the special tools necessary make this uneconomical. It will, however, give you detailed instructions to help you change your own brake pads and shoes, replace spark plugs, and perform many more jobs that can save you money and help avoid expensive problems.

A secondary purpose of this book is a reference for owners who want to understand their vehicle and/or their mechanics better.

Where to Begin

Before removing any bolts, read through the entire procedure. This will give you the overall view of what tools and supplies will be required. So read ahead and plan ahead. Each operation should be approached logically and all procedures thoroughly understood before attempting any work.

If repair of a component is not considered practical, we tell you how to remove the part and then how to install the new or rebuilt replacement. In this way, you at least save labor costs.

Avoiding Trouble

Many procedures in this book require you to "label and disconnect . . ." a group of lines, hoses or wires. Don't be think you can remember where everything goes—you won't. If you hook up vacuum or fuel lines incorrectly, the vehicle may run poorly, if at all. If you hook up electrical wiring incorrectly, you may instantly learn a very expensive lesson.

You don't need to know the proper name for each hose or line. A piece of masking tape on the hose and a piece on its fitting will allow you to assign your own label. As long as you remember your own code, the lines can be reconnected by matching your tags. Remember that tape will dissolve in gasoline or solvents; if a part is to be washed or cleaned, use another method of identification. A permanent felt-tipped marker or a metal scribe can be very handy for marking metal parts. Remove any tape or paper labels after assembly.

Maintenance or Repair?

Maintenance includes routine inspections, adjustments, and replacement of parts which show signs of normal wear. Maintenance compensates for wear or deterioration. Repair implies that something has broken or is not working. A need for a repair is often caused by lack of maintenance. for example: draining and refilling automatic transmission fluid is maintenance recommended at specific intervals. Failure to do this can shorten the life of the transmission/transaxle, requiring very expensive repairs. While no maintenance program can prevent items from eventually breaking or wearing out, a general rule is true: MAINTENANCE IS CHEAPER THAN REPAIR.

TOOLS AND EQUIPMENT

▶ **See Figures 1 thru 15**

Without the proper tools and equipment it is impossible to properly service your vehicle. It would be virtually impossible to catalog every tool that you would need to perform all of the operations in this book. It would be unwise for the amateur to rush out and buy an expensive set of tools on the theory that he/she may need one or more of them at some time.

The best approach is to proceed slowly, gathering a good quality set of those tools that are used most frequently. Don't be misled by the low cost of bargain tools. It is far better to spend a little more for better quality. Forged wrenches, 6 or 12-point sockets and fine tooth ratchets are by far preferable to their less expensive counterparts. As any good mechanic can tell you, there are few worse

Two basic mechanic's rules should be mentioned here. First, whenever the left side of the vehicle or engine is referred to, it means the driver's side. Conversely, the right side of the vehicle means the passenger's side. Second, screws and bolts are removed by turning counterclockwise, and tightened by turning clockwise unless specifically noted.

Safety is always the most important rule. Constantly be aware of the dangers involved in working on an automobile and take the proper precautions. Please refer to the information in this section regarding SERVICING YOUR VEHICLE SAFELY and the SAFETY NOTICE on the acknowledgment page.

Avoiding the Most Common Mistakes

Pay attention to the instructions provided. There are 3 common mistakes in mechanical work:

1. Incorrect order of assembly, disassembly or adjustment. When taking something apart or putting it together, performing steps in the wrong order usually just costs you extra time; however, it CAN break something. Read the entire procedure before beginning. Perform everything in the order in which the instructions say you should, even if you can't see a reason for it. When you're taking apart something that is very intricate, you might want to draw a picture of how it looks when assembled in order to make sure you get everything back in its proper position. When making adjustments, perform them in the proper order. One adjustment possibly will affect another.

2. Overtorquing (or undertorquing). While it is more common for overtorquing to cause damage, undertorquing may allow a fastener to vibrate loose causing serious damage. Especially when dealing with aluminum parts, pay attention to torque specifications and utilize a torque wrench in assembly. If a torque figure is not available, remember that if you are using the right tool to perform the job, you will probably not have to strain yourself to get a fastener tight enough. The pitch of most threads is so slight that the tension you put on the wrench will be multiplied many times in actual force on what you are tightening.

There are many commercial products available for ensuring that fasteners won't come loose, even if they are not torqued just right (a very common brand is Loctite®). If you're worried about getting something together tight enough to hold, but loose enough to avoid mechanical damage during assembly, one of these products might offer substantial insurance. Before choosing a threadlocking compound, read the label on the package and make sure the product is compatible with the materials, fluids, etc. involved.

3. Crossthreading. This occurs when a part such as a bolt is screwed into a nut or casting at the wrong angle and forced. Crossthreading is more likely to occur if access is difficult. It helps to clean and lubricate fasteners, then to start threading the bolt, spark plug, etc. with your fingers. If you encounter resistance, unscrew the part and start over again at a different angle until it can be inserted and turned several times without much effort. Keep in mind that many parts have tapered threads, so that gentle turning will automatically bring the part you're threading to the proper angle. Don't put a wrench on the part until it's been tightened a couple of turns by hand. If you suddenly encounter resistance, and the part has not seated fully, don't force it. Pull it back out to make sure it's clean and threading properly.

Be sure to take your time and be patient, and always plan ahead. Allow yourself ample time to perform repairs and maintenance.

experiences than trying to work on a vehicle with bad tools. Your monetary savings will be far outweighed by frustration and mangled knuckles.

Begin accumulating those tools that are used most frequently: those associated with routine maintenance and tune-up. In addition to the normal assortment of screwdrivers and pliers, you should have the following tools:

• Wrenches/sockets and combination open end/box end wrenches in sizes from 1/8 –3/4 in. or 3–19mm, as well as a 13/16 in. or 5/8 in. spark plug socket (depending on plug type).

➡**If possible, buy various length socket drive extensions. Universal-joint and wobble extensions can be extremely useful, but be careful when using them, as they can change the amount of torque applied to the socket.**

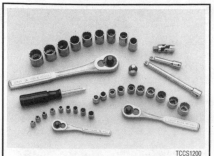

Fig. 1 All but the most basic procedures will require an assortment of ratchets and sockets

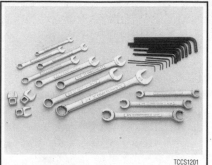

Fig. 2 In addition to ratchets, a good set of wrenches and hex keys will be necessary

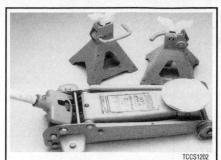

Fig. 3 A hydraulic floor jack and a set of jackstands are essential for lifting and supporting the vehicle

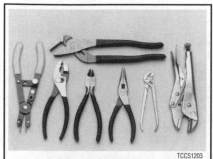

Fig. 4 An assortment of pliers, grippers and cutters will be handy for old rusted parts and stripped bolt heads

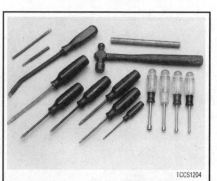

Fig. 5 Various drivers, chisels and prybars are great tools to have in your toolbox

Fig. 6 Many repairs will require the use of a torque wrench to assure the components are properly fastened

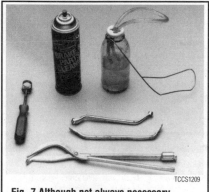

Fig. 7 Although not always necessary, using specialized brake tools will save time

Fig. 8 A few inexpensive lubrication tools will make maintenance easier

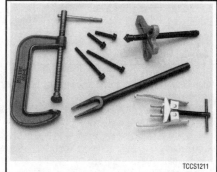

Fig. 9 Various pullers, clamps and separator tools are needed for many larger, more complicated repairs

- Jackstands for support.
- Oil filter wrench.
- Spout or funnel for pouring fluids.
- Grease gun for chassis lubrication (unless your vehicle is not equipped with any grease fittings)
- Hydrometer for checking the battery (unless equipped with a sealed, maintenance-free battery).
- A container for draining oil and other fluids.
- Rags for wiping up the inevitable mess.

In addition to the above items there are several others that are not absolutely necessary, but handy to have around. These include an equivalent oil absorbent gravel, like cat litter, and the usual supply of lubricants, antifreeze and fluids. This is a basic list for routine maintenance, but only your personal needs and desire can accurately determine your list of tools.

After performing a few projects on the vehicle, you'll be amazed at the other tools and non-tools on your workbench. Some useful household items are: a large turkey baster or siphon, empty coffee cans and ice trays (to store parts), a ball of twine, electrical tape for wiring, small rolls of colored tape for tagging lines or hoses, markers and pens, a note pad, golf tees (for plugging vacuum lines), metal coat hangers or a roll of mechanic's wire (to hold things out of the way), dental pick or similar long, pointed probe, a strong magnet, and a small mirror (to see into recesses and under manifolds).

A more advanced set of tools, suitable for tune-up work, can be drawn up easily. While the tools are slightly more sophisticated, they need not be outrageously expensive. There are several inexpensive tach/dwell meters on the market that are every bit as good for the average mechanic as a professional model. Just be sure that it goes to a least 1200–1500 rpm on the tach scale and that it works on 4, 6 and 8-cylinder engines. The key to these purchases is to make them with an eye towards adaptability and wide range. A basic list of tune-up tools could include:

- Tach/dwell meter.
- Spark plug wrench and gapping tool.
- Feeler gauges for valve adjustment.
- Timing light.

The choice of a timing light should be made carefully. A light which works on the DC current supplied by the vehicle's battery is the best choice; it should have a xenon tube for brightness. On any vehicle with an electronic ignition sys-

Fig. 10 A variety of tools and gauges should be used for spark plug gapping and installation

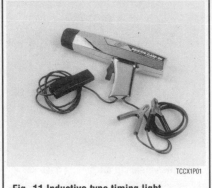

Fig. 11 Inductive type timing light

Fig. 12 A screw-in type compression gauge is recommended for compression testing

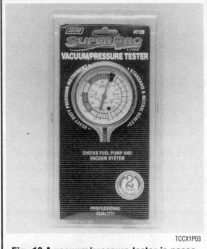

Fig. 13 A vacuum/pressure tester is necessary for many testing procedures

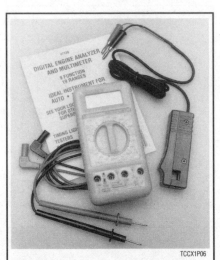

Fig. 14 Most modern automotive multimeters incorporate many helpful features

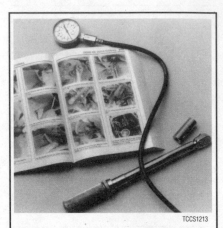

Fig. 15 Proper information is vital, so always have a Chilton Total Car Care manual handy

tem, a timing light with an inductive pickup that clamps around the No. 1 spark plug cable is preferred.

In addition to these basic tools, there are several other tools and gauges you may find useful. These include:

- Compression gauge. The screw-in type is slower to use, but eliminates the possibility of a faulty reading due to escaping pressure.
- Manifold vacuum gauge.
- 12V test light.
- A combination volt/ohmmeter
- Induction Ammeter. This is used for determining whether or not there is current in a wire. These are handy for use if a wire is broken somewhere in a wiring harness.

As a final note, you will probably find a torque wrench necessary for all but the most basic work. The beam type models are perfectly adequate, although the newer click types (breakaway) are easier to use. The click type torque wrenches tend to be more expensive. Also keep in mind that all types of torque wrenches should be periodically checked and/or recalibrated. You will have to decide for yourself which better fits your pocketbook, and purpose.

Special Tools

Normally, the use of special factory tools is avoided for repair procedures, since these are not readily available for the do-it-yourself mechanic. When it is possible to perform the job with more commonly available tools, it will be pointed out, but occasionally, a special tool was designed to perform a specific function and should be used. Before substituting another tool, you should be convinced that neither your safety nor the performance of the vehicle will be compromised.

Special tools can usually be purchased from an automotive parts store or from your dealer. In some cases special tools may be available directly from the tool manufacturer.

SERVICING YOUR VEHICLE SAFELY

♦ **See Figures 16, 17 and 18**

It is virtually impossible to anticipate all of the hazards involved with automotive maintenance and service, but care and common sense will prevent most accidents.

The rules of safety for mechanics range from "don't smoke around gasoline," to "use the proper tool(s) for the job." The trick to avoiding injuries is to develop safe work habits and to take every possible precaution.

Do's

- Do keep a fire extinguisher and first aid kit handy.
- Do wear safety glasses or goggles when cutting, drilling, grinding or prying, even if you have 20–20 vision. If you wear glasses for the sake of vision, wear safety goggles over your regular glasses.
- Do shield your eyes whenever you work around the battery. Batteries contain sulfuric acid. In case of contact with, flush the area with water or a mixture of water and baking soda, then seek immediate medical attention.
- Do use safety stands (jackstands) for any undervehicle service. Jacks are for raising vehicles; jackstands are for making sure the vehicle stays raised until you want it to come down.
- Do use adequate ventilation when working with any chemicals or hazardous materials. Like carbon monoxide, the asbestos dust resulting from some brake lining wear can be hazardous in sufficient quantities.
- Do disconnect the negative battery cable when working on the electrical

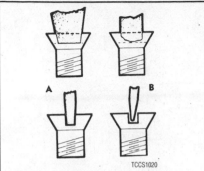

Fig. 16 Screwdrivers should be kept in good condition to prevent injury or damage which could result if the blade slips from the screw

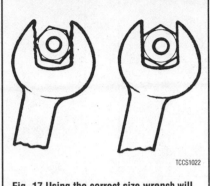

Fig. 17 Using the correct size wrench will help prevent the possibility of rounding off a nut

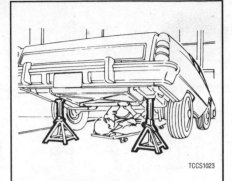

Fig. 18 NEVER work under a vehicle unless it is supported using safety stands (jackstands)

system. The secondary ignition system contains EXTREMELY HIGH VOLTAGE. In some cases it can even exceed 50,000 volts.

• Do follow manufacturer's directions whenever working with potentially hazardous materials. Most chemicals and fluids are poisonous.

• Do properly maintain your tools. Loose hammerheads, mushroomed punches and chisels, frayed or poorly grounded electrical cords, excessively worn screwdrivers, spread wrenches (open end), cracked sockets, slipping ratchets, or faulty droplight sockets can cause accidents.

• Likewise, keep your tools clean; a greasy wrench can slip off a bolt head, ruining the bolt and often harming your knuckles in the process.

• Do use the proper size and type of tool for the job at hand. Do select a wrench or socket that fits the nut or bolt. The wrench or socket should sit straight, not cocked.

• Do, when possible, pull on a wrench handle rather than push on it, and adjust your stance to prevent a fall.

• Do be sure that adjustable wrenches are tightly closed on the nut or bolt and pulled so that the force is on the side of the fixed jaw.

• Do strike squarely with a hammer; avoid glancing blows.

• Do set the parking brake and block the drive wheels if the work requires a running engine.

Don'ts

• Don't run the engine in a garage or anywhere else without proper ventilation—EVER! Carbon monoxide is poisonous; it takes a long time to leave the human body and you can build up a deadly supply of it in your system by simply breathing in a little at a time. You may not realize you are slowly poisoning yourself. Always use power vents, windows, fans and/or open the garage door.

• Don't work around moving parts while wearing loose clothing. Short sleeves are much safer than long, loose sleeves. Hard-toed shoes with neoprene soles protect your toes and give a better grip on slippery surfaces. Watches and jewelry is not safe working around a vehicle. Long hair should be tied back under a hat or cap.

• Don't use pockets for toolboxes. A fall or bump can drive a screwdriver deep into your body. Even a rag hanging from your back pocket can wrap around a spinning shaft or fan.

• Don't smoke when working around gasoline, cleaning solvent or other flammable material.

• Don't smoke when working around the battery. When the battery is being charged, it gives off explosive hydrogen gas.

• Don't use gasoline to wash your hands; there are excellent soaps available. Gasoline contains dangerous additives which can enter the body through a cut or through your pores. Gasoline also removes all the natural oils from the skin so that bone dry hands will suck up oil and grease.

• Don't service the air conditioning system unless you are equipped with the necessary tools and training. When liquid or compressed gas refrigerant is released to atmospheric pressure it will absorb heat from whatever it contacts. This will chill or freeze anything it touches.

• Don't use screwdrivers for anything other than driving screws! A screwdriver used as an prying tool can snap when you least expect it, causing injuries. At the very least, you'll ruin a good screwdriver.

• Don't use an emergency jack (that little ratchet, scissors, or pantograph jack supplied with the vehicle) for anything other than changing a flat! These jacks are only intended for emergency use out on the road; they are NOT designed as a maintenance tool. If you are serious about maintaining your vehicle yourself, invest in a hydraulic floor jack of at least a 1½ ton capacity, and at least two sturdy jackstands.

FASTENERS, MEASUREMENTS AND CONVERSIONS

Bolts, Nuts and Other Threaded Retainers

◆ **See Figures 19 and 20**

Although there are a great variety of fasteners found in the modern car or truck, the most commonly used retainer is the threaded fastener (nuts, bolts, screws, studs, etc.). Most threaded retainers may be reused, provided that they are not damaged in use or during the repair. Some retainers (such as stretch bolts or torque prevailing nuts) are designed to deform when tightened or in use and should not be reinstalled.

Whenever possible, we will note any special retainers which should be replaced during a procedure. But you should always inspect the condition of a retainer when it is removed and replace any that show signs of damage. Check all threads for rust or corrosion which can increase the torque necessary to achieve the desired clamp load for which that fastener was originally selected. Additionally, be sure that the driver surface of the fastener has not been compromised by rounding or other damage. In some cases a driver surface may become only partially rounded, allowing the driver to catch in only one direction. In many of these occurrences, a fastener may be installed and tightened, but the driver would not be able to grip and loosen the fastener again.

If you must replace a fastener, whether due to design or damage, you must ALWAYS be sure to use the proper replacement. In all cases, a retainer of the same design, material and strength should be used. Markings on the heads of most bolts will help determine the proper strength of the fastener. The same material, thread and pitch must be selected to assure proper installation and safe operation of the vehicle afterwards.

Thread gauges are available to help measure a bolt or stud's thread. Most automotive and hardware stores keep gauges available to help you select the proper size. In a pinch, you can use another nut or bolt for a thread gauge. If the bolt you are replacing is not too badly damaged, you can select a match by finding another bolt which will thread in its place. If you find a nut which threads properly onto the damaged bolt, then use that nut to help select the replacement bolt.

✳✳ WARNING

Be aware that when you find a bolt with damaged threads, you may also find the nut or drilled hole it was threaded into has also been damaged. If this is the case, you may have to drill and tap the hole, replace the nut or otherwise repair the threads. NEVER try to force a replacement bolt to fit into the damaged threads.

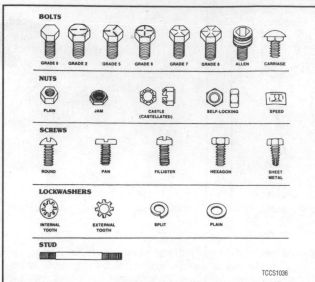

Fig. 19 There are many different types of threaded retainers found on vehicles

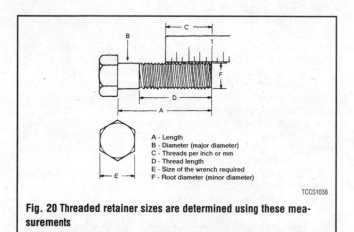

A - Length
B - Diameter (major diameter)
C - Threads per inch or mm
D - Thread length
E - Size of the wrench required
F - Root diameter (minor diameter)

Fig. 20 Threaded retainer sizes are determined using these measurements

Torque

Torque is defined as the measurement of resistance to turning or rotating. It tends to twist a body about an axis of rotation. A common example of this would be tightening a threaded retainer such as a nut, bolt or screw. Measuring torque is one of the most common ways to help assure that a threaded retainer has been properly fastened.

When tightening a threaded fastener, torque is applied in three distinct areas, the head, the bearing surface and the clamp load. About 50 percent of the measured torque is used in overcoming bearing friction. This is the friction between the bearing surface of the bolt head, screw head or nut face and the base material or washer (the surface on which the fastener is rotating). Approximately 40 percent of the applied torque is used in overcoming thread friction. This leaves only about 10 percent of the applied torque to develop a useful clamp load (the force which holds a joint together). This means that friction can account for as much as 90 percent of the applied torque on a fastener.

TORQUE WRENCHES

♦ See Figure 21

In most applications, a torque wrench can be used to assure proper installation of a fastener. Torque wrenches come in various designs and most automotive supply stores will carry a variety to suit your needs. A torque wrench should be used any time we supply a specific torque value for a fastener. Again, the general rule of "if you are using the right tool for the job, you should not have to strain to tighten a fastener" applies here.

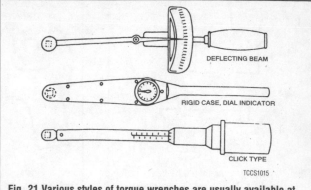

Fig. 21 Various styles of torque wrenches are usually available at your local automotive supply store

Beam Type

The beam type torque wrench is one of the most popular types. It consists of a pointer attached to the head that runs the length of the flexible beam (shaft) to a scale located near the handle. As the wrench is pulled, the beam bends and the pointer indicates the torque using the scale.

Click (Breakaway) Type

Another popular design of torque wrench is the click type. To use the click type wrench you pre-adjust it to a torque setting. Once the torque is reached, the wrench has a reflex signaling feature that causes a momentary breakaway of the torque wrench body, sending an impulse to the operator's hand.

Pivot Head Type

♦ See Figure 22

Some torque wrenches (usually of the click type) may be equipped with a pivot head which can allow it to be used in areas of limited access. BUT, it must be used properly. To hold a pivot head wrench, grasp the handle lightly, and as you pull on the handle, it should be floated on the pivot point. If the handle comes in contact with the yoke extension during the process of pulling, there is a very good chance the torque readings will be inaccurate because this could alter the wrench loading point. The design of the handle is usually such as to make it inconvenient to deliberately misuse the wrench.

➡ It should be mentioned that the use of any U-joint, wobble or extension will have an effect on the torque readings, no matter what type of wrench you are using. For the most accurate readings, install the socket directly on the wrench driver. If necessary, straight extensions (which

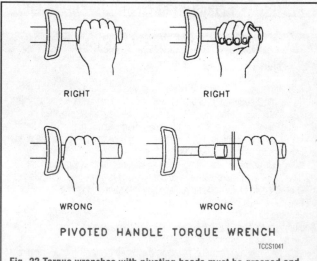

PIVOTED HANDLE TORQUE WRENCH

Fig. 22 Torque wrenches with pivoting heads must be grasped and used properly to prevent an incorrect reading

hold a socket directly under the wrench driver) will have the least effect on the torque reading. Avoid any extension that alters the length of the wrench from the handle to the head/driving point (such as a crow's foot). U-joint or wobble extensions can greatly affect the readings; avoid their use at all times.

Rigid Case (Direct Reading)

A rigid case or direct reading torque wrench is equipped with a dial indicator to show torque values. One advantage of these wrenches is that they can be held at any position on the wrench without affecting accuracy. These wrenches are often preferred because they tend to be compact, easy to read and have a great degree of accuracy.

TORQUE ANGLE METERS

Because the frictional characteristics of each fastener or threaded hole will vary, clamp loads which are based strictly on torque will vary as well. In most applications, this variance is not significant enough to cause worry. But, in certain applications, a manufacturer's engineers may determine that more precise clamp loads are necessary (such is the case with many aluminum cylinder heads). In these cases, a torque angle method of installation would be specified. When installing fasteners which are torque angle tightened, a predetermined seating torque and standard torque wrench are usually used first to remove any compliance from the joint. The fastener is then tightened the specified additional portion of a turn measured in degrees. A torque angle gauge (mechanical protractor) is used for these applications.

Standard and Metric Measurements

Throughout this manual, specifications are given to help you determine the condition of various components on your vehicle, or to assist you in their installation. Some of the most common measurements include length (in. or cm/mm), torque (ft. lbs., inch lbs. or Nm) and pressure (psi, in. Hg, kPa or mm Hg). In most cases, we strive to provide the proper measurement as determined by the manufacturer's engineers.

Though, in some cases, that value may not be conveniently measured with what is available in your toolbox. Luckily, many of the measuring devices which are available today will have two scales so the Standard or Metric measurements may easily be taken. If any of the various measuring tools which are available to you do not contain the same scale as listed in the specifications, use the accompanying conversion factors to determine the proper value.

The conversion factor chart is used by taking the given specification and multiplying it by the necessary conversion factor. For instance, looking at the first line, if you have a measurement in inches such as "free-play should be 2 in." but your ruler reads only in millimeters, multiply 2 in. by the conversion factor of 25.4 to get the metric equivalent of 50.8mm. Likewise, if the specification was given only in a Metric measurement, for example in Newton Meters (Nm), then look at the center column first. If the measurement is 100 Nm, multiply it by the conversion factor of 0.738 to get 73.8 ft. lbs.

MODEL IDENTIFICATION

The full line of Isuzu trucks and sport utility vehicles from 1981–96 is comprised of four models: Pick-up (the earlier models were known as P'UP), the Trooper/Trooper II, the Amigo, and the Rodeo.

The Pick-up truck is a 2-door conventional style pick-up vehicle with an open rear bed designed for transport of materials. The Pick-up is the only truck in the Isuzu line of trucks which has been produced since 1981. Throughout the Pick-up's production years, it has been available with several engines, including the 4-cylinder 1.8L, 2.2L diesel, 2.0L, 2.3L and 2.6L engines, as well as the V6 3.1L, which was manufactured by General Motors. The Pick-up truck has been available with 2-wheel or 4-wheel drive. The Isuzu manufactured Pick-up was last available in 1995.

The Trooper/Trooper II, which is the second vehicle to enter the Isuzu truck line-up, was introduced in 1985. The Trooper and Trooper II are the same vehicle; in 1992 the Trooper II dropped the II and simply became the Trooper. The Trooper is a large, 2 or 4-door sport utility vehicle with a squared back end (in contrast to the Rodeo). The rear doors are of the conventional swing open-type, with the right-hand door being smaller than the left-hand door. The Trooper is also equipped with 2-wheel or 4-wheel drive. The Trooper has come equipped with a 2.2L diesel, 2.3L, 2.6L, 2.8L V6 (manufactured by General Motors), and 3.2L V6 engine.

The Amigo, which was introduced in 1989, is a short wheel based, 2-door sport utility vehicle. The Amigo is equipped with a removable top and a has a rear bed which accommodates a rear seat. The rear seat could be removed to carry additional cargo. The Amigo is only available with 2 engines: the 2.3L and the 2.6L. The last year the Amigo was available is 1994.

The Rodeo, at first glance, seems to be a merging of the Trooper and the Amigo models. The Rodeo is a large, 4-door sport utility vehicle much like the Trooper. The rear end on the Rodeo is slanted and the rear door is a hatch, which swings up. The Rodeo was first introduced by Isuzu in 1991 and is still produced. This vehicle has been available with three engines. In 1991 the Rodeo was available with 2.6L and 3.1L engines, whereas in 1992–96 the vehicle came equipped with the 3.2L V6. The Rodeo also comes available with 2-wheel and 4-wheel drive.

SERIAL NUMBER IDENTIFICATION

Vehicle

▶ See Figures 23 thru 28

The vehicles covered by this manual can be identified by their Vehicle Identification Number (VIN); which is embossed on a plate attached to the top left corner of the instrument panel. The number is visible through the windshield from the outside of the vehicle. The VIN can be broken down into segments in order to ascertain certain information about the truck, as can be seen in the accompanying chart. The VIN is comprised of 17 digits. The digits are broken down into different codes, as follows:

• Digits 1, 2 and 3—Vehicle Make Identification (in this case, it is always Isuzu)
• Digit 4—Gross Vehicle Weight Rating (GVWR) range in lbs. (B=3001–4000, C=4001–5000, D=5001–6000, E=6001–7000, F=7001–8000, G=8001–9000)
• Digit 5—Chassis Type
• Digit 6 and 7—Vehicle Line Model (01=Amigo, 11=½ ton, short bed Pick-up, 14=½ ton, long bed Pick-up, 16=Space CB Pick-up, 34=1 ton Pick-up, 55=2-door Trooper II, 57=2-door Trooper, 58=Rodeo or 4-door Trooper and Trooper II)

• Digit 8—Engine Identification (B=1981–83 1.8L, S=1981–87 2.2L diesel, A=1984–87 2.0L, L=1986–95 2.3L, U=1986–87 2.2L turbocharged diesel, E=1988–96 2.6L, R=1989–91 2.8L, Z=1991–94 3.1L, V and W=1992–96 3.2L

86861P01

Fig. 23 The VIN code number is located on a plate attached to the upper left-hand of the dashboard

- Digit 9—Check Digit
- Digit 10—Model Year (B=1981, C=1982, D=1983, E=1984, F=1985, G=1986, H=1987, J=1988, K=1989, L=1990, M=1991, N=1992, P=1993, R=1994, S=1995, T=1996)
- Digit 11—Manufacturer Plant
- Digit 12—Destination
- Digits 13–17—Production Sequence Number

The 1981–88 models are equipped with a paint color code identification plate, located on the upper radiator support near the radiator. This label includes the type of paint and the color number used for the vehicle's original paint from the factory. The 1989–96 Isuzu trucks and sport utility vehicles are equipped with a Vehicle Information Plate instead. The VIP is located on either the center or the right-hand side of the dash wall, inside the engine compartment. The plate lists the VIN, paint information and all production options, as well as special equipment on the vehicle when it was shipped from the factory.

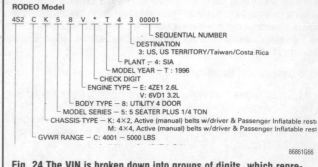

Fig. 24 The VIN is broken down into groups of digits, which represent various aspects of the vehicle—Rodeo model VIN shown, others are very similar

Fig. 25 The VIN and additional data is stamped on a plate in the engine compartment—91 Trooper shown

Fig. 26 The engine plate on newer vehicles, such as this late-model Rodeo, is actually a stick-on label

Fig. 27 Other labels located throughout the vehicle can tell about the vehicle and how to care for it . . .

Fig. 28 . . . such as the important Vehicle Emission Control Information (VECI) label

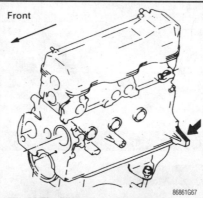

Fig. 29 The EIN is stamped on the rear end raised area of the left-hand side of the cylinder block—2.6L engines

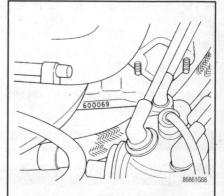

Fig. 30 The EIN is located on the front, upper area of the engine block near the distributor—1.8L and 2.0L engines

Engine

♦ See Figures 29, 30, 31, 32 and 33

The vehicle's engine can either be identified by the 8th digit in the VIN, or by the Engine Identification Number (EIN), which is stamped onto the engine itself. The location of the EIN depends on the particular engine, with which the vehicle is equipped. Refer to the following list for the specific location:

- 1.8L and 2.0L engines—The EIN is stamped onto the upper, center of the engine block, near the distributor mounting boss.
- 2.2L diesel engine—The EIN is stamped on the upper, front of the engine block, near the combination manifold mounting area.
- 2.6L and 2.8L engines—The EIN is stamped on the rear end raised area of the left-hand side of the cylinder block.
- 3.1L engine—The EIN is stamped on the front top of the engine block. The optional engine serial number is stamped on the right and left-hand rocker arm covers.

VEHICLE IDENTIFICATION CHART

VIN Code	Engine ID Code	Liters	Cu. In. (cc)	Cyl.	Fuel Sys.	Eng. Mfg.
A	G200Z	2.0	118 (1949)	4	2 BBL	Isuzu
E	4ZE1	2.6	156 (2559)	4	MFI	Isuzu
L	4ZD1	2.3	137 (2254)	4	①	Isuzu
N	G180Z	1.8	112 (1816)	4	2 BBL	Isuzu
R	LL2	2.8	173 (2828)	6	TFI	GM
S	C223	2.2	137 (2238)	4	DSL	Isuzu
U	C223-T	2.2	137 (2238)	4	DSL-Turbo	Isuzu
V	6VD1-V	3.2	193 (3165)	6	MFI	Isuzu
W	6VD1-W	3.2	193 (3165)	6	MFI	Isuzu
Z	CPC	3.1	189 (3098)	6	TFI	GM

Model Year	
VIN Code	Year
B	1981
C	1982
D	1983
E	1984
F	1985
G	1986
H	1987
J	1988
K	1989
L	1990
M	1991
N	1992
P	1993
R	1994
S	1995
T	1996

MFI - Multi-port fuel injection

TFI - Throttle body fuel injection

DSL – Diesel engine

DSL-Turbo – Turbocharged Diesel engine

2 BBL – 2 barrel carburetor

① 2 BBL or MFI, depending on year of manufacture or model

86861C09

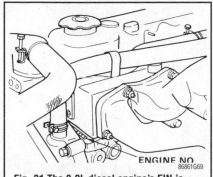

Fig. 31 The 2.2L diesel engine's EIN is stamped on the engine block near where the combination manifold mounts to the cylinder head

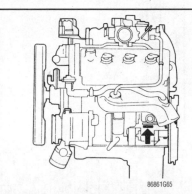

Fig. 32 The 3.2L V6's EIN is stamped on the boss directly above the starter motor mounting position

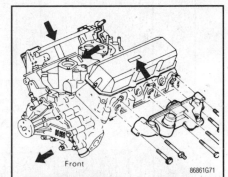

Fig. 33 The 3.1L V6 is equipped with many EIN labels, two of which are mounted directly on the top of the rocker arm covers

• 3.2L engine—The EIN is stamped on the left-hand rear lower area of the engine block, above the starter motor.

Often, the EIN can be seen most easily through the left-hand, front wheel housing once the inner mud guard is removed.

Transmission

Throughout production of the 1981–96 Isuzu trucks and sport utility vehicles, there have been 9 manual transmissions available: MSG-4, MSG-4L, MSG-5, MSG-5C, MSG-5L, MUA-5, MUA-5C, and T5R. Most of these transmissions, with the exception of the T5R are simply slight alterations of the Isuzu manual transmission. The T5R is manufactured by General Motors. The T5R is only available on the 1991–96 Rodeo with the V6 engine (either the 3.1L in 1991 or the 3.2L from 1992–96). The Transmission Identification Numbers (TIN) on all of these transmissions are located on the left-hand side of the transmission body, mounted either on a label or stamped directly into the case.

The Isuzu line of trucks and sport utility vehicles have come with a total of 5 automatic transmissions: AW03–55, AW03–75, AW03–72L, AW30–80LE and 4L30-E. The first two are 3-speed transmissions, and the latter three are 4-speed models. As with the manual transmissions, the TIN is located on the side of the transmission case.

Drive Axle

Rear axles on the Isuzu trucks are identified by a broadcast code on the right axle tube near the carrier. The rear axle identification code and manufacturer's code must be known before attempting to adjust or repair axle shafts or the rear axle case assembly. Rear axle ratio, differential type, manufacturer and build date information are stamped on the right axle tube on the front side.

The Salisbury rear axle on Pick-up models utilizes a coding convention, which can be deciphered as follows:

• Digits 1 and 2—The rear axle ratio code

• Digits 3 and 4—Differential type

• Digits 5, 6 and 7—Build date (in Julian Date form—the code represents the number of the day in the year. Therefore, 76 would represent March 17th, the 76th day of the year)

• Digit 8—Build shift (D=day shift, N=night shift)

The front drive axles on Isuzu trucks do not use an externally stamped axle identification code.

ENGINE IDENTIFICATION

All measurements are given in inches.

Year	Model	Engine Displacement Liters (cc)	Engine Series (ID Code)	Fuel System	No. of Cylinders	Engine Type
1994	Amigo	2.6 (2559)	4ZE1	MFI	4	SOHC
	Pick-up	2.3 (2254)	4ZD1	2 BBL	4	SOHC
		2.3 (2254)	4ZD1	MFI	4	SOHC
		2.6 (2559)	4ZE1	MFI	4	SOHC
	Rodeo	3.1 (3098)	CPC	TFI	6	OHV
		2.6 (2559)	4ZE1	MFI	4	SOHC
		3.2 (3165)	6VD1	MFI	6	SOHC
	Trooper	3.2 (3165)	6VD1	MFI	6	SOHC
		3.2 (3165)	6VD1	MFI	6	DOHC
1995	Pick-up	2.3 (2254)	4ZD1	MFI	4	SOHC
		2.6 (2559)	4ZE1	MFI	4	SOHC
	Rodeo	3.2 (3165)	6VD1	MFI	6	SOHC
	Trooper	3.2 (3165)	6VD1	MFI	6	DOHC
1996	Rodeo	2.6 (2559)	4ZE1	MFI	4	SOHC
		3.2 (3165)	6VD1	MFI	6	SOHC
	Trooper	3.2 (3165)	6VD1	MFI	6	SOHC

MFI - Multi-port fuel injection
BBL - Barrel carburetor
TFI - Throttle body fuel injection
SOHC - Single overhead camshaft
OHV - Overhead valve
DOHC - Double overhead camshaft
DSL - Diesel

86861C01

ENGINE IDENTIFICATION

All measurements are given in inches.

Year	Model	Engine Displacement Liters (cc)	Engine Series (ID Code)	Fuel System	No. of Cylinders	Engine Type
1981-83	Pick-up	1.8 (1816)	G180Z	2 BBL	4	SOHC
		2.2 (2238)	C223	DSL	4	OHV
1984	Pick-up	2.0 (1950)	G200Z	2 BBL	4	SOHC
		2.2 (2238)	C223	DSL	4	OHV
1985	Pick-up	2.0 (1950)	G200Z	2 BBL	4	SOHC
		2.2 (2238)	C223	DSL	4	OHV
	Trooper II	2.0 (1950)	G200Z	2 BBL	4	SOHC
1986-87	Pick-up	2.0 (1950)	G200Z	2 BBL	4	SOHC
		2.2 (2238)	C223	DSL	4	OHV
		2.2 (2238)	C223T	DSL	4	OHV
		2.3 (2254)	4ZD1	2 BBL	4	SOHC
	Trooper II	2.2 (2238)	C223T	DSL	4	OHV
		2.3 (2254)	4ZD1	2 BBL	4	SOHC
1988	Pick-up	2.3 (2254)	4ZD1	2 BBL	4	SOHC
		2.6 (2559)	4ZE1	MFI	4	SOHC
	Trooper II	2.6 (2559)	4ZE1	MFI	4	SOHC
1989-90	Amigo	2.3 (2254)	4ZD1	2 BBL	4	SOHC
		2.6 (2559)	4ZE1	MFI	4	SOHC
	Pick-up	2.3 (2254)	4ZD1	2 BBL	4	SOHC
		2.6 (2559)	4ZE1	MFI	4	SOHC
	Trooper II	2.8 (2828)	LL2	TFI	6	SOHC
1991	Amigo	2.3 (2254)	4ZD1	2 BBL	4	SOHC
		2.6 (2559)	4ZE1	MFI	4	SOHC
	Pick-up	2.3 (2254)	4ZD1	2 BBL	4	SOHC
		2.6 (2559)	4ZE1	MFI	4	SOHC
	Rodeo	3.1 (3098)	CPC	TFI	6	OHV
		2.6 (2559)	4ZE1	MFI	4	SOHC
	Trooper II	3.1 (3098)	CPC	TFI	6	OHV
		2.6 (2559)	4ZE1	MFI	4	SOHC
		2.8 (2828)	LL2	TFI	6	SOHC
1992-93	Amigo	2.3 (2254)	4ZD1	2 BBL	4	SOHC
		2.6 (2559)	4ZE1	MFI	4	SOHC
	Pick-up	2.3 (2254)	4ZD1	2 BBL	4	SOHC
		2.6 (2559)	4ZE1	MFI	4	SOHC
	Rodeo	3.1 (3098)	CPC	TFI	6	OHV
		2.6 (2559)	4ZE1	MFI	4	SOHC
	Trooper	3.2 (3165)	6VD1	MFI	6	SOHC
		3.2 (3165)	6VD1	MFI	6	SOHC
		3.2 (3165)	6VD1	MFI	6	DOHC

86861C00

ROUTINE MAINTENANCE AND TUNE-UP

GENERAL MAINTENANCE AND TUNE-UP COMPONENTS - 1996 RODEO WITH 3.2L V6 ENGINE AND AUTOMATIC TRANSMISSION SHOWN

1. Air cleaner housing
2. Power steering fluids reservoir
3. Brake master cylinder fluid reservoir
4. Coolant overflow reservoir
5. Caution/Warning label
6. Radiator fill cap
7. Battery
8. Windshield washer fluid reservoir
9. Fuse box
10. Transmission fluid dipstick
11. Engine oil fill cap
12. Ignition coil/spark plug assemblies
13. Engine oil dipstick
14. Upper radiator hose
15. Lower radiator hose
16. PCV valve

86861C20

GENERAL MAINTENANCE AND TUNE-UP COMPONENTS - 1991 TROOPER WITH 2.8L V6 ENGINE AND AUTOMATIC TRANSMISSION SHOWN.

1. Air cleaner housing
2. Brake master cylinder fluid reservoir
3. Engine oil dipstick
4. Charcoal canister
5. Power steering fluid dipstick/pump cap
6. Accessory drive belts
7. Radiator fill cap
8. Coolant overflow reservoir
9. Battery
10. Upper radiator hose
11. Windshield washer fluid reservoir
12. Heater hoses
13. Accessory drive belt tensioner pulley
14. Fuse box
15. Transmission dipstick

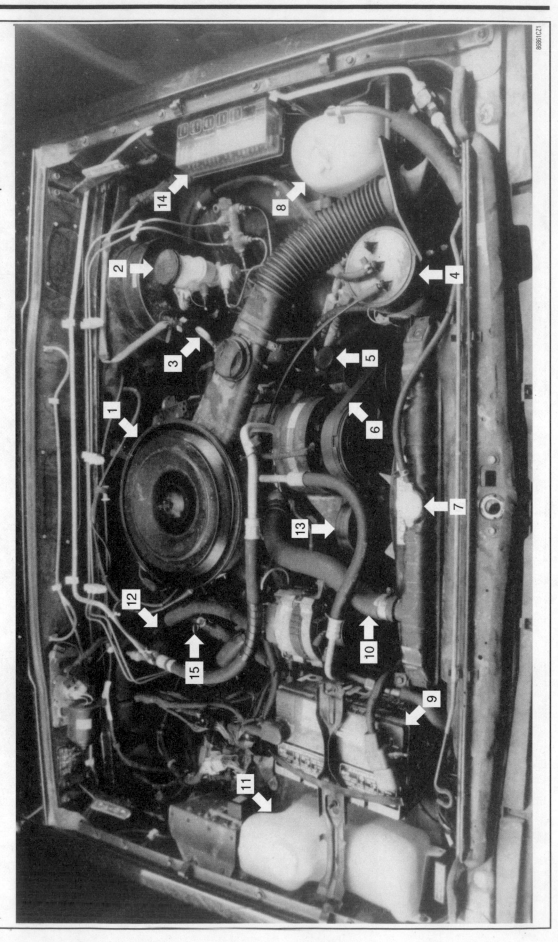

Proper maintenance and tune-up is the key to long and trouble-free vehicle life, and the work can yield its own rewards. Studies have shown that a properly tuned and maintained vehicle can achieve better gas mileage than an out-of-tune vehicle. As a conscientious owner and driver, set aside a Saturday morning, say once a month, to check or replace items which could cause major problems later. Keep your own personal log to jot down which services you performed, how much the parts cost you, the date, and the exact odometer reading at the time. Keep all receipts for such items as engine oil and filters, so that they may be referred to in case of related problems or to determine operating expenses. As a do-it-yourselfer, these receipts are the only proof you have that the required maintenance was performed. In the event of a warranty problem, these receipts will be invaluable.

The literature provided with your vehicle when it was originally delivered includes the factory recommended maintenance schedule. If you no longer have this literature, replacement copies are usually available from the dealer. A maintenance schedule is provided later in this section, in case you do not have the factory literature.

Air Cleaner (Element)

An air cleaner is used to keep airborne dirt and dust out of the air flowing through the engine. This material, if allowed to enter the engine, would form an abrasive compound in conjunction with the engine oil and drastically shorten engine life. For this reason, you should never run the engine without the air cleaner in place except for a very brief period if required for trouble diagnosis. You should also be sure to use the proper replacement part to avoid poor fit and consequent air leakage.

Proper maintenance is important since a clogged air filter will allow an ever-decreasing amount of air to enter the engine and, therefore, will increasingly enrichen the fuel/air mixture, causing poor fuel economy, a drastic increase in emissions and even serious damage to the catalytic converter system.

SERVICING

Under ordinary driving conditions, inspect the air cleaner filter element every 15,000 miles (24,000 km), and replace it every 30,000 miles (48,000 km) or sooner, if necessary. If you drive under severe conditions (stop-and-go driving in dusty conditions, extensive idling, frequent short trips, operating at sustained high speeds during hot weather above 90°F/32°C, commercial type operation, or trailer towing), inspect the filter every 15,000 miles (24,000 km) and replace it whenever necessary.

When opening up the air cleaner housing to replace the air filter, wipe dust out of the air cleaner with a clean rag. Work carefully, to prevent the entry of dirt, dust, or foreign objects. Also, after you have reassembled the housing, inspect it to make sure the air cleaner is properly installed and sealed tightly. A vacuum leak here could allow dust to enter the engine and cause severely accelerated wear.

REMOVAL & INSTALLATION

The Isuzu truck and sport utility vehicles come equipped with one of two types of air cleaners. Fuel injected vehicles are equipped with a remote located square, or rectangular air filter assembly. This type of air cleaner is attached to the throttle body via an air inlet hose. Carbureted vehicles are equipped with a round air filter assembly mounted directly onto the top of the carburetor throat.

✳✳ WARNING

Do not immerse the paper air filter element or temperature sensor in cleaning solvents, as damage can result.

Carbureted Vehicles

▶ See Figures 34 and 35

1. Raise the hood of the vehicle and inspect all of the air cleaner components for damage or improper attachment.
2. Remove the air cleaner cover.
3. Remove the paper air filter element from the air cleaner body. Hold a light on the throttle body side of the element and view the filter from the other side. If light is visible through the element, blow the dust from the element and reuse. If the element is saturated with oil or light is not visible, replace the filter with a new one. If the air filter element is saturated with oil, perform crankcase ventilation system tests, which are located in Section 4.

To install:

4. Remove the fiber crankcase filter, if equipped, and clean it with solvent. Squeeze the filter dry and apply a small amount of engine oil to it. If a metallic mesh is used to retain the fiber filter, clean the mesh with solvent and reuse.
5. Clean the inside of the air cleaner housing with compressed air. If the housing is oily, wash it with solvent.
6. Place the filter element in the cleaner body and install the air cleaner cover. Retain the cover in place with the center wingnut; tighten until snug.
7. Make certain all of the parts are correctly connected and in their proper positions.

Fuel Injected Vehicles

▶ See Figures 36, 37 and 38

1. Raise the hood of the vehicle and inspect all of the air cleaner components for damage or improper attachment.
2. Loosen the throttle body-to-air cleaner assembly air inlet hose clamps, then remove the inlet hose from the vehicle.
3. Unfasten the hold-down clamps on the air cleaner assembly, then lift the lid of the assembly off of the box.

Fig. 34 First remove the air cleaner lid by removing the wingnut . . .

Fig. 35 . . . then lift the old air filter out of the air cleaner housing—carbureted vehicles

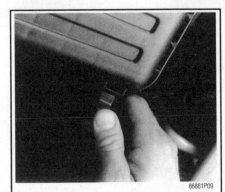

Fig. 36 The air filter cover is held in place with snap clamps—fuel injected models

4. Remove the paper air filter element from the air cleaner body. Hold a light on the throttle body side of the element and view the filter from the other side. If light is visible through the element, blow the dust from the element and reuse. If the element is saturated with oil or light is not visible, replace the filter with a new one. If the air filter element is saturated with oil, perform crankcase ventilation system inspection, as described in Section 4.

To install:

5. Clean the inside of the air cleaner housing with compressed air, then wipe with a shop rag. If the housing is oily, wash it with solvent.

6. Place the filter element in the cleaner body and install the air cleaner cover. Retain the cover in place with the hold-down clips.

7. Install the air inlet hose onto the throttle body and the air cleaner assemblies. Tighten the air inlet hose clamps until snug.

8. Make certain all parts are correctly connected and in their proper positions.

9. Close the hood.

Gasoline Fuel Filter

➡ The Pick-up (P'UP), Amigo and Rodeo models are equipped with the fuel filter located directly in front of the fuel tank, whereas on the Trooper/Trooper II models, the fuel filter is located along the inner side of the right frame rail, near the rear of the vehicle.

REMOVAL & INSTALLATION

✳✳ CAUTION

To reduce the risk of fire and personal injury, it is necessary to relieve the fuel system pressure before servicing fuel system components. Unless this procedure is followed before servicing fuel lines or connections, fuel spray could occur.

Inline Fuel Filter

▶ **See Figures 39, 40, 41 and 42**

1. Properly relieve the fuel system pressure, as described in Section 5.
2. Remove the fuel tank filler cap.
3. Raise and safely support the vehicle.
4. Using fuel line/vacuum line sealing clamps, pinch off the fuel line on each side of the fuel filter. On filters that use hex fittings, use a backup and flare nut wrench to loosen the inlet and outlet fittings.
5. Remove the fuel hose clamps and the fuel hoses from each side of the filter.
6. Remove the mounting bolt and the filter.

To install:

7. Using a new filter, install it to the vehicle. Make certain that the fuel filter is positioned so that the flow arrow points in the correct direction.
8. Install the fuel hoses and fuel hose clamps to the filter. Tighten the fuel clamps until snug.
9. Remove the fuel line sealing clamps.
10. Lower the vehicle to the ground.
11. Install the fuel tank filler cap. .
12. Start the engine and check for leaks at the filter.

In-Tank Fuel Filter

A woven plastic filter is located on the lower end of the fuel pickup tube in the fuel tank. This filter prevents dirt from entering the fuel line and also stops water, unless the filter becomes completely submerged in water. This filter is self-cleaning and normally requires no maintenance. Fuel stoppage at this point indicates that the fuel tank contains an abnormal amount of sediment or water, and the tank should therefore be thoroughly cleaned. For more information regarding the removal and installation of this filter, please refer to the Fuel Tank or Fuel Gauge Sending Unit procedures in Section 5.

Fig. 37 After removing the clamps, lift the air filter cover off . . .

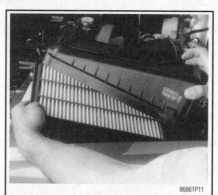

Fig. 38 . . . and lift the filter out of the filter housing—fuel injected models

Fig. 39 The in-line fuel filter is mounted in a bracket, attached to the vehicle's frame rail

Fig. 40 Use fuel line clamps on both hoses to reduce the amount of spilled fuel . . .

Fig. 41 . . . then, while compressing the hose clamps, slide them away from the fuel filter

Fig. 42 The hose can now be removed— once both hoses are detached, remove the filter

Diesel Fuel Filter/Water Separator

The fuel filter is mounted on the right-hand side of the engine compartment, near the battery.

REMOVAL & INSTALLATION

◆ See Figure 43

1. Properly relieve the fuel system pressure. For more details refer to Section 5.
2. Disconnect the negative battery cable.
3. Detach the water separator sensor wire (2) from the connector.
4. Remove the rubber fuel lines (1) from the filter/separator assembly.
5. Remove the two filter/separator assembly-to-bracket bolts (3).

➡**When removing the fuel filter, be careful not to spill the fuel from the cartridge.**

6. Remove the lower plug (4) from the filter/separator assembly and drain the residual fuel into a small container, then pull the sensor assembly (5) off the filter/separator.
7. Remove the O-ring (6) from the filter/separator cartridge.
8. Remove the filter/separator cartridge (7) from the cartridge adapter. Discard the used cartridge.

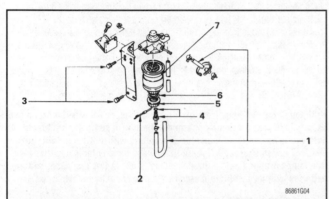

Fig. 43 Exploded view of the diesel fuel filter/separator assembly, located near the battery in the engine compartment

To install:
9. Lubricate the new sensor O-ring with diesel fuel and install the sensor onto the cartridge.
10. Lubricate the cartridge O-ring with diesel fuel. Install the cartridge until the O-ring contacts the sealing surface face, then tighten the cartridge an additional ⅔ of a turn with a filter wrench.
11. Position the filter/separator assembly against the mounting bracket with the attaching holes aligned, then install the mounting bolts until snug.
12. Attach the electrical wiring harness connector to the sensor.
13. Install the rubber hose onto the filter/separator and the adapter assembly.
14. Depress the priming pump, located on top of the cartridge, 30–40 times to fill the cartridge with fuel.

➡**The pumping force will increase as the filter/separator becomes filled.**

15. Connect the negative battery cable.
16. Start the engine and check for fuel leaks around the sealing joints (hose ends, filter/separator-to-adapter and drain plug).

DRAINING WATER

◆ See Figure 44

1. Position a 1 pt. (approximately 0.2L) container at the end of the vinyl hose, located under the drain plug of the separator.
2. Loosen the drain plug 5 turns.

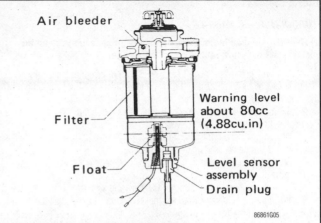

Fig. 44 The fuel filter/separator assembly will filter water out of the fuel and store it until approximately 4.88 c.i. (80cc) are accumulated, at this point the warning light in the instrument panel will illuminate

3. Depress the priming pump about 7–8 times until the water is drained from the filter.
4. Tighten the drain plug until closed.
5. Depress the priming pump several additional times to check that no fuel leaks out of the fuel filter/separator assembly.
6. Start the engine and, once again, check for leakage around the drain plug.
7. Make sure the **FILTER** warning light remains out or turns off.

Positive Crankcase Ventilation (PCV) Valve

REMOVAL & INSTALLATION

Gasoline Engines

◆ See Figure 45

➡**The PCV valve is mounted in the rocker arm cover for I4 engines, and usually in the left rocker arm cover for V6 engines. The PCV valve is connected to the intake manifold or throttle body by a vacuum hose.**

1. Using a pair of pliers, squeeze the tabs on the vacuum hose clamp together, then slide the clamp down the vacuum hose away from the PCV valve.
2. Pull the vacuum hose off of the PCV valve outlet nipple.
3. Pull the PCV valve out of the rocker arm cover grommet with a twisting motion. Take care not to damage the PCV valve mounting grommet.
4. Shake the valve and listen for the rattle of the needle inside the valve. If the valve does not rattle, replace the valve with a new one.
To install:
5. Push the PCV valve into the rubber grommet in the rocker arm cover.
6. Slide the end of the vacuum hose over the PCV valve outlet nipple. Slide the hose clamp up over the nipple bulge to hold the hose in place.

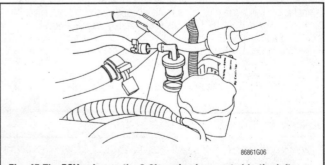

Fig. 45 The PCV valve on the 3.2L engine is mounted in the left rocker arm cover near the oil filler cap

Diesel Engines

TURBOCHARGED ENGINES

➡**The PCV valve on turbocharged diesel engines is mounted on the rocker arm cover toward the rear of the engine.**

1. Disconnect the PCV hose from the PCV valve by either loosening the clamp screw, or by compressing the clamp tabs together. Slide the clamp down the hose, away from the valve. Pull the hose from the PCV valve.
2. Remove the PCV valve-to-rocker arm cover mounting bolts, then lift the PCV valve off of the rocker arm cover.
3. Disconnect the oil drain hose from the PCV valve in the same manner as the PCV hose, once access is gained.
4. Remove the PCV valve from the engine compartment.

To install:

5. Slide the oil drain hose onto the PCV valve and secure with the hose clamp.
6. Position the PCV valve onto the rocker arm cover and install the mounting bolts. Tighten the bolts until snug.
7. Connect the PCV hose to the PCV valve and position the hose clamp to secure the hose in place.

NON-TURBOCHARGED ENGINES

➡**The PCV valve on non-turbocharged diesel engines is mounted above the rocker arm cover toward the rear of the engine.**

1. Disconnect the PCV pipe from the PCV valve by pulling it off of the PCV valve outlet nipple.
2. Detach the oil drain hose and the breather pipe-to-PCV valve hose by either loosening the clamp screw, or by compressing the clamp tabs together. Slide the clamp down the hose, away from the valve. Pull the hoses from the PCV valve.
3. Remove the PCV valve from the engine compartment.

To install:

4. Slide the oil drain hose and the breather pipe hose onto the PCV valve and secure with the hose clamps.
5. Connect the PCV pipe to the PCV valve.

Evaporative Canister

SERVICING

The charcoal canister is a sealed unit which requires no periodic maintenance. If the charcoal canister is malfunctioning, it must be replaced with a new one.

Battery

PRECAUTIONS

Always use caution when working on or near the battery. Never allow a tool to bridge the gap between the negative and positive battery terminals. Also, be careful not to allow a tool to provide a ground between the positive cable/terminal and any metal component on the vehicle. Either of these conditions will cause a short circuit, leading to sparks and possible personal injury.

Do not smoke or all open flames/sparks near a battery; the gases contained in the battery are very explosive and, if ignited, could cause severe injury or death.

All batteries, regardless of type, should be carefully secured by a battery hold-down device. If not, the terminals or casing may crack from stress during vehicle operation. A battery which is not secured may allow acid to leak, making it discharge faster. The acid can also eat away at components under the hood.

Always inspect the battery case for cracks, leakage and corrosion. A white corrosive substance on the battery case or on nearby components would indicate a leaking or cracked battery. If the battery is cracked, it should be replaced immediately.

GENERAL MAINTENANCE

Always keep the battery cables and terminals free of corrosion. Check and clean these components about once a year.

Keep the top of the battery clean, as a film of dirt can help discharge a bat-

tery that is not used for long periods. A solution of baking soda and water may be used for cleaning, but be careful to flush this off with clear water. DO NOT let any of the solution into the filler holes. Baking soda neutralizes battery acid and will de-activate a battery cell.

Batteries in vehicles which are not operated on a regular basis can fall victim to parasitic loads (small current drains which are constantly drawing current from the battery). Normal parasitic loads may drain a battery on a vehicle that is in storage and not used for 6–8 weeks. Vehicles that have additional accessories such as a phone or an alarm system may discharge a battery sooner. If the vehicle is to be stored for longer periods in a secure area and the alarm system is not necessary, the negative battery cable should be disconnected to protect the battery.

Remember that constantly deep cycling a battery (completely discharging and recharging it) will shorten battery life.

BATTERY FLUID

◆ **See Figure 46**

Check the battery electrolyte level at least once a month, or more often in hot weather or during periods of extended vehicle operation. On non-sealed batteries, the level can be checked either through the case (if translucent) or by removing the cell caps. The electrolyte level in each cell should be kept filled to the split ring inside each cell, or the line marked on the outside of the case.

If the level is low, add only distilled water through the opening until the level is correct. Each cell must be checked and filled individually. Distilled water should be used, because the chemicals and minerals found in most drinking water are harmful to the battery and could significantly shorten its life.

If water is added in freezing weather, the vehicle should be driven several miles to allow the water to mix with the electrolyte. Otherwise, the battery could freeze.

Although some maintenance-free batteries have removable cell caps, the electrolyte condition and level on all sealed maintenance-free batteries must be checked using the built-in hydrometer "eye." The exact type of eye will vary. But, most battery manufacturers, apply a sticker to the battery itself explaining the readings.

➡**Although the readings from built-in hydrometers will vary, a green eye usually indicates a properly charged battery with sufficient fluid level. A dark eye is normally an indicator of a battery with sufficient fluid, but which is low in charge. A light or yellow eye usually indicates that electrolyte has dropped below the necessary level. In this last case, sealed batteries with an insufficient electrolyte must usually be discarded.**

Checking the Specific Gravity

◆ **See Figures 47, 48 and 49**

A hydrometer is required to check the specific gravity on all batteries that are not maintenance-free. On batteries that are maintenance-free, the specific gravity is checked by observing the built-in hydrometer "eye" on the top of the battery case.

✳✳ CAUTION

Battery electrolyte contains sulfuric acid. If you should splash any on your skin or in your eyes, flush the affected area with plenty of clear water. If it lands in your eyes, get medical help immediately.

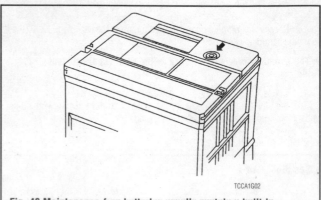

TCCA1G02

Fig. 40 Maintenance-free batteries usually contain a built-in hydrometer to check fluid level

Fig. 47 On non-sealed batteries, the fluid level can be checked by removing the cell caps

Fig. 48 If the fluid level is low, add only distilled water until the level is correct

Fig. 49 Check the specific gravity of the battery's electrolyte with a hydrometer

The fluid (sulfuric acid solution) contained in the battery cells will tell you many things about the condition of the battery. Because the cell plates must be kept submerged below the fluid level in order to operate, the fluid level is extremely important. And, because the specific gravity of the acid is an indication of electrical charge, testing the fluid can be an aid in determining if the battery must be replaced. A battery in a vehicle with a properly operating charging system should require little maintenance, but careful, periodic inspection should reveal problems before they leave you stranded.

At least once a year, check the specific gravity of the battery. It should be between 1.20 and 1.26 on the gravity scale. Most auto stores carry a variety of inexpensive battery hydrometers. These can be used on any non-sealed battery to test the specific gravity in each cell.

The battery testing hydrometer has a squeeze bulb at one end and a nozzle at the other. Battery electrolyte is sucked into the hydrometer until the float is lifted from its seat. The specific gravity is then read by noting the position of the float. If gravity is low in one or more cells, the battery should be slowly charged and checked again to see if the gravity has come up. Generally, if after charging, the specific gravity between any two cells varies more than 50 points (0.50), the battery should be replaced, as it can no longer produce sufficient voltage to guarantee proper operation.

CABLES

▶ **See Figures 50, 51, 52 and 53**

Once a year (or as necessary), the battery terminals and the cable clamps should be cleaned. Loosen the clamps and remove the cables, negative cable first. On top post batteries, the use of a puller specially made for this purpose is recommended. These are inexpensive and available in most parts stores. Side terminal battery cables are secured with a small bolt.

Clean the cable clamps and the battery terminal with a wire brush, until all corrosion, grease, etc., is removed and the metal is shiny. It is especially important to clean the inside of the clamp thoroughly (an old knife is useful here), since a small deposit of oxidation there will prevent a sound connection and inhibit starting or charging. Special tools are available for cleaning these parts,

one type for conventional top post batteries and another type for side terminal batteries. It is also a good idea to apply some dielectric grease to the terminal, as this will aid in the prevention of corrosion.

After the clamps and terminals are clean, reinstall the cables, negative cable last; DO NOT hammer the clamps onto battery posts. Tighten the clamps securely, but do not distort them. Give the clamps and terminals a thin external coating of grease after installation, to retard corrosion.

Check the cables at the same time that the terminals are cleaned. If the cable insulation is cracked or broken, or if the ends are frayed, the cable should be replaced with a new cable of the same length and gauge.

CHARGING

✳✳ CAUTION

The chemical reaction which takes place in all batteries generates explosive hydrogen gas. A spark can cause the battery to explode and splash acid. To avoid personal injury, be sure there is proper ventilation and take appropriate fire safety precautions when working with or near a battery.

A battery should be charged at a slow rate to keep the plates inside from getting too hot. However, if some maintenance-free batteries are allowed to discharge until they are almost "dead," they may have to be charged at a high rate to bring them back to "life." Always follow the charger manufacturer's instructions on charging the battery.

REPLACEMENT

When it becomes necessary to replace the battery, select one with an amperage rating equal to or greater than the battery originally installed. Deterioration and just plain aging of the battery cables, starter motor, and associated wires makes the battery's job harder in successive years. This makes it prudent to install a new battery with a greater capacity than the old.

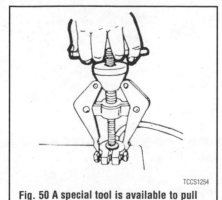

Fig. 50 A special tool is available to pull the clamp from the post

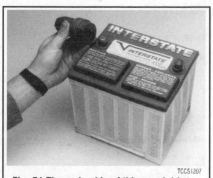

Fig. 51 The underside of this special battery tool has a wire brush to clean post terminals

Fig. 52 Place the tool over the battery posts and twist to clean until the metal is shiny

Belts

INSPECTION

▶ **See Figures 54, 55, 56, 57 and 58**

Inspect the belts for signs of glazing or cracking. A glazed belt will be perfectly smooth from slippage, while a good belt will have a slight texture of fabric visible. Cracks will usually start at the inner edge of the belt and run outward. All worn or damaged drive belts should be replaced immediately. It is best to replace all drive belts at one time, as a preventive maintenance measure, during this service operation.

ADJUSTMENT

V-Belts

▶ **See Figures 59, 60, 61 and 62**

Determine belt tension at a point halfway between the pulleys by pressing on the belt with moderate thumb pressure. If the distance between the pulleys, measured at the center of each pulley, is 13–16 in. (33–40cm), the belt should deflect ½ in. (13mm) at the halfway point of its longest straight run; ¼ in. (6mm) if the distance is 7–12 in. (18–30cm). If the defection is found to be too much or too little, loosen the mounting bolts and make the adjustments.

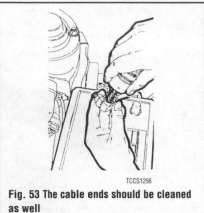

Fig. 53 The cable ends should be cleaned as well

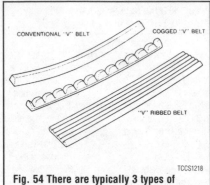

Fig. 54 There are typically 3 types of accessory drive belts found on vehicles today

Fig. 55 An example of a healthy drive belt

Fig. 56 Deep cracks in this belt will cause flex, building up heat that will eventually lead to belt failure

Fig. 57 The cover of this belt is worn, exposing the critical reinforcing cords to excessive wear

Fig. 58 Installing too wide a belt can result in serious belt wear and/or breakage

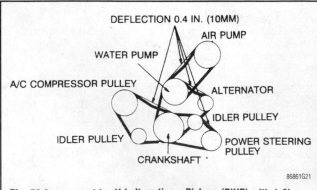

Fig. 59 Accessory drive V-belt routing—Pick-up (P'UP) with 1.8L and 1.9L engines

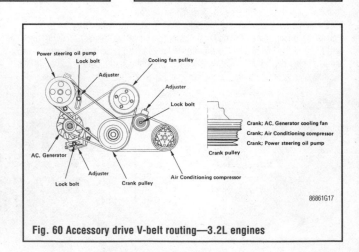

Fig. 60 Accessory drive V-belt routing—3.2L engines

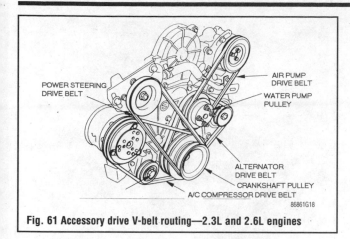

Fig. 61 Accessory drive V-belt routing—2.3L and 2.6L engines

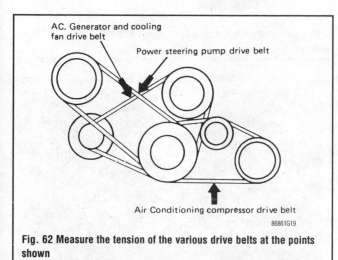

Fig. 62 Measure the tension of the various drive belts at the points shown

Before you attempt to adjust any of your engine's belts, you should take an old rag soaked in solvent and clean the mounting bolts of any road grime which has accumulated there. On some of the harder-to-reach bolts, an application of penetrating oil will make them easier to loosen. When you're adjusting belts, especially on 4-cylinder engines with air conditioning and power steering, it would be especially helpful to have a variety of socket extensions and universals to get at those hard-to-reach bolts.

➡ **When adjusting the air pump belt, if you are using a prybar, make sure that you pry against the cast iron end cover and not against the aluminum housing. Excessive force on the housing will damage it.**

Serpentine Belts

▶ **See Figures 63 and 64**

After 1989, some of the V6 engines are equipped with a serpentine belt and automatic belt tensioner. The tension is maintained by a spring loaded pulley/tensioner. The indicator mark on the moveable portion of the tensioner must be within the limits of the slotted area on the stationary portion of the tensioner. Any reading outside the limits indicates either a defective belt or tensioner.

REMOVAL & INSPECTION

V-Belts and Non-Serpentine Ribbed Belts

▶ **See Figure 65**

ALTERNATOR DRIVE BELT

The alternator is equipped with a pivot bolt, an adjusting bolt and an adjusting side lockbolt. The adjusting bolt is what loosens or tightens the drive belt. The adjusting bolt and locking bolt are on the same side of the alternator, whereas the alternator pivot bolt is opposite these two.

1. Depending on the location of the alternator in the vehicle, it may be helpful to raise and safely support the vehicle on jackstands.
2. If the alternator drive belt is located behind other belts, they will have to be removed first to facilitate removal of the alternator belt.
3. Loosen the pivot bolt only enough to allow the alternator to move.
4. Loosen the lockbolt, then turn the adjusting bolt to attain the maximum amount of slack in the drive belt.
5. Remove the drive belt from the alternator pulley, then remove it from crankshaft and cooling fan pulleys.
   To install:
6. Position the belt onto the cooling fan and crankshaft pulleys, then position it around the alternator pulley.
7. Turn the adjusting bolt until the proper amount of tension is exhibited by the belt. Tighten the locking bolt and pivot bolt securely.
8. Install any other belts which were removed, then lower the vehicle, if applicable.

AIR CONDITIONING COMPRESSOR DRIVE BELT

The A/C compressor drive belt uses a separate adjusting idler pulley assembly to tension the drive belt.

1. Depending on the location of the A/C compressor (usually toward the bottom of the engine) in the vehicle, it may be helpful to raise and safely support the vehicle on jackstands.
2. If the A/C compressor drive belt is located behind other belts, they will have to be removed first to facilitate removal of the alternator belt.

➡ **None of the A/C compressor mounting bolts should be loosened or removed—the adjusting idler pulley assembly is solely responsible for keeping the drive belt tight.**

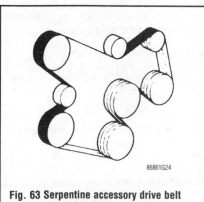

Fig. 63 Serpentine accessory drive belt routing—2.8L engines

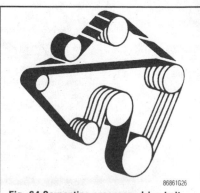

Fig. 64 Serpentine accessory drive belt routing—3.1L engine

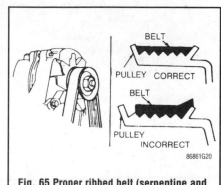

Fig. 65 Proper ribbed belt (serpentine and non-serpentine) positioning on the accessory pulleys

3. Loosen the lockbolt (at the center of the idler pulley), then turn the adjusting bolt to attain the maximum amount of slack in the drive belt.

4. Remove the drive belt from the A/C compressor pulley, then remove it from the crankshaft pulley.

To install:

5. Position the belt onto the crankshaft pulley, then position it around the A/C compressor pulley.

6. Turn the adjusting bolt until the proper amount of tension is exhibited by the belt. Tighten the locking bolt securely.

7. Install any other belts which were removed, then lower the vehicle, if applicable.

POWER STEERING PUMP DRIVE BELT

Unlike the other two belts, the power steering pump drive belt usually does not have an adjusting bolt or adjusting idler assembly. If it does, simply use the A/C compressor belt procedure instead.

1. Depending on the location of the power steering pump in the vehicle, it may be helpful to raise and safely support the vehicle on jackstands.

2. If the power steering pump drive belt is located behind other belts, they will have to be removed first to facilitate removal of the alternator belt.

3. Loosen the pivot bolt only enough to allow movement of the power steering pump.

4. Loosen the sliding bolt (the bolt whose bracket is equipped with a groove to allow adjustment of the pump). The pump should move toward the engine and the drive belt will slacken.

5. Push the pump toward the engine until enough slack is gained to allow removal of the belt from the pump pulley.

6. Remove the drive belt from the steering pump pulley, then remove it from the crankshaft pulley.

To install:

7. Position the belt onto the crankshaft pulley, then position it around the power steering pump pulley.

8. Use a padded prybar to pry against the iron housing of the steering pump. Pry the pump away from the engine until the proper amount of tension is felt in the belt, then tighten the sliding bolt. Having an assistant at hand is helpful when performing this procedure.

9. With the sliding bolt tight, check the belt tension. If the belt tension is incorrect, the sliding bolt must be loosened and the steering pump repositioned with the prybar.

10. Tighten the pivot bolt until secure.

11. Install any other belts which were removed, then lower the vehicle, if applicable.

Serpentine Belts

▶ See Figures 65, 66 and 67

1. It is helpful to note the routing of the serpentine belt before removal, since the routing may differ drastically, depending on the options with which the vehicle is equipped. If the belt is installed incorrectly, this could cause one or more components to be rotated in the opposite direction than intended; this could lead to damage.

2. Install a ½ in. drive ratchet handle, or breaker bar, into the square hole in the automatic tensioner. Pry the tensioner until the belt becomes loose on the pulleys.

3. While holding the tensioner in that position, slide the serpentine belt off of one or two of the accessory pulleys.

4. Slowly allow the tensioner to move back into its resting position. Do not allow the tensioner to quickly snap back in place; this could damage the automatic tensioner.

5. Remove the breaker bar or ratchet wrench from the tensioner assembly and remove the accessory drive belt from the remaining pulleys.

To install:

6. Position the drive belt on all of the pulleys but the one closest to the tensioner.

7. Once again, retract the tensioner using the breaker bar or ratchet wrench and slide the belt over the last pulley. Make sure that the drive belt ribs or grooves are settled into the pulleys completely.

8. Slowly release the tensioner to take up all slack in the drive belt.

9. Remove the breaker bar or ratchet wrench from the tensioner.

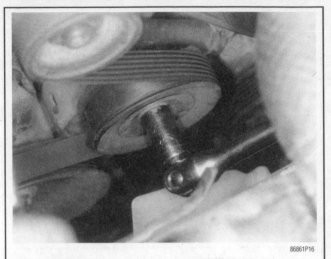

Fig. 66 To remove serpentine belts, first swing the tensioner to slacken the belt . . .

Fig. 67 . . . then remove the belt from the various pulleys

Timing Belt

Of the eight engines available for 1981–96 Isuzu trucks and sport utility vehicles, only four of them are equipped with timing belts, rather than timing chains. Timing chains generally do not need routine replacement or inspection, unless engine repairs are being done and inspection would be easy to do at the time. The timing belts on the 2.2L diesel, 2.3L, 2.6L and 3.2L engines do, however, need to be replaced at the 60,000 mile (96,000 km) and 120,000 mile (192,000 km) marks. If the timing belt is inspected earlier or more frequently than suggested, and shows signs of wear or defects, the belt should be replaced at that time.

Inspect both sides of the timing belt. Replace the belt with a new one if any of the following conditions exist:

• Hardening of black rubber; back side is glossy without resilience and leaves no indentation when pressed with a fingernail.
• Cracks on rubber backing.
• Cracks or peeling of the canvas.
• Cracks on rib root.
• Cracks on belt sides.
• Missing teeth.
• Abnormal wear of belt sides. The sides are normal if they are sharp, as if cut by a knife

If none of these conditions exist, the belt does not need replacement, unless it is at the recommended interval. The belt MUST be replaced at the recommended interval.

❄❄ WARNING

It is very important to replace the timing belt at the recommended intervals, otherwise expensive engine damage will likely result if the belt fails.

If the timing belt is not replaced at the recommended intervals, the engine will likely be damaged. Damage occurs since the valves and pistons come in contact with each other when the timing belt breaks. This can cause damage to the valves and pistons, necessitating extensive engine work.

For removal and installation procedures of the timing belt, please refer to Section 3.

Hoses

INSPECTION

▶ **See Figures 68, 69, 70 and 71**

Upper and lower radiator hoses, along with the heater hoses, should be checked for deterioration, leaks and loose hose clamps at least every 15,000 miles (24,000 km). It is also wise to check the hoses periodically in early spring and at the beginning of the fall or winter when you are performing other maintenance. A quick visual inspection could discover a weakened hose which might have left you stranded if it had remained unrepaired.

Whenever you are checking the hoses, make sure the engine and cooling system are cold. Visually inspect for cracking, rotting or collapsed hoses, and replace as necessary. Run your hand along the length of the hose. If a weak or swollen spot is noted when squeezing the hose wall, the hose should be replaced.

REMOVAL & INSTALLATION

1. Remove the radiator pressure cap.

❄❄ CAUTION

Never remove the pressure cap while the engine is running, or personal injury from scalding hot coolant or steam may result. If possible, wait until the engine has cooled to remove the pressure cap. If this is not possible, wrap a thick cloth around the pressure cap and turn it slowly to the stop. Step back while the pressure is released from the cooling system. When you are sure all the pressure has been released, use the cloth to turn and remove the cap.

2. Position a clean container under the radiator and/or engine draincock or plug, then open the drain and allow the cooling system to drain to an appropriate level. For some upper hoses, only a little coolant must be drained. To remove hoses positioned lower on the engine, such as a lower radiator hose, the entire cooling system must be emptied.

❄❄ CAUTION

When draining coolant, keep in mind that cats and dogs are attracted by ethylene glycol antifreeze, and are quite likely to drink any that is left in an uncovered container or in puddles on the ground. This will prove fatal in sufficient quantity. Always drain coolant into a sealable container. Coolant may be reused unless it is contaminated or several years old.

3. Loosen the hose clamps at each end of the hose requiring replacement. Clamps are usually either of the spring tension type (which require pliers to squeeze the tabs and loosen) or of the screw tension type (which require screw or hex drivers to loosen). Pull the clamps back on the hose away from the connection.

4. Twist, pull and slide the hose off the fitting, taking care not to damage the neck of the component from which the hose is being removed.

➡**If the hose is stuck at the connection, do not try to insert a screwdriver or other sharp tool under the hose end in an effort to free it, as the connection and/or hose may become damaged. Heater connections especially may be easily damaged by such a procedure. If the hose is to be replaced, use a single-edged razor blade to make a slice along the portion of the hose which is stuck on the connection, perpendicular to the end of the hose. Do not cut deep, so as to prevent damaging the connection. The hose can then be peeled from the connection and discarded.**

5. Clean both hose mounting connections. Inspect the condition of the hose clamps and replace them, if necessary.

To install:

6. Dip the ends of the new hose into clean engine coolant to ease installation.

7. Slide the clamps over the replacement hose, then slide the hose ends over the connections into position.

8. Position and secure the clamps at least ¼ in. (6.35mm) from the ends of the hose. Make sure they are located beyond the raised beads of the connectors.

9. Close the radiator or engine drains and properly refill the cooling system with the clean drained engine coolant or a mixture of ethylene glycol, or other suitable coolant and water.

10. If available, install a pressure tester and check for leaks. If a pressure tester is not available, run the engine until normal operating temperature is reached (allowing the system to naturally pressurize), then check for leaks.

❄❄ CAUTION

If you are checking for leaks with the system at normal operating temperature, BE EXTREMELY CAREFUL not to touch any moving or hot engine parts. Once operating temperature has been reached, shut the engine OFF, and check for leaks around the hose fittings and connections which were removed earlier.

TCCS1219

Fig. 68 The cracks developing along this hose are a result of age-related hardening

TCCS1220

Fig. 69 A hose clamp that is too tight can cause older hoses to separate and tear on either side of the clamp

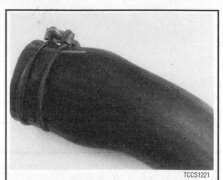

TCCS1221

Fig. 70 A soft spongy hose (identifiable by the swollen section) will eventually burst and should be replaced

CV-Boots

INSPECTION

▶ See Figures 72 and 73

The CV (Constant Velocity) boots should be checked for damage each time the oil is changed and any other time the vehicle is raised for service. These boots keep water, grime, dirt and other damaging matter from entering the CV-joints. Any of these could cause early CV-joint failure which can be expensive to repair. Heavy grease thrown around the inside of the front wheel(s) and on the brake caliper can be an indication of a torn boot. Thoroughly check the boots for missing clamps and tears. If the boot is damaged, it should be replaced immediately. Please refer to Section 7 for procedures.

Fig. 71 Hoses are likely to deteriorate from the inside if the cooling system is not periodically flushed

Fig. 72 CV-boots must be inspected periodically for damage

Fig. 73 A torn boot should be replaced immediately

Spark Plugs

▶ See Figure 74

A typical spark plug consists of a metal shell surrounding a ceramic insulator. A metal electrode extends downward through the center of the insulator and protrudes a small distance. Located at the end of the plug and attached to the side of the outer metal shell is the side electrode. The side electrode bends in at a 90° angle so that its tip is just past and parallel to the tip of the center electrode. The distance between these two electrodes (measured in thousandths of an inch or hundredths of a millimeter) is called the spark plug gap.

The spark plug does not produce a spark but instead provides a gap across which the current can arc. The coil produces anywhere from 20,000 to 50,000 volts (depending on the type and application) which travels through the wires to the spark plugs. The current passes along the center electrode and jumps the gap to the side electrode, and in doing so, ignites the air/fuel mixture in the combustion chamber.

SPARK PLUG HEAT RANGE

▶ See Figure 75

Spark plug heat range is the ability of the plug to dissipate heat. The longer the insulator (or the farther it extends into the engine), the hotter the plug will operate; the shorter the insulator (the closer the electrode is to the block's cooling passages) the cooler it will operate. A plug that absorbs little heat and remains too cool will quickly accumulate deposits of oil and carbon since it is not hot enough to burn them off. This leads to plug fouling and consequently to misfiring. A plug that absorbs too much heat will have no deposits but, due to the excessive heat, the electrodes will burn away quickly and might possibly lead to preignition or other ignition problems. Preignition takes place when plug tips get so hot that they glow sufficiently to ignite the air/fuel mixture before the actual spark occurs. This early ignition will usually cause a pinging during low speeds and heavy loads.

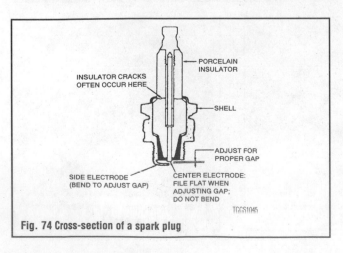
Fig. 74 Cross-section of a spark plug

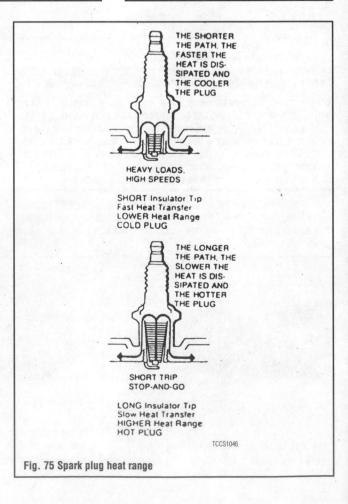
Fig. 75 Spark plug heat range

The general rule of thumb for choosing the correct heat range when picking a spark plug is: if most of your driving is long distance, high speed travel, use a colder plug; if most of your driving is stop and go, use a hotter plug. Original equipment plugs are generally a good compromise between the 2 styles and most people never have the need to change their plugs from the factory-recommended heat range.

REMOVAL & INSTALLATION

A set of spark plugs usually requires replacement by 30,000 miles (48,000 km), depending on your style of driving. In normal operation plug gap increases about 0.001 in (0.025mm) for every 2,500 miles (4,000 km). As the gap increases, the plug's voltage requirement also increases. It requires a greater voltage to jump the wider gap and about two to three times as much voltage to fire the plug at high speeds than at idle. The improved air/fuel ratio control of modern fuel injection combined with the higher voltage output of modern ignition systems will often allow an engine to run significantly longer on a set of standard spark plugs, but keep in mind that efficiency will drop as the gap widens (along with fuel economy and power).

When you're removing spark plugs, work on one at a time. Don't start by removing the plug wires all at once, because, unless you number them, they may become mixed up. Take a minute before you begin and number the wires with tape.

Except 3.2L Engine

▶ **See Figures 76, 77, 78, 79 and 80**

1. Disconnect the negative battery cable, and if the vehicle has been run recently, allow the engine to thoroughly cool.
2. Carefully twist the spark plug wire boot to loosen it, then pull upward and remove the boot from the plug. Be sure to pull on the boot and not on the wire, otherwise the connector located inside the boot may become separated.
3. Using compressed air, blow any water or debris from the spark plug well to assure that no harmful contaminants are allowed to enter the combustion chamber when the spark plug is removed. If compressed air is not available, use a rag or a brush to clean the area.

➡**Remove the spark plugs when the engine is cold, if possible, to prevent damage to the threads. If removal of the plugs is difficult, apply a few drops of penetrating oil or silicone spray to the area around the base of the plug, and allow it a few minutes to work.**

4. Using a spark plug socket that is equipped with a rubber insert to properly hold the plug, turn the spark plug counterclockwise to loosen and remove the spark plug from the bore.

✳✳ WARNING

Be sure not to use a flexible extension on the socket. Use of a flexible extension may allow a shear force to be applied to the plug. A shear force could break the plug off in the cylinder head, leading to costly and frustrating repairs.

To install:

5. Inspect the spark plug boot for tears or damage. If a damaged boot is found, the spark plug wire must be replaced.
6. Using a wire feeler gauge, check and adjust the spark plug gap. When using a gauge, the proper size should pass between the electrodes with a slight drag. The next larger size should not be able to pass, while the next smaller size should pass freely.
7. Carefully thread the plug into the bore by hand. If resistance is felt before the plug is almost completely threaded, back the plug out and begin threading again. In small, hard to reach areas, an old spark plug wire and boot could be used as a threading tool. The boot will hold the plug while you twist the end of the wire, and the wire is supple enough to twist before it would allow the plug to crossthread.

✳✳ WARNING

Do not use the spark plug socket to thread the plugs. Always carefully thread the plug by hand or using an old plug wire to prevent the possibility of crossthreading and damaging the cylinder head bore.

8. Carefully tighten the spark plug. If the plug you are installing is equipped with a crush washer, seat the plug, then tighten about ¼ turn to crush the washer. If you are installing a tapered seat plug, tighten the spark plug to 14–18 ft. lbs. (19–24 Nm).
9. Apply a small amount of silicone dielectric compound to the end of the spark plug lead or inside the spark plug boot to prevent sticking, then install the boot to the spark plug and push until it clicks into place. The click may be felt or heard, then gently pull back on the boot to assure proper contact.

3.2L Engine

▶ **See Figure 81**

➡**The 3.2L engine's spark plugs are mounted inside of the rocker arm covers. A spark plug socket (one with a rubber plug holder mounted in it) is necessary.**

1. Disconnect the negative battery cable.
2. On 1996 models, remove the 2 coil pack hold-down screws from each coil pack on the rocker arm covers. Pull the coil pack off of the spark plug and rocker arm cover.
3. On other 3.2L engines, label and remove the spark plug cables.
4. Using a spark plug socket and a long extension, situate the socket onto the spark plug. Make sure that the rubber section of the socket grips the spark plug firmly.
5. Loosen the spark plug and extract it from the rocker arm cover. If the spark plug falls out of the spark plug socket, removal of the rocker arm cover is necessary.

To install:

6. Gap the spark plug to be installed, then insert it firmly into the spark plug socket.
7. Using only the socket and extension, start the spark plug into its hole with your fingers. Make sure not to crossthread the spark plug. The spark plug should turn in easily; if a binding is felt while turning the spark plug, stop immediately. Loosen the spark plug and try installing it again.

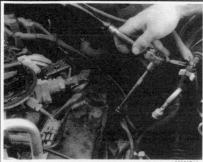

Fig. 76 To remove the spark plugs, first disconnect the plug wire holders from the rocker arm cover . . .

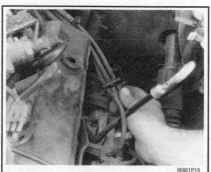

Fig. 77 . . . then pull the wires away from the engine to gain access—a 2.8L engine shown

Fig. 78 Detach the spark plug cables from the spark plugs, then . . .

Fig. 79 . . . use a spark plug socket and extension to remove the plugs—a 2.8L engine shown

Fig. 80 Notice that the spark plug socket is equipped with flats on it, so that a wrench can be used also

Fig. 81 The spark plugs on the 3.2L engine are located inside the rocker arm covers

8. Once the spark plug is adequately threaded into the bore (finger-tight), tighten it to 13 ft. lbs. (18 Nm).

9. On 1996 models, install the individual coil pack onto its spark plug, making sure that the coil extension is seated on the spark plug properly. Install the 2 hold-down screws until snug.

10. On other 3.2L engines, install the spark plug cables onto the spark plugs. Make sure that the cable is seated completely on the spark plug and in the rocker arm cover hole.

11. Connect the negative battery cable.

INSPECTION & GAPPING

▶ See Figures 82 thru 86

Check the plugs for deposits and wear. If they are not going to be replaced, clean the plugs thoroughly. Remember that any kind of deposit will decrease the efficiency of the plug. Plugs can be cleaned on a spark plug cleaning machine, which can sometimes be found in service stations, or you can do an acceptable

job of cleaning with a stiff brush. If the plugs are cleaned, the electrodes must be filed flat. Use an ignition points file, not an emery board or the like, which will leave deposits. The electrodes must be filed perfectly flat with sharp edges; rounded edges reduce the spark plug voltage by as much as 50 percent.

Check spark plug gap before installation. The ground electrode (the L-shaped one connected to the body of the plug) must be parallel to the center electrode, and the specified size wire gauge (please refer to the Tune-Up Specifications chart for specific gap specifications) must pass between the electrodes with a slight drag.

➡NEVER adjust the gap on a used platinum type spark plug.

Always check the gap on new plugs as they are not always set correctly at the factory. Do not use a flat feeler gauge when measuring the gap on a used plug, because the reading may be inaccurate. A round-wire type gapping tool is the best way to check the gap. The correct gauge should pass through the electrode gap with a slight drag. If you're in doubt, try one size smaller and one larger. The smaller gauge should go through easily, while the larger one shouldn't go through at all. Wire gapping tools usually have a bending tool attached. Use that to adjust the side electrode until the proper distance is obtained. Absolutely never attempt to bend the center electrode. Also, be careful not to bend the side electrode too far or too often as it may weaken and break off within the engine, requiring removal of the cylinder head to retrieve it.

Spark Plug Wires

➡The 1996 3.2L engine does not utilize spark plug wires; it uses individual coil packs, which mount directly on top of the spark plugs.

TESTING

▶ See Figures 87 and 88

At every tune-up/inspection, visually check the spark plug cables for burns, cuts, or breaks in the insulation. Check the boots and the nipples on the distributor cap and/or coil. Replace any damaged wiring.

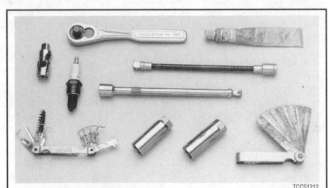

Fig. 82 A variety of tools and gauges are needed for spark plug service

Fig. 83 Checking the spark plug gap with a feeler gauge

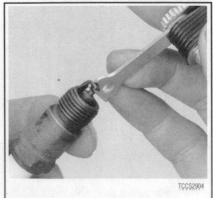

Fig. 84 Adjusting the spark plug gap

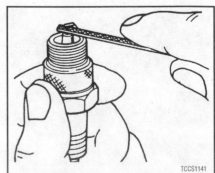

Fig. 85 If the plug is in good condition, the center electrode may be filed flat and reused

A normally worn spark plug should have light tan or gray deposits on the firing tip.

A carbon fouled plug, identified by soft, sooty, black deposits, may indicate an improperly tuned vehicle. Check the air cleaner, ignition components and engine control system.

This spark plug has been **left in the engine too long,** as evidenced by the extreme gap- Plugs with such an extreme gap can cause misfiring and stumbling accompanied by a noticeable lack of power.

An oil fouled spark plug indicates an engine with worn poston rings and/or bad valve seals allowing excessive oil to enter the chamber.

A physically damaged spark plug may be evidence of severe detonation in that cylinder. Watch that cylinder carefully between services, as a continued detonation will not only damage the plug, but could also damage the engine.

A bridged or almost bridged spark plug, identified by a build-up between the electrodes caused by excessive carbon or oil build-up on the plug.

TCCA1P40

Fig. 86 Inspect the spark plug to determine engine running conditions

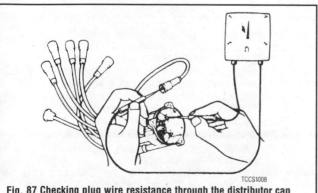

TCCS1008

Fig. 87 Checking plug wire resistance through the distributor cap with an ohmmeter

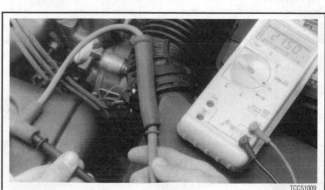

TCCS1009

Fig. 88 Checking individual plug wire resistance with a digital ohmmeter

Every 50,000 miles (80,000 km) or 60 months (whichever occurs first), the resistance of the wires should be checked with an ohmmeter. Wires with excessive resistance will cause misfiring, and may make the engine difficult to start in damp weather.

To check spark plug wire resistance on vehicles equipped with distributor ignition systems:

1. Disconnect the negative battery cable.
2. Remove the distributor cap from the distributor assembly.
3. Visually inspect the spark plug wires for burns, cuts or breaks in the insulation. Check the spark plug boots and the nipples on the distributor cap and coil. Replace any damaged wiring.
4. Inspect the spark plug wires to insure that they are firmly seated on the distributor cap.
5. Disconnect the spark plug wire(s) thought to be defective at the spark plug.
6. Using an ohmmeter, measure the resistance between the distributor cap terminal and the spark plug terminal.

➡**Make certain that a good connection exists between the distributor cap and the spark plug wire. Never, under any circumstances, measure resistance by puncturing the spark plug wire.**

7. If the measured resistance is less than 7000 ohms per foot (30.5cm) of wire, the wire is good. If the measured resistance is greater than 7000 ohms per foot (30.5cm), the wire is defective and should be replaced.
8. Connect the negative battery cable.

To inspect the spark plug wire resistance on vehicles equipped with distributorless ignition systems:

9. Disconnect the negative battery cable.
10. Remove the spark plug wires from the spark plugs by grasping the spark plug wire boot, then pulling and twisting the boot at the same time. Detach the spark plug wires from the ignition coils in the same manner.
11. Visually inspect the spark plug wires for burns, cuts or breaks in the insulation. Check the spark plug boots and the nipples on the coil unit(s). Replace any damaged wiring.
12. Using an ohmmeter, measure the resistance between both ends of the plug wire.

➡**Never, under any circumstances, measure resistance by puncturing the spark plug wire.**

13. If the measured resistance is less than 7000 ohms per foot (30.5cm) of wire, the wire is good. If the measured resistance is greater than 7000 ohms per foot (30.5cm), the wire is defective and should be replaced.
14. Install the spark plug wires.
15. Connect the negative battery cable.

REMOVAL & INSTALLATION

1. Disconnect the negative (-) battery cable.

➡**To prevent possible incorrect spark plug wire installation, remove and install spark plug wires one at a time. Refer to the engine firing order diagrams in Section 2, if any confusion arises.**

2. If equipped, remove the spark plug wires from the wire brackets.
3. Grasp the spark plug wire by the boot, then twist the boot back and forth several times to free it from the plug. Pull the boot from the spark plug.

✳✳ WARNING

DO NOT tug on the wire to remove it.

4. Remove the other end of the spark plug wire from the distributor or ignition coil units, depending on which ignition system the vehicle has.

To install:
5. Before reconnecting the spark plug wire, lubricate the entire inside surface of the boot with dielectric compound.
6. When installing a new set of spark plug wires, make sure the boot is installed firmly over the spark plug and distributor cap tower, or ignition coil tower.
7. Route the wire exactly the same way as the original and fasten the wire loom clips securely when done.

Distributor Cap and Rotor

INSPECTION

Remove the distributor cap and inspect the inside for flash over, cracking of the carbon button, lack of spring tension on the carbon button, cracking of the cap, and burned, worn terminals. Also check for broken distributer cap towers. If any of these conditions are present, the distributor cap and/or cables should be replaced.

When replacing the distributor cap, transfer cables from the original cap to the new cap one at a time. Ensure each cable is installed into the corresponding tower of the new cap. Fully seat the wires into the towers. If necessary, refer to the appropriate engine firing order diagram.

Light scaling of the terminals can be cleaned with a sharp knife. If the terminals are heavily scaled, replace the distributor cap.

A cap that is greasy, dirty or has a powder-like substance on the inside should be cleaned with a solution of warm water and mild detergent. Scrub the cap with a soft brush. Thoroughly rinse the cap and dry it with a clean, soft cloth.

Replace the rotor with a new one if it is cracked, the tip is excessively burned or heavily scaled. If the spring terminal does not have adequate tension, replace the rotor with a new one.

REMOVAL & INSTALLATION

1. Disconnect the negative battery cable.
2. If necessary for additional clearance, remove the air cleaner assembly.
3. Unplug the engine wiring harness connector from the distributor, or from the distributor wiring connector.
4. Loosen the distributor cap retaining screws or release the distributor hold-down spring clamps, depending on the specific engine being serviced.
5. Label and disconnect the spark plug cables from the distributor cap.
6. Lift the cap off of the distributor.
7. Note in which direction the rotor head is pointing.
8. Depending on the particular engine, it may be necessary to remove a rotor retaining setscrew, then pull the rotor off of the distributor shaft.
9. Remove and discard the distributor cap-to-distributor body gasket or O-ring.

To install:
10. Push the new rotor onto the distributor shaft. Make certain it is pointing in the same direction. If applicable, install the rotor retaining setscrew until snug.
11. Install a new gasket or O-ring onto the distributor housing, making sure that it is seated correctly.
12. Set the distributor cap back onto the distributor.
13. Tighten the distributor cap retaining screws until they are snug, or engage the distributor cap hold-down spring clamps.
14. Connect the spark plug cables back onto the distributor cap. Make sure that they are fully seated on the distributor towers.
15. Attach the engine harness wiring to the distributor, then connect the negative battery cable.
16. Install the air cleaner, if applicable.

Ignition Timing

GENERAL INFORMATION

Ignition timing is the measurement of crankshaft rotation, of the point at which the spark plugs fire in each of the cylinders. It is measured in degrees before or after Top Dead Center (TDC) of the compression stroke.

Because it takes a fraction of a second for the spark plug to ignite the mixture in the cylinder, the spark plug must fire a little before the piston reaches TDC. Otherwise, the mixture will not be completely ignited as the piston passes TDC and the full power of the explosion will not be used by the engine.

The timing measurement is given in degrees of crankshaft rotation before the piston reaches TDC (BTDC). If the setting for the ignition timing is 5° BTDC, the spark plug must fire 5° before each piston reaches TDC. This only holds true, however, when the engine is at idle speed.

As the engine speed increases, the pistons go faster. The spark plugs have to ignite the fuel even sooner if it is to be completely ignited when the piston reaches TDC. To do this, distributors have various means of advancing the spark timing as the engine speed increases. On some earlier model vehicles, this is accomplished by centrifugal weights within the distributor along with a vacuum diaphragm mounted on the side of the distributor. Later model vehicles are equipped with Electronic Spark Timing (EST) in which no vacuum or mechanical advance is used. Instead, the EST system makes all timing changes electronically based on signals from various sensors.

If the ignition is set too far advanced (BTDC), the ignition and expansion of the fuel in the cylinder will occur too soon and tend to force the piston down while it is still traveling up. This causes engine ping. If the ignition spark is set too far retarded, after TDC (ATDC), the piston will have already passed TDC and have started on its way down when the fuel is ignited. This will cause the piston to be forced down for only a portion of its travel. This will result in poor engine performance and lack of power.

Timing marks consist of a notch on the rim of the crankshaft pulley and a scale of degrees attached to the front of the engine (often on the engine front cover). The notch corresponds to the position of the piston in the number 1 cylinder. A stroboscopic (dynamic) timing light is used, which is hooked into the circuit of the No. 1 cylinder spark plug. Every time the spark plug fires, the timing light flashes. By aiming the timing light at the timing marks while the engine is running, the exact position of the piston within the cylinder can be easily read since the stroboscopic flash makes the mark on the pulley appear to be standing still. Proper timing is indicated when the notch is aligned with the correct number on the scale.

There are three basic types of timing lights available. The first is a simple neon bulb with two wire connections (one for the spark plug and one for the plug wire, connecting the light in series). This type of light is quite dim, and must be held closely to the marks to be seen, but it is quite inexpensive. The second type of light is powered by the car's battery. Two alligator clips connect to the battery terminals, while a third wire connects to the spark plug with an adapter. This type of light is more expensive, but the xenon bulb provides a nice bright flash which can even be seen in sunlight. The third type replaces the battery source with 110 volt house current, but still attaches to the No. 1 spark plug wire in order to determine when the plug is fired. Some timing lights have other functions built into them, such as dwell meters, tachometers, or remote starting switches. These are convenient, in that they reduce the tangle of wires under the hood, but may duplicate the functions of tools you already have.

➡ **Never pierce a spark plug wire in order to attach a timing light or perform tests. The pierced insulation will eventually lead to an electrical arc and related ignition troubles.**

Since your truck has electronic ignition, you should use a timing light with an inductive pickup. This pickup simply clamps onto the No. 1 spark plug wire, eliminating the adapter. It is not susceptible to cross-firing or false triggering, which may occur with a conventional light, due to the greater voltages produced by electronic ignition.

INSPECTION & ADJUSTMENT

➡ **The specific timing values and idle speeds can be found either on the vehicle's Vehicle Emission Control Information (VECI) label or in the Gasoline Engine Tune-up Specification chart, later in this section.**

1.8L and 2.0L Engines

▸ See Figure 89

1. Set the parking brake and block the front wheels.
2. Connect a timing light to the number 1 spark plug wire and connect a tachometer to the ignition coil.

✳✳ WARNING

Make sure that the tachometer and timing light wires are out of the way of any moving engine components, especially the cooling fan.

3. Start the engine and allow it to warm up.
4. Make sure the air conditioner switch is OFF.

✳✳ WARNING

When pointing the timing light at the timing marks, make certain that the timing light and wires are not struck by the cooling fan.

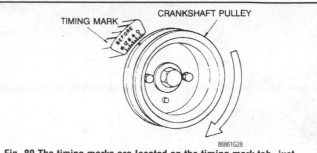

Fig. 89 The timing marks are located on the timing mark tab, just above the crankshaft pulley—1.8L, 2.0L, 2.3L and 2.6L engines

5. While the engine is idling, point the timing light at the crankshaft pulley notched line and timing marks.
6. The timing should be set to the specific values found in the Gasoline Engine Tune-up Specification chart, later in this section.
7. If adjustment is needed, loosen the distributor adjusting bolts and turn the distributor counterclockwise to advance the timing or clockwise to retard the timing.
8. Tighten the distributor adjusting bolts and recheck the timing and idle.

➡ **When tightening the distributor mounting bolt, make sure that the distributor body does not move.**

9. After everything has been rechecked, reconnect the vacuum lines and remove the timing light.

2.3L Carbureted Engines

▸ See Figure 89

➡ **Set the air gap in the distributor before timing the engine; the air gap adjustment procedure is located in Section 2. The timing marks are located near the front crankshaft pulley and consist of a pointer with graduations attached to the engine block and a mark on the crankshaft pulley.**

1. Check and correct the air gap in the distributor. Proper air gap should be 0.012–0.020 in. (0.30–0.50mm).
2. Locate and clean the timing marks on the crankshaft pulley and the front of the engine.
3. Using an inductive pickup timing light, connect it to the No. 1 spark plug wire.
4. If the distributor is equipped with a vacuum advance, disconnect and plug the vacuum line.
5. Make sure all wires from the timing light and tachometer are clear of the fan and belts. Start the engine and allow it to come to normal operating temperature.
6. Adjust the idle to 900 RPM for automatic transmission vehicles or 800 RPM for manual transmission vehicles.
7. Loosen the distributor hold-down nut.
8. Aim the timing light at the timing marks. Rotate the distributor housing until the timing marks are aligned at 6 degrees BTDC.
9. Tighten the distributor hold-down nut and check the timing again.
10. Turn the engine **OFF** and remove the timing light and tachometer. Connect the distributor vacuum line.

2.3L MFI and 2.6L Engines

▸ See Figures 89 and 90

1. Connect a timing light to the No. 1 spark plug wire.
2. Set the parking brake and block the wheels.
3. Start the engine and allow it to warm up to normal operating temperature.
4. Make sure the air conditioner is OFF.
5. Disconnect and plug the evaporative emission canister purge line.
6. Disconnect and plug the exhaust gas recirculation vacuum lines.
7. While the engine idles, point the timing light at the notched line on the crankshaft pulley.
8. Make sure the ignition timing is set at the value shown in the Gasoline Engine Tune-up Specification chart.
9. If adjustment is needed, loosen the distributor mounting bolt and turn the distributor counterclockwise to advance the timing or clockwise to retard the timing.
10. Tighten the distributor mounting bolt and recheck the timing and the idle.

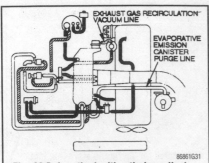

Fig. 90 Before the ignition timing adjustment can be performed, these vacuum hoses must be disconnected and plugged—2.3L MFI and 2.6L engines

Fig. 91 The timing marks are located on the crankshaft pulley and the timing mark tab, attached to the front of the engine block—2.8L and 3.1L engines

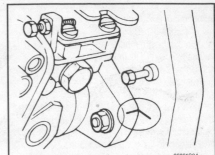

Fig. 92 Before adjusting the injection timing, make certain that the injection pump and mounting bracket are aligned—2.2L diesel engine

➡When tightening the distributor mounting bolt, make sure that the distributor body does not turn with the mounting bolt.

11. After the timing and idle have been rechecked, reconnect the vacuum lines and remove the timing light.

2.8L and 3.1L Engines

♦ **See Figure 91**

1. Warm up the engine to normal operating temperature. Stop the engine and connect the timing light to the No. 1 (left front) spark plug wire. You can also use the No. 6 wire, if it is more convenient.

➡Do not pierce the plug wire insulation on vehicles with High Energy Ignition (HEI); doing so will cause a miss. The best method is an inductive pickup timing light.

2. Clean off the timing marks, then mark the pulley or damper notch and timing scale with white chalk.

3. Disconnect the timing connector which comes out of the harness conduit next to the distributor; this will put the IC system in the bypass mode. Check the underhood emission sticker for any other hoses or wires which may need to be disconnected.

4. Start the engine and adjust the idle speed to that specified on the Vehicle Emission Control Information (VECI) label. If equipped with an automatic transmission, set the specified idle speed while in Park. It will be too high, since it is normally (in most cases) adjusted in Drive. You can disconnect the idle solenoid, if any, to get the speed down. Otherwise, adjust the idle speed screw. This is done to prevent any centrifugal (mechanical) advance.

The tachometer connects to the **TACH** terminal on the distributor and to a ground on models with a carburetor. On models with fuel injection, the tachometer connects to the **TACH** terminal on the ignition coil. Some tachometers must connect to the **TACH** terminal and to the positive battery terminal. Also, some tachometers won't work with HEI.

✳✳ WARNING

Never ground the HEI TACH terminal, otherwise serious system damage will result.

5. Aim the timing light at the pointer marks. Be careful not to touch the fan, because it may appear to be standing still. If the pulley or damper notch isn't aligned with the proper timing mark (see the underhood emissions label), the timing will have to be adjusted.

6. Loosen the distributor base clamp locknut. Turn the distributor slowly to adjust the timing, holding it by the body and not the cap. Turn the distributor in the direction of rotor rotation to retard, and against the direction of rotation to advance.

7. Tighten the locknut. Check the timing again, in case the distributor moved slightly as you tightened it. Readjust if necessary.

8. Reconnect the timing connector. Correct the idle speed if necessary.

9. Stop the engine and disconnect the timing light.

3.2L Engine

Vehicles with the 3.2L engine are equipped with a Distributorless Ignition System (DIS). The ignition timing is controlled by the ECM through the input of engine control system sensors. The ignition timing is set at 5 degrees BTDC for vehicles equipped with manual or automatic transmissions. The ignition timing cannot be adjusted.

Diesel Injection Timing

ADJUSTMENT

♦ **See Figures 92, 93 and 94**

1. Check to see if the notched lines on the injection pump and mounting plate are aligned.

2. Bring the No. 1 piston to Top Dead Center (TDC) on the compression stroke by turning the crankshaft. The correct notch must be used for alignment as the damper pulley is provided with a total of seven notches.

3. Remove the front upper timing belt cover, then check the timing belt for proper tension and alignment of the timing marks.

4. Remove the rocker arm cover and rear camshaft plug, then check that fixing plate J-29761, or equivalent, fits smoothly into the slit at the rear end of the camshaft, then remove the fixing plate.

5. Disconnect the injection pipe from the injection pump and remove the distributor head screw and gasket, then install a static timing gauge. Set the lift about 0.040 in. (1mm) from the plunger.

6. Bring the piston in No. 1 cylinder to a point 45°–60° before TDC by turning the crankshaft, then calibrate the dial indicator to zero.

7. The damper is provided with notched lines as illustrated. The four lines at one side are for static timing and should be used for service purposes. The three lines are for dynamic timing and are used only at the factory.

8. Turn the crankshaft until the line 12° on the damper is brought into alignment with the pointer, then take a reading of the dial indicator. The standard reading is 0.020 in. (0.5mm).

9. If the reading on the dial indicator deviates from the specified range, hold the crankshaft to the "Injection Pump Setting" in the diesel tune-up specifications chart. Loosen the two nuts on the injection pump flange.

10. Move the pump to a point where the dial indicator gives a reading of 0.020 in. (0.5mm). Tighten the flange nuts.

Valve Lash

ADJUSTMENT

1.8L and 2.0L Engines

♦ **See Figure 95**

➡The valves are adjusted with the engine COLD. It is best to allow an engine to sit overnight before beginning a valve adjustment. While all

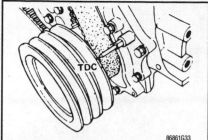

Fig. 93 The crankshaft pulley notch must be aligned with the timing pointer attached to the engine block when the No. 1 piston is at TDC on the power stroke—2.2L diesel engine

Fig. 94 Move the injection pump as shown to retard or advance the injection timing—2.2L diesel engine

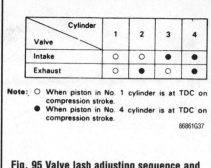

	Cylinder Valve	1	2	3	4
Intake		○	○	●	●
Exhaust		○	●	○	●

Note: ○ When piston in No. 1 cylinder is at TDC on compression stroke.
● When piston in No. 4 cylinder is at TDC on compression stroke.

Fig. 95 Valve lash adjusting sequence and cylinder head valve arrangement—1.8L, 2.0L, 2.3L and 2.6L engines

valve adjustments must be made as accurately as possible, it is better to have the valve adjustment slightly loose rather than slightly tight. A burned valve may result from overly tight valve adjustments.

1. Remove the rocker arm cover and discard the gasket.
2. Make sure both the cylinder head and camshaft retaining bolts are tightened to the proper torque.
3. Rotate the crankshaft pulley until the No. 1 piston is at TDC of the compression stroke.

➡To make sure the piston is on the correct stroke; remove the spark plug and place a finger over the hole. Feel for air being forced out of the spark plug hole. Both valves on No. 1 cylinder will be closed. Stop turning the crankshaft when the TDC timing mark on the crankshaft pulley is directly aligned with the timing mark pointer.

4. With the No. 1 piston at TDC of the compression stroke, adjust the clearances according to the "Valve Adjusting Sequence" illustrations in this section.
5. Adjust the clearance by loosening the locknut and turning the adjusting screw. Retighten the locknut when the proper thickness feeler gauge passes between the camshaft and valve stem, and has a slight drag when the clearance is corrected.
6. Rotate the crankshaft 1 complete revolution (360°) to position the No. 4 piston at TDC of its compression stroke and adjust the clearances as shown in the illustration.
7. After adjustment, use a new gasket and sealant to install the rocker arm cover.

2.2L Diesel Engine

◆ See Figure 96

1. Disconnect the negative battery cable.
2. Remove the rocker arm cover.
3. Rotate the crankshaft until No. 1 piston is at TDC of the compression stroke (firing position). To determine if the No. 1 cylinder is on the compression stroke, place fingers on the No. 1 cylinder's valves as the mark on the damper comes near the timing mark pointer. If the rocker arms are not moving, the engine is in the No. 1 firing position. If the rocker arms are moving, turn the crankshaft one complete revolution until the timing marks align again.
4. With the engine in the No. 1 firing position, adjust the following valves to 0.016 in. (0.40mm) on a cold engine:
   a. Cylinder No. 1: Intake and Exhaust
   b. Cylinder No. 2: Intake
   c. Cylinder No. 3: Exhaust
5. As before, rotate the crankshaft until No. 4-cylinder is at TDC of the compression stroke (firing position). To determine if the No. 4 piston is on the compression stroke, place fingers on the No. 4-cylinder's valves as the mark on the damper comes near the timing mark pointer. If the rocker arms are not moving, the engine is in the No. 4 firing position. If the rocker arms are moving, turn the crankshaft one complete turn until the timing marks align again.
6. With the engine in the No. 4 firing position, adjust the following valves to 0.016 in. (0.40mm) on a cold engine:
   a. Cylinder No. 2: Exhaust
   b. Cylinder No. 3: Intake
   c. Cylinder No. 4: Intake and Exhaust

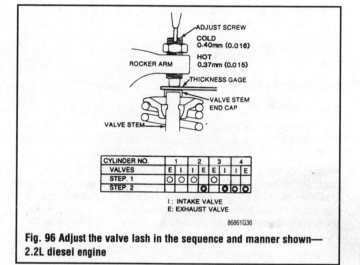

CYLINDER NO.	1		2		3		4	
VALVES	E	I	I	E	E	I	I	E
STEP. 1	○	○	○		○			
STEP. 2				○		○	○	○

I: INTAKE VALVE
E: EXHAUST VALVE

Fig. 96 Adjust the valve lash in the sequence and manner shown—2.2L diesel engine

7. Make sure the rocker arm cover gasket surface is clean and free of nicks, scratches or damage. Using a new gasket, install the rocker arm cover. Tighten the hold-down bolts to 12–17 ft. lbs. (16–23 Nm).
8. Connect the negative battery cable.

2.3L and 2.6L Engines

◆ See Figures 95 and 97

➡The valves are adjusted with the engine COLD. It is best to allow an engine to sit overnight before beginning a valve adjustment. While all valve adjustments must be made as accurately as possible, it is better to have the valve adjustment slightly loose rather than slightly tight. A burned valve may result from overly tight valve adjustments.

1. Remove the rocker arm cover and discard the gasket.
2. Rotate the crankshaft pulley until the No. 1 piston is at TDC of the compression stroke.

➡To make sure the piston is on the correct stroke, remove the spark plug and place your finger over the hole. Feel for air being forced out of the spark plug hole. Both valves on No. 1 cylinder will be closed. Stop turning the crankshaft when the TDC timing mark on the crankshaft pulley is directly aligned with the timing mark pointer.

3. With the No. 1 piston at TDC of the compression stroke, adjust the clearances of the following valves: Intake 1 and 2; Exhaust 1 and 3.
4. Adjust the clearance by loosening the locknut and turning the adjusting screw. Retighten the locknut when the proper thickness feeler gauge passes between the rocker arm and valve stem, and has a slight drag when the clearance is corrected. Clearance is 0.006 in. (0.15mm) for intake and 0.010 (0.25mm) for exhaust.
5. Rotate the crankshaft 1 complete revolution (360 degrees) to position the No. 4 piston at TDC of its compression stroke and adjust the clearances of the following valves: Intake 3 and 4; Exhaust 2 and 4.

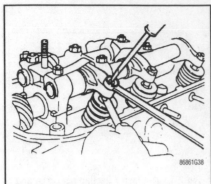

Fig. 97 Adjust the valve lash as shown—2.3L and 2.6L engines

Fig. 98 Tighten the rocker arm pivot bolt and twist the pushrod with your fingers; once the pushrod becomes slightly more difficult to turn, tighten the bolt an additional one-half of a turn—2.8L and 3.1L engines

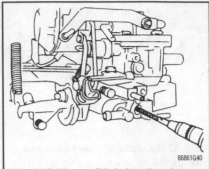

Fig. 99 Drill a small hole into the mixture screw cover, then pull it out with a small screw—carbureted engines

6. After each valve is adjusted, tighten its locknut to 10 ft. lbs. (13 Nm).

7. After adjustment, install the rocker arm cover using a new gasket and sealant.

8. Retighten the crankshaft pulley if it was loosened during the valve adjustment.

2.8L and 3.1L Engines

▶ See Figure 98

1. Remove the valve covers.
2. Rotate the crankshaft until the No. 1 piston is at TDC of its compression stroke.

➡**When the notch on the damper pulley is aligned with the 0 timing mark and the rocker arms of the No. 1 cylinder do not move, the engine is at the TDC of the compression stroke of the No. 1 cylinder. If the rocker arms move as the timing mark approaches the "0" mark, rotate the crankshaft one full revolution until the timing mark aligns with "0" again.**

3. The cylinders in the engine are arranged from the front of the cylinder head to the back, as follows:
   - Right-hand cylinder head—Cylinder No. 1, No. 3 and No. 5
   - Left-hand cylinder head—Cylinder No. 2, No. 4 and No. 6
4. The engine's valves are arranged from the front of the cylinder head to the back, as follows:
   - Right-hand cylinder head—Exhaust, intake, exhaust, intake, intake, exhaust
   - Left-hand cylinder head—Exhaust, intake, intake, exhaust, intake, exhaust
5. With the engine at TDC of the No. 1 cylinder, adjust the following valves: Exhaust 1, 2 and 3; Intake: 1, 5 and 6
6. Back out the adjusting nut until lash is felt.
7. Tighten the adjusting nut until the lash is removed, then tighten the nut an additional 1½ turns to center the lifter plunger.
8. Rotate the engine 1 complete revolution and reposition the notch on the damper pulley with the **0** mark on the timing tab; this is the No. 4-cylinder firing position.
9. With the engine at TDC of the No. 4-cylinder, adjust the following valves: Exhaust 4, 5 and 6; Intake 2, 3 and 4
10. Back out the adjusting nut until lash is felt.
11. Tighten the adjusting nut until the lash is removed, plus, turn the nut 1½ additional turns to center the lifter plunger.
12. Using new gaskets and sealant, install the rocker arm covers.

3.2L Engines

Isuzu 3.2L SOHC and DOHC engines are equipped with hydraulic lash adjusters. No valve adjustments are necessary.

Idle Speed and Mixture Adjustment

AIR/FUEL MIXTURE

1.8L, 2.0L, 2.3L and 2.6L Carbureted Engines

▶ See Figure 99

EXCEPT CALIFORNIA ENGINES

1. Set the parking brake and block the front wheels.
2. Remove the carburetor.
3. Remove the plug for the idle mixture screw. The plug can be removed by drilling a hole and inserting a screw to pull out the plug.
4. Reinstall the carburetor assembly.
5. Connect a tachometer to the engine according to the manufacturer's instructions.

➡**Make the idle speed adjustment with the engine at normal operating temperature.**

6. Make sure that the air cleaner is installed and that the choke valve is open.
7. Disconnect and plug the EGR valve, canister purge line, idle compensator line, and distributor vacuum lines.
8. Adjust the idle speed to 800 rpm.
9. Turn the idle mixture screw all the way in and then back out 3 turns.
10. Adjust the setting of the idle mixture screw to achieve the maximum speed.
11. Reset the throttle screw to 850 rpm.
12. Turn the idle mixture screw clockwise until the engine speed is down to 800 rpm.
13. Insert a new plug for the idle mixture screw.
14. Remove the tachometer and unblock the wheels.

CALIFORNIA ENGINES

1. Firmly set the parking brake and block the drive wheels.
2. Place the transmission in Neutral.
3. Remove the carburetor assembly.
4. Using a drill, drill a hole through the sealing plug covering the idle mixture screw and pry the plug from the carburetor.
5. Reinstall the carburetor.
6. Connect a tachometer according to the manufacturer's instructions.
7. Operate the engine until it reaches normal operating temperatures. Be sure the choke is fully open and the air cleaner is installed. If equipped, turn the air conditioning OFF.
8. Disconnect and plug the distributor vacuum, the canister purge and EGR vacuum lines. Shut off the vacuum to the idle compensator by bending the rubber hose.
9. Connect a dwell meter (4-cylinder scale) or duty meter to the duty monitor lead.

10. Turn the idle mixture screw all the way in and back out 1½ turns.

11. Turn the throttle adjusting screw until the engine speed is 950 rpm (1986–87) or 900 rpm (1988–90). Also refer to the Gasoline Engine Tune-up Specification chart in this section.

12. Adjust the idle mixture screw to achieve an average dwell of 36° or duty of 40 percent.

➡ **The dwell or duty reading specified is the average of the most constant variation.**

13. Reset the throttle adjusting screw until the engine speed is 850–950 rpm.

14. Reinstall a mixture adjustment plug.

15. Remove the tachometer and unblock the wheels.

2.3L MFI, 2.6L MFI, 2.8L, 3.1L and 3.2L Engines

The air/fuel mixture is computer controlled according to the needs of the engine and is not adjustable. If the air/fuel mixture is too lean or too rich, other problems with the engine and/or engine control system exist.

IDLE SPEED

1.8L, 2.0L, 2.3L and 2.6L Carbureted Engines

▶ **See Figures 100 and 101**

1. Set the parking brake and block the wheels.
2. Place the transmission in neutral.
3. Let the engine warm up to normal operating temperature.
4. Make sure that the choke is fully open and the air cleaner is installed.
5. Connect a tachometer to the engine according to the manufacturer's instructions.

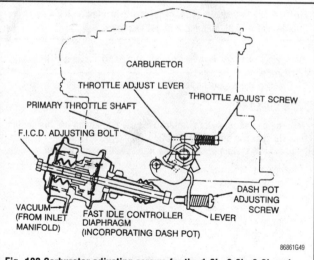

Fig. 100 Carburetor adjusting screws for the 1.8L, 2.0L, 2.3L and 2.6L carbureted engines

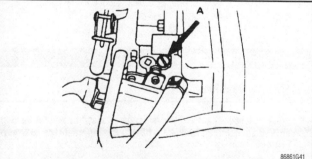

Fig. 101 Idle speed adjusting screw (A) location on the carburetor— 1.8L, 2.0L, 2.3L and 2.6L engines

6. Make sure that the air conditioner is OFF.
7. Disconnect and plug the distributor vacuum, the canister purge, and EGR vacuum lines.
8. Shut off the vacuum to the idle compensator by bending the hose.
9. Turn the throttle adjusting screw to adjust the idle speed to the specific value shown on the VECI label on the vehicle, or in the Gasoline Engine Tune-up Specification chart, later in this section.
10. If the vehicle is equipped with an air conditioner, turn it ON and set the blower to the highest position.
11. Use the FICD adjusting screw (refer to accompanying illustration) at the tip of the carburetor throttle lever to set the fast idle to the specified value.
12. Remove the tachometer and unblock the wheels.

2.2L Diesel Engine

▶ **See Figures 102, 103 and 104**

IDLE SPEED ADJUSTMENT

1. Set the parking brake and block the drive wheels.
2. With the transmission in Neutral, start the vehicle and warm to normal operating temperature. Make sure the air conditioner is turned off.
3. Connect a tachometer in accordance with the manufacturer's instructions.
4. The proper idle speed is between 700–800 rpm on manual transmission equipped vehicles, and between 800–900 rpm on automatic transmissions.
5. If the idle speed deviates from the proper range, loosen the idle adjusting screw locknut, and turn the screw in or out until the idle speed is correct. Remove the tachometer and unblock the wheels.

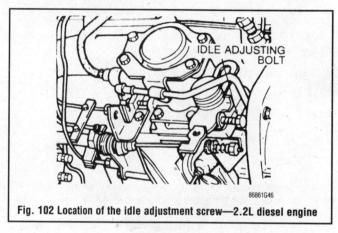

Fig. 102 Location of the idle adjustment screw—2.2L diesel engine

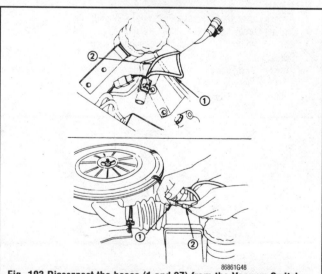

Fig. 103 Disconnect the hoses (1 and 2Z) from the Vacuum Switching Valve (VSV), then insert a small piece of tubing between the two hoses to connect them together—2.2L diesel engine

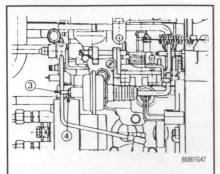

Fig. 104 The location of the fast idle adjusting bolt (3) and nut (4)—2.2L diesel engine

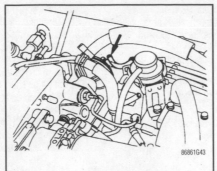

Fig. 105 Before adjusting the idle speed, make sure to detach the EGR vacuum hose . . .

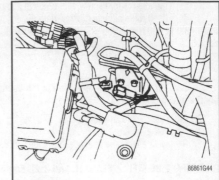

Fig. 106 . . . as well as the pressure regulator VSV connector and the . . .

FAST IDLE SPEED ADJUSTMENT

1. Start the vehicle and warm to normal operating temperature.
2. Connect a tachometer in accordance with the manufacturer's instructions.
3. Disconnect the hoses from the Vacuum Switching Valve (VSV), then connect a 4mm diameter pipe in position between the hoses.
4. Loosen the adjusting nut, and adjust the fast idle speed to 900–950 rpm.
5. Tighten the adjusting nut, and remove the tachometer.

3.1L and 3.2L Engines

The idle speed is controlled by the Idle Air Control (IAC) motor which, is also controlled by the Powertrain Control Module (PCM) or Electronic Control Module (ECM). Since the PCM/ECM regulates the idle speed under all conditions, the idle speed is not adjustable.

2.3L MFI, 2.6L MFI and 2.8L Engines

1988–95 MODELS

▶ See Figures 105, 106, 107 and 108

1. Apply the parking brake.
2. The idle speed must be adjusted with the engine running under the following conditions;
  - Engine at normal operating temperature
  - Throttle valve closed and the throttle valve switch idle contact on
  - Front wheels straight ahead. if equipped with power steering
  - Air conditioner turned off
  - Manual transmission in **NEUTRAL** or automatic transmission in **PARK** or **NEUTRAL**
  - Harness connector for pressure regulator VSV unplugged
  - Canister purge vacuum hose disconnected and plugged
  - EGR vacuum hose disconnected and plugged
3. Connect a tachometer to the engine.
4. If the idle speed does not match the value shown on the VECI label, or in the Gasoline Engine Tune-up Specification chart later in this section, it is incorrect. Turn the adjustment screw on the throttle body to obtain the correct idle speed.

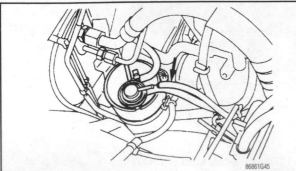

Fig. 107 . . . canister purge vacuum hose—2.3L MFI, 2.6L MFI and 2.8L engines

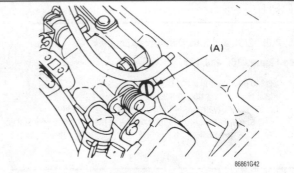

Fig. 108 The idle speed adjusting screw is located on the side of the throttle body—2.3L MFI and 2.6L MFI engines

5. Connect the pressure regulator VSV harness connector and disconnect the tachometer from the engine.
6. Connect the vacuum hoses for the EGR and the charcoal canister.

1996 MODELS

➡The engine control system determines the idle speed for this engine. If the idle speed is out of specification, it may be a symptom of an engine control system problem. The idle speed cannot be adjusted.

1. Apply the parking brake.
2. The idle speed must be inspected with the engine running under the following conditions;
  - Engine at normal operating temperature
  - Throttle valve closed and the throttle valve switch idle contact on
  - Front wheels in the straight ahead position, if equipped with power steering
  - Air conditioner and all electrical accessories turned OFF
  - Manual transmission in **N** or automatic transmission in the **P** or **N** position
3. Connect a tachometer to the engine.
4. If the idle speed does not match that of the VECI label on the vehicle or the Gasoline Engine Tune-up Specification chart later in this section, it is out of adjustment and the engine control system must be inspected.
5. Disconnect the tachometer from the engine.

Air Conditioning System

SYSTEM SERVICE & REPAIR

➡It is recommended that the A/C system be serviced by an EPA Section 609 certified automotive technician utilizing a refrigerant recovery/recycling machine.

The do-it-yourselfer should not service his/her own vehicle's A/C system for many reasons, including legal concerns, personal injury, environmental damage and cost.

DIESEL ENGINE TUNE-UP SPECIFICATIONS

Year	Engine ID/VIN	Engine Displacement cu. in. (cc)	Valve Clearance Intake (in.)	Valve Clearance Exhaust (in.)	Intake Valve Opens (deg.)	Injection Pump Setting (deg.)	Injection Nozzle Pressure (psi) New	Injection Nozzle Pressure (psi) Used	Idle Speed (rpm)	Cranking Compression Pressure (psi)
1985	C223	2.2 (2238)	0.016	0.016	16B	①	1493	NA	②	441
1986	C223	2.2 (2238)	0.016	0.016	16B	①	1493	NA	②	441
	C223T	2.2 (2238)	0.016	0.016	16B	10B	1920	NA	②	441
1987	C223	2.2 (2238)	0.016	0.016	16B	①	1493	NA	②	441
	C223T	2.2 (2238)	0.016	0.016	16B	10B	1920	NA	②	441

NOTE: The Vehicle Emission Control Information label often reflects specification changes made during production. The label figures must be used if they differ from those in this chart.

B – Before Top Dead Center
NA – Not Available
① Federal: 13B
   California: 13B
② Manual transmission: 750
   Automatic transmission: 850

86861C02

GASOLINE ENGINE TUNE-UP SPECIFICATIONS

Year	Engine ID/VIN	Engine Displacement Liters (cc)	Spark Plugs Gap (in.)	Ignition Timing (deg.) MT	Ignition Timing (deg.) AT	Fuel Pump (psi)	Idle Speed (rpm) MT	Idle Speed (rpm) AT	Valve Clearance In.	Valve Clearance Ex.
1981-83	G180Z	1.8 (1816)	0.039-0.043	6B	6B	3.5	①	850-950	0.006	0.010 ③
1984	G200Z	1.9 (1949)	0.041	6B	6B	3.5	①	850-950	0.006 ②	0.010 ③
1985	G200Z	1.9 (1949)	0.041	6B	6B	3.5	①	850-950	0.006 ②	0.010 ③
1986	G200Z	2.0 (1950)	0.040	6B	6B	3.5	①	850-950	0.006	0.010 ③
	4ZD1	2.3 (2254)	0.041	6B	6B	3.5	④	⑤	0.006	0.010
1987	G200Z	2.0 (1950)	0.041	6B	6B	3.5	④	⑤	0.006 ②	0.010 ③
	4ZD1	2.3 (2254)	0.040	6B	6B	3.5	④	900	0.006 ②	0.010
1988	4ZD1	2.3 (2254)	0.040	6B	6B	3.5	350-950	850-950	0.006	0.010
	4ZE1	2.6 (2559)	0.040	12B	12B	35	900	900	0.008	0.008
1989	4ZD1	2.3 (2254)	0.040	6B	6B	3.5	850-950	850-950	0.006	0.008
	4ZE1	2.6 (2559)	0.040	12B	12B	35	860	800	0.008	0.008
	CPC	2.8 (2828)	0.045	10B	10B	9-13	800	800	HYD	HYD
1990	4ZD1	2.3 (2254)	0.040	6B	6B	3.5	850	950	0.006	0.010
	4ZE1	2.6 (2559)	0.040	12B	12B	35	850	950	0.008	0.008
	CPC	2.8 (2828)	0.045	10B	10B	9-13	800	800	⑥	⑥
1991	4ZD1	2.3 (2254)	0.040	6B	6B	3.5	850	950	0.006	0.010
	4ZE1	2.6 (2559)	0.040	12B	12B	35	850	950	0.008	0.008
	CPC	2.8 (2828)	0.045	10B	10B	9-13	800	800	⑥	⑥
1992	4ZD1	2.3 (2254)	0.040	6B	6B	3.5	850	950	0.006	0.010
	4ZE1	2.6 (2559)	0.040	12B	12B	35	850	950	0.008	0.008
	CPC	3.1 (3098)	0.040	10B	10B	9-13	800	800	⑥	⑥
	6VD1	3.2 (3165)	0.040-0.043	5B	5B	41-46	750	750	—	—
1993	4ZD1	2.3 (2254)	0.040	6B	6B	3.5	850	950	0.006	0.010
	4ZE1	2.6 (2559)	0.040	12B	12B	35	850	950	0.008	0.008
	CPC	3.1 (3098)	0.040	10B	10B	9-13	800	800	⑥	⑥
	6VD1	3.2 (3165)	0.040-0.043	5B	5B	41-46	750	750	—	—
1994	4ZD1	2.3 (2254)	0.040	6B	⑦	3.5	850	950	0.006	0.010
	4ZE1	2.6 (2559)	0.040	12B	12B	35	850	950	0.008	0.008
	CPC	3.1 (3098)	0.040	10B	10B	9-13	800	800	⑥	⑥
	6VD1	3.2 (3165)	0.040-0.043	5B	5B	41-46	750	750	—	—
1995	4ZD1	2.3 (2254)	0.040	12B	—	35	850	850	0.006	0.010
	4ZE1	2.6 (2559)	0.040	12B	12B	35	850	950	0.006	0.010
	6VD1	3.2 (3165)	0.040-0.043	5B	5B	41-46	750	750	—	—
1996	4ZE1	2.6 (2559)	0.040	12B ⑨	12B ⑨	35	900 ⑨	900 ⑨	0.006	0.010
	6VD1	3.2 (3165)	0.040	5B ⑨	5B ⑨	41-46	750 ⑨	750 ⑨	—	—

NOTE: The Vehicle Emission Control Information label often reflects specification changes made during production. The label figures must be used if they differ from those in this chart.

NA - Not Available
B - Before Top Dead Center
① Federal models: 750-850; California models: 850-950
② Adjusted cold: 0.008 in.; 0.012 in. if adjusted hot
③ If adjusted cold: 0.012 in. if adjusted hot
④ Federal models: 800; California models: 900

⑤ Federal Pick-up models: 800
   California models: 900
   Trooper models: 900
⑥ Zero lash plus 1 1/4 turns
⑦ Carbureted models: 6B
⑧ Fuel-injected models: 12B
⑧ Carbureted models: 3.5 psi
⑨ Fuel-injected models: 35 psi
⑨ Controlled by the ECM and is not adjustable

86861C05

According to the U.S. Clean Air Act, it is a federal crime to service or repair (involving the refrigerant) a Motor Vehicle Air Conditioning (MVAC) system for money without being EPA certified. It is also illegal to vent R-12 and R-134a refrigerants into the atmosphere. State and/or local laws may be more strict than the federal regulations, so be sure to check with your state and/or local authorities for further information.

➡**Federal law dictates that a fine of up to $25,000 may be levied on people convicted of venting refrigerant into the atmosphere.**

When servicing an A/C system you run the risk of handling or coming in contact with refrigerant, which may result in skin or eye irritation or frostbite. Although low in toxicity (due to chemical stability), inhalation of concentrated refrigerant fumes is dangerous and can result in death; cases of fatal cardiac arrhythmia have been reported in people accidentally subjected to high levels of refrigerant. Some early symptoms include loss of concentration and drowsiness.

➡**Generally, the limit for exposure is lower for R-134a than it is for R-12. Exceptional care must be practiced when handling R-134a.**

Also, some refrigerants can decompose at high temperatures (near gas heaters or open flame), which may result in hydrofluoric acid, hydrochloric acid and phosgene (a fatal nerve gas).

It is usually more economically feasible to have a certified MVAC automotive technician perform A/C system service on your vehicle.

R-12 Refrigerant Conversion

If your vehicle still uses R-12 refrigerant, one way to save A/C system costs down the road is to investigate the possibility of having your system converted to R-134a. The older R-12 systems can be easily converted to R-134a refrigerant by a certified automotive technician by installing a few new components and changing the system oil.

The cost of R-12 is steadily rising and will continue to increase, because it is no longer imported or manufactured in the United States. Therefore, it is often possible to have an R-12 system converted to R-134a and recharged for less than it would cost to just charge the system with R-12.

If you are interested in having your system converted, contact local automotive service stations for more details and information.

PREVENTIVE MAINTENANCE

Although the A/C system should not be serviced by the do-it-yourselfer, preventive maintenance should be practiced to help maintain the efficiency of the vehicle's A/C system. Be sure to perform the following:
* The easiest and most important preventive maintenance for your A/C system is to be sure that it is used on a regular basis. Running the system for five minutes each month (no matter what the season) will help ensure that the seals and all internal components remain lubricated.

➡**Some vehicles automatically operate the A/C system compressor whenever the windshield defroster is activated. Therefore, the A/C system would not need to be operated each month if the defroster was used.**

* In order to prevent heater core freeze-up during A/C operation, it is necessary to maintain proper antifreeze protection. Be sure to properly maintain the engine cooling system.
* Any obstruction of or damage to the condenser configuration will restrict air flow which is essential to its efficient operation. Keep this unit clean and in proper physical shape.

➡**Bug screens which are mounted in front of the condenser (unless they are original equipment) are regarded as obstructions.**

* The condensation drain tube expels any water which accumulates on the bottom of the evaporator housing into the engine compartment. If this tube is obstructed, the air conditioning performance can be restricted and condensation buildup can spill over onto the vehicle's floor.

SYSTEM INSPECTION

Although the A/C system should not be serviced by the do-it-yourselfer, system inspections should be performed to help maintain the efficiency of the vehicle's A/C system. Be sure to perform the following:

The easiest and often most important check for the air conditioning system consists of a visual inspection of the system components. Visually inspect the system for refrigerant leaks, damaged compressor clutch, abnormal compressor drive belt tension and/or condition, plugged evaporator drain tube, blocked condenser fins, disconnected or broken wires, blown fuses, corroded connections and poor insulation.

A refrigerant leak will usually appear as an oily residue at the leakage point in the system. The oily residue soon picks up dust or dirt particles from the surrounding air and appears greasy. Through time, this will build up and appear to be a heavy dirt impregnated grease.

For a thorough visual and operational inspection, check the following:
* Check the surface of the radiator and condenser for dirt, leaves or other material which might block air flow.
* Check for kinks in hoses and lines. Check the system for leaks.
* Make sure the drive belt is properly tensioned. During operation, make sure the belt is free of noise or slippage.
* Make sure the blower motor operates at all appropriate positions, then check for distribution of the air from all outlets.

➡**Remember that in high humidity, air discharged from the vents may not feel as cold as expected, even if the system is working properly. This is because moisture in humid air retains heat more effectively than dry air, thereby making humid air more difficult to cool.**

Windshield Wipers

ELEMENT (REFILL) CARE & REPLACEMENT

▶ See Figures 109, 110 and 111

For maximum effectiveness and longest element life, the windshield and wiper blades should be kept clean. Dirt, tree sap, road tar and so on will cause streaking, smearing and blade deterioration if left on the glass. It is advisable to wash the windshield carefully with a commercial glass cleaner at least once a month. Wipe off the rubber blades with the wet rag afterwards. Do not attempt to move wipers across the windshield by hand; damage to the motor and drive mechanism will result.

To inspect and/or replace the wiper blade elements, place the wiper switch in the **LOW** speed position and the ignition switch in the **ACC** position. When the

Fig. 109 Most aftermarket blades are available with multiple adapters to fit different vehicles

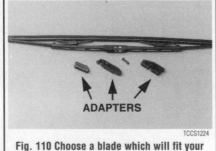

Fig. 110 Choose a blade which will fit your vehicle, and that will be readily available next time you need blades

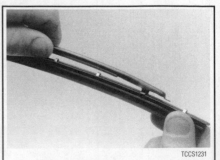

Fig. 111 When installed, be certain the blade is fully inserted into the backing

wiper blades are approximately vertical on the windshield, turn the ignition switch to **OFF**.

Examine the wiper blade elements. If they are found to be cracked, broken or torn, they should be replaced immediately. Replacement intervals will vary with usage, although ozone deterioration usually limits element life to about one year. If the wiper pattern is smeared or streaked, or if the blade chatters across the glass, the elements should be replaced. It is easiest and most sensible to replace the elements in pairs.

If your vehicle is equipped with aftermarket blades, there are several different types of refills and your vehicle might have any kind. Aftermarket blades and arms rarely use the exact same type blade or refill as the original equipment.

Regardless of the type of refill used, be sure to follow the part manufacturer's instructions closely. Make sure that all of the frame jaws are engaged as the refill is pushed into place and locked. If the metal blade holder and frame are allowed to touch the glass during wiper operation, the glass will be scratched.

Tires and Wheels

Common sense and good driving habits will afford maximum tire life. Make sure that you don't overload the vehicle or run with incorrect pressure in the tires. Either of these will increase tread wear. Fast starts, sudden stops and sharp cornering are hard on tires and will shorten their useful life span.

➡**For optimum tire life, keep the tires properly inflated, rotate them often and have the wheel alignment checked periodically.**

Inspect your tires frequently. Be especially careful to watch for bubbles in the tread or sidewall, deep cuts or underinflation. Replace any tires with bubbles in the sidewall. If cuts are so deep that they penetrate to the cords, discard the tire. Any cut in the sidewall of a radial tire renders it unsafe. Also look for uneven tread wear patterns that may indicate the front end is out of alignment or that the tires are out of balance.

TIRE ROTATION

▶ **See Figure 112**

Tires must be rotated periodically to equalize wear patterns that vary with a tire's position on the vehicle. Tires will also wear in an uneven way as the front steering/suspension system wears to the point where the alignment should be reset.

Rotating the tires will ensure maximum life for the tires as a set, so you will not have to discard a tire early due to wear on only part of the tread. Regular rotation is required to equalize wear.

When rotating "unidirectional tires," make sure that they always roll in the same direction. This means that a tire used on the left side of the vehicle must not be switched to the right side and vice-versa. Such tires should only be rotated front-to-rear or rear-to-front, while always remaining on the same side of the vehicle. These tires are marked on the sidewall as to the direction of rotation; observe the marks when reinstalling the tire(s).

Some styled or "mag" wheels may have different offsets front to rear. In these cases, the rear wheels must not be used up front and vice-versa. Furthermore, if these wheels are equipped with unidirectional tires, they cannot be rotated unless the tire is remounted for the proper direction of rotation.

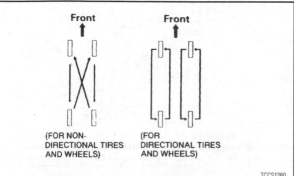

Fig. 112 Compact spare tires must NEVER be used in the rotation pattern

➡**The compact or space-saver spare is strictly for emergency use. It must never be included in the tire rotation or placed on the vehicle for everyday use.**

TIRE DESIGN

▶ **See Figure 113**

For maximum satisfaction, tires should be used in sets of four. Mixing of different brands or types (radial, bias-belted, fiberglass belted) should be avoided. In most cases, the vehicle manufacturer has designated a type of tire on which the vehicle will perform best. Your first choice when replacing tires should be to use the same type of tire that the manufacturer recommends.

When radial tires are used, tire sizes and wheel diameters should be selected to maintain ground clearance and tire load capacity equivalent to the original specified tire. Radial tires should always be used in sets of four.

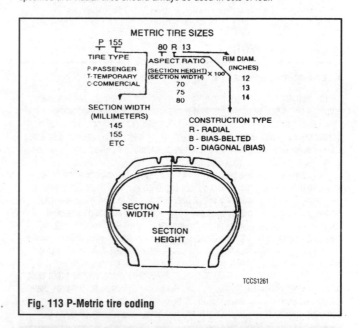

Fig. 113 P-Metric tire coding

> **⚹⚹⚹ CAUTION**
>
> **Radial tires should never be used on only the front axle.**

When selecting tires, pay attention to the original size as marked on the tire. Most tires are described using an industry size code sometimes referred to as P-Metric. This allows the exact identification of the tire specifications, regardless of the manufacturer. If selecting a different tire size or brand, remember to check the installed tire for any sign of interference with the body or suspension while the vehicle is stopping, turning sharply or heavily loaded.

Snow Tires

Good radial tires can produce a big advantage in slippery weather, but in snow, a street radial tire does not have sufficient tread to provide traction and control. The small grooves of a street tire quickly pack with snow and the tire behaves like a billiard ball on a marble floor. The more open, chunky tread of a snow tire will self-clean as the tire turns, providing much better grip on snowy surfaces.

To satisfy municipalities requiring snow tires during weather emergencies, most snow tires carry either an M + S designation after the tire size stamped on the sidewall, or the designation "all-season." In general, no change in tire size is necessary when buying snow tires.

Most manufacturers strongly recommend the use of 4 snow tires on their vehicles for reasons of stability. If snow tires are fitted only to the drive wheels, the opposite end of the vehicle may become very unstable when braking or turning on slippery surfaces. This instability can lead to unpleasant endings if the driver can't counteract the slide in time.

Note that snow tires, whether 2 or 4, will affect vehicle handling in all non-snow situations. The stiffer, heavier snow tires will noticeably change the turning and braking characteristics of the vehicle. Once the snow tires are installed, you must re-learn the behavior of the vehicle and drive accordingly.

➡Consider buying extra wheels on which to mount the snow tires. Once done, the "snow wheels" can be installed and removed as needed. This eliminates the potential damage to tires or wheels from seasonal removal and installation. Even if your vehicle has styled wheels, see if inexpensive steel wheels are available. Although the look of the vehicle will change, the expensive wheels will be protected from salt, curb hits and pothole damage.

TIRE STORAGE

If they are mounted on wheels, store the tires at proper inflation pressure. All tires should be kept in a cool, dry place. If they are stored in the garage or basement, do not let them stand on a concrete floor; set them on strips of wood, a mat or a large stack of newspaper. Keeping them away from direct moisture is of paramount importance. Tires should not be stored upright, but in a flat position.

INFLATION & INSPECTION

♦ See Figures 114 thru 119

The importance of proper tire inflation cannot be overemphasized. A tire employs air as part of its structure. It is designed around the supporting strength of the air at a specified pressure. For this reason, improper inflation drastically reduces the tire's ability to perform as intended. A tire will lose some air in day-to-day use; having to add a few pounds of air periodically is not necessarily a sign of a leaking tire.

Two items should be a permanent fixture in every glove compartment: an accurate tire pressure gauge and a tread depth gauge. Check the tire pressure (including the spare) regularly with a pocket type gauge. Too often, the gauge on the end of the air hose at your corner garage is not accurate because it suffers too much abuse. Always check tire pressure when the tires are cold, as pressure increases with temperature. If you must move the vehicle to check the tire inflation, do not drive more than a mile before checking. A cold tire is generally one that has not been driven for more than three hours.

A plate or sticker is normally provided somewhere in the vehicle (door post, hood, tailgate or trunk lid) which shows the proper pressure for the tires. Never counteract excessive pressure build-up by bleeding off air pressure (letting some air out). This will cause the tire to run hotter and wear quicker.

✳✳ CAUTION

Never exceed the maximum tire pressure embossed on the tire! This is the pressure to be used when the tire is at maximum load-

ing, but it is rarely the correct pressure for everyday driving. Consult the owner's manual or the tire pressure sticker for the correct tire pressure.

Once you've maintained the correct tire pressures for several weeks, you'll be familiar with the vehicle's braking and handling personality. Slight adjust-

Fig. 114 Tires with deep cuts, or cuts which bulge, should be replaced immediately

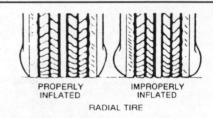

PROPERLY INFLATED — IMPROPERLY INFLATED

RADIAL TIRE

Fig. 115 Radial tires have a characteristic sidewall bulge; don't try to measure pressure by looking at the tire. Use a quality air pressure gauge

CONDITION	RAPID WEAR AT SHOULDERS	RAPID WEAR AT CENTER	CRACKED TREADS	WEAR ON ONE SIDE	FEATHERED EDGE	BALD SPOTS	SCALLOPED WEAR
EFFECT							
CAUSE	UNDER-INFLATION OR LACK OF ROTATION	OVER-INFLATION OR LACK OF ROTATION	UNDER-INFLATION OR EXCESSIVE SPEED*	EXCESSIVE CAMBER	INCORRECT TOE	UNBALANCED WHEEL OR TIRE DEFECT *	LACK OF ROTATION OF TIRES OR WORN OR OUT-OF-ALIGNMENT SUSPENSION.
CORRECTION	ADJUST PRESSURE TO SPECIFICATIONS WHEN TIRES ARE COOL ROTATE TIRES			ADJUST CAMBER TO SPECIFICATIONS	ADJUST TOE-IN TO SPECIFICATIONS	DYNAMIC OR STATIC BALANCE WHEELS	ROTATE TIRES AND INSPECT SUSPENSION

*HAVE TIRE INSPECTED FOR FURTHER USE.

Fig. 116 Common tire wear patterns and causes

ments in tire pressures can fine-tune these characteristics, but never change the cold pressure specification by more than 2 psi. A slightly softer tire pressure will give a softer ride but also yield lower fuel mileage. A slightly harder tire will give crisper dry road handling but can cause skidding on wet surfaces. Unless you're fully attuned to the vehicle, stick to the recommended inflation pressures.

All automotive tires have built-in tread wear indicator bars that show up as ½ in. (13mm) wide smooth bands across the tire when ⅟₁₆ in. (1.5mm) of tread remains. The appearance of tread wear indicators means that the tires should be replaced. In fact, many states have laws prohibiting the use of tires with less than this amount of tread.

You can check your own tread depth with an inexpensive gauge or by using a Lincoln head penny. Slip the Lincoln penny (with Lincoln's head upside-down) into several tread grooves. If you can see the top of Lincoln's head in 2 adjacent grooves, the tire has less than ⅟₁₆ in. (1.5mm) tread left and should be replaced. You can measure snow tires in the same manner by using the "tails" side of the Lincoln penny. If you can see the top of the Lincoln memorial, it's time to replace the snow tire(s).

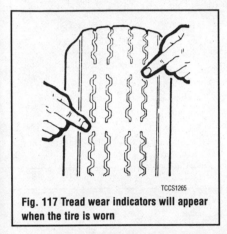

Fig. 117 Tread wear indicators will appear when the tire is worn

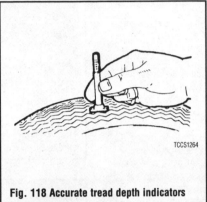

Fig. 118 Accurate tread depth indicators are inexpensive and handy

Fig. 119 A penny works well for a quick check of tread depth

FLUIDS AND LUBRICANTS

Fluid Disposal

Used fluids such as engine oil, transmission fluid, antifreeze and brake fluid are hazardous wastes and must be disposed of properly. Before draining any fluids, consult with your local authorities; in many areas waste oil, etc. is being accepted as a part of recycling programs. A number of service stations and auto parts stores are also accepting waste fluids for recycling.

Be sure of the recycling center's policies before draining any fluids, as many will not accept different fluids that have been mixed together.

Fuel and Engine Oil Recommendations

FUEL

Gasoline Engines

The engine is designed to operate on unleaded gasoline ONLY and is essential for the proper operation of the emission control system. The use of unleaded fuel will reduce spark plug fouling, exhaust system corrosion and engine oil deterioration.

In most parts of the United States, fuel with an octane rating of 87 should be used; in high altitude areas, fuel with an octane rating as low as 85 may be used. However, the high performance engines are recommended to use a fuel with an octane rating of 93 or greater. Using fuels with a lower octane may decrease engine performance, increase emissions and engine wear.

In some areas, fuel consisting of a blend of alcohol may be used; this blend of gasoline and alcohol is known as gasohol. When using gasohol, never use blends exceeding 10% ethanol or 5% methanol.

➡**The use of fuel with excessive amounts of alcohol may jeopardize the new truck warranties.**

Diesel Engines

Fuel manufacturers produce two grades of diesel fuel, No. 1 and No. 2, for use in automotive diesel engines. Generally speaking, No. 2 fuel is recommended over No. 1 for driving in temperatures above 20°F (7°C). In fact, in many areas, No. 2 diesel is the only fuel available. By comparison, No. 2 diesel fuel is less volatile than No. 1 fuel, and gives better fuel economy. No. 2 fuel is also a better injection pump lubricant.

Two important characteristics of diesel fuel are its cetane number and its viscosity.

The cetane number of a diesel fuel refers to the ease with which a diesel fuel ignites. High cetane numbers mean that the fuel will ignite with relative ease so that it ignites well in an engine being cranked at low temperatures. Naturally, the lower the cetane number, the higher the temperature must be to ignite the fuel. Most commercial fuels have cetane numbers that range from 35 to 65. No. 1 diesel fuel generally has a higher cetane rating than No. 2 fuel.

Viscosity is the ability of a liquid, in this case diesel fuel, to flow. Using straight No. 2 diesel fuel below 20°F (7°C) can cause problems, because this fuel tends to become cloudy, meaning wax crystals begin forming in the fuel. 20°F (7°C) is often called the cloud point for No. 2 fuel. In extreme cold weather, No. 2 fuel can stop flowing altogether. In either case, fuel flow is restricted, which can result in a no start condition or poor engine performance. Fuel manufacturers often winterize No. 2 diesel fuel by using various fuel additives and blends (No. 1 diesel fuel, kerosene, etc.) to lower its winter time viscosity. Generally speaking, though, No. 1 diesel fuel is more satisfactory in extremely cold weather.

➡**No. 1 and No. 2 diesel fuels will mix and burn with no ill effects, although the engine manufacturer will undoubtedly recommend one or the other. Consult the owner's manual for information.**

Depending on local climate, most fuel manufacturers make winterized No. 2 fuel available seasonally.

Many automobile manufacturers (Oldsmobile, for example) publish pamphlets giving the locations of diesel fuel stations nationwide. Contact the local dealer for information.

Do not substitute home heating oil for automotive diesel fuel. While basic characteristics of these oils are similar, the heating oil is not capable of meeting diesel cetane ratings. This means that using it might offer not only hard starting but engine knock; even under warm operating conditions. This could result in unnecessary engine wear or damage.

Further, furnace oil is not blended for operation at colder temperatures as most heating oil filters are located indoors. It could easily clog fuel filters with wax.

The equipment used in burning furnace oil does not contain the extremely fine machined surfaces or extremely tiny nozzle openings used in a diesel engine fuel system. Very small amounts of dirt and abrasives that will pass right through a heating oil fuel system could play havoc with your diesel's injection system. Finally, minimum standards regarding sulphur and ash that help keep deposits out of your diesel engine and minimize corrosion may not be met by furnace oil.

One more word on diesel fuels. Don't thin diesel fuel with gasoline. The result is the most highly explosive mixture possible in your fuel tank and unwarranted danger. Fuel thinned with gasoline may not adequately lubricate the injection system, leading to premature pump and nozzle failure and need for an expensive overhaul. Cetane rating will also be effected in an undesirable way.

It's best to buy No. 1 or blended No. 2 fuel for wintertime use. If you must use some means to keep No. 2 fuel from waxing, blend it with No. 1 or use a quality anti-waxing agent.

OIL

When adding oil to the crankcase or changing the oil or filter, it is important that oil of an equal quality to original equipment be used in your vehicle. The use of inferior oils may void the warranty, damage your engine, or both.

The SAE (Society of Automotive Engineers) grade number of oil indicates the viscosity of the oil (its ability to lubricate at a given temperature). The lower the SAE number, the lighter the oil; the lower the viscosity, the easier it is to crank the engine in cold weather but the less the oil will lubricate and protect the engine at high temperatures. This number is marked on every oil container.

Oil viscosities should be chosen from those oils recommended for the lowest anticipated temperatures during the oil change interval. Multigrade oils have been developed because of the need for an oil that embodies both good lubrication at high temperatures and easy cranking in cold weather. All oils are thick at low temperatures and thin out as the temperature rises. Basically, a multigrade oil is thinner at lower temperatures and thicker at high temperatures relative to straight weight oils. For example, a 10W-40 oil (the W stands for weight) exhibits the characteristics of a 10 weight (SAE 10) oil when the vehicle is first started and the oil is cold. Its lighter weight allows it to travel to the lubricating surfaces quicker and offer less resistance to starter motor cranking than, say, a straight 30 weight (SAE 30) oil. But after the engine reaches operating temperature, the 10W-40 oil begins acting like straight 40 weight (SAE 40) oil, its heavier weight providing greater lubrication with less chance of foaming than a straight 30 weight oil would **at that particular temperature**.

➡**Single grade (straight weight) oils such as SAE 30 are more satisfactory than multi-viscosity oils for highway driving in diesel engines.**

Synthetic Oil

There are excellent synthetic and fuel efficient oils available that, under the right circumstances, can help provide better fuel mileage and better engine protection. However, these advantages come at a price, which can be three or four times the price per quart of conventional motor oils.

Before pouring any synthetic oils into your vehicle's engine, you should consider the condition of the engine and the type of driving you do. Also, check the vehicle's warranty conditions regarding the use of synthetics.

Generally, it is best to avoid the use of synthetic oil in both brand new and older, high mileage engines. New engines require a proper break-in, and the synthetics are so slippery that they can prevent this; most manufacturers recommend that you wait at least 5,000 miles before switching to a synthetic oil. Conversely, older engines with worn seals may tend to loose oil; synthetics will slip past worn parts more readily than regular oil, and will be lost faster. If your vehicle already leaks oil (due to worn seals or gaskets), it will probably leak more with a synthetic inside.

Consider your type of driving. If most of your accumulated mileage is on the highway at higher, steadier speeds, a synthetic oil will reduce friction and probably help delivery better fuel mileage. Under such ideal highway conditions, the oil change interval can be extended, as long as the oil filter will operate effectively for the extended life of the oil. If the filter can't do its job for this extended period, dirt and sludge will build up in your engine's crankcase, sump, oil pump and lines, no matter what type of oil is used. If using synthetic oil in this manner, you should continue to change the oil filter at the recommended intervals.

Vehicles used under harder, stop-and-go, short hop circumstances should always be serviced more frequently and for these vehicles synthetic oil may not be a wise investment. Because of the necessary shorter change interval needed for this type of driving, you cannot take advantage of the long recommended change interval of most synthetic oils.

Gasoline Engines

♦ **See Figures 120 and 121**

The API (American Petroleum Institute) designation, also found on the oil container, indicates the classification of engine oil used under certain given

Fig. 120 Look for the API oil identification label when choosing your engine oil

TCCS1235

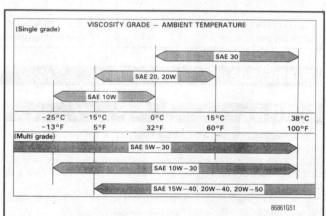

Fig. 121 When filling a gasoline engine with oil, refer to this chart for the proper viscosity rating requirement

86861G51

operating conditions. Only oils designated for use Service **SE, SF, SG, SH** heavy duty detergent or ILSAC **GF-1** should be used in your vehicle. Oils of the SE, SF, SG, SH or GF-1 type perform many functions inside the engine besides their basic function of lubrication. Through a balanced system of metallic detergents and polymeric dispersants, the oil prevents high and low temperature deposits and also keeps sludge and dirt particles in suspension. Acids, particularly sulfuric acid, as well as other by-products of engine combustion are neutralized by the oil. If these acids are allowed to concentrate, they can cause corrosion and rapid wear of the internal engine parts.

✸✸ WARNING

Non-detergent or straight mineral oils should not be used in your engine.

Diesel Engines

♦ **See Figures 120 and 122**

Diesel engines require different engine oil than those used in gasoline engines. Besides doing the things gasoline engine oil does, diesel oil must also deal with increased engine heat and the diesel blow-by gases, which create sulfuric acid, a highly corrosive compound.

Under the American Petroleum Institute (API) classifications, gasoline engine oil codes begin with an **S**, and diesel engine oil codes begin with a **C**. This first letter designation is followed by a second letter code which explains what type of service (heavy, moderate, light) the oil is meant for. For example, the top of a typical oil container will include: **API SERVICES SC, SD, SE, CA, CB, CC**.

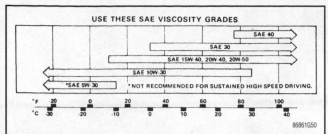

Fig. 122 When filling a diesel engine, refer to this chart for the proper oil rating requirement

This means the oil in the container is a good, moderate duty engine oil when used in a diesel engine.

It should be noted here that the further down the alphabet the second letter of the API classification is, the greater the oil's protective qualities are (CD is the severest duty diesel engine oil, CA is the lightest duty oil, etc.) The same is true for gasoline engine oil classifications (SH is the severest duty gasoline engine oil, SA is the lightest duty oil, etc.).

Many diesel manufacturers recommend an oil with both gasoline and diesel engine API classifications. Consult the owner's manual for specifications.

The top of the oil container will also contain an SAE (Society of Automotive Engineers) designation, which gives the oil's viscosity. A typical designation will be: SAE 10W-30, which indicates that the oil is a winter viscosity oil, meaning it will flow and give protection at low temperatures.

On the diesel engine, oil viscosity is critical, because the diesel is much harder to start (due to its higher compression) than a gasoline engine. Obviously, if you fill the crankcase with a very heavy oil during the winter (SAE 20W-50, for example) the starter is going to require a lot of current from the battery to turn the engine. And, since batteries don't function well in cold weather in the first place, you may find yourself stranded some morning. Consult the owner's manual for recommended oil specifications for the climate you live in.

Engine

OIL LEVEL CHECK

▶ **See Figures 123, 124, 125, 126 and 127**

As often as you stop for fuel, check the engine oil as follows:

1. Park the vehicle on a level surface (if the vehicle is not level, the reading will not be completely accurate).

2. If the vehicle has been running, stop the engine and allow it to sit for a couple of minutes. If the engine is cold, check the oil before starting it. It does not matter whether the oil is hot or cold, as long as it has had time to drain out of the engine itself and into the oil pan.

3. Open the hood and locate the dipstick which will be on either the right or left side of the engine, depending upon your particular engine. Pull the dipstick out and wipe all the oil off the bottom with a clean rag. If this is not done, you will not get an accurate reading of the oil level.

4. Re-insert the dipstick and make sure it goes all the way into the tube. Pull the dipstick out again and, holding it horizontally, read the oil level. The oil should be between the "FULL" and "ADD" marks or dots, or in the checkered area on the dipstick.

 a. If the oil level is above the lower line, although the oil level is high enough, you should still add enough oil to bring the level up to the upper mark. Usually the amount of oil needed to bring the level from the lower mark to the upper mark is one quart (0.946l), however you should fill the oil slowly and check often. It is important not to overfill the engine.

 b. If it is right near or at the lower line, add oil slowly (⅓ or ½ quart) and check the level often. Fill the oil up to the upper mark, but do not over-fill.

 c. If the oil is below the lower line, add ⅓ or ½ qt. (0.32–0.47l) at a time, until the level is at the upper mark. A beginning level below the lower line indicates that either you are not checking the oil level frequently enough or that the engine is using (leaking or burning) too much oil.

➡ **Running the engine with the oil below the lower line may contribute to excessive heat and dirt in the oil, and will leave you with insufficient reserve to allow for normal oil consumption—you could run out on the road. However, you should not add oil to the point where the level is significantly above the upper line. Under these conditions, the rotating crankshaft will cause the oil to foam, which can be damaging to the engine and will sometimes cause valve train noise.**

5. To add oil, unscrew the cap on the valve cover on top of the engine and pour the oil into the engine. Avoid letting any dirt get into the engine, and make sure to reinstall the cap before starting the engine.

➡ **Do not overfill the crankcase. This will cause oil aeration and loss of oil pressure.**

OIL AND FILTER CHANGE

▶ **See Figure 128**

✳✳ CAUTION

The EPA warns that prolonged contact with used engine oil may cause a number of skin disorders, including cancer! You should make every effort to minimize your exposure to used engine oil. Protective gloves should be worn when changing the oil. Wash your hands and any other exposed skin areas as soon as possible after exposure to used engine oil. Soap and water, or waterless hand cleaner, should be used.

➡ **The manufacturer recommends that the oil filter be changed at every other oil change, after the initial change, which can be effective maintenance. Chilton, however, recommends changing the filter with every oil change to ensure longer engine life by lowering the chance of filter clogging and the increased engine wear this would cause. Further, replacing the filter removes a substantial amount of dirty oil whose additives are depleted—an amount that otherwise remains in the system.**

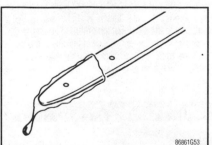

Fig. 123 The oil level should fall between the marked area on the dipstick—late 4-cylinder engines shown (others similar but may use a cross-hatched area or ADD and FULL marks)

Fig. 124 To inspect the oil level, remove the dipstick and . . .

Fig. 125 If the engine requires oil, remove the filler cap—a 3.2L engine shown

Fig. 126 Often the filler cap will have the recommended grade of oil labelled on it—a 2.8L engine shown

Fig. 127 Pour the correct amount of oil through the filler hole—using a funnel helps avoid spills

Fig. 128 Before installing a new oil filter, lightly coat the rubber gasket with clean oil

Always drain the oil after the engine has been running long enough to bring it to operating temperature. It's best to actually drive the vehicle until the temperature gauge reaches normal operating temperature to help ensure the oil will be as warm as possible. Hot oil will flow out of the oil pan more easily and will keep contaminants in suspension so that they will be removed with the oil instead of staying in the pan. You will need a large capacity drain pan—usually about a 6 qt. (6.4 l) capacity is best. Just make sure the capacity of the drain pan is greater than that of the oil pan and filter as shown in the Capacities chart, located at the end of this section. You will also need a strap-type or cap-type wrench to loosen the filter, and an ordinary set of open-end wrenches. You can purchase tools and supplies at any store which sells automotive parts. It is also necessary for you to have some dry rags available to clean up the inevitable spills.

You should also make plans to dispose of the used oil properly. Sometimes a local service station or garage will sell its used oil to a reprocessor. You may be able to add your used oil to his oil drain tank. Also, some local townships or municipalities may have an oil drop-off container for recycling; check with your local authorities.

1. Warm the engine to normal operating temperature.
2. Turn the engine **OFF** and remove the oil filler cap.
3. Support the vehicle securely on jackstands or ramps. If you can work under the vehicle at its normal height, this is okay provided the wheels are chocked.

❋❋ CAUTION

Never crawl under the vehicle while it is only supported by a jack designed for tire changing.

4. Place the drain pan under the oil pan. It should be located where the stream of oil running out of the drain hole will run into the pan—not just directly below the drain hole.
5. Loosen the drain plug using a box wrench or a ratchet, short extension and socket. Turn the plug out slowly by hand, using a rag to shield your fingers from the hot oil. By keeping inward pressure on the plug with your fingers as you unscrew it, oil won't escape past the threads and you can remove it without being burned by hot oil.
6. Quickly withdraw the drain plug and move your hands out of the way, but make sure you keep hold of the plug so that it does not drop into the pan. Wipe the plug with a clean rag. Put it in a safe place—one where it won't get kicked or bumped out of sight. As the oil drains, the stream may shift as the level in the pan changes or as the wind "kicks up." Keep your eye on the stream and shift the pan as needed.

❋❋ CAUTION

Be careful! The oil can be extremely hot and cause painful burns. Use rubber gloves, if handy.

7. Allow the oil to drain completely in the pan, then install and carefully tighten the drain plug. Use a new drain plug washer, if applicable. Be careful not to overtighten the drain plug, otherwise you will be buying a new pan or a replacement plug for stripped threads.
8. Move the pan under the oil filter. Use a strap-type or cap-type wrench to loosen the oil filter. Cover your hand with a rag and spin the filter off by hand;

turn it slowly. Keep in mind that it's holding about one quart (0.946l) of dirty, hot oil. Empty the filter into the drain pan.

➡**If the oil filter cannot be loosened by conventional methods, punch a hole through both sides at the mounting base of the filter, insert a punch and use it to break the oil filter loose. After the oil filter is loosened, remove the oil filter from the engine with an oil filter wrench or by hand.**

9. With a clean rag, wipe off the filter adapter on the engine block. Make sure that no lint from the rag remains on the adapter as it could clog an oil passage. Also make sure the rubber gasket from the old filter did not remain on the adapter.
10. Using your finger, apply a film of new oil to the rubber gasket on the top of the new oil filter. Read the directions on the side of the filter, or on the box it came in, to ascertain how tightly it should be installed. Carefully screw the new filter onto the oil filter mounting pad. If the filter becomes immediately difficult to turn, it is probably crossthreaded. Remove the filter and continue to install it until the filter goes on and turns easily. Once the threads do start, turn the filter gently until it just touches the engine block; it will suddenly get harder to turn at this point.
11. You may want to mark the filter at this point so you will know just how far to turn it. By hand, turn it an additional ½–¾ turn, or as specified by the filter manufacturer. If the filter is turned past this point, the rubber gasket may leak.
12. Wipe the drain plug area on the oil pan and carefully reinstall the drain plug. Just as with the filter, be careful not to crossthread the plug. It will easily turn well past the point where the threads have started if it's not crossthreaded. Tighten the drain plug to 20 ft. lbs. (27 Nm).
13. If raised, lower the vehicle back down to the ground.
14. Pour in oil to the full capacity of the oil pan and filter, as specified in the Capacities chart. Reinstall the filler cap. Remove the dipstick and check the oil level. If the oil level is slightly over the upper mark on the dipstick, this is alright because the new filter has not yet been filled with oil. (After the engine has been run, however, the oil level should have dropped to below the upper mark.)
15. Once the engine has enough oil, start the engine, preferably without touching the throttle, as there will be no oil pressure for 10 seconds or more while the oil pump fills the filter and engine oil passages. Allow the engine to idle at the lowest possible speed until the oil light goes out or the gauge shows that oil pressure has been established. If you do not get oil pressure within 15 to 30 seconds, stop the engine and investigate. Once oil pressure is established, leave the engine running and inspect the filter and oil plug for leaks. If there is slight leakage around the filter, you might want to try to tighten it just a bit more to stop the leaks. Usually, if you've tightened it properly, the only cause of leakage is a defective filter or gasket, which would have to be replaced before you drive the truck.
16. Turn the engine **OFF** and allow the oil to drain into the pan. Recheck the level and add oil as needed.

Manual Transmission

FLUID RECOMMENDATION

♦ See Figure 129

Use engine oil for all of the manual transmissions, except for the Borg-Warner T5R. Make sure to use engine oil of the correct viscosity for these transmissions, as follows:

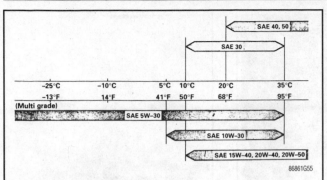

Fig. 129 Before refilling the manual transmission, decide which temperature span will be encountered until the next transmission fluid change—except B-W T5R

- Except 1992–96 Rodeo and Trooper, high temperature—SAE 40
- Except 1992–96 Rodeo and Trooper, normal temperature—SAE 5W-30SF
- 1992–96 Rodeo and Trooper, high temperature—SAE 15W-40, 20W-40 or 20W-50
- 1992–96 Rodeo and Trooper, normal temperature—SAE 5W-30

➡**High temperature refers to areas where ambient temperatures of 90°F (32°C) and higher are regularly encountered.**

The Borg-Warner (B-W) T5R is found on Rodeo models with the V6 engine. The 1991–93 B-W T5R uses DEXRON®II automatic transmission fluid, whereas the 1994–96 B-W transmission uses DEXRON® III automatic transmission fluid.

FLUID LEVEL CHECK

The oil in the manual transmission should be checked every 12 months or 15,000 miles (24,000 km).

1. Allow the engine to reach normal operating temperature. Raise the vehicle and safely support with jackstands, then remove the filler plug from the side of the transmission housing.
2. If lubricant begins to trickle out of the hole, there is enough and you need not go any further. Otherwise, carefully insert your finger (watch out for sharp threads) and check to see if the oil is up to the edge of the hole.
3. If not, add oil through the hole until the level is at the edge of the hole. Most engine oils come in a plastic bottle with a neck, making additions simple. Use a turkey baster if the area does not permit access.
4. Install the filler plug and tighten to 20 ft. lbs. (27 Nm). Lower the vehicle, then run the engine and check for leaks.

DRAIN AND REFILL

▶ **See Figures 130, 131 and 132**

➡**Before draining the fluid from the transmission, drive the vehicle until the engine reaches normal operating temperature. This ensures that the fluid in the transmission is warm, which helps the fluid drain easier and hold the sediment in suspension.**

For all transmissions except for the Borg-Warner T5R, replace the transmission fluid at the first 15,000 miles (24,000 km) and then every 30,000 miles (48,000 km) thereafter. The Borg-Warner T5R transmission does not require periodic changing of the transmission fluid.

1. Raise the vehicle and support safely on jackstands. Place a fluid catch pan under the transmission drain plug.
2. Remove the fill plug from the side of the transmission, then remove the drain plug. Be cautious when removing the drain plug: the transmission fluid can be very hot. Allow the transmission fluid to drain into the pan.
3. Install the drain plug and tighten to 20 ft. lbs. (27 Nm).
4. Refer to the manual transmission fluid recommendations for the proper viscosity of engine oil, or type of transmission fluid to be used for the T5R transmission. Fill the transmission by pouring the new fluid through the fill plug hole in the side of the transmission. Fill until the fluid starts to dribble out of the filler hole. Install the fill plug to 17 ft. lbs. (23 Nm), then lower the vehicle.

Automatic Transmission

FLUID RECOMMENDATIONS

The automatic transmissions used in the 1981–93 Isuzu trucks and sport utility vehicles should be filled with DEXRON® II automatic transmission fluid. The 1994–96 models require DEXRON® III automatic transmission fluid.

➡**Just because the automatic transmission requires DEXRON® II or III transmission fluid, does not mean that the transfer case uses the same fluid. Refer to the transfer case recommendations later in this section.**

LEVEL CHECK

Except 1996 Models

▶ **See Figures 133, 134, 135 and 136**

Check the automatic transmission fluid level at least every 15,000 miles (24,000 km) or 12 months. The dipstick can be found in the rear of the engine compartment.

1. Park the vehicle on a level surface with the engine idling. Shift the transmission into Park and set the parking brake.

➡**If you have driven for a prolonged period of time or in city traffic in hot weather, wait until the fluid cools down, about 30 minutes before checking the fluid level.**

2. Remove the dipstick and carefully touch the wet end of the dipstick, with your finger, to find out if the fluid is cool, warm or hot (if the fluid is hot, allow the vehicle to sit a while longer). Wipe the dipstick clean and then reinsert it firmly. Be sure that it has been pushed all the way in. Remove the dipstick again and check the fluid level while holding it horizontally.
- If the fluid feels cool, about room temperature—the level should be in the COLD range
- If the fluid feels warm, about normal operating temperature of 122–176°F (50–80°C)—the level should be in the HOT range

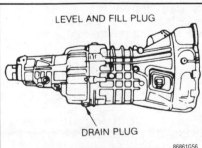

Fig. 130 The location of the drain and fill plugs on the manual transmission—2WD manual transmission, except B-W T5R

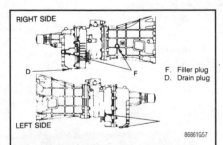

Fig. 131 The location of the drain and fill plug for the transmission and transfer case—4WD manual transmission, except B-W T5R

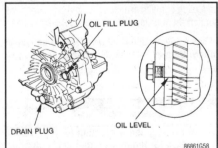

Fig. 132 The location of the drain and fill plugs on the Borg-Warner T5R manual transmission

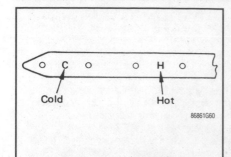

Fig. 133 Depending on the temperature of the transmission fluid, the fluid should fall within the appropriate range on the dipstick—automatic transmissions

Fig. 134 To check the transmission fluid level, remove the dipstick, then . . .

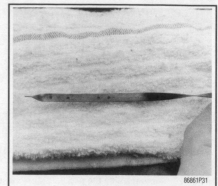

Fig. 135 . . . inspect the level on the dipstick in relation to the markings

➡Overfilling the transmission can cause foaming, loss of fluid, seal damage and overheating, whereas a low fluid level can cause slipping or loss of power. In either case, transmission damage may result.

3. Add just enough of the appropriate DEXRON® II or III transmission fluid through the dipstick tube to fill the transmission to the proper level. Use of a funnel will help prevent automatic transmission fluid spills. Check the fluid level often so that the transmission is not overfilled.

➡The fluid on the dipstick should always be a bright red color. If it is discolored (brown or black), or smells burnt, serious transmission troubles, probably due to overheating, should be suspected. The transmission should be inspected by a qualified technician to locate the cause of the burnt fluid.

4. Install the transmission dipstick and shut the hood.

1996 Models
◗ See Figure 137

The 1996 models equipped with automatic transmissions (Rodeo and Trooper) use a version of the 4L30-E transmission, which is equipped with a fill plug rather than a dipstick.

➡When adding or changing the transmission fluid, use only DEXRON® III. Also, the transmission fluid temperature is very important for this procedure; an accurate, quick thermometer, or a diagnostic read-out box scan tool, is necessary.

1. Do not check the transmission fluid immediately after driving at sustained highway speeds, after heavy city driving in hot weather, or after towing a trailer. If the vehicle has been operated under these conditions, shut the engine off and allow the vehicle to cool down for 30 minutes. After the cool-down period, restart the engine and continue with this procedure.

✳✳ WARNING

Do not overfill the transmission. Overfilling will cause foaming, loss of fluid, abnormal shifting and possible damage to the transmission.

2. Park the vehicle on level ground and apply the parking brake firmly. If the underside of the transmission cannot be reached with the vehicle on the ground, support the vehicle safely on jackstands as level as possible.

➡The transmission fluid level should be checked with the vehicle idling. Be sure that the fluid temperature is below 86°F (30°C).

3. Move the gear selector through all gear ranges.
4. Place the vehicle in Park.

✳✳ WARNING

Do not mistake the drain plug for the overfill plug. Refer to the illustration for the overfill and drain plug locations.

5. Let the engine idle for 3 minutes, then open the overfill plug on the underside of the transmission.

✳✳ WARNING

Do not open the overfill plug with the engine stopped.

6. Add transmission fluid through the overfill plug hole until the fluid starts to trickle out of the plug hole.
7. Let the engine idle until the transmission fluid has reached a temperature between 90°F (32°C) and 135°F (57°C), then install the overfill plug. Tighten the plug to 28 ft. lbs. (38 Nm).

DRAIN, FILTER CHANGE AND REFILL

Except 1996 Models
◗ See Figures 138 thru 144

1. Drive the vehicle until it has reached normal operating temperature. Raise and safely support the vehicle on jackstands. Place an drain pan under the transmission.

➡Some models have a transmission oil pan drain plug; if so, remove the plug and allow the fluid to drain into the catch pan. If not, the oil pan must be removed to drain the fluid.

2. For transmissions equipped with a fluid drain plug, remove the drain plug and allow the fluid to completely empty from the transmission. After all of the fluid is drained, remove the transmission oil pan by removing the mounting bolts and lowering the pan.
3. If there is no drain plug on your transmission oil pan, remove the pan by first loosening all of the pan bolts a few turns. However, do not completely remove the oil pan mounting bolts at this time. Place a large container under the oil pan. Tap one corner of the pan with a soft hammer to break the seal. Once the pan seal is broken loose, support it, remove all the bolts, and then tilt it to one side to drain the fluid.

➡Check the fluid in the drain pan; it should always be a bright red color. It if is discolored (brown or black), or smells burnt, serious transmission problems, probably due to overheating, should be suspected. The transmission should be inspected by a qualified service technician to locate the cause of the burnt fluid.

4. Remove the attaching bolts, then the filter assembly. This is located on the underside of the transmission in the area covered by the transmission pan. Most filters are held in place by five bolts, however the actual number of bolts may be different. Strainers may be cleaned in a safe solvent and air dried. Foam filters must be replaced.

To install:
5. Install the filter or strainer and tighten the bolts alternately (diagonally) to 35–43 inch lbs. (4–5 Nm).
6. If equipped, position the oil pan magnet on the oil pan so that it is placed immediately below the oil screen.
7. Clean all the gasket surfaces thoroughly. Then, position the pan and new gasket in place with bolt holes aligned. Reinstall the bolts, tightening them very gently with your fingers.
8. Tighten the bolts to 120 inch lbs. (10 Nm).
9. If equipped, install the transmission fluid drain plug and tighten to 11–15 ft. lbs. (15–20 Nm).

10. Add the correct type and amount (refer to the Capacities chart at the end of this section) of new transmission fluid through the dipstick tube. Set the parking brake, then start the engine and shift the transmission through the gears while depressing the brake pedal. Fill the transmission to the COLD level and check for leaks. Drive the vehicle and adjust the level to the HOT line once the vehicle reaches normal operating temperature. DO NOT overfill; for more details refer to the transmission fluid level check procedure.

1996 Models

♦ See Figure 137

FLUID DRAIN AND REFILL

➡When adding or changing the transmission fluid, use only DEXRON® III. Also, the transmission fluid temperature is very important for this procedure; an accurate, quick thermometer, or a diagnostic read-out box scan tool, is necessary.

There is no need to change the transmission fluid unless the transmission is used under one or more of the following heavy duty conditions:
  • Repeated short trips
  • Driving on rough roads
  • Driving on dusty roads
  • Towing a trailer
If the vehicle is used under these conditions, change the fluid every 20,000 miles (32,000 km), as follows:
  1. If necessary, raise and support the vehicle safely on jackstands.
  2. Place a large drain pan under the transmission fluid pan.
  3. Remove the transmission oil drain plug and allow the fluid to drain into the catch pan.

Fig. 136 To fill the transmission, a funnel is extremely helpful to avoid messy spills

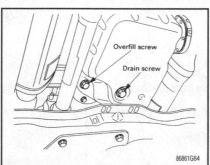

Fig. 137 Make sure to remove the overfill plug, not the drain plug, when checking the transmission fluid—1996 Rodeo and Trooper models with the 4L30-E automatic transmission

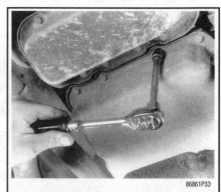

Fig. 138 To drain the transmission fluid, remove all but two bolts, which should be loosened

Fig. 139 As you can see, this procedure can cause a large mess—be prepared

Fig. 140 Once the initial amount of fluid drains, remove the last two bolts and lower the pan

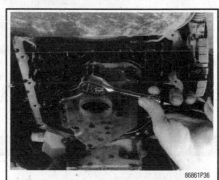

Fig. 141 Once the pan is lowered, the filter can be replaced by removing the mounting bolts . . .

Fig. 142 . . . and pulling the filter off of the transmission

Fig. 143 Before installing the components, clean the pan-to-transmission mounting flange

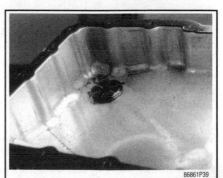

Fig. 144 When cleaning the fluid pan, make sure to remove all metal filings from the pan magnet

4. Once all of the fluid is drained, install the drain plug to 28 ft. lbs. (38 Nm).

5. Remove the transmission overfill plug and fill the transmission through the overfill plug opening. Make sure to use only DEXRON® III Automatic Transmission Fluid (ATF).

→**Add transmission fluid until it flows out the overfill plug opening.**

6. Let the engine idle until a transmission fluid temperature of 90–135°F (32–57°C) is reached, then install the overfill plug to 28 ft. lbs. (38 Nm).

7. Lower the vehicle, if necessary.

8. Properly dispose of the used transmission fluid.

OIL PAN AND FILTER SERVICE

♦ **See Figures 138 thru 144**

The transmission fluid filter only needs to be changed if the vehicle is driven under severe conditions, or if the transmission fluid appears brown or burnt.

1. If necessary for under vehicle access, raise and safely support the vehicle on jackstands.

2. Drain the transmission fluid, as described earlier in this section.

3. Remove the sixteen 10mm bolts, then lower the fluid pan from the transmission. The fluid pan may need to be broken loose from the transmission mounting flange with a rubber mallet or similar tool.

4. Remove the fluid pan magnet and clean all traces of old fluid pan gasket from the transmission and pan flanges.

5. Remove the three 13mm bolts, then separate the oil filter and old gasket from the transmission.

To install:

6. Install the new oil filter to the transmission body with a new gasket. Install the three oil filter-to-transmission body 13mm bolts to 15 ft. lbs. (20 Nm).

7. Position the pan magnet, then install the fluid pan to the transmission case with a new pan gasket.

8. Install the sixteen 10mm fluid pan-to-transmission mounting bolts to 96 inch lbs. (11 Nm) in a crisscross (alternating) manner.

9. Install the drain plug to 28 ft. lbs. (38 Nm).

10. Remove the transmission overfill plug and fill the transmission through the overfill plug opening until the transmission fluid flows out of the overfill plug opening. Make sure to use only DEXRON® III Automatic Transmission Fluid (ATF).

11. Let the engine idle until a transmission fluid temperature of 90–135°F (32–57°C) is reached, then install the overfill plug to 28 ft. lbs. (38 Nm).

12. Lower the vehicle, if necessary.

13. Properly dispose of the used transmission fluid and filter.

Transfer Case

FLUID RECOMMENDATIONS

♦ **See Figure 129**

In the earlier models (1981–90 vehicles), the manual transmission/transfer case is a complete unit and the fluid from the transmission lubricates the transfer case. On newer vehicles, the transfer case and the transmission have separate fluid systems which require separate draining and refilling. Use engine oil to refill the transfer case. Refer to the oil viscosity chart in the manual transmission section.

→**Although automatic transmissions use Automatic Transmission Fluid (ATF), transfer cases utilize the same engine oil as do manual transmissions.**

LEVEL CHECK

1981–90 Manual Transmission/Transfer Cases

Since these transfer cases share the fluid with the transmissions, refer to the manual transmission procedures earlier in this section.

Automatic Transmission and 1991–96 Manual Transmisison Transfer Cases

♦ **See Figure 145**

To check the level of the transfer case fluid, regardless of whether it is attached to an automatic or manual transmission, perform the following:

1. If necessary for access, raise and safely support the vehicle on jackstands as level as possible.

⁂ CAUTION

If the vehicle was just driven, the fluid may be very hot; be careful when checking the fluid with your finger.

86861P40

Fig. 145 The filler plug on the transfer case is located on the upper right-hand side of the assembly

2. Open the fluid fill plug and feel inside the fill plug opening with your finger. The fluid should come to the bottom edge of the hole.

3. If the level is satisfactory, reinstall the plug and tighten it securely.

4. Otherwise, add fluid through the fill plug hole until it begins to run out of the hole. Reinstall the plug securely.

5. Lower the vehicle, if necessary.

DRAIN AND REFILL

1. Raise the vehicle and support safely with jackstands. Place a catch pan under the transfer case.

2. Remove the filler plug from the transfer case.

3. Remove the drain plug at the bottom of the transfer case. Allow all of the fluid to drain into the pan.

4. Install the drain plug to 20 ft. lbs. (27 Nm).

5. Refill the transfer case with the proper amount and type of engine oil. Install the fill plug and torque to 20 ft. lbs. (26 Nm).

Differential (Drive Axle)

FLUID RECOMMENDATION

Use only standard GL-5 hypoid type gear oil in the following viscosities (depending on the ambient temperature):

Front Axle
- All temperatures—SAE 75W-90

Rear Axle
- Ambient temperature usually above 50°F (10°C)—SAE 140W
- Ambient temperature usually below 50°F (10°C)—SAE 80W or SAE 80W/90
- Ambient temperature usually between 0° and 90°F (-18° to 32°C)—SAE 90 or SAE 80W-90

If the vehicle is equipped with the optional limited slip differential rear axle, use GL-5 Limited Slip Differential Gear Lubricant or Friction Modifier Additive (Organic Additive) of the correct viscosity for the existing ambient temperatures (as listed above).

FLUID LEVEL CHECK

▶ **See Figure 146**

With the vehicle parked on a level surface, remove the filler plug from the differential housing. Check to see if the fluid is level with the bottom of the filler hole. If the fluid is at the bottom edge of the filler plug hole, reinstall the plug. Otherwise add axle fluid through the filler plug opening until the fluid starts to trickle out of the filler plug hole.

DRAIN AND REFILL

▶ **See Figures 146 thru 151**

1. Raise and support the vehicle safely on jackstands as level as possible. Place a container under the differential carrier to catch the fluid.
2. Make certain that the filler plug is removable (not rusted closed) by turning it loose. Be sure to do this **before** removing the drain plug. It would be extremely aggravating to drain the differential fluid only to discover that the filler plug required soaking with a penetrant oil overnight.
3. For vehicles with an axle drain plug, perform the following:
   a. Remove the drain plug.
   b. Remove the filler plug, if not already done. By first removing the drain plug, not as much oil will drain initially. This will help prevent any excessive spills while "fine tuning" the location of the catch pan.
   c. Allow the fluid to completely drain.
4. For vehicles without drain plugs, perform the following:
   a. Remove the bolts retaining the cover to the housing.
   b. Pry the cover from the differential housing and allow the fluid to drain

into the catch pan. A suction pump can also be used to remove the fluid through the filler hole, if available.
   c. Clean and inspect the differential cover. With the cover and housing washed free of oil, apply sealer to the mating surfaces.
   d. Using a new gasket, install the cover and tighten the bolts to 30 ft. lbs. (40 Nm).
5. If equipped, install the drain plug.
6. Fill the differential with fluid through the filler plug hole until it starts to trickle out of the opening.
7. Lower the vehicle and inspect for leaks.

Cooling System

▶ **See Figure 152**

❉❉ CAUTION

Never remove the radiator cap under any conditions while the engine is hot! Failure to follow these instructions could result in damage to the cooling system, engine and/or personal injury. To avoid having scalding hot coolant or steam blow out of the radiator, use extreme care whenever you are removing the radiator cap. Wait until the engine has cooled, then wrap a thick cloth around the radiator cap and turn it slowly to the first stop. Step back while the pressure is released from the cooling system. When you are sure the pressure has been released, press down on the radiator cap (with the cloth still in position), turn and remove the radiator cap.

Dealing with the cooling system can be a dangerous matter unless the proper precautions are observed. It is best to check the coolant level in the radiator when the engine is cold. All vehicles covered by this manual should be equipped with a coolant recovery tank. If the coolant level is at or near the MIN line (engine cold) or the MAX line (engine hot), the level is satisfactory. Always

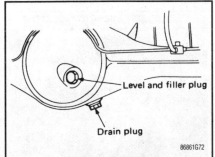

Fig. 146 The fill/level plug and drain plug locations on differentials so equipped—the differential is full if the fluid just trickles out of the fill plug hole

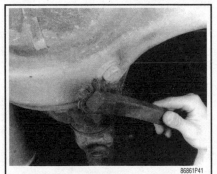

Fig. 147 Before removing the drain or filler plugs from the differentials, clean all loose dirt from the area

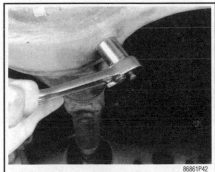

Fig. 148 After making sure the filler plug is not frozen, remove the drain plug and . . .

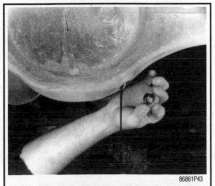

Fig. 149 . . . allow the differential fluid to drain into the catch pan, then . . .

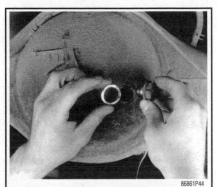

Fig. 150 . . . remove the filler plug and washer

Fig. 151 The location of the filler plug on the front differential is the same as the rear

be certain that the filler caps on both the radiator and the recovery tank are closed tightly.

In the event that the coolant level must be checked when the engine is hot and the vehicle is not equipped with a coolant recovery tank, place a thick rag over the radiator cap and slowly turn the cap counterclockwise until it reaches the first detent. Allow all hot steam to escape. This will allow the pressure in the system to drop gradually, preventing an explosion of hot coolant. When the hissing noise stops, carefully remove the cap the rest of the way.

If the coolant level is found to be low, add a 50/50 mixture of ethylene glycol-based, or ther suitable, antifreeze and clean water. If not equipped with a recovery tank, coolant must be added through the radiator filler neck. On most models, which are equipped with a recovery tank, coolant may be added either through the filler neck on the radiator or directly into the recovery tank.

✳✳ CAUTION

Never add coolant to a hot engine unless it is running. If it is not running, you run the risk of cracking the engine block.

It is wise to pressure check the cooling system at least once per year. If the coolant level is chronically low or rusty, the system should be thoroughly checked for leaks.

At least once every 2 years or 30,000 miles (48,000 km), the engine cooling system should be inspected, flushed and refilled with fresh coolant. If the coolant is left in the system too long, it loses its ability to prevent rust and corrosion. If the coolant has too much water, it won't protect against freezing.

The pressure cap should be examined for signs of age or deterioration. Fan belt and other drive belts should be inspected and adjusted to the proper tension.

Hose clamps should be tightened, and soft or cracked hoses replaced. Damp spots, or accumulations of rust or dye near hoses, water pump or other areas, indicate possible leakage, which must be corrected before filling the system with fresh coolant.

FLUID RECOMMENDATIONS

Whenever adding or changing fluid, use a good quality of ethylene glycol, or other suitable, antifreeze (one that will not affect aluminum), mix it with water until a 50/50 antifreeze solution is attained.

LEVEL CHECK

On most late model vehicles, the fluid level may be checked by observing the fluid level marks of the recovery tank (see-through plastic bottle). The level should be near the MIN mark, as applicable, when the system is cold. At normal operating temperatures, the level should be at the MAX mark or between the MIN and the MAX marks. Only add coolant to the recovery tank as necessary to bring the system up to a proper level.

✳✳ CAUTION

Should it be necessary to remove the radiator cap, make sure that the system has had time to cool, reducing the internal pressure.

On any vehicle that is not equipped with a coolant recovery or overflow tank, the level must be checked by removing the radiator cap. This should only be done when the cooling system has had time to sufficiently cool after the engine has been run. The coolant level should be within ½ in. (13mm) of the base of the radiator filler neck. If necessary, coolant can then be added directly to the radiator.

DRAIN AND REFILL

▸ **See Figures 153 thru 159**

✳✳ CAUTION

To avoid injuries from scalding fluid and steam, DO NOT remove the radiator cap while the engine and radiator are still HOT.

Fig. 152 Cooling systems should be pressure tested for leaks periodically

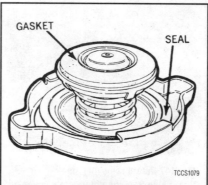

Fig. 153 Be sure the rubber gasket on the radiator cap has a tight seal

Fig. 154 Before draining the coolant, heed any warnings or cautions regarding the cooling system

Fig. 155 To drain the coolant, first remove the radiator cap, then . . .

Fig. 156 . . . remove the drain plug from the radiator and drain the coolant into a catch pan

Fig. 157 Install the drain plug, then fill the radiator with the proper mixture of antifreeze and water

1. Make sure the engine is cool and the vehicle is parked on a level surface, then remove the radiator neck cap and, if equipped, the recovery tank cap in order to relieve system pressure.

2. Position a large drain pan under the vehicle, then drain the existing antifreeze (coolant) by opening the radiator petcock and, if necessary, by removing the engine block drain plug(s). It its also possible to drain the system by disconnecting the lower radiator hose from the bottom radiator outlet.

✳✳ CAUTION

When draining coolant, keep in mind that cats and dogs are attracted by ethylene glycol antifreeze, and are quite likely to drink any that is left in an uncovered container or in puddles on the ground. This will prove fatal in sufficient quantity. Always drain the coolant into a sealable container. Coolant should be reused unless it is contaminated or several years old at which point it should be returned to a coolant recycling or hazardous waste disposal sight. Check your local laws for proper disposal methods.

3. Close the radiator/engine drains or reconnect the lower hose.

4. If necessary, empty the coolant reservoir and flush it. This is most easily done by removing the reservoir tank from the vehicle.

5. Determine the capacity of your coolant system (see capacities specifications). Through the radiator filler neck, add a 50/50 mix of quality antifreeze (ethylene glycol or other suitable formulation) and water to provide the desired protection.

6. Leave the radiator pressure cap off, then start and run the engine until the thermostat heats up and opens; this will allow air to bleed from the system and provide room for additional coolant to be added to the radiator.

7. Add additional coolant to the radiator, as necessary, until the level is within ½ in. (13mm) of the radiator's filler neck base.

8. Stop the engine and check the coolant level.

9. Check the level of protection with an antifreeze tester, then install the radiator pressure cap.

10. If equipped with a coolant recovery/overflow tank, add coolant to the tank, as necessary, to achieve the proper level.

11. Start and run the engine to normal operating temperature, then check the system for leaks.

FLUSHING AND CLEANING THE SYSTEM

♦ See Figure 160

The cooling system should be drained, thoroughly flushed and refilled at least every 30,000 miles (48,000 km) or 24 months. These operations should be done with the engine cold, especially if a backpressure flushing kit is being used. Completely draining, flushing and refilling the cooling system at least every two years will remove accumulated rust, scale and other deposits. Coolant in late model vehicles is typically a 50/50 mixture of ethylene glycol and water for year round use. Use a good quality antifreeze with water pump lubricants, rust inhibitors and other corrosion inhibitors along with acid neutralizers.

There are many products available for cooling system flushing. If a backpressure flushing kit is used, it is recommended that the thermostat be temporarily removed in order to allow free flow to the system with cold water. Always follow the kit or cleaner manufacturer's instructions and make sure the product is compatible with your vehicle.

1. Make sure the engine is cool and the vehicle is parked on a level surface, then remove the radiator neck cap and, if equipped, the recovery tank cap in order to relieve system pressure.

2. Position a large drain pan under the vehicle, then drain the existing coolant by opening the radiator petcock and/or engine drains. It is also possible to drain the system by disconnecting the lower radiator hose, from the bottom radiator outlet.

✳✳ CAUTION

When draining coolant, keep in mind that cats and dogs are attracted by ethylene glycol antifreeze, and are quite likely to drink any that is left in an uncovered container or in puddles on the ground. This will prove fatal in sufficient quantity. Always drain the coolant into a sealable container. Coolant should be reused unless it is contaminated or several years old at which point it should be returned to a coolant recycling or hazardous waste disposal sight. Check your local laws for proper disposal methods.

3. Close the radiator/engine drains or reconnect the lower hose, as applicable, and fill the system with water.

4. Add a can of quality radiator flush.

5. Idle the engine until the upper radiator hose gets hot and the thermostat has opened. This will allow the solution to fully circulate through the system.

6. Drain the system again.

7. Repeat this process until the drained water is clear and free of scale.

8. Close all drains and connect all the hoses.

9. If equipped with a coolant recovery system, flush the reservoir with water and leave empty.

10. Determine the capacity of your coolant system (see capacities specifications). Through the radiator filler neck, add a 50/50 mix of quality antifreeze (ethylene glycol or other suitable formulation) and water to provide the desired protection.

11. Leave the radiator pressure cap off, then start and run the engine until the thermostat heats up and opens; this will allow air to bleed from the system and provide room for additional coolant to be added to the radiator.

12. Add additional coolant to the radiator, as necessary, until the level is within ½ in. (13mm) of the radiator's filler neck base.

13. Stop the engine and check the coolant level.

14. Check the level of protection with an antifreeze tester, then install the radiator pressure cap.

15. If equipped with a coolant recovery/overflow tank, add coolant to the tank, as necessary to achieve the proper level.

16. Start and run the engine to normal operating temperature, then check the system for leaks.

Brake Master Cylinder

FLUID RECOMMENDATION

When adding or replacing the brake fluid, always use DOT-3 brake fluid. Do not allow the brake fluid container or master cylinder reservoir to remain open for long periods of time; brake fluid absorbs moisture from the air, reducing its

Fig. 158 Once the radiator and engine are full, top of the coolant reservoir—Trooper shown

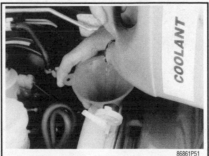

Fig. 159 The coolant reservoir on this Rodeo is more towards the back of the engine compartment

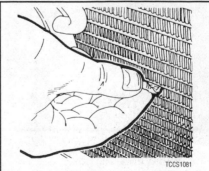

Fig. 160 Periodically remove all debris from the radiator fins

effectiveness and causing corrosion in the lines. Isuzu recommends that silicone brake should not be used in the brake system. Damage to the rubber parts may result.

When making additions of brake fluid, use only fresh, uncontaminated brake fluid which meets or exceeds DOT-3 standards. Be careful not to spill any brake fluid on painted surfaces, as it will quickly eat the paint.

LEVEL CHECK

▶ **See Figures 161, 162 and 163**

➡**Any sudden decrease in the brake system fluid level indicates a possible leak in the system and should be inspected immediately.**

The master cylinder is located in the left rear section of the engine compartment. It should be obvious how important the brake system is to safe operation of your vehicle. The brake fluid is key to the proper operation of the brake system. Low levels of fluid indicate a need for service (there may be a leak in the system or the brake pads may just be worn and in need of replacement). In any case, the brake fluid level should be inspected at least during every oil change, but more often is desirable. Every time you open the hood is a good time to glance at the master cylinder reservoir.

To check the fluid level on most vehicles covered by this manual, you may peer through the sidewall of the reservoir and observe the level in relation to the markings. If the reservoir is opaque, simply unsnap and lift off the reservoir cover, to check the fluid level; it should be within ¼ in. (6mm) of the top of the MAX marks. When making additions of brake fluid, use only fresh, uncontaminated brake fluid which meets or exceeds DOT-3 standards. Be careful not to spill any brake fluid on painted surfaces, as it will quickly eat the paint. Do not allow the brake fluid container or the master cylinder reservoir to remain open any longer than necessary; brake fluid absorbs moisture from the air, reducing its effectiveness and causing corrosion in the lines.

Clutch Master Cylinder

FLUID RECOMMENDATIONS

When adding or replacing the clutch fluid, always use a top quality brake fluid, such as Delco Supreme II or DOT-3. DO NOT allow the clutch fluid container or cylinder reservoir to remain open for long periods of time; brake fluid absorbs moisture from the air, reducing its effectiveness and causing corrosion in the lines. Isuzu recommends that silicone brake should not be used in the clutch system. Damage to the rubber parts may result.

LEVEL CHECK

➡**Any sudden decrease in the clutch system fluid level indicates a possible leak in the system and should be inspected immediately.**

The clutch master cylinder, located in the left rear section of the engine compartment near the brake master cylinder, consists of an aluminum body and a translucent nylon reservoir with minimum and maximum fill indicators. The fluid level of the reservoirs should be kept near the top of the MAX marks.

If fluid must be added, twist the reservoir cap off. (It screws on.) Add the fluid and wipe any dripping fluid from the reservoir or engine component; remember, brake fluid will eat through paint. Screw the cap back on the reservoir until snug.

➡**Be careful not to spill any brake fluid on painted surfaces; it will eat the vehicle's paint.**

Power Steering Pump

FLUID RECOMMENDATION

When filling or replacing the fluid of the power steering pump or reservoir, use Dexron®II (1981–93 models) or II-E (1994–96 models) automatic transmission fluid only. Any other fluid may cause damage to the internal power steering components.

LEVEL CHECK

Vehicles With a Separate Reservoir

▶ **See Figures 164 and 165**

Power steering fluid level should be checked at least once every 12 months or 7,500 miles (12,000 km). To prevent possible overfilling, check the fluid level only when the fluid has warmed to operating temperatures and the wheels are turned straight ahead. If the level is low, fill the pump reservoir until the fluid level reaches "Full" or "Max" in the reservoir. Low fluid level usually produces a moaning sound as the wheels are turned (especially when standing still or parking) and increases steering wheel effort.

Vehicles Without a Separate Reservoir

▶ **See Figure 166**

Power steering fluid level should be checked at least once every 12 months or 7,500 miles (12,000 km). To prevent possible overfilling, check the fluid level only when the fluid has warmed to operating temperatures and the wheels are turned straight ahead.
1. Open the hood.
2. Remove the power steering dipstick from the power steering pump and wipe the steering fluid off of it.
3. Reinsert the dipstick completely in the pump, then remove it again.
4. While holding the dipstick horizontally, read the level of the fluid on the end of the dipstick. Make sure that the fluid level is within the allowable marks on the dipstick.
5. If the fluid level is too low, add fluid until it is at the correct level.
Low fluid level usually produces a moaning sound as the wheels are turned (especially when standing still or parking) and increases steering wheel effort.

Manual Steering Gear

Use chassis grease to lubricate the manual rack and pinion assembly during overhaul.

Fig. 161 The brake fluid level can be read through the translucent master cylinder reservoir

Fig. 162 If, for some reason, the fluid can't be seen through the plastic, remove the lid to check the level

Fig. 163 If necessary, add clean DOT 3 brake fluid until the level is at the MAX level

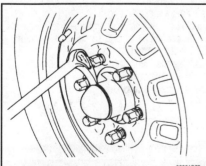

Fig. 164 The power steering fluid level can be seen through the plastic reservoir—a 3.2L engine shown

Fig. 165 If the level is low, fill the reservoir with the proper recommended fluid for your vehicle

Fig. 166 When filling the power steering pump, use a funnel to avoid messy spills—2.8L engine shown

Use SAE 80W-90 GL-5 gear lubricant in the Pick-up manual steering box. Remove the fill plug on the side cover to refill the steering box with lubricant.

Chassis Greasing

All original suspension components have no provision for grease fittings. Some replacement components do have grease fittings. If equipped with fittings, use a pressurized grease gun to inject a small amount of chassis grease about every 15,000 miles (24,000 km). Do not overfill the components, otherwise grease seal damage may occur. Use spray lithium grease to lubricate the stabilizer and strut rod bushings.

Front Wheel Bearings

→This procedure is accurate for 2-wheel drive Isuzu trucks and sport utility vehicles. For the bearings on 4-wheel drive vehicles, refer to Section 7.

Once every 30,000 miles (48,000 km), clean and repack wheel bearings with a high temperature multipurpose grease (NLPI No. 2) grease for the Pick-up, Amigo and Rodeo (the Trooper is only available with 4-wheel drive). It is wise to perform this service more often if the vehicle is subject to heavy use such as towing a trailer. Use only enough grease to completely coat the rollers.

It is important that wheel bearings be properly adjusted after installation. Improperly adjusted wheel bearings can cause steering instability, front-end shimmy and wander, and increased tire wear. Properly adjusted bearings have a slightly loose feeling. Wheel bearings must never be preloaded in service. Preloading will damage the bearings and eventually the spindles. If the bearings are too loose, they should be cleaned, inspected and then adjusted.

Hold the tire at the top and bottom and move the wheel in and out of the spindle. If the movement is greater than 0.005 in. (0.127mm), the bearings are too loose and must be adjusted.

Before handling the bearings, there are a few things that you should remember to do and and few things you should not.

Always remember to DO the following:
- Remove all outside dirt from the housing before exposing the bearing.

- Treat a used bearing as gently as you would a new one.
- Work with clean tools in clean surroundings.
- Use clean, dry canvas gloves, or at least clean, dry hands.
- Clean solvents and flushing fluids are a must.
- Use clean paper when laying out the bearings to dry.
- Protect disassembled bearings from rust and dirt. Cover them up.
- Use clean rags to wipe bearings.
- Keep the bearings in oil-proof paper when they are to be stored or are not in use.
- Clean the inside of the housing before replacing the bearing.

There are also a few things NOT to do:
- Don't work in dirty surroundings.
- Don't use dirty, chipped or damaged tools.
- Try not to work on wooden work benches or use wooden mallets.
- Don't handle bearings with dirty or moist hands.
- Do not use gasoline for cleaning; use a safe solvent.
- Do not spin-dry bearings with compressed air. They will be damaged.
- Do not spin dirty bearings.
- Avoid using cotton waste or dirty cloths to wipe bearings.
- Try not to scratch or nick bearing surfaces.
- Do not allow the bearing to come in contact with dirt or rust at any time.

REMOVAL, REPACKING AND INSTALLATION

Pick-up

♦ See Figures 167 thru 172

⁂ CAUTION

Brake pads may contain asbestos, which has been determined to be a cancer causing agent. Never clean the brake surfaces with compressed air! Avoid inhaling any dust from any brake surface! When cleaning brake surfaces, use a commercially available brake cleaning fluid.

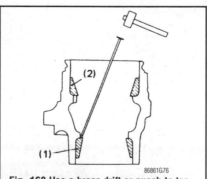

Fig. 167 Use a prytool to remove the dust cover from the hub assembly—take care not to distort it

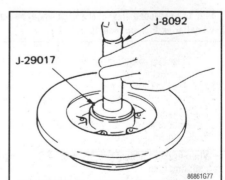

Fig. 168 Use a brass drift or punch to tap out the outer (1) and inner (2) wheel bearing races

Fig. 169 Use the special tools J-29017 and J-8092, or their equivalents, to install the new oil seal—2-wheel drive Pick-up models

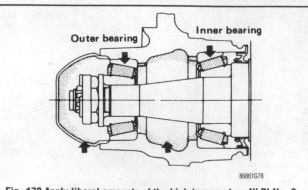

Fig. 170 Apply liberal amounts of the high temperature NLPI No. 2 grease to the shaded areas of the hub and bearings

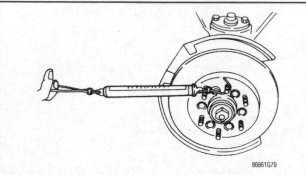

Fig. 171 To properly adjust the bearing preload, the use of a spring scale is essential

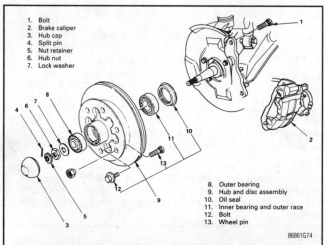

1. Bolt
2. Brake caliper
3. Hub cap
4. Split pin
5. Nut retainer
6. Hub nut
7. Lock washer

8. Outer bearing
9. Hub and disc assembly
10. Oil seal
11. Inner bearing and outer race
12. Bolt
13. Wheel pin

Fig. 172 Exploded view of the front wheel hub and bearings—2-wheel drive Pick-up models

1. Raise and safely support the vehicle. Remove the wheel assembly.
2. Remove the front disc brake caliper, as outlined in Section 9 of this manual. The brake caliper need only be removed from the rotor; suspend it from the vehicle's frame with strong cord or wire and with the hydraulic brake fluid lines attached.
3. Remove the dust cap from the rotor/hub assembly by prying a little at a time, moving around the cap.

➡ When prying the dust cap off of the hub, be careful not to distort the cap sealing face.

4. Remove the cotter pin, nut retainer (if equipped), hub nut, lockwasher and outer roller bearing assembly from the hub. Carefully pull the hub off of the spindle without dragging the inner bearings against the smooth area of the spindle.

5. Using a prytool, pry the inner bearing lip seal out of the inboard side of the hub, then remove the inner bearing assembly with your fingers.
6. Wash all parts in a cleaning solvent and dry with compressed air. Do NOT allow the bearings to spin while drying them with the compressed air.
7. Check the bearings for pitting or scoring. Also check for smooth rotation and lack of noise as follows:
   a. Once the bearings and bearing races, located in the hub assembly, have been cleaned of all old grease and build up, oil the bearings with regular, clean engine oil.
   b. Position each bearing, one at a time, in its respective bearing race. Provide slight inward pressure and turn the bearings.
   c. While pressing in and rotating the bearings, note how they turn in the bearing races. The bearings should turn smoothly and evenly.
   d. If the bearings turn irregularly or make noises while rotating, they must be replaced with new ones. Any time the bearings are replaced, the bearing races should also be replaced.

➡ Special installation tools (J-29016 and J-29015 or equivalents) are necessary to assemble new bearing races into the hub assembly.

8. If necessary, remove the bearing races as follows:
   a. Place the hub assembly on a piece of clean cardboard with the outboard side facing down.
   b. Using a long, brass drift pin or punch, tap the outer bearing race out of the hub assembly. It will be necessary to work the punch around the bearing in a circular motion, otherwise the bearing race can become excessive cocked in the hub bore; this makes removal almost impossible. If this happens, simply tap on the opposite side of the bearing race until it has leveled out in the bore.
   c. After the outer bearing race is removed, flip the hub over and perform the same with the inner bearing race.

To install:
9. If necessary, install the new inner and outer bearing races as follows:
   a. Position the hub assembly with the outboard face down.
   b. Insert the bearing race into the hub bore as level as possible.
   c. Drive the new inner bearing race into the bore with special tool J-29016 and J-8092, or equivalent, until completely seated.
   d. Flip the hub assembly over and drive the outer bearing race into the hub using special tool J-29015 and J-8092, or equivalents.
10. Pressure pack the bearings with high temperature wheel bearing grease. If a bearing packer is not available, pack the bearings with your hands. Make sure that the bearings are completely packed with as much grease as possible; work the grease into the bearings and cage until full.
11. Position the inner bearing in the bearing race.
12. Using special tools J-29017 and J-8092, or equivalents, install the inner oil seal into the hub assembly.
13. Apply grease to the spindle and inside surface of the hub (shaded areas in the illustration).
14. Install the hub assembly on the spindle.
15. Install the outer wheel bearing, lockwasher and adjust the hub nut as follows:
   a. Tighten the hub nut to 22 ft. lbs. (30 Nm).
   b. Turn the hub 2 or 3 times, then loosen the hub nut just enough so that it can be turned with your fingers.
   c. Tighten the nut as much as possible using only your fingers.
   d. Grasp the rotor and wiggle to ensure that there is no bearing free-play. If free-play is evident, tighten it more with your fingers.
   e. Measure the bearing preload by pulling on one of the wheel hub studs with a spring scale. Measure the amount force necessary to rotate the hub. The force required should be 1.8–2.2 lbs. (0.8–1.0 kg).
   f. Tighten the hub nut until the specified bearing preload is obtained.
16. Install a new cotter pin and the dust cap on the hub.
17. Install the brake caliper and support assembly.
18. Install the wheel assembly.

Amigo and Rodeo

♦ See Figures 168, 171, 173, 174 and 175

✳✳ CAUTION

Brake pads may contain asbestos, which has been determined to be a cancer causing agent. Never clean the brake surfaces with com-

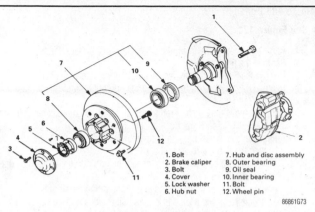

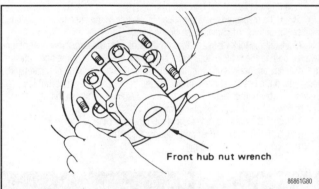

Fig. 173 Exploded view of the front wheel bearings and hub assembly—2-wheel drive Amigo and Rodeo models

1. Bolt	7. Hub and disc assembly
2. Brake caliper	8. Outer bearing
3. Bolt	9. Oil seal
4. Cover	10. Inner bearing
5. Lock washer	11. Bolt
6. Hub nut	12. Wheel pin

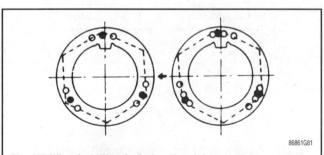

Front hub nut wrench

Fig. 174 The special hub nut wrench is needed to remove the hub nut—2-wheel drive Amigo and Rodeo models

Fig. 175 When installing the lockwasher, it is essential to properly align it with the hub nut—2-wheel drive Amigo and Rodeo models

pressed air! Avoid inhaling any dust from any brake surface! When cleaning brake surfaces, use a commercially available brake cleaning fluid.

1. Raise and safely support the vehicle. Remove the wheel assembly.
2. Remove the front disc brake caliper, as outlined in Section 9 of this manual. The brake caliper need only be removed from the rotor; suspend it from the vehicle's frame with strong cord or wire and with the hydraulic brake fluid lines attached.
3. Remove the 6 hub end cover retaining bolts, then remove the hub end cover.
4. Remove the lockwasher, then remove the hub nut using the front hub nut wrench J-36827, or equivalent. Carefully pull the hub off of the spindle without dragging the bearings against the smooth area of the spindle.
5. Remove the outer bearings with your fingers.
6. Using a prytool, pry the inner bearing lip oil seal out of the inboard side of the hub, then remove the inner bearing assembly with your fingers.

7. Wash all parts in a cleaning solvent and dry with compressed air. Do NOT allow the bearings to spin while drying them with the compressed air.
8. Check the bearings for pitting or scoring. Also check for smooth rotation and lack of noise as follows:
   a. Once the bearings and bearing races, located in the hub assembly, have been cleaned of all old grease and build up, oil the bearings with regular, clean engine oil.
   b. Position each bearing, one at a time, in its respective bearing race. Provide slight inward pressure and turn the bearings.
   c. While pressing in and rotating the bearings, note how they turn in the bearing races. The bearings should turn smoothly and evenly.
   d. If the bearings turn irregularly or make noises while rotating, they must be replaced with new ones. Any time the bearings are replaced, the bearing races should also be replaced.

➡**Special installation tools (J-29016 and J-29015 or equivalents) are necessary to assemble new bearing races into the hub assembly.**

9. Inspect the bearing races for excessive wear or scratching. If any damage is evident, the bearing races and bearings must be replaced.
10. To remove the bearing races, proceed as follows:
   a. Place the hub assembly on a piece of clean cardboard with the outboard side facing down.
   b. Using a long, brass drift pin or punch, tap the outer bearing race out of the hub assembly. It will be necessary to work the punch around the bearing in a circular motion, otherwise the bearing race can become excessive cocked in the hub bore; this makes removal almost impossible. If this happens, simply tap on the opposite side of the bearing race until it has leveled out in the bore.
   c. After the outer bearing race is removed, flip the hub over and perform the same with the inner bearing race.

To install:
11. If necessary, install the new inner and outer bearing races as follows:
   a. Position the hub assembly with the outboard face down.
   b. Insert the bearing race into the hub bore as level as possible.
   c. Drive the new inner bearing race into the bore with special tool J-36829 and J-8092, or equivalent, until completely seated.
   d. Flip the hub assembly over and drive the outer bearing race into the backside of the hub using special tool J-29015 and J-8092, or equivalents.
12. Pressure pack the bearings with high temperature wheel bearing grease (NLGI No. 2). If a bearing packer is not available, pack the bearings with your hands. Make sure that the bearings are completely packed with as much grease as possible; work the grease into the bearings and cage until full.
13. Position the inner bearing in the bearing race.
14. Using special tools J-36830 and J-8092, or equivalents, install the inner oil seal into the hub assembly. Apply the multipurpose grease to the lip of the oil seal.
15. Apply an ample amount of grease to the spindle and inside surface of the hub (shaded areas in the illustration).
16. Install the hub assembly on the spindle.
17. Install the outer wheel bearing, then install the hub nut by turning the place where there is a chamfer in the tapped hole to the outer side and install the nut. Use the special wrench J-36827, or equivalent, to tighten the hub nut.
18. Adjust the front wheel bearing preload as follows:
   a. Tighten the hub nut to 22 ft. lbs. (30 Nm).
   b. Turn the hub 2 or 3 times, then loosen the hub nut just enough so that it can be turned with your fingers.
   c. Tighten the nut as much as possible using only your fingers.
   d. Grasp the rotor and wiggle to ensure that there is no bearing free-play. If free-play is evident, tighten it more with your fingers.
   e. Measure the bearing preload by pulling on one of the wheel hub studs with a spring scale. Measure the amount force necessary to rotate the hub. The force required should be 4.4–5.5 lbs. (2.0–2.5 kg) for new bearings, or 2.6–4.0 lbs. (1.2–1.8 kg) for used bearings.
   f. If the measured bearing preload is outside of the specifications, adjust it by loosening or tightening the bearing nut.
19. Install the lockwasher by turning the side with the larger diameter of the tapered bore to the vehicle outer side, and attach the washer. If the bolt holes in the lockplate are not aligned with the corresponding holes in the nut, reverse the lockplate. If the bolt holes are still out of alignment, turn in the hub nut just enough to obtain alignment. The bolt is to be fastened tightly so that its head will be lower than the surface of the washer.

20. Install the hub end cover and the 6 retaining bolts.
21. Install the brake caliper and support assembly.
22. Install the wheel assembly.

ADJUSTMENT

Pick-up

▶ See Figure 171

1. Raise and safely support the vehicle. Remove the wheel assembly.
2. Remove the dust cap from the rotor/hub assembly by prying a little at a time, moving around the cap.

➡**When prying the dust cap off of the hub, be careful not to distort the cap sealing face.**

3. Remove the cotter pin, nut retainer (if equipped) and loosen the hub nut.
4. Adjust the bearing preload as follows:
    a. Tighten the hub nut to 22 ft. lbs. (30 Nm).
    b. Turn the hub 2 or 3 times, then loosen the hub nut just enough so that it can be turned with your fingers.
    c. Tighten the nut as much as possible using only your fingers.
    d. Grasp the rotor and wiggle to ensure that there is no bearing free-play. If free-play is evident, tighten it more with your fingers.
    e. Measure the bearing preload by pulling on one of the wheel hub studs with a spring scale. Measure the amount force necessary to rotate the hub. The force required should be 1.8–2.2 lbs. (0.8–1.0 kg).
    f. Tighten the hub nut until the specified bearing preload is obtained.
5. Install a new cotter pin and the dust cap on the hub.
6. Install the brake caliper and support assembly.
7. Install the wheel assembly.

Amigo and Rodeo

▶ See Figure 171

1. Raise and support the front of the vehicle safely on jackstands.
2. Remove the front wheels.
3. Remove the 6 hub end cover retaining bolts, then remove the hub end cover.
4. Remove the lockwasher, then loosen the hub nut using the front hub nut wrench J-36827, or equivalent.
5. Carefully move the hub and rotor back and forth to gain clearance from the brake calipers. Make sure that the hub can spin freely.
6. Adjust the front wheel bearing preload as follows:
    a. Tighten the hub nut to 22 ft. lbs. (30 Nm).
    b. Turn the hub 2 or 3 times, then loosen the hub nut just enough so that it can be turned with your fingers.
    c. Tighten the nut as much as possible using only your fingers.
    d. Grasp the rotor and wiggle to ensure that there is no bearing free-play. If free-play is evident, tighten it more with your fingers.
    e. Measure the bearing preload by pulling on one of the wheel hub studs with a spring scale. Measure the amount force necessary to rotate the hub. The force required should be 4.4–5.5 lbs. (2.0–2.5 kg) for new bearings, or 2.6–4.0 lbs. (1.2–1.8 kg) for used bearings.
    f. If the measured bearing preload is outside of the specifications, adjust it by loosening or tightening the bearing nut.
7. Install the lockwasher by turning the side with the larger diameter of the tapered bore to the vehicle outer side, and attach the washer. If the bolt holes in the lockplate are not aligned with the corresponding holes in the nut, reverse the lockplate. If the bolt holes are still out of alignment, turn in the hub nut just enough to obtain alignment. The bolt is to be fastened tightly so that its head will be lower than the surface of the washer.
8. Install the hub end cover and the 6 retaining bolts.
9. Install the brake caliper and support assembly.
10. Install the wheel assembly.

TRAILER TOWING

▶ See Figure 176

General Recommendations

Your vehicle was primarily designed to carry passengers and cargo. It is important to remember that towing a trailer will place additional loads on your vehicle's engine, drive train, steering, braking and other systems. However, if you decide to tow a trailer, using the proper equipment is a must.

Local laws may require specific equipment such as trailer brakes or fender mounted mirrors. Check your local laws.

Information on trailer towing, special equipment and optional equipment is available at your local dealership. You can write to American Isuzu Motors Inc. 2300 Pellissier Place, Whittier, CA 90601–9979

Trailer Weight

The weight of the trailer is the most important factor. A good weight-to-horsepower ratio is about 35:1, 35 lbs. of Gross Combined Weight (GCW) for every horsepower your engine develops. Multiply the engine's rated horsepower by 35 and subtract the weight of the vehicle passengers and luggage. The number remaining is the approximate ideal maximum weight you should tow, although a numerically higher axle ratio can help compensate for heavier weight.

Hitch (Tongue) Weight

Calculate the hitch weight in order to select a proper hitch. The weight of the hitch is usually 9–11% of the trailer gross weight and should be measured with the trailer loaded. Hitches fall into various categories: those that mount on the frame and rear bumper, the bolt-on type, or the weld-on distribution type used for larger trailers. Axle mounted or clamp-on bumper hitches should never be used.

Check the gross weight rating of your trailer. Tongue weight is usually figured as 10% of gross trailer weight. Therefore, a trailer with a maximum gross weight of 2000 lbs. will have a maximum tongue weight of 200 lbs. Class I trailers fall into this category. Class II trailers are those with a gross weight rating of 2000–3000

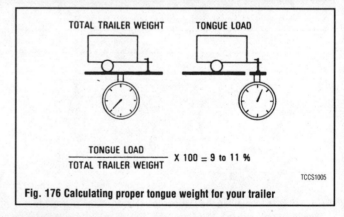

Fig. 176 Calculating proper tongue weight for your trailer

lbs., while Class III trailers fall into the 3500–6000 lbs. category. Class IV trailers are those over 6000 lbs. and are for use with fifth wheel trucks, only.

When you've determined the hitch that you'll need, follow the manufacturer's installation instructions, exactly, especially when it comes to fastener torques. The hitch will subjected to a lot of stress and good hitches come with hardened bolts. Never substitute an inferior bolt for a hardened bolt.

Cooling

ENGINE

Overflow Tank

One of the most common, if not THE most common, problems associated with trailer towing is engine overheating. If you have a cooling system without an expansion tank, you'll definitely need to get an aftermarket expansion tank kit, preferably one with at least a 2 quart capacity. These kits are easily installed on the radiator's overflow hose, and come with a pressure cap designed for expansion tanks.

Flex Fan

Another helpful accessory for vehicles using a belt-driven radiator fan is a flex fan. These fans are large diameter units designed to provide more airflow at low speeds, by using fan blades that have deeply cupped surfaces. The blades then flex, or flatten out, at high speed, when less cooling air is needed. These fans are far lighter in weight than stock fans, requiring less horsepower to drive them. Also, they are far quieter than stock fans. If you do decide to replace your stock fan with a flex fan, note that if your vehicle has a fan clutch, a spacer will be needed between the flex fan and water pump hub.

Oil Cooler

Aftermarket engine oil coolers are helpful for prolonging engine oil life and reducing overall engine temperatures. Both of these factors increase engine life. While not absolutely necessary in towing Class I and some Class II trailers, they are recommended for heavier Class II and all Class III towing. Engine oil cooler systems usually consist of an adapter, screwed on in place of the oil filter, a remote filter mounting and a multi-tube, finned heat exchanger, which is mounted in front of the radiator or air conditioning condenser.

TRANSMISSION

An automatic transmission is usually recommended for trailer towing. Modern automatics have proven reliable and, of course, easy to operate, in trailer towing. The increased load of a trailer, however, causes an increase in the temperature of the automatic transmission fluid. Heat is the worst enemy of an automatic transmission. As the temperature of the fluid increases, the life of the fluid decreases.

It is essential, therefore, that you install an automatic transmission cooler. The cooler, which consists of a multi-tube, finned heat exchanger, is usually installed in front of the radiator or air conditioning compressor, and hooked in-line with the transmission cooler tank inlet line. Follow the cooler manufacturer's installation instructions.

Select a cooler of at least adequate capacity, based upon the combined gross weights of the vehicle and trailer.

Cooler manufacturers recommend that you use an aftermarket cooler in addition to, and not instead of, the present cooling tank in your radiator. If you do want to use it in place of the radiator cooling tank, get a cooler at least two sizes larger than normally necessary.

➡️**A transmission cooler can, sometimes, cause slow or harsh shifting in the transmission during cold weather, until the fluid has a chance to come up to normal operating temperature. Some coolers can be purchased with or retrofitted with a temperature bypass valve which will allow fluid flow through the cooler only when the fluid has reached above a certain operating temperature.**

Handling A Trailer

Towing a trailer with ease and safety requires a certain amount of experience. It's a good idea to learn the feel of a trailer by practicing turning, stopping and backing in an open area such as an empty parking lot.

JUMP STARTING A DEAD BATTERY

◆ **See Figure 177**

Whenever a vehicle is jump started, precautions must be followed in order to prevent the possibility of personal injury. Remember that batteries contain a small amount of explosive hydrogen gas which is a by-product of battery charging. Sparks should always be avoided when working around batteries, especially when attaching jumper cables. To minimize the possibility of accidental sparks, follow the procedure carefully.

❊❊ WARNING

NEVER hook the batteries up in a series circuit or the entire electrical system will go up in smoke, including the starter!

Vehicles equipped with a diesel engine may utilize two 12 volt batteries. If so, the batteries are connected in a parallel circuit (positive terminal to positive terminal, negative terminal to negative terminal). Hooking the batteries up in parallel circuit increases battery cranking power without increasing total battery voltage output. Output remains at 12 volts. On the other hand, hooking two 12 volt batteries up in a series circuit (positive terminal to negative terminal, positive terminal to negative terminal) increases total battery output to 24 volts (12 volts plus 12 volts).

Jump Starting Precautions

- Be sure that both batteries are of the same voltage. Vehicles covered by this manual and most vehicles on the road today utilize a 12 volt charging system.
- Be sure that both batteries are of the same polarity (have the same terminal, in most cases NEGATIVE grounded).
- Be sure that the vehicles are not touching or a short could occur.
- On serviceable batteries, be sure the vent cap holes are not obstructed.
- Do not smoke or allow sparks anywhere near the batteries.
- In cold weather, make sure the battery electrolyte is not frozen. This can occur more readily in a battery that has been in a state of discharge.
- Do not allow electrolyte to contact your skin or clothing.

Jump Starting Procedure

1. Make sure that the voltages of the 2 batteries are the same. Most batteries and charging systems are of the 12 volt variety.

2. Pull the jumping vehicle (with the good battery) into a position so the jumper cables can reach the dead battery and that vehicle's engine. Make sure that the vehicles do NOT touch.

3. Place the transmissions of both vehicles in **Neutral** (M/T) or **P** (A/T), as applicable, then firmly set their parking brakes.

➡️**If necessary for safety reasons, the hazard lights on both vehicles may be operated throughout the entire procedure without significantly increasing the difficulty of jumping the dead battery.**

4. Turn all lights and accessories OFF on both vehicles. Make sure the ignition switches on both vehicles are turned to the **OFF** position.

5. Cover the battery cell caps with a rag, but do not cover the terminals.

6. Make sure the terminals on both batteries are clean and free of corrosion or proper electrical connection will be impeded. If necessary, clean the battery terminals before proceeding.

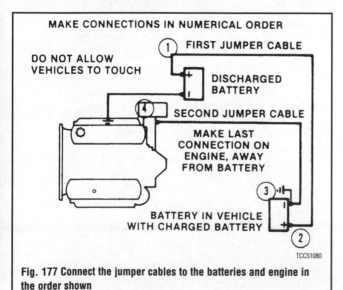

Fig. 177 Connect the jumper cables to the batteries and engine in the order shown

Within the figure:
MAKE CONNECTIONS IN NUMERICAL ORDER
① FIRST JUMPER CABLE
DO NOT ALLOW VEHICLES TO TOUCH
DISCHARGED BATTERY
④ SECOND JUMPER CABLE
MAKE LAST CONNECTION ON ENGINE, AWAY FROM BATTERY
③
② BATTERY IN VEHICLE WITH CHARGED BATTERY
TCCS1080

7. Identify the positive (+) and negative (−) terminals on both batteries.

8. Connect the first jumper cable to the positive (+) terminal of the dead battery, then connect the other end of that cable to the positive (+) terminal of the booster (good) battery.

9. Connect one end of the other jumper cable to the negative (−) terminal on the booster battery and the final cable clamp to an engine bolt head, alternator bracket or other solid, metallic point on the engine with the dead battery. Try to pick a ground on the engine that is positioned away from the battery in order to minimize the possibility of the 2 clamps touching should one loosen during the procedure. DO NOT connect this clamp to the negative (−) terminal of the bad battery.

✳✳ CAUTION

Be very careful to keep the jumper cables away from moving parts (cooling fan, belts, etc.) on both engines.

10. Check to make sure that the cables are routed away from any moving parts, then start the donor vehicle's engine. Run the engine at moderate speed for several minutes to allow the dead battery a chance to receive some initial charge.

11. With the donor vehicle's engine still running slightly above idle, try to start the vehicle with the dead battery. Crank the engine for no more than 10 seconds at a time and let the starter cool for at least 20 seconds between tries. If the vehicle does not start in 3 tries, it is likely that something else is also wrong or that the battery needs additional time to charge.

12. Once the vehicle is started, allow it to run at idle for a few seconds to make sure that it is operating properly.

13. Turn ON the headlights, heater blower and, if equipped, the rear defroster of both vehicles in order to reduce the severity of voltage spikes and subsequent risk of damage to the vehicles' electrical systems when the cables are disconnected. This step is especially important to any vehicle equipped with computer control modules.

14. Carefully disconnect the cables in the reverse order of connection. Start with the negative cable that is attached to the engine ground, then the negative cable on the donor battery. Disconnect the positive cable from the donor battery and finally, disconnect the positive cable from the formerly dead battery. Be careful when disconnecting the cables from the positive terminals not to allow the alligator clips to touch any metal on either vehicle or a short and sparks will occur.

JACKING

General Information

♦ **See Figures 178 thru 186**

Your vehicle was supplied with a jack for emergency road repairs. This jack is fine for changing a flat tire or other short term procedures not requiring you to go beneath the vehicle. If it is used in an emergency situation, carefully follow the instructions provided either with the jack or in your owner's manual. Do not attempt to use the jack on any portions of the vehicle other than specified by the vehicle manufacturer. Always block the diagonally opposite wheel when using a jack.

A more convenient way of jacking is the use of a garage or floor jack. Refer to the various jacking diagrams for the jacking and supporting sections of the Isuzu truck and sport utility vehicles' frames.

Never place the jack under the radiator, engine or transmission components. Severe and expensive damage will result when the jack is raised. Additionally, never jack under the floorpan or bodywork; the metal will deform.

Whenever you plan to work under the vehicle, you must support it on jackstands or ramps. Never use cinder blocks or stacks of wood to support the vehicle, even if you're only going to be under it for a few minutes. Never crawl under the vehicle when it is supported only by the tire-changing jack or other floor jack.

➡ **Always position a block of wood or small rubber pad on top of the jack or jackstand to protect the lifting point's finish when lifting or supporting the vehicle.**

Small hydraulic, screw, or scissors jacks are satisfactory for raising the vehicle. Drive-on trestles or ramps are also a handy and safe way to both raise and support the vehicle. Be careful though, some ramps may be too steep to drive your vehicle onto without scraping the front bottom panels. Never support the vehicle on any suspension member (unless specifically instructed to do so by a repair manual) or by an underbody panel.

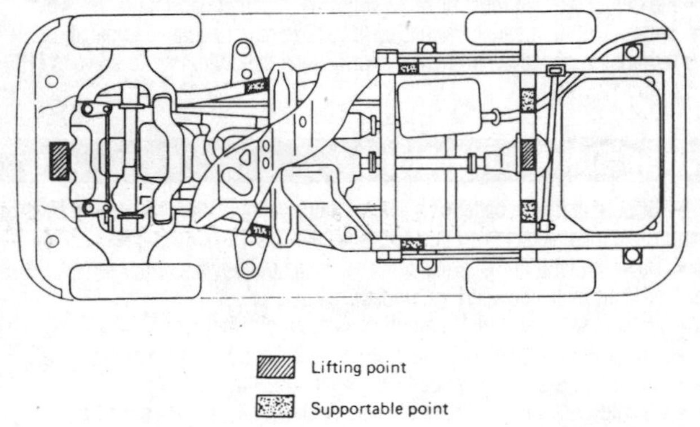

Jacking Precautions

The following safety points cannot be overemphasized:

• Always block the opposite wheel or wheels to keep the vehicle from rolling off the jack.

Lifting point

Supportable point

86861G86

Fig. 178 Make certain to support the vehicle at the points shown in the illustration—Rodeo and Trooper (short wheel base models)

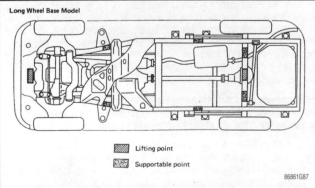

Long Wheel Base Model

Lifting point

Supportable point

86861G87

Fig. 179 Recommended vehicle jacking and support points—Trooper (long wheel base models)

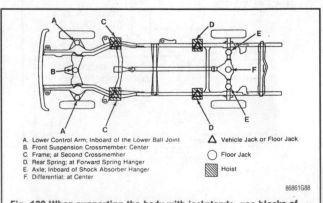

A. Lower Control Arm; Inboard of the Lower Ball Joint
B. Front Suspension Crossmember: Center
C. Frame; at Second Crossmember
D. Rear Spring; at Forward Spring Hanger
E. Axle; Inboard of Shock Absorber Hanger
F. Differential; at Center

△ Vehicle Jack or Floor Jack
○ Floor Jack
▨ Hoist

86861G88

Fig. 180 When supporting the body with jackstands, use blocks of wood to protect the frame—Pick-up models

86861P58

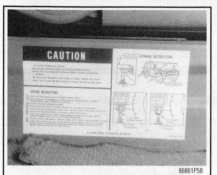

Fig. 181 Often the vehicle is equipped with a label showing the jacking positions and cautions

86861P59

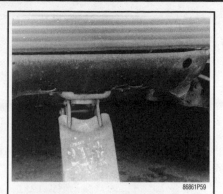

Fig. 182 Use a hydraulic floor jack on the front lower crossmember or . . .

86861P60

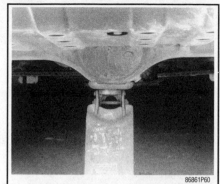

Fig. 183 . . . on the rear differential case to raise or lower the vehicle

86861P61

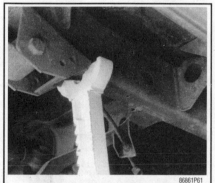

Fig. 184 Jackstands should always be supporting the vehicle by the frame and . . .

86861P62

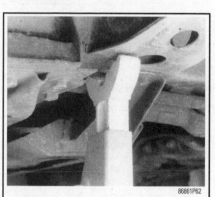

Fig. 185 . . . make sure that they are securely situated and stable

86861P00

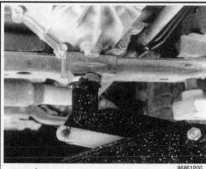

Fig. 186 If instructions call for jacking the engine, transmission or transfer case, use a block of wood

- When raising the front of the vehicle, firmly apply the parking brake.
- When the drive wheels are to remain on the ground, leave the vehicle in gear to help prevent it from rolling.
- Always use jackstands to support the vehicle when you are working underneath. Place the stands beneath the vehicle's jacking brackets. Before climbing underneath, rock the vehicle a bit to make sure it is firmly supported.

MAINTENANCE INTERVALS CHARTS

The maintenance intervals charts are designed to let you know how often to perform certain maintenance procedures to your Isuzu truck or sport utility vehicle. Adhering to these maintenance charts will help ensure that your vehicle performs the best it can for the longest amount of time possible. Vehicles which are maintained very well often last 10, 20 or even 30 years.

***SEVERE DRIVING CONDITIONS**

A: Repeated short trips
B: Driving on rough roads
C: Driving on dusty roads
D: Towing a trailer

ITEM		INTERVAL	A	B	C	D
AUTOMATIC TRANSMISSION FLUID		CHANGE EVERY 20,000 MILES	•	•	•	•
REAR AXLE OIL		CHANGE EVERY 15,000 MILES	•	•	•	•
ENGINE OIL AND FILTER	V6-3.2L	CHANGE EVERY 3,000 MILES OR 3 MONTHS	•	•	•	•
	L4-2.6L	CHANGE EVERY 3,750 MILES	•	•	•	•

86861G90

Fig. 187 Often, certain maintenance procedures must be performed more frequently when the vehicle is driven under severe conditions—make certain to adhere to these intervals

MAINTENANCE SCHEDULE LIST

COMPLETE VEHICLE MAINTENANCE SCHEDULE (MILEAGE ONLY ITEMS)

No.	ITEM	7.5	15	22.5	30	37.5	45	52.5	60	67.5	75	82.5	90	97.5	105	112.5	120	DESCRIPTION
1	*(1) CHANGE FRONT & REAR AXLE OIL																	
2	CHANGE MANUAL TRANSMISSION AND TRANSFER CASE OIL (V6-3.2L only)																	
3	ADJUST ENGINE IDLE SPEED (L4-2.6L engine)								*(3)		*(3)		*(3)		*(3)		*(3)	
4	ADJUST VALVE CLEARANCE (L4-2.6L engine)																	
5	REPLACE AIR CLEANER FILTER																	
6	REPLACE SPARK PLUGS																	
7	CHANGE ENGINE COOLANT																	
8	*(2) REPLACE TIMING BELT																	
9	ROTATE TIRES																	
10	CHANGE POWER STEERING FLUID																	
11	REPACK FRONT WHEEL BEARINGS AND FREE WHEELING HUBS																	
12	CLEAN RADIATOR CORE AND A/C CONDENSER																	
13	CHECK SPARK PLUG WIRE																	

SHADED AREAS INDICATE SERVICE TO BE PERFORMED.

*(1) : Under severe driving conditions, additional maintenance is required.
Refer to "Severe driving conditions".

*(2) : Replacement of the timing belt is recommended at every 60,000 miles (96,000 km).
Failure to replace the timing belt may result in damage to the engine.

*(3) : This service is recommended for vehicles sold in California, and it is required
for vehicles sold in other areas.

COMPLETE VEHICLE MAINTENANCE SCHEDULE (MILEAGE/MONTHS whichever comes first)

No.	ITEM	EVERY MONTHS OR	7.5	15	22.5	30	37.5	45	52.5	60	67.5	75	82.5	90	97.5	105	112.5	120	DESCRIPTION
1	CHECK BATTERY FLUID LEVEL	12																	
2	CHECK ENGINE COOLANT LEVEL	12																	
3	CHECK BRAKE FLUID LEVEL	12																	
4	CHECK CLUTCH FLUID LEVEL	12																	
5	CHECK FOR FLUID LEAKS	12																	
6	*(1) CHANGE ENGINE OIL	12																	
7	*(1) REPLACE ENGINE OIL FILTER	12																	
8	CHECK COOLING AND HEATER HOSES	12																	
9	*(2) CHECK EXHAUST SYSTEM	12																	
10	*(2) CHECK FUEL LINE AND FUEL TANK/CAP	12																	
11	CHECK ENGINE DRIVE BELTS	24																	
12	CHECK TIRES AND WHEELS	12																	
13	ADJUST STEERING GEAR PLAY	24																	
14	CHECK BRAKE LINES AND HOSES	12																	
15	CHECK DRUM AND DISC BRAKES	12																	
16	CHECK PARKING BRAKE	12																	
17	ADJUST BRAKE PEDAL PLAY	12																	
18	LUBE ACCELERATOR LINKAGE	6																	
19	LUBE BODY AND CHASSIS	6																	
20	LUBE FRONT AND REAR PROPELLER SHAFT	6																	
21	CHECK CLUTCH LINES AND HOSES	12																	
22	LUBE CLUTCH PEDAL SPRING, BUSHING AND CLEVIS PIN	6																	
23	CHECK CLUTCH PEDAL FREE PLAY	12																	
24	CHECK PROPELLER SHAFT FLANGE TORQUE	12																	
25	CHECK STARTER SAFETY SWITCH	12																	
26	CHECK THROTTLE LINKAGE	12																	
27	CHECK SUSPENSION AND STEERING	12																	
28	*(1) CHECK AUTOMATIC TRANSMISSION FLUID	12																	
29	CHECK AUTO CRUISE CONTROL LINKAGE AND HOSES	12																	

SHADED AREAS INDICATE SERVICE TO BE PERFORMED

*(1) : Under severe driving conditions, additional maintenance is required.
Refer to "Severe driving conditions".

*(2) : This service is recommended for vehicles sold in California, and it is required
for vehicles sold in other areas.

86861G89

CAPACITIES

Year	Model	Engine ID/VIN	Engine Displacement Liters (cc)	Oil with Filter (qts.)	Engine Transmission (pts.)			Transfer Case (pts.)	Drive Axle		Fuel Tank (gal.)	Cooling System (qts.)
					4-Spd	5-Spd	Auto.		Front (pts.)	Rear (pts.)		
1981–83	Pick-up	G180Z	1.8 (1816)	4.2	2.7	2.7	14	5.2	1.7	1.7	13.0	①
		C223	2.2 (2238)	6.7	2.6	3.3	12.6	2.0	2.1	3.2	21.5	8.5
1984	Pick-up	G200Z	2.0 (1950)	4.1	2.7	2.7	13.3	5.2	1.7	1.7	②	③
		C223	2.2 (2238)	6.7	2.6	3.3	12.6	2.0	2.1	3.2	21.5	8.5
1985	Pick-up	G200Z	2.0 (1950)	4.1	2.6	3.3	—	2.0	2.1	3.2	④	8.5
		C223	2.2 (2238)	6.7	2.6	3.3	12.6	2.0	2.1	3.2	21.5	8.5
	Trooper	G200Z	2.0 (1950)	4.1	2.6	3.3	—	2.0	2.1	3.2	13.2	8.5
1986–87	Pick-up	G200Z	2.0 (1950)	4.1	2.6	3.3	—	2.0	2.1	3.2	④	8.5
		C223	2.2 (2238)	6.7	2.6	3.3	12.6	2.0	2.1	3.2	21.5	⑥
		C223T	2.2 (2238)	6.7	2.6	3.3	12.6	2.0	2.1	3.2	21.5	11.2
		4ZD1	2.3 (2254)	4.1	2.6	3.3	13.4	2.0	2.1	3.2	④	8.5
	Trooper	C223	2.2 (2238)	6.7	—	9.7	—	⑤	2.1	3.2	21.5	11.2
		4ZD1	2.3 (2254)	4.1	—	9.7	—	⑤	2.1	3.2	13.2	8.5
1988	Pick-up	4ZD1	2.3 (2254)	4.2	—	3.2	—	—	—	3.2	⑧	9.5
		4ZE1	2.6 (2559)	5.2	—	6.2	13.8	3.0	3.2	3.8	⑧	9.5
	Trooper	4ZE1	2.6 (2559)	5.2	—	6.2	24	⑦	3.2	3.8	21.9	8.5
1989–90	Amigo	4ZD1	2.3 (2254)	4.2	—	3.2	—	—	—	3.2	21.9	9.5
		4ZE1	2.6 (2559)	5.2	—	6.2	13.8	3.0	3.2	3.8	21.9	9.5
	Pick-up	4ZD1	2.3 (2254)	4.2	—	3.2	—	—	—	3.2	⑧	9.5
		4ZE1	2.6 (2559)	5.2	—	6.2	13.8	3.0	3.2	3.8	⑧	9.5
	Trooper	4ZE1	2.6 (2559)	5.2	—	6.2	24	⑦	3.2	3.8	21.9	8.5
		CPC	2.8 (2828)	4.5	—	6.2	18.6	3,0	3.2	3.8	21.9	10.6
1991	Amigo	4ZD1	2.3 (2254)	4.2	—	3.2	—	—	—	3.2	21.9	9.5
		4ZE1	2.6 (2559)	5.2	—	6.2	13.8	3.0	3.2	3.8	21.9	9.5
	Pick-up	4ZD1	2.3 (2254)	4.2	—	3.2	—	—	—	3.2	⑧	9.5
		4ZE1	2.6 (2559)	5.2	—	6.2	13.8	3.0	3.2	3.8	⑧	9.5
		CPC	3.1 (3098)	4.5	—	6.2	—	3.0	3.2	3.8	21.9	11.4
	Rodeo	4ZE1	2.6 (2559)	5.8	—	6.2	19.0	3.0	3.2	3.9	21.9	9.5
		CPC	3.1 (3098)	4.5	—	4.8	19.0	3.0	3.2	3.9	21.9	11.4
	Trooper	4ZE1	2.6 (2559)	5.2	—	6.2	24.0	⑨	3.2	3.8	21.9	8.5
		CPC	2.8 (2828)	4.5	—	6.2	18.6	3.0	3.2	3.8	21.9	10.6
1992–93	Amigo	4ZD1	2.3 (2254)	4.2	—	3.2	—	—	—	3.2	21.9	9.5
		4ZE1	2.6 (2559)	5.2	—	6.2	13.8	3.0	3.2	3.8	21.9	9.5
	Pick-up	4ZD1	2.3 (2254)	4.2	—	3.2	—	—	—	3.2	⑧	9.5
		4ZE1	2.6 (2559)	5.2	—	6.2	13.8	3.0	3.2	3.8	⑧	9.5
		CPC	3.1 (3098)	4.5	—	6.2	—	3.0	3.2	3.8	21.9	11.4
	Rodeo	4ZE1	2.6 (2559)	5.8	—	⑩	19.0	3.0	3.2	3.9	21.9	9.5
		6VD1	3.2 (3165)	6.2	—	⑩	18.2	3.0	3.2	3.9	21.9	⑪
	Trooper	6VD1	3.2 (3165)	6.3	—	6.2	18.2	3.0	3.2	3.9	22.5	⑫
		6VD1	3.2 (3165)	6.3	—	6.2	18.2	3.0	3.2	3.9	22.5	⑫
1994	Amigo	4ZE1	2.6 (2559)	5.2	—	6.2	13.8	3.0	3.2	3.8	21.9	9.5
	Pick-up	4ZD1	2.3 (2254)	4.2	—	3.2	—	—	—	3.2	⑧	9.5
		4ZE1	2.6 (2559)	5.2	—	6.2	13.8	3.0	3.2	3.2	⑧	9.5
		CPC	3.1 (3098)	4.5	—	6.2	—	3.0	3.2	3.2	21.9	11.4
	Rodeo	4ZE1	2.6 (2559)	5.8	—	⑩	19.0	3.0	3.2	3.9	21.9	9.5
		6VD1	3.2 (3165)	6.2	—	⑩	18.2	3.0	3.2	3.9	21.9	⑪
	Trooper	6VD1	3.2 (3165)	6.3	—	6.2	18.2	3.0	3.2	3.9	22.5	⑫
		6VD1	3.2 (3165)	6.3	—	6.2	18.2	3.0	3.2	3.9	22.5	⑫
1995	Pick-up	4ZD1	2.3 (2254)	3.7	—	3.2	—	—	—	3.2	⑧	9.5
		4ZE1	2.6 (2559)	4.4	—	6.2	—	3.0	3.2	3.8	⑧	9.5
	Rodeo	4ZE1	2.6 (2559)	4.4	—	⑩	—	—	—	⑬	21.9	9.5
		6VD1	3.2 (3165)	6.2	—	⑩	18.2	3.0	3.2	⑬	21.9	⑪
	Trooper	6VD1	3.2 (3165)	5.7	—	6.2	18.2	3.0	3.2	3.8	22.5	⑫
		6VD1	3.2 (3165)	5.7	—	6.2	18.2	3.0	3.2	3.8	22.6	⑫
1996	Rodeo	4ZE1	2.6 (2559)	4.4	—	⑩	—	—	—	⑬	21.9	9.5
		6VD1	3.2 (3165)	5.7	—	⑩	18.2	3.0	3.2	⑬	21.9	⑪
	Trooper	6VD1	3.2 (3165)	5.7	—	6.2	18.2	3.0	3.2	3.8	22.5	⑫

① 6.7 qts. with manual transmission
　 6.4 qts. with automatic transmission
② 13.2 gallons with standard body, 19.1 gallons with long body
③ 8.6 qts. with manual transmission
　 8.3 qts. with automatic transmission
④ Standard: 13.2
　 Optional: 19.1
⑤ Quantity included transmission
⑥ Manual transmission: 9.5
　 Automatic transmission: 11.2
⑦ Manual transmission: 3.0
　 Automatic transmission: 2.4
⑧ Standard bed: 14.0
　 Spacecab and long bed: 19.8
⑨ Manual transmission: 7.3
　 Automatic transmission: 7.8
⑩ MUA transmission: 6.2
　 Borg-Warner transmission: 4.8
⑪ Manual transmission: 9.7
　 Automatic transmission: 9.3
⑫ Manual transmission: 9.3
　 Automatic transmission: 9.0
⑬ Saginaw differential unit: 4.0
　 Dana differential unit: 3.8

86861C3A

ENGLISH TO METRIC CONVERSION: MASS (WEIGHT)

Current **mass** measurement is expressed in pounds and ounces (lbs. & ozs.). The metric unit of mass (or weight) is the kilogram (kg). Even although this table does not show conversion of masses (weights) larger than 15 lbs, it is easy to calculate larger units by following the data immediately below.

To convert ounces (oz.) to grams (g): multiply th number of ozs. by 28
To convert grams (g) to ounces (oz.): multiply the number of grams by .035

To convert pounds (lbs.) to kilograms (kg): multiply the number of lbs. by .45
To convert kilograms (kg) to pounds (lbs.): multiply the number of kilograms by 2.2

lbs	kg	lbs	kg	oz	kg	oz	kg
0.1	0.04	0.9	0.41	0.1	0.003	0.9	0.024
0.2	0.09	1	0.4	0.2	0.005	1	0.03
0.3	0.14	2	0.9	0.3	0.008	2	0.06
0.4	0.18	3	1.4	0.4	0.011	3	0.08
0.5	0.23	4	1.8	0.5	0.014	4	0.11
0.6	0.27	5	2.3	0.6	0.017	5	0.14
0.7	0.32	10	4.5	0.7	0.020	10	0.28
0.8	0.36	15	6.8	0.8	0.023	15	0.42

ENGLISH TO METRIC CONVERSION: TEMPERATURE

To convert Fahrenheit (°F) to Celsius (°C): take number of °F and subtract 32; multiply result by 5; divide result by 9

To convert Celsius (°C) to Fahrenheit (°F): take number of °C and multiply by 9; divide result by 5; add 32 to total

Fahrenheit (F)		Celsius (C)		Fahrenheit (F)		Celsius (C)		Fahrenheit (F)		Celsius (C)	
°F	°C	°C	°F	°F	°C	°C	°F	°F	°C	°C	°F
−40	−40	−38	−36.4	80	26.7	18	64.4	215	101.7	80	176
−35	−37.2	−36	−32.8	85	29.4	20	68	220	104.4	85	185
−30	−34.4	−34	−29.2	90	32.2	22	71.6	225	107.2	90	194
−25	−31.7	−32	−25.6	95	35.0	24	75.2	230	110.0	95	202
−20	−28.9	−30	−22	100	37.8	26	78.8	235	112.8	100	212
−15	−26.1	−28	−18.4	105	40.6	28	82.4	240	115.6	105	221
−10	−23.3	−26	−14.8	110	43.3	30	86	245	118.3	110	230
−5	−20.6	−24	−11.2	115	46.1	32	89.6	250	121.1	115	239
0	−17.8	−22	−7.6	120	48.9	34	93.2	255	123.9	120	248
1	−17.2	−20	−4	125	51.7	36	96.8	260	126.6	125	257
2	−16.7	−18	−0.4	130	54.4	38	100.4	265	129.4	130	266
3	−16.1	−16	3.2	135	57.2	40	104	270	132.2	135	275
4	−15.6	−14	6.8	140	60.0	42	107.6	275	135.0	140	284
5	−15.0	−12	10.4	145	62.8	44	112.2	280	137.8	145	293
10	−12.2	−10	14	150	65.6	46	114.8	285	140.6	150	302
15	−9.4	−8	17.6	155	68.3	48	118.4	290	143.3	155	311
20	−6.7	−6	21.2	160	71.1	50	122	295	146.1	160	320
25	−3.9	−4	24.8	165	73.9	52	125.6	300	148.9	165	329
30	−1.1	−2	28.4	170	76.7	54	129.2	305	151.7	170	338
35	1.7	0	32	175	79.4	56	132.8	310	154.4	175	347
40	4.4	2	35.6	180	82.2	58	136.4	315	157.2	180	356
45	7.2	4	39.2	185	85.0	60	140	320	160.0	185	365
50	10.0	6	42.8	190	87.8	62	143.6	325	162.8	190	374
55	12.8	8	46.4	195	90.6	64	147.2	330	165.6	195	383
60	15.6	10	50	200	93.3	66	150.8	335	168.3	200	392
65	18.3	12	53.6	205	96.1	68	154.4	340	171.1	205	401
70	21.1	14	57.2	210	98.9	70	158	345	173.9	210	410
75	23.9	16	60.8	212	100.0	75	167	350	176.7	215	414

TCCS1C01

ENGLISH TO METRIC CONVERSION: LENGTH

To convert inches (ins.) to millimeters (mm): multiply number of inches by 25.4

To convert millimeters (mm) to inches (ins.): multiply number of millimeters by .04

Inches		Decimals	Milli-meters	Inches to millimeters		Inches		Decimals	Milli-meters	Inches to millimeters	
				inches	mm					inches	mm
	1/64	0.051625	0.3969	0.0001	0.00254		33/64	0.515625	13.0969	0.6	15.24
	1/32	0.03125	0.7937	0.0002	0.00508	17/32		0.53125	13.4937	0.7	17.78
	3/64	0.046875	1.1906	0.0003	0.00762		35/64	0.546875	13.8906	0.8	20.32
1/16		0.0625	1.5875	0.0004	0.01016	9/16		0.5625	14.2875	0.9	22.86
	5/64	0.078125	1.9844	0.0005	0.01270		37/64	0.578125	14.6844	1	25.4
	3/32	0.09375	2.3812	0.0006	0.01524	19/32		0.59375	15.0812	2	50.8
	7/64	0.109375	2.7781	0.0007	0.01778		39/64	0.609375	15.4781	3	76.2
1/8		0.125	3.1750	0.0008	0.02032	5/8		0.625	15.8750	4	101.6
	9/64	0.140625	3.5719	0.0009	0.02286		41/64	0.640625	16.2719	5	127.0
	5/32	0.15625	3.9687	0.001	0.0254	21/32		0.65625	16.6687	6	152.4
	11/64	0.171875	4.3656	0.002	0.0508		43/64	0.671875	17.0656	7	177.8
3/16		0.1875	4.7625	0.003	0.0762	11/16		0.6875	17.4625	8	203.2
	13/64	0.203125	5.1594	0.004	0.1016		45/64	0.703125	17.8594	9	228.6
	7/32	0.21875	5.5562	0.005	0.1270	23/32		0.71875	18.2562	10	254.0
	15/64	0.234375	5.9531	0.006	0.1524		47/64	0.734375	18.6531	11	279.4
1/4		0.25	6.3500	0.007	0.1778	3/4		0.75	19.0500	12	304.8
	17/64	0.265625	6.7469	0.008	0.2032		49/64	0.765625	19.4469	13	330.2
	9/32	0.28125	7.1437	0.009	0.2286	25/32		0.78125	19.8437	14	355.6
	19/64	0.296875	7.5406	0.01	0.254		51/64	0.796875	20.2406	15	381.0
5/16		0.3125	7.9375	0.02	0.508	13/16		0.8125	20.6375	16	406.4
	21/64	0.328125	8.3344	0.03	0.762		53/64	0.828125	21.0344	17	431.8
	11/32	0.34375	8.7312	0.04	1.016	27/32		0.84375	21.4312	18	457.2
	23/64	0.359375	9.1281	0.05	1.270		55/64	0.859375	21.8281	19	482.6
3/8		0.375	9.5250	0.06	1.524	7/8		0.875	22.2250	20	508.0
	25/64	0.390625	9.9219	0.07	1.778		57/64	0.890625	22.6219	21	533.4
	13/32	0.40625	10.3187	0.08	2.032	29/32		0.90625	23.0187	22	558.8
	27/64	0.421875	10.7156	0.09	2.286		59/64	0.921875	23.4156	23	584.2
7/16		0.4375	11.1125	0.1	2.54	15/16		0.9375	23.8125	24	609.6
	29/64	0.453125	11.5094	0.2	5.08		61/64	0.953125	24.2094	25	635.0
	15/32	0.46875	11.9062	0.3	7.62	31/32		0.96875	24.6062	26	660.4
	31/64	0.484375	12.3031	0.4	10.16		63/64	0.984375	25.0031	27	690.6
1/2		0.5	12.7000	0.5	12.70						

ENGLISH TO METRIC CONVERSION: TORQUE

To convert foot-pounds (ft. lbs.) to Newton-meters: multiply the number of ft. lbs. by 1.3

To convert inch-pounds (in. lbs.) to Newton-meters: multiply the number of in. lbs. by .11

in lbs	N-m	in lbs	N-m	in lbs	N-m	in lbs	N-m	in lbs	N-m
0.1	0.01	1	0.11	10	1.13	19	2.15	28	3.16
0.2	0.02	2	0.23	11	1.24	20	2.26	29	3.28
0.3	0.03	3	0.34	12	1.36	21	2.37	30	3.39
0.4	0.04	4	0.45	13	1.47	22	2.49	31	3.50
0.5	0.06	5	0.56	14	1.58	23	2.60	32	3.62
0.6	0.07	6	0.68	15	1.70	24	2.71	33	3.73
0.7	0.08	7	0.78	16	1.81	25	2.82	34	3.84
0.8	0.09	8	0.90	17	1.92	26	2.94	35	3.95
0.9	0.10	9	1.02	18	2.03	27	3.05	36	4.0

ENGLISH TO METRIC CONVERSION: TORQUE

Torque is now expressed as either foot-pounds (ft./lbs.) or inch-pounds (in./lbs.). The metric measurement unit for torque is the Newton-meter (Nm). This unit—the Nm—will be used for all SI metric torque references, both the present ft./lbs. and in./lbs.

ft lbs	N-m	ft lbs	N-m	ft lbs	N-m	ft lbs	N-m
0.1	0.1	33	44.7	74	100.3	115	155.9
0.2	0.3	34	46.1	75	101.7	116	157.3
0.3	0.4	35	47.4	76	103.0	117	158.6
0.4	0.5	36	48.8	77	104.4	118	160.0
0.5	0.7	37	50.7	78	105.8	119	161.3
0.6	0.8	38	51.5	79	107.1	120	162.7
0.7	1.0	39	52.9	80	108.5	121	164.0
0.8	1.1	40	54.2	81	109.8	122	165.4
0.9	1.2	41	55.6	82	111.2	123	166.8
1	1.3	42	56.9	83	112.5	124	168.1
2	2.7	43	58.3	84	113.9	125	169.5
3	4.1	44	59.7	85	115.2	126	170.8
4	5.4	45	61.0	86	116.6	127	172.2
5	6.8	46	62.4	87	118.0	128	173.5
6	8.1	47	63.7	88	119.3	129	174.9
7	9.5	48	65.1	89	120.7	130	176.2
8	10.8	49	66.4	90	122.0	131	177.6
9	12.2	50	67.8	91	123.4	132	179.0
10	13.6	51	69.2	92	124.7	133	180.3
11	14.9	52	70.5	93	126.1	134	181.7
12	16.3	53	71.9	94	127.4	135	183.0
13	17.6	54	73.2	95	128.8	136	184.4
14	18.9	55	74.6	96	130.2	137	185.7
15	20.3	56	75.9	97	131.5	138	187.1
16	21.7	57	77.3	98	132.9	139	188.5
17	23.0	58	78.6	99	134.2	140	189.8
18	24.4	59	80.0	100	135.6	141	191.2
19	25.8	60	81.4	101	136.9	142	192.5
20	27.1	61	82.7	102	138.3	143	193.9
21	28.5	62	84.1	103	139.6	144	195.2
22	29.8	63	85.4	104	141.0	145	196.6
23	31.2	64	86.8	105	142.4	146	198.0
24	32.5	65	88.1	106	143.7	147	199.3
25	33.9	66	89.5	107	145.1	148	200.7
26	35.2	67	90.8	108	146.4	149	202.0
27	36.6	68	92.2	109	147.8	150	203.4
28	38.0	69	93.6	110	149.1	151	204.7
29	39.3	70	94.9	111	150.5	152	206.1
30	40.7	71	96.3	112	151.8	153	207.4
31	42.0	72	97.6	113	153.2	154	208.8
32	43.4	73	99.0	114	154.6	155	210.2

TCCS1C03

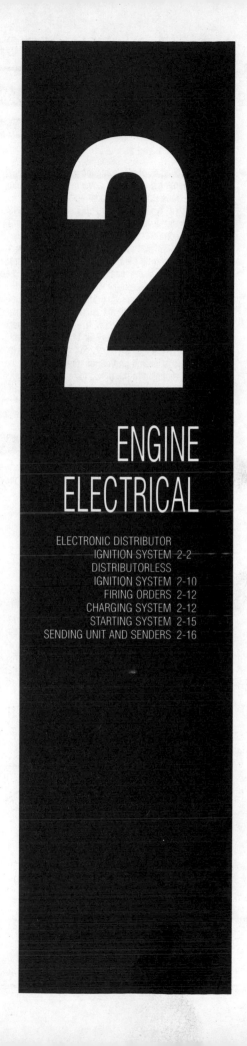

2

ENGINE
ELECTRICAL

ELECTRONIC DISTRIBUTOR IGNITION SYSTEM

General Information

▶ **See Figures 1 and 2**

There are 2 types of electronic ignition systems used on Isuzu trucks: one uses a conventional centrifugal advance type distributor. The second system uses a fully transistorized type distributor.

Conventional type distributors are made up of the distributor shaft, rotor shaft, rotor head, breaker assembly, reluctor, governor flyweight, pinion gear and vacuum control unit.

Transistorized distributors consist of dust bushing, rotor, pinion and a crank angle sensor built into the distributor housing. The crank angle sensor uses a photo-electric pick-up to measure piston position and engine speed.

The computer, or Electronic Control Module (ECM), monitors the information from the engine sensor network. The ECM uses this information to calculate the proper spark timing and tell the distributor when to make timing modifications.

Some engines are equipped with an Electronic Spark Control (ESC) system. At the heart of the ESC system is the knock sensor which is mounted to the engine block. The knock sensor is connected to the electronic spark control module which is located on the right fender panel in the engine compartment or on a bracket mounted to the block. In response to engine knock, the sensor transmits a signal to the electronic spark module ("half function box"). The spark control module sends the signal to the ECM which in turn tells the distributor to retard the spark timing up to 20° to reduce spark knock in the engine.

Diagnosis and Testing

Before beginning any diagnosis and testing procedures, visually inspect the components of the ignition system and engine control systems. Check for the following:

- Discharged battery
- Damaged or loose connections
- Damaged electrical insulation
- Poor coil and spark plug connections
- Ignition module connections
- Blown fuses
- Damaged vacuum hoses
- Damaged spark plugs

Check the spark plug wires and boots for signs of poor insulation that could cause crossfiring. Make sure the battery is fully charged and that all accessories are off during diagnosis and testing. Make sure the idle speed is within specification.

You will need a good quality volt-ohmmeter and a spark tester in order to check the ignition system. A spark tester resembles a spark plug without threads and the side electrode removed. Using a modified spark plug is as a spark tester is not recommended.

When attempting to search for ignition troubles, keep in mind the various sensor inputs which the control module uses to calculate timing may affect engine performance. The PCM will alter timing based on sensor inputs as follows:

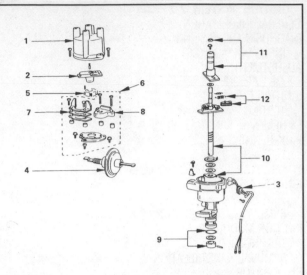

Disassembly steps

▲ 1. Distributor cap and seal	7. Stator and magnet
2. Distributor rotor	8. IC igniter
3. Harness connecter	▲ 9. Pin collar and ring
▲ 4. Vacuum advance	10. Governor shaft
▲ 5. Retractor	11. Rotor shaft
6. IC igniter and breaker plate assembly	▲ 12. Springs and weights

86862G03

Fig. 2 Vacuum advance type distributor and components—Pick-up models

- Low MAP output voltage = More spark advance
- Cold engine = More spark advance
- High MAP output voltage = Less spark advance
- Hot engine = Less spark advance

With this in mind, DETONATION could be caused by low MAP output or high resistance in the coolant sensor circuit. POOR PERFORMANCE could be caused by a high MAP output or low resistance in the coolant sensor circuit.

INPUT VOLTAGE TEST

▶ **See Figure 3**

1. Place the ignition switch in the **ON** position.
2. Using a suitable voltmeter, measure the voltage between the positive (+) terminal of the coil and a ground.

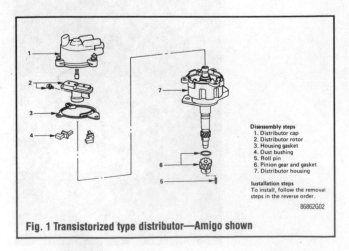

Disassembly steps
1. Distributor cap
2. Distributor rotor
3. Housing gasket
4. Dust bushing
5. Roll pin
6. Pinion gear and gasket
7. Distributor housing

Iustallation steps
To install, follow the removal steps in the reverse order.

86862G02

Fig. 1 Transistorized type distributor—Amigo shown

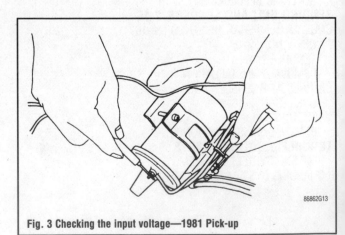

86862G13

Fig. 3 Checking the input voltage—1981 Pick-up

3. The standard voltage should be approximately 12 volts. If the voltage is not within specification, check the wiring and connectors. As long as the wiring and connectors are OK, replace the coil if testing deems it to be defective.

Adjustments

AIR GAP

♦ See Figures 4, 5 and 6

On all 4-cylinder engines using the conventional distributor with vacuum advance, the air gap setting in the distributor should be checked and adjusted before the ignition timing is adjusted.
1. Disconnect the negative battery cable.
2. Remove the distributor cap, O-ring and rotor.
3. Use a feeler gauge to measure the air gap at the pick up coil projection. The gap should be 0.008-0.016 in. (0.20-0.40mm) for the G200Z engine, or 0.012-0.020 in. (0.30-0.50mm) for the 4ZD1 engine; adjust it if necessary.

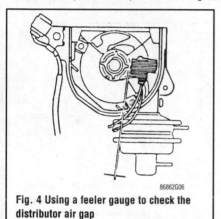

Fig. 4 Using a feeler gauge to check the distributor air gap

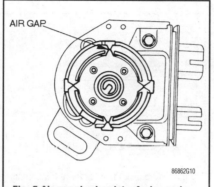

Fig. 5 Air gap check point—Amigo and Pick-up models

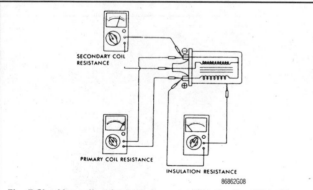

Fig. 7 Checking coil resistance of a conventional coil—1981–85 models

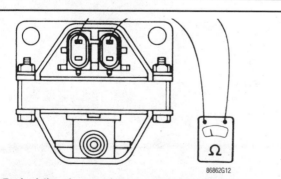

Fig. 9 To check the primary resistance, connect an ohmmeter between the indicated terminals—6-cylinder engines

4. Loosen the screws and move the signal generator until the gap is correct. Tighten the screws and recheck the gap.

➡The electrical parts in this system are not repairable. If found to be defective, they must be replaced.

Ignition Coil

TESTING

Primary Coil Resistance

♦ See Figures 7, 8 and 9

1. Place the ignition switch in the **OFF** position.
2. Tad and disconnect the ignition coil terminals.
3. Using a suitable ohmmeter, measure the resistance between the ignition coil positive terminal and the ignition coil negative terminal.

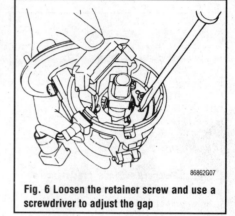

Fig. 6 Loosen the retainer screw and use a screwdriver to adjust the gap

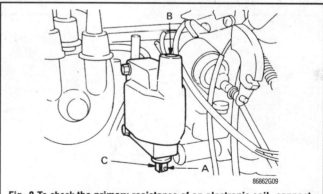

Fig. 8 To check the primary resistance of an electronic coil, connect an ohmmeter between points A and C—4-cylinder engines

4. The standard resistance should be 1.130–1.529 ohms. If the resistance is not within specification, check the wiring and connectors. Replace the coil if found defective.

Secondary Coil Resistance

♦ See Figures 10 and 11

1. Place the ignition switch in the **OFF** position.
2. Tag and disconnect the ignition coil terminals.
3. Using a suitable ohmmeter, measure the resistance between the ignition coil positive terminal and the high voltage terminal.
4. The standard resistance should be 10.20–13.80 kilo-ohms. If the resistance is not within specification, check the wiring and connectors. Replace the coil if found defective.

Insulation Resistance

▶ **See Figure 12**

1. Place the ignition switch in the **OFF** position.
2. Tag and disconnect the ignition coil terminals.
3. Using a suitable ohmmeter, measure the resistance between the ignition coil positive terminal and the body of the coil.
4. The standard resistance should be more than 10 milo-ohms. If the resistance is not within specification, check the wiring and connectors. Replace the coil if found defective.

REMOVAL & INSTALLATION

▶ **See Figures 13 thru 20**

1. Disconnect the negative battery cable.
2. Tag and disconnect any applicable connectors and leads.
3. Remove the coil and bracket assembly. Remove the bracket assembly from the coil.

To install:

4. Install the bracket to the coil and tighten the retaining screw.
5. Install the assembly to the vehicle and tighten the mounting bolts.
6. Connect all coil wires, then connect the negative battery cable.
7. Check for proper vehicle operation.

Pick-up Coil

TESTING

4-Cylinder Models

1. Place the ignition switch in the **OFF** position.
2. Disconnect the ignition coil terminals.
3. Using a suitable ohmmeter, measure the pick-up coil resistance between the pick-up coil terminals.
4. The standard resistance should be 140–180 ohms. If the resistance is not within specification, check the wiring and connectors. Replace the pick-up coil if defective.

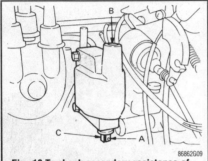

Fig. 10 To check secondary resistance of an electronic coil, connect an ohmmeter between points A and B—4-cylinder engines

86862G09

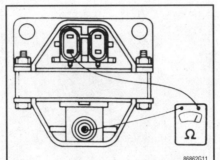

Fig. 11 To check the secondary resistance, attach an ohmmeter between the coil high tension terminal and the indicated connection—6-cylinder engines

86862G11

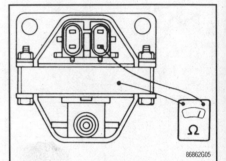

Fig. 12 To check the insulator resistance, connect an ohmmeter between the coil positive terminal and the body of the coil—1993 6-cylinder engine

86862G05

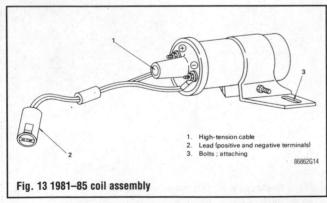

1. High-tension cable
2. Lead (positive and negative terminals)
3. Bolts ; attaching

86862G14

Fig. 13 1981–85 coil assembly

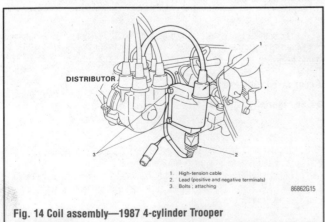

DISTRIBUTOR

1. High-tension cable
2. Lead (positive and negative terminals)
3. Bolts ; attaching

86862G15

Fig. 14 Coil assembly—1987 4-cylinder Trooper

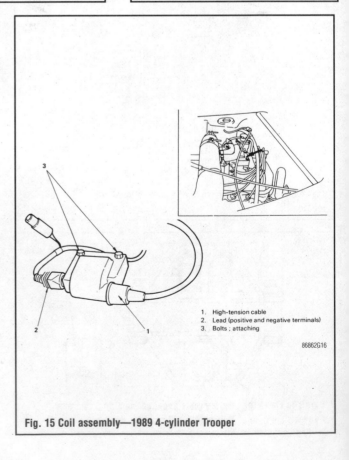

1. High-tension cable
2. Lead (positive and negative terminals)
3. Bolts ; attaching

86862G16

Fig. 15 Coil assembly—1989 4-cylinder Trooper

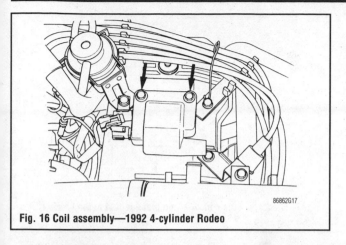

Fig. 16 Coil assembly—1992 4-cylinder Rodeo

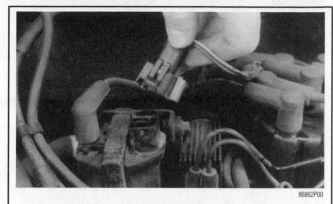

Fig. 17 Unfasten the coil harness—Trooper shown

Fig. 18 Remove the coil high tension wire

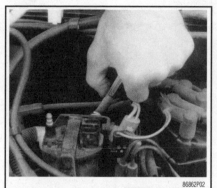

Fig. 19 Loosen and remove the coil retainer bolts

Fig. 20 Remove the coil from the retainer bracket

6-Cylinder Models

♦ See Figures 21 and 22

1. Disconnect the pick-up coil wiring.
2. Switch the ohmmeter to the middle ohms scale.
3. Measure the coil resistance between either of the pick-up coil leads and the housing. Infinite resistance should be read.
4. Connect the ohmmeter probes across the coil leads and measure the resistance. It should read 500–1000 ohms. Flex the lead wires at the coil and connector by hand to check for intermittent opens in the wiring.
5. If the resistance readings are not within specifications, replace the coil.

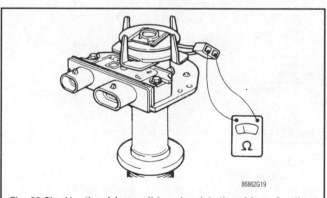

Fig. 22 Checking the pick-up coil for a break in the wiring—6-cylinder models

REMOVAL & INSTALLATION

♦ See Figures 23 and 24

1. Disconnect the negative battery cable.
2. Remove the distributor cap, with the spark plug wires attached, and place aside. Remove the rotor cap.
3. Unfasten the harness attached to the distributor and pick-up coil.
4. Remove the pick-up coil retainer. Unfasten the pick-up coil wire harness plastic connector at the side of the distributor. Slide the pick-up coil off the distributor shaft.

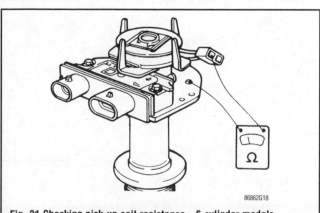

Fig. 21 Checking pick-up coil resistance—6-cylinder models

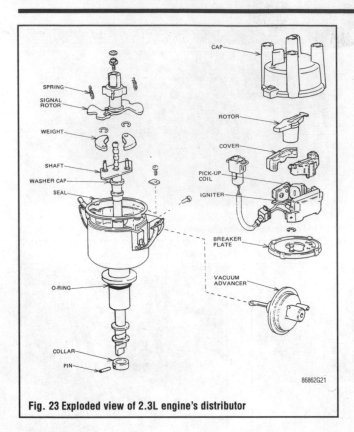

Fig. 23 Exploded view of 2.3L engine's distributor

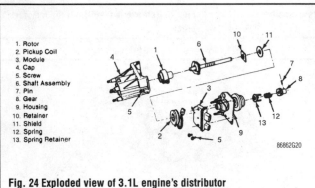

1. Rotor
2. Pickup Coil
3. Module
4. Cap
5. Screw
6. Shaft Assembly
7. Pin
8. Gear
9. Housing
10. Retainer
11. Shield
12. Spring
13. Spring Retainer

Fig. 24 Exploded view of 3.1L engine's distributor

To install:

5. Lubricate the distributor shaft lightly with oil. Slide the pick-up coil down the shaft and position in place. Install the pick-up coil retainer clip to secure the coil in place.

6. Attach the wire harness to the side of the distributor body, making sure none of the wires could get caught in the distributor while it rotates.

7. Attach the wire harness to the distributor and pick-up coil.

8. Install the rotor and distributor cap.

9. Connect the negative battery cable.

10. Check for proper vehicle operation.

Igniter

TESTING

▶ **See Figures 25 and 26**

1. Remove the distributor cap.

2. Disconnect the ignition coil high tension cable at the distributor side. Move the high tension cable end to the coil retainer screw/bolt and maintain a ¼ in. (6mm) clearance.

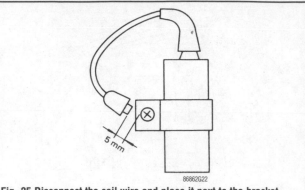

Fig. 25 Disconnect the coil wire and place it next to the bracket screw

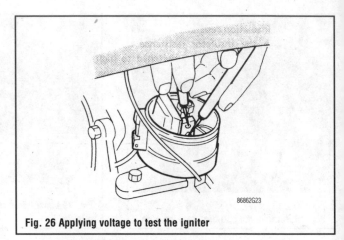

Fig. 26 Applying voltage to test the igniter

3. Place the ignition switch in the **ON** position.

4. Connect a 1.5 volt dry cell to the red igniter wiring terminal at the positive side, and the white wiring terminal to the negative side.

➡ **Do not apply voltage to the igniter for more than three seconds at a time to avoid destroying the power transistor in the igniter.**

5. The igniter is normal when sparks are generated between the high tension cable and ground.

6. If the igniter fails this test (no sparks), replace it.

7. Reconnect all disconnected wiring and install all removed parts.

REMOVAL & INSTALLATION

1981–85 Models

WITHOUT VACUUM ADVANCE

1. Disconnect the negative battery cable.

2. Remove the distributor cap, seal and rotor.

3. Remove the igniter cover and igniter assembly.

To install:

4. Install the igniter and adjust the gap between the pick-up coil and coil projections with a feeler gauge. The measurement should be 0.008–0.016 in. (0.2–0.4mm).

5. Install the igniter cover, rotor, seal and cap.

6. Connect the battery cable and check vehicle operation.

WITH VACUUM ADVANCE

1. Disconnect the negative battery cable.

2. Remove the distributor cap, rotor and seal.

3. Remove the vacuum control screw and vacuum advance canister.

4. Disconnect the wiring harness.

5. Remove the retractor roll pin. Pry loose the retractor outer cover, then insert a suitable prybar into the lower side of the retractor and pull it free.

6. Remove the igniter and breaker plate assembly. Remove the stator, magnet and igniter.

To install:

7. Install the igniter, stator and magnet.

8. Install the retractor with the roll pin notch and retractor notch in parallel alignment.

9. Install the harness, vacuum advance, distributor cap, seal and rotor.

10. Connect the negative battery cable.

11. Check the vacuum canister by applying vacuum to the vacuum port. The breaker plate should move freely and hold vacuum.

1986–91 4-Cylinder Models

♦ See Figures 27 and 28

1. Disconnect the negative battery cable.

2. Remove the distributor cap retaining screws and cap.

3. Remove the rotor.

4. Disconnect the module electrical harness.

5. Remove the module retaining screws and module assembly.

To install:

6. Clean the module mating surfaces. Apply a coat of dielectric compound to both module and mating surfaces. This compound helps absorb heat and is essential for long module life.

7. Install the igniter module and tighten the retaining screws.

8. Connect the electrical harness.

9. Install the rotor and distributor cap.

10. Connect the battery cable and check vehicle operation.

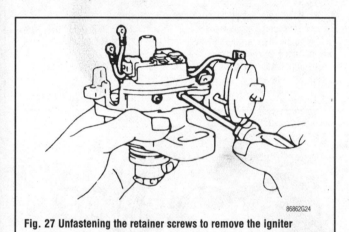

Fig. 27 Unfastening the retainer screws to remove the igniter

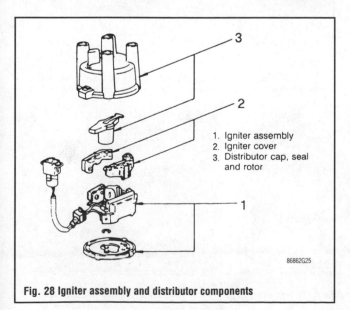

Fig. 28 Igniter assembly and distributor components

1. Igniter assembly
2. Igniter cover
3. Distributor cap, seal and rotor

Ignition Module

TESTING

Most ignition modules cannot be tested using basic tools and equipment. Therefore, if you suspect a defective ignition module, it must be removed and taken to a qualified shop with the necessary diagnostic equipment.

REMOVAL & INSTALLATION

6-Cylinder Engines

♦ See Figure 29

➡Some distributors may require partial disassembly in order to remove and replace the ignition module. Though most modules are replaceable without disassembling the distributor, removing the distributor assembly from the engine will make access to the components easier. If you wish to avoid removing the distributor from the engine, remove the cap and rotor to see if access to the module retainers and connectors is possible, then decide if you want to remove the distributor.

1. Disconnect the negative battery cable.

2. Remove the distributor cap and position aside with the wires attached.

3. If necessary, remove the distributor from the engine and place it on a clean work surface.

4. If necessary, remove the rotor from the distributor assembly. If needed, remove the packing ring and the cover.

5. If applicable, remove the electrical harness-to-distributor screw.

6. Disengage the electrical harness from the ignition module.

7. Remove the ignition module retaining screws, then lift the module from the distributor. If equipped, be sure to remove the spacers from the module.

To install:

8. Apply a coat of silicone lubricant to the base of the ignition module to aid in heat dissipation.

9. Install the ignition module to the distributor assembly and secure using the retainer screws. If equipped, be sure to properly position the spacers during installation.

10. Attach the harness to the ignition module, then if equipped, install the harness retaining screw.

11. If applicable, install the packing ring and cover.

12. Install the rotor to the distributor assembly.

13. If removed, install the distributor.

14. Install the cap to the distributor assembly. If any wiring was disconnected, be sure to engage it as tagged or noted during removal.

15. Connect the negative battery cable.

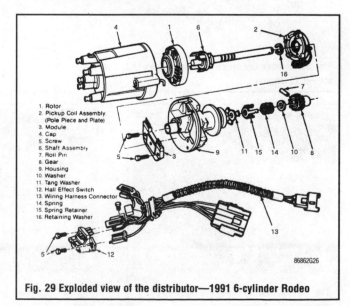

1. Rotor
2. Pickup Coil Assembly (Pole Piece and Plate)
3. Module
4. Cap
5. Screw
6. Shaft Assembly
7. Roll Pin
8. Gear
9. Housing
10. Washer
11. Tang Washer
12. Hall Effect Switch
13. Wiring Harness Connector
14. Spring
15. Spring Retainer
16. Retaining Washer

Fig. 29 Exploded view of the distributor—1991 6-cylinder Rodeo

Distributor

REMOVAL

♦ **See Figures 30 thru 38**

1. Disconnect the negative battery cable.
2. Remove the air cleaner and hoses, if additional working space is needed.
3. Tag and disconnect the electrical harnesses either from the distributor or from the ignition coil, depending on model and coil location.
4. Remove the distributor cap from the distributor and position aside. If possible, do not remove the coil or spark plug wires.

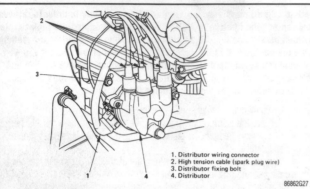

1. Distributor wiring connector
2. High tension cable (spark plug wire)
3. Distributor fixing bolt
4. Distributor

86862G27

Fig. 30 Distributor mounted to the side of the engine—2.3L and 2.6L engines

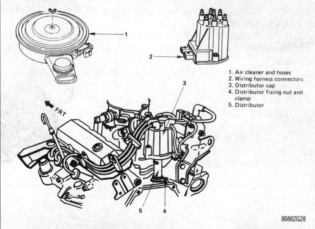

1. Air cleaner and hoses
2. Wiring harness connectors
3. Distributor cap
4. Distributor fixing nut and clamp
5. Distributor

86862G28

Fig. 31 Remove the air cleaner and hoses to access the distributor—3.1L engine

5. If equipped, disconnect the vacuum hose from the distributor vacuum advance module.
6. Using paint or equivalent, scribe alignment marks on the rotor-to-distributor and distributor housing-to-engine head or block.
7. Loosen and remove the distributor hold-down bolt and clamp, then carefully lift the distributor out of the engine. Note the position of the rotor alignment.
8. Remove the distributor housing seal and discard.

INSTALLATION

Undisturbed Engine

This condition exists if the engine has not been rotated while the distributor was removed.

1. Lubricate a new housing seal with oil and install on the distributor.
2. With the rotor aligned with the mark on the housing, install the distributor, taking care to align the distributor body mark with the mark scribed on the engine. It may be necessary to lift the distributor and turn the rotor slightly to properly align the gears and the oil pump driveshaft.
3. With the respective marks aligned, install the hold-down clamp and bolt finger-tight.
4. If equipped, connect the vacuum hose to the distributor vacuum advance module.
5. Install and secure the distributor cap to the distributor body.
6. Attach the electrical harness(es) to the distributor or coil, depending on engine and coil location.
7. If removed, connect the spark plug and coil wires.
8. If removed, install the air cleaner and hoses.
9. Connect the negative battery cable. Connect a timing light to the engine (following the manufacturer's instructions), then start the engine and check the timing. Adjust, as necessary.
10. Turn the engine **OFF** and tighten the distributor clamp bolt.
11. Start the engine and recheck the timing.

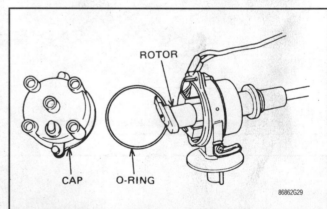

ROTOR

CAP   O-RING

86862G29

Fig. 32 On 1.8L and 2.0L engines, remove the distributor cap O-ring

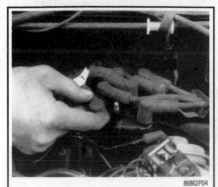

86862P04

Fig. 33 If removing the spark plug wires, tag each wire before disconnecting

86862P05

Fig. 34 Loosen the distributor cap retainer clips

86862P06

Fig. 35 Lift the distributor cap off and place aside

Fig. 36 Place alignment marks on the rotor cap, distributor body . . .

Fig. 37 . . . and cylinder head

Fig. 38 With the distributor hold-down clamp removed, carefully lift the assembly out of the mounting hole

Disturbed Engine

♦ See Figures 39 and 40

This condition exists when the engine has been rotated with the distributor removed.

1. Lubricate a new housing seal with oil and install on the distributor.
2. Rotate the crankshaft to position the No. 1 piston at Top Dead Center (TDC) of the compression stroke. This may be determined by removing the No. 1 spark plug and inserting a rag into the No. 1 spark plug hole, then slowly turning the engine crankshaft. When the timing mark on the crankshaft pulley aligns with the 0° mark on the timing scale and the rag is blown out by the compression, the No. 1 piston is close to TDC.

➡If you are unsure when TDC is reached, remove the valve cover and watch the rocker arms for the No. 1 cylinder. If the valves move as the crankshaft timing marker approaches the scale, the No. 1 piston is on its exhaust stroke. If the valves remain closed as the timing mark approaches the scale, then the No. 1 piston is approaching TDC of the compression stroke.

3. Turn the rotor so that it will point to the No. 1 terminal of the distributor cap.
4. Install the distributor into the engine block. It may be necessary to turn the rotor to engage the distributor and oil pump drive gears.
5. Rotate the engine two revolutions and bring the No. 1 piston to TDC again, then check to see that the rotor is pointing toward the No. 1 terminal of the cap.
6. With the marks aligned, install the hold-down clamp and bolt finger-tight.
7. Install and secure the distributor cap.
8. Attach the electrical harness(es) to the distributor and, if equipped, the vacuum advance hose.
9. If removed, connect the spark plug and coil wires.
10. If removed, be sure to install the air cleaner and hoses.
11. Connect the negative battery cable.
12. Connect a timing light to the engine (following the manufacturer's instructions). Start the engine, then check and adjust the timing, as necessary.
13. Turn the engine **OFF** and tighten the distributor clamp bolt.
14. Start the engine and recheck the timing to verify that it did not change while tightening the hold-down bolt, then stop the engine and remove the timing light.

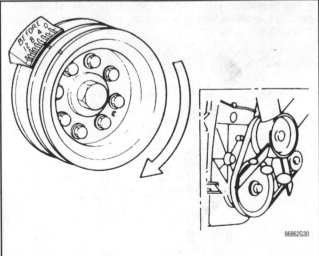

Fig. 39 Aligning the 2.3L and 2.6L engines' crankshaft pulley and timing marks

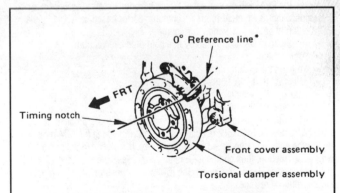

NOTE: With #1 cyl at T.D.C. as determined by positioning #3 cyl 0.7mm below #5 cyl, "0" reference line of pointer must align with center of timing notch on torsional damper within 0.5mm after assembling securely.

Fig. 40 Aligning the crankshaft pulley on a 3.1L engine

DISTRIBUTORLESS IGNITION SYSTEM

General Information

This electronic system is designed to provide spark for air/fuel combustion in response to timing commands from the Powertrain Control Module (PCM). System components include the PCM, the Ignition Control Module or ICM (which contains the coil packs), and the Crankshaft Position (CKP) sensor. Each coil pack is made up of 2 spark towers. Spark plug wires deliver voltage from the towers to the spark plugs located in the cylinder head bores. The ICM receives inputs from the crankshaft position sensor in order to monitor engine position and rotation. The module provides output signals, based on the CKP signal, which are used by the PCM to determine engine timing.

The crankshaft position sensor is mounted in the side of the engine block and protrudes within approximately 0.050 in. (1.27mm) of the crankshaft reluctor ring. The reluctor is a special wheel which is cast into the crankshaft with slots that are machined into it. Most of the slots are evenly spaced while a single slot is spaced several degrees from one of the other slots. As the reluctor rotates with the crankshaft, the slots change the magnetic field of the sensor, creating an induced voltage pulse. The unevenly spaced slot is used as a reference point so the ICM can tell the PCM what cylinder is next approaching TDC.

A distributorless ignition system such as this one operates based on the "waste spark" method of spark distribution. Each cylinder is paired with the cylinder that is opposite it (1 and 4; 2 and 3) in the firing order. The spark occurs simultaneously in the cylinder coming up on the compression stroke and in the cylinder coming up on the exhaust stroke. Since the cylinder on the exhaust stroke requires very little of the available energy to fire the spark plug, most of the voltage will go to fire the cylinder on compression. As the process is repeated, the cylinders reverse roles.

When the ignition is switched to the **ON** (or **RUN**) position, battery voltage is applied to the ICM, but no spark occurs because the CKP sensor shows no engine rotation. When the engine begins to rotate and reference signals are received, the ICM will control spark by triggering each of the 2 ignition coils at a pre-determined interval based only on engine speed. This ignition operation during engine cranking is known as bypass timing mode.

Once engine speed rises above 400 rpm, the PCM will take over control of the ignition control circuit in order to compensate for all driving conditions. This is known as Ignition Control (IC) mode. During normal engine operation in IC mode, the PCM will control spark timing advance or retard according to various sensor inputs, in order to obtain optimum performance. In IC mode, the PCM will rely on the following information:

- Engine load (as determined by manifold pressure/vacuum)
- Atmospheric pressure
- Engine temperature
- Manifold air temperature
- Crankshaft position
- Engine speed (rpm)

PCM control of the ignition timing will continue unless a problem occurs and the bypass timing mode is again entered, during which the ICM module will determine engine timing based on preset values. If the vehicle stalls, the engine will cease rotation, thus ending CKP reference pulses. The PCM and ICM will cut the ignition. Should this occur, the ICM will not resume plug firing until engine rotation resumes.

Diagnosis and Testing

Before beginning any diagnosis and testing procedures, visually inspect the components of the ignition system and engine control systems. Check for the following:

- Discharged battery
- Damaged or loose connections
- Damaged electrical insulation
- Poor coil and spark plug connections
- Ignition module connections
- Blown fuses

- Damaged vacuum hoses
- Damaged spark plugs

Check the spark plug wires and boots for signs of poor insulation that could cause cross-firing. Make sure the battery is fully charged and that all accessories are off during diagnosis and testing. Make sure the idle speed is within specification.

You will need a good quality volt-ohmmeter and a spark tester (such as ST-125) in order to check the ignition system. A spark tester resembles a spark plug without threads or a side electrode. Using a modified spark plug is as a spark tester is not recommended.

If an open or ground in the Ignition Control (IC) circuit occurs during engine operation, the engine will continue to run, but using a back-up timing mode (controlled by the ICM) based on preset timing values. The Malfunction Indicator Lamp (MIL) or SERVICE ENGINE SOON light will not illuminate at the first appearance of a break in the circuit. However, if the IC fault is still present once the engine is restarted, a code will set in the PCM and the MIL will illuminate. Poor performance and fuel economy may be noticed while the engine is running under back-up timing.

When attempting to search for ignition troubles, keep in mind that the various sensor inputs which the PCM uses to calculate timing may affect engine performance. The PCM will alter timing based on sensor inputs as follows:

- Low MAP output voltage = More spark advance
- Cold engine = More spark advance
- High MAP output voltage = Less spark advance
- Hot engine = Less spark advance

With this in mind, DETONATION could be caused by low MAP output or high resistance in the coolant sensor circuit. POOR PERFORMANCE could be caused by a high MAP output or low resistance in the coolant sensor circuit.

Ignition Coil Pack

REMOVAL & INSTALLATION

▶ See Figure 41

➡ **Disconnecting the negative battery cable on some vehicles may interfere with the functions of the on-board computer systems and may require the computer to undergo a relearning process, once the negative battery cable is reconnected.**

The coil pack is located on the top of the engine (3.1L), or directly over the individual spark plugs (3.2L).

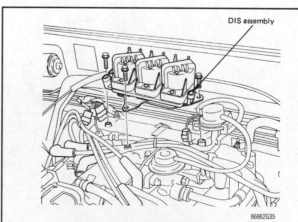

Fig. 41 Coil pack mounted on top of the engine—3.2L engine

3.1L Engine

1. Disconnect the negative battery cable.
2. Remove the coil pack protective cover, if equipped.
3. Tag and disconnect the spark plug wires from the coil pack on the top or side of the engine.
4. Remove the coil pack retaining screws.
5. Separate the coil pack from the ignition module.
6. Clean any dirt or debris between the module and coil pack.

To install:

7. Install the coil pack to the ignition module assembly.
8. Attach the coil retaining screws and tighten to 17 ft. lbs. (24 Nm).

✳✳ WARNING

Do not overtighten the retainer screws, otherwise the module or coil pack could be damaged.

9. Attach the spark plug wires to the coil pack in the correct order.
10. Attach the coil pack protective cover, if equipped.
11. Connect the negative battery cable.
12. Start the vehicle and check for correct operation.

3.2L Engine

▶ See Figures 42, 43 and 44

1. Disconnect the negative battery cable.
2. Disconnect the coil harness from the coil pack on the top of the spark plug.
3. Remove the coil pack retaining screws.
4. Separate the coil pack from the spark plug.

To install:

5. Install the coil pack on to the spark plug.
6. Attach the coil retaining screws and tighten snugly.

✳✳ WARNING

Do not overtighten the retainer screws or the coil pack could be damaged.

7. Attach the wire harness to the coil pack.
8. Connect the negative battery cable.
9. Start the vehicle and check for correct operation.

Ignition Module

REMOVAL & INSTALLATION

▶ See Figure 41

➡Disconnecting the negative battery cable on some vehicles may interfere with the functions of the on-board computer systems and may require the computer to undergo a relearning process, once the negative battery cable is reconnected.

The ignition module is sandwiched between the coil pack and retainer bracket.

1. Disconnect the negative battery cable.
2. Remove the coil pack protective cover, if equipped.
3. Unfasten the ignition module electrical harness.
4. Tag and disconnect the spark plug wiring from the coil pack.
5. Remove the ignition module/coil pack assembly retainer bracket screws, then remove the assembly from the engine.
6. Remove the coil pack from the ignition module by removing the retainer screws. Separate the ignition module from the coil pack and bracket.

To install:

7. Install the module to the bracket, and place the ignition coil pack on top of the module.
8. Secure the module and coil pack to the bracket using the retainer screws. Tighten the retainer screws to 17 ft. lbs. (24 Nm).
9. Install the module/coil assembly to the engine block and tighten the retaining bolts to 15–22 ft. lbs. (20–30 Nm).
10. Attach the spark plug wires to the proper coil towers.
11. Attach the module electrical connectors.
12. Install the protective cover over the coil pack, if equipped.
13. Connect the negative battery cable.
14. Start the vehicle and check for proper engine operation.

Crankshaft Position Sensor

REMOVAL & INSTALLATION

Refer to Section 4 for removal, installation and testing procedures.

Fig. 42 Unfasten the wire harness from the coil pack on top of the spark plug

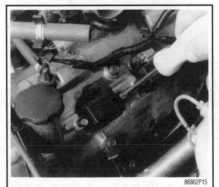

Fig. 43 Remove the coil pack retainer screws

Fig. 44 Detach the coil pack from the spark plug

FIRING ORDERS

▶ **See Figures 45, 46, 47 and 48**

➡ To avoid confusion, remove and tag the spark plug wires one at a time, for replacement.

If a distributor is not keyed for installation with only one orientation, it could have been removed previously and rewired. The resultant wiring would hold the correct firing order, but could change the relative placement of the plug towers in relation to the engine. For this reason it is imperative that you label all wires before disconnecting any of them. Also, before removal, compare the current wiring with the accompanying illustrations. If the current wiring does not match, make notes in your book to reflect how your engine is wired.

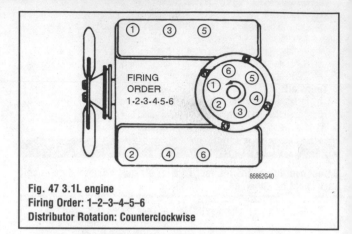

Fig. 47 3.1L engine
Firing Order: 1–2–3–4–5–6
Distributor Rotation: Counterclockwise

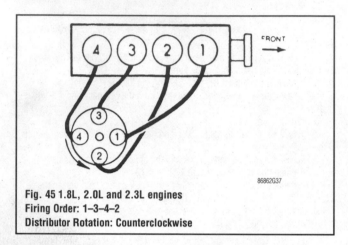

Fig. 45 1.8L, 2.0L and 2.3L engines
Firing Order: 1–3–4–2
Distributor Rotation: Counterclockwise

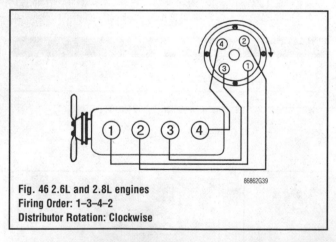

Fig. 46 2.6L and 2.8L engines
Firing Order: 1–3–4–2
Distributor Rotation: Clockwise

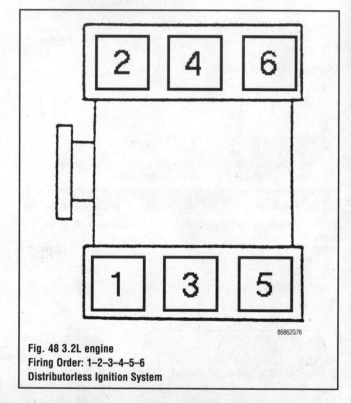

Fig. 48 3.2L engine
Firing Order: 1–2–3–4–5–6
Distributorless Ignition System

CHARGING SYSTEM

Alternator

ALTERNATOR PRECAUTIONS

To prevent damage to the on-board computer, alternator and regulator, the following precautionary measures must be taken when working with the electrical system.

• If the battery is removed for any reason, make sure it is reconnected with the correct polarity. Reversing the battery connections may result in damage to the one-way rectifiers. Always check the battery polarity visually. This is to be done before any connections are made to be sure that all of the connections correspond to the battery ground polarity.

• When utilizing a booster battery as a starting aid, always connect the positive to positive terminals and the negative terminal from the booster battery to a good engine ground on the vehicle being started.

• Never use a fast charger as a booster to start vehicles.

• Disconnect the battery cables when charging the battery with a fast charger; the charger has a tendency to force current through the diodes in the opposite direction for which they were designed. This burns out the diodes.

• Make sure the ignition switch is **OFF** when connecting or disconnecting any electrical component, especially on trucks equipped with an on-board computer control system.

• Never attempt to polarize the alternator.

• Do not use test lights of more than 12 volts when checking diode continuity.

• Do not short across or ground any of the alternator terminals.

• The polarity of the battery, alternator and regulator must be matched and considered before making any electrical connections within the system.

• Never separate the alternator on an open circuit. Make sure all connections within the circuit are clean and tight.

• Disconnect the battery ground terminal when performing any service on electrical components.

• Disconnect the battery if arc welding is to be done on the vehicle.

TESTING

Voltage Test

1. Make sure the engine is **OFF**, and turn the headlights on for 15–20 seconds to remove any surface charge from the battery.
2. Using a DVOM set to volts DC, probe across the battery terminals.
3. Measure the battery voltage.
4. Write down the voltage reading and proceed to the next test.

No-Load Test

1. Connect a tachometer to the engine.

✳✳ CAUTION

Ensure that the transmission is in PARK and the emergency brake is set. Blocking a wheel is optional and an added safety measure.

2. Turn off all electrical loads (radio, blower motor, wipers, etc.)
3. Start the engine and increase engine speed to approximately 1500 rpm.
4. Measure the voltage reading at the battery with the engine holding a steady 1500 rpm. Voltage should have raised at least 0.5 volts, but no more than 2.5 volts.
5. If the voltage does not go up more than 0.5 volts, the alternator is not charging. If the voltage goes up more than 2.5 volts, the alternator is overcharging.

➡Usually under and overcharging is caused by a defective alternator, or its related parts (regulator), and replacement will fix the problem; however, faulty wiring and other problems can cause the charging system to malfunction. Further testing, which is not covered by this book, will reveal the exact component failure. Many automotive parts stores have alternator bench testers available for use by customers. An alternator bench test is the most definitive way to determine the condition of your alternator.

6. If the voltage is within specifications, proceed to the next test.

Load Test

1. With the engine running, turn on the blower motor and the high beams (or other electrical accessories to place a load on the charging system).
2. Increase and hold engine speed to 2000 rpm.
3. Measure the voltage reading at the battery.
4. The voltage should increase at least 0.5 volts from the voltage test. If the voltage does not meet specifications, the charging system is malfunctioning.

➡Usually under and overcharging is caused by a defective alternator, or its related parts (regulator), and replacement will fix the problem; however, faulty wiring and other problems can cause the charging system to malfunction. Further testing, which is not covered by this book, will reveal the exact component failure. Many automotive parts stores have alternator bench testers available for use by customers. An alternator bench test is the most definitive way to determine the condition of your alternator.

REMOVAL & INSTALLATION

1981–85 Vehicles

▶ **See Figure 49**

1. Disconnect the negative battery cable.
2. If equipped with an air pump, remove it for additional working space.
3. Disconnect and label the alternator wiring.
4. Remove the alternator pivot bolt on the lower part of the alternator. Remove the drive belt from the pulley.
5. Remove the alternator mounting bolt(s) and the alternator from the engine.
   To install:
6. Install the alternator.
7. Adjust the belt tension and tighten the alternator mounting bolts.
8. Connect the alternator wiring.

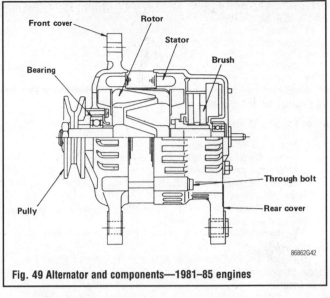

Fig. 49 Alternator and components—1981–85 engines

9. Connect the negative battery cable.
10. Start the vehicle and check for proper voltage output.

1986–96 Models With V-Belts

▶ **See Figure 50**

1. Disconnect the negative battery cable.
2. Remove the terminal plug and the battery lead from the rear of the alternator.
3. Loosen the alternator pivot and retainer bolts.
4. Remove the drive belt.
5. Remove the air pump bracket bolt from the rear of the alternator, if equipped.
6. Remove the pivot bolts and bracket from the front of the alternator, then remove the lower alternator retainer nut and bolt.
7. Remove the alternator from the vehicle.
   To install:
8. Position the alternator to the bracket on the engine.
9. Install the lower retainer nut and bolt. Attach the adjusting bracket and pivot bolts.
10. Install the air pump bracket, if removed.
11. Install the drive belt.
12. Tension the drive belt.

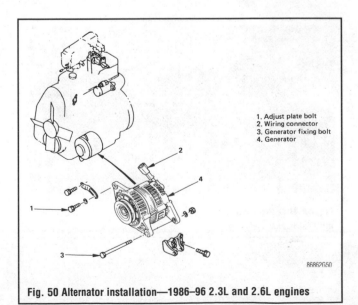

1. Adjust plate bolt
2. Wiring connector
3. Generator fixing bolt
4. Generator

Fig. 50 Alternator installation—1986–96 2.3L and 2.6L engines

13. Tighten the lower mounting bolt to 26 ft. lbs. (35 Nm), and the pivot bolts to 18 ft. lbs. (25 Nm).
14. Tighten the air pump bracket bolt to 18 ft. lbs. (25 Nm).
15. Connect the alternator terminal wires.
16. Connector the battery lead wire to the rear of the alternator.
17. Connect the negative battery cable.
18. Start the vehicle and check for proper alternator operation.

V6 Engines With Serpentine Belt

▶ See Figures 51 thru 55

1. Disconnect the negative battery cable.
2. Remove the serpentine belt.
3. Raise and support the front of the vehicle.
4. Remove the right front tire and wheel assembly for access through the wheelwell.
5. Working through the wheelwell, remove the alternator bracket-to-block bolt, then remove the brace-to-intake nut.
6. Unfasten the alternator wiring connector, then remove the battery terminal nut and wire.
7. Loosen the alternator retaining bolts, then support the alternator and remove the fasteners. Remove the alternator from the vehicle.
To install:
8. Position the alternator in the vehicle and loosely install the retaining bolts.
9. Tighten the left alternator bolt to 22 ft. lbs. (30 Nm) and the right bolt to 32 ft. lbs. (43 Nm).

10. Install the battery terminal wire and tighten the retaining nut, then engage the alternator wiring connector.
11. Install the alternator brace, then tighten the retaining nuts and bolts to 22 ft. lbs. (30 Nm).
12. Hold the serpentine drive belt tensioner, back off the belt while slipping the belt over the alternator pulley. Gradually lower the tensioner into contact with the belt, then check for proper alignment and tension.
13. Install the wheel and tire assembly. Lower the vehicle.
14. Connect the negative battery cable.
15. Start the vehicle and check for proper alternator operation.

External Voltage Regulator

An external voltage regulator is used with the early 4-cylinder engines. The regulator is mounted on the left inner fender.

REMOVAL & INSTALLATION

1. Disconnect the negative battery cable.
2. Tag and disconnect the electrical leads at the voltage.
3. Remove the regulator mounting screws and remove the regulator.
To install:
4. Install the voltage regulator and secure with the retainer screws.
5. Connect the electrical leads to the regulator.
6. Connect the negative battery cable.
7. Start the vehicle and check for proper voltage.

Fig. 51 Unfasten the control harness from the rear of the alternator assembly—1991 Trooper

Fig. 52 Remove the protective plate over the main power connection

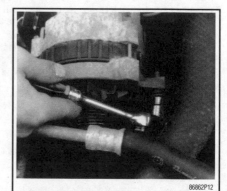

Fig. 53 Loosen and remove the upper adjusting bolt

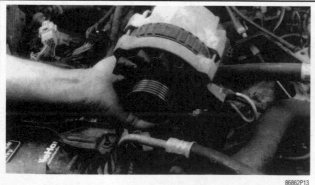

Fig. 54 After the lower retainer bolt has been removed, lift out the alternator assembly

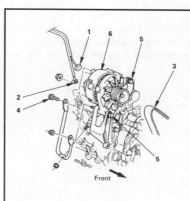

Fig. 55 V6 alternator installation

Removal steps
1. Wiring connector
2. Battery lead wire
3. Drive belt
4. Rear bracket fixing bolt
5. Mounting bolts
6. Generator

Installation steps
To install, follow the removal steps in the reverse order.

Front

STARTING SYSTEM

Starter

TESTING

Voltage Drop Test

➡**The battery must be in good condition and fully charged prior to performing this test.**

1. Disable the ignition system by unplugging the coil pack. Verify that the vehicle will not start.
2. Connect a voltmeter between the positive terminal of the battery and the starter **B+** circuit.
3. Turn the ignition key to the **START** position and note the voltage on the meter.
4. If voltage reads 0.5 volts or more, there is high resistance in the starter cables or the cable ground, repair as necessary. If the voltage reading is ok proceed to the next step.
5. Connect a voltmeter between the positive terminal of the battery and the starter **M** circuit.
6. Turn the ignition key to the **START** position and note the voltage on the meter.
7. If voltage reads 0.5 volts or more, there is high resistance in the starter. Repair or replace the starter as necessary.

➡**Many automotive parts stores have starter bench testers available for use by customers. A starter bench test is the most definitive way to determine the condition of your starter.**

REMOVAL & INSTALLATION

4-Cylinder Engines

▶ **See Figure 56**

1. Disconnect the negative battery cable.
2. Raise and safely support the vehicle on jackstands.
3. If equipped, it may be necessary to disconnect and remove the EGR pipe to access all the starter bolts.
4. Tag and disconnect the starter battery and control wiring at the starter.
5. If equipped, remove the starter bracket and/or heat shield.

6. Remove the starter-to-engine bolts.
7. Move the starter away from the engine and down to remove from the vehicle. Some starter may be installed with shims between the starter and engine. When the starter is removed, these shims may fall out. Do not loose them.

To install:

8. Install the starter and shims, if equipped to the engine. Align the mounting bolt holes and insert the bolts. Hand-tighten the bolts.
9. Tighten the starter mounting bolts to 30–34 ft. lbs. (39–44 Nm).
10. Install the starter bracket and/or heat shield, if equipped.
11. Connect the battery and starter control electrical wires to the starter.
12. If the EGR pipe was removed, install it.
13. Lower the vehicle.
14. Connect the negative battery cable.
15. Start the vehicle to make sure the starter functions correctly.

V6 Engine

▶ **See Figure 57**

1. Disconnect the negative battery cable.
2. Raise and safely support the vehicle on jackstands.
3. Label and disconnect the battery and starter control wires from the starter.
4. If equipped, remove the starter bracket and/or heat shield.
5. Remove the starter-to-engine mounting bolts.
6. Lower the starter from the engine. If any shims are present, keep them for reinstallation purposes.

To install:

7. Install the starter and shims, if equipped, to the engine. Tighten the mounting bolts to 30–34 ft. lbs. (39–44 Nm).
8. Install the starter bracket and/or heat shield, if equipped.
9. Reconnect the electrical connectors to the starter.
10. Lower the vehicle.
11. Connect the negative battery cable.
12. Start the vehicle to make sure the starter functions correctly.

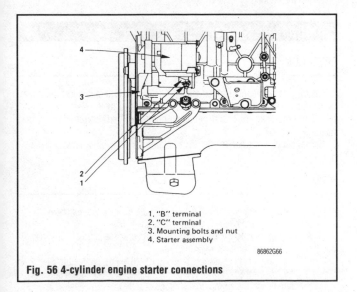

1. "B" terminal
2. "C" terminal
3. Mounting bolts and nut
4. Starter assembly

86862G66

Fig. 56 4-cylinder engine starter connections

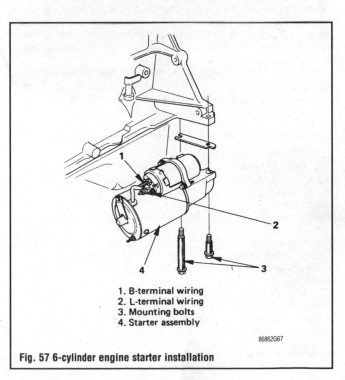

1. B-terminal wiring
2. L-terminal wiring
3. Mounting bolts
4. Starter assembly

86862G67

Fig. 57 6-cylinder engine starter installation

SOLENOID REPLACEMENT

♦ **See Figure 58**

1. Disconnect the negative battery cable.
2. Remove the starter motor from the vehicle and place on a clean work surface.
3. Disconnect the solenoid-to-starter lead wire.
4. Remove the solenoid mounting bolts and slide out the solenoid. Pull out the solenoid torsion spring, if so equipped. On some models, it may be necessary to remove the starter assembly through bolts from the yoke to remove the solenoid.
5. If equipped with shims between the solenoid and starter, remove and place aside.

To install:

6. Install the solenoid with any adjustment shims.
7. Torque the bolts to 15 ft. lbs. (20 Nm).
8. Connect the starter-to-solenoid electrical lead.
9. Install the starter through-bolts if removed.
10. Install the starter motor.
11. Check for proper operation.

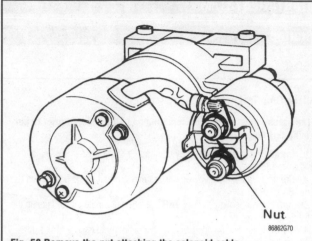

Nut

86862G70

Fig. 58 Remove the nut attaching the solenoid cable

SENDING UNIT AND SENDERS

The following sending units and sensors are not related to engine control. These sensors are only used for the instrument panel warning lights and gauges. For electronic engine control related sensors, please refer to Section 4.

Coolant Temperature Sensor

OPERATION

The coolant temperature sensor is a thermistor where as the coolant temperature increases or decreases, the resistance inside the sensor unit changes accordingly. The coolant sensors' resistance changes inversely as the temperature of the coolant changes. The resistance in the sender unit increases as the fluid temperature decreases and vice versa. When the engine is cold, the resistance of the sender unit is approximately 130 ohms. As the engine warms up to operating temperature, the resistance inside the sender gradually and smoothly decreases to a minimum resistance of 26.7 ohms. At 180° the resistance level is approximately 48.5 ohms.

Depending on the production year, model and trim level, the coolant information gathered by the sensor is relayed to either an "idiot light" or gauge in the instrument cluster or a gauge in the center of the dash panel.

TESTING

1. Remove the coolant temperature sensor from the engine block.
2. Clean any residue from the sensor probe.
3. Attach an ohmmeter to the sensor unit as follows:
   a. Attach one lead to the metal body of the sensor unit (near the sender unit's threads).
   b. Attach the other lead to the sensor unit's wiring harness connector terminal.
4. With the leads still attached, place the sensor unit in a pot of ice water, such that none of the leads are immersed in the water. The probe section of the sensor unit which normally makes contact with the engine coolant should be submerged.
5. Measure the resistance. The resistance should be 98–130 ohms.
6. Slowly heat the pot up (on the stove) and observe the resistance. The resistance should evenly and steadily decrease as the water temperature increases. The resistance should not jump decrease erratically.
7. When the water reaches 190–210° F (88–99° C) the resistance of the sensor unit should be on, or near, 39–26.7 ohms.
8. If the sensor unit did not function as described, replace the sensor.

REMOVAL & INSTALLATION

♦ **See Figures 59 and 60**

1. Disconnect the wire at the sending unit.
2. Drain the cooling system to a level below the sending unit.

✸✸ CAUTION

When draining the coolant, keep in mind that cats and dogs are attracted to ethylene glycol antifreeze, and could drink any that is left in an uncovered container or in puddles on the ground. This will prove fatal in sufficient quantity. Always drain the coolant into a sealable container. Coolant should be reused unless it is contaminated or several years old.

3. Unscrew the sender.
4. Coat the threads of the new sender with sealer and screw it into place. Tighten the sender to 15 ft. lbs. (20 Nm).
5. Connect the wire.
6. Fill the cooling system.

Oil Pressure Sensor

OPERATION

The oil pressure sensor functions by the opening and closing of the contact points in the sensor. This action is controlled by the rising and falling oil pressure, which is dependant upon the oil temperature and engine speed.

The sensor closes when the oil pressure drops to between 4–7 psi (28–48 kPa).

TESTING

This test should be performed if the oil pressure gauge does not show correct oil pressure and the cause is thought to be the sender.

1. Turn the ignition to the **ON** position (do not start the engine). Observe the oil pressure gauge or dash indicator light.
   a. If the gauge reads between 0–30 psi (0–207 kPa), proceed to Step 2.
   b. If the gauge reads 0 or below or the indicator light does not come on, the problem lies in the wiring, to the gauge or indicator.

Fig. 59 Coolant temperature sensor in the intake manifold—2.8L engine

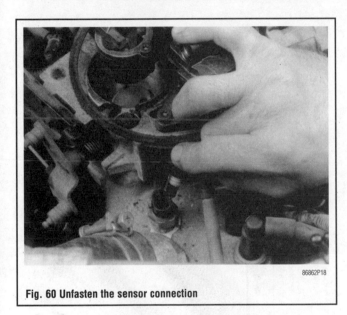

Fig. 60 Unfasten the sensor connection

2. Disconnect the oil pressure switch/sender and short the lead to an engine ground.

    a. If the gauge indicates approximately mid-scale or slightly above mid-scale, replace the oil pressure switch/sender. Retest the system after repairs are complete.

    b. If the gauge does not perform as described above, the problem lies in the wiring, the gauge itself or the instrument cluster.

REMOVAL & INSTALLATION

▶ **See Figures 61 and 62**

➡**The pressure switch type unit used with the indicator lamp system is not interchangeable with the variable resistance type unit used with the gauge system. Installation of the wrong part will result in an inoperative oil pressure indicating system and a damaged switch unit or gauge.**

1. Disconnect the negative battery cable.

2. Locate the sensor at the side of the engine block.
3. Disconnect the wire at the sending/switch unit.
4. Place a drain pan below the sensor to catch any oil which may spill out.
5. Remove the sending unit from the engine block.
To install:
6. Wrap the threads of the new sending unit with Teflon® tape and carefully screw it into place. Make sure not to cross-thread the sending unit.
7. Tighten the sending unit to 15 ft. lbs. (20 Nm).
8. Attach the wire to the sending unit.
9. Connect the negative battery cable.

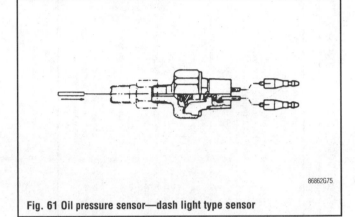

Fig. 61 Oil pressure sensor—dash light type sensor

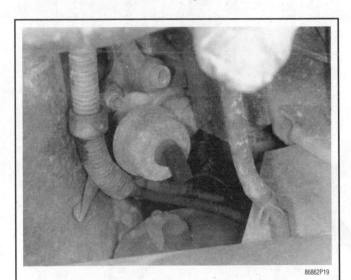

Fig. 62 Oil pressure sensor—gauge type sensor

Troubleshooting Basic Starting System Problems

Problem	Cause	Solution
Starter motor rotates engine slowly	• Battery charge low or battery defective	• Charge or replace battery
	• Defective circuit between battery and starter motor	• Clean and tighten, or replace cables
	• Low load current	• Bench-test starter motor. Inspect for worn brushes and weak brush springs.
	• High load current	• Bench-test starter motor. Check engine for friction, drag or coolant in cylinders. Check ring gear-to-pinion gear clearance.
Starter motor will not rotate engine	• Battery charge low or battery defective	• Charge or replace battery
	• Faulty solenoid	• Check solenoid ground. Repair or replace as necessary.
	• Damaged drive pinion gear or ring gear	• Replace damaged gear(s)
	• Starter motor engagement weak	• Bench-test starter motor
	• Starter motor rotates slowly with high load current	• Inspect drive yoke pull-down and point gap, check for worn end bushings, check ring gear clearance
	• Engine seized	• Repair engine
Starter motor drive will not engage (solenoid known to be good)	• Defective contact point assembly	• Repair or replace contact point assembly
	• Inadequate contact point assembly ground	• Repair connection at ground screw
	• Defective hold-in coil	• Replace field winding assembly
Starter motor drive will not disengage	• Starter motor loose on flywheel housing	• Tighten mounting bolts
	• Worn drive end busing	• Replace bushing
	• Damaged ring gear teeth	• Replace ring gear or driveplate
	• Drive yoke return spring broken or missing	• Replace spring
Starter motor drive disengages prematurely	• Weak drive assembly thrust spring	• Replace drive mechanism
	• Hold-in coil defective	• Replace field winding assembly
Low load current	• Worn brushes	• Replace brushes
	• Weak brush springs	• Replace springs

TCCS2C01

Troubleshooting Basic Charging System Problems

Problem	Cause	Solution
Noisy alternator	• Loose mountings	• Tighten mounting bolts
	• Loose drive pulley	• Tighten pulley
	• Worn bearings	• Replace alternator
	• Brush noise	• Replace alternator
	• Internal circuits shorted (High pitched whine)	• Replace alternator
Squeal when starting engine or accelerating	• Glazed or loose belt	• Replace or adjust belt
Indicator light remains on or ammeter indicates discharge (engine running)	• Broken belt	• Install belt
	• Broken or disconnected wires	• Repair or connect wiring
	• Internal alternator problems	• Replace alternator
	• Defective voltage regulator	• Replace voltage regulator/alternator
Car light bulbs continually burn out—battery needs water continually	• Alternator/regulator overcharging	• Replace voltage regulator/alternator
Car lights flare on acceleration	• Battery low	• Charge or replace battery
	• Internal alternator/regulator problems	• Replace alternator/regulator
Low voltage output (alternator light flickers continually or ammeter needle wanders)	• Loose or worn belt	• Replace or adjust belt
	• Dirty or corroded connections	• Clean or replace connections
	• Internal alternator/regulator problems	• Replace alternator/regulator

TCCS2C02

3

ENGINE AND ENGINE OVERHAUL

ENGINE MECHANICAL

VALVE SPECIFICATIONS

Year	Engine ID/VIN	Engine Displacement Liters (cc)	Seat Angle (deg.)	Face Angle (deg.)	Spring Test Pressure (lbs.@in.)	Spring Installed Height (in.)	Stem-to-Guide Clearance (in.) Intake	Stem-to-Guide Clearance (in.) Exhaust	Stem Diameter (in.) Intake	Stem Diameter (in.) Exhaust
1981	G180Z	1.8 (1816)				[3]	0.0009-0.0022	0.0015-0.0031	0.3150	0.3150
	C223	2.2 (2238)	45	45	[2]	[4]	0.0015-0.0027	0.0025-0.0037	0.3150	0.3150
1982	G180Z	1.8 (1816)	45	45	[1]	[3]	0.0009-0.0022	0.0015-0.0031	0.3150	0.3150
	C223	2.2 (2238)	45	45	[2]	[4]	0.0015-0.0027	0.0025-0.0037	0.3150	0.3150
1983	G200Z	2.0 (1949)	45	45	56@1.60	1.60	0.0009-0.0022	0.0015-0.0031	0.3150	0.3150
	C223	2.2 (2238)	45	45	[2]	[4]	0.0015-0.0027	0.0025-0.0037	0.3150	0.3150
1984	G200Z	2.0 (1949)	45	45	56@1.60	1.60	0.0009-0.0022	0.0015-0.0031	0.3150	0.3150
	C223	2.2 (2238)	45	45	[2]	[4]	0.0015-0.0027	0.0025-0.0037	0.3150	0.3150
1985	G200Z	2.0 (1949)	45	45	56@1.60	1.60	0.0009-0.0022	0.0015-0.0031	0.3150	0.3150
	C223	2.2 (2238)	45	45	[2]	[4]	0.0015-0.0027	0.0025-0.0037	0.3150	0.3150
1986	G200Z	2.0 (1949)	45	45	56@1.60	1.60	0.0009-0.0022	0.0015-0.0031	0.3150	0.3150
	C223	2.2 (2238)	45	45	[2]	[4]	0.0015-0.0027	0.0025-0.0037	0.3150	0.3150
	C223T	2.2 (2238)	45	45	[2]	[4]	0.0015-0.0027	0.0025-0.0037	0.3150	0.3150
1987	4ZD1	2.3 (2254)	45	45	55.3@1.62	1.62	0.0009-0.0022	0.0015-0.0037	0.3150	0.3410-0.3420
	G200Z	2.0 (1949)	45	45	56@1.60	1.60	0.0009-0.0022	0.0015-0.0031	0.3150	0.3150
	C223	2.2 (2238)	45	45	[2]	[4]	0.0015-0.0027	0.0025-0.0037	0.3150	0.3150
	C223T	2.2 (2238)	45	45	[2]	[4]	0.0015-0.0027	0.0025-0.0037	0.3150	0.3150
1988	4ZD1	2.3 (2254)	45	45	55.3@1.62	1.62	0.0009-0.0022	0.0015-0.0037	0.3150	0.3410-0.3420
	4ZE1	2.6 (2559)	45	45	55.3@1.62	1.62	0.0009-0.0022	0.0015-0.0031	0.3150	0.3150
1989	4ZD1	2.3 (2254)	45	45	49-56@1.61	1.62	0.0009-0.0022	0.0015-0.0031	0.3150	0.3150
	4ZE1	2.6 (2559)	45	45	49-56@1.61	1.62	0.0009-0.0022	0.0015-0.0031	0.3150	0.3150
	CPC	2.8 (2828)	46	45	175@1.26	1.72	0.0010-0.0027	0.0010-0.0027	0.3410-0.3420	0.3410-0.3420
1990	4ZD1	2.3 (2254)	45	45	49-56@1.61	1.62	0.0009-0.0022	0.0015-0.0031	0.3150	0.3150
	4ZE1	2.6 (2559)	45	45	49-56@1.61	1.62	0.0009-0.0022	0.0015-0.0031	0.3150	0.3150
	CPC	2.8 (2828)	46	45	175@1.26	1.72	0.0010-0.0027	0.0010-0.0027	0.3410-0.3420	0.3410-0.3420

86863C02

GENERAL ENGINE SPECIFICATIONS

Year	Engine ID/VIN	Engine Displacement Liters (cc)	Fuel System Type	Net Horsepower @ rpm	Net Torque @ rpm (ft. lbs.)	Bore x Stroke (in.)	Compression Ratio	Oil Pressure @ rpm
1981	G180Z	1.8 (1816)	2 BBL	80@4600	95@3000	3.31x3.23	8.5:1	57@1400
1982	C223	2.2 (2238)	DSL	56@4300	93@2200	3.46x3.62	21.1:1	55@1400
	G180Z	1.8 (1816)	2 BBL	80@4600	95@3000	3.31x3.23	8.5:1	57@1400
1983	C223	2.2 (2238)	DSL	58@4300	93@2200	3.46x3.62	21.1:1	55@1400
	G200Z	2.0 (1949)	2 BBL	82@4600	101@3000	3.42x3.23	8.4:1	57@1400
1984	C223	2.2 (2238)	DSL	56@4300	93@2200	3.46x3.62	21.1:1	55@1400
	G200Z	2.0 (1949)	2 BBL	82@4600	101@3000	3.42x3.23	8.4:1	57@1400
1985	C223	2.2 (2238)	DSL	56@4300	93@2200	3.46x3.62	21.1:1	55@1400
	G200Z	2.0 (1949)	2 BBL	82@4600	101@3000	3.42x3.23	8.4:1	57@1400
1986	C223	2.2 (2238)	DSL	58@4300	93@2200	3.46x3.62	21.1:1	55@1400
	G200Z	2.0 (1949)	2 BBL	80@4000	128@2200	3.46x3.62	21.1:1	55@1400
	C223	2.2 (2238)	DSL	80@4000	128@2200	3.46x3.62	21.1:1	55@1400
	C223T	2.3 (2254)	MFI	96@4600	123@2600	3.52x3.54	8.3:1	57@3000
1987	4ZD1	2.0 (1949)	2 BBL	82@4600	101@3000	3.42x3.23	8.4:1	57@1400
	G200Z	2.2 (2238)	DSL	58@4300	93@2200	3.46x3.62	21.1:1	55@1400
	C223	2.2 (2238)	DSL	80@4000	128@2200	3.46x3.62	21.1:1	55@1400
	C223T	2.3 (2254)	MFI	96@4600	123@2600	3.52x3.54	8.3:1	57@3000
1988	4ZD1	2.3 (2254)	MFI	120@4600	150@2600	3.65x3.74	8.6:1	57-71@4000
	4ZE1	2.6 (2559)	MFI	96@4600	123@2600	3.52x3.54	8.3:1	57@3000
1989	4ZD1	2.3 (2254)	MFI	120@4600	150@2600	3.65x3.74	8.6:1	57-71@4000
	4ZE1	2.6 (2559)	MFI	125@4800	150@2400	3.50x2.99	8.9:1	30-55@2000
	CPC	2.8 (2828)	TFI	96@4600	123@2600	3.52x3.54	8.3:1	57@3000
1990	4ZD1	2.3 (2254)	MFI	120@4600	150@2600	3.65x3.74	8.6:1	57-71@4000
	4ZE1	2.6 (2559)	MFI	125@4800	150@2400	3.50x2.99	8.9:1	30-55@2000
	CPC	2.8 (2828)	TFI	120@4400	150@2600	3.65x3.74	8.6:1	57-71@4000
	6VD1 [1]	3.1 (3098)	MFI	125@5200	165@2800	3.50x3.31	8.9:1	57-80@3000
	6VD1 [2]	3.2 (3165)	MFI	96@4600	123@2600	3.52x3.54	8.3:1	57@3000
1991	4ZD1	2.3 (2254)	MFI	120@4600	150@2600	3.65x3.74	8.6:1	57-71@4000
	4ZE1	2.6 (2559)	MFI	125@4800	150@2400	3.50x2.99	8.9:1	30-55@2000
	CPC	2.8 (2828)	TFI	120@4400	150@2600	3.65x3.74	8.6:1	57-71@4000
	6VD1 [1]	3.1 (3098)	MFI	175@5200	188@4000	3.67x3.03	9.3:1	57-80@3000
	6VD1 [2]	3.2 (3165)	MFI	96@4600	123@2600	3.52x3.54	8.3:1	57@3000
1992	4ZD1	2.3 (2254)	MFI	120@4600	150@2600	3.65x3.74	8.6:1	57-71@4000
	4ZE1	2.6 (2559)	MFI	125@4800	150@2400	3.50x2.99	8.9:1	30-55@2000
	CPC	2.8 (2828)	TFI	120@4400	165@2800	3.50x3.31	8.5:1	57-71@4000
	6VD1 [1]	3.1 (3098)	MFI	175@5200	188@4000	3.67x3.03	9.3:1	57-80@3000
	6VD1 [2]	3.2 (3165)	MFI	100@4600	125@2600	3.52x3.54	8.3:1	57@3000
1993	4ZD1	2.3 (2243)	MFI	120@4600	150@2600	3.65x3.74	8.6:1	57-71@4000
	4ZE1	2.6 (2559)	MFI	175@5200	188@4000	3.67x3.03	9.3:1	57-80@3000
	6VD1 [1]	3.1 (3098)	MFI	190@5600	195@3800	3.67x3.03	9.8:1	57-80@3000
	6VD1 [2]	3.2 (3165)	MFI	120@4600	150@2600	3.65x3.74	8.6:1	57-71@4000
1994	4ZE1	2.6 (2559)	MFI	175@5200	188@4000	3.67x3.03	9.3:1	57-80@3000
	6VD1 [1]	3.2 (3165)	MFI	190@5600	195@3800	3.67x3.03	9.8:1	57-80@3000
	6VD1 [2]	3.2 (3165)	MFI	120@4600	150@2600	3.65x3.74	8.6:1	57-71@4000
1995	4ZE1	2.6 (2559)	MFI	175@5200	188@4000	3.67x3.03	9.3:1	57-80@3000
	6VD1 [1]	3.2 (3165)	MFI	190@5600	188@4000	3.68x3.03	9.1:1	57-80@3000
1996	6VD1 [2]	3.2 (3165)	MFI	190@5600	188@4000	3.68x3.03	9.1:1	57-80@3000

MFI - Multi-port Fuel Injection
BBL - Barrel carburetor
DSL - Diesel
TFI - Throttle body Fuel Injection
[1] Single Overhead Camshaft (SOHC)
[2] Double Overhead Camshaft (DOHC)

86863C01

CAMSHAFT SPECIFICATIONS
All measurements given in inches.

Year	Engine ID/VIN	Engine Displacement Liters (cc)	Journal Diameter 1	2	3	4	5	Elevation In.	Elevation Ex.	Bearing Clearance	Camshaft End-Play
1981	G180Z	1.8 (1816)	1.3362-1.3368	1.3362-1.3368	1.3362-1.3368	1.3362-1.3368	1.3362-1.3368	1.4510	1.4510	0.0016-0.0035	0.0020-0.0059
	C223	2.2 (2238)	1.8900	1.8900	1.8900	-	-	NA	NA	0.0020	0.0080
1982	G180Z	1.8 (1816)	1.3362-1.3368	1.3362-1.3368	1.3362-1.3368	1.3362-1.3368	1.3362-1.3368	1.4510	1.4510	0.0016-0.0035	0.0020-0.0059
	C223	2.2 (2238)	1.8900	1.8900	1.8900	-	-	NA	NA	0.0020	0.0080
1983	G200Z	2.0 (1949)	1.3390	1.3390	1.3390	1.3390	1.3390	1.4510	1.4510	0.0030-0.0043	0.0020-0.0060
	C223	2.2 (2238)	1.8900	1.8900	1.8900	-	-	NA	NA	0.0020	0.0080
1984	G200Z	2.0 (1949)	1.3390	1.3390	1.3390	1.3390	1.3390	1.4510	1.4510	0.0030-0.0043	0.0020-0.0060
	C223	2.2 (2238)	1.8900	1.8900	1.8900	-	-	NA	NA	0.0020	0.0080
1985	G200Z	2.0 (1949)	1.3390	1.3390	1.3390	1.3390	1.3390	1.4510	1.4510	0.0030-0.0043	0.0020-0.0060
	C223	2.2 (2238)	1.8900	1.8900	1.8900	-	-	NA	NA	0.0020	0.0080
1986	G200Z	2.0 (1949)	1.3390	1.3390	1.3390	1.3390	1.3390	1.4510	1.4510	0.0030-0.0043	0.0020-0.0060
	C223	2.2 (2238)	1.8900	1.8900	1.8900	-	-	NA	NA	0.0020	0.0080
	C223T	2.2 (2238)	1.8900	1.8900	1.8900	-	-	NA	NA	0.0020	0.0080
	4ZD1	2.3 (2254)	1.3390	1.3390	1.3390	1.3390	1.3390	1.4510	1.4510	0.0033-0.0051	0.0020-0.0059
1987	G200Z	2.0 (1949)	1.3390	1.3390	1.3390	1.3390	1.3390	1.4510	1.4510	0.0030-0.0043	0.0020-0.0060
	C223	2.2 (2238)	1.8900	1.8900	1.8900	-	-	NA	NA	0.0020	0.0080
	C223T	2.2 (2238)	1.8900	1.8900	1.8900	-	-	NA	NA	0.0020	0.0080
	4ZD1	2.3 (2254)	1.3390	1.3390	1.3390	1.3390	1.3390	1.4510	1.4510	0.0033-0.0051	0.0020-0.0059
1988	4ZD1	2.3 (2254)	1.3390	1.3390	1.3390	1.3390	1.3390	1.4510	1.4510	0.0033-0.0051	0.0020-0.0059
	4ZE1	2.6 (2559)	1.3390	1.3390	1.3390	1.3390	1.3390	1.4510	1.4510	0.0026-0.0043	0.0020-0.0080
1989	4ZD1	2.3 (2254)	1.3390	1.3390	1.3390	1.3390	1.3390	1.4510	1.4510	0.0033-0.0051	0.0020-0.0059
	4ZE1	2.6 (2559)	1.3390	1.3390	1.3390	1.3390	1.3390	1.4510	1.4510	0.0026-0.0043	0.0020-0.0080
	CPC	2.8 (2828)	1.8670-1.8810	1.8670-1.8810	1.8670-1.8810	1.8670-1.8810	-	0.2620-0.2730	0.2620-0.2730	0.0010-0.0040	NA
1990	4ZD1	2.3 (2254)	1.3390	1.3390	1.3390	1.3390	1.3390	1.4510	1.4510	0.0033-0.0051	0.0002-0.0069
	4ZE1	2.6 (2559)	1.3390	1.3390	1.3390	1.3390	1.3390	1.4510	1.4510	0.0026-0.0043	0.0020-0.0080
	CPC	2.8 (2828)	1.8670-1.8810	1.8670-1.8810	1.8670-1.8810	1.8670-1.8810	-	0.2620-0.2730	0.2620-0.2730	0.0010-0.0040	NA

NA - Not Available

86863C04

VALVE SPECIFICATIONS

Year	Engine ID/VIN	Engine Displacement Liters (cc)	Seat Angle (deg.)	Face Angle (deg.)	Spring Test Pressure (lbs. @ in.)	Spring Installed Height (in.)	Stem-to-Guide Clearance Intake	Exhaust	Stem Diameter Intake	Exhaust
1991	4ZD1	2.3 (2245)	45	45	49-56@1.61	1.61	0.0009-0.0080	0.0015-0.0098	0.3102-0.3134	0.3091-0.3124
	4ZE1	2.6 (2559)	45	45	49-56@1.61	1.61	0.0009-0.0080	0.0015-0.0098	0.3102-0.3134	0.3091-0.3124
	CPC	2.8 (2828)	46	45	175@1.26	1.72	0.0010-0.0080	0.0015-0.0098	0.3102-0.3134	0.3091-0.3124
	CPC	3.1 (3098)	46	45	82@1.58	1.58	0.0010-0.0027	0.0010-0.0027	0.3410-0.3420	0.3410-0.3420
1992	4ZD1	2.3 (2254)	45	45	49-56@1.61	1.61	0.0009-0.0080	0.0015-0.0098	0.3102-0.3134	0.3091-0.3124
	4ZE1	2.6 (2559)	45	45	49-56@1.61	1.61	0.0009-0.0080	0.0015-0.0098	0.3102-0.3134	0.3091-0.3124
	CPC	3.1 (3098)	46	45	82@1.58	1.58	0.0010-0.0027	0.0010-0.0027	0.3410-0.3420	0.3410-0.3420
	6VD1	3.2 (3165)	45	45	45-55@1.54	1.54	0.0009-0.0078	0.0012-0.0078	0.2323-0.2346	0.2323-0.2350
1993	4ZD1	2.3 (2254)	45	45	49-56@1.61	1.61	0.0009-0.0080	0.0015-0.0098	0.3102-0.3134	0.3091-0.3124
	4ZE1	2.6 (2559)	45	45	49-56@1.61	1.61	0.0009-0.0080	0.0015-0.0098	0.3102-0.3134	0.3091-0.3124
	CPC	3.1 (3098)	46	45	82@1.58	1.58	0.0010-0.0027	0.0010-0.0027	0.3410-0.3420	0.3410-0.3420
	6VD1	3.2 (3165)	45	45	45-55@1.54	1.54	0.0009-0.0078	0.0012-0.0078	0.2323-0.2346	0.2323-0.2350
1994	4ZD1	2.3 (2254)	45	45	49-56@1.61	1.61	0.0009-0.0080	0.0015-0.0098	0.3102-0.3134	0.3091-0.3124
	4ZE1	2.6 (2559)	45	45	49-56@1.61	1.61	0.0009-0.0080	0.0015-0.0098	0.3102-0.3134	0.3091-0.3124
	CPC	3.1 (3098)	46	45	82@1.58	1.58	0.0010-0.0027	0.0010-0.0027	0.3410-0.3420	0.3410-0.3420
	6VD1	3.2 (3165)	45	45	45-55@1.54	1.54	0.0009-0.0078	0.0012-0.0078	0.2323-0.2346	0.2323-0.2350
1995	4ZD1	2.3 (2254)	45	45	49-56@1.61	1.61	0.0009-0.0080	0.0015-0.0098	0.3102-0.3134	0.3091-0.3124
	4ZE1	2.6 (2559)	45	45	45-55@1.61	1.61	0.0009-0.0080	0.0015-0.0098	0.3102-0.3134	0.3091-0.3124
	6VD1	3.2 (3165)	45	45	45-55@1.54	1.54	0.0009-0.0078	0.0012-0.0078	0.2323-0.2353	0.2323-0.2350
1996	4ZE1	2.6 (2559)	45	45	45-55@1.61	1.61	0.0009-0.0079	0.0015-0.0098	0.3102-0.3134	0.3091-0.3124
	6VD1	3.2 (3165)	45	45	45-55@1.54	1.54	0.0009-0.0079	0.0012-0.0079	0.2323-0.2353	0.2323-0.2350

1 Inner: 20@1.516
   Outer: 34.5@1.614
2 Inner: 12-14@1.45
   Outer: 43-49@1.53
3 Inner: 1.51
   Outer: 1.61
4 Inner: 1.45
   Outer: 1.53

NA - Not Available

86863C03

CRANKSHAFT AND CONNECTING ROD SPECIFICATIONS

All measurements are given in inches.

Year	Engine ID/VIN	Engine Displacement Liters (cc)	Crankshaft Main Brg. Journal Dia.	Crankshaft Main Brg. Oil Clearance	Crankshaft Shaft End-Play	Crankshaft Thrust on No.	Connecting Rod Journal Diameter	Connecting Rod Oil Clearance	Connecting Rod Side Clearance
1981	G180Z	1.8 (1816)	2.2016-2.2022	0.0008-0.0025	0.0024-0.0094	3	1.9290	0.0007-0.0030	0.0137
	C223	2.2 (2238)	2.3591-2.3594	0.0011-0.0033	0.0039	3	2.0635-2.0839	0.0016	0.0137
1982	G180Z	1.8 (1816)	2.2016-2.2022	0.0008-0.0025	0.0024-0.0094	3	1.9290	0.0007-0.0030	0.0137
	C223	2.2 (2238)	2.3591-2.3594	0.0011-0.0033	0.0039	3	2.0635-2.0839	0.0016	0.0137
1983	G200Z	2.0 (1949)	2.2016-2.2022	0.0008-0.0025	0.0024-0.0094	3	1.9290	0.0007-0.0029	0.0078-0.0130
	C223	2.2 (2238)	2.3591-2.3594	0.0011-0.0033	0.0039	3	2.0635-2.0839	0.0016	0.0137
1984	G200Z	2.0 (1949)	2.2016-2.2022	0.0008-0.0025	0.0024-0.0094	3	1.9290	0.0007-0.0029	0.0078-0.0130
	C223	2.2 (2238)	2.3591-2.3594	0.0011-0.0033	0.0039	3	2.0635-2.0839	0.0016	0.0137
1985	G200Z	2.0 (1949)	2.2016-2.2022	0.0008-0.0025	0.0024-0.0094	3	1.9290	0.0007-0.0029	0.0078-0.0130
	C223	2.2 (2238)	2.3591-2.3594	0.0011-0.0033	0.0039	3	2.0635-2.0839	0.0016	0.0137
1986	G200Z	2.0 (1949)	2.2016-2.2022	0.0008-0.0025	0.0024-0.0094	3	1.9290	0.0007-0.0029	0.0078-0.0130
	C223	2.2 (2238)	2.3591-2.3594	0.0011-0.0033	0.0039	3	2.0635-2.0839	0.0016	0.0137
	C223T	2.2 (2238)	2.3591-2.3594	0.0011-0.0033	0.0039	3	2.0635-2.0839	0.0016	0.0137
	4ZD1	2.3 (2254)	2.2032-2.2038	0.0009-0.0020	0.0024-0.0099	3	1.9276-1.9282	0.0012-0.0024	0.0078-0.0130
1987	G200Z	2.0 (1949)	2.2016-2.2022	0.0008-0.0025	0.0024-0.0094	3	1.9290	0.0007-0.0029	0.0078-0.0130
	C223	2.2 (2238)	2.3591-2.3594	0.0011-0.0033	0.0039	3	2.0635-2.0839	0.0016	0.0137
	C223T	2.2 (2238)	2.3591-2.3594	0.0011-0.0033	0.0039	3	2.0635-2.0839	0.0016	0.0137
1988	4ZD1	2.3 (2254)	2.2032-2.2038	0.0009-0.0020	0.0024-0.0099	3	1.9276-1.9282	0.0012-0.0024	0.0078-0.0130
	4ZE1	2.6 (2559)	2.1819-2.2016	0.0009-0.0047	0.0024-0.0118	3	1.9065-1.9262	0.0008-0.0020	0.0078-0.0130
1989	4ZD1	2.3 (2254)	2.2032-2.2038	0.0009-0.0020	0.0024-0.0099	3	1.9276-1.9282	0.0012-0.0024	0.0078-0.0130
	4ZE1	2.6 (2559)	2.1819-2.2016	0.0009-0.0047	0.0024-0.0118	3	1.9065-1.9262	0.0008-0.0020	0.0078-0.0130
	CPC	2.8 (2828)	2.6473-2.6483	0.0016-0.0033	0.0020-0.0080	3	1.9993-1.9993	0.0013-0.0026	0.0060-0.0170
1990	4ZD1	2.3 (2254)	2.2032-2.2038	0.0009-0.0020	0.0024-0.0099	3	1.9262	0.0012-0.0024	0.0078-0.0130
	4ZE1	2.6 (2559)	2.1819-2.2016	0.0009-0.0047	0.0024-0.0118	3	1.9262	0.0008-0.0020	0.0078-0.0130
	CPC	2.8 (2828)	2.6473-2.6483	0.0016-0.0033	0.0020-0.0080	3	1.9993-1.9993	0.0013-0.0026	0.0060-0.0170

86863C06

CAMSHAFT SPECIFICATIONS

All measurements given in inches.

Year	Engine ID/VIN	Engine Displacement Liters (cc)	Journal Diameter 1	2	3	4	5	Elevation In.	Elevation Ex.	Bearing Clearance	Camshaft End-Play
1991	4ZD1	2.3 (2254)	1.3390	1.3390	1.3390	1.3390	1.3390	1.4510	1.4510	0.0033-0.0061	0.0002-0.0059
	4ZE1	2.6 (2559)	1.3390	1.3390	1.3390	1.3390	1.3390	NA	NA	0.0026-0.0043	0.0059-0.0080
	CPC	2.8 (2828)	1.8670-1.8810	1.8670-1.8810	1.8670-1.8810	1.8670-1.8810	NA	0.2620-0.2730	0.2620-0.2730	0.0010-0.0040	NA
	CPC	3.1 (3098)	1.8670-1.8810	1.8670-1.8810	1.8670-1.8810	1.8670-1.8810	NA	0.2300-0.2670	0.2300-0.2670	0.0010-0.0040	NA
1992	4ZD1	2.3 (2254)	1.3310-1.3390	1.3310-1.3390	1.3310-1.3390	1.3310-1.3390	1.3310-1.3390	1.4320-1.4560	1.4320-1.4560	0.0033-0.0051	0.0002-0.0059
	4ZE1	2.6 (2559)	1.3310-1.3390	1.3310-1.3390	1.3310-1.3390	1.3310-1.3390	1.3310-1.3390	NA	NA	0.0026-0.0043	0.0080[5]
	CPC	3.1 (3098)	1.8670-1.8810	1.8670-1.8810	1.8670-1.8810	1.8670-1.8810	NA	0.2300-0.2670	0.2300-0.2670	0.0010-0.0040	NA
	6VD1 [1]	3.2 (3165)	1.7634-1.7701	1.7634-1.7701	1.7634-1.7701	1.7634-1.7701	1.7634-1.7701	[3]	[3]	0.0016-0.0197	0.0020-0.0079
	6VD1 [2]	3.2 (3165)	1.0555-1.0618	1.0555-1.0618	1.0555-1.0618	1.0500-1.0510	1.0500-1.0510	[4]	[4]	0.0019-0.0069	0.0020-0.0079
1993	4ZD1	2.3 (2254)	1.3310-1.3390	1.3310-1.3390	1.3310-1.3390	1.3310-1.3390	1.3310-1.3390	1.4320-1.4560	1.4320-1.4560	0.0033-0.0051	0.0002-0.0059
	4ZE1	2.6 (2559)	1.3390	1.3390	1.3390	1.3390	1.3390	NA	NA	0.0026-0.0043	0.0059-0.0080
	CPC	3.1 (3098)	1.8670-1.8810	1.8670-1.8810	1.8670-1.8810	1.8670-1.8810	NA	0.2300-0.2670	0.2300-0.2670	0.0010-0.0040	NA
	6VD1 [1]	3.2 (3165)	1.7634-1.7701	1.7634-1.7701	1.7634-1.7701	1.7634-1.7701	1.7634-1.7701	[3]	[3]	0.0016-0.0197	0.0020-0.0079
	6VD1 [2]	3.2 (3165)	1.0555-1.0618	1.0555-1.0618	1.0555-1.0618	1.0500-1.0510	1.0500-1.0510	[4]	[4]	0.0019-0.0059	0.0020-0.0060
1994	4ZD1	2.3 (2254)	1.3310-1.3390	1.3310-1.3390	1.3310-1.3390	1.3310-1.3390	1.3310-1.3390	1.4320-1.4560	1.4320-1.4560	0.0033-0.0051	0.0002-0.0059
	4ZE1	2.6 (2559)	1.3390	1.3390	1.3390	1.3390	1.3390	NA	NA	0.0026-0.0043	0.0080[5]
	CPC	3.1 (3098)	1.8670-1.8810	1.8670-1.8810	1.8670-1.8810	1.8670-1.8810	NA	0.2300-0.2670	0.2300-0.2670	0.0010-0.0040	NA
	6VD1 [1]	3.2 (3165)	1.7634-1.7701	1.7634-1.7701	1.7634-1.7701	1.7634-1.7701	1.7634-1.7701	1.5030	1.5030	0.0011-0.0031	0.0020-0.0060
	6VD1 [2]	3.2 (3165)	1.0500-1.0510	1.0500-1.0510	1.0500-1.0510	1.0500-1.0510	1.0500-1.0510	1.5030	1.5030	0.0011-0.0031	0.0020-0.0060
1995	4ZD1	2.3 (2254)	1.3310-1.3390	1.3310-1.3390	1.3310-1.3390	1.3310-1.3390	1.3310-1.3390	1.4320-1.4560	1.4320-1.4560	0.0033-0.0051	0.0002-0.0059
	4ZE1	2.6 (2559)	1.3307-1.3386	1.3307-1.3386	1.3307-1.3386	1.3307-1.3386	1.3307-1.3386	1.4311-1.4331	1.4311-1.4331	0.0033-0.0059	0.0020-0.0079
	6VD1 [1]	3.2 (3165)	1.7634-1.7701	1.7634-1.7701	1.7634-1.7701	1.7634-1.7701	1.7634-1.7701	1.3480-1.3500	1.4638-1.4658	0.0016-0.0197	0.0028-0.0098
	6VD1 [2]	3.2 (3165)	1.0555-1.0618	1.0555-1.0618	1.0555-1.0618	1.0555-1.0618	1.0555-1.0618	1.3437-1.3457	1.3437-1.3457	0.0019-0.0059	0.0020-0.0079
1996	4ZE1	2.6 (2559)	1.3307-1.3386	1.3307-1.3386	1.3307-1.3386	1.3307-1.3386	1.3386	1.4291-1.4311	1.4291-1.4311	0.0033	0.0020-0.0079
	6VD1	3.2 (3165)	1.7634-1.7701	1.7634-1.7701	1.7634-1.7701	1.7634-1.7701	1.7701	1.3460-1.3480	1.4618-1.4638	0.0016-0.0197	0.0028-0.0098

NA - Not Available
1 Single overhead camshaft
2 Double overhead camshaft
3 Intake or exhaust: 1.6732-1.6870
4 Intake: 1.7441-1.7579 Exhaust: 1.7429-1.7567
5 Limit

86863C05

PISTON AND RING SPECIFICATIONS

All measurements are given in inches.

Year	Engine ID/VIN	Engine Displacement Liters (cc)	Piston Clearance	Ring Gap Top Compression	Ring Gap Bottom Compression	Ring Gap Oil Control	Ring Side Top Compression	Ring Side Bottom Compression	Ring Side Oil Control
1981	G180Z	1.8 (1816)	0.0018-0.0026	0.0120-0.0180	0.0120-0.0180	0.0080-0.0350	0.0059	0.0059	0.0059
	C223	2.2 (2238)	0.0014-0.0022	0.0079-0.0158	0.0079-0.0158	0.0079-0.0158	0.0018-0.0028	0.0012-0.0021	0.0008-0.0021
1982	G180Z	1.8 (1816)	0.0018-0.0026	0.0120-0.0180	0.0120-0.0180	0.0080-0.0350	0.0059	0.0059	0.0059
	C223	2.2 (2238)	0.0014-0.0022	0.0079-0.0158	0.0079-0.0158	0.0079-0.0158	0.0018-0.0028	0.0012-0.0021	0.0008-0.0021
1983	G200Z	2.0 (1949)	0.0018-0.0026	0.0120-0.0180	0.0100-0.0160	0.0080-0.0280	0.0010-0.0024	0.0010-0.0024	0.0008
	C223	2.2 (2238)	0.0014-0.0022	0.0079-0.0158	0.0079-0.0158	0.0079-0.0158	0.0018-0.0028	0.0012-0.0021	0.0008-0.0021
1984	G200Z	2.0 (1949)	0.0018-0.0026	0.0120-0.0180	0.0100-0.0160	0.0080-0.0280	0.0010-0.0024	0.0010-0.0024	0.0008
	C223	2.2 (2238)	0.0014-0.0022	0.0079-0.0158	0.0079-0.0158	0.0079-0.0158	0.0018-0.0028	0.0012-0.0021	0.0008-0.0021
1985	G200Z	2.0 (1949)	0.0018-0.0026	0.0120-0.0180	0.0100-0.0160	0.0080-0.0280	0.0010-0.0024	0.0010-0.0024	0.0008
	C223	2.2 (2238)	0.0014-0.0022	0.0079-0.0158	0.0079-0.0158	0.0079-0.0158	0.0018-0.0028	0.0012-0.0021	0.0008-0.0021
1986	G200Z	2.0 (1949)	0.0018-0.0026	0.0120-0.0180	0.0100-0.0160	0.0080-0.0280	0.0010-0.0024	0.0010-0.0024	0.0008
	C223	2.2 (2238)	0.0014-0.0022	0.0079-0.0158	0.0079-0.0158	0.0079-0.0158	0.0018-0.0028	0.0012-0.0021	0.0008-0.0021
	C223T	2.2 (2238)	0.0014-0.0022	0.0079-0.0158	0.0079-0.0158	0.0079-0.0158	0.0018-0.0028	0.0012-0.0021	0.0008-0.0021
1987	4ZD1	2.3 (2254)	0.0016-0.0024	0.0120-0.0180	0.0120-0.0180	0.0080-0.0280	0.0010-0.0024	0.0010-0.0024	NA
	G200Z	2.0 (1949)	0.0018-0.0026	0.0120-0.0180	0.0100-0.0160	0.0080-0.0280	0.0010-0.0024	0.0010-0.0024	0.0008
	C223	2.2 (2238)	0.0014-0.0022	0.0079-0.0158	0.0079-0.0158	0.0079-0.0158	0.0018-0.0028	0.0012-0.0021	0.0008-0.0021
	C223T	2.2 (2238)	0.0014-0.0022	0.0079-0.0158	0.0079-0.0158	0.0079-0.0158	0.0018-0.0028	0.0012-0.0021	0.0008-0.0021
1988	4ZD1	2.3 (2254)	0.0016-0.0024	0.0120-0.0180	0.0120-0.0180	0.0080-0.0280	0.0010-0.0024	0.0010-0.0024	NA
	4ZE1	2.6 (2559)	0.0016-0.0024	0.0120-0.0180	0.0120-0.0180	0.0080-0.0280	0.0010-0.0024	0.0010-0.0024	NA
1989	4ZD1	2.3 (2254)	0.0016-0.0024	0.0120-0.0180	0.0120-0.0180	0.0080-0.0280	0.0010-0.0024	0.0010-0.0024	NA
	4ZE1	2.6 (2559)	0.0010-0.0018	0.0120-0.0240	0.0120-0.0240	0.0080-0.0590	0.0010-0.0024	0.0008-0.0024	0.0008-0.0021
	CPC	2.8 (2828)	0.0007-0.0017	0.0590	0.0590	0.0590	0.0059	0.0059	NA
1990	4ZD1	2.3 (2254)	0.0008-0.0016	0.0120-0.0240	0.0120-0.0240	0.0080-0.0590	0.0010-0.0024	0.0008-0.0059	NA
	4ZE1	2.6 (2559)	0.0010-0.0018	0.0590	0.0590	0.0590	0.0059	0.0059	NA
	CPC	2.8 (2828)	0.0007-0.0017	0.0011-0.0027	0.0098-0.0196	0.0020-0.0550	0.0011-0.0027	0.0015-0.0037	0.0080 MAX

86863C08

CRANKSHAFT AND CONNECTING ROD SPECIFICATIONS

All measurements are given in inches.

Year	Engine ID/VIN	Engine Displacement Liters (cc)	Crankshaft Main Brg. Journal Dia.	Crankshaft Main Brg. Oil Clearance	Crankshaft Shaft End-Play	Thrust on No.	Journal Diameter	Connecting Rod Oil Clearance	Connecting Rod Side Clearance
1991	4ZD1	2.3 (2254)	2.1819-2.2016	0.0009-0.0047	0.0024-0.0118	3	1.9065-1.9262	0.0012-0.0024	0.0078-0.0130
	4ZE1	2.6 (2559)	2.1819-2.2016	0.0009-0.0047	0.0024-0.0118	3	1.9065-1.9262	0.0008-0.0020	0.0078-0.0130
	CPC	2.8 (2828)	2.6473-2.6483	0.0016-0.0033	0.0020-0.0080	3	1.9983-1.9993	0.0013-0.0026	0.0060-0.0170
	CPC	3.1 (3098)	2.6473-2.6483	0.0012-0.0027	0.0024-0.0083	3	1.9983-1.9994	0.0011-0.0032	0.0140-0.0267
	6VD1	3.2 (3165)	2.5165-2.5170	0.0010-0.0050	0.0020-0.0120	3	2.2434-2.2441	0.0010-0.0047	0.0060-0.0160
1992	4ZD1	2.3 (2254)	2.1819-2.2016	0.0009-0.0047	0.0024-0.0118	3	1.9065-1.9262	0.0012-0.0024	0.0078-0.0130
	4ZE1	2.6 (2559)	2.1819-2.2016	0.0009-0.0047	0.0024-0.0118	3	1.9065-1.9262	0.0012-0.0470	0.0078-0.0130
	CPC	3.1 (3098)	2.6473-2.6483	0.0012-0.0027	0.0024-0.0083	3	1.9983-1.9994	0.0011-0.0032	0.0140-0.0267
	6VD1	3.2 (3165)	2.5165-2.5170	0.0010-0.0050	0.0020-0.0120	3	2.2434-2.2441	0.0010-0.0047	0.0060-0.0160
1993	4ZD1	2.3 (2254)	2.1819-2.2016	0.0009-0.0047	0.0024-0.0118	3	1.9065-1.9262	0.0012-0.0470	0.0078-0.0130
	4ZE1	2.6 (2559)	2.1819-2.2016	0.0009-0.0047	0.0024-0.0118	3	1.9065-1.9262	0.0012-0.0470	0.0078-0.0130
	CPC	3.1 (3098)	2.6473-2.6483	0.0012-0.0027	0.0024-0.0083	3	1.9983-1.9994	0.0010-0.0047	0.0140-0.0267
	6VD1	3.2 (3165)	2.5165-2.5170	0.0010-0.0050	0.0020-0.0120	3	2.2434-2.2441	0.0010-0.0047	0.0060-0.0160
1994	4ZD1	2.3 (2254)	2.1819-2.2016	0.0009-0.0047	0.0024-0.0118	3	1.9065-1.9262	0.0012-0.0470	0.0078-0.0130
	4ZE1	2.6 (2559)	2.1819-2.2016	0.0009-0.0047	0.0024-0.0118	3	1.9065-1.9262	0.0012-0.0470	0.0078-0.0130
	CPC	3.1 (3098)	2.6473-2.6483	0.0012-0.0027	0.0024-0.0083	3	1.9994	0.0010-0.0047	0.0140-0.0267
	6VD1	3.2 (3165)	2.5165-2.5170	0.0010-0.0050	0.0020-0.0120	3	2.2434-2.2441	0.0010-0.0047	0.0060-0.0160
1995	4ZD1	2.3 (2254)	2.2016-2.2022	0.0009-0.0047	0.0024-0.0118	3	1.9262-1.9268	0.0012-0.0470	0.0079-0.0130
	4ZE1	2.6 (2559)	2.2016-2.2022	0.0009-0.0047	0.0024-0.0118	3	1.9262-1.9268	0.0012-0.0470	0.0079-0.0130
	6VD1	3.2 (3165)	2.5165-2.5170	0.0010-0.0047	0.0023-0.0094	3	2.1229-2.1235	0.0010-0.0047	0.0063-0.0157
1996	4ZE1	2.6 (2559)	2.2016-2.2022	[1]	0.0024-0.0118	3	1.9276-1.9282	0.0012-0.0470	0.0079-0.0157
	6VD1	3.2 (3165)	2.5165-2.5170	[2]	0.0023-0.0094	3	1.8888-1.8898	0.0010-0.0047	0.0063-0.0157

1 Crankshaft bearing size marks:
Blue: 0.0010-0.0020
Black: 0.0009-0.0019
Brown: 0.0009-0.0018
2 Crankshaft bearing size marks:
Brown: 0.0012-0.0019
Green: 0.0011-0.0019
Yellow: 0.0011-0.0018
Pink: 0.0010-0.0018

86863C07

TORQUE SPECIFICATIONS

All readings in ft. lbs.

Year	Engine ID/VIN	Engine Displacement Liters (cc)	Cylinder Head Bolts	Main Bearing Bolts	Rod Bearing Bolts	Crankshaft Damper Bolts	Flywheel Bolts	Manifold Intake	Manifold Exhaust	Spark Plugs	Lug Nut
1981	G180Z	1.8 (1816)	[2]	72	43	87	76	16	15	11-14	80-94
	C223	2.2 (2238)	[1]	123	61	136	82	15	15	-	80-94
1982	G180Z	1.8 (1816)	[2]	72	43	87	76	16	15	11-14	80-94
	C223	2.2 (2238)	[1]	123	61	136	82	16	15	-	80-94
1983	G200Z	2.0 (1949)	[2]	65-79	42-45	87	72-79	16	16	11-14	80-94
	C223	2.2 (2238)	[1]	123	61	136	82	15	15	-	80-94
1984	G200Z	2.0 (1949)	[2]	65-79	42-45	87	72-79	16	16	11-14	80-94
	C223	2.2 (2238)	[1]	123	61	136	82	15	15	-	80-94
1985	G200Z	2.0 (1949)	[2]	65-79	42-45	87	72-79	15	16	11-14	80-94
	C223	2.2 (2238)	[1]	123	61	136	82	15	15	-	80-94
1986	G200Z	2.0 (1949)	[3]	65-79	42-45	87	72-79	16	16	-	58-87
	C223	2.2 (2238)	[3]	123	61	136	82	15	15	-	7
	C223T	2.2 (2238)	[3]	65-80	61	136	82	16	16	10-17	7
1987	G200Z	2.0 (1949)	[2]	65-79	42-45	87	72-79	16	16	11-14	58-87
	C223	2.2 (2238)	[3]	123	61	136	68	15	15	-	7
	C223T	2.3 (2254)	[2]	123	61	136	82	15	15	10-17	7
1988	4ZD1	2.3 (2254)	[2]	65-80	42-45	76-98	40-47	16	16	10-17	7
	4ZE1	2.3 (2254)	[2]	65-80	42-45	76-98	40-47	16	16	22	7
1989	4ZD1	2.3 (2254)	[2]	65-80	42-45	76-98	40-47	16	16	10-17	7
	4ZE1	2.6 (2559)	[2]	65-80	42-45	79-102	40-47	16	16	22	7
	CPC	2.8 (2828)	[4]	70	39	79-102	52	23	25	22	7
1990	4ZD1	2.3 (2254)	[2]	65-80	42-45	76-98	40-47	16	16	10-17	7
	CPC	2.8 (2828)	[4]	70	39	79-102	52	23	25	22	7
1991	4ZD1	2.3 (2254)	[2]	65-80	42-45	76-98	40-47	16	16	10-17	7
	4ZE1	2.6 (2559)	[2]	65-80	42-45	79-102	40-47	16	16	22	7
	CPC	3.1 (3098)	[4]	70	39	70	52	23	25	14	7
1992	4ZD1	2.3 (2254)	[2]	72	43	87	40	16	16	14	7
	4ZE1	2.6 (2559)	[2]	72	43	87	40	16	16	14	7
	CPC	3.1 (3098)	[4]	72	39	70	52	19	25	14	7
	6VD1	3.2 (3165)	[5]	29 [6]	49	123	40	17	42	13	87
1993	4ZD1	2.3 (2254)	[2]	72	43	87	40	16	16	14	7
	4ZE1	2.6 (2559)	[2]	72	43	87	40	16	16	13	7
	CPC	3.1 (3098)	[2]	72	39	70	52	19	25	14	7
	6VD1	3.2 (3165)	[5]	29 [6]	49	123	40	17	42	13	87
1994	4ZD1	2.3 (2254)	[2]	72	43	87	40	16	16	14	7
	4ZE1	2.6 (2559)	[2]	72	43	87	40	16	16	14	7
	6VD1	3.2 (3165)	[5]	29 [6]	49	123	40	17	42	13	87
1995	4ZD1	2.3 (2254)	[2]	72	43	87	40	16	16	14	7
	4ZE1	2.6 (2559)	[2]	72	43	87	40	16	16	14	7
	6VD1	3.2 (3165)	[5]	29 [6]	49	123	40	17	42	13	87
1996	4ZE1	2.6 (2559)	[2]	72	43	87	40	16	33	14	7
	6VD1	3.2 (3165)	[5]	29 [6]	49	123	40	17	42	13	87

1 Torque in sequence
  New bolts: 54 ft. lbs.
  Used bolts: 65 ft. lbs.
2 Step 1: 60 ft. lbs.
  Step 2: 72 ft. lbs.
3 Step 1: 44 ft. lbs.
  Step 2: 65 ft. lbs.
4 Step 1: 41 ft. lbs.
  Step 2: Turn an additional 90 degrees
5 8x1.25 bolts: 15 ft. lbs.
  11x1.5 bolts: 47 ft. lbs.
6 Main bearing cap bolts: 29 ft. lbs. plus 55-65 degrees
  Oil gallery bolts: 29 ft. lbs.
  Buttress bolts: 29 ft. lbs.
7 Steel wheels: 58-72 ft. lbs.
  Aluminum wheels: 80-94 ft. lbs.

86863C10

PISTON AND RING SPECIFICATIONS

All measurements are given in inches.

Year	Engine ID/VIN	Engine Displacement Liters (cc)	Piston Clearance	Ring Gap Top Compression	Ring Gap Bottom Compression	Ring Gap Oil Control	Ring Side Clearance Top Compression	Ring Side Clearance Bottom Compression	Ring Side Clearance Oil Control
1991	4ZD1	2.3 (2254)	0.0008-0.0016	0.0120-0.0590	0.0240-0.0590	0.0080-0.0590	0.0010-0.0069	0.0008-0.0059	NA
	4ZE1	2.6 (2559)	0.0010-0.0016	0.0120-0.0590	0.0240-0.0590	0.0080-0.0590	0.0010-0.0069	0.0008-0.0059	NA
	CPC	2.8 (2828)	0.0007-0.0017	0.0098-0.0196	0.0098-0.0196	0.0020-0.0550	0.0011-0.0027	0.0015-0.0037	0.0080 MAX
	CPC	3.1 (3098)	0.0009-0.0022	0.0100-0.0200	0.0200-0.0280	0.0100-0.0300	0.0020-0.0035	0.0020-0.0035	0.0080 MAX
	6VD1	3.2 (3165)	0.0016-0.0023	0.0138-0.0185	0.0177-0.0236	0.0059-0.0177	0.0006-0.0015	0.0006-0.0015	NA
1992	4ZD1	2.3 (2254)	0.0008-0.0016	0.0120-0.0180	0.0240-0.0280	0.0080-0.0280	0.0010-0.0024	0.0008-0.0022	NA
	4ZE1	2.6 (2559)	0.0010-0.0018	0.0120-0.0180	0.0240-0.0280	0.0080-0.0280	0.0010-0.0024	0.0008-0.0022	NA
	CPC	3.1 (3098)	0.0009-0.0022	0.0100-0.0200	0.0200-0.0280	0.0100-0.0300	0.0020-0.0035	0.0020-0.0035	NA
	6VD1	3.2 (3165)	0.0016-0.0023	0.0138-0.0185	0.0177-0.0236	0.0059-0.0177	0.0006-0.0015	0.0006-0.0015	NA
1993	4ZD1	2.3 (2254)	0.0008-0.0016	0.0120-0.0180	0.0240-0.0280	0.0080-0.0280	0.0010-0.0024	0.0008-0.0022	NA
	4ZE1	2.6 (2559)	0.0010-0.0018	0.0118-0.0177	0.0236-0.0283	0.0079-0.0276	0.0010-0.0024	0.0008-0.0022	NA
	CPC	3.1 (3098)	0.0009-0.0022	0.0100-0.0200	0.0200-0.0280	0.0100-0.0300	0.0020-0.0035	0.0020-0.0035	NA
	6VD1	3.2 (3165)	0.0016-0.0023	0.0138-0.0185	0.0177-0.0236	0.0059-0.0177	0.0006-0.0015	0.0006-0.0015	NA
1994	4ZD1	2.3 (2254)	0.0008-0.0016	0.0118-0.0177	0.0236-0.0283	0.0079-0.0276	0.0010-0.0024	0.0008-0.0022	NA
	4ZE1	2.6 (2559)	0.0010-0.0018	0.0118-0.0177	0.0236-0.0283	0.0079-0.0276	0.0010-0.0024	0.0008-0.0022	NA
	6VD1	3.2 (3165)	0.0016-0.0023	0.0138-0.0185	0.0177-0.0236	0.0059-0.0177	0.0006-0.0015	0.0006-0.0015	NA
1995	4ZD1	2.3 (2254)	0.0008-0.0016	0.0118-0.0177	0.0236-0.0283	0.0079-0.0276	0.0010-0.0024	0.0008-0.0022	NA
	4ZE1	2.6 (2559)	[1]	0.0118-0.0177	0.0236-0.0283	0.0079-0.0276	0.0010-0.0024	0.0008-0.0022	NA
	6VD1	3.2 (3165)	0.0016-0.0023	0.0138-0.0185	0.0177-0.0236	0.0059-0.0177	0.0006-0.0015	0.0006-0.0015	NA
1996	4ZE1	2.6 (2559)	0.0010-0.0018	0.0138-0.0177	0.0177-0.0236	0.0059-0.0177	0.0006-0.0024	0.0006-0.0022	NA
	6VD1	3.2 (3165)	[2]	0.0138-0.0185	0.0177-0.0236	0.0059-0.0177	0.0006-0.0015	0.0006-0.0015	NA

1 Size mark A pistons: 0.0010-0.0018
  Size mark B and C pistons: 0.0010-0.0017
2 Size mark A pistons: 0.0009-0.0017
  Size mark B and C pistons: 0.0016-0.0024
  Size mark B and C pistons: 0.0016-0.0023
NA - Not Available

86863C09

Engine

REMOVAL & INSTALLATION

1981–91 Vehicles

GASOLINE ENGINES

1. Disconnect both battery cables, the negative cable first.
2. Matchmark the hood-to-hinges and remove the hood.
3. Remove the undercover. Open the drain plugs on the radiator and the cylinder and drain the cooling system.

> **✳✳ CAUTION**
>
> When draining the coolant, keep in mind that cats and dogs are attracted by ethylene glycol antifreeze, and are quite likely to drink any that is left in an uncovered container or in puddles on the ground. This will prove fatal in sufficient quantity. Always drain the coolant into a sealable container. Coolant should be reused unless it is contaminated or several years old.

4. Remove the air cleaner by performing the following procedures:
   a. Disconnect the air duct and PCV hose from the air cleaner.
   b. Disconnect the air hose from the AIR pump.
   c. Remove the air cleaner-to-bracket bolts and wing nut.
   d. Lift the air cleaner, disconnect the vacuum hose(s) from the underside and remove the air cleaner.
   e. Using a clean shop cloth, cover the air cleaner port to prevent dirt from entering the engine.
5. Disconnect the TCA hot air hose and remove the manifold cover.
6. Label and disconnect the electrical connector(s) from the alternator.
7. Remove the exhaust pipe-to-exhaust manifold nuts and separate the pipe from the manifold.
8. Loosen the clutch cable adjusting nut and relieve the tension, if equipped with a manual transmission.
9. Disconnect the heater hoses from the heater core.
10. If equipped with an oxygen sensor, disconnect the electrical connector.
11. If equipped with a vacuum switching valve, disconnect the rubber hose from the valve.
12. Disconnect the engine-to-chassis ground cable.
13. Disconnect the fuel hoses from the carburetor.
14. Disconnect the high-tension wire from the ignition coil, the vacuum hose from the rear connector of the intake manifold and the rubber hoses from the canister.
15. Disconnect the accelerator cable from the carburetor. Disconnect the electrical connectors from the starter, the thermo-unit, the oil pressure switch and distributor harness.
16. Disconnect the hose from the vacuum switch, if equipped, and the solenoid valve.
17. Disconnect the electrical connectors from the EFE heater, the carburetor solenoid valve and the electric choke.
18. From the rear of the engine, disconnect the back-up light switch and transmission wiring at the connector.
19. Using an engine hoist, connect it to the engine hangers and support the engine.
20. Remove the engine-to-mount nut. Raise the engine slightly and remove the left side engine mount stopper plate.
21. If equipped with air conditioning, remove the compressor from the engine and move it aside; do not disconnect the pressure hoses.
22. Disconnect the upper and lower radiator hoses and the reservoir tank hose.
23. Remove the radiator and fan blade assembly.
24. Raise and support the vehicle safely. Drain the oil from the engine.

> **✳✳ CAUTION**
>
> The EPA warns that prolonged contact with used engine oil may cause a number of skin disorders, including cancer! You should make every effort to minimize your exposure to used engine oil. Protective gloves should be worn when changing the oil. Wash your hands and any other exposed skin areas as soon as possible after exposure to used engine oil. Soap and water, or waterless hand cleaner should be used.

25. Remove the starter motor and the flywheel cover pan.
26. Remove the bell housing-to-engine bolts and support the transmission.
27. Lift the engine slightly. Remove the exhaust pipe bracket from the transmission and the engine-to-mount nuts.

➡ **Make certain that all lines, hoses, cables and wires have been disconnected from the engine and frame.**

28. Lift the engine from the vehicle with the front of the engine raised slightly to clear the transmission input shaft.
    To install:
29. Lower the engine into the vehicle, align it transmission assembly and install the nuts/bolts.
30. Install the starter motor and the flywheel cover pan.
31. If equipped with a manual transmission, install the clutch cable and clutch return spring.
32. Lower the vehicle.
33. The balance of the installation is the reverse of removal.

DIESEL ENGINES 1981–87 ONLY

1. Matchmark hinges to the hood and remove the hood.
2. Disconnect the battery cables, negative first and remove the battery from the vehicle.
3. Drain the cooling system.

➡ **On 4WD vehicles, the transmission and transfer case must be removed or detached from the engine before the engine is raised from under the hood.**

> **✳✳ CAUTION**
>
> When draining the coolant, keep in mind that cats and dogs are attracted by ethylene glycol antifreeze, and are quite likely to drink any that is left in an uncovered container or in puddles on the ground. This will prove fatal in sufficient quantity. Always drain the coolant into a sealable container. Coolant should be reused unless it is contaminated or several years old.

4. Remove the air cleaner assembly as follows: Remove the intake silencer. Remove the bolts mounting the air cleaner and loosen the clamp bolt. Lift the air cleaner slightly and disconnect the breather hose. Remove the air cleaner assembly.
5. Disconnect the upper radiator hose at the engine.
6. Loosen the air conditioning compressor drive belts by moving the power steering pump or idler.
7. Remove the cooling fan and fan shroud.
8. Disconnect the lower radiator hose at the engine.
9. Remove the radiator grille.
10. Remove the radiator attaching bolts and remove the radiator.
11. Disconnect the accelerator control cable from the injection pump.
12. If equipped with air conditioning, disconnect the air conditioning compressor control cable.
13. Disconnect and plug the fuel hoses from the injection pump.
14. Disconnect the ground cable from the engine.
15. Raise and safely support the vehicle. Disconnect and label the transmission wiring. Drain the engine oil.

> **✳✳ CAUTION**
>
> The EPA warns that prolonged contact with used engine oil may cause a number of skin disorders, including cancer! You should make every effort to minimize your exposure to used engine oil. Protective gloves should be worn when changing the oil. Wash your hands and any other exposed skin areas as soon as possible after exposure to used engine oil. Soap and water, or waterless hand cleaner should be used.

16. Disconnect the vacuum hose from the fast idle actuator.
17. Disconnect the fuel cut solenoid wiring.

18. Disconnect the air conditioning compressor wiring, sensing resistor and thermoswitch connectors.

19. Disconnect the heater hoses extending from the heater unit from the dash panel side.

20. Disconnect the hose for power brake booster from the vacuum pump.

21. Disconnect vacuum hose from the vacuum pump.

22. Disconnect the alternator wiring.

23. Disconnect the exhaust pipe from the exhaust manifold at the flange.

24. Remove the exhaust pipe mounting bracket from the engine.

25. Disconnect and label the starter motor wiring.

26. Pull the gearshift lever boot upwards on the lever. Remove the 2 gearshift lever bolts and the lever.

27. Disconnect speedometer and ground cables from the transmission.

28. Matchmark and remove the driveshaft(s).

29. Remove or detach the transmission and transfer case from the engine.

30. Remove the clutch fork return spring from the clutch fork.

31. Disconnect clutch cable from the hooked portion of clutch fork and pull it out forward through the stiffener bracket.

32. Remove 2 bracket-to-transmission rear mount bolts and nuts.

33. Raise the engine and transmission and remove the crossmember-to-frame bracket bolts.

34. Remove the rear mounting nuts from the transmission rear extension.

35. Remove or detach the transmission and transfer case from the engine.

36. Disconnect electrical connectors at CRS switch and back-up lamp switch.

37. Raise the engine and remove the engine mounting bolts and nuts.

38. Remove the engine towards the front of the vehicle making sure the front of the engine is slightly above the level.

To install:

39. Install the engine towards the front of the vehicle making sure the front of the engine is slightly above the level.

40. Lower the engine and install the engine mounting bolts and nuts.

41. The balance of the installation is the reverse of removal.

1992–96 2.3L, 2.6L and 3.1L Engines

➡The transmission or transmission and transfer case assembly should be completely removed from the vehicle before the engine is removed. If you chose to leave the transmission in the vehicle after separating it from the engine, it must be securely supported. The transfer case shouldn't be separated from the transmission.

1. Relieve the fuel pressure.

2. Disconnect the negative and positive battery cables. Remove the battery.

3. Remove the radiator skid plate.

4. Drain the coolant from the radiator and engine block.

5. Remove the air cleaner box and the intake air duct. Cover the throttle body port with a shop towel to prevent dirt from entering the engine.

6. Disconnect the throttle cable from the throttle body linkage.

7. Label and disconnect the following:
   a. Air switch valve hose.
   b. Oxygen sensor harness.
   c. Power booster vacuum hose.
   d. Alternator wiring harness.
   e. Fuel pressure regulator vacuum hose.
   f. Canister hose.
   g. Engine wiring harness connectors located on the right wheel well.
   h. Inlet and return fuel lines.
   i. Starter motor cables.
   j. Engine ground cables.
   k. Oil pressure switch connectors.

8. Remove the radiator grille from the deflector panel.

9. Disconnect the upper and lower radiator hoses and the reservoir tank hose.

10. Remove the fan shroud and fan blade assembly.

11. Remove the radiator.

12. If equipped with air conditioning, remove the compressor from the engine and move it aside. Do not disconnect the A/C lines.

13. If equipped with a manual transmission, remove the gear shift lever by performing the following procedures:

a. Place the gear shift lever in **N**.
b. Remove the front console.
c. Pull the shift lever boot and grommet upward.
d. Remove the shift lever cover bolts and the shift lever.

14. If equipped with four–wheel drive, remove the transfer case shift lever by performing the following procedures:

a. Place the transfer shift lever in **2H**.
b. Pull the shift lever boot and dust cover upward.
c. Remove the shift lever retaining bolts.
d. Pull the shift lever from the transfer case.

15. Raise and safely support the vehicle. Remove the front wheels.

16. Disconnect the backup light switch connector and the vehicle speed sensor cable from the transmission.

17. Remove the transmission and transfer case skid plates.

18. Drain the oil from the engine.

19. Drain the transmission and transfer case fluid.

20. If equipped with an automatic transmission, perform the following procedures:

a. Remove the dipstick and the tube.
b. Disconnect the shift select control link rod from the select lever.
c. Disconnect the downshift cable from the transmission.
d. Disconnect and plug the fluid coolant lines from the transmission.

21. Matchmark the front and rear drive shaft flanges.

22. If equipped with a one-piece driveshaft, remove the driveshaft flange-to-pinion nuts, lower the driveshaft and pull it from the transmission.

23. If equipped with a two-piece driveshaft, perform the following procedures:

a. Remove the rear driveshaft flange-to-pinion nuts.
b. Remove the rear driveshaft flange-to-transfer case flange bolts and the rear driveshaft.
c. Remove the center bearing-to-chassis bolts, move the front driveshaft rearward and from the transmission.

24. Unbolt and remove the starter.

25. If equipped with a clutch slave cylinder, remove it from the transmission and move it aside.

26. Unbolt the front exhaust pipe flanges and separate the front pipe from the exhaust system.

27. Attach engine hangers to the engine.

28. Connect a chain hoist to the engine hangers and support the engine.

29. Remove the transmission or transmission and transfer case assembly by performing the following procedures:

a. Support the transmission with a jack.
b. Remove the rear mount-to-transmission nuts.
c. Remove the rear mount-to-side mount member nuts/bolts and the mount.
d. Remove the transmission-to-engine bolts.
e. Move the transmission assembly rearward.
f. Carefully lower the transmission from the vehicle.

30. Support the weight of the engine with the chain hoist. Unbolt the engine mounts.

31. Verify that all wiring harnesses and vacuum lines have been disconnected.

32. Using the hoist, slowly lift the engine from the vehicle; be sure to hold the front of the engine higher than the rear.

33. Place the engine on a workstand.

To install:

34. Using the hoist, slowly lower the engine into the vehicle. Be sure to hold the front of the engine higher than the rear.

35. Install the engine mount nuts and bolts. Tighten the engine mount and transmission mount bolts to 30 ft. lbs. (41 Nm). Tighten the engine mount nuts to 62 ft. lbs. (83 Nm). Tighten the transmission mount nuts to 30 ft. lbs. (41 Nm).

36. Install the transmission or transmission and transfer assembly by performing the following procedures:

a. Raise the transmission into position.
b. Move the transmission forward. Engage the output shaft and dowel pins with the engine.
c. Install the transmission case bolts. Tighten the upper six bolts to 56 ft. lbs. (76 Nm). Tighten the lower right two bolts to 35 ft. lbs. (48 Nm). Tighten

the lower left bolt to 20 ft. lbs. (27 Nm). Tighten the remaining bolts to 53 inch lbs. (6 Nm).

    d. Install the rear mount and the rear mount-to-side mount member nuts/bolts.

    e. Install the rear mount-to-transmission nuts.

    f. Remove the transmission jack.

37. Remove the engine hoist and the engine hangers from the engine.

38. The balance of the installation is the reverse of removal.

1992–96 3.2L Engine

> **⁂ WARNING**
>
> **The transmission and transfer case assembly may be completely removed from the vehicle before the engine is removed. If you chose to leave the transmission and transfer case assembly in the vehicle, it must be securely supported.**

1. Shift the transmission into the **N** or neutral position. If equipped with four–wheel drive, shift the transfer case into the **2H** position and verify that the front axle and hubs are not engaged. Set the parking brake and securely block the rear wheels while the vehicle is on the ground.

2. Relieve the fuel pressure.

3. Disconnect the negative and positive battery cables. Remove the battery.

4. Use a felt–tipped marker to matchmark the hood hinge plates. Remove the hood.

5. If equipped with a manual transmission, remove the gear shift lever:

    a. Verify that the transmission is in **N**.

    b. Remove retaining screws from the front console.

    c. Remove the shift knob.

    d. Pull the shift lever boot and grommet upward.

    e. Remove the shift lever cover bolts and the shift lever.

6. If equipped with an automatic transmission:

    a. Verify that the transmission is in **N**.

    b. Remove the retaining screws from the front console.

    c. Disconnect the shift lock cable.

    d. Label and uncouple the wiring connectors.

    e. After the vehicle has been raised and supported, disconnect the shift control rod from the selector lever linkage.

7. If equipped with four–wheel drive, remove the transfer case shift lever:

    a. Verify that the transfer case is in **2H**.

    b. Pull the shift lever boot and dust cover upward.

    c. Remove the shift lever retaining bolts.

    d. Pull the shift lever from the transfer case.

8. If equipped, remove the radiator skid plate.

9. Drain the engine coolant into a container.

10. Remove the air cleaner and the intake air duct. Use a clean shop cloth to plug the throttle body port to prevent dirt from entering the engine.

11. If necessary, remove the vehicle's grille to prevent it from being damaged.

12. Disconnect the upper and lower radiator hoses from the engine. Disconnect the coolant reservoir hose from the radiator.

13. Disconnect the heater hoses from the engine. Catch any coolant that drains out.

14. Remove the radiator fan shroud and cooling fan blade.

15. Remove the radiator.

16. Release the accessory drive belt tensions, and then remove the drive belts.

17. If equipped with air conditioning, unbolt the compressor from the engine and move it out of the work area. Don't disconnect the A/C lines.

18. Unbolt the power steering pump from its bracket. Move the pump out of the way with the hydraulic line connected.

19. Disconnect the starter wiring harness.

20. Disconnect the battery ground cables from the power steering pump bracket.

21. Disconnect the throttle cable from the throttle body linkage.

22. Label and disconnect the following vacuum hoses from the intake manifold chamber:

    a. PCV hose

    b. EVAP canister vacuum hose

    c. Brake booster hose

23. Label and disconnect the following sensor connectors from the rear of the intake manifold chamber:

    a. Ignition control module connectors

    b. Linear EGR valve

    c. MAP sensor

    d. EVAP purge valve

    e. Throttle position sensor

    f. Idle air control valve

    g. Intake air temperature sensor

24. Disconnect the EGR valve supply tube and bracket.

25. Disconnect the MAP sensor tube, and then unbolt the MAP sensor bracket.

26. If necessary, the intake manifold chamber may be removed to avoid damage. If removed, cover the intake ports to keep dirt or foreign objects out.

27. If necessary, the ignition coil assembly may be removed to avoid damaged. Label the spark plug wires to avoid confusion.

28. If necessary, the cruise control actuator and cable brackets may be unbolted to move the actuator and cable out of the work area.

29. Raise and safely support the vehicle. Remove the front wheels.

30. Drain the oil from the engine.

31. Drain the transmission and transfer case fluid.

32. Disconnect the backup light switch connector and the speed sensor connector from the transmission.

33. If equipped with an automatic transmission, perform the following procedures:

    a. Remove the dipstick and the tube.

    b. Disconnect the shift select control link rod from the select lever.

    c. Disconnect the downshift cable from the transmission.

    d. Disconnect and plug the fluid coolant lines from the transmission.

34. Unbolt and remove the rear driveshaft. Unbolt the center bearing and lower the driveshaft from the vehicle.

35. If equipped, remove the front driveshaft's splined yoke flange-to-transfer case bolts and separate the front driveshaft from the transfer case; do not allow the splined flange to fall away from the driveshaft.

36. If equipped with a clutch slave cylinder, remove it from the transmission and move it aside.

37. Label and disconnect the oxygen sensor connectors.

38. Unbolt the front exhaust pipe flanges from the exhaust manifolds and catalytic converters. Separate the exhaust system from the engine, and move it out of the work area. If necessary, the front part of the exhaust system may be removed from the vehicle.

39. Attach a engine lifting chain to the engine hangers. The engine hangers are located on the right and left sides of the engine below the valve covers.

40. Make sure the engine is safely supported.

➡ **Make sure that no engine components will be damaged by the lifting chain.**

41. Remove the transmission/transfer case assembly:

    a. Place a transmission jack under the transmission for support.

    b. Unbolt the transmission rear mount from the frame crossmember.

    c. Remove the rear mount.

    d. Remove the transmission-to-engine bolts.

    e. Move the transmission assembly rearward slightly to disengage it from the engine.

    f. Carefully lower the transmission from the vehicle.

42. Unbolt the engine mounts.

43. Raise the engine slightly. Verify that all vacuum lines and electrical connectors have been disconnected so that the engine removal is not obstructed.

44. Raise the chain hoist to lift the engine out of the vehicle. If necessary, keep the front of the engine higher than the rear to clear the bulkhead.

45. Secure the engine to a workstand.

To install:

46. Using the chain hoist, slowly lower the engine into the vehicle. Be sure to hold the front of the engine higher than the rear.

47. Install the engine mount nuts and bolts. Tighten the engine mount bolts to 30 ft. lbs. (41 Nm). Tighten the engine mount nuts to 37 ft. lbs. (50 Nm).

> **⁂ WARNING**
>
> **Make sure that the transmission mounting dowels are in the correct locations for the type of transmission (M/T or A/T). Incorrect dowel positioning can crack the transmission case.**

48. Install the transmission/transfer case assembly:
   a. Raise the transmission into position.
   b. Move the transmission forward. Engage the output shaft and dowel pins with the engine.
   c. Install the engine-to-transmission bolts. Tighten the upper six bolts to 56 ft. lbs. (76 Nm). Tighten the lower right two bolts to 35 ft. lbs. (48 Nm). Tighten the lower left bolt to 20 ft. lbs. (27 Nm). Tighten the remaining bolts to 4.4 ft. lbs. (6 Nm).
   d. Install the rear mount. Tighten the nuts to 37 ft. lbs. (50 Nm). Tighten the bolts to 37–43 ft. lbs. (50–59 Nm).
   e. Install the crossmember and tighten its bolts to 56 ft. lbs. (76 Nm).
   f. Remove the transmission jack.
49. The balance of the installation is the reverse of removal.

Rocker Arm Cover

REMOVAL & INSTALLATION

4-Cylinder Gasoline Engines

♦ **See Figure 1**

1. Disconnect the negative battery cable.
2. Remove the air cleaner (carbureted) and air inlet hose (EFI).
3. Remove the PCV hose.
4. Label and remove the spark plug wires.
5. Remove the timing belt cover attaching bolts, if so equipped.
6. Disconnect the power brake booster hose and throttle cable if in the way.
7. Remove the rocker arm cover bolts and cover.
8. If the cover will not come loose, tap the sides with a rubber hammer to dislodge.

To install:

9. Clean the gasket mating surfaces with a scraper and solvent.
10. Install a new gasket and apply a 0.08–0.12 in. (2–3mm) bead of RTV sealer around the gasket surface.
11. Install the rocker arm cover and torque the bolts to 89 inch lbs. (10 Nm).
12. Install the spark plug wires, PCV hose, brake booster hose and throttle cable if removed.
13. Install the air cleaner or air inlet hose.
14. Connect the battery cable, start the engine and check for leaks.

Diesel Engine

1. Disconnect the negative battery cable.
2. Remove the PCV valve from the rocker arm cover and the PCV valve hose.

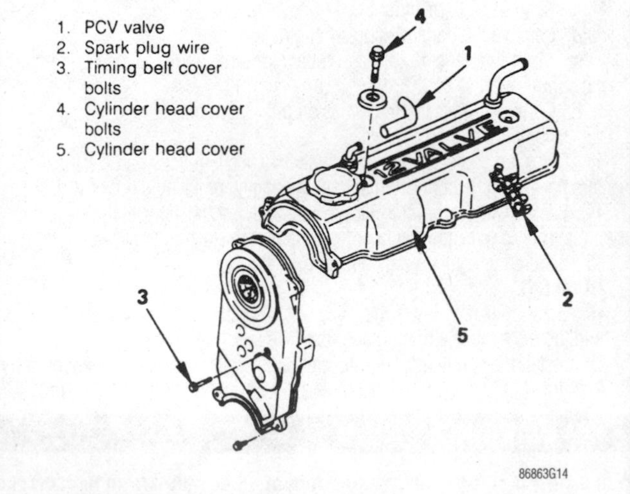

3. Remove the air cleaner assembly.
4. Remove the rocker arm cover-to-cylinder head bolts and remove the cover from the engine.

➠**DO NOT pry on the cover to remove it. If it sticks, use your palm or a rubber mallet to bump it rearwards, from the front.**

5. Using a putty knife, carefully clean the gasket mounting surfaces. Keep debris out of the engine.
6. To install, use a new gasket and reverse the removal procedures. Torque the rocker arm cover-to-cylinder head bolts to 9–13 ft. lbs. (12–18 Nm). Be careful not to overtighten the fasteners and either distort the valve cover (causing and leak) or break the fastener (causing more work).

2.8L and 3.1L Engines

♦ **See Figures 2, 3 and 4**

1. Disconnect the negative battery cable.
2. Remove the air cleaner.

Fig. 2 Rocker arm cover removal may involve removal of hoses, brackets and other components

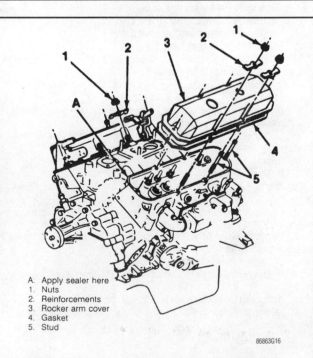

1. PCV valve
2. Spark plug wire
3. Timing belt cover bolts
4. Cylinder head cover bolts
5. Cylinder head cover

86863G14

Fig. 1 Rocker arm cover removal on a single overhead camshaft 4-cylinder engine

A. Apply sealer here
1. Nuts
2. Reinforcements
3. Rocker arm cover
4. Gasket
5. Stud

86863G16

Fig. 3 Rocker arm cover removal on a V6, 2.8L engine shown

Fig. 4 Removing the rocker arm cover—2.8L engine

3. Remove the ignition coil and bracket (RH) or the crankcase ventilation valve (LH).

4. Label and remove the spark plug wires from the bracket at the rocker arm cover stud.

5. Remove the PCV valve (RH).

6. Remove the throttle cable and alternator (RH only).

7. Remove the rocker arm cover nuts, reinforcements, cover and gasket. If the cover sticks to the head, bump the end of the cover with a rubber hammer. Do NOT damage the sealing flange.

To install:

8. Clean the gasket mating surfaces with a scraper and solvent.

9. Install the rocker arm cover with a new gasket. Apply RTV sealer to the cylinder head-to-intake manifold contact points.

10. Install the rocker arm cover nuts and reinforcements. Torque the cover bolts to 72 inch lbs. (8 Nm).

11. Install the throttle cable and alternator (RH only).

12. Install the PCV valve (RH).

13. Install the spark plug wires to the bracket at the rocker arm cover stud.

14. Install the ignition coil and bracket (RH) or the crankcase ventilation valve (LH).

15. Install the air cleaner.

16. Connect the negative battery cable, start the engine and check for leaks.

3.2L Engine

▶ **See Figure 5**

1. Disconnect the negative battery cable.
2. Remove the air cleaner.
3. Remove the EGR pipe.
4. Remove the (PCV) crankcase ventilation valve (LH).
5. Label and remove the spark plug wires from the bracket at the rocker arm cover stud.
6. Remove the camshaft angle sensor (LH) or fuel hose (RH).
7. Remove the throttle cable (LH) or heater pipe (RH).
8. Remove the rocker arm cover nuts, reinforcements, cover and gasket. If the cover sticks to the head, bump the end of the cover with a rubber hammer. Do NOT damage the sealing flange.

To install:

9. Clean the gasket mating surfaces with a scraper and solvent.

10. Install the rocker arm cover with a new gasket. Apply RTV sealer to the cylinder head-to-intake manifold contact points.

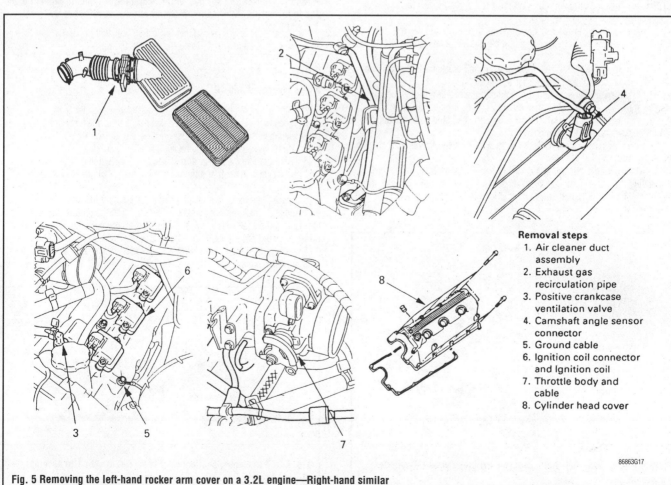

Removal steps
1. Air cleaner duct assembly
2. Exhaust gas recirculation pipe
3. Positive crankcase ventilation valve
4. Camshaft angle sensor connector
5. Ground cable
6. Ignition coil connector and Ignition coil
7. Throttle body and cable
8. Cylinder head cover

Fig. 5 Removing the left-hand rocker arm cover on a 3.2L engine—Right-hand similar

11. Install the rocker arm cover nuts and reinforcements. Torque the cover bolts to 72 inch lbs. (8 Nm).

12. Install the throttle cable. Torque the body and cable bolts to 14 ft. lbs. (19 Nm).

13. Install the PCV valve.

14. Install the EGR pipe; torque the manifold side to 20 ft. lbs. (28 Nm) and the head cover side to 4.5 ft. lbs. (6 Nm).

15. Install the spark plug wires to the bracket at the rocker arm cover stud.

16. Install the ignition coil and bracket and crankcase ventilation valve.

17. Install the air cleaner.

18. Connect the negative battery cable, start the engine and check for leaks.

Rocker Arms/Shafts

REMOVAL & INSTALLATION

4-Cylinder Gasoline Engines

▶ See Figures 6, 7 and 8

1. Disconnect the negative battery cable. Remove the rocker cover.

2. Loosen the rocker arm shaft bracket nuts a little at a time, in sequence, starting with the outer nuts.

3. Remove the nuts from the rocker arm shaft brackets. Remove shaft assembly.

4. To disassemble the rockers and shafts; remove the spring from the rocker arm shaft, the rocker brackets and arms. Keep parts in order for reassembly.

5. Before installing apply a generous amount of clean engine oil to the rocker arm shaft, rocker arms and valve stems.

To install:

6. Install the longer shaft on the exhaust valve side and the shorter shaft on the intake side so the aligning marks on the shafts are turned on the front side of the engine.

7. Assemble the rocker arm shaft brackets and rocker arms to the shafts so the cylinder number, on the upper face of the brackets, points toward the front of the engine.

8. Align the mark on the No. 1 rocker arm shaft bracket with the mark on the intake and exhaust valve side rocker arm shaft.

9. Make certain the amount of projection of the rocker arm shaft beyond the face of the No. 1 rocker arm shaft bracket, is longer on the exhaust side shaft than on the intake shaft when the rocker arm shaft stud holes are aligned with the rocker arm shaft bracket stud holes.

10. Place the rocker arm shaft springs in position between the shaft bracket and rocker arm.

11. Check that the punch mark on the rocker arm shaft is facing upward, then, install the rocker arm shaft bracket assembly onto the cylinder head studs. Align the mark on the camshaft with the mark on the No. 1 rocker arm shaft bracket.

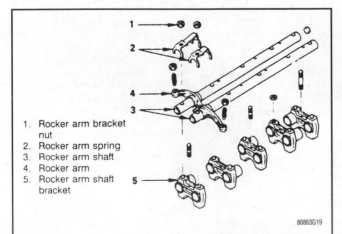

1. Rocker arm bracket nut
2. Rocker arm spring
3. Rocker arm shaft
4. Rocker arm
5. Rocker arm shaft bracket

Fig. 6 Rocker arm and shaft assembly exploded view—4-cylinder gasoline engine

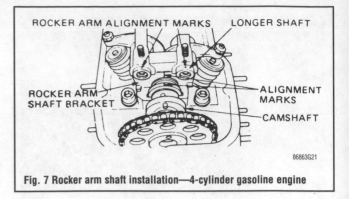

Fig. 7 Rocker arm shaft installation—4-cylinder gasoline engine

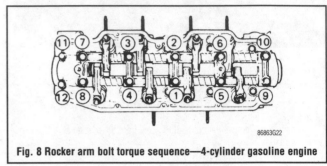

Fig. 8 Rocker arm bolt torque sequence—4-cylinder gasoline engine

12. Torque the rocker arm shaft brackets-to-cylinder head nuts to 16 ft. lbs. (21 Nm) and bolts to 72 inch lbs. (8 Nm).

➡**Hold the rocker arm springs while tightening the nuts to prevent damage to the spring. Start with the center nut and work outward.**

13. Adjust the valves as outlined in Section 1. Install the rocker arm cover, with a new gasket and sealer. Check the ignition timing.

Diesel Engine

▶ See Figures 9 and 10

1. Disconnect the negative battery cable. Remove the cam cover.

2. Loosen the rocker arm shaft bracket nuts a little at a time, in sequence, commencing with the outer brackets.

3. Remove the nuts from the rocker arm shaft brackets.

4. Disassemble the rocker arm shaft assembly by removing the spring from the rocker arm shaft and then removing the rocker arm brackets and arms.

5. Inspect the rocker arm shaft for run-out. Support the shaft on V-blocks at each end and check run-out by slowly turning it with the probe of a dial indicator. Replace the shaft with a new one if the run-out exceeds 0.0156 in. (0.4mm). Run-out should not exceed 0.0079 in. (0.2mm).

6. Inspect the rocker arm shaft for wear, replace the shaft if obvious signs of wear are encountered.

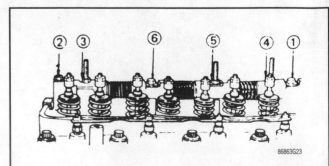

Fig. 9 Bolt loosening sequence for removing rocker arm assembly—diesel engine

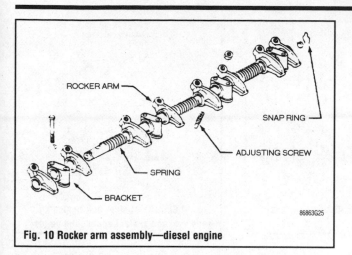

Fig. 10 Rocker arm assembly—diesel engine

To install:

7. Use a liberal amount of clean engine oil to coat the shaft, rocker arms and valve stems. Install the longer shaft on the exhaust valve side, shorter shaft on the intake side, so that the aligning marks on the shafts are turned to the front of the engine.

8. Torque the rocker arm shaft bracket and stud nuts to 15–22 ft. lbs. (20–27 Nm). Hold the rocker arm springs with an adjustable wrench while tightening the nuts to prevent damage to the springs. Torque the nuts a little at a time in sequence, beginning with the center bracket and working outward.

9. Adjust valve clearances, reinstall the cam cover and check for leaks.

2.8L and 3.1L Engines

▶ See Figure 11

1. Disconnect the negative battery cable.
2. Remove the rocker arm covers.
3. Remove the rocker arm nut, the pivot balls, the rocker arm and the pushrods. Keep all components separated so they may be reinstalled in the same location.

→The intake and exhaust pushrods are of different lengths.

To install:

4. Install the pushrods in their original location; be sure the lower ends are seated in the lifter.
5. Coat the bearing surfaces of the rocker arms and pivot balls with Molykote® or equivalent.
6. Install the rocker arm nuts and tighten until spring use starts to move. Loosen bolt until slight lash is felt. On compression stroke, nut should be turned one and one-half turns after lash is removed.
7. Adjust the valve lash as outlined in Section 1.

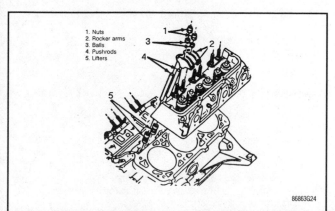

1. Nuts
2. Rocker arms
3. Balls
4. Pushrods
5. Lifters

Fig. 11 Rocker arms and cylinder head assembly—2.8L and 3.1L engines

3.2L Engine

1993–95 VEHICLES

▶ See Figures 12, 13 and 14

→Isuzu has issued a recall notice for 1993–94 Rodeos equipped with 3.2L engines. This is campaign number 94V–094, and involves faulty camshaft end plugs. The plugs may dislodge from the cylinder heads and can cause rapid oil loss. Remember this when ordering parts: a service kit is available for affected vehicles.

1. Disconnect negative battery cable.
2. Remove the air cleaner assembly.
3. Disconnect the accelerator pedal cable from the throttle body and cable brackets.
4. Disconnect the canister vacuum hose from the Vacuum Switch Valve (VSV).
5. Disconnect the vacuum booster hose from the common chamber duct.
6. Disconnect the electrical connectors from the Idle Air Control Valve, Throttle Position sensor, Manifold Absolute Pressure sensor, canister VSV, EGR VSV, Intake Air Temperature sensor and VSV.
7. Remove the high tension cable from the cylinder heads.
8. Disconnect the connectors from the ignition module.
9. Remove the three bolts from the electronic ignition bracket and assembly.
10. Remove the four bolts from the throttle body and remove the throttle body.
11. Disconnect the canister VSV and the EGR VSV vacuum hose from the throttle body.
12. Disconnect the fuel pressure control valve vacuum hose from the common chamber duct.
13. Disconnect the PCV hose from the common chamber duct.
14. Disconnect the evaporative emission canister purge hose from the common chamber duct.
15. Remove the four bolts from the EGR valve assembly common chamber duct and remove the exhaust manifold.
16. Remove the four bolts, four nuts and three manifold bracket fixing bolts from the common chamber duct.
17. Remove the ground cable fixing bolt from the rear of the common chamber duct.
18. Remove the six bolts and two nuts from the common chamber duct.
19. Remove the common chamber duct bracket fixing bolts from the rear of the common chamber duct.
20. Remove the following components, and then remove the timing belt:
    a. Remove the upper fan shroud from the radiator.
    b. Remove the four nuts retaining the cooling fan assembly. Remove the cooling fan.
    c. Remove the power steering drive belt.
    d. Remove the air conditioning compressor drive belt.
    e. Remove the generator drive belt.
    f. Remove the fan pulley assembly.
    g. Make sure the timing belt is set at TDC: all the timing marks must align. On 1994–1995 vehicles, the engine will be at TDC/compression for the No. 2 cylinder. On earlier engines, no cylinders are at TDC/compression when the marks are aligned.
    h. Remove the crankshaft pulley center bolt. Remove the crankshaft pulley.
    i. Remove the two oil cooler hose bracket fixing bolts on the timing cover. Remove the oil cooler hose.
    j. Remove the timing belt cover.
    k. Remove the pusher. The rod must always be facing upward.
    l. Mark the timing belt, cam pulley and crankshaft pulley. Remove the timing belt.
21. Remove the cylinder head cover.
22. Remove the camshaft holders and camshaft.

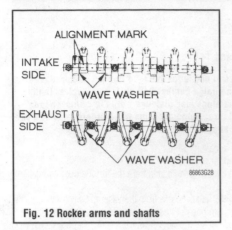

Fig. 12 Rocker arms and shafts

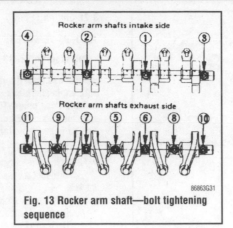

Fig. 13 Rocker arm shaft—bolt tightening sequence

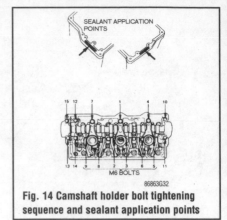

Fig. 14 Camshaft holder bolt tightening sequence and sealant application points

23. Remove the rocker arm shaft bolts. Lift the rocker arm assembly from the cylinder head.

24. The hydraulic lifters are attached to the rocker arms. Remove them and inspect, bleed, or replace as necessary.

To install:

25. Install new camshaft seals and retaining plates onto the cylinder head. Tighten the right camshaft seal retaining plate 6mm bolts to 65 inch lbs. (7.5 Nm). Tighten the left camshaft seal retaining plate 8mm bolts to 191 inch lbs. (21.5 Nm).

26. Install the rocker arm assembly and tighten the bolts in sequence to 13 ft. lbs. (18 Nm).

27. Oil the camshaft bearing journals, camshaft lobes, and rocker arm contact areas.

28. Install the camshaft. Apply sealant to the contact edges of the camshaft holders. Tighten the camshaft 6mm holder bolts to 69 inch lbs. (8 Nm). Tighten the remaining bolts to 13 ft. lbs. (18 Nm).

29. Install the cylinder head covers and carefully tighten the bolts to 69 inch lbs. (8 Nm). Do not overtighten the head cover bolts: they crack very easily.

30. Install the timing belt:

   a. Align the groove on the crankshaft timing pulley with mark on the oil pump.

   b. Align the marks on the camshaft timing pulleys with the dots on the front plate.

   c. Install the timing belt. Align the dotted marks on the timing belt with the mark on the crankshaft gear.

   d. Align the white line on the timing belt with the alignment mark on the right bank camshaft timing pulley. Secure the belt with a double clip.

   e. Turn the crankshaft counterclockwise to remove the slack between the crankshaft pulley and the right camshaft timing pulley.

   f. Install the belt on the water pump pulley.

   g. Install the belt on the idler pulley.

   h. Align the white alignment mark on the timing belt with the alignment mark on the left bank camshaft timing pulley.

   i. Install the crankshaft pulley and tighten the center bolt by hand. Turn the crankshaft pulley clockwise to give slack between the crankshaft timing pulley and the right bank camshaft timing pulley.

   j. Install the pusher while pushing the tension pulley to the belt.

   k. Pull the pin out from the pusher.

   l. Remove the double clips from the pulleys. Turn the crankshaft pulley clockwise 2 turns. Measure the rod protrusion to be sure it is between 0.16–0.24 in. (4–6mm).

   m. Tighten the adjusting bolt to 31 ft. lbs. (42 Nm).

   n. Tighten the pusher bolt to 14 ft. lbs. (19 Nm).

   o. Remove crankshaft pulley. Install the timing belt cover and tighten bolts to 12 ft. lbs. (17 Nm).

   p. Install the oil cooler hose and tighten brackets to 16 ft. lbs. (22 Nm).

   q. Install the crankshaft pulley and tighten the bolt to 123 ft. lbs. (167 Nm).

   r. Install the fan pulley assembly and tighten the bolts to 16 ft. lbs. (22 Nm).

   s. Engage and adjust the alternator drive belt.

   t. Engage and adjust the air conditioning drive belt.

   u. Engage and adjust the power steering pump drive belt.

   v. Install the cooling fan assembly and tighten bolts to 69 inch lbs. (8 Nm).

   w. Install the upper fan shroud to the radiator.

31. Install the common chamber duct bracket bolts to the rear of the common chamber duct.

32. Install the six bolts and two nuts to the common chamber duct.

33. Install the ground cable fixing bolt to the rear of the common chamber duct.

34. Install the four bolts, four nuts and three manifold bracket bolts to the common chamber duct.

35. Install the exhaust manifold and install the four bolts to the EGR valve assembly and common chamber duct.

36. Connect the evaporative emission canister purge hose to the common chamber duct.

37. Connect the PCV hose to the common chamber duct.

38. Connect the fuel pressure control valve vacuum hose to the common chamber duct.

39. Connect the canister VSV and the EGR VSV vacuum hose to the throttle-body.

40. Install the throttle body and install the four bolts to the throttle body and remove the throttle body.

41. Install the electronic ignition assembly and its bracket.

42. Connect the three connectors to the electronic ignition module.

43. Connect the high tension cable to the cylinder head cover clips.

44. Connect the electrical connectors to the Idle Air Control Valve, Throttle Position sensor, Manifold Absolute Pressure sensor, canister VSV, EGR VSV, Intake Air Temperature sensor and VSV.

45. Connect the vacuum booster hose to the common chamber duct.

46. Connect the canister vacuum hose to the Vacuum Switch Valve (VSV).

47. Connect the accelerator pedal cable to the throttle body and cable brackets.

48. Verify that all vacuum hoses, lines, and wiring harnesses are reconnected.

49. Install the air cleaner assembly.

50. Connect the negative battery cable.

1996 VEHICLES

▶ See Figures 15, 16, 17 and 18

1. Relieve the fuel system pressure:

   a. Remove the fuel filler cap.

   b. Remove the fuel pump relay from the underhood relay box.

   c. Start the engine and let it run until it stalls. Then, crank the engine for an additional 30 seconds.

   d. Turn the ignition switch to the **OFF** position.

2. Disconnect the negative battery cable and reinstall the fuel pump relay.

3. Drain the coolant into a sealable container.

4. Support the hood as far open as possible.

5. Remove the air intake duct and the air cleaner box.

6. Disconnect and remove the upper and lower radiator hoses. Catch any coolant that runs out.

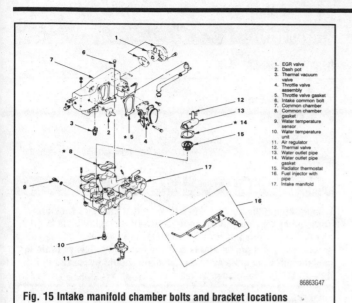

1. EGR valve
2. Dash pot
3. Thermal vacuum valve
4. Throttle valve assembly
5. Throttle valve gasket
6. Intake common bolt
7. Common chamber
8. Common chamber gasket
9. Water temperature sensor
10. Water temperature unit
11. Air regulator
12. Thermal valve
13. Water outlet pipe
14. Water outlet pipe gasket
15. Radiator thermostat
16. Fuel injector with pipe
17. Intake manifold

Fig. 15 Intake manifold chamber bolts and bracket locations

7. Loosen and remove the power steering pump, A/C compressor, and alternator drive belts.

8. Remove the cooling fan and its pulley assembly.

9. Unbolt the power steering pump mounting bracket. Move the pump and bracket out of the way without disconnecting the hydraulic lines.

10. Disconnect the throttle cable from the throttle body linkage.

11. Label and disconnect the following vacuum hoses from the intake manifold chamber:

   a. PCV hose

   b. EVAP canister vacuum hose

   c. Brake booster hose

12. Label and disconnect the following sensor connectors from the rear of the intake manifold chamber:

   a. Ignition control module connectors

   b. Linear EGR valve

   c. MAP sensor

   d. EVAP purge valve

   e. Throttle position sensor

   f. Idle air control valve

   g. Intake air temperature sensor

13. Disconnect the EGR valve supply tube and bracket.

14. First, remove the throttle body, and then remove the intake manifold chamber.

15. Carefully clean any dirt from the fuel rail and fuel fittings.

✳✳ CAUTION

Fuel injection systems remain under pressure even after the engine has been turned off. The fuel system pressure must be relieved before disconnecting any fuel lines. Failure to do so may result in fire and personal injury.

16. Disconnect the fuel feed and return lines from the front of the fuel rail. Clean up any spilled fuel.

17. Remove the intake manifold gaskets. Be careful not to drop any pieces of the gaskets into the engine. Don't scratch or gouge the machined aluminum mating surfaces of the intake manifold and engine block.

18. Cover the intake openings with a sheet of plastic or clean shop towels to keep out dirt and foreign objects.

19. Label the ignition coil assemblies and disconnect them from the wiring harness. Remove the coil assemblies so they won't be damaged.

20. Unbolt the oil cooler line brackets from the timing belt covers.

21. Remove the upper timing belt covers.

22. Rotate the crankshaft to align the camshaft timing marks with the pointer dots on the back covers. When the timing marks are aligned, the No. 2 piston is at TDC/compression.

23. Remove the crankshaft pulley. Remove the lower timing belt cover.

24. Remove the pusher assembly (tensioner) from below the timing belt tensioner pulley. The pusher rod must always be facing upward to prevent oil leakage. Push the pusher rod in, and insert a wire pin into the hole to keep the pusher rod retracted.

25. Remove the timing belt.

✳✳ WARNING

If the timing belt is worn, damaged, or shows signs of oil or coolant contamination, it must be replaced.

26. Loosen the valve cover bolts in a crisscross sequence. Remove the valve covers.

27. Remove the camshaft sprockets and back covers.

28. Loosen the camshaft holder bolts in a crisscross sequence to prevent warping.

29. Remove the camshaft and camshaft holders from the cylinder head.

30. Inspect the camshaft lobes and journals for signs of wear or damage.

31. Loosen the exhaust and intake rocker shaft bolts in a crisscross sequence to prevent warping.

32. Remove the intake and exhaust rocker shafts from the cylinder head.

33. If the rocker arms and shafts must be disassembled, label the parts and wave washers so that they can be reassembled in the same positions.

34. If necessary, remove the hydraulic valve lash adjusters from the rocker arms.

35. Inspect the hydraulic lash adjusters for excess movement and replace if necessary. The hydraulic lash adjusters are designed to be self-bleeding, but new adjusters must be primed before installation.

   a. Use a small–diameter rod (0.08 in. or 2mm) to push in the adjuster's check ball.

   b. Submerge the adjuster in a tub of clean engine oil.

   c. Pump the plunger with your finger to fill the adjuster with oil and displace any air.

   d. Keep pumping the plunger until it's hard and no more air bubbles come out. Then, remove the rod to release the check ball.

To install:

36. Reassemble the rocker arm, shaft, and hydraulic lash adjuster components. Assemble the hydraulic lash adjusters to the rockers before removing them from the tub of oil. The intake rocker arms all face the same direction when installed.

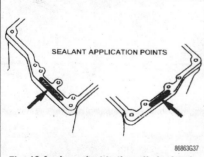

Fig. 16 Apply sealant to the cylinder head at the camshaft holder mounts

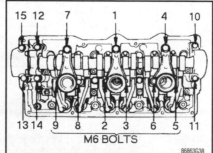

M6 BOLTS

Fig. 17 Camshaft mounting bolts—tightening sequence

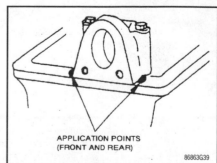

APPLICATION POINTS
(FRONT AND REAR)

Fig. 18 Apply sealant to the camshaft holders

37. Lubricate the rocker arms and shafts with clean engine oil.

38. Install the intake and exhaust rocker arms and shaft assemblies. Tighten the rocker shaft holder bolts to 13 ft. lbs. (18 Nm), starting with the intake shaft and then moving to the exhaust shaft. Make sure the intake and exhaust rockers contact each other properly.

39. Make sure all mating surfaces are clean and free of oil, coolant, or gasket residue.

40. Lubricate the camshaft lobes and journals with clean engine oil.

41. Apply a bead of sealant to the front and rear camshaft holder mating surfaces on the cylinder head.

42. Install the camshaft and holder assembly onto the cylinder head before the sealant cures. Install the camshaft holder bolts, but don't tighten them yet.

43. Use a crisscross sequence to tighten the camshaft holder bolts. Tighten the 8mm bolts to 13 ft. lbs. (18 Nm). Tighten the 6mm bolts to 6 ft. lbs. (8 Nm).

44. Use a seal driver to install a new camshaft seal.

45. Install the camshaft sprocket back covers and tighten their bolts to 12 ft. lbs. (17 Nm).

46. Install the camshaft sprockets so that the timing marks are aligned. Tighten the bolts to 46 ft. lbs. (64 Nm).

47. Apply a 2–3mm bead of sealant to the joint were the camshaft holders meet the cylinder head. Install the valve cover with a new gasket before the sealant cures.

48. Tighten the valve cover bolts to 6 ft. lbs. (8 Nm) in crisscross pattern.

49. Verify that the camshaft and crankshaft timing marks are properly aligned.

50. Install and tension the timing belt. Tighten the pusher bolts to 14 ft. lbs. (19 Nm).

51. Install the lower timing belt covers and tighten the bolts to 13 ft. lbs. (18 Nm). Install the crankshaft pulley. Tighten the pulley bolt to 123 ft. lbs. (167 Nm).

52. Install the upper timing belt covers and tighten the bolts to 13 ft. lbs. (18 Nm).

53. Fit the oil cooler line brackets onto the timing cover and tighten the bolts to 13 ft. lbs. (18 Nm).

54. Reconnect the fuel feed and return lines.

55. Install and reconnect the ignition coil assemblies.

56. Install the intake manifold chamber and throttle body with new gaskets. Tighten the nuts and bolts to 17 ft. lbs. (24 Nm).

57. Reconnect the throttle cable to the throttle body linkage.

58. Reconnect the EGR valve supply tube and bracket.

59. Reconnect the following vacuum to the intake manifold chamber:
    a. PCV hose
    b. EVAP canister vacuum hose
    c. Brake booster hose

60. Reconnect the following sensor connectors to the rear of the intake manifold chamber:
    a. Ignition control module connectors
    b. Linear EGR valve
    c. MAP sensor
    d. EVAP purge valve
    e. Throttle position sensor
    f. Idle air control valve
    g. Intake air temperature sensor

61. Install the power steering pump and mounting bracket.

62. Install the cooling fan and its pulley assembly.

63. Install and tension the alternator, A/C compressor, and power steering pump drive belts.

64. Install and reconnect the upper and lower radiator hoses.

65. Install the air cleaner box and air intake duct.

66. Verify that all fuel lines, vacuum and coolant hoses, and wiring harness have been reconnected.

67. Refill the engine with fresh coolant.

68. Crank the engine until it starts. A longer than normal starting time may be necessary due to air in the fuel lines. Check all fuel line connections for leaks.

69. Bleed any air from the cooling system.

70. Bleed the power steering system if necessary.

71. Check the throttle cable operation and adjustment.

72. Check the engine oil level and add if necessary.

Thermostat

REMOVAL & INSTALLATION

1.8L and 2.0L Engines

▶ See Figure 19

1. Disconnect the negative battery cable.
2. Drain the cooling system. Disconnect the upper radiator hose from the thermostat housing.

✳✳ CAUTION

When draining the coolant, keep in mind that cats and dogs are attracted by ethylene glycol antifreeze, and are quite likely to drink any that is left in an uncovered container or in puddles on the ground. This will prove fatal in sufficient quantity. Always drain the coolant into a sealable container. Coolant should be reused unless it is contaminated or several years old.

3. Remove the air cleaner assembly.
4. Remove the thermostat housing from the intake manifold.
5. Remove the gasket and the thermostat.

To install:

6. Install the thermostat, with the spring facing the engine.
7. Using a new gasket, install the thermostat housing. Torque the bolts to 15 ft. lbs. (20 Nm).
8. Connect the radiator hose to the thermostat housing and refill the cooling system.
9. Install the air cleaner.
10. Connect the negative battery cable.
11. Operate the engine until normal operating temperatures are reached and check the thermostat operation.

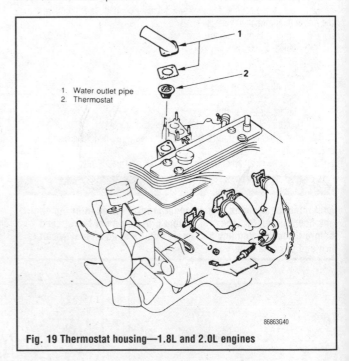

1. Water outlet pipe
2. Thermostat

86863G40

Fig. 19 Thermostat housing—1.8L and 2.0L engines

Diesel Engine

The thermostat is located under the thermostat housing, at the upper front of the engine.

1. Disconnect the negative battery cable.
2. Drain the cooling system.

When draining the coolant, keep in mind that cats and dogs are attracted by ethylene glycol antifreeze, and are quite likely to drink any that is left in an uncovered container or in puddles on the ground. This will prove fatal in sufficient quantity. Always drain the coolant into a sealable container. Coolant should be reused unless it is contaminated or several years old.

3. Disconnect the electrical connectors from the thermostat housing.
4. Remove the upper thermostat housing-to-lower housing bolts and the upper housing.
5. Remove the gasket and the thermostat.
6. Clean the gasket mounting surfaces.
   To install:
7. Install the thermostat, with the spring facing the engine.
8. Using a new gasket, install the upper thermostat housing and torque the upper housing-to-lower housing bolts to 10–17 ft. lbs. (14–24 Nm).
9. Connect the electrical connectors.
10. Connect the radiator hose to the thermostat housing and refill the cooling system.
11. Connect the negative battery cable.
12. Operate the engine until normal operating temperatures are reached and check the thermostat operation.

2.3L and 2.6L Engines

1. Disconnect the negative battery cable.
2. Drain the coolant into a sealable container. Reuse the coolant if it isn't old or contaminated.
3. Disconnect the upper radiator hose from the thermostat housing on the intake manifold.
4. Unbolt and remove the thermostat housing.
5. Remove the thermostat and its gasket.
   To install:
6. Clean the sealing surface thoroughly.
7. Install the thermostat and a new gasket. The thermostat's pin faces outward. Tighten the thermostat housing mounting bolts to 18 ft. lbs. (25 Nm).
8. Connect the upper radiator hose to the thermostat housing.
9. Refill and bleed the cooling system.
10. Connect the negative battery cable.
11. Warm the engine up to normal operating temperature and test the operation of the thermostat. Check for coolant leaks.

2.8L and 3.1L Engines

▶ See Figures 20, 21 and 22

1. Disconnect the negative battery cable.
2. Drain the coolant into a clean container so it can be reused.

3. Remove the upper radiator hose from the thermostat housing.
4. Remove the thermostat housing mounting bolts and remove the thermostat.
   To install:
5. Clean the sealing surface, use a new gasket and install the thermostat with the spring toward the engine. Torque the thermostat housing mounting bolts to 18 ft. lbs. (24 Nm).
6. Connect the radiator hose to the thermostat housing.
7. Refill the cooling system and connect the negative battery cable.
8. Start the engine and add coolant as needed until the level stabilizes below the radiator cap.
9. Install the radiator cap and check for leaks.

3.2L Engine

▶ See Figure 23

1. Disconnect the negative battery cable.
2. Drain the coolant into a clean container so it can be reused.
3. Disconnect the upper radiator hose from the thermostat housing.
4. Unbolt and remove the thermostat housing. Remove the thermostat and its gasket.
   To install:
5. Clean the sealing surface. Use a new gasket and install the thermostat with the spring toward the engine. Torque the thermostat housing mounting bolts to 14 ft. lbs. (19 Nm).
6. Connect the radiator hose to the thermostat housing.
7. Refill and bleed the cooling system.
8. Connect the negative battery cable.
9. Start the engine and add coolant as needed until the level stabilizes below the radiator cap.
10. Install the radiator cap and check for leaks.

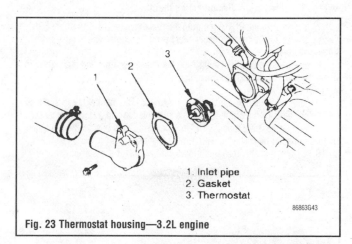

1. Inlet pipe
2. Gasket
3. Thermostat

86863G43

Fig. 23 Thermostat housing—3.2L engine

86863P01

Fig. 20 Removing the thermostat housing bolts—2.8L engine

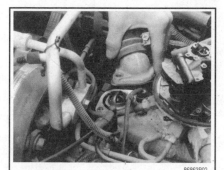

86863P02

Fig. 21 Place the hose and housing aside to gain access to the thermostat—2.8L engine

86863P03

Fig. 22 When installing the thermostat the spring side must be in the block—2.8L engine

Intake Manifold

REMOVAL & INSTALLATION

1.8L and 2.0L Engines

▶ See Figure 24

1. Drain the cooling system and disconnect the battery cables.

❊❊❊ CAUTION

When draining the coolant, keep in mind that cats and dogs are attracted by ethylene glycol antifreeze, and are quite likely to drink any that is left in an uncovered container or in puddles on the ground. This will prove fatal in sufficient quantity. Always drain the coolant into a sealable container. Coolant should be reused unless it is contaminated or several years old.

➡**Before removing the intake manifold, check to make certain the engine coolant is completely drained. If any water remains in the block it will flow into the cylinders when the intake manifold is removed.**

2. Remove the air cleaner assembly.
3. Disconnect the radiator hose from the front part of the intake manifold.
4. Disconnect the fuel lines, all vacuum lines and the carburetor control cable.
5. Disconnect the heater hoses from the rear part of the manifold and from the connector under the dashboard.
6. Disconnect the distributor vacuum hose and all thermo-valve wiring. Disconnect the electric choke or solenoid wires.

➡**Tag all wires before disconnecting them.**

7. Disconnect the PCV hose from the rocker cover. Disconnect the EGR valve from the EGR pipe and disconnect the air injection vacuum hose from the three-way connector.
8. Remove the eight nuts attaching the intake manifold and lift it clear, being careful not to snag any loose lines.
   To install:
9. Check the manifold for cracks or damage. The manifold head surfaces can be checked for distortion by using a straightedge and a feeler gauge. Distortion should be no more than 0.0157 in. (0.4mm), if it is beyond the limit, the distortion has to be corrected with a surface grinder.
10. Clean all gasket mating surfaces with a scraper and solvent.

11. Replace all gaskets and torque all nuts in sequence to 25–32 ft. lbs. (34–43 Nm).
12. Connect the PCV hose to the rocker cover. Connect the EGR valve to the EGR pipe and connect the air injection vacuum hose to the three-way connector.
13. Connect the distributor vacuum hose and all thermo-valve wiring. Connect the electric choke or solenoid wires.
14. Connect the heater hoses to the rear part of the manifold and to the connector under the dashboard.
15. Connect the fuel lines, all vacuum lines and the carburetor control cable.
16. Connect the radiator hose to the front part of the intake manifold.
17. Install the air cleaner assembly.
18. Refill the cooling system, connect the battery cables and check for leaks.

Diesel Engine

▶ See Figure 25

1. Open the hood and disconnect the battery. Remove the air cleaner assembly.
2. Remove the connecting hose and PCV hose.
3. Remove the sensing resistor assembly.
4. Remove the 6 screws attaching the injection pipe clips and remove the injection pipe.
5. Remove the 10 bolts attaching the upper dust cover and remove the upper dust cover.
6. Remove the 2 bolts attaching the engine hanger and remove the engine hanger.
7. Remove the 2 bolts attaching the stay and remove the stay. Remove the three bolts and two nuts attaching the intake manifold and lift off the manifold.
   To install:
8. Clean the gasket mating surfaces with a scraper and solvent. Inspect the components for warpage, distortion and damage.
9. Using a new manifold gasket, install the manifold and torque the bolts to 13–18 ft. lbs. (19–25 Nm).
10. Install the 2 bolts attaching the engine hanger and hanger.
11. Install the 10 bolts attaching the upper dust cover and the upper dust cover.
12. Install the 6 screws attaching the injection pipe clips and the injection pipe.
13. Install the sensing resistor assembly.
14. Install the connecting hose and PCV hose.
15. Connect the battery cable, install the air cleaner assembly, start the engine and check for leaks.

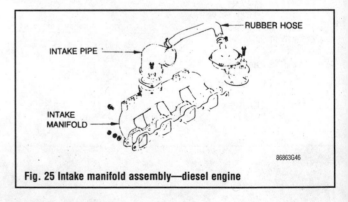

Fig. 25 Intake manifold assembly—diesel engine

2.3L and 2.6L Engines

▶ See Figures 26 and 27

AMIGO AND PICK-UP

➡**Wait until the engine has cooled to ambient air temperature before removing the intake manifold.**

1. Relieve the fuel pressure.

❊❊❊ CAUTION

Fuel injection systems remain under pressure even after the engine has been turned off. The fuel system pressure must be relieved before disconnecting any fuel lines. Failure to do so may result in fire and personal injury.

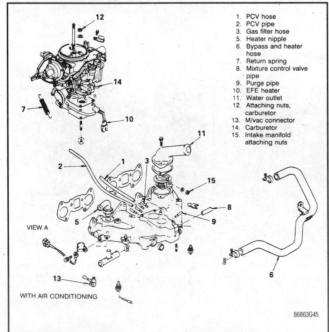

1. PCV hose
2. PCV pipe
3. Gas filter hose
5. Heater nipple
6. Bypass and heater hose
7. Return spring
8. Mixture control valve pipe
9. Purge pipe
10. EFE heater
11. Water outlet
12. Attaching nuts, carburetor
13. M/vac connector
14. Carburetor
15. Intake manifold attaching nuts

Fig. 24 Intake manifold assembly—1.8L and 2.0L engines

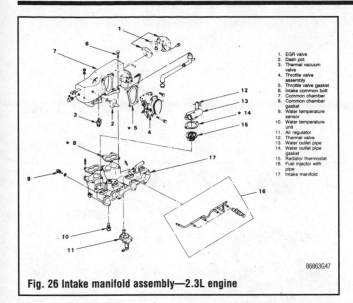

Fig. 26 Intake manifold assembly—2.3L engine

1. EGR valve
2. Dash pot
3. Thermal vacuum valve
4. Throttle valve assembly
5. Throttle valve gasket
6. Intake common bolt
7. Common chamber
8. Common chamber gasket
9. Water temperature sensor
10. Water temperature unit
11. Air regulator
12. Thermal valve
13. Water outlet pipe
14. Water outlet pipe gasket
15. Radiator thermostat
16. Fuel injector with pipe
17. Intake manifold

86863G47

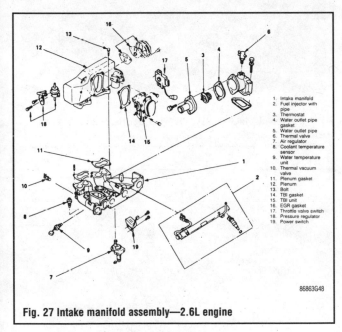

Fig. 27 Intake manifold assembly—2.6L engine

1. Intake manifold
2. Fuel injector with pipe
3. Thermostat
4. Water outlet pipe gasket
5. Water outlet pipe
6. Thermal valve
7. Air regulator
8. Coolant temperature sensor
9. Water temperature unit
10. Thermal vacuum valve
11. Plenum gasket
12. Plenum
13. Bolt
14. TBI gasket
15. TBI unit
16. EGR gasket
17. Throttle valve switch
18. Pressure regulator
19. Power switch

86863G48

Torque the mounting nuts and bolts to 16 ft. lbs. (22 Nm) starting in the center and working towards the ends.

15. Install new O–rings and cushion rings onto the fuel injectors and there mounting ports. Install the fuel injector rail with the injectors onto the manifold. Tighten the fuel injector rail securing bolts to 14 ft. lbs. (19 Nm).

16. Using a new gasket, install the upper intake manifold plenum to the intake manifold. Tighten the upper intake manifold plenum attaching bolts to 20 ft. lbs. (27 Nm).

17. Using a new gasket, install the throttle body to the plenum. Tighten the throttle body attaching bolts to 14 ft. lbs. (19 Nm).

18. Connect the accelerator linkage, vacuum lines, and electrical wiring.

19. Reconnect the fuel line using new washers.

20. Using a new gasket, install the EGR valve and bracket assembly to the intake manifold. Tighten the 22mm nut to 33 ft. lbs. (44 Nm), and the 8mm nut to 17 ft. lbs. (24 Nm).

21. Install the air regulator hose to the upper intake manifold plenum.

22. Install the upper coolant hoses to the manifold.

23. Install the air duct and connect the negative battery cable.

24. Refill and bleed the cooling system and check for leaks.

25. Adjust the accelerator linkage cable so there is 0.078 in. (2mm) of clearance.

26. Check for fuel leaks.

RODEO

1. Support the hood as far open as possible.
2. Relieve the fuel pressure:
   a. Remove the fuel filler cap.
   b. Remove the fuel pump primary relay from the underhood relay box.
   c. Start the engine and allow it to stall. After the engine stalls, crank it for an additional 30 seconds.
3. Disconnect the negative battery cable.
4. Drain the engine coolant.
5. Disconnect the throttle cable from the throttle body linkage.
6. Disconnect and remove the air intake duct.
7. Disconnect the vacuum hose from the EGR valve. If equipped, disconnect the EGR temperature sensor connector.
8. Disconnect the EGR fuel pressure control rubber hose.
9. Use a flare wrench to disconnect the EGR pipe fitting from the intake manifold.

❋❋ CAUTION

Fuel injection systems remain under pressure after the engine has been turned OFF. Properly relieve fuel pressure before disconnecting any fuel lines. Failure to do so may result in fire or personal injury.

10. Disconnect the fuel feed hose from the fuel rail.

11. Label and disconnect the coolant hoses from the intake manifold. Use a drain pan to catch any spilled coolant.

12. Disconnect the air regulator hose and connector from the lower rear of the intake manifold chamber.

13. Disconnect the throttle position sensor connector and disconnect the coolant hoses from the throttle body.

14. Loosen the throttle body mounting bolts, and then remove the throttle body from the intake manifold chamber.

15. Loosen the intake manifold chamber mounting nuts and bolts; then, remove the intake manifold chamber from the lower part of the manifold.

16. Disconnect the fuel injector wire harness clip (plastic wire tie).

17. Remove the fuel injector rail attaching bolts.

18. Label and disconnect the fuel injector wiring harness connectors.

19. Carefully lift the fuel rail and injectors from the intake manifold as an assembly.

20. Loosen the intake manifold mounting bolts and nuts in a crisscross sequence.

21. Remove the intake manifold from the engine. Clean any old gasket material from the cylinder head and intake manifold mating surfaces.

To install:

22. Install a new intake manifold gasket onto the cylinder head. Next, position the intake manifold onto its cylinder head mounting studs.

23. Install the intake manifold attaching bolts and nuts. Tighten the bolts

2. Disconnect the negative battery cable and remove the air duct.

3. Drain the cooling system. Disconnect the upper radiator hose from the manifold. Disconnect the coolant hoses from the throttle body.

4. Remove the air regulator hose from the intake plenum.

5. Remove the EGR valve and bracket assembly from the intake manifold.

6. Disconnect the accelerator linkage. Disconnect and tag the vacuum lines and electrical connections.

7. Disconnect the fuel injector wiring harnesses. Disconnect the fuel line from the fuel rail.

8. Loosen the throttle body attaching nuts in a crisscross pattern. Remove the throttle body.

9. Loosen the upper intake manifold plenum nuts in a crisscross pattern. Remove the upper intake manifold plenum.

10. Remove the fuel injector rail and fuel injectors as an assembly.

11. Loosen the intake manifold nuts and bolts in a crisscross pattern. Then, remove the intake manifold nuts and bolts.

12. Remove the manifold from the cylinder head. If it sticks, tap it with a soft–faced mallet.

To install:

13. Inspect all intake manifold mating surfaces for warpage and other signs of damage. Replace or machine as necessary.

14. Using a new gasket, install the intake manifold to the cylinder head.

and nuts in a two–step crisscross pattern beginning in the center and working outward. The final torque specification is 16 ft. lbs. (22 Nm).

24. Lubricate new O–rings with a small amount of clean engine oil; then, install them onto the fuel injectors. Next, install the fuel injectors into the fuel rail, if they were removed. Install the fuel injectors and fuel rail assembly onto the intake manifold. Tighten the fuel rail attaching bolts to 14 ft. lbs. (19 Nm).

25. Reconnect the fuel injector wiring harness connectors.

26. Install the fuel injector wiring harness clip wire tie.

27. Install the intake manifold chamber to the lower part of the manifold using a new gasket. Tighten the bolts and nuts to 20 ft. lbs. (27 Nm) in a two–step crisscross pattern.

28. Install a new throttle body gasket and then install the throttle body. Tighten the mounting bolts to 14 ft. lbs. (19 Nm).

29. Reconnect the throttle position sensor connector. Reconnect the coolant hoses to the throttle body.

30. Connect the EGR pipe to the intake manifold, torque the flange nut to 33 ft. lbs. (44 Nm).

31. Connect the EGR fuel pressure control rubber hose. If equipped, reconnect the EGR temperature sensor connector.

32. Connect the vacuum hose to the EGR valve.

33. Connect the air regulator hose and the air regulator connector.

34. Connect the coolant hoses to the intake manifold.

35. Connect the fuel feed hose to the fuel rail using new sealing washers.

36. Install the air intake duct and reconnect the vacuum hose.

37. Connect the throttle cable to the throttle body linkage and adjust as necessary.

38. Refill and bleed the cooling system.

39. Connect the negative battery cable.

40. Turn the ignition switch **ON** and check for fuel leaks at the fuel rail.

41. Check the manifold coolant hoses for leaks. Check the intake manifold mating surfaces for leaks.

2.8L Engine

▶ See Figures 28, 29 and 30

1. Relieve the fuel pressure. Disconnect the negative battery cable.
2. Remove the air cleaner. Drain the cooling system.

✳✳ CAUTION

When draining the coolant, keep in mind that cats and dogs are attracted by ethylene glycol antifreeze, and are quite likely to drink any that is left in an uncovered container or in puddles on the ground. This will prove fatal in sufficient quantity. Always drain the coolant into a sealable container. Coolant should be reused unless it is contaminated or several years old.

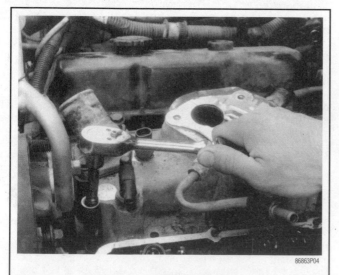

Fig. 28 Removing the intake manifold bolts—2.8L engine

3. Label and disconnect the wires and hoses from the TBI unit and the intake manifold.

4. Disconnect and plug the fuel lines from the TBI unit.

5. Disconnect the accelerator cables from the TBI unit.

6. Disconnect the ignition wires from the spark plugs and the wires from the coil.

7. Remove the distributor cap with the wires.

8. Mark the location of the rotor to the distributor housing and the distributor housing to the intake manifold.

9. Remove the distributor hold-down clamp and the distributor.

Fig. 29 Carefully lift the intake manifold make sure all hoses and wires are disconnected—2.8L engine

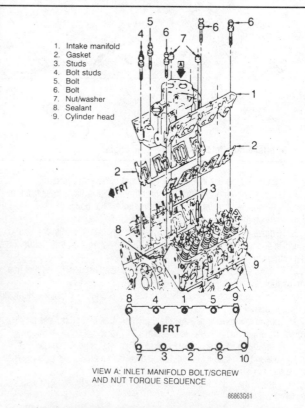

1. Intake manifold
2. Gasket
3. Studs
4. Bolt studs
5. Bolt
6. Bolt
7. Nut/washer
8. Sealant
9. Cylinder head

VIEW A: INLET MANIFOLD BOLT/SCREW AND NUT TORQUE SEQUENCE

Fig. 30 Intake manifold installation and manifold torque sequence— 2.8L and 3.1L engines

10. Label and disconnect the EGR vacuum line and the emission hoses.
11. Remove the pipe brackets from the rocker arm covers.
12. Remove the rocker arm covers.
13. Remove the upper radiator hose and the heater hose.
14. Disconnect the electrical connectors from the coolant sensors.
15. Remove the intake manifold nuts/bolts, the manifold and gaskets.
16. Clean the gasket mounting surfaces.

To install:

17. Using RTV sealant, apply a ⅛ in. (3mm) bead to the front and rear of the block; make sure no water or oil is present.
18. Using new gaskets, marked right and left side, apply a ¼ in. (6mm) bead of sealant to hold them in place and install them onto the cylinder heads; the gaskets may have to be cut to be installed around the pushrods.
19. Install the intake manifold and torque the nuts/bolts, in sequence, to 23 ft. lbs. (31 Nm) and retorque using the same sequence.

→**Make sure the areas between the case ridges and the intake manifold are completely sealed.**

20. Install the heater hose and the radiator to the manifold.
21. Using new gaskets, install the rocker arm covers.
22. Connect the electrical connectors to the coolant sensors.
23. Install the pipe brackets.
24. Align the matchmarks and install the distributor and the distributor cap.
25. Connect the fuel lines and the accelerator cables to the TBI unit.
26. Connect all the wires and vacuum hoses.
27. Install the air cleaner. Connect the negative battery cable. Refill the cooling system.

3.1L Engine

♦ **See Figure 31**

1. Relieve the fuel pressure. Disconnect the negative battery cable.
2. Remove the air cleaner. Drain the cooling system.
3. Label and disconnect the wires and hoses from the TBI unit and the intake manifold.
4. Disconnect and plug the fuel lines from the TBI unit.
5. Disconnect the accelerator cables from the TBI unit.
6. Disconnect the ignition wires from the spark plugs and the wires from the coil.
7. Remove the distributor cap with the wires.
8. Mark the location of the rotor to the distributor housing and the distributor housing to the intake manifold.
9. Remove the distributor hold-down clamp and the distributor.
10. Label and disconnect the EGR vacuum line and the emission hoses.
11. Remove the pipe brackets from the rocker arm covers.
12. Remove the rocker arm covers.
13. Remove the upper radiator hose and the heater hose.
14. Disconnect the electrical connectors from the coolant sensors.
15. Remove the intake manifold nuts/bolts, the manifold and gaskets.
16. Clean the gasket mounting surfaces.

To install:

17. Using RTV sealant, apply a ⅛ in. (3mm) bead to the front and rear of the block; make sure no water or oil is present.
18. Using new gaskets, marked right and left side, apply a ¼ in. (6mm) bead of sealant to hold them in place and install them onto the cylinder heads; the gaskets may have to be cut to be installed around the pushrods.

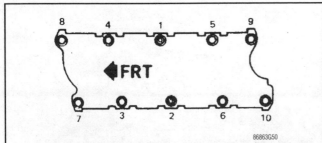

Fig. 31 Intake manifold bolt tightening sequence—3.1L engine

19. Install the intake manifold and torque the nuts/bolts, in sequence, to 19 ft. lbs. (26 Nm) and retorque using the same sequence.

→**Make sure the areas between the case ridges and the intake manifold are completely sealed.**

20. Install the heater and radiator hose to the manifold.
21. Using new gaskets, install the rocker arm covers.
22. Connect the electrical connectors to the coolant sensor.
23. Install the pipe brackets.
24. Align the matchmarks and install the distributor and the distributor cap.
25. Connect the fuel lines and the accelerator cables to the TBI unit.
26. Connect all the wires and vacuum hoses.
27. Install the air cleaner. Connect the negative battery cable. Refill the cooling system.

3.2L Engine

1993–95 VEHICLES

✳✳ CAUTION

Fuel injection systems remain under pressure even after the engine has been turned off. The fuel system pressure must be relieved before disconnecting any fuel lines. Failure to do so may result in fire and personal injury.

1. Relieve the fuel pressure:
   a. Remove the fuel filler cap.
   b. Remove the fuel pump relay from the underhood relay box.
   c. Start the engine and let it run until it stalls. Then, crank the engine for an additional 30 seconds.
   d. Turn the ignition switch to the **OFF** position.
2. Disconnect the negative battery cable. Reinstall the fuel pump relay.
3. Remove the air cleaner assembly.
4. Disconnect the accelerator pedal cable from the throttle body and bracket.
5. Disconnect the charcoal canister vacuum hose from the vacuum pipe.
6. Disconnect the air vacuum hose and the vacuum booster hose from the common chamber.
7. Disconnect the following electrical connectors:
   a. MAP sensor
   b. Charcoal canister vacuum switching valve (VSV)
   c. Exhaust Gas Recirculation VSV
   d. Intake Air Temperature sensor
   e. Engine ground cable
   f. Fuel injector connectors
   g. Thermo sensor connector
8. Tag and then disconnect the spark plug wires.
9. Remove the ignition module assembly with the spark plug wires attached.
10. Tag and then disconnect the vacuum hoses from the throttle body.
11. Remove the four throttle body mounting bolts. Then, remove the throttle body.
12. Disconnect the PCV hose from the common chamber.
13. Disconnect the fuel pressure control valve vacuum hose from the common chamber.
14. Disconnect the Evaporative Emission Canister Purge hose from the common chamber.
15. Remove the EGR valve assembly from the common chamber.
16. Remove the common chamber (six bolts, two nuts, and three brackets).
17. Disconnect the fuel feed and return hoses from the fuel rail. Remove the bracket mounting bolts from the cylinder head cover.
18. Remove the two bolts and four nuts to remove the intake manifold from the engine.

To install:

→**Use new self-locking nuts when installing the intake manifold. Use new manifold gaskets. Use new sealing washers when reconnecting the fuel lines.**

19. Install the intake manifold on the engine. Torque the bolts and nuts to 17 ft. lbs. (24 Nm). Tighten the bolts from the center towards the ends.

20. Connect the electrical connectors to the fuel injectors and the thermo sensor.
21. Connect the fuel return and feed hoses to the fuel rail.
22. Install the common chamber. Torque the bolts and nuts to 17 ft. lbs. (24 Nm).
23. Install the EGR assembly. Torque the bolts to 78 inch lbs. (9 Nm).
24. Connect the charcoal canister purge and fuel pressure regulator vacuum hoses to the common chamber.
25. Connect the PCV hose to the common chamber.
26. Install the throttle body assembly and connect the vacuum hoses to the throttle body. Torque the throttle body mounting bolts to 16 ft. lbs. (22 Nm).
27. Install the ignition module assembly. Torque the mounting bolts to 16 ft. lbs. (22 Nm).
28. Reconnect the spark plug wires.
29. Reconnect the following electrical connectors:
   a. MAP sensor
   b. Charcoal canister vacuum switching valve (VSV)
   c. Exhaust Gas Recirculation VSV
   d. Intake Air Temperature sensor
   e. Engine ground cable
30. Connect the air vacuum hose and the vacuum booster hose to the common chamber.
31. Connect the charcoal canister vacuum hose to the vacuum pipe.
32. Connect the accelerator cable to the throttle body and bracket. Adjust the cable so that the linkage rests against the stop when moved by hand.
33. Install the air cleaner assembly.
34. Verify that all electrical connectors and vacuum lines have been reconnected.
35. Connect the negative battery cable.
36. Turn the ignition key to the ON position for two seconds, then off. Turn the ignition ON again to pressurize the fuel system and check for leaks.

1996 VEHICLES

▶ See Figures 32, 33, 34, 35 and 36

1. Relieve the fuel system pressure:
   a. Remove the fuel filler cap.
   b. Remove the fuel pump relay from the underhood relay box.
   c. Start the engine and let it run until it stalls. Then, crank the engine for an additional 30 seconds.
   d. Turn the ignition switch to the **OFF** position.
2. Disconnect the negative battery cable and reinstall the fuel pump relay.
3. Remove the air cleaner and air intake duct.
4. Drain the engine coolant to a level below the upper radiator hose. Catch the coolant in a clean drain pan if it is to be reused.
5. Disconnect the throttle cable from the throttle body linkage.
6. Label and disconnect the following vacuum hoses from the intake manifold chamber:

   a. PCV hose
   b. EVAP canister vacuum hose
   c. Brake booster hose
7. Label and disconnect the following sensor connectors from the rear of the intake manifold chamber:
   a. Ignition control module connectors
   b. Linear EGR valve
   c. MAP sensor
   d. EVAP purge valve

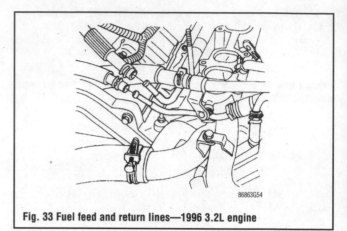
Fig. 33 Fuel feed and return lines—1996 3.2L engine

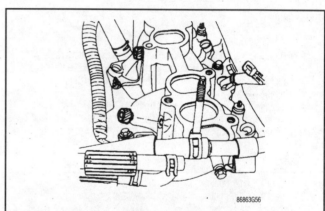
Fig. 34 Fuel rail spacer grommets must be installed in the correct position—1996 3.2L engine

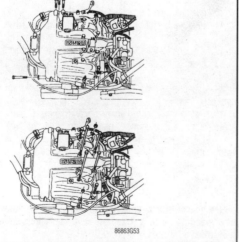
Fig. 32 Intake manifold chamber bolts and bracket locations—1996 3.2L engine

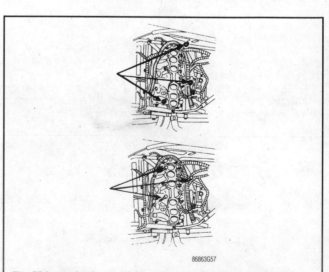
Fig. 35 Lower intake manifold nut and bolt locations—1996 3.2L engine

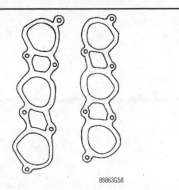

Fig. 36 Lower intake manifold chamber gaskets position—1996 3.2L engine

e. Throttle position sensor
f. Idle air control valve
g. Intake air temperature sensor
8. Disconnect the EGR valve supply tube and bracket.
9. Remove the throttle body.

❋❋ WARNING

Don't use solvent of any type when cleaning the gasket mating surfaces of the throttle body and intake manifold. Solvent may damage the machined surfaces of these components. Be careful not to scratch the mating surfaces.

10. Disconnect the MAP sensor tube, and then unbolt the MAP sensor bracket.
11. Unbolt the intake manifold chamber from its brackets which are located at its front and rear edges.
12. Loosen the six manifold mounting bolts and two nuts in a crisscross sequence.
13. Remove the bolts and nuts, and then lift the chamber off of the base of the intake manifold. Note the positions of the long and short bolts.
14. Cover the intake manifold with a sheet of plastic, or clean shop towels to keep out dirt and foreign objects.
15. Carefully clean any dirt from the fuel rail and fuel fittings.

❋❋ CAUTION

Fuel injection systems remain under pressure even after the engine has been turned off. The fuel system pressure must be relieved before disconnecting any fuel lines. Failure to do so may result in fire and personal injury.

16. Disconnect the fuel feed and return lines from the front of the fuel rail. Clean up any spilled fuel.
17. Label and disconnect the fuel injector wiring harness.
18. Unbolt the fuel return line bracket from the front of the intake manifold.
19. Unbolt the fuel rail from the intake manifold.
20. Carefully lift the fuel rail and injectors off of the intake manifold as an assembly. Move the fuel rail out of the work are so it won't be damaged; then, clean up any spilled fuel.
21. Remove the fuel rail spacer grommets from the sides of the intake manifold. Replace the spacer grommets if they are cracked or ripped.
22. Loosen the intake manifold nuts and bolts in a crisscross sequence working from the outer edges of the manifold toward the center.
23. Push the engine wiring harnesses aside and lift the intake manifold up and off of the engine block.
24. Remove the intake manifold gaskets. Be careful not to drop any pieces of the gaskets into the engine. Don't scratch or gouge the machined aluminum mating surfaces of the intake manifold and engine block.
25. Cover the intake openings with a sheet of plastic or clean shop towels to keep out dirt and foreign objects.
To install:
26. Remove the covers from the intake openings. Install new intake manifold gaskets.

27. Fit the intake manifold into position. Move the wiring harness back into position.
28. Install the intake manifold nuts and bolts. Tighten them in a two–step crisscross pattern to 15 ft. lbs. (20.5 Nm) working from the center of the manifold toward the outer edges.
29. Install the fuel rail spacer grommets.
30. Install the fuel rail assembly onto the intake manifold. Make sure all the fuel injectors are properly seated. Tighten the fuel rail bolts to 62 inch lbs. (7 Nm).
31. Reconnect the fuel feed and return lines. Install the return line bracket bolt.
32. Reconnect the fuel injector wiring harness.
33. Install a new intake manifold chamber gasket. Install the intake manifold chamber.
34. Install the six intake manifold chamber bolts and two nuts. Tighten the nuts and bolts to 15 ft. lbs. (20.5 Nm) in a crisscross sequence.
35. Install the intake manifold chamber bracket bolts.
36. Reconnect the MAP sensor tube and bracket.
37. Reconnect the EGR supply tube and bracket.
38. Install the throttle body with a new gasket. Tighten the bolts to 10 ft. lbs. (13.5 Nm) in a crisscross sequence.
39. Reconnect the following sensor connectors to the rear of the intake manifold chamber:
    a. Ignition control module connectors
    b. Linear EGR valve
    c. MAP sensor
    d. EVAP purge valve
    e. Throttle position sensor
    f. Idle air control valve
    g. Intake air temperature sensor
40. Reconnect the following vacuum hoses to the intake manifold chamber:
    a. PCV hose
    b. EVAP canister vacuum hose
    c. Brake booster hose
41. Reconnect the throttle cable to the throttle body linkage.
42. Install the air cleaner and air intake duct.
43. Reconnect the negative battery cable.
44. Refill and bleed the cooling system.
45. Crank the engine until it starts. Air trapped in the fuel lines may cause the engine to crank for a longer period of time than normal.
46. Check the fuel lines, fuel rail, and injectors for any signs of leakage.
47. Warm the engine up to normal operating temperature and check the operation of the throttle cable and linkage. Adjust if necessary.
48. Check the manifold and throttle body mating surfaces for vacuum leaks.

Combination Manifold

REMOVAL & INSTALLATION

Diesel Engine

◗ **See Figure 37**

Although the intake and exhaust manifolds are individual parts, they must be remove at the same time so the 1-piece gasket may be replaced.
1. Disconnect the negative battery cable.
2. Remove the air cleaner and air duct, if necessary.
3. Disconnect the accelerator cable from the throttle body.
4. Label and disconnect the necessary vacuum hoses and electrical connectors.
5. If not equipped with a turbocharger, disconnect the exhaust manifold from the exhaust pipe.
6. If equipped with a turbocharger, perform the following procedures:
    a. Disconnect the intake and exhaust hoses from the turbocharger.
    b. Disconnect the oil lines from the turbocharger.
    c. Remove the turbocharger-to-exhaust manifold nuts, the turbocharger assembly-to-exhaust pipe nuts and the turbocharger assembly.
7. Remove the intake manifold-to-cylinder head bolts and the intake manifold.
8. Remove the exhaust manifold-to-cylinder head bolts, the exhaust manifold and discard the gasket.

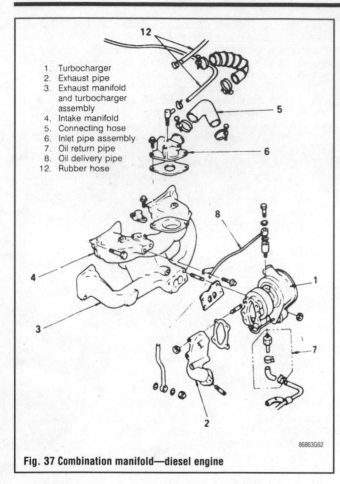

1. Turbocharger
2. Exhaust pipe
3. Exhaust manifold and turbocharger assembly
4. Intake manifold
5. Connecting hose
6. Inlet pipe assembly
7. Oil return pipe
8. Oil delivery pipe
12. Rubber hose

86863G62

Fig. 37 Combination manifold—diesel engine

9. Clean the gasket mounting surfaces.

To install:

10. Using a new gasket, install it onto the cylinder head with the center mark facing outward and upward.

11. Install the exhaust and intake manifolds onto the cylinder head and torque the nuts/bolts to 10–17 ft. lbs. (14–25 Nm) for a non-turbocharged engine or 13–17 ft. lbs. (17–25 Nm) for a turbocharged engine.

12. If not equipped with a turbocharger, install the exhaust manifold to the exhaust pipe.

13. If equipped with a turbocharger, perform the following procedures:

    a. Refill the turbocharger with clean engine oil.

    b. Install the turbocharger-to-exhaust manifold nuts to 16–23 ft. lbs. (24–32 Nm) and the turbocharger assembly-to-exhaust pipe nuts to 16–23 ft. lbs. (24–32 Nm).

    c. Connect the oil feed lines to the turbocharger.

Exhaust Manifold

REMOVAL & INSTALLATION

1.8L, 2.0L and 2.3L Engines

▸ **See Figure 38**

1. Disconnect the negative battery cable and remove the air cleaner assembly.

2. Remove the EGR pipe clamp bolt at the rear of the cylinder head.

3. Raise and safely support the vehicle. Remove the EGR pipe from the intake and exhaust manifolds.

4. Disconnect the exhaust pipe from the exhaust manifold. Disconnect the electrical connector from the oxygen sensor.

5. Remove the manifold shield and heat stove.

6. Remove the manifold retaining nuts and remove the manifold from the engine.

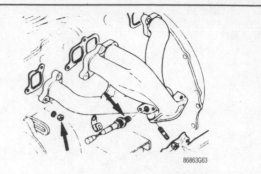

86863G63

Fig. 38 Exhaust manifold for 1.8L, 2.0L, 2.3L and 2.6L engines. Always apply anti-seize compound to nuts, studs and oxygen sensor threads during assembly

To install:

7. Using a new gasket, install the exhaust manifold and torque the nuts to 14–18 ft. lbs. (20–25 Nm).

8. Install the heat stove and shield.

9. Connect the exhaust pipe to the exhaust manifold. Connect the electrical connector to the oxygen sensor.

10. Install the EGR pipe to the intake and exhaust manifolds and lower the vehicle.

11. Install the EGR pipe clamp bolt to the rear of the cylinder head.

12. Install the air cleaner. Connect the negative battery cable.

2.6L Engine

▸ **See Figure 38**

✳ CAUTION

Allow the engine to cool to ambient temperature before removing the exhaust manifold.

1. Disconnect the negative battery cable.

2. Remove the intake air duct.

3. Label and disconnect the hoses from the air pump.

4. Release the air pump drive belt tension.

5. Remove the air pump mounting bolts. Slip the drive belt off the pulley and remove the air pump.

6. Remove the manifold heat shield.

7. Remove the EGR pipe clamp bolt from the rear of the cylinder head.

8. Raise and safely support the vehicle.

9. Disconnect the EGR pipe from the exhaust manifold.

➡ **The dipstick and tube may be removed for extra access to the oxygen sensor and EGR pipe.**

10. Disconnect the front exhaust pipe from the exhaust manifold.

11. Uncouple the oxygen sensor electrical connector.

12. Loosen the exhaust manifold nuts in a crisscross pattern.

13. Remove the exhaust manifold from the cylinder head. If it sticks, tap it with a soft-faced mallet.

To install:

➡ **Install the new exhaust manifold gasket with the stamped mark facing outward.**

14. Inspect the exhaust manifold mating surfaces for warpage or other damage. Replace if necessary. The warpage limit is 0.016 in. (0.4mm).

15. Using a new gasket, install the exhaust manifold. Tighten the manifold nuts in a crisscross pattern starting in the center and working outward to 33 ft. lbs. (44 Nm).

16. Install the tube and the dipstick if they were removed.

17. Connect the exhaust pipe to the exhaust manifold. Tighten the nuts to 49 ft. lbs. (67 Nm).

18. If the oxygen sensor was removed, coat its threads with small amount anti-seize compound. Don't get any anti–seize on the sensor's tip. Install the sensor and tighten its fitting to 31 ft. lbs. (42 Nm).

19. Connect the electrical connector to the oxygen sensor.

20. Install the EGR pipe to the intake and exhaust manifolds and tighten the bolts to 17 ft. lbs. (24 Nm).
21. Lower the vehicle.
22. Install the manifold heat shield.
23. Install the EGR pipe clamp bolt to the rear of the cylinder head.
24. Install the air pump and drive belt.
25. Connect the hoses to the air pump.
26. Install the intake air duct.
27. Connect the negative battery cable.

2.8L Engine

▶ **See Figures 39 and 40**

1. Disconnect the negative battery cable.
2. Raise and safely support the vehicle.
3. Remove the exhaust pipe from the manifold.
4. Lower the vehicle and remove the rear manifold bolts.
5. On the right side, remove the diverter valve, the heat shield, the AIR pump bracket and alternator bracket.
6. On the left side, remove the heat stove tube and the power steering bracket.
7. Remove the exhaust manifold-to-cylinder head bolts and the manifold.
8. Clean the gasket mounting surfaces.

Fig. 39 Removing the exhaust manifold bolts—2.8L engine

Fig. 40 Lifting the exhaust manifold from the cylinder head—2.8L engine

To install:
9. Using a new gasket, install the exhaust manifold-to-cylinder head bolts and torque the bolts to 25 ft. lbs. (34 Nm).
10. On the left side, install the power steering bracket and heat stove tube.
11. On the right side, install the AIR pump bracket, the alternator bracket, the diverter valve and the heat shield.
12. Raise and safely support the vehicle.
13. Install the exhaust pipe-to-manifold bolts.
14. Lower the vehicle and connect the negative battery cable.

3.1L Engine

▶ **See Figure 41**

LEFT EXHAUST MANIFOLD

1. Disconnect the negative battery cable.
2. Raise and safely support the vehicle.
3. Remove the front wheels.
4. Remove the dust cover.
5. Disconnect the exhaust pipe from the exhaust manifold.
6. Remove the power steering pump bracket.
7. Remove the exhaust manifold mounting bolts.
8. Remove the exhaust manifold.

To install:
9. Install the exhaust manifold. Torque the mounting bolts to 25 ft. lbs. (34 Nm).
10. Install the power steering pump bracket.
11. Connect the exhaust pipe to the exhaust manifold.
12. Install the dust cover and the front wheels.
13. Lower the vehicle to the floor.
14. Connect the negative battery cable, start the engine and check for leaks.

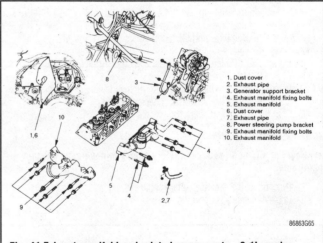

1. Dust cover
2. Exhaust pipe
3. Generator support bracket
4. Exhaust manifold fixing bolts
5. Exhaust manifold
6. Dust cover
7. Exhaust pipe
8. Power steering pump bracket
9. Exhaust manifold fixing bolts
10. Exhaust manifold

Fig. 41 Exhaust manifold and related components—3.1L engine

RIGHT EXHAUST MANIFOLD

1. Disconnect the negative battery cable.
2. Raise and safely support the vehicle.
3. Remove the front wheels.
4. Remove the dust cover.
5. Disconnect the exhaust pipe from the exhaust manifold.
6. Remove the generator support bracket.
7. Using a 6 point socket, remove the exhaust manifold mounting bolts.
8. Remove the exhaust manifold.

To install:
9. Install the exhaust manifold. Torque the mounting bolts to 25 ft. lbs. (34 Nm).
10. Install the generator support bracket.
11. Connect the exhaust pipe to the exhaust manifold.
12. Install the dust cover and the front wheels.
13. Lower the vehicle to the floor.
14. Connect the negative battery cable, start the engine and check for leaks.

3.2L Engine

♦ See Figure 42

LEFT EXHAUST MANIFOLD

➡Allow the engine to cool completely before removing the exhaust manifolds.

1. Disconnect the negative battery cable.
2. Remove the air duct.
3. Remove the EGR pipe mounting bolts from the exhaust manifold.
4. Raise and safely support the vehicle.
5. If necessary to gain extra working room, remove the transfer case skid plate.
6. Label and disconnect the oxygen sensor connectors.
7. Remove the two stud nuts and two bolts and nuts and separate the front exhaust pipes from the exhaust manifold. Be careful not to damage the oxygen sensors when working around the exhaust pipes.
8. Lower the vehicle.
9. Remove the engine hanger and the heat shield.
10. Remove the seven nuts and then remove the exhaust manifold from the cylinder head.

To install:

➡Use new self-locking nuts and new gaskets when installing the exhaust manifolds.

11. Install the exhaust manifold and gasket to the cylinder head using new nuts. Tighten the new nuts to 42 ft. lbs. (57 Nm) in a crisscross sequence.
12. Install the heat shield and the engine hanger.
13. Raise and safely support the vehicle.
14. Install the front exhaust pipes and reconnect the exhaust system. Tighten the exhaust fasteners to the following specifications:
    a. Stud nuts: 49 ft. lbs. (67 Nm)
    b. Flange nuts and bolts: 32–37 ft. lbs. (43–50 Nm)
15. Reconnect the oxygen sensor connectors.
16. Install the skid plate and tighten the bolts to 27 ft. lbs. (37 Nm).
17. Lower the vehicle.
18. Install the EGR pipe to the exhaust manifold. Tighten the mounting bolts to 21 ft. lbs. (28 Nm).
19. Install the air duct and connect the negative battery cable. Verify that all wires and vacuum lines have been reconnected.
20. Start the engine and check for exhaust leaks.

RIGHT EXHAUST MANIFOLD

➡Allow the engine to cool completely before removing the exhaust manifolds.

1. Disconnect the negative battery cable.
2. Raise and safely support the vehicle.
3. If necessary to gain extra working room, remove the transfer case skid plate.
4. Label and disconnect the oxygen sensor connectors.
5. Remove the two stud nuts and two bolts and nuts and separate the front exhaust pipes from the exhaust manifold. Be careful not to damage the oxygen sensors when working around the exhaust pipes.
6. Lower the vehicle.
7. Remove the engine hanger.
8. Remove the five heat shield mounting bolts and then remove the heat shield.
9. Remove the seven nuts and then remove the exhaust manifold from the cylinder head.

To install:

➡Use new self-locking nuts and new gaskets when installing the exhaust manifolds.

10. Install the exhaust manifold and gasket to the cylinder head using new nuts. Tighten the new nuts to 42 ft. lbs. (57 Nm) in a crisscross sequence.
11. Install the heat shield and the engine hanger.
12. Raise and safely support the vehicle.
13. Install the front exhaust pipes and reconnect the exhaust system. Tighten the exhaust fasteners to the following specifications:
    a. Stud nuts: 49 ft. lbs. (67 Nm)
    b. Flange nuts and bolts: 32–37 ft. lbs. (43–50 Nm)
14. Reconnect the oxygen sensor connectors.
15. Install the skid plate and tighten the bolts to 27 ft. lbs. (37 Nm).
16. Lower the vehicle.
17. Verify that all wires and vacuum lines have been reconnected.
18. Reconnect the negative battery cable.
19. Start the engine and check for exhaust leaks.

Turbocharger

REMOVAL & INSTALLATION

♦ See Figure 43

1. Disconnect the negative battery cable.
2. Remove the air cleaner and air duct.
3. Disconnect the intake and exhaust hoses from the turbocharger.
4. Disconnect the oil lines from the turbocharger.
5. Remove the turbocharger-to-exhaust manifold nuts, the turbocharger assembly-to-exhaust pipe nuts and the turbocharger assembly.
6. Clean the gasket mounting surfaces. Refill the turbocharger with clean engine oil.

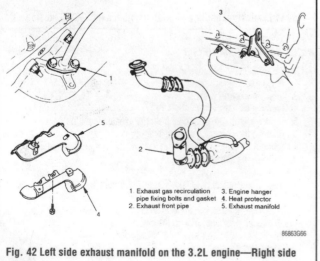

1. Exhaust gas recirculation pipe fixing bolts and gasket
2. Exhaust front pipe
3. Engine hanger
4. Heat protector
5. Exhaust manifold

86863G66

Fig. 42 Left side exhaust manifold on the 3.2L engine—Right side similar

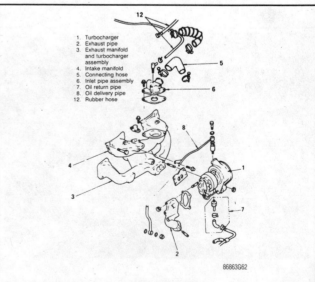

1. Turbocharger
2. Exhaust pipe
3. Exhaust manifold and turbocharger assembly
4. Intake manifold
5. Connecting hose
6. Inlet pipe assembly
7. Oil return pipe
8. Oil delivery pipe
12. Rubber hose

86863G62

Fig. 43 Turbocharger and combination manifold assembly—diesel engine

7. Using a new gasket, install the turbocharger-to-exhaust manifold nuts to 16–23 ft. lbs. (21–33 Nm) and the turbocharger assembly-to-exhaust pipe nuts to 16–23 ft. lbs. (21–33 Nm).

8. Connect the oil feed lines to the turbocharger.

9. Connect the intake and exhaust hoses to the turbocharger.

10. Install the air cleaner and air duct.

11. Connect the negative battery cable.

Radiator

REMOVAL & INSTALLATION

▶ **See Figures 44 and 45**

1981–92 Vehicles

1. Disconnect the negative battery cable.

✳✳ CAUTION

When draining the coolant, keep in mind that cats and dogs are attracted by ethylene glycol antifreeze, and are quite likely to drink any that is left in an uncovered container or in puddles on the ground. This will prove fatal in sufficient quantity. Always drain the coolant into a sealable container. Coolant should be reused unless it is contaminated or several years old.

2. Drain the cooling system.

3. Remove the upper, lower and reservoir hoses from the radiator.

4. Remove the fan shroud-to-radiator bolts and the shroud. Remove the electric fan and shroud, if so equipped.

5. Remove the radiator-to-chassis bolts and the radiator.

To install:

6. Install the radiator and the radiator-to-chassis bolts.

7. Install the fan shroud and the shroud-to-radiator bolts. Install and connect the electric fan, if so equipped.

8. Reconnect the radiator hoses.

9. Refill the cooling system.

10. Connect the negative battery cable.

1993–94 Vehicles

1. Disconnect the negative battery cable.

2. Drain the cooling system into a clean container so it can be reused.

3. Remove the upper, lower, and reservoir hoses from the radiator.

4. Disconnect the oil cooling lines from the radiator if equipped with automatic transmission.

5. Remove the fan shroud attaching bolts and the shroud.

6. Remove the radiator attaching bolts and the radiator.

To install:

7. Install the radiator and its attaching bolts.

8. Install the fan shroud and the shroud attaching bolts.

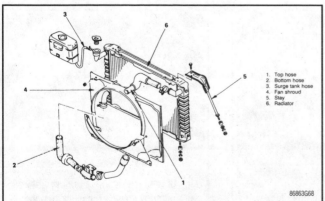

Fig. 44 Radiator assembly used with mechanical fan assembly

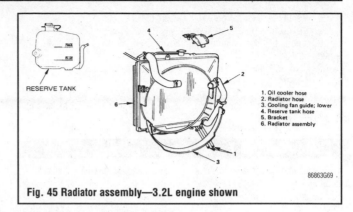

Fig. 45 Radiator assembly—3.2L engine shown

9. Reconnect the radiator hoses.

10. Connect the oil cooling lines, if removed.

11. Refill the cooling system.

12. Connect the negative battery cable and check for coolant system leaks.

1995–96 Vehicles

4-CYLINDER ENGINES

1. Disconnect the negative battery cable.

2. Loosen the drain plug on the bottom of the radiator and drain the coolant into a container.

3. Remove the upper radiator hose.

4. Remove the two air intake duct mounting bolts; then, move the duct and deflector out of the way.

5. Disconnect the lower radiator hose from the radiator.

6. Disconnect the coolant recovery hose from the radiator.

7. Disconnect the lower fan guide clips and the bottom lock, then remove the lower fan shroud from the vehicle.

8. Remove the four upper fan shroud attaching bolts and remove the shroud.

9. Remove the four radiator bolts and carefully remove the radiator.

To install:

10. Carefully lower the radiator into the vehicle, take care not to damage the radiator or the fan blades.

11. Position the radiator and install the four bolts.

12. Install the upper fan shroud and its attaching bolts.

13. Install the lower fan guide, make sure that the clips are fully engaged.

14. Connect the coolant recovery hose to the radiator.

15. Connect the lower radiator hose to the radiator.

16. Install the air intake duct assembly and the two mounting bolts.

17. Install the upper radiator hose.

18. Refill and bleed the air from the cooling system.

19. Connect the negative battery cable.

3.2L ENGINE

1. Disconnect the negative battery cable.

2. Loosen the drain plug on the bottom of the radiator and drain the coolant.

3. If equipped with an automatic transmission, disconnect and plug the ATF cooler hoses.

4. Disconnect the upper and lower radiator hoses from the engine.

5. Disconnect the lower fan guide clips and the bottom lock, then remove the lower fan guide from the vehicle.

6. Disconnect the reserve tank hose from the radiator.

7. Remove the radiator bracket.

8. Lift the radiator from the vehicle with the hoses attached. Remove the cushions from the bottom of the radiator.

9. Remove the upper and lower hoses from the radiator.

To install:

10. Install the rubber cushions to the bottom of the radiator. Install the upper and lower radiator hoses to the radiator.

11. Carefully lower the radiator into the vehicle, take care not to damage the radiator or the fan blades.

12. Install the radiator bracket.

13. Connect the reserve tank hose to the radiator.

14. Install the lower fan guide, make sure that the clips are fully engaged.
15. Connect the upper and lower radiator hoses to the engine.
16. If equipped with an automatic transmission, connect the ATF cooler hoses.
17. Refill and bleed the air from the cooling system.
18. Connect the negative battery cable.
19. Warm up the vehicle and check the operation of the cooling system and heater. Check the transmission fluid level on automatic-equipped vehicles and add ATF If necessary.

Engine Cooling Fan/Clutch Fan

The vehicles covered by this manual are either equipped with a standard cooling fan (early models) or a clutch fan assembly (most later model vehicles). Standard cooling fans are simply bolted to the water pump hub, while on clutch fans, the fan blade assembly is bolted to a clutch assembly which is secured to water pump hub studs. Both fans are removed in a similar manner, but the clutch assembly requires a little more effort.

CLUTCH FAN DIAGNOSIS

Start the engine and listen for fan noise. Fan noise is usually evident during the first few minutes after start-up and when the clutch is engaged for maximum cooling (during idle). If fan noise is excessive, the fan cannot be rotated by hand while the engine is stopped, or there is a rough, grating feel as the fan is turned, replace the clutch.

Check a loose fan assembly for wear and replace as necessary. Under certain conditions, the fan may flex up to ¼ in. (6mm). This is not cause for replacement.

The fan clutch is not affected by small fluid leaks which may occur in the area around the bearing assembly. If leakage appears excessive, replace the fan clutch.

If the fan clutch free-wheels with no drag (revolves more than five times when spun by hand), replace the clutch.

REMOVAL & INSTALLATION

▶ **See Figures 46, 47 and 48**

➡**DO NOT use or repair a damaged fan assembly. An unbalanced fan assembly could fly apart and cause personal injury or property damage. Replace damaged assemblies with new ones.**

1. Disconnect the negative battery cable.
2. Remove the upper radiator shroud and, if desired for additional clearance, remove the radiator from the vehicle.

➡**Although it is not necessary in most cases, the radiator may be removed from the vehicle for easier access to the fan retainers. If the radiator is left in place, use extra caution to prevent damage to the fragile radiator fins.**

3. Remove the fan assembly attaching nuts (clutch type) or bolts (standard type), then remove the fan assembly from the engine.

➡**Some vehicles use a space between the fan and the water pump pulley. If used, be sure to retain the spacer for installation.**

4. If necessary, the clutch may be removed from the fan by removing the attaching nuts or bolts (as applicable).
   To install:
5. If removed, install the fan to the clutch and secure using the fasteners.
6. Position the spacer (if used) and fan assembly to the water pump pulley and secure using the fasteners.
7. If removed for clearance, install the radiator.
8. Install the upper fan shroud.
9. Connect the negative battery cable.
10. If the radiator was removed, properly refill the engine cooling system.

Electric Cooling Fan

REMOVAL & INSTALLATION

▶ **See Figure 49**

1. Disconnect the negative battery cable.
2. Remove the radiator dynamic damper.
3. On some models it may be necessary to drain some engine coolant and remove the upper radiator hose.

✳✳ CAUTION

When draining the coolant, keep in mind that cats and dogs are attracted by ethylene glycol antifreeze, and are quite likely to drink any that is left in an uncovered container or in puddles on the ground. This will prove fatal in sufficient quantity. Always drain the coolant into a sealable container. Coolant should be reused unless it is contaminated or several years old.

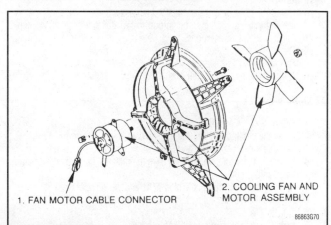

1. FAN MOTOR CABLE CONNECTOR
2. COOLING FAN AND MOTOR ASSEMBLY

86863G70

Fig. 49 Electric fan assembly

Fig. 46 Although usually not necessary, removing the radiator will often make fan removal easier

85383156

Fig. 47 For non-clutch type fans, loosen and remove the retaining bolts

85383157

Fig. 48 With the retainers removed, the fan assembly may be removed from the water pump pulley

85383158

4. Disconnect the fan electrical connector.
5. Remove the fan guide, fan and motor assembly.

To install:

6. Install the fan guide, fan and motor assembly.
7. Connect the fan electrical connector.
8. Install the radiator hoses and refill the engine coolant.
9. Install the radiator dynamic damper.
10. Connect the negative battery cable, start the engine and check for leaks.

Water Pump

REMOVAL & INSTALLATION

1.8L and 2.0L Engines

▶ See Figure 50

➡This procedure may be easier if the radiator and shroud is removed. If the radiator is not removed, place cardboard in front so not to damage the radiator core

1. Open the hood and disconnect the battery. Remove the lower engine cover.
2. Drain the cooling system.

✻✻ CAUTION

When draining the coolant, keep in mind that cats and dogs are attracted by ethylene glycol antifreeze, and are quite likely to drink any that is left in an uncovered container or in puddles on the ground. This will prove fatal in sufficient quantity. Always drain the coolant into a sealable container. Coolant should be reused unless it is contaminated or several years old.

3. On cars without air conditioning, remove the fan.
4. On cars with air conditioning, remove the air pump and generator mounting bolts, then remove the fan and air pump drive belt (pivot the generator and air pump in toward the engine). Remove the fan and pulley with set plate. Remove the hoses to the pump.
5. Remove the 6 bolts attaching the water pump and remove the water pump assembly. Clean all gasket surfaces carefully.

To install:

6. Install the 6 bolts attaching the water pump with a new gasket.
7. On cars with air conditioning, install the air pump and generator mounting bolts, then install the fan and air pump drive belt (pivot the generator and air pump in toward the engine). Install the fan and pulley with set plate. Install the hoses to the pump.
8. On cars without air conditioning, install the fan.
9. Refill the cooling system.
10. Connect the battery, start the engine and check for leaks.

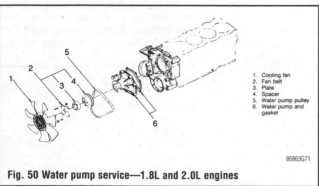

1.	Cooling fan
2.	Fan belt
3.	Plate
4.	Spacer
5.	Water pump pulley
6.	Water pump and gasket

86863G71

Fig. 50 Water pump service—1.8L and 2.0L engines

Diesel Engine

▶ See Figure 51

1. Open the hood and disconnect the battery. Remove the radiator cap.
2. Drain the cooling system and remove the hoses from the pump.

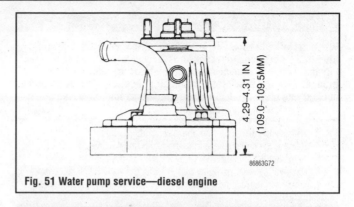

4.29–4.31 IN.
(109.0–109.5MM)

86863G72

Fig. 51 Water pump service—diesel engine

✻✻ CAUTION

When draining the coolant, keep in mind that cats and dogs are attracted by ethylene glycol antifreeze, and are quite likely to drink any that is left in an uncovered container or in puddles on the ground. This will prove fatal in sufficient quantity. Always drain the coolant into a sealable container. Coolant should be reused unless it is contaminated or several years old.

3. Remove the fan and pulley.
4. Remove the four attaching bolts holding the damper pulley. Remove the damper pulley.
5. Remove the engine dust covers.
6. Remove the bypass hose.
7. Remove the five bolts attaching the water pump and remove the pump and gasket.

To install:

8. Clean all gasket surfaces carefully and inspect for nicks, cracks or deep scratches.
9. Use a new gasket. Torque all water pump mounting bolts to 11–18 ft. lbs. (15–23 Nm).
10. Install the bypass hose.
11. Install the engine dust covers.
12. Install the four attaching bolts holding the damper pulley and damper pulley.
13. Install the fan and pulley.
14. Install the hoses to the water pump and refill the cooling system.
15. Connect the battery, install the radiator cap, start the engine and check for leaks.

1986–92 2.3L Engine

1. Disconnect the battery and drain the radiator.

✻✻ CAUTION

When draining the coolant, keep in mind that cats and dogs are attracted by ethylene glycol antifreeze, and are quite likely to drink any that is left in an uncovered container or in puddles on the ground. This will prove fatal in sufficient quantity. Always drain the coolant into a sealable container. Coolant should be reused unless it is contaminated or several years old.

2. Remove the fan belt, plate, spacer, and pulley.
3. Remove the water pump and gasket.

To install:

4. Before installation, clean the gasket surfaces carefully and torque the water pump retaining bolts to 18 ft. lbs. (25 Nm).
5. Install the fan belt, plate, spacer, and pulley.
6. Connect the battery, refill the radiator, start the engine and check for leaks.

1988–92 2.6L Engine

1. Disconnect the negative battery cable.
2. Remove the undercover, if equipped, and drain the cooling system.

✳✳ CAUTION

When draining the coolant, keep in mind that cats and dogs are attracted by ethylene glycol antifreeze, and are quite likely to drink any that is left in an uncovered container or in puddles on the ground. This will prove fatal in sufficient quantity. Always drain the coolant into a sealable container. Coolant should be reused unless it is contaminated or several years old.

3. Remove the drive belt from the water pump pulley.
4. Remove the coolant hose from the pump body, if so equipped.
5. Remove the fan blade and pulley from the pump hub.
6. Remove the water pump-to-engine bolts, the water pump and gasket.
7. Clean and inspect the mounting surfaces of the water pump and engine.

To install:
8. Install a new gasket and the water pump; torque the water pump-to-engine bolts to 24–38 ft. lbs. (33–52 Nm).
9. Install the fan blade and pulley to the water pump.
10. Connect the water hose to the pump, if so equipped.
11. Install and adjust the drive belt.
12. Refill the cooling system and install the undercover, if equipped.
13. Connect the negative battery cable.
14. Operate the engine to normal operating temperatures and check for leaks.

1993–94 2.3L and 2.6L Engines

1. Disconnect the negative battery cable.
2. Remove the undercover, if equipped, and drain the cooling system into a clean container so it can be reused.
3. Remove the drive belt from the water pump pulley.
4. Remove the fan blade and pulley from the pump hub.
5. Remove the water pump-to-engine bolts, the water pump and gasket.
6. Clean and inspect the mounting surfaces of the water pump and engine.

To install:
7. Install a new gasket and the water pump; torque the water pump-to-engine bolts to 13.7 ft. lbs. (18 Nm).
8. Install the fan blade and pulley to the water pump.
9. Install and adjust the drive belt.
10. Refill the cooling system and install the undercover, if equipped.
11. Connect the negative battery cable.
12. Operate the engine to normal operating temperatures and check for leaks.

1995–96 4-Cylinder Engines

▶ **See Figure 52**

1. Disconnect the negative battery cable.
2. Drain the coolant from the radiator by loosening the drain plug on the bottom of the radiator. Drain the coolant into a sealable container.
3. Disconnect the radiator hoses from the radiator.
4. Remove the air duct assembly.
5. Remove the lower fan guide clips and the bottom lock. Then, remove the lower fan shroud from the vehicle.

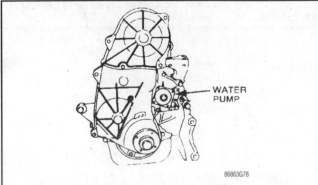

Fig. 52 Water pump assembly—4-cylinder engine

6. Remove the four upper fan shroud attaching bolts and remove the shroud.
7. Remove the four nuts attaching the fan to the water pump; then, remove the fan.
8. If equipped with power steering, remove the power steering belt.
9. If equipped with air conditioning, loosen the air conditioner idler pulley nuts; then, remove the two mounting bolts and the idler pulley. Remove the air conditioning compressor belt.
10. Remove the alternator belt.
11. Remove the pulley from the water pump.
12. Rotate the crankshaft to align the crankshaft pulley timing marks.
13. Remove the starter and install the flywheel holder (part No. J-38674).
14. Remove the crankshaft pulley bolt. Remove the crankshaft pulley.
15. Remove the upper and lower timing belt covers.
16. Remove the four bolts and one nut from the water pump. Remove the pump from the engine.

To install:
17. Clean the water pump mounting surface.
18. Install the water pump with a new gasket. Tighten the mounting bolts to 14 ft. lbs. (19 Nm), and torque the nut to 20 ft. lbs. (25 Nm).
19. Install the timing belt lower and upper covers. Tighten the timing belt cover bolts to 4 ft. lbs. (6 Nm).
20. Install the crankshaft pulley, tighten the bolt to 90 ft. lbs. (122 Nm).
21. Install the starter motor. Tighten mounting bolts to 30 ft. lbs. (40 Nm).
22. Install the water pump pulley.
23. Install the alternator belt to the pulleys, do not tension the belt at this time.
24. If equipped with air conditioning, install the air conditioning belt and idler pulley, then adjust the belt tension.
25. If equipped with power steering, install and adjust the power steering belt.
26. Install the fan pulley to the water pump, and adjust the alternator belt tension. Tighten the fan attaching nuts to 20 ft. lbs. (27 Nm). Install the cooling fan.
27. Install the upper fan shroud.
28. Install the lower fan shroud.
29. Install the air duct assembly.
30. Connect the radiator hoses to the radiator.
31. Fill and bleed the air from the cooling system.
32. Connect the negative battery cable.

2.8L Engine

▶ **See Figures 53, 54, 55 and 56**

1. Disconnect the negative battery terminal.
2. Drain the cooling system.

✳✳ CAUTION

When draining the coolant, keep in mind that cats and dogs are attracted by ethylene glycol antifreeze, and are quite likely to drink any that is left in an uncovered container or in puddles on the ground. This will prove fatal in sufficient quantity. Always drain the coolant into a sealable container. Coolant should be reused unless it is contaminated or several years old.

3. Remove the fan shroud and/or radiator support, as applicable.
4. Remove all drive belts.
5. Remove the fan and pulley from the water pump.
6. Remove the alternator upper and lower brackets. Remove the power steering pump lower bracket and swing aside.
7. Remove the bottom radiator hose and heater hose from the pump.
8. Remove the water pump.

To install:
9. Clean the gasket mating surfaces with solvent and a scraper.
10. Coat the new gasket with RTV Sealer.
11. Install the gasket, pump and bolts. Torque the pump bolts 15–25 ft. lbs. (20–34 Nm).
12. Install the bottom radiator hose and heater hose to the pump.
13. Install the alternator upper and lower brackets. Install the power steering pump lower bracket.

Fig. 53 After removing the fan, the belt pulley will slide off—2.8L engine

Fig. 54 Since the heater hoses will be disconnected, it's a good time to replace them with new hoses and clamps—2.8L engine

Fig. 55 Removing the water pump retaining bolt—2.8L engine

Fig. 56 The water pump mating surface must be completely free of dirt and old gasket, or the new pump will leak—2.8L engine

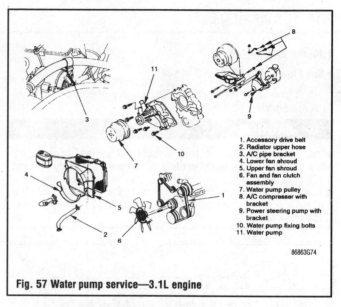

1. Accessory drive belt
2. Radiator upper hose
3. A/C pipe bracket
4. Lower fan shroud
5. Upper fan shroud
6. Fan and fan clutch assembly
7. Water pump pulley
8. A/C compresser with bracket
9. Power steering pump with bracket
10. Water pump fixing bolts
11. Water pump

Fig. 57 Water pump service—3.1L engine

14. Install the fan and pulley to the water pump.
15. Install all drive belts.
16. Install the fan shroud and/or radiator support, as applicable.
17. Refill the cooling system.
18. Connect the negative battery terminal. Start the engine and check for leaks.

3.1L Engine

▶ **See Figure 57**

1. Disconnect the negative battery terminal.
2. Drain the cooling system.
3. Remove the upper and lower fan shroud.
4. Remove all drive belts.
5. Remove the fan and pulley from the water pump.
6. Remove the alternator upper and lower brackets. Remove the power steering pump lower bracket and swing aside.
7. Remove the bottom radiator hose and heater hose from the pump.
8. Remove the water pump.

To install:

9. Clean the gasket mating surfaces with solvent and a scraper.
10. Coat the new gasket with RTV Sealer.
11. Install the gasket, pump and bolts. Torque the pump bolts 22 ft. lbs. (30 Nm).
12. Install the bottom radiator hose and heater hose to the pump.
13. Install the alternator upper and lower brackets. Install the power steering pump lower bracket.
14. Install the fan and pulley to the water pump.
15. Install all drive belts.

16. Install the upper and lower fan shroud.
17. Refill the cooling system.
18. Connect the negative battery terminal. Start the engine and check for leaks.

3.2L Engine

▶ **See Figure 58**

1. Disconnect the negative battery cable.
2. Drain the engine coolant into a clean container.

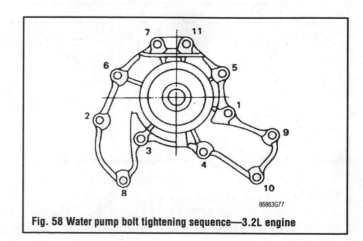

Fig. 58 Water pump bolt tightening sequence—3.2L engine

3. Remove the upper radiator hose.

4. Remove the timing belt and the idler pulley. The timing belt must be replaced if it has been contaminated by oil or coolant.

5. Unbolt and remove the water pump.

6. Remove the water pump gasket. Clean any gasket material or sealant residue from the water pump mating sealing surfaces.

To install:

7. Install the water pump using a new gasket. Tighten the mounting bolts to 13 ft. lbs. (18 Nm) in a two-step crisscross sequence.

8. Install the idler pulley. Tighten the mounting bolt to 31 ft. lbs. (42 Nm).

9. Install and tension the timing belt.

10. Install the upper radiator hose.

11. Refill and bleed the cooling system.

12. Connect the negative battery cable. Start the engine and check for coolant leaks.

Cylinder Head

REMOVAL & INSTALLATION

1.8L and 2.0L Engines

▶ See Figures 59, 60, 61, 62 and 63

1. Disconnect the negative battery cable and drain the engine coolant. Remove the rocker cover.

☀ CAUTION

When draining the coolant, keep in mind that cats and dogs are attracted by ethylene glycol antifreeze, and are quite likely to drink any that is left in an uncovered container or in puddles on the ground. This will prove fatal in sufficient quantity. Always drain the coolant into a sealable container. Coolant should be reused unless it is contaminated or several years old.

2. Remove the EGR pipe clamp bolt at the rear of the cylinder head.

3. Raise and support the vehicle safely. Disconnect the exhaust pipe at the exhaust manifold.

4. Lower the vehicle.

5. Disconnect the heater hoses at the intake manifold and at the rear of the cylinder head. Remove the air conditioning compressor and/or power steering pump with hoses attached and support them aside.

6. Disconnect the accelerator linkage and fuel line at the carburetor. Disconnect and label the electrical connections, spark plug wires and vacuum lines at the cylinder head.

7. Rotate the engine until the No. 4 cylinder is in the firing position. Remove the distributor cap and mark the rotor to housing relationship. Remove distributor and the fuel pump.

8. Lock the timing chain adjuster by depressing and turning the automatic adjuster side pin 90° clockwise.

9. Remove the timing sprocket-to-camshaft bolt and remove the sprocket from the camshaft.

➡**Keep the sprocket on the chain damper and chain.**

10. Disconnect the AIR hose and the check valve at the exhaust manifold.

11. Remove the cylinder head to timing cover bolts.

12. Starting with the outer bolts and working inward, remove the cylinder head bolts.

13. Remove the cylinder head, intake and exhaust manifold as a unit. Remove all accessories if the manifold has to be serviced.

To install:

14. Clean the gasket mating surfaces with scraper and solvent. Check the cylinder head and block for warpage using a straightedge and feeler gauge. Refer to Cylinder Head Inspection procedure in this section.

15. Use a new gasket and install the cylinder head on the engine.

16. Torque the bolts to specifications. Refer to the Torque Specifications chart earlier in this section.

17. Install the timing chain by performing the following procedures:

a. Install the timing sprocket and pinion gear with the groove side toward the front cover. Align the key grooves with the key on the crankshaft, then drive into position.

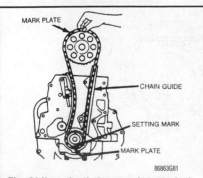

FRONT COVER FIXING SCREW

86863G79

Fig. 59 Cylinder head bolt torque sequence—1.8L and 2.0L engines

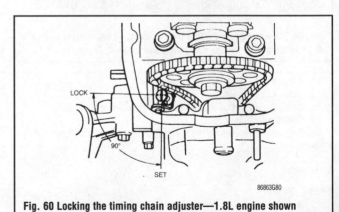

LOCK

90°

SET

86863G80

Fig. 60 Locking the timing chain adjuster—1.8L engine shown

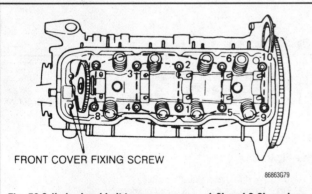

MARK PLATE

CHAIN GUIDE

SETTING MARK

MARK PLATE

86863G81

Fig. 61 Keep the timing sprocket attached to the chain while aligning or removing. A piece of mechanics wire may be helpful

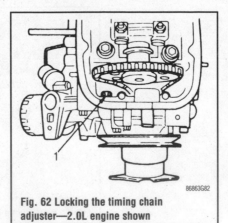

1

86863G82

Fig. 62 Locking the timing chain adjuster—2.0L engine shown

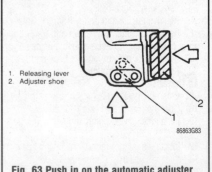

1. Releasing lever
2. Adjuster shoe

86863G83

Fig. 63 Push in on the automatic adjuster shoe (1) and lock it in the retracted position by releasing lever (2)—2.0L engine

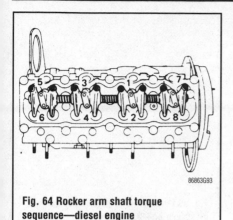

Fig. 64 Rocker arm shaft torque sequence—diesel engine

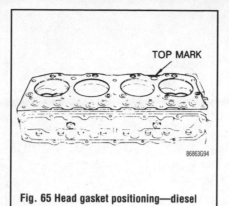

Fig. 65 Head gasket positioning—diesel engine

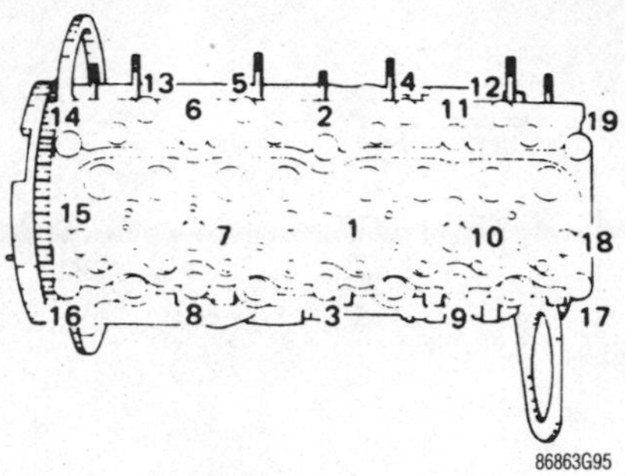

Fig. 66 Cylinder head bolt torque sequence—diesel engine

b. Confirm that the No. 1 piston is at TDC. If not, turn the crankshaft so the key is turned toward the cylinder head side (No. 1 and No. 4 pistons at top dead center).

c. Install the timing chain by aligning the mark plate on the chain with the mark on the crankshaft timing sprocket. The side of the chain with the mark plate is on the front side and the side of the chain with the most links between the mark plates is on the chain guide side.

d. Install the camshaft timing sprocket so the mark side of the sprocket faces forward and so the triangular mark aligns with the chain mark plate.

➡**Keep the timing chain engaged with the camshaft timing sprocket until the sprocket is installed on the camshaft.**

18. Install the front cover assembly, using a new gasket and sealer.
19. Connect the AIR hose and the check valve at the exhaust manifold.
20. Connect the accelerator linkage and fuel line to the carburetor. Connect the electrical connections, the spark plug wires and the vacuum lines.
21. Connect the heater hoses to the intake manifold and the rear of the cylinder head. Install the air conditioner compressor and/or power steering pump.
22. Connect the exhaust pipe to the exhaust manifold.
23. Install the EGR pipe clamp bolt to the rear of the cylinder head.
24. Install the rocker arm cover and connect the negative battery cable.
25. Refill the engine with coolant. Start the engine and check for leaks.

Diesel Engine

◆ **See Figures 64, 65 and 66**

1. Relieve the fuel pressure. Disconnect the negative battery cable. Drain the cooling system.

❊❊ CAUTION

When draining the coolant, keep in mind that cats and dogs are attracted by ethylene glycol antifreeze, and are quite likely to drink any that is left in an uncovered container or in puddles on the ground. This will prove fatal in sufficient quantity. Always drain the coolant into a sealable container. Coolant should be reused unless it is contaminated or several years old.

2. Remove the cooling fan assembly and the drive belt. Remove the alternator and bracket.
3. Remove the upper radiator hose and heater hose(s).
4. Remove the air cleaner and intake duct.
5. Label and disconnect the necessary vacuum hoses and electrical connectors.
6. Remove the fuel injector pipe, the clip and the nozzle holder assembly.
7. Remove the glow plugs and sensing resister.
8. If equipped with a turbocharger, remove the turbocharger cover and the turbocharger.
9. Remove the intake and exhaust manifolds from the cylinder head; discard the gaskets.
10. Remove the rocker arm cover, the valve tappet chamber cover and rocker oil feed pipe.

11. Back off the rocker arm adjustments. Remove the rocker arm assembly-to-cylinder head bolts and the rocker arm assembly.
12. Remove the pushrods and keep them in order for reinstallation purposes.
13. Remove the cylinder head-to-engine bolts, a little at a time, by reversing the torquing sequence. Remove the cylinder head; it may be necessary to use a mallet to tap the cylinder head loose from the engine.
14. Match the old gasket to the new cylinder head gasket and clean the gasket mounting surfaces.

To install:
15. Using a new gasket, position it onto the engine with the work **TOP** facing upwards.
16. Refill the turbocharger with clean engine oil before installation.
17. Install the cylinder head onto the engine. Lubricate the cylinder head bolts with engine oil and torque them, in sequence, using the following procedure;
Turbocharged Engine:
• 1st step: 33–40 ft. lbs. (45–54 Nm)
• 2nd step: 120–150°
Non-Turbocharged Engine:
• 1st step: 40–47 ft. lbs. (54–63 Nm)
• 2nd step: 54–61 ft. lbs. (74–81 Nm) for a new bolt or 61–69 ft. lbs. (81–95 Nm) for a used bolt
18. Install the pushrods and make sure they are positioned in the tappets.
19. Install the rocker arm assembly and torque the rocker arm-to-cylinder head bolts to 10–17 ft. lbs. (14–24 Nm) Adjust the valve lash.
20. Using new gaskets, reverse the removal procedures.
21. Refill the cooling system. Connect the negative battery cable. Start the engine and check for leaks.

2.3L Engine

◆ **See Figures 67, 68, 69 and 70**

1. Disconnect negative battery cable and drain cooling system.

❊❊ CAUTION

When draining the coolant, keep in mind that cats and dogs are attracted by ethylene glycol antifreeze, and are quite likely to drink any that is left in an uncovered container or in puddles on the ground. This will prove fatal in sufficient quantity. Always drain the coolant into a sealable container. Coolant should be reused unless it is contaminated or several years old.

2. Rotate the engine until the engine is at TDC on the compression stroke of the No. 1 cylinder, make sure timing mark is on the scale. Remove distributor cap and mark the distributor rotor to housing position and housing to cylinder head. Remove the distributor hold down bolt and remove the distributor.
3. Disconnect radiator inlet and outlet hoses and remove the radiator.
4. Remove the alternator and the air conditioner drive belts. Remove engine fan.
5. Remove the crankshaft pulley center bolt and remove the pulley and hub assembly.

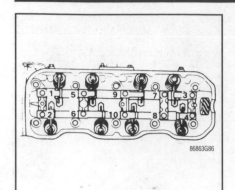

Fig. 67 Rocker arm shaft bolt removal sequence—2.3L and 2.6L engines

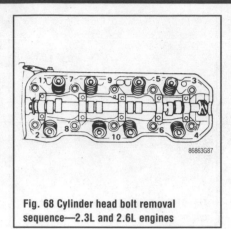

Fig. 68 Cylinder head bolt removal sequence—2.3L and 2.6L engines

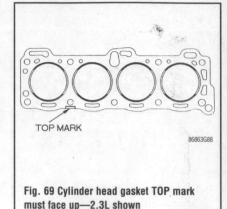

Fig. 69 Cylinder head gasket TOP mark must face up—2.3L shown

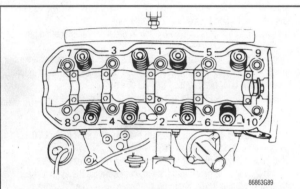

Fig. 70 Cylinder head bolt tightening sequence—2.3L and 2.6L engines

6. Remove the air pump belt and move the air pump out of the way. Remove the air conditioning compressor and lay it to one side (if equipped with air conditioning). Remove the compressor mounting bracket.

7. Remove the water pump pulley. Remove the top section of the front cover and the water pump.

8. Remove the lower section of the front cover.

9. Remove the tension spring. Loosen the top bolt of the tension pulley and draw the tension pulley fully to the water pump side.

10. Remove the timing belt.

11. Remove cam cover.

12. Sequentially loosen and remove the rocker arm shaft tightening nuts from the outermost one and remove the rocker arm shaft with the bracket as an assembly.

13. Raise vehicle and disconnect the exhaust pipe at the exhaust manifold. On turbocharged model disconnect exhaust pipe from wastegate manifold and remove control cable for turbocharger.

14. Lower vehicle disconnect all lines, hoses, electrical connections and spark plug wires.

➡ Tag all wires and hoses before disconnecting them from the engine.

15. Disconnect the accelerator linkage, on turbocharged model remove engine wiring harness assembly from fuel injectors and fuel line from fuel injector pipe.

16. Remove the cylinder head bolts using an extension bar with socket. Remove bolts in progressive sequence, beginning with the outer bolts.

➡ Use light oil to free frozen bolts.

17. With the aid of an assistant, remove the cylinder head, intake and exhaust manifolds as an assembly.

To install:

18. Clean all gasket material from the cylinder head and block surfaces. Check for nicks or heavy scratches on the mating surfaces.

19. Cylinder bolt threads in the block and threads on the bolts must be cleaned. Dirt will affect head torque.

20. Match up the old gasket with the new gasket to make sure it is an exact fit.

21. Install the gasket and cylinder head with the help of an assistant. Torque in sequence and 2 steps first step 57 ft. lbs. (76 Nm) and second step 72 ft. lbs. (96 Nm).

22. Connect the accelerator linkage, on turbocharged model install engine wiring harness assembly to fuel injectors and fuel line to fuel injector pipe.

23. Connect all lines, hoses, electrical connections and spark plug wires.

24. Raise vehicle and connect the exhaust pipe at the exhaust manifold. On turbocharged model connect exhaust pipe to wastegate manifold and install control cable for turbocharger.

25. Sequentially install and torque the rocker arm shaft tightening nuts from the outermost one and install the rocker arm shaft with the bracket as an assembly. Refer to the appropriate illustration.

26. Install the rocker arm cover.

27. Install the timing belt.

28. Install the tension spring. Tighten the top bolt of the tension pulley.

29. Install the lower section of the front cover.

30. Install the water pump pulley. Install the top section of the front cover and the water pump.

31. Install the air pump and belt. Install the air conditioning compressor bracket and compressor.

32. Install the crankshaft pulley and center bolt.

33. Install the alternator and the air conditioner drive belts. Install engine fan.

34. Connect radiator inlet and outlet hoses and after installing the radiator.

35. Install the distributor, hold down bolt and cap.

36. Connect negative battery cable, refill the cooling system and check for leaks.

2.6L Engine

◆ See Figures 67 thru 70

1. Relieve the fuel pressure. Disconnect the negative battery cable. Drain the cooling system.

✳✳ CAUTION

When draining the coolant, keep in mind that cats and dogs are attracted by ethylene glycol antifreeze, and are quite likely to drink any that is left in an uncovered container or in puddles on the ground. This will prove fatal in sufficient quantity. Always drain the coolant into a sealable container. Coolant should be reused unless it is contaminated or several years old.

2. Remove the drive belts from the power steering pump, the air pump, the air conditioning compressor (if equipped) and the cooling fan.

3. Rotate the engine to position the No. 1 cylinder on TDC.

4. Remove the distributor cap, high tension cables and the distributor.

5. Remove the exhaust manifold-to-exhaust pipe bolts.

6. Label and disconnect the electrical connectors and vacuum hoses which may be in the way.

7. Remove the coolant hoses, the radiator and the cooling fan assembly.

8. Remove the crankshaft pulley bolt and the pulley.

9. Remove the upper and lower timing belt covers, the tension spring and the timing belt.

10. Remove the camshaft pulley bolt, the pulley and the camshaft boss.

11. Remove the timing belt guide plate and the cylinder head front plate.
12. Remove the rocker arm cover and gasket.
13. Remove the cylinder head-to-engine bolts, the cylinder head and gasket.
14. Clean the gasket mounting surfaces.

To install:

15. Using a new gasket, install the cylinder head and torque the bolts, in sequence to 57 ft. lbs. (76 Nm) in the 1st step and to 65–79 ft. lbs. (88–108 Nm) in the final step.
16. Install the camshaft pulley.
17. Using a new gasket, install the rocker arm cover.
18. Align the camshaft pulley mark with the mark on the front plate. Make sure the keyway on the crankshaft if facing upward, aimed at the pointer on the engine block.
19. Install the timing belt in the following order: crankshaft pulley, the oil pump pulley, the camshaft and the tensioner.
20. Install the timing belt covers, using a new gasket.
21. Install the crankshaft pulley.
22. Install the cooling fan assembly, the radiator and the coolant hoses.
23. Connect the electrical connectors and vacuum hoses.
24. Install the exhaust manifold-to-exhaust pipe bolts.
25. Install the distributor, the distributor cap, and the high tension cables.
26. Install the drive belts to the power steering pump, the air pump, the air conditioning compressor (if equipped) and the cooling fan.
27. Connect the negative battery cable. Refill the cooling system.
28. Start the engine and check for leaks.

2.8L Engine

♦ **See Figures 71 thru 76**

LEFT SIDE

1. Relieve the fuel pressure. Disconnect the negative battery cable. Drain the cooling system.

✳✳ CAUTION

When draining the coolant, keep in mind that cats and dogs are attracted by ethylene glycol antifreeze, and are quite likely to drink any that is left in an uncovered container or in puddles on the ground. This will prove fatal in sufficient quantity. Always drain the coolant into a sealable container. Coolant should be reused unless it is contaminated or several years old.

2. Remove the intake manifold.
3. Raise and safely support the vehicle.
4. Disconnect the exhaust pipe from the exhaust manifold and remove the exhaust manifold-to-cylinder head bolts.
5. Remove the dipstick tube from the engine.
6. Lower the vehicle.
7. Loosen the rocker arm nuts, turn the rocker arms and remove the pushrods; keep the pushrods in the same order as removed.
8. Remove the cylinder head bolts in stages and in the reverse order of torquing.
9. Remove the cylinder head; do not pry on the head to loosen it.
10. Clean the gasket mounting surfaces.

To install:

11. Position a new cylinder head gasket over the dowel pins with the words **This Side Up** facing upwards. Carefully, guide the cylinder head into place.
12. Install the pushrods; make sure the lower ends are in the lifter heads. Torque the rocker arm nuts to 14–20 ft. lbs. (20–27 Nm).
13. Install the intake manifold.
14. Install the dipstick tube to the engine.
15. Install the exhaust manifold-to-cylinder head bolts and the exhaust pipe-to-exhaust manifold nuts.
16. Refill the cooling system. Start the engine and check for leaks.

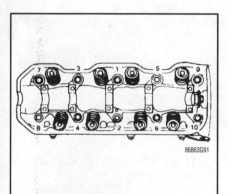

Fig. 71 Cylinder head bolt removal sequence—2.8L engine

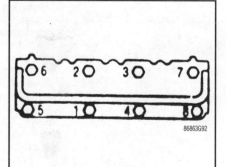

Fig. 72 Cylinder head bolt tightening sequence—2.8L engine

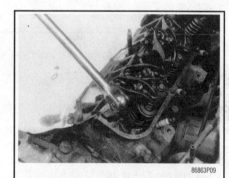

Fig. 73 Loosen the cylinder head bolts by stages, in the reverse order of the tighten sequence—2.8L engine

Fig. 74 Remember to cover the engine to keep old gasket material and dirt from getting inside—2.8L engine

Fig. 75 Place cylinder head aside, make certain all mating surfaces are clean of dirt and gasket material—2.8L engine

Fig. 76 Removing the cylinder head gasket—2.8L engine

RIGHT SIDE

1. Relieve the fuel pressure. Disconnect the negative battery cable. Drain the cooling system.

❄❄ CAUTION

When draining the coolant, keep in mind that cats and dogs are attracted by ethylene glycol antifreeze, and are quite likely to drink any that is left in an uncovered container or in puddles on the ground. This will prove fatal in sufficient quantity. Always drain the coolant into a sealable container. Coolant should be reused unless it is contaminated or several years old.

2. Remove the intake manifold.
3. If equipped, remove the cruise control servo bracket, the air management valve and hose.
4. Raise and safely support the vehicle.
5. Disconnect the exhaust pipe from the exhaust manifold and remove the exhaust manifold-to-cylinder head bolts.
6. Remove the exhaust pipe at crossover, the crossover and the heat shield, if equipped.
7. Lower the vehicle.
8. Label and disconnect the electrical wiring and vacuum hoses that may interfere with the removal of the right cylinder head.
9. Loosen the rocker arm nuts, turn the rocker arms and remove the pushrods; keep the pushrods in the same order as removed.
10. Remove the cylinder head bolts in stages and in the reverse order of torquing.
11. Remove the cylinder head; do not pry on the head to loosen it.
12. Clean the gasket mounting surfaces.
To install:
13. Position a new cylinder head gasket over the dowel pins with the words **This Side Up** facing upwards. Carefully, guide the cylinder head into place.
14. Install the pushrods; make sure the lower ends are in the lifter heads. Torque the rocker arm nuts to 14–20 ft. lbs. (20–27 Nm).
15. Install the intake manifold.
16. Install the exhaust pipe at crossover, the crossover and the heat shield, if equipped.
17. Install the exhaust manifold-to-cylinder head bolts and the exhaust pipe-to-exhaust manifold nuts.
18. Connect the electrical wiring and vacuum hoses to the right cylinder head.
19. If equipped, install the cruise control servo bracket, the air management valve and hose.
20. Refill the cooling system. Start the engine and check for leaks.

3.1L Engine

♦ **See Figures 77 and 78**

LEFT SIDE

1. Relieve the fuel pressure. Disconnect the negative battery cable. Drain the cooling system.
2. Remove the intake manifold.
3. Raise and safely support the vehicle.
4. Disconnect the exhaust pipe from the exhaust manifold and remove the exhaust manifold-to-cylinder head bolts.
5. Remove the dipstick tube from the engine.

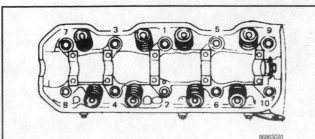

Fig. 77 Cylinder head bolt removal sequence—3.1L engine

86863G91

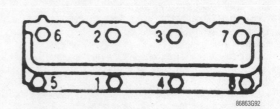

86863G92

Fig. 78 Cylinder head bolt tightening sequence—3.1L engine

6. Lower the vehicle.
7. Loosen the rocker arm nuts, turn the rocker arms and remove the pushrods; keep the pushrods in the same order as removed.
8. Remove the cylinder head bolts in stages and in the reverse order of torquing.
9. Remove the cylinder head; do not pry on the head to loosen it.
10. Clean the gasket mounting surfaces thoroughly.
To install:
11. Position a new cylinder head gasket over the dowel pins with the words **This Side Up** facing upwards. Carefully, guide the cylinder head into place.
12. Torque the cylinder head bolts in sequence to 41 ft. lbs. (55 Nm) then go back and turn each bolt an additional 90 degrees.
13. Install the pushrods; make sure the lower ends are in the lifter heads. Torque the rocker arm nuts to 14–20 ft. lbs. (20–27 Nm).
14. Install the intake manifold.
15. Install the dipstick tube to the engine.
16. Install exhaust manifold-to-cylinder head bolts and the exhaust pipe-to-exhaust manifold nuts.
17. Refill the cooling system. Start the engine and check for leaks.

RIGHT SIDE

1. Relieve the fuel pressure. Disconnect the negative battery cable. Drain the cooling system.
2. Remove the intake manifold.
3. If equipped, remove the cruise control servo bracket, the air management valve and hose.
4. Raise and safely support the vehicle.
5. Disconnect the exhaust pipe from the exhaust manifold and remove the exhaust manifold-to-cylinder head bolts.
6. Remove the exhaust pipe at crossover, the crossover and the heat shield, if equipped.
7. Lower the vehicle.
8. Label and disconnect the electrical wiring and vacuum hoses that may interfere with the removal of the right cylinder head.
9. Loosen the rocker arm nuts, turn the rocker arms and remove the pushrods; keep the pushrods in the same order as removed.
10. Remove the cylinder head bolts in stages and in the reverse order of torquing.
11. Remove the cylinder head; do not pry on the head to loosen it.
12. Clean the gasket mounting surfaces thoroughly.
To install:
13. Position a new cylinder head gasket over the dowel pins with the words **This Side Up** facing upwards. Carefully, guide the cylinder head into place.
14. Torque the cylinder head bolts in sequence to 41 ft. lbs. (55 Nm) then go back and turn each bolt an additional 90 degrees.
15. Install the pushrods; make sure the lower ends are in the lifter heads. Torque the rocker arm nuts to 14–20 ft. lbs. (20–27 Nm).
16. Install the intake manifold.
17. Install the exhaust pipe at crossover, the crossover and the heat shield, if equipped.
18. Install the exhaust manifold-to-cylinder head bolts and the exhaust pipe-to-exhaust manifold nuts.
19. Connect the electrical wiring and vacuum hoses to the right cylinder head.
20. If equipped, install the cruise control servo bracket, the air management valve and hose.
21. Refill the cooling system. Start the engine and check for leaks.

3.2L Engine

1993–95 VEHICLES

▶ **See Figures 79 and 80**

➡Isuzu has issued a recall notice for 1993–94 Rodeos equipped with 3.2L engines. This is campaign number 94V–094, and involves faulty camshaft end plugs. The plugs may dislodge from the cylinder heads and can cause rapid oil loss. Remember this when ordering parts: a service kit is available for affected vehicles.

1. Matchmark the hood hinge to the hood and remove the hood.
2. Relieve the fuel system pressure and disconnect the negative battery cable.
3. Remove the air cleaner assembly.
4. Remove the upper cooling fan shroud.
5. Remove the cooling fan assembly.
6. Disconnect the accelerator cable from the throttle body and the bracket.
7. Disconnect the canister vacuum hose from the vacuum pipe.
8. Disconnect the air vacuum hose from the common chamber.
9. Disconnect the vacuum booster hose from the common chamber.
10. Disconnect the MAP sensor; Canister vacuum switching valve (VSV); Exhaust gas recirculation (VSV); Intake air temperature sensor and ground connectors.
11. Remove the spark plug wires from the cylinder head cover.
12. Remove the ignition control module assembly.
13. Remove the four bolts and the throttle body from the common chamber.
14. Disconnect the vacuum hoses from the throttle body.
15. Disconnect the positive crankcase ventilation hose from the common chamber.
16. Disconnect the fuel pressure control valve vacuum hose from the common chamber.
17. Disconnect the evaporative emission canister purge hose from the common chamber.
18. Remove the EGR valve assembly.
19. Remove the common chamber from the intake manifold.
20. Disconnect the fuel feed and return hoses from the fuel rail assembly.
21. Disconnect the connectors to the fuel injectors and the thermo sensor.
22. Remove the intake manifold.
23. Remove the engine coolant manifold by removing the heater hose and four mounting bolts.
24. Remove the accessory drive belts.
25. Remove the power steering pump.
26. Remove the fan pulley assembly.
27. Remove the crankshaft pulley and damper.
28. Remove the oil cooler hoses and bracket on the timing belt cover.
29. Remove the timing belt cover.
30. Align the timing marks.
31. Remove the timing belt auto tensioner (pusher). The pusher prevents air from entering the oil chamber. Its rod must always be facing upward.
32. Remove the timing belt.
33. Remove the cylinder head cover.
34. Remove the power steering pump bracket.
35. Remove the front exhaust pipes from the exhaust manifolds.
36. Remove the dipstick tube bracket from the cylinder head.

✳✳ WARNING

The cylinder head and engine block must be at room temperature before removing the cylinder head.

37. Remove the cylinder head bolts in sequence, gradually and in two steps.
38. Remove the cylinder head.

To install:

39. Install new camshaft seals and retaining plates onto the cylinder. Tighten the right camshaft seal retaining plate 6mm bolts to 65 inch lbs. Tighten the left camshaft seal retaining plate 8mm bolts to 191 inch lbs.
40. Thoroughly clean the cylinder head and engine block sealing surfaces.
41. Place a new head gasket on the engine block and carefully position the cylinder head on top of the new gasket.

➡**Do not reuse or apply oil to the cylinder head bolts.**

42. Install new cylinder head bolts and torque them in sequence to 47 ft. lbs. (64 Nm) for the M11 bolts and 15 ft. lbs. (21 Nm) for the M8 bolts.
43. Install the dipstick tube bracket to the cylinder head.
44. Connect the front exhaust pipes to the exhaust manifolds. Tighten the exhaust bolts to 48 ft. lbs. (67 Nm).
45. Install the power steering pump bracket. Torque the mounting bolts to 34 ft. lbs. (46 Nm).
46. Install the cylinder head covers.
47. Install the timing belt and the auto tensioner (pusher). Torque the mounting bolt to 14 ft. lbs. (19 Nm).
48. Install the timing belt cover and oil cooler hoses and bracket.
49. Install the crankshaft pulley. Torque the center bolt to 123 ft. lbs. (167 Nm).
50. Install the fan pulley assembly.
51. Install the power steering pump.
52. Install the accessory drive belts.
53. Install the engine coolant manifold and the heater hose.
54. Install the intake manifold. Torque the nuts and bolts to 17 ft. lbs. (24 Nm) in a crisscross pattern.
55. Install the fuel injector connectors and the fuel hoses to the fuel rail.
56. Install the common chamber. Torque the nuts and bolts to 17 ft. lbs. (24 Nm).
57. Install the EGR valve assembly. Torque the mounting bolts on the valve side to 69 inch lbs. (8 Nm) and the bolts on the exhaust side to 21 ft. lbs. (28 Nm).
58. Connect the evaporative emission canister purge hose.
59. Connect the fuel pressure control valve vacuum hose.
60. Connect the positive crankcase ventilation hose.
61. Install the throttle body assembly. Torque the mounting bolts to 14 ft. lbs. (19 Nm).
62. Connect the vacuum hoses to the throttle body.
63. Install the ignition control module and the spark plug wires.
64. Connect the MAP sensor; Canister vacuum switching valve (VSV); Exhaust gas recirculation (VSV); Intake air temperature sensor and ground connectors.
65. Connect the vacuum booster hose.
66. Connect the air vacuum hose.
67. Connect the accelerator cable. Adjust the accelerator cable by pulling the cable housing while closing the throttle valve and tightening the adjusting nut and screw cap by hand temporarily. Now loosen the adjusting nut by three

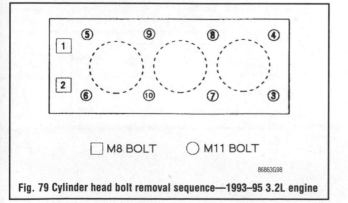

□ M8 BOLT   ○ M11 BOLT

86863G98

Fig. 79 Cylinder head bolt removal sequence—1993–95 3.2L engine

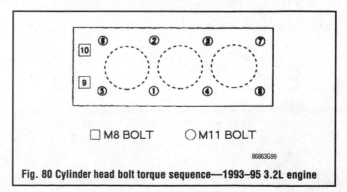

□ M8 BOLT   ○ M11 BOLT

86863G99

Fig. 80 Cylinder head bolt torque sequence—1993–95 3.2L engine

turns and then tightening the screw cap. Make sure the throttle valve reaches the screw stop when the throttle is closed.

68. Install the cooling fan assembly and the upper fan shroud.
69. Install the air cleaner assembly.
70. Connect the negative battery cable.
71. Refill and bleed the cooling system.
72. Refill and bleed the power steering pump if necessary.
73. Refill the engine with fresh oil.
74. Run the engine and check for leaks and proper compression.

1996 VEHICLES

▶ **See Figures 81 and 82**

> **⁂ WARNING**
>
> **The cylinder head should be cool to the touch before it is removed. If the head bolts are loosened on a hot engine, the cylinder head may warp.**

1. Relieve the fuel system pressure:
   a. Remove the fuel filler cap.
   b. Remove the fuel pump relay from the underhood relay box.
   c. Start the engine and let it run until it stalls. Then, crank the engine for an additional 30 seconds.
   d. Turn the ignition switch to the **OFF** position.

> **⁂ CAUTION**
>
> **Fuel injection systems remain under pressure even after the engine has been turned off. The fuel system pressure must be relieved before disconnecting any fuel lines. Failure to do so may result in fire and personal injury.**

2. Disconnect the negative battery cable and reinstall the fuel pump relay.
3. Raise and support the vehicle safely.
4. Disconnect the front exhaust pipes from the exhaust manifolds. If necessary, separate the front exhaust pipes from the crossover pipe. Label and disconnect the oxygen sensors.
5. Lower the vehicle.
6. Drain the coolant into a sealable container.
7. Use a felt–tipped marker to matchmark the hood hinge plates. Remove the hood.
8. Remove the air intake duct and the air cleaner box.
9. Disconnect and remove the upper and lower radiator hoses. Catch the coolant that runs out.
10. Loosen and remove the power steering pump, A/C compressor, and alternator drive belts.
11. Remove the cooling fan and its pulley assembly.
12. Unbolt the power steering pump mounting bracket. Move the pump and bracket out of the way without disconnecting the hydraulic lines.
13. Disconnect the throttle cable from the throttle body linkage.
14. Label and disconnect the following vacuum hoses from the intake manifold chamber:

   a. PCV hose
   b. EVAP canister vacuum hose
   c. Brake booster hose
15. Label and disconnect the following sensor connectors from the rear of the intake manifold chamber:
   a. Ignition control module connectors
   b. Linear EGR valve
   c. MAP sensor
   d. EVAP purge valve
   e. Throttle position sensor
   f. Idle air control valve
   g. Intake air temperature sensor
16. Disconnect the EGR valve supply tube and bracket.
17. First, remove the throttle body, and then remove the intake manifold chamber.
18. Carefully clean any dirt from the fuel rail and fuel fittings.
19. Disconnect the fuel feed and return lines from the front of the fuel rail. Clean up any spilled fuel.
20. Label and disconnect the fuel injector wiring harness.
21. Remove the fuel injectors and lower intake manifold as an assembly. If desired, the fuel rail and injectors may be removed separately as an assembly.
22. Remove the intake manifold gaskets. Be careful not to drop any pieces of the gaskets into the engine. Don't scratch or gouge the machined aluminum mating surfaces of the intake manifold and engine block.
23. Cover the intake openings with a sheet of plastic or clean shop towels to keep out dirt and foreign objects.
24. Label the ignition coil assemblies and disconnect them from the wiring harness. Remove the coil assemblies so they won't be damaged.
25. Unbolt the oil cooler line brackets from the timing belt covers.
26. Rotate the crankshaft to align the camshaft timing marks with the pointer dots on the back covers. When the timing marks are aligned, the No. 2 piston is at TDC/compression.
27. Remove the crankshaft pulley. Remove the lower timing belt cover.
28. Remove the pusher assembly (tensioner) from below the timing belt tensioner pulley. The pusher rod must always be facing upward to prevent oil leakage. Push the pusher rod in, and insert a wire pin into the hole to keep the pusher rod retracted.
29. Remove the timing belt.

> **⁂ WARNING**
>
> **If the timing belt is worn, damaged, or shows signs of oil or coolant contamination, it must be replaced.**

30. Disconnect the heater hoses from the engine; then, unbolt and remove the engine coolant manifold.
31. Unbolt the dipstick tube from the cylinder head.
32. Loosen the valve cover bolts in a crisscross sequence. Remove the valve covers.
33. Loosen the cylinder head bolts in a two–step crisscross pattern working from the outer bolts to those at the center of the head. First, partially loosen the 11mm bolts, then partially loosen the 8mm bolts. Finally loosen all the bolts and then remove them.
34. Remove the cylinder head. If it sticks, tap it with a wooden or plastic–faced mallet.
35. Remove the head gasket.
36. Inspect the cylinder head for cracking or warpage. Inspect the engine

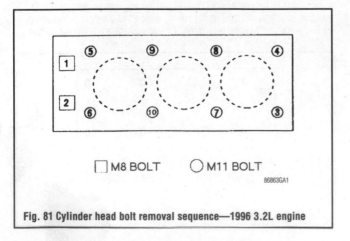

☐ M8 BOLT ◯ M11 BOLT

86863GA1

Fig. 81 Cylinder head bolt removal sequence—1996 3.2L engine

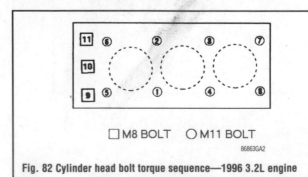

☐ M8 BOLT ◯ M11 BOLT

86863GA2

Fig. 82 Cylinder head bolt torque sequence—1996 3.2L engine

block for any signs of damage. Carefully clean the head gasket mating surfaces, don't scratch or gouge the machined aluminum surfaces.

37. Cover the engine block with a sheet of plastic or clean shop towels to keep any dirt and foreign objects out of the combustion chambers.

To install:

➡ **Use new head bolts when installing the cylinder head. Do not apply oil to the head bolt threads.**

38. Make sure all mating surfaces are clean and free of oil, coolant, or gasket residue.

39. Install new cylinder head gaskets.

40. Install the cylinder head. Install the new head bolts and tighten them by hand only.

41. Follow these steps to tighten the cylinder head bolts to their final torque specification:

   a. Use a two-step crisscross pattern to tighten the 11mm bolts to 47 ft. lbs. (64 Nm). Start tightening with the center bolts, and work toward the outer bolts.

   b. Tighten the 8mm bolts to 15 ft. lbs. (21 Nm). Start with the bolt closest to the exhaust side of the head and work toward the intake side.

42. Apply a 2–3mm bead of sealant to the joint were the camshaft holders meet the cylinder head. Install the valve cover with a new gasket before the sealant cures.

43. Tighten the valve cover bolts to 6 ft. lbs. (8 Nm) in crisscross pattern.

44. Verify that the camshaft and crankshaft timing marks are properly aligned.

45. Install and tension the timing belt. Tighten the pusher bolts to 14 ft. lbs. (19 Nm).

46. Install the lower timing belt covers and tighten the bolts to 13 ft. lbs. (18 Nm). Install the crankshaft pulley. Tighten the pulley bolt to 123 ft. lbs. (167 Nm).

47. Install the upper timing belt covers and tighten the bolts to 13 ft. lbs. (18 Nm).

48. Fit the oil cooler line brackets onto the timing cover and tighten the bolts to 13 ft. lbs. (18 Nm).

49. Install the engine coolant manifold and reconnect the heater hoses. Tighten the bolts to 16 ft. lbs. (22 Nm).

50. Install the dipstick tube bracket.

51. Raise and safely support the vehicle. Install and reconnect the front exhaust pipes. Reconnect the oxygen sensors. Lower the vehicle.

52. Install the intake manifold with a new gasket. Tighten the bolts and nuts to 17 ft. lbs. (24 Nm).

53. Reconnect the fuel injector wiring harness. Reconnect the fuel feed and return lines.

54. Install and reconnect the ignition coil assemblies.

55. Install the intake manifold chamber and throttle body with new gaskets. Tighten the nuts and bolts to 17 ft. lbs. (24 Nm).

56. Reconnect the throttle cable to the throttle body linkage.

57. Reconnect the EGR valve supply tube and bracket.

58. Reconnect the following vacuum to the intake manifold chamber:

   a. PCV hose
   b. EVAP canister vacuum hose
   c. Brake booster hose

59. Reconnect the following sensor connectors to the rear of the intake manifold chamber:

   a. Ignition control module connectors
   b. Linear EGR valve
   c. MAP sensor
   d. EVAP purge valve
   e. Throttle position sensor
   f. Idle air control valve
   g. Intake air temperature sensor

60. Install the power steering pump and mounting bracket.

61. Install the cooling fan and its pulley assembly.

62. Install and tension the alternator, A/C compressor, and power steering pump drive belts.

63. Install and reconnect the upper and lower radiator hoses.

64. Install the air cleaner box and air intake duct.

65. Install the hood.

66. Verify that all fuel lines, vacuum and coolant hoses, and wiring harness have been reconnected.

67. Refill the engine with fresh coolant.

68. Drain the engine oil. Install a new oil filter and refill the engine with fresh oil. If the engine oil was severely contaminated with coolant, a second oil and filter change may be necessary.

69. Crank the engine until it starts. A longer than normal starting time may be necessary due to air in the fuel lines. Check all fuel line connections for leaks.

70. Bleed any air from the cooling system.

71. Bleed the power steering system if necessary.

72. Warm the engine up to normal operating temperature and check the operation of the thermostat and water pump.

73. Check the throttle cable operation and adjustment.

74. Check the engine oil level and add if necessary.

Valve Lifters (Tappets)

REMOVAL & INSTALLATION

Diesel Engine

1. Disconnect the negative battery cable.
2. Remove the engine from the vehicle as outlined in this section.
3. Remove the rocker arm cover and rocker arm assembly.
4. Label and remove the pushrods.
5. Remove the tappet chamber cover and oil feed pipe.
6. Remove the camshaft oil seal retainer.
7. Remove the timing pulley housing.
8. Remove the camshaft as outlined in this section.
9. Remove and label the tappets.

To install:

10. Install the tappets into their original locations.
11. Install the camshaft as outlined in this section.
12. Install the timing pulley housing.
13. Install the camshaft oil seal retainer.
14. Install the tappet chamber cover and oil feed pipe.
15. Install the pushrods into their original locations.
16. Install the rocker arm assembly and cover.
17. Install the engine into the vehicle as outlined in this section.
18. Connect the negative battery cable, refill all engine fluids, start the engine and check for leaks.

2.8L and 3.1L Engines

▶ **See Figures 83 thru 88**

Some engines may have either standard size and 0.010 in. (0.25mm) or oversize valve lifters. The cylinder block will be marked with a white paint mark and 0.25mm O.S. stamp where the oversize lifters are used. If lifters replacement is necessary, use new lifters with a narrow flat along the lower ¾ of the body length. This provides additional oil to the cam lobe and lifter surfaces.

Using a Hydraulic Lifter Remover tool J-9290-1 (slide hammer type) or J-3049-A (plier type) will greatly ease the removal of stuck lifters.

1. Remove the rocker arm covers.
2. Remove the intake manifold.

Fig. 83 Oversize lifter marking—2.8L engine shown

86863GC7

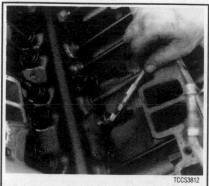

Fig. 84 A magnet is useful in removing lifters from their bores

Fig. 85 Stuck lifters must be freed using a slide hammer type lifter removal tool

Fig. 86 Loosen the rocker arms and remove the pushrods bolts—2.8L engine

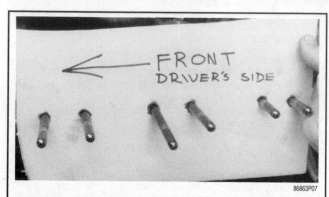

Fig. 87 All of the valve train parts must be keep in correct order for installation. A piece of cardboard works for pushrods

Fig. 88 Removing the lifter—2.8L engine

3. Remove the rocker arm nuts and balls.
4. Remove the rocker arms and pushrods.

➡️If any valve train components (lifters, pushrods, rocker arms) are to be reused, they must be tagged or arranged during removal to assure installation in their original locations.

5. Remove the lifters from the bores.
To install:
6. For proper rotation during engine operation, the lifter bottom must be convex. Check the lifter bottom for proper shape using a straightedge. If the lifter bottom is not convex, replace the lifter. Chances are if lifters are in need of replacement, so is the camshaft.
7. Lubricate and install the lifters. If installing new lifters, coat the lifter body and foot using Molykote® or an equivalent prelube, then add 1051396 or an equivalent engine oil supplement to the crankcase.
8. Install the pushrods, rocker arms, rocker arm nuts and balls, then properly adjust the valve lash.
9. Install the intake manifold.
10. Install the rocker arm covers.

Overhead Camshaft Engines

The camshaft directly actuates the rocker arms or the valve on the overhead shaft engine. Refer to camshaft and rocker arm shaft procedures for valve train service on these type engines.

Oil Pan

♦ **See Figure 89**

Pan removal is possible with the engine in the vehicle on some of the power-train combinations covered by this manual. If it is possible, it will often require

the removal or repositioning of components including, the steering linkage assembly, the forward drive axle and crossmember (4WD) and/or the engine mounts. It is a difficult and tedious task to remove the oil pan with the engine in the vehicle. The chances of contaminating the bearing surfaces or damaging other internal engine components is great. Also, working under the vehicle with the engine jacked up in the frame puts you at great risk for great personal injury. Therefore, it is desirable in most cases to remove the engine in order to gain access to the oil pan.

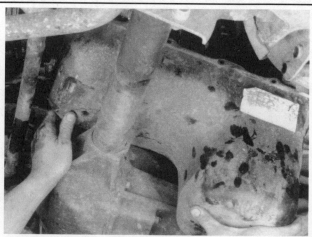

Fig. 89 Oil pan removal may necessitate removal of suspension, drive train or steering components

REMOVAL & INSTALLATION

Diesel Engine

UPPER OIL PAN

1. Disconnect the negative battery cable.
2. Remove the engine from the vehicle.
3. Drain the engine oil. Remove the dipstick and the dipstick tube.

※※ CAUTION

The EPA warns that prolonged contact with used engine oil may cause a number of skin disorders, including cancer! You should make every effort to minimize your exposure to used engine oil. Protective gloves should be worn when changing the oil. Wash your hands and any other exposed skin areas as soon as possible after exposure to used engine oil. Soap and water, or waterless hand cleaner should be used.

4. Remove the upper oil pan-to-engine bolts and the oil pan.
To install:
5. Clean the gasket mounting surfaces.
6. Using a new gasket and sealant, install the oil pan. Torque the oil pan-to-engine bolts to 120–185 inch lbs. (14–18 Nm).
7. Install the engine into the vehicle as outlined in this section.
8. Connect the battery cable, start the engine and check for leaks.

LOWER OIL PAN

1. Raise and safely support the vehicle.
2. Drain the crankcase.

※※ CAUTION

The EPA warns that prolonged contact with used engine oil may cause a number of skin disorders, including cancer! You should make every effort to minimize your exposure to used engine oil. Protective gloves should be worn when changing the oil. Wash your hands and any other exposed skin areas as soon as possible after exposure to used engine oil. Soap and water, or waterless hand cleaner should be used.

3. Remove the lower oil pan-to-upper oil pan bolts and the lower pan.
To install:
4. Clean the gasket mounting surfaces.
5. Using a new gasket and sealant, install the lower oil pan and torque the bolts to 24–96 inch lbs. (3–11 Nm).
6. Refill the crankcase, connect the negative battery cable, start the engine and check for leaks.

1986–94 2.3L and 2.6L Engines

▶ See Figures 90 and 91

UPPER OIL PAN

➡ **On 4WD gasoline engines, the engine must be removed before removing the oil pan.**

1. Disconnect the negative battery cable.
2. Raise and safely support the vehicle.
3. Drain the engine oil. Remove the dipstick and the dipstick tube.
4. Remove the front splash shield, if equipped.
5. Remove the flywheel cover.
6. Disconnect the engine mount nuts and bolts. Raise the engine off the mounts to provide clearance for pan removal.
7. Remove the oil pan bolts and remove the oil pan. Use oil pan seal cutter J–37228 or equivalent if needed to break the oil pan-to-block sealant.
To install:
8. Clean the gasket mounting surfaces.
9. Apply sealant to the oil pan flange and install the oil pan. Torque the oil pan-to-engine bolts to 13 ft. lbs. (18 Nm).
10. Lower the engine and install the engine mounts. Torque the engine mount bolts to 41 ft. lbs. (55 Nm).

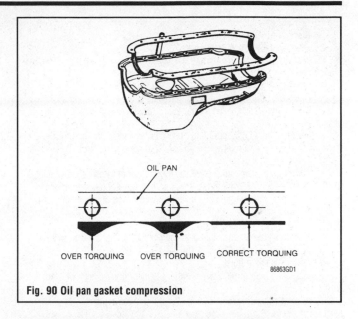

Fig. 90 Oil pan gasket compression

OIL PAN

OVER TORQUING   OVER TORQUING   CORRECT TORQUING

86863GD1

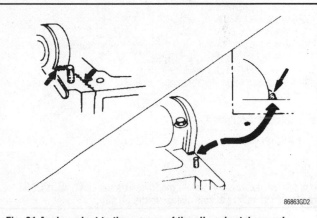

Fig. 91 Apply sealant to the corners of the oil seal retainer and bearing cap

86863GD2

11. Install the flywheel cover.
12. Install the dipstick and tube.
13. Install the engine under cover, if equipped.
14. Refill the crankcase with engine oil.
15. Connect the negative battery cable, start the engine and check for leaks.

LOWER OIL PAN (4WD)

1. Raise and safely support the vehicle.
2. Drain the crankcase.
3. Remove the lower oil pan-to-upper oil pan bolts and the lower pan.
4. Clean the gasket mounting surfaces.
To install:
5. Using a new gasket and sealant, install the lower oil pan and torque the bolts to 4–8 ft. lbs. (5–11 Nm).
6. Refill the crankcase.
7. Lower the vehicle to the floor.
8. Start the engine and check for leaks.

1995 2.3L Engine

▶ See Figure 90

1. Disconnect the negative battery cable.
2. Drain the engine oil.
3. Attach a chain hoist to the engine lifting hooks.
4. Raise and safely support the vehicle.
5. Remove the front wheels.

6. Remove the dipstick from the dipstick tube.
7. Remove the lower radiator shroud.
8. Remove the flywheel dust cover.
9. Matchmark the Pitman arm to the steering shaft. Use a puller to remove the Pitman arm.
10. Unbolt the idler arm assembly from the frame.
11. Raise the chain hoist to take the engine's weight off the mounts.
12. Unbolt the engine mounts from their brackets on either side of the oil pan.
13. Remove the oil pan mounting bolts and bolt retainers. Use a sealer cutter to break the seal and remove the oil pan from the engine block.

To install:

14. Thoroughly clean and dry the sealing surface of the oil pan and engine block. Apply beads of sealant to the front and rear oil seal retainer surfaces. Install the oil pan to the engine block within five minutes of sealer application. Install the bolt retainers and all the mounting bolts. Then, torque the mounting bolts in sequence to 4 ft. lbs. (5.4 Nm).
15. Reconnect the engine mounts to their brackets. Tighten the mount–to–bracket nuts to 41 ft. lbs. (55 Nm).
16. Lower the chain hoist.
17. Install the idler arm bracket. Torque the mounting bolts to 33 ft. lbs. (45 Nm).
18. Align the matchmark and install the Pitman arm on the sector shaft. Torque the nut to 160 ft. lbs. (216 Nm).
19. Install the flywheel dust cover.
20. Install the lower fan shroud.
21. Lower the vehicle to the floor.
22. Install the dipstick and refill the engine with the proper amount of oil.
23. Connect the negative battery cable.
24. Start the engine and check for leaks.
25. Check and adjust the front wheel alignment and the steering wheel spoke angle.

1995–96 2.6L Engine

♦ See Figure 91

PICK-UP

➡**On four–wheel drive vehicles, the front axle assembly must be lowered from its mounts to gain access to the oil pan.**

1. Disconnect the negative battery cable.
2. Drain the engine oil.
3. Attach a chain hoist to the engine lifting hooks.
4. Raise and safely support the vehicle.
5. Remove the front wheels.
6. Remove the dipstick from the dipstick tube.
7. Remove the radiator skid plate and the radiator lower shroud.
8. Remove the suspension crossmember.
9. Remove the flywheel dust cover.
10. Matchmark the Pitman arm to the steering shaft. Use a puller to remove the Pitman arm.
11. Unbolt the idler arm assembly from the frame.
12. If equipped with four wheel drive; support the axle assembly with a jack and remove the mounting bolts on both sides of the axle assembly. Lower the axle assembly to gain access to the oil pan. After lowering the axle, support it with jackstands.
13. Raise the chain hoist to take the engine's weight off the mounts.
14. Unbolt and remove the engine mounts and mount brackets on either side of the oil pan.

➡**The lower section of the oil pan may be separated and removed from the upper section of the oil pan.**

15. Remove the oil pan mounting bolts. Use a sealer cutter to break the seal and remove the oil pan from the engine block.

To install:

16. Thoroughly clean and dry the sealing surface of the oil pan and engine block. Apply a continuous bead of sealant to the oil pan flange. Install the oil pan to the engine block within five minutes of sealer application. Torque the mounting bolts to 13 inch lbs. (18 Nm).
17. Install the engine mounts. Tighten the mount bracket bolts to 37 ft. lbs. (50 Nm). Tighten the mount–to–bracket nuts to 62 ft. lbs. (83 Nm).

18. Lower the chain hoist.
19. On four wheel drive vehicles; raise the axle housing assembly into position. Torque the axle–to–frame mounting bolts and nuts to 112 ft. lbs. (152 Nm).
20. Install the idler arm bracket. Torque the mounting bolts to 33 ft. lbs. (45 Nm).
21. Align the matchmark and install the Pitman arm on the sector shaft. Torque the nut to 160 ft. lbs. (216 Nm).
22. Install the flywheel dust cover.
23. Install the suspension crossmember. Torque the mounting bolts to 58 ft. lbs. (78 Nm).
24. Install the lower fan shroud.
25. Install the skid plate and tighten its bolts to 27 ft. lbs. (37 Nm).
26. Lower the vehicle to the floor.
27. Install the dipstick and refill the engine with the proper amount of oil.
28. Connect the negative battery cable.
29. Start the engine and check for leaks.
30. Check and adjust the front wheel alignment and the steering wheel spoke angle.

RODEO

➡**On 4WD vehicles, the front axle assembly must be lowered from its mounts to gain access to the oil pan.**

1. Disconnect the negative battery cable.
2. Drain the engine oil.
3. Attach a chain hoist to the engine lifting hooks.
4. Raise and safely support the vehicle.
5. Remove the front wheels.
6. Remove the dipstick from the dipstick tube.
7. Remove the radiator skid plate and the radiator lower shroud.
8. Remove the suspension crossmember.
9. Remove the flywheel dust cover.
10. Matchmark the Pitman arm to the steering shaft. Use a puller to remove the Pitman arm from the steering box.
11. Unbolt the idler arm assembly from the frame.
12. If equipped with four wheel drive; support the axle assembly with a jack and remove the mounting bolts on both sides of the axle assembly. Lower the axle assembly to gain access to the oil pan. After lowering the axle, support it with jackstands.
13. Raise the chain hoist to take the engine's weight off the mounts. The engine must be securely supported.
14. Unbolt and remove the engine mounts and mount brackets on either side of the oil pan.

➡**The lower section of the oil pan may be separated and removed from the upper section of the oil pan.**

15. Remove the oil pan mounting bolts. Use a seal cutter to break the seal and separate the oil pan from the engine block.

To install:

16. Thoroughly clean and dry the sealing surface of the oil pan and engine block. Apply a continuous bead of sealant to the oil pan flange. Install the oil pan to the engine block within five minutes of sealer application. Allow the sealant to cure before refilling the engine with oil.
17. Tighten the oil pan mounting bolts and nuts:
    a. First step: Tighten the two bolts at the middle of the oil pan to 6 ft. lbs. (9 Nm).
    b. Second step: Tighten the all the mounting bolts and nuts to 13 inch lbs. (18 Nm) in a crisscross pattern starting in the middle of the oil pan and working toward the outer edges.
18. Install the engine mounts. Tighten the mount bracket bolts to 37 ft. lbs. (50 Nm). Tighten the mount and bracket nuts to 62 ft. lbs. (83 Nm).
19. Lower the chain hoist.
20. On 4WD vehicles, raise the axle housing assembly into position. Tighten the axle mounting bracket bolts and nuts to 112 ft. lbs. (152 Nm).
21. Install the idler arm bracket. Tighten the mounting bolts to 33 ft. lbs. (45 Nm).
22. Align the matchmark and install the Pitman arm on the sector shaft. Tighten the nut to 160 ft. lbs. (216 Nm).
23. Install the flywheel dust cover.
24. Install the suspension crossmember. Tighten the mounting bolts to 58 ft. lbs. (78 Nm).

25. Install the lower fan shroud.
26. Install the skid plate and tighten its bolts to 27 ft. lbs. (37 Nm).
27. Lower the vehicle to the floor.
28. Install the dipstick and refill the engine with the proper amount of oil.
29. Connect the negative battery cable.
30. Start the engine and check for leaks.
31. Check and adjust the front wheel alignment.

2.8L Engine

1. Disconnect the negative battery cable.
2. Remove the dipstick. Raise and safely support the vehicle. Drain the crankcase.

✳✳ CAUTION

The EPA warns that prolonged contact with used engine oil may cause a number of skin disorders, including cancer! You should make every effort to minimize your exposure to used engine oil. Protective gloves should be worn when changing the oil. Wash your hands and any other exposed skin areas as soon as possible after exposure to used engine oil. Soap and water, or waterless hand cleaner should be used.

3. Remove the front skid plate and the crossmember.
4. Remove the exhaust pipe-to-catalytic converter bolts, the exhaust pipe-to-manifolds bolts and the Y-exhaust pipe.
5. Remove the front driveshaft from the front differential.
6. Remove the braces from the flywheel cover.
7. Disconnect the electrical connectors from the starter. Remove the starter-to-engine bolts and the starter.
8. Remove the flywheel inspection cover.
9. Matchmark the Pitman arm-to-Pitman shaft for reassembly. Remove the Pitman arm-to-Pitman arm shaft nut and separate the Pitman arm from the Pitman shaft.
10. Remove the idler arm-to-shaft nut and separate the idler arm from the shaft.
11. Remove the rubber hose from the front axle vent and support the axle housing assembly.
12. Remove both bolts from the left axle housing isolator and the right axle housing isolator, then, lower the front axle housing assembly.
13. Remove the oil pan-to-engine bolts, the oil pan and discard the gasket.
14. Clean the gasket mounting surfaces.

To install:

15. Using a new gasket and sealant, install the oil pan. Torque both rear pan-to-engine bolts to 18 ft. lbs. (25 Nm) and the other bolts/nuts/studs to 7 ft. lbs. (10 Nm).
16. To complete the installation, reverse the removal procedures. Torque the Pitman arm-to-Pitman shaft nut to 159 ft. lbs. (215 Nm), idler arm-to-shaft nut to 86 ft. lbs. (117 Nm) and the front drive axle shaft bolts to 46 ft. lbs. (62 Nm).
17. Refill the crankcase. Connect the negative battery cable.
18. Start the engine and check for leaks.

3.1L Engine

1. Disconnect the negative battery cable.
2. Remove the dipstick. Raise and safely support the vehicle. Drain the crankcase.
3. Remove the front skid plate and the crossmember.
4. Remove the front driveshaft from the front differential.
5. Remove the braces from the flywheel cover.
6. Disconnect the electrical connectors from the starter. Remove the starter-to-engine bolts and the starter.
7. Remove the flywheel inspection cover.
8. Matchmark the Pitman arm-to-Pitman shaft for reassembly. Remove the Pitman arm-to-Pitman arm shaft nut and separate the Pitman arm from the Pitman shaft.
9. Remove the idler arm-to-shaft nut and separate the idler arm from the shaft.
10. Remove the rubber hose from the front axle vent and support the axle housing assembly.
11. Remove both bolts from the left axle housing isolator and the right axle housing isolator, then, lower the front axle housing assembly.

12. Remove the oil pan-to-engine bolts, the oil pan and discard the gasket.
13. Clean the gasket mounting surfaces.

To install:

14. Using a new gasket and sealant, install the oil pan. Torque both rear pan-to-engine bolts to 18 ft. lbs. (25 Nm) and the other bolts/nuts/studs to 7 ft. lbs. (10 Nm).
15. Install the front axle housing assembly. Torque the front drive axle mounting bolts to 112 ft. lbs. (152 Nm).
16. Install the Pitman arm and the idler arm. Torque the Pitman arm nut to 159 ft. lbs. (215 Nm) and the idler arm nut to 86 ft. lbs. (117 Nm).
17. Install the flywheel dust cover.
18. Install the starter motor. Torque the bolts to 27 ft. lbs. (36 Nm).
19. Install the driveshaft. Torque the driveshaft bolts to 46 ft. lbs. (63 Nm.).
20. Install the suspension crossmember. Torque the bolts to 58 ft. lbs. (78 Nm).
21. Install the under cover and the stone guard.
22. Install the dipstick and refill the crankcase with oil.
23. Connect the negative battery cable, start the engine and check for leaks.

3.2L Engine

▶ See Figure 92

1. Disconnect the negative battery cable.
2. Drain the engine oil.
3. Raise and safely support the vehicle.
4. Remove the front wheels.
5. Remove the dipstick from the dipstick tube.
6. Remove the radiator skid plate and the radiator lower shroud.
7. Remove the suspension crossmember from below the oil pan.
8. Remove the flywheel dust cover.
9. Remove the outer tie rod end cotter pins and castle nuts. Use a ball joint separator tool to disconnect the tie rod ends from the steering knuckles.
10. Matchmark the Pitman arm to the steering shaft and use a puller, (tool No. J–29107, or equivalent) to remove the Pitman arm.
11. Unbolt the idler arm bracket from the frame. Then, remove the steering linkage from the vehicle as an assembly.
12. If equipped with four wheel drive, perform the following steps:
    a. Support the axle assembly with a jack and safety stands.
    b. Remove the mounting bolts and nuts from the axle assembly mounting brackets on both sides of the axle assembly.
    c. Lower the axle assembly to gain access to the oil pan. Support the axle assembly so that the halfshafts aren't stressed.
13. Remove the oil pan mounting bolts. Use a sealer cutter to break the seal and separate the oil pan from the engine block.

To install:

14. Thoroughly clean and dry the sealing surface of the oil pan and engine block. Apply a continuous bead of sealant to the oil pan flange and install the oil pan to the engine block. Do not allow the sealant to cure before installation. Tighten the mounting bolts to 7.4 ft. lbs. (10 Nm) in a two–step crisscross sequence.
15. Install the axle housing assembly. Tighten the axle mounting bracket bolts and nut to 112 ft. lbs. (152 Nm). If the axle housing flange bolts at the

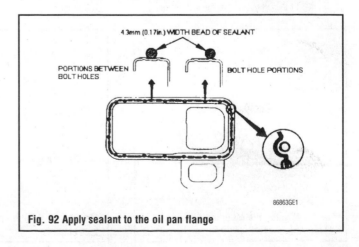

Fig. 92 Apply sealant to the oil pan flange

mounting brackets were loosened or removed, tighten them to 61 ft. lbs. (82 Nm).

16. Install the idler arm. Tighten the mounting bolts to 33 ft. lbs. (45 Nm).

17. Align the matchmark and install the Pitman arm on the sector shaft. Tighten the nut to 160 ft. lbs. (216 Nm).

18. Install the flywheel dust cover.

19. Install the suspension crossmember. Tighten the mounting bolts to 58 ft. lbs. (78 Nm).

20. Install the steering linkage, Pitman arm, and idler arm assembly. Tighten the castle nuts to the following specifications:

    a. Tie rod end castle nuts: 73 ft. lbs. (98 Nm)

    b. Idler arm bracket bolts: 33 ft. lbs. (44 Nm)

    c. Pitman arm nuts: 159 ft. lbs. (216 Nm).

21. Install the lower fan shroud.

22. Install the radiator skid plate. Tighten the bolts to 27 ft. lbs. (37 Nm).

23. Verify that the front axle and any suspension components have been correctly installed.

24. Lower the vehicle to the floor.

25. Install the dipstick and refill the engine with the proper amount of oil.

26. Connect the negative battery cable.

27. Start the engine and check for oil leaks.

Oil Pump

REMOVAL & INSTALLATION

1.8L and 2.0L Engines

♦ See Figures 93, 94 and 95

The oil pump is located in the oil pan and is attached to the front cover.

1. Disconnect the negative battery cable. Raise and safely support the vehicle.

2. Rotate the crankshaft to position the No. 1 or No. 4 cylinder at the TDC of its compression stroke.

3. Drain the crankcase and remove the oil pan as outlined in this section.

✳✳ CAUTION

The EPA warns that prolonged contact with used engine oil may cause a number of skin disorders, including cancer! You should make every effort to minimize your exposure to used engine oil. Protective gloves should be worn when changing the oil. Wash your hands and any other exposed skin areas as soon as possible after exposure to used engine oil. Soap and water, or waterless hand cleaner should be used.

4. Remove the oil pick-up-to-engine bolt and the oil pick-up tube from the oil pump.

5. Remove the oil pump-to-front cover bolts and the oil pump.

To install:

6. Turn the punch mark on the oil pump drive gear toward the oil filter and align the center of the oil pump's drive gear with the mark on the oil pump case.

7. Insert the oil pump into the front cover.

➡When installing the oil pump, turn the oil pump shaft so the drive gear engages with the drive pinion. When installed, the punch mark on the drive gear should be facing the main bearings and the shaft tang must be engaged with the distributor shaft.

8. Install the oil pump and pump-to-front cover bolts.

9. Remove the oil pick-up-to-engine bolt and the oil pick-up tube from the oil pump.

10. Install the oil pan as outlined in this section.

11. Connect the negative battery cable. Lower the vehicle.

12. Refill the crankcase. Connect the negative battery cable.

13. Start the engine and check for leaks.

Diesel Engine

♦ See Figure 96

1. Disconnect the negative battery cable and drain the engine oil.

✳✳ CAUTION

The EPA warns that prolonged contact with used engine oil may cause a number of skin disorders, including cancer! You should make every effort to minimize your exposure to used engine oil. Protective gloves should be worn when changing the oil. Wash your hands and any other exposed skin areas as soon as possible after exposure to used engine oil. Soap and water, or waterless hand cleaner should be used.

2. Remove the engine from the vehicle as outlined in this section.

3. Remove the oil pan as outlined in this section.

4. Remove the oil pipe from the oil pump. Remove the oil pump-to-engine bolts and the oil pump.

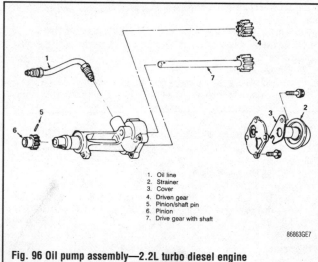

1. Oil line
2. Strainer
3. Cover
4. Driven gear
5. Pinion/shaft pin
6. Pinion
7. Drive gear with shaft

86863GE7

Fig. 96 Oil pump assembly—2.2L turbo diesel engine

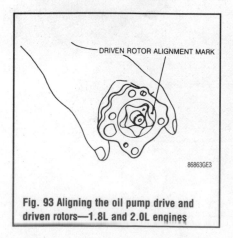

86863GE3

Fig. 93 Aligning the oil pump drive and driven rotors—1.8L and 2.0L engines

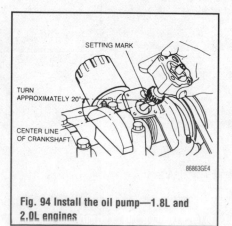

86863GE4

Fig. 94 Install the oil pump—1.8L and 2.0L engines

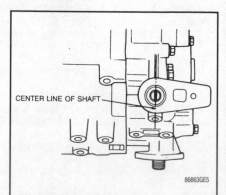

86863GE5

Fig. 95 Aligning the oil pump drive shaft—1.8L and 2.0L engines

To install:

5. Clean the gasket mounting surfaces.

6.. Using a new gasket, install the oil pump and connect the oil pipe to the oil pump. Install and torque the oil pan-to-engine bolts to 10–17 ft. lbs. (14–22 Nm).

7. Install the oil pan.

8. Install the engine into the vehicle.

9. Connect the negative battery cable, refill the engine oil, start the engine and check for leaks.

2.3L and 2.6L Engines

♦ **See Figure 97**

1. Disconnect the negative battery cable.

2. Drain the engine oil.

3. Loosen and remove the engine accessory drive belts.

4. Unbolt and remove the cooling fan assembly.

5. If equipped with A/C, remove the belt tensioner.

6. Remove the water pump pulley.

7. Remove the power steering pump from its mount. Don't disconnect the hydraulic lines.

8. Disconnect and remove the starter motor if a flywheel holding tool is to be used.

9. Remove the upper timing belt cover.

10. Rotate the crankshaft to set the engine at TDC/compression for the No. 1 cylinder. The mark on the camshaft sprocket will align with the mark on the rear timing cover.

11. Remove the crankshaft pulley.

12. Remove the lower timing belt cover. Verify that the engine is set at TDC/compression for the No. 1 cylinder; the pointer on the crankshaft sprocket aligns with the pointer on the oil seal retainer.

13. Loosen the timing belt tensioner and relax the tension and remove the timing belt from the crankshaft sprocket.

14. Use tool No. J–22888 or an equivalent puller to remove the oil pump sprocket.

15. Unbolt the oil pump and remove it from the engine.

16. Remove the O–ring seal from the oil pump housing.

To install:

❊❊ WARNING

The timing belt must be replaced if it is damaged, or has come in contact with oil or coolant.

17. Inspect the oil pump and its rotors for signs of scoring and damage. Replace the pump or any damaged parts.

18. Lubricate and install a new O–ring seal.

19. Install the oil pump and tighten the bolts to 14 ft. lbs. (19 Nm).

20. Align the timing marks and install the oil pump sprocket. Apply a small amount of thread locking compound to the nut threads and tighten it to 56 ft. lbs. (76 Nm).

21. Verify that the engine is at TDC/compression for the No. 1 cylinder.

22. Install the timing belt.

23. If a flywheel holder tool was used, remove it.

24. Apply the tensioner pulley spring pressure to the timing belt.

➡**Remove the crankshaft holder before rotating the crankshaft to tension the timing belt.**

25. Rotate the crankshaft counterclockwise for two complete revolutions and realign the timing marks.

26. Loosen tensioner pulley bolt to allow the spring to adjust the correct tension. Torque the tensioner pulley bolt to 14 ft. lbs. (19 Nm).

27. Install the lower timing cover and tighten the bolts to 4.4 ft. lbs. (6 Nm).

28. Install the crankshaft pulley and tighten the bolt to 87 ft. lbs. (118 Nm).

29. Install the upper timing cover.

30. Install the starter motor and tighten the mounting bolts to 30 ft. lbs. (40 Nm).

31. Install the power steering pump. If the hydraulic lines were disconnected, refill and bleed the power steering system.

32. Install the cooling fan and tighten the bolts to 20 ft. lbs. (26 Nm).

33. Install and adjust the accessory drive belts.

34. Refill the engine with fresh oil.

35. Reconnect the negative battery cable.

36. Start the engine and check for leaks.

37. Check the engine's oil pressure.

2.8L Engine

♦ **See Figure 98**

The oil pump is attached to the cylinder block and is located in the oil pan.

1. Disconnect the negative battery cable. Raise and safely support the vehicle.

2. Drain the crankcase. Remove the oil pan as outlined in this section.

❊❊ CAUTION

The EPA warns that prolonged contact with used engine oil may cause a number of skin disorders, including cancer! You should make every effort to minimize your exposure to used engine oil. Protective gloves should be worn when changing the oil. Wash your hands and any other exposed skin areas as soon as possible after exposure to used engine oil. Soap and water, or waterless hand cleaner should be used.

3. Remove the oil pump-to-engine bolts and the oil pump.

To install:

4. Align the oil pump shaft with the hexagon socket and install the pump. Torque the oil pump-to-engine bolts to 30 ft. lbs. (41 Nm).

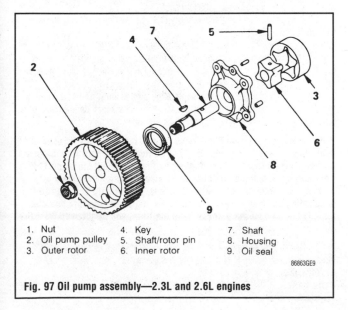

1. Nut	4. Key	7. Shaft
2. Oil pump pulley	5. Shaft/rotor pin	8. Housing
3. Outer rotor	6. Inner rotor	9. Oil seal

86863GE9

Fig. 97 Oil pump assembly—2.3L and 2.6L engines

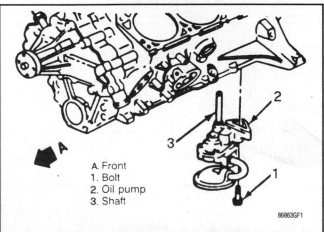

A. Front
1. Bolt
2. Oil pump
3. Shaft

86863GF1

Fig. 98 Exploded view of the oil pump assembly mounting—2.8L engine

5. Install the oil pan.

6. Connect the negative battery cable. Start the engine and check for leaks.

3.1L Engine

▶ See Figure 99

The oil pump is attached to the cylinder block and is located under the oil pan.

1. Disconnect the negative battery cable. Raise and safely support the vehicle.

2. Drain the crankcase and remove the oil pan.

3. Remove the oil pump-to-engine bolts and the oil pump.

To install:

4. Align the oil pump shaft with the hexagon socket and install the pump. Torque the oil pump-to-engine bolts to 30 ft. lbs. (41 Nm).

5. Install the oil pan.

6. Refill the crankcase with oil.

7. Connect the negative battery cable. Start the engine and check for leaks.

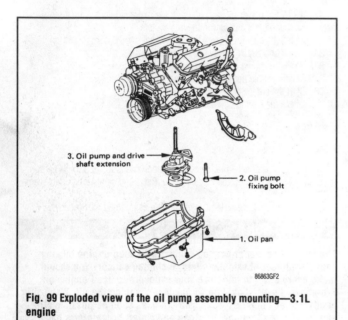

3. Oil pump and drive shaft extension

2. Oil pump fixing bolt

1. Oil pan

86863GF2

Fig. 99 Exploded view of the oil pump assembly mounting—3.1L engine

3.2L Engine

▶ See Figure 100

1. Disconnect the negative battery cable.

2. Remove the timing belt. If the timing belt is damaged or has been contaminated with oil or coolant, it must be replaced.

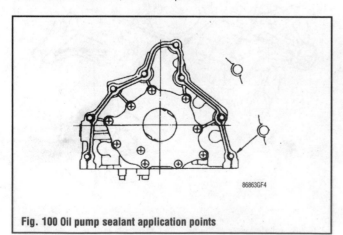

86863GF4

Fig. 100 Oil pump sealant application points

3. Remove the crankshaft timing pulley.

4. Raise and safely support the vehicle.

5. Drain the engine oil.

6. Remove the oil pan.

7. Remove the oil pipe and O-ring.

8. Remove the oil strainer and O-ring.

9. Remove the oil cooler assembly.

10. Remove the oil pump mounting bolts, and then remove the oil pump from the engine block.

To install:

11. Install a new oil seal into the oil pump housing.

12. Thoroughly clean the sealing surface of the oil pump and the engine block.

13. Apply sealant to the oil pump. Be careful not to block the oil ports.

14. Apply engine oil to the seal lip and install the oil pump on the engine block. Tighten the mounting bolts to 13 ft. lbs. (18 Nm). Take care not to drop the garter spring from the seal lid during installation.

15. Install the oil cooler assembly.

16. Install the oil pipe and O-ring.

17. Install the oil strainer and O-ring.

18. Install the oil pan.

19. Install the crankshaft timing pulley.

20. Install the timing belt.

21. Install the remaining accessories and drive belts.

22. Lower the vehicle.

23. Refill the engine with oil.

24. Connect the negative battery cable, start the engine and check for proper oil pressure.

➡**If the oil pressure does not build up almost immediately, stop the engine and investigate the cause.**

25. Check for oil leaks.

Crankshaft Damper

REMOVAL & INSTALLATION

Except Diesel Engine

▶ See Figures 101, 102, 103, 104 and 105

Most of the engines covered in this manual are equipped with a crankshaft hub and pulley assembly. The pulley is usually mounted to the hub using 3 or so bolts around the inner circle of the pulley. The center mounting bolt is used to retain the hub to the crankshaft, but may also be used to retain the pulley. If the center mounting bolt also retains the pulley, a washer can normally be seen between the bolt head and the inner lip of the pulley.

1. Disconnect the negative battery cable.

2. Loosen and remove the accessory drive belts or serpentine drive belt from the crankshaft damper.

3. If necessary for access on certain models, remove the fan assembly.

4. Remove the pulley mounting bolts from the pulley and damper assembly. If the center mounting bolt is not used to retain the pulley, it may be separated from the hub at this time and removed from the engine.

5. Spray the damper bolt with penetrating oil and allow it to soak in for at least a few minutes. Loosen and remove the center crankshaft damper bolt. If the pulley was not removed earlier, it should be free now.

➡**If damper bolt removal is difficult, various methods may be used to hold the crankshaft while loosening or tightening the bolt. One method involves installing a flywheel holding fixture to prevent the crankshaft from turning. A holding tool may be available for some dampers which threads into the pulley bolt holes. But most importantly of all, allow the penetrating oil to do the work when loosening an old damper bolt and reapply oil, as necessary. If you have the time, you might even want the oil to sit overnight.**

6. Remove the damper from the end of the crankshaft using a suitable threaded damper puller, NOT a jawed-type puller which would most likely destroy dampers with bonded hubs.

Fig. 101 Loosen the pulley and/or damper retaining bolts—in this case all must be removed before the pulley can be separated

Fig. 102 The damper retaining bolt is threaded into the center of the hub

Fig. 103 With the bolts removed, separate the pulley from the hub

Fig. 104 Use a threaded damper puller to draw the hub from the end of the crankshaft

Fig. 105 Once the hub is loosened carefully withdraw the hub from the end of the crankshaft

✳✳ WARNING

The use of any other type of puller, such as a universal claw type which pulls on the outside of the hub, can destroy the balancer on some of these engines. Many of the vehicles covered in this manual use a balancer, the outside ring of which is bonded in rubber to the hub. Pulling on the outside will break the bond.

To install:

7. If removal of the damper was difficult, check the damper inner diameter and the crankshaft outer diameter for corrosion. A small amount of corrosion may be removed using steel wool, then the surface may be lubricated lightly using clean engine oil.

8. Coat the front cover seal contact edge of the damper lightly with clean engine oil, then apply a small amount of RTV sealant to the keyway in the damper hub. Install the damper on the end of the crankshaft (along with the pulley if the share the center retaining bolt), but DO NOT hammer it into position, instead use a damper installation tool to slowly draw the hub into position. If the damper can be positioned far enough over the end of the crankshaft, the damper bolt may be used to draw it into position, but be careful that sufficient threads are in contact to prevent stripping the bolt or crankshaft.

9. Once the damper is fully seated, install and tighten the retaining bolt to specification.

10. If not done earlier, install the pulley and secure using the outer retaining bolts.

11. If removed for access, install the fan assembly.

12. Install the drive belt(s) to the crankshaft pulley.

13. Connect the negative battery cable.

Diesel Engine

The 2.2L diesel engine utilizes an exposed crankshaft pulley and a hidden crankshaft timing pulley/damper. The following procedure may be used to remove the exposed crankshaft pulley.

1. Disconnect the negative battery cable.

2. Loosen and remove the accessory drive belts.

3. Turn the crankshaft pulley to align the timing mark with the engine pointer. This should be done if any further procedures are being performed which might disturb valve timing.

4. Remove the retaining bolts, then remove the crankshaft pulley.

To install:

5. Align and install the crankshaft pulley.

6. Install the retaining bolts, then tighten to 10–17 ft. lbs. (14–23 Nm).

7. Install the accessory drive belts, then properly adjust their tension.

8. Connect the negative battery cable.

Timing Belt Front Cover

REMOVAL & INSTALLATION

Diesel Engine

1. Disconnect the negative battery cable. Drain the cooling system.

✳✳ CAUTION

When draining the coolant, keep in mind that cats and dogs are attracted by ethylene glycol antifreeze, and are quite likely to drink any that is left in an uncovered container or in puddles on the ground. This will prove fatal in sufficient quantity. Always drain the coolant into a sealable container. Coolant should be reused unless it is contaminated or several years old.

2. Remove the cooling fan assembly and the drive belt(s). Remove the alternator and bracket.

3. Remove the radiator hoses and the radiator.

4. Label and disconnect the necessary vacuum hoses and electrical connectors.

5. Remove the crankshaft pulley.

6. Remove the timing belt cover-to-engine bolts and the cover.

To install:

7. Install the timing belt cover-to-engine bolts and the cover.

8. Install the crankshaft pulley.

9. Connect the necessary vacuum hoses and electrical connectors.

10. Install the radiator hoses and the radiator.

11. Install the cooling fan assembly and the drive belt(s). Install the alternator and bracket.

12. Connect the negative battery cable.

13. Refill the cooling system.

14. Start the engine, allow it to reach normal operating temperatures and check for leaks.

2.3L and 2.6L Engines

1. Disconnect the negative battery cable.

2. Remove all accessory drive belts.

3. Remove the cooling fan and pulley.

4. If equipped, remove the power steering pump from its mount and unbolt the hydraulic line from the upper timing cover. Move the pump and hydraulics lines out of the work area. If the lines must be disconnect, plug them to prevent fluid loss and contamination.

5. Remove the upper timing cover.

6. Rotate the crankshaft to set the engine at TDC/compression for the No. 1 cylinder. The arrow mark on the camshaft timing sprocket aligns with the mark on the back timing cover.

7. Use a suitable holder tool to remove the crankshaft pulley bolt.

➡**The starter motor can be removed and a bar–type crankshaft holder tool installed in its opening.**

8. Remove the crankshaft pulley.

9. Remove the lower timing belt cover.

To install:

10. Clean any oil, coolant, or excess sealant from the timing belt covers before installation.

11. Install the lower timing belt covers. Tighten the bolts to 4.4 ft. lbs. (6 Nm).

12. Install the crankshaft pulley and bolt. Tighten the bolt to 87 ft. lbs. (118 Nm).

13. Remove the crankshaft holder tool. Install the starter motor if it was removed and tighten its bolts to 30 ft. lbs. (40 Nm).

14. Install the upper timing belt cover.

15. If removed, install the power steering pump. Tighten the mounting bolts to 27 ft. lbs. (37 Nm). Reconnect the fluid line fittings with new washers and tighten the banjo bolt to 14 ft. lbs. (19 Nm).

16. Install the cooling fan and pulley and tighten the pulley mounting bolts to 20 ft. lbs. (26 Nm).

17. Install and adjust the accessory drive belts.

18. Verify that all wiring harnesses and vacuum lines have reconnected correctly.

19. Connect the negative battery cable.

20. Refill and bleed the power steering system.

3.2L Engine

1992–95 VEHICLES

▶ See Figure 106

1. Disconnect the negative battery cable.

2. Drain the engine coolant.

3. Remove the air cleaner assembly.

4. Remove the upper fan shroud from the radiator.

5. Remove the four nuts retaining the cooling fan assembly. Remove the cooling fan.

6. Loosen and remove the power steering drive belt.

7. Loosen and remove the air conditioning compressor drive belt.

8. Loosen and remove the alternator drive belt.

9. Remove the fan pulley assembly.

10. Remove the crankshaft pulley center bolt. Remove the crankshaft pulley.

11. Remove the two oil cooler hose bracket bolts on the timing cover. Remove the oil cooler hose.

12. Remove the timing belt cover.

To install:

13. Install the timing belt cover and tighten bolts to 12 ft. lbs. (17 Nm).

14. Install the oil cooler hose and tighten brackets to 16 ft. lbs. (22 Nm).

15. Install the crankshaft pulley. Use tool No. J–8614–01, or an equivalent pulley holder and tighten the bolts to 123 ft. lbs. (167 Nm).

16. Install fan pulley assembly and tighten the bolts to 16 ft. lbs. (22 Nm).

17. Install and adjust the alternator drive belt.

18. Install and adjust the air conditioning compressor drive belt.

19. Install and adjust the power steering pump drive belt.

20. Install cooling fan assembly and tighten bolts to 69 inch lbs. (8 Nm).

21. Install upper fan shroud to the radiator.

22. Install air cleaner assembly.

23. Refill the engine with fresh coolant. Bleed the cooling system.

24. Connect the negative battery cable.

1996 VEHICLES

▶ See Figure 106

1. Disconnect the negative battery cable.

2. Drain the engine coolant.

3. Remove the air cleaner assembly and intake air duct.

4. Remove the upper fan shroud from the radiator.

5. Remove the four nuts retaining the cooling fan assembly. Remove the cooling fan.

6. Loosen and remove the power steering drive belt.

7. Loosen and remove the air conditioning compressor drive belt.

8. Loosen and remove the alternator drive belt.

9. Remove the fan pulley assembly.

10. Remove the two oil cooler hose bracket bolts on the timing cover. Move the oil cooler hose off of the lower timing cover.

11. Remove the upper timing belt covers.

12. Rotate the crankshaft to align the camshaft timing marks with the pointer dots on the back covers. When the timing marks are aligned, the No. 2 piston is at TDC/compression.

13. Use tool No. J–8614–01, or a suitable pulley holding tool to remove the crankshaft pulley center bolt. Remove the crankshaft pulley.

14. Remove the lower timing belt cover.

To install:

15. Install the lower timing belt cover and tighten bolts to 12 ft. lbs. (17 Nm).

16. Install the crankshaft pulley. Use tool No. J–8614–01, or an equivalent pulley holder and tighten the bolts to 123 ft. lbs. (167 Nm).

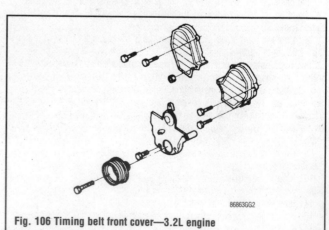

Fig. 106 Timing belt front cover—3.2L engine

86863GG2

17. Verify that the timing marks align and that the No. 2 piston is at TDC/compression.

18. Install the upper timing belt covers and tighten the bolts to 12 ft. lbs. (17 Nm).

19. Fit oil cooler hose onto the timing cover and tighten the bracket bolts to 16 ft. lbs. (22 Nm).

20. Install fan pulley assembly and tighten the bolts to 16 ft. lbs. (22 Nm).

21. Install and adjust the alternator drive belt.

22. Install and adjust the air conditioning compressor drive belt.

23. Install and adjust the power steering pump drive belt.

24. Install cooling fan assembly and tighten bolts to 6 ft. lbs. (8 Nm).

25. Install upper fan shroud to the radiator.

26. Install air cleaner assembly and intake air duct.

27. Refill the engine with fresh coolant. Bleed the cooling system.

28. Connect the negative battery cable.

Timing Chain Front Cover

REMOVAL & INSTALLATION

1.8L and 2.0L Engines

1. Disconnect the negative battery cable.
2. Drain the cooling system.

> **⁂ CAUTION**
>
> **When draining the coolant, keep in mind that cats and dogs are attracted by ethylene glycol antifreeze, and are quite likely to drink any that is left in an uncovered container or in puddles on the ground. This will prove fatal in sufficient quantity. Always drain the coolant into a sealable container. Coolant should be reused unless it is contaminated or several years old.**

3. Disconnect the radiator hoses and remove the radiator.
4. Remove the air cleaner and the rocker arm cover.
5. Remove the alternator and air conditioning compressor drive belts.
6. Remove the cooling fan.
7. Raise and safely support the vehicle. Drain the engine oil.

> **⁂ CAUTION**
>
> **The EPA warns that prolonged contact with used engine oil may cause a number of skin disorders, including cancer! You should make every effort to minimize your exposure to used engine oil. Protective gloves should be worn when changing the oil. Wash your hands and any other exposed skin areas as soon as possible after exposure to used engine oil. Soap and water, or waterless hand cleaner should be used.**

8. Remove the crankshaft pulley center bolt, the pulley and balancer assembly.

9. Remove the oil pan-to-engine bolts and the oil pan.

10. Remove the oil pump pick-up tube, the oil pump-to-front cover bolts and the oil pump.

11. Remove the front cover-to-engine bolts and the front cover from the engine and discard the gasket.

12. Clean the gasket mounting surfaces.

➡ **When the front cover is removed, replace the oil seal.**

To install:

13. Using a new gasket and sealant, install the front cover to the engine and torque the bolts to 18 ft. lbs. (25 Nm).

14. Align the oil pump's slotted shaft with the tip of the distributor and install the oil pump. Install the oil pick-up tube to the oil pump.

15. Using a new gasket, install the oil pan.

16. Install the crankshaft balancer assembly, pulley and bolt. Lower the vehicle.

17. Install the cooling fan assembly.

18. Install the alternator and compressor drive belts and adjust the tension.

19. Using a new gasket, install the rocker arm cover. Install the air cleaner.

20. Refill the crankcase and the cooling system.

21. Connect the negative battery cable.

2.8L and 3.1L Engines

▶ **See Figures 107 thru 112**

1. Disconnect the negative battery cable.
2. Drain the cooling system. Remove the lower radiator hose from the front cover.

> **⁂ CAUTION**
>
> **When draining the coolant, keep in mind that cats and dogs are attracted by ethylene glycol antifreeze, and are quite likely to drink any that is left in an uncovered container or in puddles on the ground. This will prove fatal in sufficient quantity. Always drain the coolant into a sealable container. Coolant should be reused unless it is contaminated or several years old.**

3. Remove the water pump.
4. Remove the power steering bracket, if equipped.
5. Remove the crankshaft pulley.
6. Remove the front cover-to-engine bolts and the cover and discard the gasket.
7. Clean the gasket mounting surfaces.

➡ **When the front cover is removed, replace the oil seal.**

To install:

8. Using a new gasket and sealant, install the front cover.
9. Install the water pump and the lower radiator hose.
10. Install the crankshaft pulley.
11. Install the power steering pump bracket, if equipped.
12. Install the drive belt(s).
13. Connect the negative battery cable and refill the cooling system.

Fig. 107 Removing the lower pulley—2.8L engine

Fig. 108 Using a puller to removing the damper—2.8L engine

Fig. 109 The key slot must be aligned when installing the crankshaft damper—2.8L engine

Fig. 110 After the damper has been removed, remove the timing chain cover bolts—2.8L engine

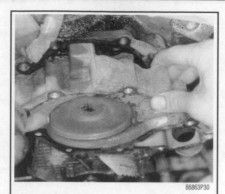

Fig. 111 Removing the timing chain cover from the engine block—2.8L engine

Fig. 112 Both sides of the timing chain cover must be cleaned of gasket material and dirt—2.8L engine

Front Cover Oil Seal

REMOVAL & INSTALLATION

▶ See Figures 113 and 114

Timing Chain Engines

1. Disconnect the negative battery cable.
2. Drain the cooling system.

✳✳ CAUTION

When draining the coolant, keep in mind that cats and dogs are attracted by ethylene glycol antifreeze, and are quite likely to drink any that is left in an uncovered container or in puddles on the ground. This will prove fatal in sufficient quantity. Always drain the coolant into a sealable container. Coolant should be reused unless it is contaminated or several years old.

3. Disconnect the radiator hoses and remove the radiator.
4. Remove the alternator and compressor drive belts.
5. Remove the cooling fan.
6. Remove the crankshaft pulley center bolt, the pulley and balancer assembly.
7. Using a small prybar and care not to damage the crankshaft and cover sealing surfaces, carefully, pry out the timing cover seal.

To install:
8. Using engine oil, lubricate the new seal and tap it into the front cover.
9. Install the balancer assembly, the pulley and the center bolt.
10. Install the cooling fan and the drive belts.
11. Install the radiator and connect the hoses.
12. Refill the cooling system and connect the negative battery cable.

Timing Belt Engines

GASOLINE MODELS

1. Disconnect the negative battery cable. Remove the crankshaft pulley.
2. Remove the upper and lower timing belt covers.
3. Rotate the crankshaft to align the camshaft sprocket with the mark on the rear timing cover and the crankshaft sprocket keyway with the mark on the oil seal retainer cover.

➡**With the timing marks aligned, the engine is positioned at TDC of the No. 4 cylinder's compression stroke.**

4. Loosen the timing belt tensioner and relax the tension and remove the timing belt from the crankshaft sprocket.
5. Remove the crankshaft sprocket bolt, the sprocket, the key and deflector shield.
6. Using a small prybar, pry the oil seal from the oil seal retainer.
To install:
7. Using a new oil seal, lubricate it with engine oil and tap it into the retainer with an oil seal installation tool.
8. Install the deflector, the key, the crankshaft sprocket and bolt.

Fig. 113 Use a prybar to remove the old oil seal, but be careful not to distort the cover flange

Fig. 114 Install the seal to the cover using a suitable installation driver

9. With the crankshaft sprocket aligned with the timing mark, install the timing belt.

10. Apply the tensioner pulley spring pressure to the timing belt.

11. Rotate the crankshaft 2 complete revolutions in the opposite direction of rotation and realign the timing marks.

12. Loosen the tensioner pulley bolt to allow the spring to adjust the correct tension. Torque the tensioner pulley bolt to 14 ft. lbs. (20 Nm).

13. Install the timing covers and the crankshaft pulley.

14. To complete the installation, reverse the removal procedures.

DIESEL MODELS

▶ **See Figure 115**

1. Disconnect the negative battery terminal. Drain the cooling system.

☀ CAUTION

When draining the coolant, keep in mind that cats and dogs are attracted by ethylene glycol antifreeze, and are quite likely to drink any that is left in an uncovered container or in puddles on the ground. This will prove fatal in sufficient quantity. Always drain the coolant into a sealable container. Coolant should be reused unless it is contaminated or several years old.

2. Remove the timing belt.

3. Remove the crankshaft sprocket bolt.

➡ **To remove the crankshaft sprocket bolt, it may be necessary to remove the starter or the flywheel cover plate to lock the flywheel; otherwise, it may be difficult to keep the crankshaft from turning.**

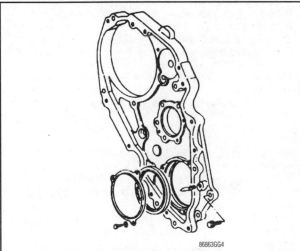

Fig. 115 Timing pulley housing, crankshaft seal and retainer—diesel engine

4. Using a puller tool press the crankshaft center and timing sprocket from the crankshaft.

5. Remove the oil seal retainer-to-rear timing cover bolts and the retainer.

6. Using a small prybar, pry the oil seal from engine housing; be careful not to damage the crankshaft or the oil seal mounting surface.

To install:

7. Using a new oil seal, lubricate the seal lips with engine oil and install it into the engine using a seal installation tool.

8. Install the oil seal retainer.

9. Install the crankshaft center and timing sprocket to the crankshaft.

10. Install the timing belt.

11. Refill the cooling system. Start the engine, check and/or adjust the timing and check for leaks.

Timing Belt

REMOVAL & INSTALLATION

Diesel Engine

▶ **See Figures 116, 117, 118 and 119**

1. Disconnect the negative battery cable. Drain the cooling system.

☀ CAUTION

When draining the coolant, keep in mind that cats and dogs are attracted by ethylene glycol antifreeze, and are quite likely to drink any that is left in an uncovered container or in puddles on the ground. This will prove fatal in sufficient quantity. Always drain the coolant into a sealable container. Coolant should be reused unless it is contaminated or several years old.

2. Remove the timing belt cover. Remove the injection pump sprocket flange.

3. Using a prybar, remove the tension spring from the timing belt tensioner.

➡ **When removing the tension spring, avoid using excessive force for the spring may become distorted.**

4. Remove the tensioner pulley bolt and the pulley.

5. Remove the timing belt and discard it.

To install:

6. Rotate the crankshaft to bring the No. 1 piston to TDC of the compression stroke.

7. Align the timing marks on the injection pump sprocket with the camshaft sprocket; the marks must be facing each other.

8. Using a new timing belt, install it in the following sequence: crankshaft sprocket, camshaft sprocket and the injection pump sprocket; the slack must be between the injection pump and camshaft sprockets.

9. Install the tension center and the tension pulley so the end of the tension center is fitted against both pins on the timing pulley housing.

10. Hand tighten the nut so the tension pulley can be rotated freely.

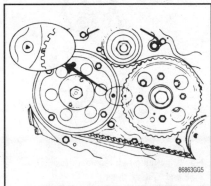

Fig. 116 Injection pump and camshaft alignment marks—diesel engine

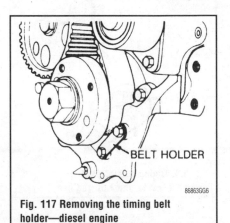

Fig. 117 Removing the timing belt holder—diesel engine

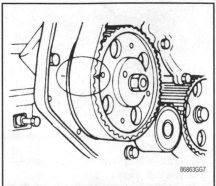

Fig. 118 Injection pump alignment marks—diesel engine

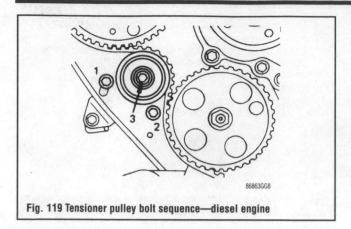

Fig. 119 Tensioner pulley bolt sequence—diesel engine

11. Install the tension spring and semi-tighten the pulley nut to 22–36 ft. lbs. (30–48 Nm).

12. Rotate the crankshaft 2 full turns clockwise to seat the belt and further turn the crankshaft 90° beyond TDC to settle the injection pump.

13. Loosen the tension pulley nut to take up the timing belt slack. Tighten the tension pulley nut to 79–94 ft. lbs. (108–128 Nm).

14. Install the injection pump sprocket flange; the hole in the outer circumference of the flange should be aligned with the triangular timing mark on the injection pump sprocket.

15. Rotate the crankshaft 2 full turns clockwise to bring the No. 1 piston to TDC of the compression stroke. Make sure the triangular timing mark on the timing sprocket is aligned with the hole in the flange, then, measure the timing belt tension; it should be 33–55 lbs.

16. Install the timing belt cover.

17. Connect the negative battery cable.

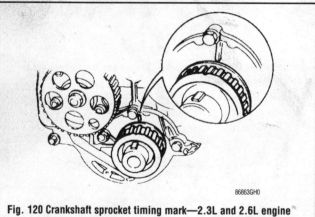

Fig. 120 Crankshaft sprocket timing mark—2.3L and 2.6L engine

1986–92 2.3L and 2.6L Engines

▶ **See Figures 120, 121, 122 and 123**

1. Disconnect the negative battery cable. Remove the crankshaft pulley.

2. Remove the upper and lower timing belt covers.

3. Rotate the crankshaft to align the camshaft sprocket with the mark on the rear timing cover and the crankshaft sprocket keyway with the mark on the oil seal retainer cover.

➡With the timing marks aligned, the engine is positioned on the TDC of the No. 4 cylinder's compression stroke.

4. Loosen the timing belt tensioner and relax the tension and remove the timing belt from the crankshaft sprocket.

To install:

5. With the crankshaft and the camshaft sprockets aligned with the timing marks, install the timing belt. Install the timing belt using the following sequence: the crankshaft sprocket, the oil pump sprocket and the camshaft sprocket.

6. Apply the tensioner pulley spring pressure to the timing belt.

7. Rotate the crankshaft 2 complete revolutions in the opposite direction of rotation and realign the timing marks.

8. Loosen the tensioner pulley bolt to allow the spring to adjust the correct tension. Torque the tensioner pulley bolt to 14 ft. lbs. (20 Nm).

9. Install the timing covers and the crankshaft pulley.

10. Connect the negative battery cable. Start the engine and check for leaks.

1993–96 2.3L and 2.6L Engines

▶ **See Figures 120, 121, 122 and 123**

1. Disconnect the negative battery cable.

2. Loosen and remove the engine accessory drive belts.

3. Remove the cooling fan assembly and the water pump pulley.

4. Drain the fluid from the power steering reservoir.

5. Unbolt and remove the power steering pump. Unbolt the hydraulic line brackets from the upper timing cover and move the pump out of the work area without disconnecting the hydraulic lines.

6. Disconnect and remove the starter motor if a flywheel holder (part No. J–38674) is to be used.

7. Remove the upper timing belt cover.

8. Rotate the crankshaft to set the engine at TDC/compression for the No. 1 cylinder. The arrow mark on camshaft sprocket aligns with mark on the rear timing cover.

9. Remove the crankshaft pulley.

10. Remove the lower timing belt cover.

11. Verify that the engine is set at TDC/compression for the No. 1 cylinder. The notch on the crankshaft sprocket aligns with the pointer on the oil seal retainer.

12. Release and remove the tensioner spring to release the timing belt's tension.

13. Remove the timing belt.

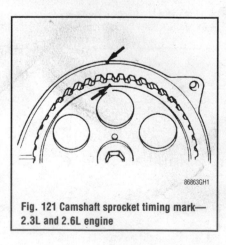

Fig. 121 Camshaft sprocket timing mark— 2.3L and 2.6L engine

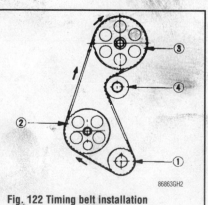

Fig. 122 Timing belt installation sequence—2.3L and 2.6L engines

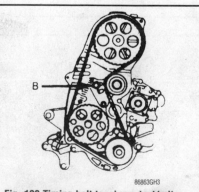

Fig. 123 Timing belt tensioner lockbolt— 2.3L and 2.6L engines

14. Unbolt the tensioner pulley bracket from the engine's front cover.
15. If necessary, unbolt and remove the camshaft sprockets. Use a puller to remove the crankshaft pulley if necessary. Don't loose the crankshaft sprocket key.

To install:

16. Install the camshaft and crankshaft sprockets if they were removed. Align the timing marks and be sure to install any keys. Tighten the camshaft sprocket bolt to 43 ft. lbs. (59 Nm).
17. Install the tensioner assembly. Tighten the tensioner mounting bolt to 14 ft. lbs. (19 Nm). Tighten the cap bolt to 9 ft. lbs. (13 Nm).
18. Make sure the crankshaft and the camshaft sprockets are aligned with their timing marks. Install the timing belt onto the sprockets using the following sequence: first, crankshaft sprocket; second, oil pump sprocket; third, camshaft sprocket.
19. Loosen the tensioner mounting bolt. This will allow the tensioner spring to apply pressure to the timing belt.
20. After the spring has pulled the timing belt as far as possible, temporarily tighten the tensioner mounting bolt to 14 ft. lbs. (19 Nm).

➡Remove the flywheel holder before rotating the crankshaft. Reinstall the holder to torque the crankshaft pulley bolt.

21. Rotate the crankshaft counterclockwise two complete revolutions to check the rotation of the belt and the alignment of the timing marks. Listen for any rubbing noises which may mean the belt is binding.
22. Loosen the tensioner pulley bolt to allow the spring to adjust the correct tension. Then, retighten the tensioner pulley bolt to 14 ft. lbs (19 Nm).
23. Install the lower timing cover and the crankshaft pulley.
24. Tighten the crankshaft pulley bolt to 87 ft. lbs. (118 Nm). Tighten the small pulley bolts to 6 ft. lbs. (8 Nm).
25. Install the upper timing cover.
26. Install the starter if it was removed. Tighten the bolts to 30 ft. lbs. (40 Nm).
27. Install the power steering pump. If the hydraulic lines were disconnected, refill and bleed the power steering system.
28. Install the water pump pulley and tighten its nut to 20 ft. lbs. (26 Nm).
29. Install the cooling fan assembly.
30. Install and adjust the accessory drive belts.
31. Connect the negative battery cable.

1992–95 3.2L Engine

➧ See Figures 124, 125, 126, 127 and 128

1. Disconnect the negative battery cable.
2. Drain the engine coolant into a sealable container.
3. Remove the air cleaner assembly.
4. Remove the upper fan shroud from the radiator.
5. Remove the four nuts retaining the cooling fan assembly. Remove the cooling fan.
6. Remove the power steering drive belt.
7. Remove the air conditioning compressor drive belt.
8. Remove the alternator drive belt.
9. Remove the fan pulley assembly.
10. Set the timing belt so that the timing marks on the sprockets align with those on the oil pump and front plate.
11. Remove the crankshaft pulley center bolt. Remove the crankshaft pulley.
12. Remove the two oil cooler hose bracket fixing bolts on the timing cover. Remove the oil cooler hoses and bracket.
13. Remove the timing belt cover.

⁂ WARNING

Set the timing sprockets so that the crankshaft and camshaft sprocket timing marks align with the timing marks on the oil pump and front plate. When the timing marks are align, no pistons are at TDC for the compression stroke. Valve damage may result if the sprockets and belt are out of alignment.

14. Remove the pusher. The rod must always be facing upward.

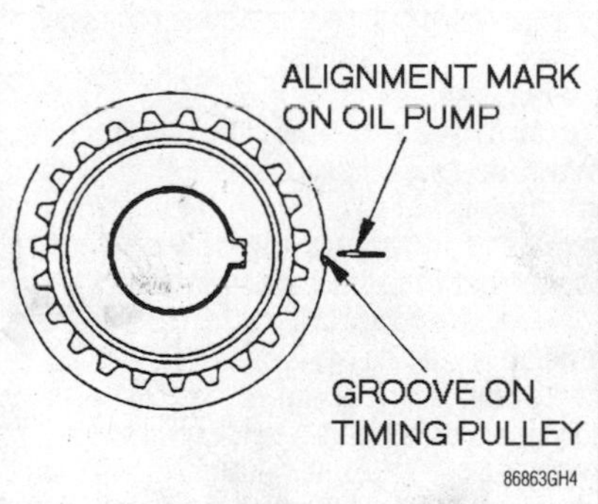

Fig. 124 Crankshaft sprocket groove and alignment marks—3.2L engine

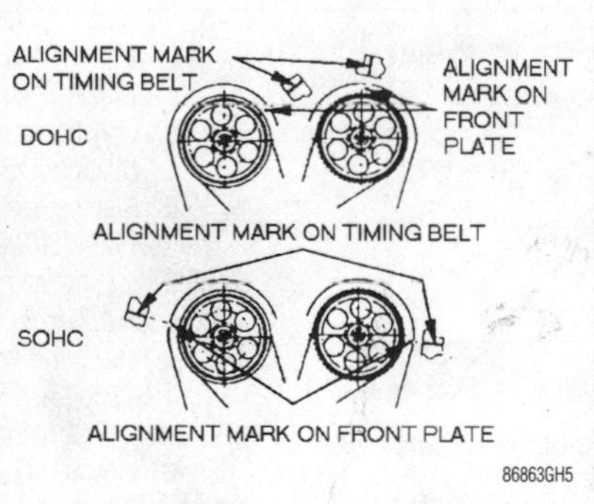

Fig. 125 Camshaft sprocket alignment marks—3.2L engine

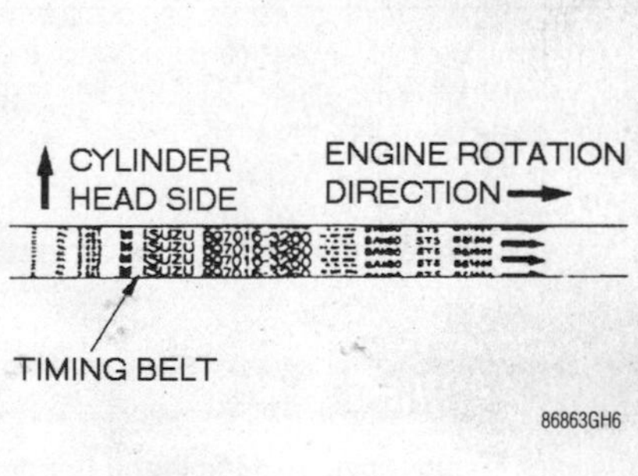

Fig. 126 Timing belt direction of installation and rotation—3.2L engine

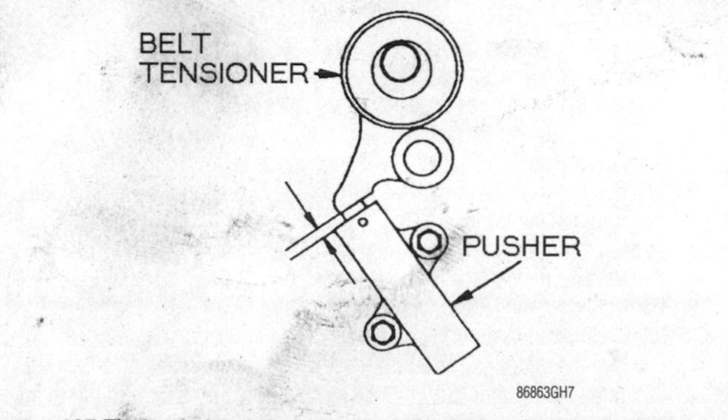

Fig. 127 Timing belt tensioner pulley with pusher installed—3.2L engine

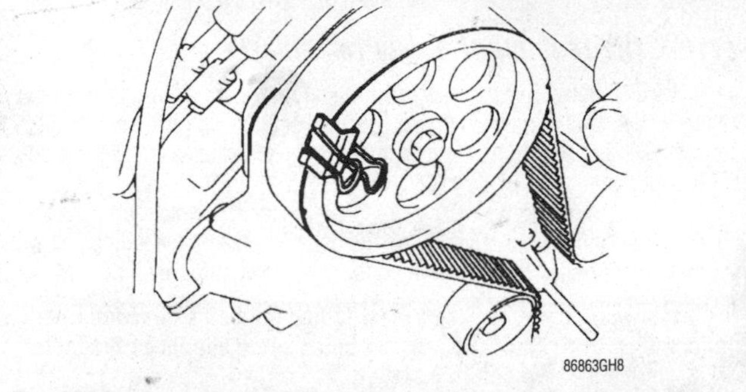

Fig. 128 Large paper clips are an excellent way to hold the belt in place during service. Timing belt tensioner pulley with pusher installed—3.2L engine

15. Mark the timing belt, cam pulley and crankshaft pulley. Remove the timing belt.

To install:

16. Align the groove on the crankshaft timing pulley with mark on the oil pump.

17. Align the marks on the camshaft timing pulleys with the dots on the front plate.

18. Install the timing belt. Align the dotted marks on the timing belt with the mark on the crankshaft pulley.

19. Align the white line on the timing belt with the alignment mark on the right bank camshaft timing pulley. Secure the belt with a small clamp.

20. Turn the crankshaft counterclockwise to remove the slack between the crankshaft pulley and the right camshaft timing pulley.

21. Install the belt on the water pump pulley.

22. Install the belt on the idler pulley.

23. Align the white alignment mark on the timing belt with the alignment mark on the left bank camshaft timing pulley.

24. Install the crankshaft pulley and tighten the center bolt by hand. Turn the crankshaft pulley clockwise to give slack between the crankshaft timing pulley and the right bank camshaft timing pulley.

25. Install the pusher while pushing the tension pulley to the belt.

26. Pull the pin out from the pusher.

27. Remove the clamps from the pulleys. Turn the crankshaft pulley clockwise two turns. Measure the rod protrusion to be sure it is between 0.16–0.24 in. (4–6mm).

28. Check the stick–out of the pusher plunger against the belt tensioner. Clearance should be 0.16–0.24 in. (4–6mm).

29. Tighten adjusting bolt to 31 ft. lbs. (42 Nm).

30. Tighten pusher bolt to 14 ft. lbs. (19 Nm).

31. Remove crankshaft pulley. Install the timing belt cover and tighten bolts to 12 ft. lbs. (17 Nm).

32. Install the oil cooler hose and tighten brackets to 16 ft. lbs. (22 Nm).

33. Install the crankshaft pulley and tighten bolts to 123 ft. lbs. (167 Nm).

34. Install fan pulley assembly and tighten fixing bolts to 16 ft. lbs. (22 Nm).

35. Install and adjust alternator drive belt.

36. Install and adjust air conditioning drive belt.

37. Install and adjust power steering pump drive belt.

38. Install cooling fan assembly and tighten bolts to 69 inch lbs. (8 Nm).

39. Install upper fan shroud to the radiator.

40. Install air cleaner assembly.

41. Refill and bleed the cooling system.

42. Reconnect the negative battery cable.

43. Check the operation of the engine and valve train.

ADJUSTMENT

✳✳ WARNING

It is very highly recommended that a timing belt be replaced any time its tension is released.

A timing belt should not be viewed as an adjustable component. The timing belt's tension cannot be increased to compensate for wear. If the engine has been disassembled for mechanical work, a new timing belt should be installed. The small cost of a new timing belt is cheap insurance against expensive engine damage which can be caused by the failure of a re–used timing belt.

SETTING THE TENSION OF A NEW TIMING BELT

1. Verify that the camshaft sprocket timing marks are aligned. The groove and the keyway on the crankshaft timing sprocket align with mark on the oil pump. The white pointers on the camshaft timing sprockets align with the dots on the front plate.

2. Install the timing belt. Use clips to secure the belt onto each sprocket until the installation is complete. Align the dotted marks on the timing belt with the timing mark opposite the groove on the crankshaft sprocket.

➡**The arrows on the timing belt must follow the belt's direction rotation. The manufacturer's trademark on the belt's spine should be readable left–to–right when the belt is installed.**

3. Align the white line on the timing belt with the alignment mark on the right bank camshaft timing pulley. Secure the belt with a clip.

4. Rotate the crankshaft counterclockwise to remove the slack between the crankshaft sprocket and the right camshaft timing sprocket.

5. Install the belt around the water pump pulley.

6. Install the belt on the idler pulley.

7. Align the white alignment mark on the timing belt with the alignment mark on the left bank camshaft timing sprocket.

8. Install the crankshaft pulley and tighten the center bolt by hand. Rotate the crankshaft pulley clockwise to give slack between the crankshaft timing pulley and the right bank camshaft timing pulley.

9. Insert a 1.4mm piece of wire through the hole in the pusher to hold the rod in. Install the pusher assembly while pushing the tension pulley toward the belt.

10. Pull the pin out from the pusher to release the rod.

11. Remove the clamps from the sprockets. Rotate the crankshaft pulley clockwise two turns. Measure the rod protrusion to be sure it is 0.16–0.24 in. (4–6mm).

12. If the tensioner pulley bracket pivot bolt was removed, tighten it to 31 ft. lbs. (42 Nm).

13. Tighten pusher bolts to 14 ft. lbs. (19 Nm).

14. Remove crankshaft pulley. Install the lower and upper timing belt covers and tighten their bolts to 12 ft. lbs. (17 Nm).

15. Install the crankshaft pulley and tighten the pulley bolt to 123 ft. lbs. (167 Nm).

TIMING BELT INSPECTION

1. Disconnect the negative and positive battery cables.

2. Label and disconnect the ignition wires and remove the spark plugs. Remove the upper timing belt cover.

3. Rotate the crankshaft to align the camshaft timing marks with the pointer dots on the back covers. Verify that the pointer on the crankshaft aligns with the mark on the lower timing cover.

➡**When the timing marks are aligned on 1994–95 vehicles, no pistons will be at TDC/compression. When the timing marks are aligned on 1995½–96 vehicles, the No. 2 piston is at TDC/compression.**

4. Rotate the crankshaft pulley to cycle the belt through its entire rotation.

5. Inspect the entire length of the timing belt. Look carefully for any signs of the following conditions:

   a. Cracked, chipped, or broken teeth.

   b. Fraying, separation, or heat damage to the belt's rubber and fiber layers.

   c. Oil or coolant leaks which may have contaminated the belt.

   d. Make sure the timing marks align. Misaligned marks may indicate that the belt has jumped one or more teeth, or has been improperly tensioned.

6. Check the camshaft and crankshaft oil seals for any signs of leakage. Also check the water pump for leakage. The source of any oil or coolant leaks must be found and corrected before a new timing belt is installed.

7. Replace the timing belt if it's damaged in any way, or if its condition or the vehicle's maintenance history is uncertain. Isuzu's recommended service interval for timing belt replacement is 60,000 miles (96,000 Km). It's also recommended to install a new water pump when the timing belt is replaced.

8. After inspection, retighten the crankshaft pulley bolt to 123 ft. lbs. (167 Nm). Install the timing belt covers and valve covers. Install the spark plugs and reconnect the ignition wires. Reconnect the battery cables.

1996 3.2L Engine

1. Disconnect the negative battery cable.

2. Drain the engine coolant into a sealable container.

3. Remove the air cleaner assembly and intake air duct.

4. Disconnect the upper radiator hose from the coolant inlet.

5. Remove the upper fan shroud from the radiator.

6. Remove the four nuts retaining the cooling fan assembly. Remove the cooling fan from the fan pulley.

7. Loosen and remove the power steering drive belt.

8. Loosen and remove the air conditioning compressor drive belt.

9. Loosen and remove the alternator drive belt.

10. Remove the upper timing belt covers.

11. Remove the fan pulley assembly.

12. Rotate the crankshaft to align the camshaft timing marks with the pointer dots on the back covers. Verify that the pointer on the crankshaft aligns with the mark on the lower timing cover.

➡When the timing marks are aligned on 1994–95 vehicles, no pistons will be at TDC/compression. When the timing marks are aligned on 1995½–96 vehicles, the No. 2 piston is at TDC/compression.

❉❉ WARNING

Align the camshaft and crankshaft sprockets with their alignment marks before removing the timing belt. Failure to align the belt and sprocket marks may result in valve damage.

13. Use tool No. J–8614–01, or a suitable pulley holding tool to remove the crankshaft pulley center bolt. Remove the crankshaft pulley.

14. Disconnect the two oil cooler hose bracket bolts on the timing cover. Move the oil cooler hoses and bracket off of the lower timing cover.

15. Remove the lower timing belt cover.

16. Remove the pusher assembly (tensioner) from below the belt tensioner pulley. The pusher rod must always be facing upward to prevent oil leakage. Push the pusher rod in, and insert a wire pin into the hole to keep the pusher rod retracted.

17. Remove the timing belt.

18. Use tool No. J–41472, or a suitable pulley holding tool to loosen and remove the camshaft sprocket bolt. Remove the camshaft sprockets.

19. Inspect the water pump and replace it if there is any doubt about its condition.

20. Repair any oil or coolant leaks before installing a new timing belt. If the timing belt has been contaminated with oil or coolant, or is damaged, it must be replaced.

To install:

21. Install the camshaft sprockets. Use a holding tool, and tighten their bolts to 41 ft. lbs. (55 Nm).

22. Verify that the sprocket timing marks are still aligned. The groove and the keyway on the crankshaft timing sprocket align with mark on the oil pump. The white pointers on the camshaft timing sprockets align with the dots on the front plate.

23. Install the timing belt. Use clips to secure the belt onto each sprocket until the installation is complete. Align the dotted marks on the timing belt with the timing mark opposite the groove on the crankshaft sprocket.

➡The arrows on the timing belt must follow the belt's direction rotation. The manufacturer's trademark on the belt's spine should be readable left–to–right when the belt is installed.

24. Align the white line on the timing belt with the alignment mark on the right bank camshaft timing pulley. Secure the belt with a clip.

25. Rotate the crankshaft counterclockwise to remove the slack between the crankshaft sprocket and the right camshaft timing sprocket.

26. Install the belt around the water pump pulley.

27. Install the belt on the idler pulley.

28. Align the white alignment mark on the timing belt with the alignment mark on the left bank camshaft timing sprocket.

29. Install the crankshaft pulley and tighten the center bolt by hand. Rotate the crankshaft pulley clockwise to give slack between the crankshaft timing pulley and the right bank camshaft timing pulley.

30. Insert a 1.4mm piece of wire through the hole in the pusher to hold the rod in. Install the pusher assembly while pushing the tension pulley toward the belt.

31. Pull the pin out from the pusher to release the rod.

32. Remove the clamps from the sprockets. Rotate the crankshaft pulley clockwise two turns. Measure the rod protrusion to be sure it is between 0.16–0.24 in. (4–6mm).

33. If the tensioner pulley bracket pivot bolt was removed, tighten it to 31 ft. lbs. (42 Nm).

34. Tighten pusher bolts to 14 ft. lbs. (19 Nm).

35. Remove the crankshaft pulley. Install the lower and upper timing belt covers and tighten their bolts to 12 ft. lbs. (17 Nm).

36. Fit the oil cooler hose onto the timing cover and tighten its mounting bracket bolts to 16 ft. lbs. (22 Nm).

37. Install the crankshaft pulley and tighten the pulley bolt to 123 ft. lbs. (167 Nm).

38. Install fan pulley assembly and tighten bolts to 16 ft. lbs. (22 Nm).

39. Install and adjust the alternator drive belt.

40. Install and adjust the air conditioning drive belt.

41. Install and adjust the power steering pump drive belt.

42. Install cooling fan assembly and tighten bolts to 6 ft. lbs. (8 Nm).

43. Install upper fan shroud.

44. Install air cleaner assembly and intake air duct.

45. Connect the upper radiator hose to the coolant inlet.

46. Refill and bleed the cooling system.

47. Connect the negative battery cable.

Timing Chain and Gears

REMOVAL & INSTALLATION

1.8L and 2.0L Engines

▶ **See Figures 129, 130, 131, 132 and 133**

1. Disconnect the negative battery cable. Rotate the engine until No. 1 piston is at TDC on the compression stroke.

2. Remove the rocker arm cover, the front cover and the oil pan.

3. Depress or lock the shoe of the automatic chain adjuster in the retracted position.

4. Remove the camshaft sprocket-to-camshaft bolts and the sprocket.

5. Remove the timing chain from the timing sprockets.

6. Using a puller, remove the sprocket and the pinion gear from the crankshaft.

7. Remove the bolt or E-clip and remove the automatic chain adjuster.

8. Inspect the adjuster pin, arm, wedge and rack teeth. Replace assembly if worn. Remove the chain tensioner.

9. Check the timing chain for wear.

10. Check the tensioner pins for wear or damage and replace if necessary.

11. Replace the chain tensioner and adjuster using the E-clips or bolt.

To install:

12. Install the timing sprocket and pinion gear with the groove side toward the front cover. Align the key grooves with the key on the crankshaft, then, drive into position.

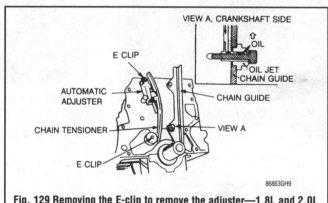

Fig. 129 Removing the E-clip to remove the adjuster—1.8L and 2.0L engines

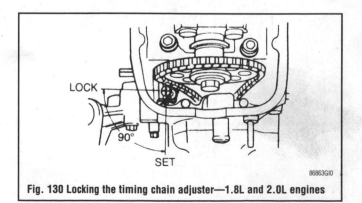

Fig. 130 Locking the timing chain adjuster—1.8L and 2.0L engines

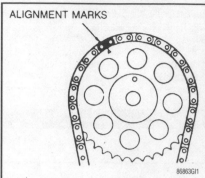

Fig. 131 Aligning the timing chain with the camshaft sprocket—1.8L and 2.0L engines

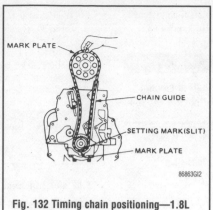

Fig. 132 Timing chain positioning—1.8L and 2.0L engines

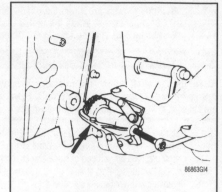

Fig. 133 Using a puller to remove the crankshaft timing gear

13. Confirm the No. 1 piston is at TDC; if not, turn the crankshaft so the key is turned toward the cylinder head side (No. 1 and No. 4 pistons at TDC).

14. Install the timing chain by aligning the mark plate on the chain with the mark on the crankshaft timing sprocket. The side of the chain with the mark plate is on the front side and the side of the chain with the most links between the mark plates is on the chain guide side.

15. Install the camshaft timing sprocket so the mark side of the sprocket faces forward and so the triangular mark aligns with the chain mark plate.

➡Keep the timing chain engaged with the camshaft timing sprocket until the sprocket is installed on the camshaft.

16. Using a new gasket and sealant, install the front cover assembly.
17. Install the rocker arm cover and oil pan.
18. Refill the cooling system and the crankcase.
19. Connect the negative battery cable.

2.8L and 3.1L Engines

♦ **See Figures 134, 135, 136, 137 and 138**

1. Disconnect the negative battery cable.
2. Rotate the crankshaft to position the No. 1 cylinder at the TDC of its compression stroke.

Fig. 134 Timing chain and gears—2.8L engine

Fig. 135 You must first remove the camshaft sprocket to get the timing chain off—2.8L engine

Fig. 136 It is recommended to replace the timing chain and gears as a set—2.8L engine

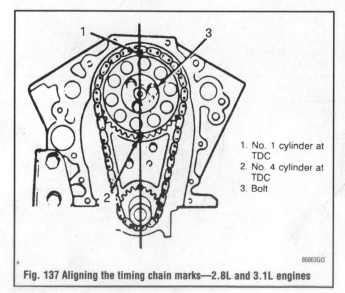

1. No. 1 cylinder at TDC
2. No. 4 cylinder at TDC
3. Bolt

Fig. 137 Aligning the timing chain marks—2.8L and 3.1L engines

3. Remove the front cover.
4. Inspect the sprocket for chipped teeth and wear.
5. Inspect the timing chain for wear; if the chain can be pulled out more than 0.374 in. (9.5mm) from the damper, replace the chain.
6. Remove camshaft sprocket-to-camshaft bolts, the sprocket and the timing chain; if necessary, use a mallet to tap the sprocket from the camshaft.
7. Using a puller tool, pull the crankshaft sprocket from the crankshaft.

To install:

8. Using an installation tool and a hammer, drive the crankshaft sprocket onto the crankshaft; make sure the timing mark faces outward.
9. Using Molykote® or equivalent, lubricate the camshaft sprocket thrust surface and install the timing chain onto the sprocket.
10. While holding the camshaft sprocket and chain vertically, align the marks on the camshaft and crankshaft sprockets.
11. Align the camshaft dowel with the camshaft sprocket hole. Install the camshaft sprocket and torque the bolts to 17 ft. lbs. (23 Nm).
12. Lubricate the timing chain with engine oil.
13. Install the front cover and crankshaft pulley.
14. Connect the negative battery cable.
15. Start the engine, then, check and/or adjust the timing.

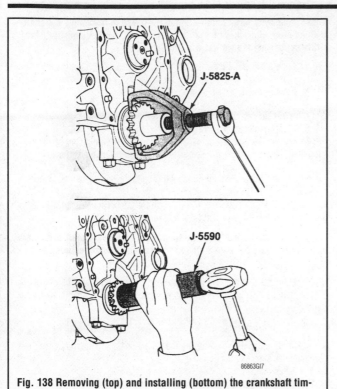

Fig. 138 Removing (top) and installing (bottom) the crankshaft timing gear

Camshaft

Most engines covered by this manual utilize lifters between the camshaft and valve train. On all engines equipped with lifters, a complete new set of lifters must be installed whenever the camshaft is replaced. Excessive camshaft and lifter wear can occur if they are not replaced as a set.

REMOVAL & INSTALLATION

1.8L and 2.0L Engines

▶ See Figure 139

1. Disconnect the negative battery cable.
2. Remove the rocker arm cover.
3. Rotate the engine until the No. 4 piston is at Top Dead Center (TDC) on the compression stroke. Remove the distributor cap and mark the rotor to housing position.
4. Release the tension on the automatic timing chain adjuster by performing the following procedures:

a. Using a small prybar, depress the lock lever on the automatic adjuster rearward.
b. Push on the automatic adjuster shoe and lock it into the retracted position by releasing the lever.
5. Remove the camshaft sprocket-to-camshaft bolt, the sprocket and suspend the assembly on the wire; allow the chain to remain on the sprocket.
6. Remove the rocker arm brackets-to-cylinder head bolts and the rocker arm bracket assembly from the cylinder head.
7. Remove the camshaft from the cylinder head.

To install:
8. Lubricate the camshaft with engine oil and install it onto the cylinder head.
9. Install the rocker arm assembly onto the cylinder head and torque the bolts to 16 ft. lbs. (21 Nm).
10. Align the camshaft sprocket hole with camshaft dowel pin and install the sprocket. Torque the camshaft sprocket-to-camshaft bolt to 50–65 ft. lbs. (68–88 Nm).
11. Set the automatic adjuster by turning the adjuster slide pin 90° counterclockwise with a small prybar.
12. Adjust the valve lash.
13. Install the rocker arm cover and make sure the alignment marks are aligned.
14. To complete the installation, reverse the removal procedures. Start the engine and check and/or adjust the timing.

Diesel Engine

▶ See Figure 140

1. Disconnect the negative battery cable.
2. Drain the crankcase. Remove the oil pan and the oil pump.

✳✳ CAUTION

The EPA warns that prolonged contact with used engine oil may cause a number of skin disorders, including cancer! You should make every effort to minimize your exposure to used engine oil. Protective gloves should be worn when changing the oil. Wash your hands and any other exposed skin areas as soon as possible after exposure to used engine oil. Soap and water, or waterless hand cleaner should be used.

3. Remove the timing belt cover, the timing belt, the camshaft sprocket.
4. Remove the rocker arm assembly, the pushrods and the valve lifters; be sure to keep the parts in order for reinstallation purposes.
5. Remove the camshaft retainer-to-engine bolts and the retainer. Using a small prybar, pry the oil seal from the cylinder block.
6. Screw a bolt into the camshaft and carefully remove the camshaft from the front of the engine; be careful not to damage the bearing surfaces.
7. Inspect the camshaft for wear, scoring and/or damage; if necessary, replace it.

To install:
8. Lubricate the camshaft with engine oil and insert it into the front of the engine.

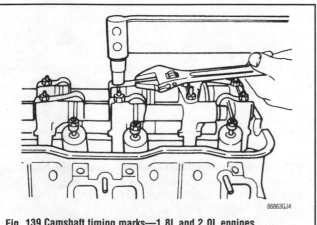

Fig. 139 Camshaft timing marks—1.8L and 2.0L engines

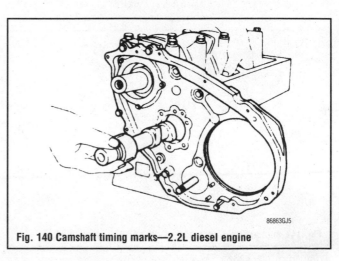

Fig. 140 Camshaft timing marks—2.2L diesel engine

9. Using a new oil seal, lubricate the seal lips with engine oil and install it into the engine.

10. Install the camshaft retainer and the camshaft sprocket.

11. Install the oil pump and the oil pan.

12. Install the valve lifters, the pushrods and the rocker arm assembly.

13. Install and adjust the timing belt. Install the timing belt cover.

14. Rotate the crankshaft to bring the No. 1 piston to TDC of the compression stroke and adjust the valve lash.

15. To complete the installation, reverse the removal procedures.

16. Refill the cooling system and the crankcase.

17. Connect the negative battery cable. Start the engine, allow it to reach normal operating temperatures.

18. Check and/or adjust the idle speed and timing.

2.3L and 2.6L Engines

Removal of the camshaft involves replacement of the timing belt and rocker arm assembly. Review those procedures first before proceeding further. It is not possible to replace the camshaft without completely disassembling the front cover, due to the need to align the timing belt marks on both the camshaft and crankshaft. The timing belt should be replaced any time the camshaft is serviced.

1. Disconnect the negative battery cable.

2. Rotate the crankshaft to position the No. 4 cylinder on the TDC of its compression stroke.

3. Remove the distributor cap and move it aside. Matchmark the rotor to the distributor housing and the distributor housing to the engine. Remove the distributor.

4. Remove the rocker arm cover, the timing belt cover and the timing belt. Refer to procedures in the section.

5. Remove the rocker arm assembly-to-cylinder head bolts, the rocker arm assembly and the camshaft. If necessary, remove the camshaft sprocket-to-camshaft bolt and the sprocket.

To install:

6. Lubricate the camshaft with engine oil and position it onto the cylinder head.

7. Install the rocker arm assembly and torque the bolts to bolts to 6 ft. lbs. (8 Nm) and the nuts to 16 ft. lbs. (22 Nm).

8. Align the timing marks and install the timing belt.

9. Using a new gasket, install the rocker arm cover.

10. Install the timing belt cover.

11. Align the matchmarks and install the distributor to the cylinder head.

12. To complete the installation, reverse the removal procedures.

13. With the timing marks aligned, start the engine, then, check and/or adjust the engine timing.

2.8L and 3.1L Engines

▶ See Figure 141

Removal of the camshaft involves replacement of the timing chain assembly and removal of the radiator and usually front grille. Review those procedures first before proceeding further. If replacing the camshaft you should always install all new hydraulic lifters, and a new timing chain and gear set.

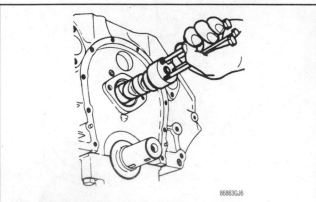

86863GJ6

Fig. 141 Replacing the camshaft—2.8L and 3.1L engines

➡ **Use long bolts threaded into the camshaft to help remove the shaft without damaging the camshaft bearings. Remove the camshaft slowly while supporting the weight with the long bolt.**

1. Relieve the fuel pressure. Disconnect the negative battery cable.

2. Remove the timing cover and the camshaft sprocket.

3. Remove the upper fan shroud and the radiator.

4. Disconnect the fuel line(s), the accelerator linkage, the vacuum hoses and electrical connectors from the throttle body unit.

5. Remove the rocker arm covers.

6. Loosen the valves, rotate them 90° and remove the pushrods; be sure to keep them aligned so they may be installed in their original positions.

7. Remove the intake manifold.

8. Using a hydraulic lifter removal tool, pull the valve lifters from the engine.

9. Using 3 long bolts, thread them into the camshaft holes. Grasp the bolts and carefully, pull the camshaft from the front of the engine.

➡ **All the camshaft bearing journals are the same diameter; exercise care in removing the camshaft so the bearings do not become damaged.**

To install:

10. Lubricate the camshaft with engine oil and install it into the engine.

11. Using a hydraulic lifter installation tool, install the hydraulic lifters into the engine.

12. Using new gaskets and sealant, install the intake manifold.

13. Install the pushrods and the rocker arms.

14. Install the camshaft sprocket, the timing chain and the front cover; be sure the timing marks are aligned.

15. Adjust the valves.

16. Using new gaskets, install the rocker arm covers.

17. To complete the installation, reverse the removal procedures. Refill the cooling system.

18. Start the engine and allow it to reach normal operating temperatures. Check and/or adjust the timing.

3.2L SOHC Engine

1992–95 VEHICLES

▶ See Figure 142

➡ **Isuzu has issued a recall notice for 1993–94 Troopers equipped with 3.2L SOHC engines. This is campaign number 94V–094, and involves faulty camshaft end plugs. The plugs may dislodge from the cylinder heads and can cause rapid oil loss. Remember this when ordering parts; a service kit is available for affected vehicles.**

1. Disconnect the negative battery cable.

2. Remove the air cleaner assembly.

3. Remove the upper cooling fan shroud.

4. Remove the cooling fan assembly.

5. Disconnect the accelerator cable from the throttle body and remove it from the bracket.

6. Disconnect the canister vacuum hose from the vacuum pipe.

7. Disconnect the vacuum booster hose from the common chamber.

8. Disconnect the MAP sensor; Canister vacuum switching valve (VSV); Exhaust gas recirculation (VSV); Intake air temperature sensor and ground connectors.

9. Remove the spark plug wires from the cylinder head cover.

10. Remove the ignition control module assembly.

11. Remove the four bolts and the throttle body from the common chamber.

12. Disconnect the vacuum hoses from the throttle body.

13. Disconnect the positive crankcase ventilation hose from the common chamber.

14. Disconnect the fuel pressure control valve vacuum hose from the common chamber.

15. Disconnect the evaporative emission canister purge hose from the common chamber.

16. Remove the EGR valve assembly.

17. Remove the common chamber from the intake manifold.

18. Disconnect the fuel feed and return hoses from the fuel rail assembly.

19. Remove the accessory drive belts.

20. Remove the power steering pump.

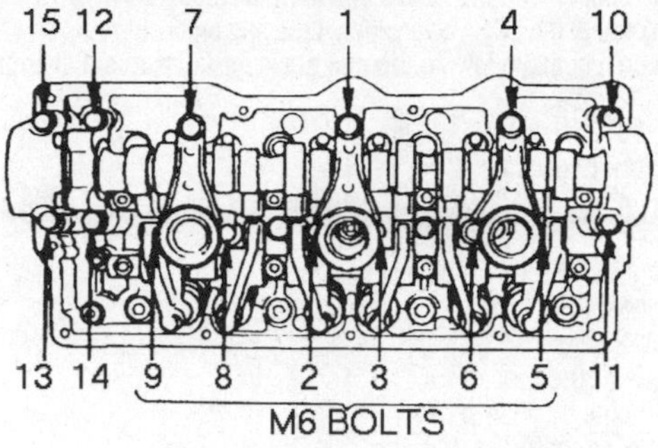

Fig. 142 Camshaft mounting bolts torque sequence—3.2L SOHC engine

21. Remove the fan pulley assembly.
22. Remove the crankshaft pulley and damper.
23. Remove the timing belt cover.
24. Remove the timing belt auto tensioner (pusher). The pusher prevents air from entering the oil chamber. Its rod must always be facing upward.
25. Align the timing marks and remove the timing belt. After the timing marks are aligned, the engine must not be disturbed.
26. Remove the cylinder head cover(s).
27. Remove the camshaft pulley.
28. Remove the camshaft front plate.
29. Remove the camshaft mounting bracket bolts and the camshaft.

To install:
30. Install new camshaft seals and retaining plates onto the cylinder. Tighten the right camshaft seal retaining plate 6mm bolts to 65 inch lbs. (7 Nm). Tighten the left camshaft seal retaining plate 8mm bolts to 191 inch lbs. (21.5 Nm).
31. Apply sealant to the mounting surfaces on the cylinder head where the front and rear camshaft mounting brackets attach to the cylinder head.
32. Install the camshaft and mounting brackets. Torque the bolts in sequence to 69 inch lbs. (8 Nm) for the M6 bolts and 13 ft. lbs. (18 Nm) for the M8 bolts.
33. Install the front plate. Torque the bolts to 12 ft. lbs. (17 Nm).
34. Install the camshaft pulley. Torque the mounting bolts to 41 ft. lbs. (55 Nm).
35. Apply sealant to both sides of the front and rear camshaft mounting brackets and install the cylinder head cover(s). Torque the bolts to 69 inch lbs. (8 Nm). Do not overtighten the cylinder head covers: they crack very easily.
36. Install the timing belt.
37. Install the timing belt auto tensioner. Torque the mounting bolts to 13 ft. lbs. (18 Nm).
38. Rotate the crankshaft by hand to verify that the timing belt is aligned properly and there is no piston–to–valve interference.
39. Install the timing belt cover.
40. Install the oil cooler hoses and bracket.
41. Install the crankshaft pulley assembly. Torque the center bolt to 123 ft. lbs. (167 Nm).
42. Install the fan pulley assembly. Torque the mounting bolts to 16 ft. lbs. (22 Nm).
43. Install the power steering pump.
44. Install the accessory drive belts.
45. Connect the fuel hoses to the fuel rail assembly.
46. Install the common chamber. Torque the bolts and nuts to 17 ft. lbs. (24 Nm) in a crisscross pattern.
47. Install the EGR valve assembly. Torque the mounting bolts on the valve side to 69 inch lbs. (8 Nm) and the bolts on the exhaust side to 21 ft. lbs. (28 Nm).
48. Connect the evaporative emission canister purge hose.
49. Connect the fuel pressure control valve vacuum hose.
50. Connect the positive crankcase ventilation hose.
51. Install the throttle body assembly. Torque the mounting bolts to 14 ft. lbs. (19 Nm).
52. Connect the vacuum hoses to the throttle body.
53. Install the ignition control module and the spark plug wires.

54. Connect the MAP sensor; Canister vacuum switching valve (VSV); Exhaust gas recirculation (VSV); Intake air temperature sensor and ground connectors.
55. Connect the vacuum booster hose.
56. Connect the air vacuum hose.
57. Connect the accelerator cable. Adjust the accelerator cable by pulling the cable housing while closing the throttle valve and tightening the adjusting nut and screw cap by hand temporarily. Now loosen the adjusting nut by three turns and then tightening the screw cap. Make sure the throttle valve reaches the screw stop when the throttle is closed.
58. Install the cooling fan assembly and the upper fan shroud.
59. Install the air cleaner assembly.
60. Connect the negative battery cable.

1996 VEHICLES

▶ See Figure 142

✳✳ CAUTION

Fuel injection systems remain under pressure even after the engine has been turned off. The fuel system pressure must be relieved before disconnecting any fuel lines. Failure to do so may result in fire and personal injury.

1. Relieve the fuel system pressure:
   a. Remove the fuel filler cap.
   b. Remove the fuel pump relay from the underhood relay box.
   c. Start the engine and let it run until it stalls. Then, crank the engine for an additional 30 seconds.
   d. Turn the ignition switch to the **OFF** position.
2. Disconnect the negative battery cable and reinstall the fuel pump relay.
3. Drain the coolant into a sealable container.
4. Support the hood as far open as possible.
5. Remove the air intake duct and the air cleaner box.
6. Disconnect and remove the upper and lower radiator hoses. Catch any coolant that runs out.
7. Loosen and remove the power steering pump, A/C compressor, and alternator drive belts.
8. Remove the cooling fan and its pulley assembly.
9. Unbolt the power steering pump mounting bracket. Move the pump and bracket out of the way without disconnecting the hydraulic lines.
10. Disconnect the throttle cable from the throttle body linkage.
11. Label and disconnect the following vacuum hoses from the intake manifold chamber:
   a. PCV hose
   b. EVAP canister vacuum hose
   c. Brake booster hose
12. Label and disconnect the following sensor connectors from the rear of the intake manifold chamber:
   a. Ignition control module connectors
   b. Linear EGR valve
   c. MAP sensor
   d. EVAP purge valve
   e. Throttle position sensor
   f. Idle air control valve
   g. Intake air temperature sensor
13. Disconnect the EGR valve supply tube and bracket.
14. First, remove the throttle body, and then remove the intake manifold chamber.
15. Carefully clean any dirt from the fuel rail and fuel fittings.
16. Disconnect the fuel feed and return lines from the front of the fuel rail. Clean up any spilled fuel.
17. Remove the intake manifold gaskets. Be careful not to drop any pieces of the gaskets into the engine. Don't scratch or gouge the machined aluminum mating surfaces of the intake manifold and engine block.
18. Cover the intake openings with a sheet of plastic or clean shop towels to keep out dirt and foreign objects.
19. Label the ignition coil assemblies and disconnect them from the wiring harness. Remove the coil assemblies so they won't be damaged.
20. Unbolt the oil cooler line brackets from the timing belt covers.
21. Remove the upper timing belt covers.

22. Rotate the crankshaft to align the camshaft timing marks with the pointer dots on the back covers. When the timing marks are aligned, the No. 2 piston is at TDC/compression.

23. Remove the crankshaft pulley. Remove the lower timing belt cover.

24. Remove the pusher assembly (tensioner) from below the timing belt tensioner pulley. The pusher rod must always be facing upward to prevent oil leakage. Push the pusher rod in, and insert a wire pin into the hole to keep the pusher rod retracted.

25. Remove the timing belt.

✸✸ WARNING

If the timing belt is worn, damaged, or shows signs of oil or coolant contamination, it must be replaced.

26. Loosen the valve cover bolts in a crisscross sequence. Remove the valve covers.

27. Remove the camshaft sprockets and back covers.

28. Loosen the camshaft holder bolts in a crisscross sequence to prevent warping.

29. Remove the camshaft and camshaft holders from the cylinder head.

30. Inspect the camshaft lobes and journals for signs of wear or damage.

To install:

31. Make sure all mating surfaces are clean and free of oil, coolant, or gasket residue.

32. Lubricate the camshaft lobes and journals with clean engine oil.

33. Apply a bead of sealant to the front and rear camshaft holder mating surfaces on the cylinder head.

34. Install the camshaft and holder assembly onto the cylinder head before the sealant cures. Install the camshaft holder bolts, but don't tighten them yet.

35. Use a crisscross sequence to tighten the camshaft holder bolts. Tighten the 8mm bolts to 13 ft. lbs. (18 Nm). Tighten the 6mm bolts to 6 ft. lbs. (8 Nm).

36. Use a seal driver to install a new camshaft seal.

37. Install the camshaft sprocket back covers and tighten their bolts to 12 ft. lbs. (17 Nm).

38. Install the camshaft sprockets so that the timing marks are aligned. Tighten the bolts to 46 ft. lbs. (64 Nm).

39. Apply a 2–3mm bead of sealant to the joint were the camshaft holders meet the cylinder head. Install the valve cover with a new gasket before the sealant cures.

40. Tighten the valve cover bolts to 6 ft. lbs. (8 Nm) in crisscross pattern.

41. Verify that the camshaft and crankshaft timing marks are properly aligned.

42. Install and tension the timing belt. Tighten the pusher bolts to 14 ft. lbs. (19 Nm).

43. Install the lower timing belt covers and tighten the bolts to 13 ft. lbs. (18 Nm). Install the crankshaft pulley. Tighten the pulley bolt to 123 ft. lbs. (167 Nm).

44. Install the upper timing belt covers and tighten the bolts to 13 ft. lbs. (18 Nm).

45. Fit the oil cooler line brackets onto the timing cover and tighten the bolts to 13 ft. lbs. (18 Nm).

46. Reconnect the fuel feed and return lines.

47. Install and reconnect the ignition coil assemblies.

48. Install the intake manifold chamber and throttle body with new gaskets. Tighten the nuts and bolts to 17 ft. lbs. (24 Nm).

49. Reconnect the throttle cable to the throttle body linkage.

50. Reconnect the EGR valve supply tube and bracket.

51. Reconnect the following vacuum to the intake manifold chamber:
   a. PCV hose
   b. EVAP canister vacuum hose
   c. Brake booster hose

52. Reconnect the following sensor connectors to the rear of the intake manifold chamber:
   a. Ignition control module connectors
   b. Linear EGR valve
   c. MAP sensor
   d. EVAP purge valve
   e. Throttle position sensor
   f. Idle air control valve
   g. Intake air temperature sensor

53. Install the power steering pump and mounting bracket.

54. Install the cooling fan and its pulley assembly.

55. Install and tension the alternator, A/C compressor, and power steering pump drive belts.

56. Install and reconnect the upper and lower radiator hoses.

57. Install the air cleaner box and air intake duct.

58. Verify that all fuel lines, vacuum and coolant hoses, and wiring harness have been reconnected.

59. Refill the engine with fresh coolant.

60. Crank the engine until it starts. A longer–than–normal starting time may be necessary due to air in the fuel lines. Check all fuel line connections for leaks.

61. Bleed any air from the cooling system.

62. Bleed the power steering system if necessary.

63. Check the throttle cable operation and adjustment.

64. Check the engine oil level and add if necessary.

3.2L DOHC Engine

▶ See Figures 143, 144 and 145

➡️**Isuzu has issued a recall notice for 1993–94 Troopers equipped with 3.2L DOHC engines. This is campaign number 94V–094, and involves faulty camshaft end plugs. The plugs may dislodge from the cylinder heads and can cause rapid oil loss. Remember this when ordering parts: a service kit is available for affected vehicles.**

1. Relieve the fuel pressure:
   a. Remove the fuel filler cap.
   b. Remove the fuel pump relay from the underhood relay box.
   c. Start the engine and let it run until it stalls. Then, crank the engine for an additional 30 seconds.
   d. Turn the ignition switch to the **OFF** position.

2. Disconnect the negative battery cable. Install the fuel pump relay.

3. Remove the air cleaner assembly.

4. Remove the upper cooling fan shroud.

5. Remove the cooling fan assembly.

6. Disconnect the accelerator cable from the throttle body and remove it from the bracket.

7. Disconnect the canister vacuum hose from the vacuum pipe.

8. Disconnect the vacuum booster hose from the common chamber.

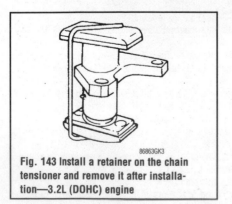

Fig. 143 Install a retainer on the chain tensioner and remove it after installation—3.2L (DOHC) engine

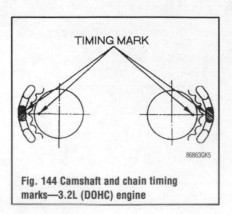

Fig. 144 Camshaft and chain timing marks—3.2L (DOHC) engine

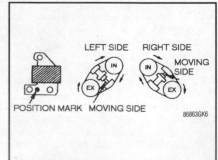

Fig. 145 Chain tensioner installed position—3.2L (DOHC) engine

9. Disconnect the following connectors:
   a. MAP sensor
   b. Canister vacuum switching valve (VSV)
   c. Exhaust gas recirculation (VSV)
   d. Intake air temperature sensor
   e. Ground cables
10. Disconnect and label the spark plug wires.
11. Remove the ignition control module assembly with the spark plug wire attached.
12. Remove the four bolts to separate the throttle body from the common chamber.
13. Disconnect the vacuum hoses from the throttle body.
14. Disconnect the positive crankcase ventilation (PCV) hose from the common chamber.
15. Disconnect the fuel pressure control valve vacuum hose from the common chamber.
16. Disconnect the evaporative emission canister purge hose from the common chamber.
17. Remove the EGR valve assembly.
18. Remove the common chamber air duct.
19. Remove the common chamber from the intake manifold.
20. Disconnect the fuel feed and return hoses from the fuel rail assembly.
21. Remove the accessory drive belts.
22. Remove the power steering pump.
23. Remove the fan pulley assembly.
24. Remove the crankshaft pulley and damper.
25. Remove the oil cooler hoses and bracket.
26. Remove the timing belt cover.
27. Align the timing marks
28. Remove the timing belt auto tensioner (pusher). The pusher prevents air from entering the oil chamber. Its rod must always be facing upward.
29. Remove the timing belt.
30. Remove the cylinder head covers.
31. Remove the camshaft pulley.
32. Remove the camshaft front plate.
33. Remove the camshaft mounting bracket bolts.
34. Remove the camshaft chain tensioner bolts.
35. Remove the camshafts with the timing chain and tensioner attached.

To install:

➡**Install a retainer on the chain tensioner to prevent the plunger from moving. Remove the retainer after installation.**

36. Apply sealant to the cylinder head mounting surface of the front and rear camshaft mounting brackets.
37. Apply clean engine oil to the camshaft journals, lobes, and sprockets.
38. Install the camshaft assembly with the chain and tensioner. Take care not to install the wrong tensioner, the left and right tensioners are different and they are marked accordingly. Make sure the timing marks on the camshaft chain sprockets are aligned with the timing marks on the chain links. Torque the camshaft holder mounting bolts to 87 inch lbs. (10 Nm).
39. Install the chain tensioner. Torque the bolts to 14 ft. lbs. (19 Nm).
40. Install new camshaft seals and retaining plates onto the cylinder. Tighten the rear camshaft seal retaining plate 6mm bolts to 70 inch lbs. (8 Nm). Tighten the front camshaft seal retaining bolts to 65 inch lbs. (7 Nm).

41. Install the camshaft pulley. Hold the camshaft with an open ended wrench to prevent it from turning and torque the pulley bolts to 41 ft. lbs. (55 Nm) for 1992–94 vehicles, or 46 ft. lbs. (63 Nm) for 1995 vehicles.
42. Apply sealant to both sides of the front and rear camshaft mounting brackets and install the cylinder head cover(s). Torque the bolts to 69 inch lbs. (8 Nm). Don't overtorque the bolts, as the head covers may crack.
43. Install the timing belt.
44. Install the timing belt auto tensioner. Torque the mounting bolts to 14 ft. lbs. (19 Nm).
45. Install the timing belt cover.
46. Install the oil cooler hoses and bracket.
47. Install the crankshaft pulley assembly. Torque the center bolt to 123 ft. lbs. (167 Nm).
48. Install the fan pulley assembly. Torque the mounting bolts to 16 ft. lbs. (22 Nm).
49. Install the power steering pump.
50. Install the accessory drive belts.
51. Connect the fuel hoses to the fuel rail assembly.
52. Install the common chamber. Torque the bolts and nuts to 17 ft. lbs. (24 Nm).
53. Install the common chamber air duct. Torque the nuts and bolts to 17 ft. lbs. (24 Nm).
54. Connect the ground cable.
55. Install the EGR valve assembly. Torque the mounting bolts on the valve side to 69 inch lbs. (8 Nm) and the bolts on the exhaust side to 21 ft. lbs. (28 Nm).
56. Connect the evaporative emission canister purge hose.
57. Connect the fuel pressure control valve vacuum hose.
58. Reconnect the fuel lines using new washers.
59. Connect the positive crankcase ventilation hose.
60. Install the throttle body assembly. Torque the mounting bolts to 14 ft. lbs. (19 Nm).
61. Connect the vacuum hoses to the throttle body.
62. Install the ignition control module and the spark plug wires.
63. Connect the MAP sensor; Canister Vacuum Switching Valve (VSV); Exhaust Gas Recirculation (EGR), the Intake air temperature sensor connectors; and ground cables.
64. Connect the vacuum booster hose.
65. Connect the air vacuum hose.
66. Connect the accelerator cable. Adjust the accelerator cable by pulling the cable housing while closing the throttle valve and tightening the adjusting nut and screw cap by hand temporarily. Now loosen the adjusting nut by three turns and then tightening the screw cap. Make sure the throttle valve reaches the screw stop when the throttle is closed.
67. Install the cooling fan assembly and the upper fan shroud.
68. Install the air cleaner assembly.
69. Connect the negative battery cable.
70. Start the engine and check for fuel leaks.

INSPECTION

◆ **See Figures 146, 147 and 148**

Using solvent, degrease the camshaft and clean out all of the oil holes. Visually inspect the cam lobes and bearing journals for excessive wear. If a lobe is

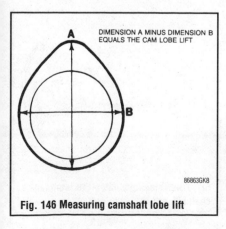

Fig. 146 Measuring camshaft lobe lift

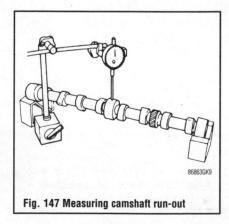

Fig. 147 Measuring camshaft run-out

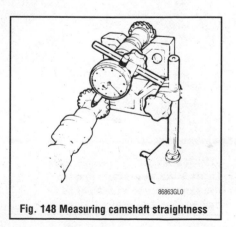

Fig. 148 Measuring camshaft straightness

questionable, check all of the lobes as indicated. If a journal or lobe is worn, the camshaft MUST BE or replaced.

➡️**If a journal is worn, there is a good chance that the bearings or journals are worn and need replacement.**

If the lobes and journals appear intact, place the front and rear journals in V-blocks and rest a dial indicator on the center journal. Rotate the camshaft to check the straightness. If deviation exceeds 0.001 in. (0.0254mm), replace the camshaft.

Check the camshaft lobes with a micrometer, by measuring the lobes from the nose to the base and again at 90° (see illustration). The lobe lift is determined by subtracting the second measurement from the first. If all of the exhaust and intake lobes are not identical, the camshaft must be reground or replace.

Camshaft Bearings

REMOVAL & INSTALLATION

▶ **See Figures 149, 150 and 151**

➡️**Overhead valve engines (2.8L, 3.1L and 2.2L diesel) are equipped with removable camshaft bearings. Overhead camshaft engines, however, do not have removable camshaft bearings; on these engines, the journal is cast into the cylinder head and also acts as the bearing.**

The camshaft, lifters, flywheel and the expansion plug (at the rear of the camshaft) must be removed. Drive the expansion plug out from the inside of the engine block. On overhead camshaft engines, have a machine shop check the heads if the bearing surface is damaged.

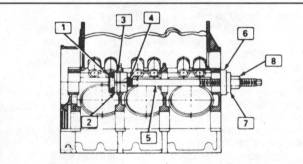

1. Backup nut
2. Expanding collet
3. Bearing
4. Expanding mandrel
5. Two piece puller
6. Pulling plate
7. Thrust gearing
8. Pulling nut

86863GL1

Fig. 149 Removal and installation of camshaft bearings—2.8L and 3.1L engines

2.8L, 3.1L and 2.2L Diesel Engines

➡️**It is recommended that the engine be removed from the vehicle before attempting this procedure. A machine shop is better equipped to replace camshaft bearings and check the bearing alignment.**

To remove the camshaft bearings, the camshaft, lifters, flywheel, rear camshaft expansion plug, and crankshaft must be removed.

Camshaft bearings can be replaced with engine completely or partially disassembled. To replace bearings without complete disassembly, remove the camshaft and crankshaft, leaving the cylinder heads attached and the pistons in place. Before removing the crankshaft, install rubber fuel hoses on the threads of the connecting rod bolts to prevent damage to the crankshaft. Fasten the connecting rods against the sides of the engine so they will not be in the way while replacing the camshaft bearings. Use rubber bands and the oil pan bolts to hold the connecting rods away from the crankshaft during removal.

If excessive wear is indicated, or if the engine is being completely rebuilt, camshaft bearings should be replaced as follows: Drive the camshaft rear plug from the block. Assemble the removal puller with its shoulder on the bearing to be removed. Gradually tighten the puller nut until bearing is removed. Remove remaining bearings, leaving the front and rear for last. To remove front and rear bearings, reverse position of the tool, so as to pull the bearings in toward the center of the block. Leave the tool in this position, pilot the new front and rear bearings on the installer, and pull them into position: Return the tool to its original position and pull remaining bearings into position.

➡️**Ensure that the oil holes align when installing the bearings.**

Replace camshaft rear plug, and stake it into position to aid retention.

Rear Main Seal

REMOVAL & INSTALLATION

One-Piece Seal

▶ **See Figure 152**

➡️**Either the engine or the transmission must be removed to replace the rear main seal. Most engines, other than the 2.3L and 2.6L, have one-piece rear crankshaft oil seals. The oil pan does not have to be removed to access the seal.**

1. Disconnect the negative battery cable. Raise and safely support the vehicle.
2. Drain the engine oil and remove the oil pan.

✳✳ CAUTION

The EPA warns that prolonged contact with used engine oil may cause a number of skin disorders, including cancer! You should make every effort to minimize your exposure to used engine oil. Protective gloves should be worn when changing the oil. Wash your hands and any other exposed skin areas as soon as possible after

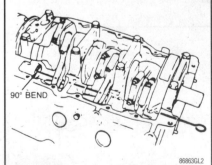

Fig. 150 Aligning the camshaft bearing oil holes with a piece of wire bent at a 90 degree angle. The holes MUST be in alignment— 2.8L and 3.1L engine

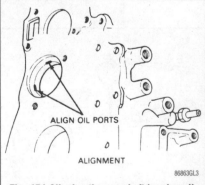

Fig. 151 Aligning the camshaft bearing oil holes. The holes MUST be in alignment— diesel engine

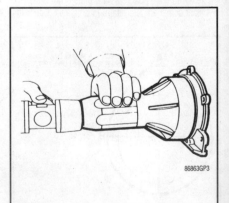

Fig. 152 Installing a one-piece rear crankshaft oil seal

exposure to used engine oil. Soap and water, or waterless hand cleaner should be used.

3. If equipped with an automatic transmission, remove the transmission. If equipped with a manual transmission, remove the transmission and clutch assembly.

4. Remove the starter without disconnecting the wires and secure it aside.

5. Remove the flywheel-to-crankshaft bolts and the flywheel.

6. Carefully, remove the oil seal, using a small prybar; work the tool around the diameter of the seal until the seal begins to lift out. Use care not to damage the seat and area around the seal.

7. Fill the space between the seal lips with grease and lubricate the seal lips with clean engine oil. Install the new oil seal.

8. Install the flywheel, transmission and starter motor.

9. Connect the battery cable, start the engine and check for leaks.

Two-Piece Seal

▶ See Figure 153

Both halves of the rear main oil seal can be replaced without removing the crankshaft. Always replace the upper and lower seal together. The lip should face the front of the engine. Be very careful that you do not break the sealing bead in the channel on the outside portion of the seal while installing it. An installation tool can be fabricated to protect the seal bead.

1. Remove the oil pan and rear main bearing cap.

2. Remove the oil seal from the bearing cap by prying it out.

3. Remove the upper half of the seal with a small punch. Drive it around far enough to be gripped with pliers. **Be very careful not to damage the crankshaft sealing surface.**

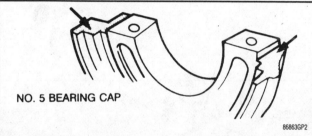

NO. 5 BEARING CAP

86863GP2

Fig. 153 Apply sealant to the rear main bearing cap at the arrowed locations—two-piece oil seal

To install:

4. Clean the crankshaft and bearing cap.

5. Coat the lips and bead of the seal with light engine oil, keeping oil from the ends of the seal.

6. Position the a suitable tool between the crankshaft and seal seat.

7. Position the seal between the crankshaft and tip of the tool so that the seal bead contacts the tip of the tool. The oil seal lip should face forward.

8. Roll the seal around the crankshaft using the tool to protect the seal bead from the sharp corners of the crankcase.

9. The installation tool should be left installed until the seal is properly positioned with both ends flush with the block.

10. Remove the tool.

11. Install the other half of the seal in the bearing cap using the tool in the same manner as before. Light thumb pressure should install the seal.

12. Install the bearing cap with sealant applied to the mating areas of the cap and block. Keep sealant from the ends of the seal.

13. Torque the rear main bearing cap to specifications.

14. Install the oil pan and refill the engine with oil. Start the engine and check for leaks.

Flywheel/Flexplate

On most of the engines covered by this manual, the flywheel and the ring gear are machined from one piece of metal and cannot be separated. On some of the engines, however, the ring gear is a separate piece and can be driven from the flywheel, once the gear is heated with a torch.

REMOVAL & INSTALLATION

1. Remove the transmission assembly from the vehicle.

2. If equipped with a manual transmission, remove the clutch and pressure plate assembly.

3. Remove the flywheel-to-crankshaft bolts, then remove the flywheel from the engine.

To install:

4. Inspect the flywheel for cracks, and inspect the ring gear for burrs or worn teeth. Replace the flywheel if any damage is apparent. Remove burrs with a mill file.

5. Install the flywheel. Most flywheels will only attach to the crankshaft in one position, as the bolt holes are unevenly spaced and/or the crankshaft is fitted with a dowel pin. Install the bolts and torque to specification using a crisscross pattern.

6. If equipped, install the clutch and pressure plate assembly.

7. Install the transmission assembly.

EXHAUST SYSTEM

General Information

Two types of pipe connections are used on most exhaust systems, they are: the ball joint (to allow angular movement for alignment purposes) and the slip joint. Gaskets are used only with the ball joint type connections.

The system is supported by free hanging rubber mountings which permit some movement of the exhaust system but do not allow the transfer of noise and vibration into the passenger compartment. Any noise vibrations or rattles in the exhaust system are usually caused by misalignment of the parts.

✳ CAUTION

Before performing any operation on the exhaust system, be sure to allow it to cool.

Whenever working on the exhaust system always keep the following in mind:

• Check the complete exhaust system for open seams, holes loose connections, or other deterioration which could permit exhaust fumes to seep into the passenger compartment.

• The exhaust system is usually supported by free-hanging rubber mountings which permit some movement of the exhaust system, but does not permit transfer of noise and vibration into the passenger compartment. Do not replace the rubber mounts with solid ones.

• Before removing any component of the exhaust system, ALWAYS squirt a

liquid rust dissolving agent onto the fasteners for ease of removal. A lot of knuckle skin will be saved by following this rule. It may even be wise to spray the fasteners and allow them to sit overnight.

✳ CAUTION

Allow the exhaust system to cool sufficiently before spraying a solvent exhaust fasteners. Some solvents are highly flammable and could ignite when sprayed on hot exhaust components.

• Annoying rattles and noise vibrations in the exhaust system are usually caused by misalignment of the parts. When aligning the system, leave all bolts and nuts loose until all parts are properly aligned, then tighten, working from front to rear.

Safety Precautions

For a number of reasons, exhaust system work can be the most dangerous type of work you can do on your car. Always observe the following precautions:

➡**Safety glasses should be worn at all times when working on or near the exhaust system. Older exhaust systems will almost always be covered with loose rust particles which will shower you when disturbed. These particles are more than a nuisance and could injure your eye.**

• When installing exhaust system parts, make sure there is enough clearance between the hot exhaust parts and pipes and hoses that would be adversely affected by excessive heat. Also make sure there is adequate clearance from the floor pan to avoid possible overheating of the floor.

• Support the vehicle extra securely. Not only will you often be working directly under it, but you'll frequently be using a lot of force, say, heavy hammer blows, to dislodge rusted parts. This can cause a vehicle that's improperly supported to shift and possibly fall.

• Wear goggles. Exhaust system parts are always rusty. Metal chips can be dislodged, even when you're only turning rusted bolts. Attempting to pry pipes apart with a chisel makes the chips fly even more frequently.

• If you're using a cutting torch, keep it a great distance from either the fuel tank or lines. Stop what you're doing and feel the temperature of the fuel bearing pipes on the tank frequently. Even slight heat can expand and/or vaporize fuel, resulting in accumulated vapor, or even a liquid leak, near your torch.

• Watch where your hammer blows fall and make sure you hit squarely. You could easily tap a brake or fuel line when you hit an exhaust system part with a glancing blow. Inspect all lines and hoses in the area where you've been working.

Special Tools

A number of special exhaust system tools can be rented from auto supply houses or local stores that rent special equipment. A common one is a tail pipe expander, designed to enable you to join pipes of identical diameter.

It may also be quite helpful to use solvents designed to loosen rusted bolts or flanges. Soaking rusted parts the night before you do the job can speed the work of freeing rusted parts considerably. Remember that these solvents are often flammable. Apply only to parts after they are cool!

System Inspection

▶ **See Figures 154, 155, 156, 157 and 158**

Check the complete exhaust system and nearby body areas for broken, damaged, missing or mispositioned parts, open seams, holes, loose connections or other deterioration which could permit exhaust fumes to seep into the trunk or passenger compartment. Dust or water in the trunk may be an indication of a problem in one of these areas. Any defects should be corrected immediately. To help insure continued integrity, the exhaust system pipe rearward of the muffler must be replaced whenever a new muffler is installed.

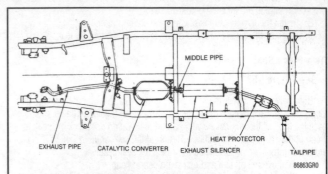

Fig. 154 Exhaust system components—1986 and earlier P'up with 4-cylinder gasoline engine

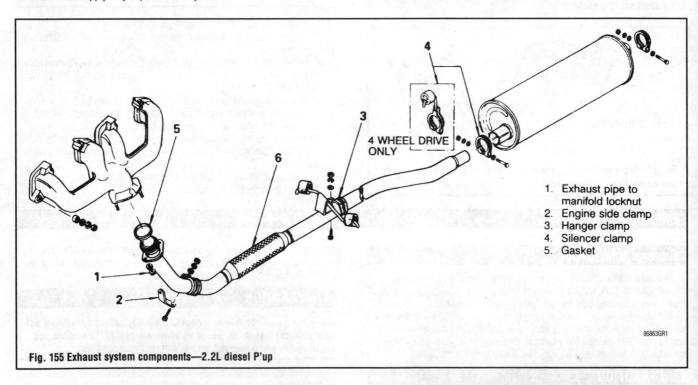

1. Exhaust pipe to manifold locknut
2. Engine side clamp
3. Hanger clamp
4. Silencer clamp
5. Gasket

Fig. 155 Exhaust system components—2.2L diesel P'up

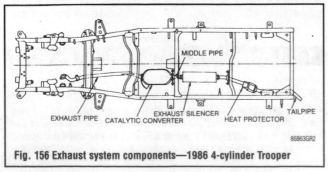

Fig. 156 Exhaust system components—1986 4-cylinder Trooper

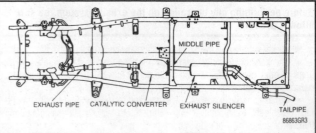

Fig. 157 Exhaust system components—1987 and later 4-cylinder P'up, Amigo and Trooper

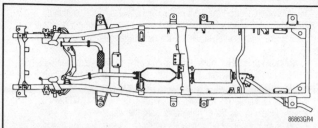

Fig. 158 Exhaust system components—V6 engine-equipped Rodeo, P'up, Amigo and Trooper

Front Pipe/Crossover Pipe

REMOVAL & INSTALLATION

▶ See Figures 159 and 160

➡Safety glasses should be worn at all times when working on or near the exhaust system. Older exhaust systems will almost always be covered with loose rust particles which will shower you when disturbed. These particles are more than a nuisance and could injure your eye.

1. Raise and support the front of the truck safely using jackstands.
2. Disconnect the oxygen sensor(s) electrical connector.
3. Remove the oxygen sensor(s). Special oxygen sensor sockets are available to help make removal easier.
4. Spray all fasteners which are to be disconnected using a penetrating oil.
5. Remove the front pipe(s)-to-manifold(s) nuts and separate (pry, if necessary) the front pipe (usually a ball joint fitting) from the exhaust manifold(s).
6. At the catalytic converter, loosen the front pipe-to-converter clamp nuts, then slide the clamp away from the converter and separate the front pipe from the converter.

➡Use a twisting motion to separate the front pipe-to-converter slip joint connection. If the front pipe cannot be removed from the catalytic converter, use a hammer (to loosen the connection) or wedge tool to separate the connection.

7. Inspect the pipe for holes, damage or deterioration; if necessary, replace the front pipe.
8. Installation is the reverse of removal.

➡Be sure to use a sealing compound, such as 1051249 or equivalent, at the slip joint connection.

Fig. 159 Removing the exhaust pipe bolts—2.8L engine

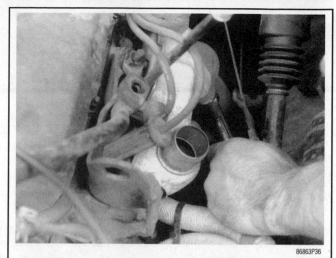

Fig. 160 Removing the oxygen sensor from the exhaust pipe—2.8L engine

9. Lubricate the front pipe-to-manifold(s) studs/nuts and the front pipe-to-converter clamp threads. Torque the front pipe-to-exhaust manifold bolts to 15 ft. lbs. (20 Nm) and the front pipe-to-converter clamp nuts to 35 ft. lbs. (47 Nm).
10. Install the oxygen sensor. Coat the threads with anti-seize compound before installing.
11. Connect the oxygen sensor(s) electrical connector.
12. Start the engine and check for exhaust leaks.

Catalytic Converter

. The catalytic converter is an emission control device added to the exhaust system to reduce the emission of hydrocarbon and carbon monoxide pollutants. Periodic maintenance of the exhaust system is not required, however, if the vehicle is raised for other service, it is advisable to check the general condition of the catalytic converter, pipes and mufflers. Check the exhaust system hangers for damage and deterioration. Replace any hardware if necessary. System damage may occur if there are broken hangers.

REMOVAL & INSTALLATION

➡Safety glasses should be worn at all times when working on or near the exhaust system. Older exhaust systems will almost always be covered with loose rust particles which will shower you when disturbed. These particles are more than a nuisance and could injure your eye.

1. Raise and support the front of the truck safely using jackstands.
2. Spray all fasteners which are to be disconnected using a penetrating oil.
3. Remove the catalytic converter-to-muffler bolts and separate the muffler from the converter.

➡The connection between the converter and the muffler is usually a ball joint type, which can be easily separated.

4. Remove the catalytic converter-to-front pipe clamp nuts and move the clamp forward.
5. Remove the converter-to-mounting bracket bolts, then twist the converter to separate it from the front pipe.
6. Inspect the condition of the catalytic converter for physical damage, replace it, if necessary.

➡When installing the catalytic converter, be sure that it is installed with adequate clearance from the floor pan, to prevent overheating of the vehicle floor.

7. Align the components and reverse the removal procedures.

➡Be sure to use a sealing compound, such as 1051249 or equivalent, at the slip joint connection.

8. Tighten the fasteners taking care not to damage the pipe sealing surfaces when tightening the retaining clamps.

9. Remove the jackstands and carefully lower the truck.

10. Start the engine and check for exhaust leaks.

Muffler

REMOVAL & INSTALLATION

➡ **Safety glasses should be worn at all times when working on or near the exhaust system. Older exhaust systems will almost always be covered with loose rust particles which will shower you when disturbed. These particles are more than a nuisance and could injure your eye.**

1. Raise and support the front of the truck safely using jackstands.

2. Spray all fasteners which are to be disconnected using a penetrating oil.

3. Remove the catalytic converter-to-muffler flange bolts and separate the items.

4. Remove the intermediate and rear tail pipe-to-bracket clamp nuts/bolts.

5. Remove the muffler bracket-to-chassis bolts and lower the muffler from the vehicle.

6. Coat the slip joints with GM type sealing compound 1051249 or equivalent, and loosely install the components onto the vehicle.

7. After aligning the components, tighten the connecting bolts and clamps, taking care not to distort the sealing surfaces.

➡ **When torquing the exhaust system connectors, be careful not to over-tighten the pipe clamps.**

8. Remove the jackstands and carefully lower the vehicle.

9. Start the engine and check for exhaust leaks.

ENGINE RECONDITIONING

Determining Engine Condition

Anything that generates heat and/or friction will eventually burn or wear out (for example, a light bulb generates heat, therefore its life span is limited). With this in mind, a running engine generates tremendous amounts of both; friction is encountered by the moving and rotating parts inside the engine and heat is created by friction and combustion of the fuel. However, the engine has systems designed to help reduce the effects of heat and friction and provide added longevity. The oiling system reduces the amount of friction encountered by the moving parts inside the engine, while the cooling system reduces heat created by friction and combustion. If either system is not maintained, a break-down will be inevitable. Therefore, you can see how regular maintenance can affect the service life of your vehicle. If you do not drain, flush and refill your cooling system at the proper intervals, deposits will begin to accumulate in the radiator, thereby reducing the amount of heat it can extract from the coolant. The same applies to your oil and filter; if it is not changed often enough it becomes laden with contaminates and is unable to properly lubricate the engine. This increases friction and wear.

There are a number of methods for evaluating the condition of your engine. A compression test can reveal the condition of your pistons, piston rings, cylinder bores, head gasket(s), valves and valve seats. An oil pressure test can warn you of possible engine bearing, or oil pump failures. Excessive oil consumption, evidence of oil in the engine air intake area and/or bluish smoke from the tailpipe may indicate worn piston rings, worn valve guides and/or valve seals. As a general rule, an engine that uses no more than one quart of oil every 1000 miles is in good condition. Engines that use one quart of oil or more in less than 1000 miles should first be checked for oil leaks. If any oil leaks are present, have them fixed before determining how much oil is consumed by the engine, especially if blue smoke is not visible at the tailpipe.

COMPRESSION TEST

A noticeable lack of engine power, excessive oil consumption and/or poor fuel mileage measured over an extended period are all indicators of internal engine wear. Worn piston rings, scored or worn cylinder bores, blown head gaskets, sticking or burnt valves, and worn valve seats are all possible culprits. A check of each cylinder's compression will help locate the problem.

Gasoline Engines

♦ See Figure 161

➡ **A screw-in type compression gauge is more accurate than the type you simply hold against the spark plug hole. Although it takes slightly longer to use, it's worth the effort to obtain a more accurate reading.**

1. Make sure that the proper amount and viscosity of engine oil is in the crankcase, then ensure the battery is fully charged.

2. Warm-up the engine to normal operating temperature, then shut the engine **OFF**.

3. Disable the ignition system.

4. Label and disconnect all of the spark plug wires from the plugs.

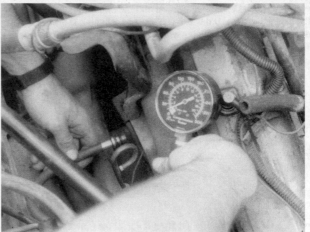

Fig. 161 A screw-in type compression gauge is more accurate and easier to use without an assistant

5. Thoroughly clean the cylinder head area around the spark plug ports, then remove the spark plugs.

6. Set the throttle plate to the fully open (wide-open throttle) position. You can block the accelerator linkage open for this, or you can have an assistant fully depress the accelerator pedal.

7. Install a screw-in type compression gauge into the No. 1 spark plug hole until the fitting is snug.

✳✳ WARNING

Be careful not to crossthread the spark plug hole.

8. According to the tool manufacturer's instructions, connect a remote starting switch to the starting circuit.

9. With the ignition switch in the **OFF** position, use the remote starting switch to crank the engine through at least five compression strokes (approximately 5 seconds of cranking) and record the highest reading on the gauge.

10. Repeat the test on each cylinder, cranking the engine approximately the same number of compression strokes and/or time as the first.

11. Compare the highest readings from each cylinder to that of the others. The indicated compression pressures are considered within specifications if the lowest reading cylinder is within 75 percent of the pressure recorded for the highest reading cylinder. For example, if your highest reading cylinder pressure was 150 psi (1034 kPa), then 75 percent of that would be 113 psi (779 kPa). So the lowest reading cylinder should be no less than 113 psi (779 kPa).

12. If a cylinder exhibits an unusually low compression reading, pour a tablespoon of clean engine oil into the cylinder through the spark plug hole and repeat the compression test. If the compression rises after adding oil, it means

that the cylinder's piston rings and/or cylinder bore are damaged or worn. If the pressure remains low, the valves may not be seating properly (a valve job is needed), or the head gasket may be blown near that cylinder. If compression in any two adjacent cylinders is low, and if the addition of oil doesn't help raise compression, there is leakage past the head gasket. Oil and coolant in the combustion chamber, combined with blue or constant white smoke from the tailpipe, are symptoms of this problem. However, don't be alarmed by the normal white smoke emitted from the tailpipe during engine warm-up or from cold weather driving. There may be evidence of water droplets on the engine dipstick and/or oil droplets in the cooling system if a head gasket is blown.

Diesel Engines

Checking cylinder compression on diesel engines is basically the same procedure as on gasoline engines except for the following:

1. A special compression gauge adapter suitable for diesel engines (because these engines have much greater compression pressures) must be used.
2. Remove the injector tubes and remove the injectors from each cylinder.

❊❊ WARNING

Do not forget to remove the washer underneath each injector. Otherwise, it may get lost when the engine is cranked.

3. When fitting the compression gauge adapter to the cylinder head, make sure the bleeder of the gauge (if equipped) is closed.
4. When reinstalling the injector assemblies, install new washers underneath each injector.

OIL PRESSURE TEST

Check for proper oil pressure at the sending unit passage with an externally mounted mechanical oil pressure gauge (as opposed to relying on a factory installed dash-mounted gauge). A tachometer may also be needed, as some specifications may require running the engine at a specific rpm.

1. With the engine cold, locate and remove the oil pressure sending unit.
2. Following the manufacturer's instructions, connect a mechanical oil pressure gauge and, if necessary, a tachometer to the engine.
3. Start the engine and allow it to idle.
4. Check the oil pressure reading when cold and record the number. You may need to run the engine at a specified rpm, so check the specifications.
5. Run the engine until normal operating temperature is reached (upper radiator hose will feel warm).
6. Check the oil pressure reading again with the engine hot and record the number. Turn the engine **OFF**.
7. Compare your hot oil pressure reading to specification. If the reading is low, check the cold pressure reading against the chart. If the cold pressure is well above the specification, and the hot reading was lower than the specification, you may have the wrong viscosity oil in the engine. Change the oil, making sure to use the proper grade and quantity, then repeat the test.

Low oil pressure readings could be attributed to internal component wear, pump related problems, a low oil level, or oil viscosity that is too low. High oil pressure readings could be caused by an overfilled crankcase, too high of an oil viscosity or a faulty pressure relief valve.

Buy or Rebuild?

Now if you have determined that your engine is worn out, you must make some decisions. The question of whether or not an engine is worth rebuilding is largely a subjective matter and one of personal worth. Is the engine a popular one, or is it an obsolete model? Are parts available? Will it get acceptable gas mileage once it is rebuilt? Is the car it's being put into worth keeping? Would it be less expensive to buy a new engine, have your engine rebuilt by a pro, rebuild it yourself or buy a used engine from a salvage yard? Or would it be simpler and less expensive to buy another car? If you have considered all these matters, and have still decided to rebuild the engine, then it is time to decide how you will rebuild it.

➡**The editors at Chilton feel that most engine machining should be performed by a professional machine shop. Think of it as an assurance that the job has been done right the first time. There are many expensive**

and specialized tools required to perform such tasks as boring and honing an engine block or having a valve job done on a cylinder head. Even inspecting the parts requires expensive micrometers and gauges to properly measure wear and clearances. A machine shop can deliver to you clean, and ready to assemble parts, saving you time and aggravation. Your maximum savings will come from performing the removal, disassembly, assembly and installation of the engine and purchasing or renting only the tools required to perform these tasks.

A complete rebuild or overhaul of an engine involves replacing all of the moving parts (pistons, rods, crankshaft, camshaft, etc.) with new ones and machining the non-moving wearing surfaces of the block and heads. Unfortunately, this may not be cost effective. For instance, your crankshaft may have been damaged or worn, but it can be machined undersize for a minimal fee.

So although you can replace everything inside the engine, it is usually wiser to replace only those parts which are really needed, and, if possible, repair the more expensive ones. Later in this section, we will break the engine down into its two main components: the cylinder head and the engine block. We will discuss each component, and the recommended parts to replace during a rebuild on each.

Engine Overhaul Tips

Most engine overhaul procedures are fairly standard. In addition to specific parts replacement procedures and specifications for your individual engine, this section is also a guide to acceptable rebuilding procedures. Examples of standard rebuilding practice are given and should be used along with specific details concerning your particular engine.

Competent and accurate machine shop services will ensure maximum performance, reliability and engine life. In most instances it is more profitable for the do-it-yourself mechanic to remove, clean and inspect the component, buy the necessary parts and deliver these to a shop for actual machine work.

Much of the assembly work (crankshaft, bearings, piston rods, and other components) is well within the scope of the do-it-yourself mechanic's tools and abilities. You will have to decide for yourself the depth of involvement you desire in an engine repair or rebuild.

TOOLS

The tools required for an engine overhaul or parts replacement will depend on the depth of your involvement. With a few exceptions, they will be the tools found in a mechanic's tool kit (see Section 1 of this manual). More in-depth work will require some or all of the following:

- A dial indicator (reading in thousandths) mounted on a universal base
- Micrometers and telescope gauges
- Jaw and screw-type pullers
- Scraper
- Valve spring compressor
- Ring groove cleaner
- Piston ring expander and compressor
- Ridge reamer
- Cylinder hone or glaze breaker
- Plastigage®
- Engine stand

The use of most of these tools is illustrated in this section. Many can be rented for a one-time use from a local parts jobber or tool supply house specializing in automotive work.

Occasionally, the use of special tools is called for. See the information on Special Tools and the Safety Notice in the front of this book before substituting another tool.

OVERHAUL TIPS

Aluminum has become extremely popular for use in engines, due to its low weight. Observe the following precautions when handling aluminum parts:

- Never hot tank aluminum parts (the caustic hot tank solution will eat the aluminum.)
- Remove all aluminum parts (identification tag, etc.) from engine parts prior to the tanking.
- Always coat threads lightly with engine oil or anti-seize compounds before installation, to prevent seizure.
- Never overtighten bolts or spark plugs especially in aluminum threads.

When assembling the engine, any parts that will be exposed to frictional contact must be prelubed to provide lubrication at initial start-up. Any product specifically formulated for this purpose can be used, but engine oil is not recommended as a prelube in most cases.

When semi-permanent (locked, but removable) installation of bolts or nuts is desired, threads should be cleaned and coated with Loctite or another similar, commercial non-hardening sealant.

CLEANING

▶ See Figures 162, 163, 164 and 165

Before the engine and its components are inspected, they must be thoroughly cleaned. You will need to remove any engine varnish, oil sludge and/or carbon deposits from all of the components to insure an accurate inspection. A crack in the engine block or cylinder head can easily become overlooked if hidden by a layer of sludge or carbon.

Most of the cleaning process can be carried out with common hand tools and readily available solvents or solutions. Carbon deposits can be chipped away using a hammer and a hard wooden chisel. Old gasket material and varnish or sludge can usually be removed using a scraper and/or cleaning solvent. Extremely stubborn deposits may require the use of a power drill with a wire brush. If using a wire brush, use extreme care around any critical machined surfaces (such as the gasket surfaces, bearing saddles, cylinder bores, etc.). USE OF A WIRE BRUSH IS NOT RECOMMENDED ON ANY ALUMINUM COMPONENTS. Always follow any safety recommendations given by the manufacturer of the tool and/or solvent.

✳✳ CAUTION

Always wear eye protection during any cleaning process involving scraping, chipping or spraying of solvents.

An alternative to the mess and hassle of cleaning the parts yourself is to drop them off at a local garage or machine shop. They should have the necessary equipment to properly clean all of the parts for a nominal fee.

Remove any oil galley plugs, freeze plugs and/or pressed-in bearings and carefully wash and degrease all of the engine components including the fasteners and bolts. Small parts such as the valves, springs, etc., should be placed in a metal basket and allowed to soak. Use pipe cleaner type brushes, and clean all passageways in the components.

Use a ring expander and remove the rings from the pistons. Clean the piston ring grooves with a special tool or a piece of broken ring. Scrape the carbon off of the top of the piston. You should never use a wire brush on the pistons. After preparing all of the piston assemblies in this manner, wash and degrease them again.

✳✳ WARNING

Use extreme care when cleaning around the cylinder head valve seats. A mistake or slip may cost you a new seat.

When cleaning the cylinder head, remove carbon from the combustion chamber with the valves installed. This will avoid damaging the valve seats.

REPAIRING DAMAGED THREADS

▶ See Figures 166, 167, 168, 169 and 170

Several methods of repairing damaged threads are available. Heli-Coil® (shown here), Keenserts® and Microdot® are among the most widely used. All involve basically the same principle—drilling out stripped threads, tapping the hole and installing a prewound insert—making welding, plugging and oversize fasteners unnecessary.

Two types of thread repair inserts are usually supplied: a standard type for most inch coarse, inch fine, metric course and metric fine thread sizes and a spark lug type to fit most spark plug port sizes. Consult the individual tool manufacturer's catalog to determine exact applications. Typical thread repair kits will contain a selection of prewound threaded inserts, a tap (corresponding to the outside diameter threads of the insert) and an installation tool. Spark plug inserts usually differ because they require a tap equipped with pilot threads and

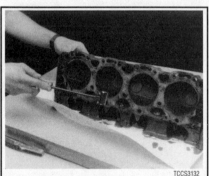
Fig. 162 Use a gasket scraper to remove the old gasket material from the mating surfaces

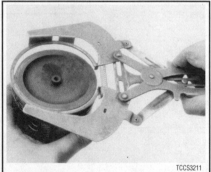
Fig. 163 Before cleaning and inspection, use a ring expander tool to remove the piston rings

Fig. 164 Clean the piston ring grooves using a ring groove cleaner tool, or . . .

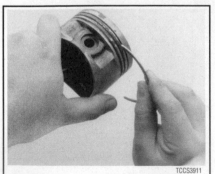
Fig. 165 . . . use a piece of an old ring to clean the grooves. Be careful, the ring can be quite sharp

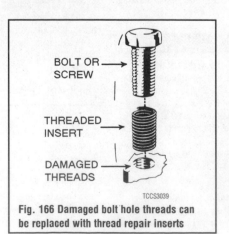
Fig. 166 Damaged bolt hole threads can be replaced with thread repair inserts

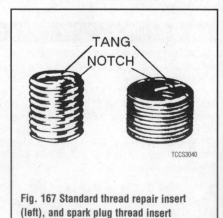
Fig. 167 Standard thread repair insert (left), and spark plug thread insert

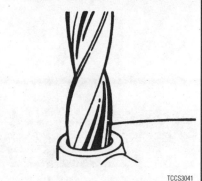

Fig. 168 Drill out the damaged threads with the specified size bit. Be sure to drill completely through the hole or to the bottom of a blind hole

TCCS3041

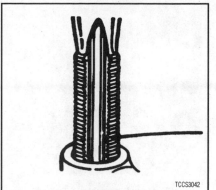

Fig. 169 Using the kit, tap the hole in order to receive the thread insert. Keep the tap well oiled and back it out frequently to avoid clogging the threads

TCCS3042

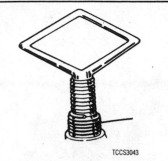

TCCS3043

Fig. 170 Screw the insert onto the installer tool until the tang engages the slot. Thread the insert into the hole until it is ¼–½ turn below the top surface, then remove the tool and break off the tang using a punch

a combined reamer/tap section. Most manufacturers also supply blister-packed thread repair inserts separately in addition to a master kit containing a variety of taps and inserts plus installation tools.

Before attempting to repair a threaded hole, remove any snapped, broken or damaged bolts or studs. Penetrating oil can be used to free frozen threads. The offending item can usually be removed with locking pliers or using a screw/stud extractor. After the hole is clear, the thread can be repaired as shown in the kit manufacturer's instructions.

Engine Preparation

To properly rebuild an engine, you must first remove it from the vehicle, then disassemble and diagnose it. Ideally you should place your engine on an engine stand. This affords you the best access to the engine components. Remove the flywheel or flexplate before installing the engine to the stand.

Now that you have the engine on a stand, and assuming that you have drained the oil and coolant from the engine, it's time to strip it of all but the necessary components. Before you start disassembling the engine, you may want to take a moment to draw some pictures, or fabricate some labels or containers to mark the locations of various components and the bolts and/or studs which fasten them. Modern day engines use a lot of little brackets and clips which hold wiring harnesses and such, and these holders are often mounted on studs and/or bolts that can be easily mixed up. The manufacturer spent a lot of time and money designing your vehicle, and they wouldn't have wasted any of it by haphazardly placing brackets, clips or fasteners on the vehicle. If it's present when you disassemble it, put it back when you assemble, you will regret not remembering that little bracket which holds a wire harness out of the path of a rotating part.

You should begin by unbolting any accessories still attached to the engine, such as the water pump, power steering pump, alternator, etc. Then, unfasten any manifolds (intake or exhaust) which were not removed during the engine removal procedure. Finally, remove any covers remaining on the engine such as the rocker arm, front or timing cover and oil pan. Some front covers may require the vibration damper and/or crank pulley to be removed beforehand. The idea is to reduce the engine to the bare necessities of cylinder head(s), valve train, engine block, crankshaft, pistons and connecting rods, plus any other `in block' components such as oil pumps, balance shafts and auxiliary shafts.

Finally, remove the cylinder head(s) from the engine block and carefully place on a bench. Disassembly instructions for each component follow later in this section.

Cylinder Head

There are two basic types of cylinder heads used on today's automobiles: the Overhead Valve (OHV) and the Overhead Camshaft (OHC). The latter can also be broken down into two subgroups: the Single Overhead Camshaft (SOHC) and the Dual Overhead Camshaft (DOHC). Generally, if there is only a single camshaft on a head, it is just referred to as an OHC head. Also, an engine with an OHV cylinder head is also known as a pushrod engine.

Most cylinder heads these days are made of an aluminum alloy due to its light weight, durability and heat transfer qualities. However, cast iron was the material of choice in the past, and is still used on many vehicles. Whether made from aluminum or iron, all cylinder heads have valves and seats. Some use two valves per cylinder, while the more hi-tech engines will utilize a multi-valve configuration using 3, 4 and even 5 valves per cylinder. When the valve contacts the seat, it does so on precision machined surfaces, which seals the combustion chamber. All cylinder heads have a valve guide for each valve. The guide centers the valve to the seat and allows it to move up and down within it. The clearance between the valve and guide can be critical. Too much clearance and the engine may consume oil, lose vacuum and/or damage the seat. Too little, and the valve can stick in the guide causing the engine to run poorly if at all, and possibly causing severe damage. The last component all automotive cylinder heads have are valve springs. The spring holds the valve against its seat. It also returns the valve to this position when the valve has been opened by the valve train or camshaft. The spring is fastened to the valve by a retainer and valve locks (sometimes called keepers). Aluminum heads will also have a valve spring shim to keep the spring from wearing away the aluminum.

An ideal method of rebuilding the cylinder head would involve replacing all of the valves, guides, seats, springs, etc. with new ones. However, depending on how the engine was maintained, often this is not necessary. A major cause of valve, guide and seat wear is an improperly tuned engine. An engine that is running too rich, will often wash the lubricating oil out of the guide with gasoline, causing it to wear rapidly. Conversely, an engine which is running too lean will place higher combustion temperatures on the valves and seats allowing them to wear or even burn. Springs fall victim to the driving habits of the individual. A driver who often runs the engine rpm to the redline will wear out or break the springs faster then one that stays well below it. Unfortunately, mileage takes it toll on all of the parts. Generally, the valves, guides, springs and seats in a cylinder head can be machined and re-used, saving you money. However, if a valve is burnt, it may be wise to replace all of the valves, since they were all operating in the same environment. The same goes for any other component on the cylinder head. Think of it as an insurance policy against future problems related to that component.

Unfortunately, the only way to find out which components need replacing, is to disassemble and carefully check each piece. After the cylinder head(s) are disassembled, thoroughly clean all of the components.

DISASSEMBLY

OHV Heads

♦ See Figures 171 thru 176

Before disassembling the cylinder head, you may want to fabricate some containers to hold the various parts, as some of them can be quite small (such as keepers) and easily lost. Also keeping yourself and the components organized will aid in assembly and reduce confusion. Where possible, try to maintain a components original location; this is especially important if there is not going to be any machine work performed on the components.

1. If you haven't already removed the rocker arms and/or shafts, do so now.
2. Position the head so that the springs are easily accessed.

Fig. 171 When removing an OHV valve spring, use a compressor tool to relieve the tension from the retainer

Fig. 172 A small magnet will help in removal of the valve locks

Fig. 173 Be careful not to lose the small valve locks (keepers)

Fig. 174 Remove the valve seal from the valve stem—O-ring type seal shown

Fig. 175 Removing an umbrella/positive type seal

Fig. 176 Invert the cylinder head and withdraw the valve from the valve guide bore

3. Use a valve spring compressor tool, and relieve spring tension from the retainer.

➡Due to engine varnish, the retainer may stick to the valve locks. A gentle tap with a hammer may help to break it loose.

4. Remove the valve locks from the valve tip and/or retainer. A small magnet may help in removing the locks.

5. Lift the valve spring, tool and all, off of the valve stem.

6. If equipped, remove the valve seal. If the seal is difficult to remove with the valve in place, try removing the valve first, then the seal. Follow the steps below for valve removal.

7. Position the head to allow access for withdrawing the valve.

➡Cylinder heads that have seen a lot of miles and/or abuse may have mushroomed the valve lock grove and/or tip, causing difficulty in removal of the valve. If this has happened, use a metal file to carefully remove the high spots around the lock grooves and/or tip. Only file it enough to allow removal.

8. Remove the valve from the cylinder head.

9. If equipped, remove the valve spring shim. A small magnetic tool or screwdriver will aid in removal.

10. Repeat Steps 3 though 9 until all of the valves have been removed.

OHC Heads

▶ **See Figures 177 and 178**

Whether it is a single or dual overhead camshaft cylinder head, the disassembly procedure is relatively unchanged. One aspect to pay attention to is careful labeling of the parts on the dual camshaft cylinder head. There will be an intake camshaft and followers as well as an exhaust camshaft and followers and they must be labeled as such. In some cases, the components are identical and could easily be installed incorrectly. DO NOT MIX THEM UP! Determining which is which is very simple; the intake camshaft and components are on the same side of the head as was the intake manifold. Conversely, the exhaust camshaft and components are on the same side of the head as was the exhaust manifold.

Fig. 177 Exploded view of a valve, seal, spring, retainer and locks from an OHC cylinder head

CUP TYPE CAMSHAFT FOLLOWERS

▶ **See Figures 179, 180 and 181**

Most cylinder heads with cup type camshaft followers will have the valve spring, retainer and locks recessed within the follower's bore. You will need a C-clamp style valve spring compressor tool, an OHC spring removal tool (or equivalent) and a small magnet to disassemble the head.

1. If not already removed, remove the camshaft(s) and/or followers. Mark their positions for assembly.

2. Position the cylinder head to allow use of a C-clamp style valve spring compressor tool.

➡It is preferred to position the cylinder head gasket surface facing you with the valve springs facing the opposite direction and the head laying horizontal.

3. With the OHC spring removal adapter tool positioned inside of the follower bore, compress the valve spring using the C-clamp style valve spring compressor.

4. Remove the valve locks. A small magnetic tool or screwdriver will aid in removal.

5. Release the compressor tool and remove the spring assembly.

6. Withdraw the valve from the cylinder head.

7. If equipped, remove the valve seal.

Fig. 178 Example of a multi-valve cylinder head. Note how it has 2 intake and 2 exhaust valve ports

Fig. 180 Most cup type follower cylinder heads retain the camshaft using bolt-on bearing caps

Fig. 179 C-clamp type spring compressor and an OHC spring removal tool (center) for cup type followers

Fig. 181 Position the OHC spring tool in the follower bore, then compress the spring with a C-clamp type tool

➡Special valve seal removal tools are available. Regular or needlenose type pliers, if used with care, will work just as well. If using ordinary pliers, be sure not to damage the follower bore. The follower and its bore are machined to close tolerances and any damage to the bore will effect this relationship.

8. If equipped, remove the valve spring shim. A small magnetic tool or screwdriver will aid in removal.

9. Repeat Steps 3 through 8 until all of the valves have been removed.

ROCKER ARM TYPE CAMSHAFT FOLLOWERS

♦ **See Figures 182 thru 190**

Most cylinder heads with rocker arm-type camshaft followers are easily disassembled using a standard valve spring compressor. However, certain models may not have enough open space around the spring for the standard tool and may require you to use a C-clamp style compressor tool instead.

1. If not already removed, remove the rocker arms and/or shafts and the camshaft. If applicable, also remove the hydraulic lash adjusters. Mark their positions for assembly.

2. Position the cylinder head to allow access to the valve spring.

3. Use a valve spring compressor tool to relieve the spring tension from the retainer.

➡Due to engine varnish, the retainer may stick to the valve locks. A gentle tap with a hammer may help to break it loose.

4. Remove the valve locks from the valve tip and/or retainer. A small magnet may help in removing the small locks.

5. Lift the valve spring, tool and all, off of the valve stem.

6. If equipped, remove the valve seal. If the seal is difficult to remove with the valve in place, try removing the valve first, then the seal. Follow the steps below for valve removal.

7. Position the head to allow access for withdrawing the valve.

Fig. 182 Example of the shaft mounted rocker arms on some OHC heads

Fig. 183 Another example of the rocker arm type OHC head. This model uses a follower under the camshaft

Fig. 184 Before the camshaft can be removed, all of the followers must first be removed . . .

Fig. 185 . . . then the camshaft can be removed by sliding it out (shown), or unbolting a bearing cap (not shown)

Fig. 186 Compress the valve spring . . .

Fig. 187 . . . then remove the valve locks from the valve stem and spring retainer

Fig. 188 Remove the valve spring and retainer from the cylinder head

Fig. 189 Remove the valve seal from the guide. Some gentle prying or pliers may help to remove stubborn ones

Fig. 190 All aluminum and some cast iron heads will have these valve spring shims. Remove all of them as well

➡Cylinder heads that have seen a lot of miles and/or abuse may have mushroomed the valve lock grove and/or tip, causing difficulty in removal of the valve. If this has happened, use a metal file to carefully remove the high spots around the lock grooves and/or tip. Only file it enough to allow removal.

8. Remove the valve from the cylinder head.
9. If equipped, remove the valve spring shim. A small magnetic tool or screwdriver will aid in removal.
10. Repeat Steps 3 though 9 until all of the valves have been removed.

INSPECTION

Now that all of the cylinder head components are clean, it's time to inspect them for wear and/or damage. To accurately inspect them, you will need some specialized tools:
• A 0–1 in. micrometer for the valves
• A dial indicator or inside diameter gauge for the valve guides
• A spring pressure test gauge
If you do not have access to the proper tools, you may want to bring the components to a shop that does.

Valves

▶ See Figures 191 and 192

The first thing to inspect are the valve heads. Look closely at the head, margin and face for any cracks, excessive wear or burning. The margin is the best place to look for burning. It should have a squared edge with an even width all around the diameter. When a valve burns, the margin will look melted and the edges

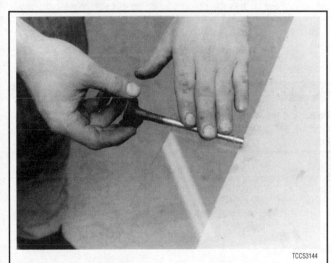

Fig. 191 Valve stems may be rolled on a flat surface to check for bends

rounded. Also inspect the valve head for any signs of tulipping. This will show as a lifting of the edges or dishing in the center of the head and will usually not occur to all of the valves. All of the heads should look the same, any that seem dished more than others are probably bad. Next, inspect the valve lock grooves and valve tips. Check for any burrs around the lock grooves, especially if you had to file them to remove the valve. Valve tips should appear flat, although slight rounding with high mileage engines is normal. Slightly worn valve tips will need to be machined flat. Last, measure the valve stem diameter with the micrometer. Measure the area that rides within the guide, especially towards the tip where most of the wear occurs. Take several measurements along its length and compare them to each other. Wear should be even along the length with little to no taper. If no minimum diameter is given in the specifications, then the stem should not read more than 0.001 in. (0.025mm) below the unworn portion of the stem. Any valves that fail these inspections should be replaced.

Springs, Retainers and Valve Locks

▶ See Figures 193 and 194

The first thing to check is the most obvious, broken springs. Next check the free length and squareness of each spring. If applicable, insure to distinguish between intake and/or exhaust springs. Use a ruler and/or carpenter's square to measure the length. A carpenter's square should be used to check the springs for squareness. If a spring pressure test gauge is available, check each springs rating and compare to the specifications chart. Check the readings against the specifications given. Any springs that fail these inspections should be replaced.

The spring retainers rarely need replacing, however they should still be checked as a precaution. Inspect the spring mating surface and the valve lock retention area for any signs of excessive wear. Also check for any signs of cracking. Replace any retainers that are questionable.

Valve locks should be inspected for excessive wear on the outside contact area as well as on the inner notched surface. Any locks which appear worn or broken and its respective valve should be replaced.

Cylinder Head

There are several things to check on the cylinder head: valve guides, seats, cylinder head surface flatness, cracks and physical damage.

VALVE GUIDES

▶ See Figure 195

Now that you know the valves are good, you can use them to check the guides, although a new valve, if available, is preferred. Before you measure anything, look at the guides carefully and inspect them for any cracks, chips or breakage. Also if the guide is a removable style (as in most aluminum heads), check them for any looseness or evidence of movement. All of the guides should appear to be at the same height from the spring seat. If any seem lower (or higher) from another, the guide has moved. Mount a dial indicator onto the spring side of the cylinder head. Lightly oil the valve stem and insert it into the cylinder head. Position the dial indicator against the valve stem near the tip and zero the gauge. Grasp the valve stem and wiggle towards and away from the dial indicator and observe the readings. Mount the dial indicator 90 degrees from the initial point and zero the gauge and again take a reading. Compare the two readings for an out of round condition.

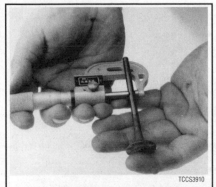

Fig. 192 Use a micrometer to check the valve stem diameter

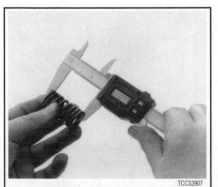

Fig. 193 Use a caliper to check the valve spring free-length

Fig. 194 Check the valve spring for squareness on a flat surface; a carpenter's square can be used

Check the readings against the specifications given. An Inside Diameter (I.D.) gauge designed for valve guides will give you an accurate valve guide bore measurement. If the I.D. gauge is used, compare the readings with the specifications given. Any guides that fail these inspections should be replaced or machined.

VALVE SEATS

A visual inspection of the valve seats should show a slightly worn and pitted surface where the valve face contacts the seat. Inspect the seat carefully for severe pitting or cracks. Also, a seat that is badly worn will be recessed into the cylinder head. A severely worn or recessed seat may need to be replaced. All cracked seats must be replaced. A seat concentricity gauge, if available, should be used to check the seat run-out. If run-out exceeds specifications the seat must be machined (if no specification is available given use 0.002 in. or 0.051mm).

CYLINDER HEAD SURFACE FLATNESS

◆ See Figures 196 and 197

After you have cleaned the gasket surface of the cylinder head of any old gasket material, check the head for flatness.

Place a straightedge across the gasket surface. Using feeler gauges, determine the clearance at the center of the straightedge and across the cylinder head at several points. Check along the centerline and diagonally on the head surface. If the warpage exceeds 0.003 in. (0.076mm) within a 6.0 in. (15.2cm) span, or 0.006 in. (0.152mm) over the total length of the head, the cylinder head must be resurfaced. After resurfacing the heads of a V-type engine, the intake manifold flange surface should be checked, and if necessary, milled proportionally to allow for the change in its mounting position.

CRACKS AND PHYSICAL DAMAGE

Generally, cracks are limited to the combustion chamber, however, it is not uncommon for the head to crack in a spark plug hole, port, outside of the head or in the valve spring/rocker arm area. The first area to inspect is always the hottest: the exhaust seat/port area.

A visual inspection should be performed, but just because you don't see a crack does not mean it is not there. Some more reliable methods for inspecting for cracks include Magnaflux®, a magnetic process or Zyglo®, a dye penetrant. Magnaflux® is used only on ferrous metal (cast iron) heads. Zyglo® uses a spray on fluorescent mixture along with a black light to reveal the cracks. It is strongly recommended to have your cylinder head checked professionally for cracks, especially if the engine was known to have overheated and/or leaked or consumed coolant. Contact a local shop for availability and pricing of these services.

Physical damage is usually very evident. For example, a broken mounting ear from dropping the head or a bent or broken stud and/or bolt. All of these defects should be fixed or, if unrepairable, the head should be replaced.

Camshaft and Followers

Inspect the camshaft(s) and followers as described earlier in this section.

REFINISHING & REPAIRING

Many of the procedures given for refinishing and repairing the cylinder head components must be performed by a machine shop. Certain steps, if the

inspected part is not worn, can be performed yourself inexpensively. However, you spent a lot of time and effort so far, why risk trying to save a couple bucks if you might have to do it all over again?

Valves

Any valves that were not replaced should be refaced and the tips ground flat. Unless you have access to a valve grinding machine, this should be done by a machine shop. If the valves are in extremely good condition, as well as the valve seats and guides, they may be lapped in without performing machine work.

It is a recommended practice to lap the valves even after machine work has been performed and/or new valves have been purchased. This insures a positive seal between the valve and seat.

LAPPING THE VALVES

➡Before lapping the valves to the seats, read the rest of the cylinder head section to insure that any related parts are in acceptable enough condition to continue. Also, remember that before any valve seat machining and/or lapping can be performed, the guides must be within factory recommended specifications.

1. Invert the cylinder head.
2. Lightly lubricate the valve stems and insert them into the cylinder head in their numbered order.
3. Raise the valve from the seat and apply a small amount of fine lapping compound to the seat.
4. Moisten the suction head of a hand-lapping tool and attach it to the head of the valve.
5. Rotate the tool between the palms of both hands, changing the position of the valve on the valve seat and lifting the tool often to prevent grooving.
6. Lap the valve until a smooth, polished circle is evident on the valve and seat.
7. Remove the tool and the valve. Wipe away all traces of the grinding compound and store the valve to maintain its lapped location.

✳✳ WARNING

Do not get the valves out of order after they have been lapped. They must be put back with the same valve seat with which they were lapped.

Springs, Retainers and Valve Locks

There is no repair or refinishing possible with the springs, retainers and valve locks. If they are found to be worn or defective, they must be replaced with new (or known good) parts.

Cylinder Head

Most refinishing procedures dealing with the cylinder head must be performed by a machine shop. Read the sections below and review your inspection data to determine whether or not machining is necessary.

TCCS3142

Fig. 195 A dial gauge may be used to check valve stem-to-guide clearance; read the gauge while moving the valve stem

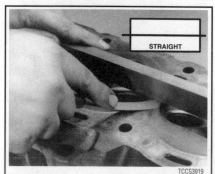

TCCS3919

Fig. 196 Check the head for flatness across the center of the head surface using a straightedge and feeler gauge

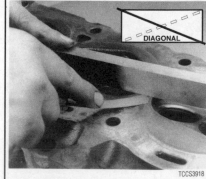

TCCS3918

Fig. 197 Checks should also be made along both diagonals of the head surface

VALVE GUIDE

→If any machining or replacements are made to the valve guides, the seats must be machined.

Unless the valve guides need machining or replacing, the only service to perform is to thoroughly clean them of any dirt or oil residue.

There are only two types of valve guides used on automobile engines: the replaceable-type (all aluminum heads) and the cast-in integral-type (most cast iron heads). There are four recommended methods for repairing worn guides.

- Knurling
- Inserts
- Reaming oversize
- Replacing

Knurling is a process in which metal is displaced and raised, thereby reducing clearance, giving a true center, and providing oil control. It is the least expensive way of repairing the valve guides. However, it is not necessarily the best, and in some cases, a knurled valve guide will not stand up for more than a short time. It requires a special knurlizer and precision reaming tools to obtain proper clearances. It would not be cost effective to purchase these tools, unless you plan on rebuilding several of the same cylinder head.

Installing a guide insert involves machining the guide to accept a bronze insert. One style is the coil-type which is installed into a threaded guide. Another is the thin-walled insert where the guide is reamed oversize to accept a split-sleeve insert. After the insert is installed, a special tool is then run through the guide to expand the insert, locking it to the guide. The insert is then reamed to the standard size for proper valve clearance.

Reaming for oversize valves restores normal clearances and provides a true valve seat. Most cast-in type guides can be reamed to accept an valve with an oversize stem. The cost factor for this can become quite high as you will need to purchase the reamer and new, oversize stem valves for all guides which were reamed. Oversizes are generally 0.003–0.030 in. (0.076–0.762mm), with 0.015 in. (0.381mm) being the most common.

To replace cast-in type valve guides, they must be drilled out, then reamed to accept replacement guides. This must be done on a fixture which will allow centering and leveling off of the original valve seat or guide, otherwise a serious guide-to-seat misalignment may occur making it impossible to properly machine the seat.

Replaceable-type guides are pressed into the cylinder head. A hammer and a stepped drift or punch may be used to install and remove the guides. Before removing the guides, measure the protrusion on the spring side of the head and record it for installation. Use the stepped drift to hammer out the old guide from the combustion chamber side of the head. When installing, determine whether or not the guide also seals a water jacket in the head, and if it does, use the recommended sealing agent. If there is no water jacket, grease the valve guide and its bore. Use the stepped drift, and hammer the new guide into the cylinder head from the spring side of the cylinder head. A stack of washers the same thickness as the measured protrusion may help the installation process.

VALVE SEATS

→Before any valve seat machining can be performed, the guides must be within factory recommended specifications. If any machining occurred or if replacements were made to the valve guides, the seats must be machined.

If the seats are in good condition, the valves can be lapped to the seats, and the cylinder head assembled. See the valves section for instructions on lapping.

If the valve seats are worn, cracked or damaged, they must be serviced by a machine shop. The valve seat must be perfectly centered to the valve guide, which requires very accurate machining.

CYLINDER HEAD SURFACE

If the cylinder head is warped, it must be machined flat. If the warpage is extremely severe, the head may need to be replaced. In some instances, it may be possible to straighten a warped head enough to allow machining. In either case, contact a professional machine shop for service.

→Any OHC cylinder head that shows excessive warpage should have the camshaft bearing journals align bored after the cylinder head has been resurfaced.

✳✳ WARNING

Failure to align bore the camshaft bearing journals could result in severe engine damage including but not limited to: valve and piston damage, connecting rod damage, camshaft and/or crankshaft breakage.

CRACKS AND PHYSICAL DAMAGE

Certain cracks can be repaired in both cast iron and aluminum heads. For cast iron, a tapered threaded insert is installed along the length of the crack. Aluminum can also use the tapered inserts, however welding is the preferred method. Some physical damage can be repaired through brazing or welding. Contact a machine shop to get expert advice for your particular dilemma.

ASSEMBLY

The first step for any assembly job is to have a clean area in which to work. Next, thoroughly clean all of the parts and components that are to be assembled. Finally, place all of the components onto a suitable work space and, if necessary, arrange the parts to their respective positions.

OHV Engines

1. Lightly lubricate the valve stems and insert all of the valves into the cylinder head. If possible, maintain their original locations.
2. If equipped, install any valve spring shims which were removed.
3. If equipped, install the new valve seals, keeping the following in mind:
- If the valve seal presses over the guide, lightly lubricate the outer guide surfaces.
- If the seal is an O-ring type, it is installed just after compressing the spring but before the valve locks.
4. Place the valve spring and retainer over the stem.
5. Position the spring compressor tool and compress the spring.
6. Assemble the valve locks to the stem.
7. Relieve the spring pressure slowly and insure that neither valve lock becomes dislodged by the retainer.
8. Remove the spring compressor tool.
9. Repeat Steps 2 through 8 until all of the springs have been installed.

OHC Engines

▶ See Figure 198

CUP TYPE CAMSHAFT FOLLOWERS

To install the springs, retainers and valve locks on heads which have these components recessed into the camshaft follower's bore, you will need a small screwdriver-type tool, some clean white grease and a lot of patience. You will also need the C-clamp style spring compressor and the OHC tool used to disassemble the head.

1. Lightly lubricate the valve stems and insert all of the valves into the cylinder head. If possible, maintain their original locations.
2. If equipped, install any valve spring shims which were removed.
3. If equipped, install the new valve seals, keeping the following in mind:
- If the valve seal presses over the guide, lightly lubricate the outer guide surfaces.
- If the seal is an O-ring type, it is installed just after compressing the spring but before the valve locks.
4. Place the valve spring and retainer over the stem.
5. Position the spring compressor and the OHC tool, then compress the spring.
6. Using a small screwdriver as a spatula, fill the valve stem side of the lock with white grease. Use the excess grease on the screwdriver to fasten the lock to the driver.
7. Carefully install the valve lock, which is stuck to the end of the screwdriver, to the valve stem then press on it with the screwdriver until the grease squeezes out. The valve lock should now be stuck to the stem.
8. Repeat Steps 6 and 7 for the remaining valve lock.
9. Relieve the spring pressure slowly and insure that neither valve lock becomes dislodged by the retainer.
10. Remove the spring compressor tool.

Fig. 198 Once assembled, check the valve clearance and correct as needed

11. Repeat Steps 2 through 10 until all of the springs have been installed.

12. Install the followers, camshaft(s) and any other components that were removed for disassembly.

ROCKER ARM TYPE CAMSHAFT FOLLOWERS

1. Lightly lubricate the valve stems and insert all of the valves into the cylinder head. If possible, maintain their original locations.

2. If equipped, install any valve spring shims which were removed.

3. If equipped, install the new valve seals, keeping the following in mind:

• If the valve seal presses over the guide, lightly lubricate the outer guide surfaces.

• If the seal is an O-ring type, it is installed just after compressing the spring but before the valve locks.

4. Place the valve spring and retainer over the stem.

5. Position the spring compressor tool and compress the spring.

6. Assemble the valve locks to the stem.

7. Relieve the spring pressure slowly and insure that neither valve lock becomes dislodged by the retainer.

8. Remove the spring compressor tool.

9. Repeat Steps 2 through 8 until all of the springs have been installed.

10. Install the camshaft(s), rockers, shafts and any other components that were removed for disassembly.

Engine Block

GENERAL INFORMATION

A thorough overhaul or rebuild of an engine block would include replacing the pistons, rings, bearings, timing belt/chain assembly and oil pump. For OHV engines also include a new camshaft and lifters. The block would then have the cylinders bored and honed oversize (or if using removable cylinder sleeves, new sleeves installed) and the crankshaft would be cut undersize to provide new wearing surfaces and perfect clearances. However, your particular engine may not have everything worn out. What if only the piston rings have worn out and the clearances on everything else are still within factory specifications? Well, you could just replace the rings and put it back together, but this would be a very rare example. Chances are, if one component in your engine is worn, other components are sure to follow, and soon. At the very least, you should always replace the rings, bearings and oil pump. This is what is commonly called a "freshen up".

Cylinder Ridge Removal

Because the top piston ring does not travel to the very top of the cylinder, a ridge is built up between the end of the travel and the top of the cylinder bore. Pushing the piston and connecting rod assembly past the ridge can be diffi-

cult, and damage to the piston ring lands could occur. If the ridge is not removed before installing a new piston or not removed at all, piston ring breakage and piston damage may occur.

➡ It is always recommended that you remove any cylinder ridges before removing the piston and connecting rod assemblies. If you know that new pistons are going to be installed and the engine block will be bored oversize, you may be able to forego this step. However, some ridges may actually prevent the assemblies from being removed, necessitating its removal.

There are several different types of ridge reamers on the market, none of which are inexpensive. Unless a great deal of engine rebuilding is anticipated, borrow or rent a reamer.

1. Turn the crankshaft until the piston is at the bottom of its travel.

2. Cover the head of the piston with a rag.

3. Follow the tool manufacturers instructions and cut away the ridge, exercising extreme care to avoid cutting too deeply.

4. Remove the ridge reamer, the rag and as many of the cuttings as possible. Continue until all of the cylinder ridges have been removed.

DISASSEMBLY

◗ See Figures 199 and 200

The engine disassembly instructions following assume that you have the engine mounted on an engine stand. If not, it is easiest to disassemble the engine on a bench or the floor with it resting on the bell housing or transmission mounting surface. You must be able to access the connecting rod fasteners and turn the crankshaft during disassembly. Also, all engine covers (timing, front, side, oil pan, whatever) should have already been removed. Engines which are seized or locked up may not be able to be completely disassembled, and a core (salvage yard) engine should be purchased.

Pushrod Engines

If not done during the cylinder head removal, remove the pushrods and lifters, keeping them in order for assembly. Remove the timing gears and/or timing chain assembly, then remove the oil pump drive assembly and withdraw the camshaft from the engine block. Remove the oil pick-up and pump assembly. If equipped, remove any balance or auxiliary shafts. If necessary, remove the cylinder ridge from the top of the bore. See the cylinder ridge removal procedure earlier in this section.

OHC Engines

If not done during the cylinder head removal, remove the timing chain/belt and/or gear/sprocket assembly. Remove the oil pick-up and pump assembly and, if necessary, the pump drive. If equipped, remove any balance or auxiliary

Fig. 199 Place rubber hose over the connecting rod studs to protect the crankshaft and cylinder bores from damage

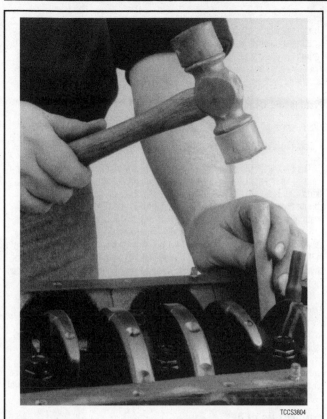

TCCS3804

Fig. 200 Carefully tap the piston out of the bore using a wooden dowel

shafts. If necessary, remove the cylinder ridge from the top of the bore. See the cylinder ridge removal procedure earlier in this section.

All Engines

Rotate the engine over so that the crankshaft is exposed. Use a number punch or scribe and mark each connecting rod with its respective cylinder number. The cylinder closest to the front of the engine is always number 1. However, depending on the engine placement, the front of the engine could either be the flywheel or damper/pulley end. Generally the front of the engine faces the front of the vehicle. Use a number punch or scribe and also mark the main bearing caps from front to rear with the front most cap being number 1 (if there are five caps, mark them 1 through 5, front to rear).

✳✳ WARNING

Take special care when pushing the connecting rod up from the crankshaft because the sharp threads of the rod bolts/studs will score the crankshaft journal. Insure that special plastic caps are installed over them, or cut two pieces of rubber hose to do the same.

Again, rotate the engine, this time to position the number one cylinder bore (head surface) up. Turn the crankshaft until the number one piston is at the bottom of its travel, this should allow the maximum access to its connecting rod. Remove the number one connecting rods fasteners and cap and place two lengths of rubber hose over the rod bolts/studs to protect the crankshaft from damage. Using a sturdy wooden dowel and a hammer, push the connecting rod up about 1 in. (25mm) from the crankshaft and remove the upper bearing insert. Continue pushing or tapping the connecting rod up until the piston rings are out of the cylinder bore. Remove the piston and rod by hand, put the upper half of the bearing insert back into the rod, install the cap with its bearing insert installed, and hand-tighten the cap fasteners. If the parts are kept in order in this manner, they will not get lost and you will be able to tell which bearings came form what cylinder if any problems are discovered and diagnosis is necessary. Remove all the other piston assemblies in the same manner.

On V-style engines, remove all of the pistons from one bank, then reposition the engine with the other cylinder bank head surface up, and remove that banks piston assemblies.

The only remaining component in the engine block should now be the crankshaft. Loosen the main bearing caps evenly until the fasteners can be turned by hand, then remove them and the caps. Remove the crankshaft from the engine block. Thoroughly clean all of the components.

INSPECTION

Now that the engine block and all of its components are clean, it's time to inspect them for wear and/or damage. To accurately inspect them, you will need some specialized tools:

- Two or three separate micrometers to measure the pistons and crankshaft journals
- A dial indicator
- Telescoping gauges for the cylinder bores
- A rod alignment fixture to check for bent connecting rods

If you do not have access to the proper tools, you may want to bring the components to a shop that does.

Generally, you shouldn't expect cracks in the engine block or its components unless it was known to leak, consume or mix engine fluids, it was severely overheated, or there was evidence of bad bearings and/or crankshaft damage. A visual inspection should be performed on all of the components, but just because you don't see a crack does not mean it is not there. Some more reliable methods for inspecting for cracks include Magnaflux®, a magnetic process or Zyglo®, a dye penetrant. Magnaflux® is used only on ferrous metal (cast iron). Zyglo® uses a spray on fluorescent mixture along with a black light to reveal the cracks. It is strongly recommended to have your engine block checked professionally for cracks, especially if the engine was known to have overheated and/or leaked or consumed coolant. Contact a local shop for availability and pricing of these services.

Engine Block

ENGINE BLOCK BEARING ALIGNMENT

Remove the main bearing caps and, if still installed, the main bearing inserts. Inspect all of the main bearing saddles and caps for damage, burrs or high spots. If damage is found, and it is caused from a spun main bearing, the block will need to be align-bored or, if severe enough, replacement. Any burrs or high spots should be carefully removed with a metal file.

Place a straightedge on the bearing saddles, in the engine block, along the centerline of the crankshaft. If any clearance exists between the straightedge and the saddles, the block must be align-bored.

Align-boring consists of machining the main bearing saddles and caps by means of a flycutter that runs through the bearing saddles.

DECK FLATNESS

The top of the engine block where the cylinder head mounts is called the deck. Insure that the deck surface is clean of dirt, carbon deposits and old gasket material. Place a straightedge across the surface of the deck along its centerline and, using feeler gauges, check the clearance along several points. Repeat the checking procedure with the straightedge placed along both diagonals of the deck surface. If the reading exceeds 0.003 in. (0.076mm) within a 6.0 in. (15.2cm) span, or 0.006 in. (0.152mm) over the total length of the deck, it must be machined.

CYLINDER BORES

◆ See Figure 201

The cylinder bores house the pistons and are slightly larger than the pistons themselves. A common piston-to-bore clearance is 0.0015–0.0025 in. (0.0381mm–0.0635mm). Inspect and measure the cylinder bores. The bore should be checked for out-of-roundness, taper and size. The results of this inspection will determine whether the cylinder can be used in its existing size and condition, or a rebore to the next oversize is required (or in the case of removable sleeves, have replacements installed).

The amount of cylinder wall wear is always greater at the top of the cylinder than at the bottom. This wear is known as taper. Any cylinder that has a taper of 0.0012 in. (0.305mm) or more, must be rebored. Measurements are taken at a

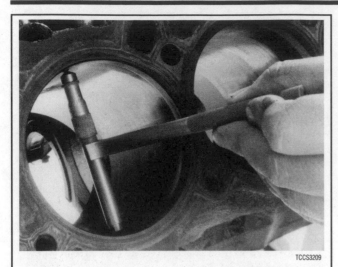

TCCS3209

Fig. 201 Use a telescoping gauge to measure the cylinder bore diameter—take several readings within the same bore

number of positions in each cylinder: at the top, middle and bottom and at two points at each position; that is, at a point 90 degrees from the crankshaft centerline, as well as a point parallel to the crankshaft centerline. The measurements are made with either a special dial indicator or a telescopic gauge and micrometer. If the necessary precision tools to check the bore are not available, take the block to a machine shop and have them mike it. Also if you don't have the tools to check the cylinder bores, chances are you will not have the necessary devices to check the pistons, connecting rods and crankshaft. Take these components with you and save yourself an extra trip.

For our procedures, we will use a telescopic gauge and a micrometer. You will need one of each, with a measuring range which covers your cylinder bore size.

1. Position the telescopic gauge in the cylinder bore, loosen the gauges lock and allow it to expand.

➡**Your first two readings will be at the top of the cylinder bore, then proceed to the middle and finally the bottom, making a total of six measurements.**

2. Hold the gauge square in the bore, 90 degrees from the crankshaft centerline, and gently tighten the lock. Tilt the gauge back to remove it from the bore.
3. Measure the gauge with the micrometer and record the reading.
4. Again, hold the gauge square in the bore, this time parallel to the crankshaft centerline, and gently tighten the lock. Again, you will tilt the gauge back to remove it from the bore.
5. Measure the gauge with the micrometer and record this reading. The difference between these two readings is the out-of-round measurement of the cylinder.
6. Repeat steps 1 through 5, each time going to the next lower position, until you reach the bottom of the cylinder. Then go to the next cylinder, and continue until all of the cylinders have been measured.

The difference between these measurements will tell you all about the wear in your cylinders. The measurements which were taken 90 degrees from the crankshaft centerline will always reflect the most wear. That is because at this position is where the engine power presses the piston against the cylinder bore the hardest. This is known as thrust wear. Take your top, 90 degree measurement and compare it to your bottom, 90 degree measurement. The difference between them is the taper. When you measure your pistons, you will compare these readings to your piston sizes and determine piston-to-wall clearance.

Crankshaft

Inspect the crankshaft for visible signs of wear or damage. All of the journals should be perfectly round and smooth. Slight scores are normal for a used crankshaft, but you should hardly feel them with your fingernail. When measuring the crankshaft with a micrometer, you will take readings at the front and rear of each journal, then turn the micrometer 90 degrees and take two more readings, front and rear. The difference between the front-to-rear readings is the journal taper and the first-to-90 degree reading is the out-of-round measurement. Generally, there should be no taper or out-of-roundness found, however,

up to 0.0005 in. (0.0127mm) for either can be overlooked. Also, the readings should fall within the factory specifications for journal diameters.

If the crankshaft journals fall within specifications, it is recommended that it be polished before being returned to service. Polishing the crankshaft insures that any minor burrs or high spots are smoothed, thereby reducing the chance of scoring the new bearings.

Pistons and Connecting Rods

PISTONS

▶ **See Figure 202**

The piston should be visually inspected for any signs of cracking or burning (caused by hot spots or detonation), and scuffing or excessive wear on the skirts. The wrist pin attaches the piston to the connecting rod. The piston should move freely on the wrist pin, both sliding and pivoting. Grasp the connecting rod securely, or mount it in a vise, and try to rock the piston back and forth along the centerline of the wrist pin. There should not be any excessive play evident between the piston and the pin. If there are C-clips retaining the pin in the piston then you have wrist pin bushings in the rods. There should not be any excessive play between the wrist pin and the rod bushing. Normal clearance for the wrist pin is approx. 0.001–0.002 in. (0.025mm–0.051mm).

Use a micrometer and measure the diameter of the piston, perpendicular to the wrist pin, on the skirt. Compare the reading to its original cylinder measurement obtained earlier. The difference between the two readings is the piston-to-wall clearance. If the clearance is within specifications, the piston may be used as is. If the piston is out of specification, but the bore is not, you will need a new piston. If both are out of specification, you will need the cylinder rebored and oversize pistons installed. Generally if two or more pistons/bores are out of specification, it is best to rebore the entire block and purchase a complete set of oversize pistons.

CONNECTING ROD

You should have the connecting rod checked for straightness at a machine shop. If the connecting rod is bent, it will unevenly wear the bearing and piston, as well as place greater stress on these components. Any bent or twisted connecting rods must be replaced. If the rods are straight and the wrist pin clearance is within specifications, then only the bearing end of the rod need be checked. Place the connecting rod into a vice, with the bearing inserts in place, install the cap to the rod and torque the fasteners to specifications. Use a telescoping gauge and carefully measure the inside diameter of the bearings. Compare this reading to the rods original crankshaft journal diameter measurement. The difference is the oil clearance. If the oil clearance is not within specifications, install new bearings in the rod and take another measurement. If the clearance is still out of specifications, and the crankshaft is not, the rod will need to be reconditioned by a machine shop.

➡**You can also use Plastigage® to check the bearing clearances. The assembling section has complete instructions on its use.**

Camshaft

Inspect the camshaft and lifters/followers as described earlier in this section.

Bearings

All of the engine bearings should be visually inspected for wear and/or damage. The bearing should look evenly worn all around with no deep scores or pits. If the bearing is severely worn, scored, pitted or heat blued, then the bearing, and the components that use it, should be brought to a machine shop for inspection. Full-circle bearings (used on most camshafts, auxiliary shafts, balance shafts, etc.) require specialized tools for removal and installation, and should be brought to a machine shop for service.

Oil Pump

➡**The oil pump is responsible for providing constant lubrication to the whole engine and so it is recommended that a new oil pump be installed when rebuilding the engine.**

Completely disassemble the oil pump and thoroughly clean all of the components. Inspect the oil pump gears and housing for wear and/or damage. Insure that the pressure relief valve operates properly and there is no binding or stick-

Fig. 202 Measure the piston's outer diameter, perpendicular to the wrist pin, with a micrometer

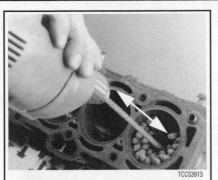

Fig. 203 Use a ball type cylinder hone to remove any glaze and provide a new surface for seating the piston rings

Fig. 204 Most pistons are marked to indicate positioning in the engine (usually a mark means the side facing the front)

ing due to varnish or debris. If all of the parts are in proper working condition, lubricate the gears and relief valve, and assemble the pump.

REFINISHING

▶ See Figure 203

Almost all engine block refinishing must be performed by a machine shop. If the cylinders are not to be rebored, then the cylinder glaze can be removed with a ball hone. When removing cylinder glaze with a ball hone, use a light or penetrating type oil to lubricate the hone. Do not allow the hone to run dry as this may cause excessive scoring of the cylinder bores and wear on the hone. If new pistons are required, they will need to be installed to the connecting rods. This should be performed by a machine shop as the pistons must be installed in the correct relationship to the rod or engine damage can occur.

Pistons and Connecting Rods

▶ See Figure 204

Only pistons with the wrist pin retained by C-clips are serviceable by the home-mechanic. Press fit pistons require special presses and/or heaters to remove/install the connecting rod and should only be performed by a machine shop.

All pistons will have a mark indicating the direction to the front of the engine and the must be installed into the engine in that manner. Usually it is a notch or arrow on the top of the piston, or it may be the letter F cast or stamped into the piston.

ASSEMBLY

Before you begin assembling the engine, first give yourself a clean, dirt free work area. Next, clean every engine component again. The key to a good assembly is cleanliness.

Mount the engine block into the engine stand and wash it one last time using water and detergent (dishwashing detergent works well). While washing it, scrub the cylinder bores with a soft bristle brush and thoroughly clean all of the oil passages. Completely dry the engine and spray the entire assembly down with an anti-rust solution such as WD-40® or similar product. Take a clean lint-free rag and wipe up any excess anti-rust solution from the bores, bearing saddles, etc. Repeat the final cleaning process on the crankshaft. Replace any freeze or oil galley plugs which were removed during disassembly.

Crankshaft

▶ See Figures 205, 206, 207 and 208

1. Remove the main bearing inserts from the block and bearing caps.
2. If the crankshaft main bearing journals have been refinished to a definite undersize, install the correct undersize bearing. Be sure that the bearing inserts and bearing bores are clean. Foreign material under inserts will distort bearing and cause failure.
3. Place the upper main bearing inserts in bores with tang in slot.

➡ The oil holes in the bearing inserts must be aligned with the oil holes in the cylinder block.

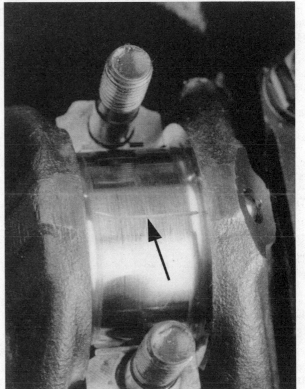

Fig. 205 Apply a strip of gauging material to the bearing journal, then install and torque the cap

4. Install the lower main bearing inserts in bearing caps.
5. Clean the mating surfaces of block and rear main bearing cap.
6. Carefully lower the crankshaft into place. Be careful not to damage bearing surfaces.
7. Check the clearance of each main bearing by using the following procedure:
   a. Place a piece of Plastigage® or its equivalent, on bearing surface across full width of bearing cap and about ¼ in. off center.
   b. Install cap and tighten bolts to specifications. Do not turn crankshaft while Plastigage® is in place.
   c. Remove the cap. Using the supplied Plastigage® scale, check width of Plastigage® at widest point to get maximum clearance. Difference between readings is taper of journal.
   d. If clearance exceeds specified limits, try a 0.001 in. or 0.002 in. undersize bearing in combination with the standard bearing. Bearing clearance must be within specified limits. If standard and 0.002 in. undersize bearing does not bring clearance within desired limits, refinish crankshaft journal, then install undersize bearings.

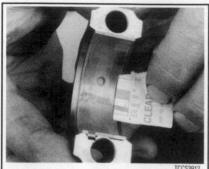

Fig. 206 After the cap is removed again, use the scale supplied with the gauging material to check the clearance

Fig. 207 A dial gauge may be used to check crankshaft end-play

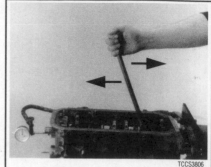

Fig. 208 Carefully pry the crankshaft back and forth while reading the dial gauge for end-play

8. After the bearings have been fitted, apply a light coat of engine oil to the journals and bearings. Install the rear main bearing cap. Install all bearing caps except the thrust bearing cap. Be sure that main bearing caps are installed in original locations. Tighten the bearing cap bolts to specifications.

9. Install the thrust bearing cap with bolts finger-tight.

10. Pry the crankshaft forward against the thrust surface of upper half of bearing.

11. Hold the crankshaft forward and pry the thrust bearing cap to the rear. This aligns the thrust surfaces of both halves of the bearing.

12. Retain the forward pressure on the crankshaft. Tighten the cap bolts to specifications.

13. Measure the crankshaft end-play as follows:

   a. Mount a dial gauge to the engine block and position the tip of the gauge to read from the crankshaft end.

   b. Carefully pry the crankshaft toward the rear of the engine and hold it there while you zero the gauge.

   c. Carefully pry the crankshaft toward the front of the engine and read the gauge.

   d. Confirm that the reading is within specifications. If not, install a new thrust bearing and repeat the procedure. If the reading is still out of specifications with a new bearing, have a machine shop inspect the thrust surfaces of the crankshaft, and if possible, repair it.

14. Rotate the crankshaft so as to position the first rod journal to the bottom of its stroke.

15. Install the rear main seal.

Pistons and Connecting Rods

▶ See Figures 209, 210, 211 and 212

1. Before installing the piston/connecting rod assembly, oil the pistons, piston rings and the cylinder walls with light engine oil. Install connecting rod bolt protectors or rubber hose onto the connecting rod bolts/studs. Also perform the following:

   a. Select the proper ring set for the size cylinder bore.

   b. Position the ring in the bore in which it is going to be used.

   c. Push the ring down into the bore area where normal ring wear is not encountered.

Fig. 209 Checking the piston ring-to-ring groove side clearance using the ring and a feeler gauge

Fig. 210 The notch on the side of the bearing cap matches the tang on the bearing insert

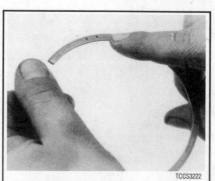

Fig. 211 Most rings are marked to show which side of the ring should face up when installed to the piston

Fig. 212 Install the piston and rod assembly into the block using a ring compressor and the handle of a hammer

d. Use the head of the piston to position the ring in the bore so that the ring is square with the cylinder wall. Use caution to avoid damage to the ring or cylinder bore.

e. Measure the gap between the ends of the ring with a feeler gauge. Ring gap in a worn cylinder is normally greater than specification. If the ring gap is greater than the specified limits, try an oversize ring set.

f. Check the ring side clearance of the compression rings with a feeler gauge inserted between the ring and its lower land according to specification. The gauge should slide freely around the entire ring circumference without binding. Any wear that occurs will form a step at the inner portion of the lower land. If the lower lands have high steps, the piston should be replaced.

2. Unless new pistons are installed, be sure to install the pistons in the cylinders from which they were removed. The numbers on the connecting rod and bearing cap must be on the same side when installed in the cylinder bore. If a connecting rod is ever transposed from one engine or cylinder to another, new bearings should be fitted and the connecting rod should be numbered to correspond with the new cylinder number. The notch on the piston head goes toward the front of the engine.

3. Install all of the rod bearing inserts into the rods and caps.

4. Install the rings to the pistons. Install the oil control ring first, then the second compression ring and finally the top compression ring. Use a piston ring expander tool to aid in installation and to help reduce the chance of breakage.

5. Make sure the ring gaps are properly spaced around the circumference of the piston. Fit a piston ring compressor around the piston and slide the piston and connecting rod assembly down into the cylinder bore, pushing it in with the wooden hammer handle. Push the piston down until it is only slightly below the top of the cylinder bore. Guide the connecting rod onto the crankshaft bearing journal carefully, to avoid damaging the crankshaft.

6. Check the bearing clearance of all the rod bearings, fitting them to the crankshaft bearing journals. Follow the procedure in the crankshaft installation above.

7. After the bearings have been fitted, apply a light coating of assembly oil to the journals and bearings.

8. Turn the crankshaft until the appropriate bearing journal is at the bottom of its stroke, then push the piston assembly all the way down until the connecting rod bearing seats on the crankshaft journal. Be careful not to allow the bearing cap screws to strike the crankshaft bearing journals and damage them.

9. After the piston and connecting rod assemblies have been installed, check the connecting rod side clearance on each crankshaft journal.

10. Prime and install the oil pump and the oil pump intake tube.

OHV Engines

CAMSHAFT, LIFTERS AND TIMING ASSEMBLY

1. Install the camshaft.
2. Install the lifters/followers into their bores.
3. Install the timing gears/chain assembly.

CYLINDER HEAD(S)

1. Install the cylinder head(s) using new gaskets.
2. Assemble the rest of the valve train (pushrods and rocker arms and/or shafts).

OHC Engines

CYLINDER HEAD(S)

1. Install the cylinder head(s) using new gaskets.
2. Install the timing sprockets/gears and the belt/chain assemblies.

Engine Covers and Components

Install the timing cover(s) and oil pan. Refer to your notes and drawings made prior to disassembly and install all of the components that were removed. Install the engine into the vehicle.

Engine Start-up and Break-in

STARTING THE ENGINE

Now that the engine is installed and every wire and hose is properly connected, go back and double check that all coolant and vacuum hoses are con-

nected. Check that your oil drain plug is installed and properly tightened. If not already done, install a new oil filter onto the engine. Fill the crankcase with the proper amount and grade of engine oil. Fill the cooling system with a 50/50 mixture of coolant/water.

1. Connect the vehicle battery.
2. Start the engine. Keep your eye on your oil pressure indicator; if it does not indicate oil pressure within 10 seconds of starting, turn the vehicle **OFF**.

✸ WARNING

Damage to the engine can result if it is allowed to run with no oil pressure. Check the engine oil level to make sure that it is full. Check for any leaks and if found, repair the leaks before continuing. If there is still no indication of oil pressure, you may need to prime the system.

3. Confirm that there are no fluid leaks (oil or other).
4. Allow the engine to reach normal operating temperature (the upper radiator hose will be hot to the touch).
5. At this point any necessary checks or adjustments can be performed, such as ignition timing.
6. Install any remaining components or body panels which were removed.

BREAKING IT IN

Make the first miles on the new engine, easy ones. Vary the speed but do not accelerate hard. Most importantly, do not lug the engine, and avoid sustained high speeds until at least 100 miles. Check the engine oil and coolant levels frequently. Expect the engine to use a little oil until the rings seat. Change the oil and filter at 500 miles, 1500 miles, then every 3000 miles past that.

KEEP IT MAINTAINED

Now that you have just gone through all of that hard work, keep yourself from doing it all over again by thoroughly maintaining it. Not that you may not have maintained it before, heck you could have had one to two hundred thousand miles on it before doing this. However, you may have bought the vehicle used, and the previous owner did not keep up on maintenance. Which is why you just went through all of that hard work. See?

**TORQUE SPECIFICATIONS
1.8L AND 2.0L ENGINE**

Component	U.S.	Metric
Intake Manifold		
1.8L	14-18ft. lbs.	19-25 Nm
2.0L	14-18ft. lbs.	19-25 Nm
Connecting Rods	42-45 ft. lbs.	57-61 Nm
Cylinder Head		
1st	40-47 ft. lbs.	54-63 Nm
2nd	65-80 ft. lbs.	88-108 Nm
Crankshaft pulley	76-97 ft. lbs.	103-132 Nm
Exhaust Manifold	14-18 ft. lbs.	19-25 Nm
Flywheel	73-80 ft. lbs.	99-108 Nm
Intake Manifold	13-18 ft. lbs.	19-25 Nm
Main Bearing Caps	65-79 ft. lbs.	88-107 Nm
Oil Pan	3-4 ft. lbs.	4-6 Nm
Rocker Arm Assembly		
Bolts	12-15 ft. lbs.	16-20 Nm
Nuts	15-17 ft. lbs.	20-23 Nm
Rocker Arm Cover	3-5 ft. lbs.	4-7 Nm
Thermostat Housing	10-17 ft. lbs.	14-24 Nm
Water Pump	16-18 ft. lbs.	12-25 Nm

86863C11

TORQUE SPECIFICATIONS
2.2L DIESEL ENGINE

Component	U.S.	Metric
Combination Manifold		
Non-turbocharged	10-17 ft. lbs.	14-25 Nm
Turbocharged engine	13-17 ft. lbs.	17-25 Nm
Connecting Rods	58-65 ft. lbs.	77-87 Nm
Cylinder Head		
1st	40-47 ft. lbs.	54-63 Nm
2nd (New Bolt)	54-61 ft. lbs.	74-81 Nm
2nd (Used Bolt)	61-69 ft. lbs.	81-95 Nm
Crankshaft pulley	124-151 ft. lbs.	248-300 Nm
Exhaust Manifold	14-18 ft. lbs.	19-25 Nm
Flywheel	83-90 ft. lbs.	113-122 Nm
Intake Manifold	13-18 ft. lbs.	19-25 Nm
Main Bearing Caps	116-130 ft. lbs.	157-176 Nm
Oil Pan	11-17 ft. lbs.	15-24 Nm
Rocker Arm Assembly	10-17 ft. lbs.	14-24 Nm
Rocker Arm Cover	9-13 ft. lbs.	12-18 Nm
Thermostat Housing	10-17 ft. lbs.	14-24 Nm
Water Pump	11-18 ft. lbs.	15-23 Nm

86863C12

TORQUE SPECIFICATIONS
2.3L AND 2.6L ENGINE

Component	U.S.	Metric
Connecting Rods	42-45 ft. lbs.	57-61 Nm
Cylinder Head *		
1st	40-47 ft. lbs.	54-63 Nm
2nd	65-80 ft. lbs.	88-108 Nm
Crankshaft pulley	76-90 ft. lbs.	103-122 Nm
Exhaust Manifold	14-18 ft. lbs.	19-25 Nm
Flywheel	40-47 ft. lbs.	55-64 Nm
Intake Manifold	14-18 ft. lbs.	19-25 Nm
Main Bearing Caps *	65-80 ft. lbs.	88-108 Nm
Oil Pan	3-4 ft. lbs.	4-6 Nm
Oil Pump	12-15 ft. lbs.	16-20 Nm
Rocker Arm Assembly		
Bolts	12-15 ft. lbs.	16-20 Nm
Nuts	15-17 ft. lbs.	20-23 Nm
Small bolts	5-7 ft. lbs.	7-10 Nm
Rocker Arm Cover	3-5 ft. lbs.	4-7 Nm
Spark Plug	10-17 ft. lbs.	14-23 Nm
Thermostat Housing	10-17 ft. lbs.	14-24 Nm
Water Pump		
Bolts	12-15 ft. lbs.	16-20 Nm
Nut	18-21 ft. lbs.	24-28 Nm

* apply oil to threads

86863C13

TORQUE SPECIFICATIONS
2.8L AND 3.1L ENGINE

Component	U.S.	Metric
A/C Compressor Bracket	58 ft. lbs.	78 Nm
Connecting Rods	38-40 ft. lbs.	52-54 Nm
Cylinder Head		
1st	40-42 ft. lbs.	54-57 Nm
2nd	tighten an additional 90 degrees	
Crankshaft pulley	68-72 ft. lbs.	93-98 Nm
Exhaust Manifold	14-18 ft. lbs.	19-25 Nm
Flywheel	40-47 ft. lbs.	55-64 Nm
Intake Manifold		
2.8L engine	23 ft. lbs.	31 Nm
3.1L engine	19 ft. lbs.	26 Nm
Main Bearing Caps		
2.8L engine	70 ft. lbs.	95 Nm
3.1L engine	72 ft. lbs.	98 Nm
Oil Pan		
Bolts	18 ft. lbs.	25 Nm
Nuts	7 ft. lbs.	10 Nm
Oil Pump	30 ft. lbs.	41 Nm
Power Steering Bracket	37 ft. lbs.	50 Nm
Rocker Arm	Follow adjustment procedure	
Rocker Arm Cover	72 inch lbs.	8 Nm
Spark Plug		
2.8L	22 ft. lbs.	29 Nm
3.1L	14 ft. lbs.	19 Nm
Thermostat Housing	18 ft. lbs.	24 Nm
Water Pump	22 ft. lbs.	30 Nm

86863C14

TORQUE SPECIFICATIONS
3.2L ENGINE

Component	U.S.	Metric
Camshaft		
Pulley	41 ft. lbs.	55 Nm
M6 Housing Bolts	70 inch lbs.	8 Nm
M8 Housing Bolts	13 ft. lbs.	18 Nm
Connecting Rods	49 ft. lbs.	67 Nm
Cooling Fan Assembly	70 inch lbs.	8 Nm
Cylinder Head *		
M8x1.5 Bolts	15 ft. lbs.	21 Nm
M11x1.5 (must use new bolts)	47 ft. lbs.	64 Nm
Crankshaft pulley	123 ft. lbs.	167 Nm
Exhaust Manifold		
Manifold	42 ft. lbs.	57 Nm
Studs	49 ft. lbs.	32 Nm
Front Pipe	32 ft. lbs.	43 Nm
EGR Pipe	21 ft. lbs.	28 Nm
Flywheel	40-47 ft. lbs.	55-64 Nm
Intake Manifold		
Nuts and Bolts	17 ft. lbs.	24 Nm
Common Chamber	17 ft. lbs.	24 Nm
Throttle Body	16 ft. lbs.	22 Nm
EGR Pipe	21 ft. lbs.	28 Nm
Main Bearing Caps *		
Main Caps Bolts	29 ft. lbs.	39 Nm
Side Galley Bolts	29 ft. lbs.	39 Nm
Oil Gallery Bolts *		
1st	29 ft. lbs	39 Nm
2nd	an additional 60 degrees	
Oil Pan	89 inch lbs.	10 Nm
Oil Pump	13 ft. lbs.	18 Nm
Oxygen Sensor	31 ft. lbs.	42 Nm
Power Steering Pump	41 ft. lbs.	56 Nm
Rocker Arm Cover	70 inch lbs.	8 Nm
Rocker Arm Shaft	13 ft. lbs.	18 Nm
Spark Plug	13 ft. lbs.	18 Nm
Thermostat Housing	14 ft. lbs.	19 Nm
Timing Belt		
Cover	12 ft. lbs.	17 Nm
Pusher	14 ft. lbs.	19 Nm
Water Pump	13 ft. lbs.	18 Nm

* apply oil to threads

86863C15

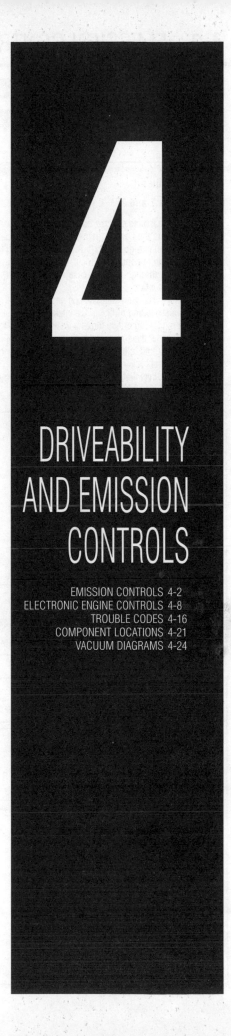

4

DRIVEABILITY AND EMISSION CONTROLS

EMISSION CONTROLS

Crankcase Ventilation System

OPERATION

Gasoline Engines

▶ **See Figures 1 and 2**

Most of the gasoline engines covered in this manual use a PCV valve. The PCV valve meters the flow at a rate depending upon the manifold vacuum. If the manifold vacuum is high, the PCV restricts the flow to the intake manifold. If abnormal, operating conditions occur, excessive amounts of internal exhaust gases back flow through the crankcase vent tube into the air filter to be burned by normal combustion.

Some early carbureted gasoline engines do not use a PCV valve. In place of the valve is a regulating orifice in the intake manifold. Blow-by gases are drawn through the regulating orifice into the intake manifold for reburning. During wide open throttle, the engine vacuum is not sufficient to draw enough vapor through the manifold, allowing part to be drawn into the air cleaner via a hose at the rear end of the rocker arm cover.

The crankcase ventilation system must be operating correctly to provide complete scavenging of the crankcase vapors.

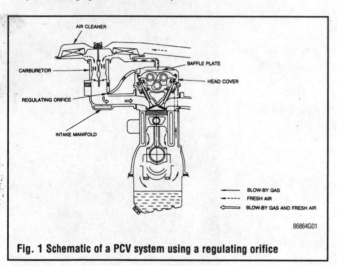

Fig. 1 Schematic of a PCV system using a regulating orifice

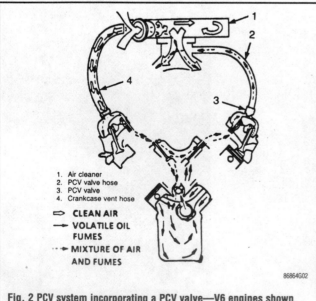

1. Air cleaner
2. PCV valve hose
3. PCV valve
4. Crankcase vent hose

⇨ **CLEAN AIR**

→ **VOLATILE OIL FUMES**

--▶ **MIXTURE OF AIR AND FUMES**

Fig. 2 PCV system incorporating a PCV valve—V6 engines shown

Diesel Engines

▶ **See Figures 3 and 4**

The crankcase ventilation system is a closed type, and is designed to force blow-by gas generated in the engine crankcase back into the intake manifold to return with the fresh air back into the combustion chamber.

When the engine is running at high speed, the high negative pressure from the intake manifold makes the diaphragm valve close, as a result, the blow-by gas passes through the regulating orifice. When the engine is running at low speed, the negative pressure from the intake manifold is so small that the cylinder head cover pressure makes the diaphragm valve open. As a result, the blow-by gas passes through both the regulating orifice and the diaphragm passage opened by the diaphragm valve.

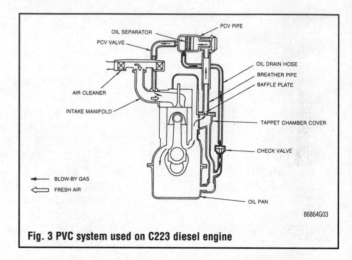

Fig. 3 PVC system used on C223 diesel engine

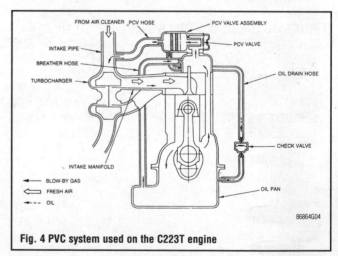

Fig. 4 PVC system used on the C223T engine

INSPECTION

PCV Valve

▶ **See Figure 5**

1. While the engine is idling, pull the PCV valve from the valve cover.
2. Place your thumb over the end of the PCV valve and check for vacuum.
3. If no vacuum exists, check for a plugged PCV valve, manifold port, hoses or deteriorated hoses. Also, check for proper routing. Refer to the vacuum diagrams at the end of this section.
4. With the engine off, remove the PCV valve and shake it. Listen for the rattle of the check needle inside the valve. If it does not rattle, replace the valve.

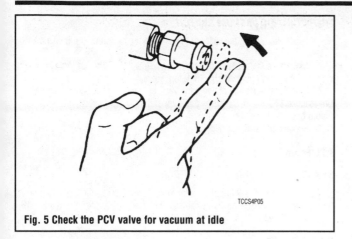

Fig. 5 Check the PCV valve for vacuum at idle

Regulating Orifice System

Clean the hoses and calibrating orifice internally. Blow away foreign matter with compressed air. Check the hoses for cracks, fatigue and swelling. Replace if necessary.

REMOVAL & INSTALLATION

1. Label the PCV valve or regulating orifice hoses before removing.
2. Disconnect the hoses and remove the valve/orifice.
3. Connect the hoses to the new valve/orifice and install the valve/orifice.

Evaporative Emission Controls

OPERATION

◆ See Figure 6

To limit gasoline vapor discharge into the air, this system is designed to trap fuel vapors, which normally escape from the fuel tank and, if equipped, the carburetor. Vapor arrest is accomplished through the use of the charcoal canister. This canister absorbs fuel vapors and stores them until they can be removed to be burned in the engine. Removal of the vapors from the canister to the engine is accomplished by a carburetor, throttle body assembly or solenoid operated bowl vent. The fuel tank requires a non-vented gas cap. The domed fuel tank positions a vent high enough above the fuel to keep the vent pipe in the vapor at all times. The single vent pipe is routed directly to the canister. From the canister, the vapors are routed to the PCV system, where they will be burned during normal combustion.

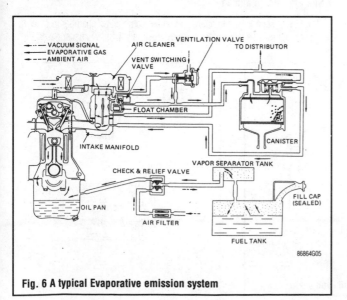

Fig. 6 A typical Evaporative emission system

TESTING

1.8L and 2.0L Engines

SYSTEM INSPECTION

Visually inspect the entire system for kinked, cracked, swollen, plugged or fatigued hoses. Replace the vapor canister if cracked, damaged or if fuel is leaking from the bottom.

CHECK AND RELIEF VALVE

Remove the check valve and inspect for leakage by blowing air into the ports in the check valve as follows. Replace if necessary.
1. When air is applied from the fuel tank side, the check valve is normal if air passes in to the check side (canister side), but not leaking into the relief side (air filter).
2. When air is applied from the check side, the valve is normal if air is restricted.
3. When air is applied from the relief side, the valve is normal if air passes into the fuel tank side but not into the check side.

ROLL OVER AND FLOAT VALVE

Check the roll over and float valve for fuel leaks, distortion, dents and orifice clogging. Replace if necessary.

CANISTER

Remove the canister and inspect the function of the purge valve as follows. Replace if necessary.
1. When 7.5 psi (51 kPa) of pressure is applied to the port marked **VC**, there should not be an air leak from the diaphragm.
2. Apply 15 in.Hg (50 kPa) of vacuum to the port marked **PURGE**. Gradually apply vacuum to the port marked **VC**.
3. If the purge control valve begins to open between 7–9 in.Hg (23–30 kPa), the purge control valve is normal.

Carbureted 2.3L Engines

SYSTEM INSPECTION

Visually inspect the entire system for kinked, cracked, swollen, plugged or fatigued hoses. Replace the vapor canister if cracked, damaged or if fuel is leaking from the bottom.

CANISTER

Remove the canister and inspect the function of the purge valve as follows. Replace if necessary.
1. When 7.5 psi (51 kPa) of pressure is applied to the port marked **VC**, there should not be an air leak from the diaphragm.
2. Apply 15 in.Hg (50 kPa) of vacuum to the port marked **PURGE**. Gradually apply vacuum to the port marked **VC**.
3. If the purge control valve begins to open between 7–9 in.Hg (23–30 kPa), the purge control valve is normal.

VACUUM SWITCHING VALVE (VSV)

◆ See Figure 7

1. Unplug the electrical connector. Using an ohmmeter check the resistance between the terminals. If should be approximately 35 ohms.
2. Using a fused jumper wire, apply battery voltage to the valve terminals.
3. Check to see that air does not flow freely through ports **X** and **Y**.
4. Remove the jumper wire from the terminals.
5. Check that air flows freely through ports **X** and **Y**. If a problem is found, replace the valve.

VENTILATION VALVE

◆ See Figure 8

1. Check to see that air flows freely through ports **B** and **C**.
2. Apply vacuum to port **A**. Check to see that air does not flow from ports **B** to **C**.
3. Replace the valve if defective.

ROLL OVER AND FLOAT VALVE

Check the roll over and float valve for fuel leaks, distortion, dents and orifice clogging. Replace if necessary.

Fuel Injected 2.3L and 2.6L Engines

SYSTEM INSPECTION

Visually inspect the entire system for kinked, cracked, swollen, plugged or fatigued hoses. Replace the vapor canister if cracked, damaged or if fuel is leaking from the bottom.

CANISTER

➡This procedure does not apply to 1996 models. On 1996 models, visually inspect the canister. Replace the vapor canister if cracked, damaged or if fuel is leaking from the bottom.

1. Unplug hose **A** from the canister. The hose should be free of restrictions and air should pass freely into the canister. Reconnect the hose.
2. Start the engine and allow it to idle.
3. Unplug hose **C** and check that vacuum is not present at ports **B** and **D**.
4. Replace the canister if necessary.

VACUUM SWITCHING VALVE (VSV)

♦ See Figure 9

➡This component is not used on 1996 models.

1. Unplug the electrical connector. Using an ohmmeter check the resistance between the terminals. If should be approximately 35 ohms.
2. Using a fused jumper wire, apply battery voltage to the valve terminals.
3. Check to see that air does not flow freely through ports **Y** and **Z**, but flows freely from **X** to **Y**.
4. Remove the jumper wire from the terminals.
5. Check that air flows freely through ports **Y** and **Z**, but not **X** and **Y**. If a problem is found, replace the valve.

PURGE VALVE

➡The purge valve is found on 1996 models only.

1. Unplug the solenoid connector.
2. Disconnect the throttle body-to-purge solenoid vacuum hose.
3. Apply 15 in. Hg (51 kPa) of vacuum. The solenoid should hold vacuum; if not replace it.
4. Apply battery voltage to the solenoid terminals. The vacuum must drop. If not, replace the solenoid.

2.8L and 3.1L Engines

SYSTEM INSPECTION

Visually inspect the entire system for kinked, cracked, swollen, plugged or fatigued hoses. Replace the vapor canister if cracked, damaged or if fuel is leaking from the bottom.

THERMOSTATIC VACUUM SWITCH

1. Label and unplug the vacuum hoses from the switch on the intake manifold.
2. Make sure the coolant temperature is below 115°F (46°C). Apply vacuum to one of the switch ports. It should hold a vacuum.
3. Start the engine and observe the vacuum gauge as the coolant temperature reaches 115°F (46°C). When this temperature is approached, the switch should begin to bleed the vacuum.
4. Replace the switch if necessary.

3.2L Engines

SYSTEM INSPECTION

Visually inspect the entire system for kinked, cracked, swollen, plugged or fatigued hoses. Replace the vapor canister if cracked, damaged or if fuel is leaking from the bottom.

PURGE VALVE

1. Unplug the solenoid connector.
2. Disconnect the throttle body-to-purge solenoid vacuum hose.
3. Apply 15 in. Hg (51 kPa) of vacuum. The solenoid should hold vacuum; if not replace it.
4. Apply battery voltage to the solenoid terminals. The vacuum must drop. If not, replace the solenoid.

PURGE VACUUM SWITCH

➡This is only used on 1996 3.2L engines.

1. Unplug the solenoid connector.
2. Disconnect the purge solenoid-to-vacuum switch vacuum hose.
3. Using an ohmmeter, check for continuity between the ohmmeter terminals. If continuity is not present, replace the switch.
4. Apply vacuum to the switch. Continuity should not be present at the switch terminals. Replace the switch if necessary.

REMOVAL & INSTALLATION

Components of the evaporative system are all removed in the same basic manner. First label, then unplug any vacuum and electrical connections from the component. Remove any hardware retaining the component to the vehicle, then remove the component from the vehicle.

Exhaust Gas Recirculation (EGR) System

OPERATION

♦ See Figures 10 and 11

The EGR system lowers temperatures in the combustion chamber in order to reduce nitrogen oxide emissions in the exhaust gas stream. Exhaust gases are

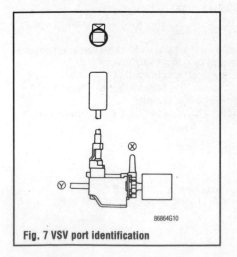
Fig. 7 VSV port identification

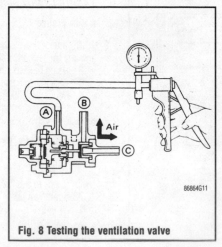
Fig. 8 Testing the ventilation valve

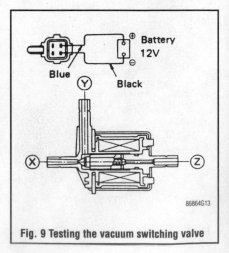
Fig. 9 Testing the vacuum switching valve

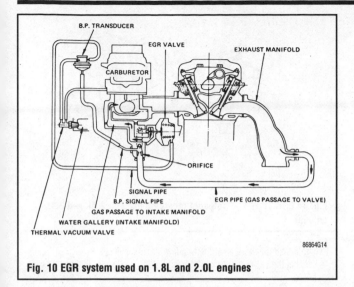

Fig. 10 EGR system used on 1.8L and 2.0L engines

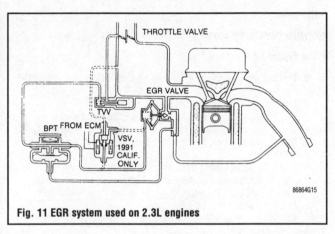

Fig. 11 EGR system used on 2.3L engines

drawn from the cylinder head exhaust port through the intake manifold riser through the cylinder head, intake manifold and EGR valve passages.

TESTING

1981–95 Gasoline Engines

BACKPRESSURE TRANSDUCER—EXCEPT 3.2L

➡This is found on 1.8L, 2.0L and 2.3L carbureted engines.

1. Blow air into the black colored hose at the lower side of the transducer. It should be closed.
2. Blow air into the EGR side signal hose. Check to see if air passes through the opposite side and air filter side of the transducer.
3. If necessary, replace the transducer.

BACKPRESSURE TRANSDUCER—3.2L

1. Label and disconnect the hoses from the transducer.
2. Place a finger over the Vacuum Switching Valve (VSV) port and blow into the EGR valve port of the transducer. Air should pass through the filter portion of the transducer.
3. Connect a vacuum gauge to the VSV port and plug the EGR port.
4. Blow air into port **S**. Vacuum should be indicated on the gauge.
5. Replace the transducer if necessary.

THERMAL VACUUM VALVE

➡This is not used on the fuel injected engines.

The thermal vacuum valve is mounted on the intake manifold and is connected in series between the vacuum port in the carburetor and EGR valve.

While the coolant temperature is below 115129°F (4654°C) the valve is closed. Above that temperature, the valve is open.

To test the thermal vacuum valve, disconnect the hoses. Check that no air flows between the hoses when the engine is cold and that the passage opens after engine warms up.

EGR CUT VALVE AND DUTY SOLENOID

➡These components are only used on the 2.3L and 2.6L fuel injected engines.

1. Label and unplug the electrical connection and hoses from the valve/solenoid.
2. Apply battery voltage between the terminals using a jumper wire.
3. Check that air flows freely from port **X** to **Y**.
4. Disconnect the jumper wire and check that air does not flow from **X** to **Y**.
5. Replace the valve/solenoid as necessary.

ELECTRONIC VACUUM REGULATOR VALVE

➡This component is found on the 2.8L and 3.1L engines.

1. Unplug the solenoid valve connector.
2. Disconnect the throttle body-to-solenoid valve vacuum hose.
3. Apply 15 in. Hg (51 kPa) of vacuum. The solenoid should hold vacuum; if not replace it.
4. Apply battery voltage to the solenoid terminals. The vacuum must drop. If not, replace the solenoid valve.

VACUUM SWITCHING VALVE (VSV)

▶ See Figure 12

➡This component is found on the 3.2L engine.

1. Label and unplug the hoses and electrical connection from the valve.
2. Check the resistance between the two terminals with an ohmmeter. It should be 33–39 ohms.
3. Blow into port **1**. Air should exhaust through the filter, not port **2**.
4. Apply battery voltage to the valve terminals. Blow into port **1**. Air should exhaust through port **2**.
5. Replace the valve if necessary.

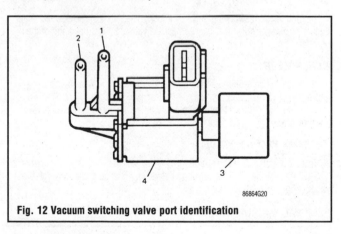

Fig. 12 Vacuum switching valve port identification

EGR VALVE

▶ See Figure 13

1. Disconnect and plug the vacuum hose from the valve.
2. Apply vacuum to the port on the valve. It should hold vacuum.
3. Release the vacuum.
4. Start the engine and allow it to idle.
5. Apply vacuum to the port on the valve. The engine should run rough or stall.
6. If the engine did not stall or run rough, shut the engine off and allow it to cool.
7. Remove the EGR valve and check for clogged passages in the valve and intake manifold.
8. Clean or replace the valve as necessary.

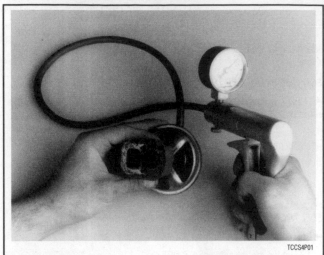

Fig. 13 Some EGR valves may be tested using a vacuum pump by watching for diaphragm movement

1996 Gasoline Engines

An OBD-II compliant scan tool is necessary to diagnose the EGR system used on 1996 models. Please follow the accompanying diagnostic charts.

Diesel Engines

➡An EGR system is used on the C223 California engine only.

EGR VALVE

With the engine off, unplug the vacuum hose from the valve. Apply vacuum to the port on the valve. The diaphragm should move smoothly and be able to hold vacuum.

VACUUM SWITCHING VALVE

Test the vacuum switching valve by applying 12V to the electrical terminals. Listen for plunger noise that is accompanied with electrical operation of the plunger.

CONTROLLER

To check the controller, connect a voltmeter to the green/black or green (+) and black/yellow (–) wire terminals at the vacuum switching valve. The controller is normal if the voltage is about 12V when the engine speed is below 3000 rpm.

THERMAL VACUUM VALVE

Test the thermal valve by submerging it in water and raise the temperature to 115–129°F (46–54°C). Blow through the valve. Air should pass through the valve, if not replace the valve.

REMOVAL & INSTALLATION

Control Solenoids

▶ See Figure 14

The various control solenoids used on the EGR systems can all be removed using the same basic procedure.
1. Unplug the electrical connection from the solenoid.
2. Label and disconnect the vacuum hoses.
3. Remove any hardware securing the solenoid to the engine.
4. When installing the solenoid, be sure to connect the vacuum hoses to the correct ports.

Thermal Vacuum Valve

1. Label and disconnect the vacuum hoses from the valve.
2. Unthread the valve from the intake manifold.

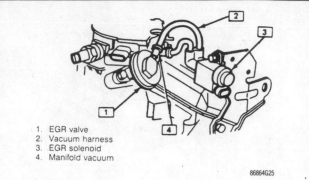

1. EGR valve
2. Vacuum harness
3. EGR solenoid
4. Manifold vacuum

86864G25

Fig. 14 EGR valve and solenoid mounting used on 2.8L and 3.1L engines

3. To install the valve, coat the first few threads with sealer.
4. Install the valve in the manifold and tighten until snug. Engage the vacuum hoses.

EGR Valve

VACUUM OPERATED VALVES

▶ See Figure 14

1. Remove any components which may interfere with removal of the EGR valve.
2. Unplug the vacuum hose from the valve.
3. If equipped, remove the exhaust crossover pipe from the valve.
4. If equipped, bend back the retaining tabs securing the mounting bolts.
5. Loosen and remove the bolts securing the valve, then remove the valve.

To install:
6. Clean the gasket mating surfaces of the manifold and valve.
7. Using a new gasket, install the valve. Tighten the bolts until snug.
8. If applicable, bend the retaining tabs to secure the mounting bolts.
9. Install the crossover pipe if equipped.
10. Connect the vacuum hose and install any remaining components removed.

LINEAR EGR VALVES

▶ See Figure 15

➡These valves are found on 1996 models.

1. Disconnect the negative battery cable.
2. Unplug the electrical connector from the valve.
3. Remove the hardware securing the valve to the intake manifold.
4. Remove the valve and gasket from the manifold.

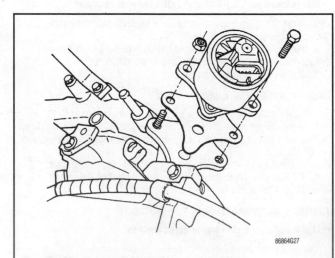

86864G27

Fig. 15 EGR valve mounting used on 3.2L engines

To install:

5. Install the valve with a new gasket. Tighten the securing hardware until snug.
6. Engage the electrical connector to the valve.
7. Connect the negative battery cable.

Early Fuel Evaporation (EFE) System

OPERATION

➡**This component is found on some carbureted models.**

The Early Fuel Evaporation (EFE) system consists of the EFE heater, electronic control module, coolant temperature sensor and the EFE relay.

The EFE heater is equipped with a ceramic ring which is located below the primary carburetor bore. The ring is an internal part of the carburetor gasket. The EFE heats the incoming air charge to improve atomization. This offers better cold start and driveaway performance.

The coolant temperature sensor is activated when the ignition switch is turned to the **ON** position and the engine is started. If the engine coolant temperature is below the specified value, the ECM will supply current from the battery to the coils in the EFE heater to heat the incoming fuel/air charge.

INSPECTION

Remove the EFE heater from under the carburetor. If any of the heating grids are cracked or if the heater plate is damaged, it must be replaced.

REMOVAL & INSTALLATION

1. Disconnect the negative (–) battery cable.
2. Remove the air cleaner assembly.
3. Remove the carburetor as outlined in Section 5.
4. Disconnect and remove the EFE heater and gaskets.

To install:

5. Install the heater with new gaskets.
6. Install the carburetor as outlined in Section 5.
7. Install the air cleaner, connect the battery cable, start the engine and check operation.

High Altitude Emission Control System

OPERATION

On the 1988 Pick-Up, the major component of the system is the altitude switch which is installed on the right side of the dash panel. This switch senses altitude to the height of 6560 ft. (2000 m). The switch is connected to the ECM and makes the check engine lamp inoperable in case of a rich oxygen sensor error at or above the designated altitude.There is no interaction between the altitude switch and the emission control system and the system does not require adjustment.

On the 1989 and later Amigo and P'Up, a Manifold Absolute Pressure (MAP) sensor is used to measure atmospheric pressure though a vacuum switching valve. The system prevents the vehicle's self-diagnostic system from generating a false rich fuel metering error at altitudes higher than the system's set point.

Thermostatically Controlled Air (TCA) Cleaner System

OPERATION

◆ **See Figure 16**

The TCA functions to maintain ambient air temperature at an optimum level so that the fuel/air ratio remains constant. This ensures fuel combustion and reduces pollutant emissions. The TCA system is mounted on the air cleaner. It consists of a vacuum motor, hot air control damper and an Inlet Temperature Compensator (ITC) valve.

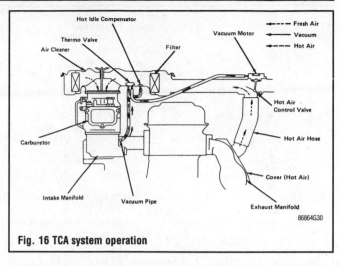

Fig. 16 TCA system operation

When the engine is running, there is no vacuum signal at either the vacuum motor or the ITC valve. In this condition the vacuum motor spring closes off the passage from the hot air duct. On a cold start, the ITC valve delivers maximum vacuum to the vacuum motor which moves the hot air control damper to the fully open position. This closes the ambient air passage and opens the hot air duct. If the engine speed increases, the system vacuum level will drop allowing the diaphragm spring to overcome the vacuum force and push the hot air control damper to the fully closed position.

When the engine is running under normal conditions, the ITC valve closes the passage to the intake manifold and opens the passage to the from the air cleaner to the vacuum motor. As fresh air is fed to the vacuum motor, the diaphragm spring forces the air control valve to close off the hot air duct and open the ambient air passage.

During conditions of extended idling, hill climbing or high speed driving, there is a substantial increase in engine and engine compartment temperatures. This results in an excessive amount of fuel vapor entering the intake manifold, causing an over-rich mixture. The over-rich mixture causes rough idling and increased CO emissions. To prevent this, the ITC valve opens the passage from the air cleaner to the intake manifold. Fresh air is allowed to enter the intake manifold and lean out the mixture.

TESTING

Vacuum Motor

1. Remove the air cleaner.
2. Unplug the vacuum hose from the motor.
3. Check that the hot air flap is completely closed.
4. Apply vacuum to the motor. Check that the flap opens and is able to hold a vacuum.
5. Replace the motor if necessary.

Thermo Sensor

◆ **See Figure 17**

1. Remove the air cleaner.
2. Apply a vacuum to the sensor. If the ambient air temperature is below 86°F (30°C) on 2.8L and 3.1L engines or 100–111° F (38–44° C) on other engines, it should hold a vacuum.
3. With a hair drier, heat the sensor to above 86°F (30°C) on 2.8L and 3.1L engines or 100–111° F (38–44° C) on other engines. The sensor should now bleed off the vacuum.
4. Replace the sensor if necessary.

Inlet Temperature Compensator

◆ **See Figure 18**

➡**This is not used on 2.8L and 3.1L engines.**

1. Remove the air cleaner.
2. Blow air through the sensor hose. If the ambient air temperature is below 115°F (46°C), air should not pass.

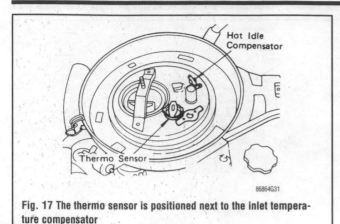

Fig. 17 The thermo sensor is positioned next to the inlet temperature compensator

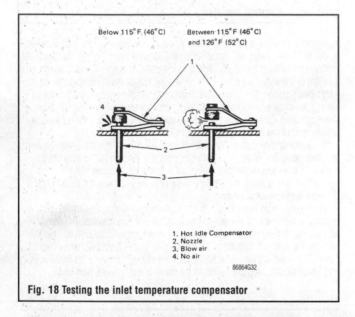

1. Hot Idle Compensator
2. Nozzle
3. Blow air
4. No air

Fig. 18 Testing the inlet temperature compensator

3. With a hair drier, heat the sensor to above 115° F (46°C). The sensor should now be able to pass air.
4. Replace the sensor if necessary.

Air Injection Reactor Systems

OPERATION

In gasoline engines, it is difficult to burn the air-fuel mixture completely through combustion that takes place with the combustion chambers. In order to reduce HC and CO emissions, the system draws air into the exhaust ports to speed up oxidation. The air management valve switches air passage from the air pump through a vacuum management valve which is actuated by an electric signal supplied from the ECM.

The air pump is belt driven by the pulley mounted on the water pump shaft of the engine. Air is drawn through the air cleaner and suction hose into the outlet chamber, where it is trapped between two vanes and the pump body. As the rotor turns, these vanes carry the air to the outlet chamber and then to the air manifold.

TESTING

1.8L and 2.0L Engines

The check valve should only allow air to flow in one direction. If air does not flow or in both directions, the valve is defective and must be replaced.

The air switching valve is designed to switch air flow from the air pump. When the manifold vacuum flows to the pipe, the air switching valve allows air from the pump to flow to the check valve. Unplug the valve electrical connector check the resistance between the terminals of the valve with an ohmmeter. It should be over 20 ohms.

2.3L, 2.6L and 2.8L Engines

The check valve should only allow air to flow in one direction. If air does not flow or in both directions, the valve is defective and must be replaced.

Unplug the valve electrical connector check the resistance between the terminals of the valve with an ohmmeter. It should be over 20 ohms.

ELECTRONIC ENGINE CONTROLS

General Information

SERVICE PRECAUTIONS

Be careful not to get water on any electronic component. Pay close attention to the relay box and throttle valve switch connector. The connector is not waterproofed and may be damaged by water.

When charging the battery be sure to remove it from the vehicle first. Never disconnect the battery cable from the battery when the engine is running. The generation of surge voltage may damage the control unit and other electrical parts.

When replacing parts or checking the system, make sure to set the starter switch to the **OFF** position. When measuring voltage at the control unit harness connector, unplug all the control unit harnesses first, then set the starter switch to the **ON** position.

When checking the electrical terminals of the control unit with a tester, do not apply the probe to terminal directly but insert a pin into the terminal from the harness side and perform the measurement through the pin. If the tester probe is held against the terminal directly, the terminal will be deformed, causing poor contact. Connect each harness correctly and firmly to insure a good contact.

The wiring connectors for the fuel injector, throttle valve switch, air regulator and water temperature sensor are provided with locked wires. To unlock the connector, pull and shake it gently.

System cables must be placed at least 4 in. (10 cm) away from the tension cables. Be careful not to apply any shock to the system components such as the air flow sensor, crank angle sensor, and control unit. Component parts of the fuel injection system are precisely set. Even a slight distortion or dent will seriously affect performance.

The fuel pump must not be operated without fuel. Since fuel lubricates the pump, noise or other serious problems such as parts seizure will result. It is also prohibited to use any fuel other than gasoline.

Electronic Control Module (ECM)

OPERATION

➡**When the term Electronic Control Module (ECM) is used in this manual it will refer to the engine control computer regardless that it may be a Vehicle Control Module (VCM), Powertrain Control Module (PCM) or Electronic Control Module (ECM).**

The Electronic Control Module (ECM) is required to maintain the exhaust emissions at acceptable levels. The module is a small, solid state computer which receives signals from many sources and sensors; it uses these data to make judgments about operating conditions and then control output signals to the fuel and emission systems to match the current requirements.

Engines coupled to electronically controlled transmissions employ a Powertrain Control Module (PCM) or Vehicle Control Module (VCM) to oversee both engine and transmission operation. The integrated functions of engine and transmission control allow accurate gear selection and improved fuel economy.

In the event of an ECM failure, the system will default to a pre-programmed set of values. These are compromise values which allow the engine to operate, although at a reduced efficiency. This is variously known as the default, limp-in or back-up mode. Driveability is almost always affected when the ECM enters this mode.

REMOVAL & INSTALLATION

♦ See Figure 19

1. Disconnect the negative battery cable. Disable the SRS system if equipped.
2. Remove any trim panel necessary to access the ECM.
3. Disengage the connectors from the ECM.
4. Remove the spring retainer off and over the rail of the ECM.
5. Slide the ECM out of the bracket at an angle.
6. Remove the ECM.

To install:

7. Install the ECM into the bracket.
8. Install the spring retainer and engage the electrical connectors.
9. Install any components removed to access the ECM.
10. Connect the negative battery cable.

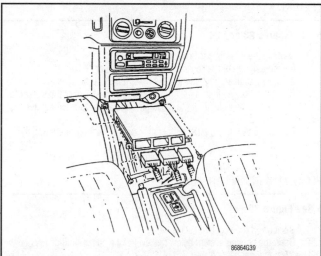

86864G39

Fig. 19 The ECM can usually be found in front of the center console, under the dash

Oxygen Sensor

OPERATION

There are two types of oxygen sensor's used in these vehicles. They are the single wire oxygen sensor (O2S) and the heated oxygen sensor (HO2S). The oxygen sensor is a spark plug shaped device that is screwed into the exhaust manifold. It monitors the oxygen content of the exhaust gases and sends a voltage signal to the Electronic Control Module (ECM). The ECM monitors this voltage and, depending on the value of the received signal, issues a command to the mixture control solenoid on the carburetor to adjust for rich or lean conditions.

The heated oxygen sensor has a heating element incorporated into the sensor to aid in the warm up to the proper operating temperature and to maintain that temperature.

The proper operation of the oxygen sensor depends upon four basic conditions:

1. Good electrical connections. Since the sensor generates low currents, good clean electrical connections at the sensor are a must.
2. Outside air supply. Air must circulate to the internal portion of the sensor. When servicing the sensor, do not restrict the air passages.
3. Proper operating temperatures. The ECM will not recognize the sensor's signals until the sensor reaches approximately 600°F (316°C).

4. Non-leaded fuel. The use of leaded gasoline will damage the sensor very quickly.

TESTING

Single Wire Sensor

1. Start the engine and bring it to normal operating temperature, then run the engine above 1200 rpm for two minutes.
2. Backprobe with a high impedance averaging voltmeter (set to the DC voltage scale) between the oxygen sensor (O2S) and battery ground.
3. Verify that the O2S voltage fluctuates rapidly between 0.40–0.60 volts.
4. If the O2S voltage is stabilized at the middle of the specified range (approximately 0.45–0.55 volts) or if the O2S voltage fluctuates very slowly between the specified range (O2S signal crosses 0.5 volts less than 5 times in ten seconds), the O2S may be faulty.
5. If the O2S voltage stabilizes at either end of the specified range, the ECM is probably not able to compensate for a mechanical problem such as a vacuum leak, faulty pressure regulator or high float level. These types of mechanical problems will cause the O2S to sense a constant lean or constant rich mixture. The mechanical problem will first have to be repaired and then the O2S test repeated.
6. Pull a vacuum hose located after the throttle plate. Voltage should drop to approximately 0.12 volts (while still fluctuating rapidly). This tests the ability of the O2S to detect a lean mixture condition. Reattach the vacuum hose.
7. Richen the mixture using a propane enrichment tool. Voltage should rise to approximately 0.90 volts (while still fluctuating rapidly). This tests the ability of the O2S to detect a rich mixture condition.
8. If the O2S voltage is above or below the specified range, the O2S and/or the O2S wiring may be faulty. Check the wiring for any breaks, repair as necessary and repeat the test.

Heated Oxygen Sensor

1. Start the engine and bring it to normal operating temperature, then run the engine above 1200 rpm for two minutes.
2. Turn the ignition **OFF** disengage the HO2S harness connector.
3. Check for battery voltage at the white/blue wire with the ignition switch **ON** and the engine off. If not, there is a problem in the black/yellow or red/green wire. Check the HO2S wiring and the fuse.
4. Next, connect a high impedance ohmmeter between the black wire and white/red wire that becomes the black/yellow wire after the connector. Verify that the resistance is 3.5–14.0 ohms.
5. If the HO2S heater resistance is not as specified, the HO2S may be faulty.
6. Start the engine and bring it to normal operating temperature, then run the engine above 1200 rpm for two minutes.
7. Backprobe with a high impedance averaging voltmeter (set to the DC voltage scale) between the oxygen sensor (O2S) and battery ground.
8. Verify that the O2S voltage fluctuates rapidly between 0.40–0.60 volts.
9. If the O2S voltage is stabilized at the middle of the specified range (approximately 0.45–0.55 volts) or if the O2S voltage fluctuates very slowly between the specified range (O2S signal crosses 0.5 volts less than 5 times in ten seconds), the O2S may be faulty.
10. If the O2S voltage stabilizes at either end of the specified range, the ECM is probably not able to compensate for a mechanical problem such as a vacuum leak or a faulty fuel pressure regulator. These types of mechanical problems will cause the O2S to sense a constant lean or constant rich mixture. The mechanical problem will first have to be repaired and then the O2S test repeated.
11. Pull a vacuum hose located after the throttle plate. Voltage should drop to approximately 0.12 volts (while still fluctuating rapidly). This tests the ability of the O2S to detect a lean mixture condition. Reattach the vacuum hose.
12. Richen the mixture using a propane enrichment tool. Voltage should rise to approximately 0.90 volts (while still fluctuating rapidly). This tests the ability of the O2S to detect a rich mixture condition.
13. If the O2S voltage is above or below the specified range, the O2S and/or the O2S wiring may be faulty. Check the wiring for any breaks, repair as necessary and repeat the test.

REMOVAL & INSTALLATION

▶ **See Figure 20**

> ⁂ **WARNING**
>
> **The sensor uses a permanently attached pigtail and connector. This pigtail should not be removed from the sensor. Damage or removal of the pigtail or connector could affect the proper operation of the sensor. Keep the electrical connector and louvered end of the sensor clean and free of grease. NEVER use cleaning solvents of any type on the sensor!**

→ **The oxygen sensor may be difficult to remove when the temperature of the engine is below 120°F (49°C). Excessive force may damage the threads in the exhaust manifold or exhaust pipe.**

1. Disconnect the negative battery cable.
2. Unplug the electrical connector and any attaching hardware.
3. Remove the sensor.

To install:

4. Coat the threads of the sensor with an anti-seize compound before installation. New sensors are precoated with this compound.

→ **DO NOT use a conventional anti-seize paste. The use of a regular paste may electrically insulate the sensor, rendering it useless. The threads MUST be coated with the proper electrically conductive anti-seize compound.**

5. Install the sensor and tighten to 30 ft. lbs. (40 Nm). Use care in making sure the silicone boot is in the correct position to avoid melting it during operation.
6. Engage the electrical connector.
7. Connect the negative battery cable.

Mass Air Flow (MAF) Sensor

OPERATION

The Mass Air Flow (MAF) Sensor measures the amount of air entering the engine during a given time. The ECM uses the mass airflow information for fuel delivery calculations. A large quantity of air entering the engine indicates an acceleration or high load situation, while a small quantity of air indicates deceleration or idle.

TESTING

▶ **See Figure 21**

1. Uncover the rubber boot on the sensor side of the harness connector.
2. Remove the intake duct from the sensor.
3. With a high impedance voltmeter, check for voltage between the white wire and ground while blowing through the sampling tube in the sensor. Voltage should be between 0.5–1.5 volts. If not, replace the sensor.
4. Turn the ignition **OFF**. Install the intake dust and recover the connector with the rubber boot.

REMOVAL & INSTALLATION

▶ **See Figure 22**

1. Unplug the connector from the sensor.
2. Remove the air intake duct from the sensor.
3. Remove the bolts securing the sensor, then remove it from the vehicle.
4. To install the sensor, position it in place, then secure it with the mounting bolts. Install the duct and engage the electrical connection.

Engine Coolant Temperature (ECT) Sensor

OPERATION

The Engine Coolant Temperature (ECT) sensor is mounted in the intake manifold and sends engine temperature information to the ECM. The ECM supplies 5 volts to the coolant temperature sensor circuit. The sensor is a thermistor which changes internal resistance as temperature changes. When the sensor is cold (internal resistance high), the ECM monitors a high signal voltage which it interprets as a cold engine. As the sensor warms (internal resistance low), the ECM monitors a low signal voltage which it interprets as warm engine.

TESTING

▶ **See Figures 23 and 24**

1. Remove the ECT sensor from the vehicle.
2. Immerse the tip of the sensor in container of water.
3. Connect a digital ohmmeter to the two terminals of the sensor.
4. Using a calibrated thermometer, compare the resistance of the sensor to the temperature of the water. Refer to the engine coolant sensor temperature vs. resistance illustration.
5. Repeat the test at two other temperature points, heating or cooling the water as necessary.
6. If the sensor does not meet specification, it must be replaced.

REMOVAL & INSTALLATION

▶ **See Figure 25**

1. Disconnect the negative battery cable.
2. Drain the cooling system below the level of the sensor and disengage the sensor electrical connection.
3. Remove the coolant sensor.

To install:

4. Install the sensor and engage the electrical connector.
5. Refill the cooling system and connect the negative battery cable.

Intake Air Temperature (IAT) Sensor

OPERATION

the Intake Air Temperature (IAT) Sensor is a thermistor which changes value based on the temperature of the air entering the engine. Low temperature pro-

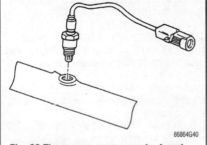

Fig. 20 The oxygen sensor can be found on the exhaust manifold or exhaust pipe

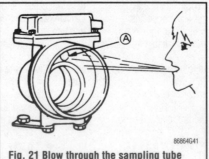

Fig. 21 Blow through the sampling tube (A) when testing the MAF sensor

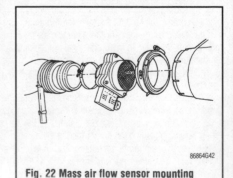

Fig. 22 Mass air flow sensor mounting

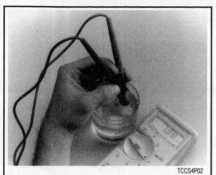

Fig. 23 Submerge the end of the temperature sensor in cold or hot water and check the resistance

°C	°F	OHMS
Temperature vs. Resistance Values (approximate)		
100	212	177
80	176	332
60	140	667
45	113	1188
35	95	1802
25	77	2796
15	59	4450
5	41	7280
−5	23	12300
−15	5	21450
−30	−22	52700
−40	−40	100700

Fig. 24 Temperature sensor resistance values

Fig. 25 The coolant temperature sensor can be found threaded into the coolant crossover tube or intake manifold

duces a high resistance, while a high temperature causes a low resistance. The ECM supplies a 5 volt signal to the sensor through a resistor in the ECM and measures the voltage. The voltage will be high when the incoming air is cold, and low when the air is hot. By measuring the voltage, the ECM calculates the incoming air temperature.

the IAT sensor signal is used to adjust spark timing according to incoming air density.

TESTING

◆ See Figures 23 and 24

1. Remove the Intake Air Temperature (IAT) sensor.
2. Connect a digital ohmmeter to the two terminals of the sensor.
3. Using a calibrated thermometer, compare the resistance of the sensor to the temperature of the ambient air. Refer to the temperature vs. resistance illustration.
4. Repeat the test at two other temperature points, heating or cooling the air as necessary with a hair dryer or other suitable tool.
5. If the sensor does not meet specification, it must be replaced.

REMOVAL & INSTALLATION

◆ See Figure 26

1. Disconnect the negative battery cable.
2. Disengage the sensor electrical connection.
3. Loosen and remove the IAT sensor.
4. Installation is the reverse of removal.

Wide Open Throttle (WOT) Switch

OPERATION

The WOT switch relays to the ECM when the throttle valve is in the wide open throttle position. The ECM uses this information for air/fuel ratio enrich-

ment, air conditioning clutch cutout, as well as disabling certain emission components such as EGR.

TESTING

1.8L and 2.0L Engines

◆ See Figure 27

1. Unplug the switch connector.
2. Check resistance between terminals **A** and **B**, then **C** and **D**. Resistance should be 0 ohms.
3. Unplug the vacuum hoses from the switch and connect a vacuum pump.
4. Apply 4 in.Hg of vacuum to the switch. Check resistance between terminals **A** and **B**, then **C** and **D**. Resistance should be over 100k ohms. Vacuum should hold.
5. Replace the switch if necessary.

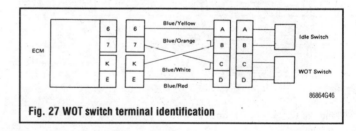

Fig. 27 WOT switch terminal identification

Fuel Injected 2.3L and 2.6L Engines

◆ See Figure 28

1. Unplug the switch connector.
2. Using an ohmmeter, check for continuity between terminals **I** and **P** with the throttle valve in the following positions.
- Not depressed—0 ohms
- Slightly depressed—infinite resistance
- Fully depressed—infinite resistance

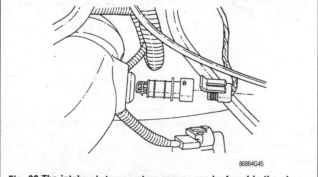

Fig. 26 The intake air temperature sensor can be found in the air intake duct, or threaded into the intake manifold

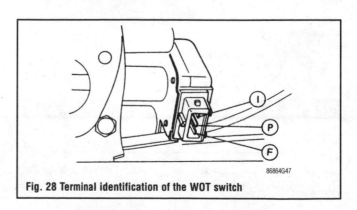

Fig. 28 Terminal identification of the WOT switch

3. Using an ohmmeter, check for continuity between terminals **P** and **F** with the throttle valve in the following positions.
- Not depressed—infinite resistance
- Slightly depressed—infinite resistance
- Fully depressed—0 ohms

4. Replace the switch if necessary.

Mixture Control Solenoid

OPERATION

The mixture control solenoid is used on carbureted engines to meter the air/fuel mixture. The ECM sends a varying signal to the mixture control solenoid. This signal is determined by the ECM according to information it receives from other sensors, such as the coolant temperature sensor, wide open throttle switch and oxygen sensor.

TESTING

▶ **See Figure 29**

1. Unplug the mixture control solenoid connector.
2. Using an ohmmeter, check resistance between the terminals.
3. Resistance should be over 20 ohms. If not, replace the sensor.

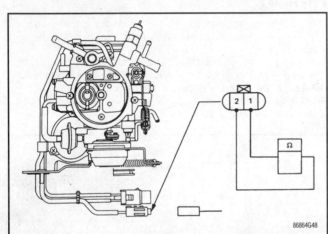

Fig. 29 Check the resistance between the mixture control solenoid terminals

Fuel Cut Solenoid

OPERATION

The fuel cut solenoid is used on carbureted engines. It's purpose is to shut fuel supply in the carburetor off during deceleration to improve emissions.

TESTING

▶ **See Figure 30**

1. Unplug the fuel cut solenoid connector.
2. Using an ohmmeter, check resistance between terminals **1** and **3**.
3. Resistance should be over 15 ohms. If not, replace the sensor.

Throttle Position Sensor (TPS)

OPERATION

The Throttle Position Sensor (TPS) is connected to the throttle shaft on the throttle body. It is a potentiometer with one end connected to 5 volts from the ECM and the other to ground.

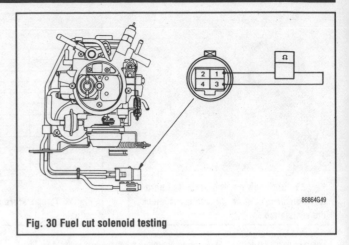

Fig. 30 Fuel cut solenoid testing

A third wire is connected to the ECM to measure the voltage from the TPS. As the throttle valve angle is changed (accelerator pedal moved), the output of the TPS also changes. At a closed throttle position, the output of the TPS is low (approximately .5 volts). As the throttle valve opens, the output increases so that, at wide-open throttle, the output voltage should be approximately 4.5 volts.

By monitoring the output voltage from the TPS, the ECM can determine fuel delivery based on throttle valve angle (driver demand).

TESTING

▶ **See Figure 31**

1. Backprobe with a high impedance voltmeter at the outside TPS terminals (**A** and **B**).
2. With the key **ON** and engine off, the voltmeter reading should be approximately 5.0 volts.
3. If the voltage is not as specified, either the wiring to the TPS or the ECM may be faulty. Correct any wiring or ECM faults before continuing test.
4. Backprobe with a high impedance voltmeter at center and lower terminals (**C** and **B**).
5. With the key **ON** and engine off and the throttle closed, the TPS voltage should be approximately 0.5–1.2 volts.
6. Verify that the TPS voltage increases or decreases smoothly as the throttle is opened or closed. Make sure to open and close the throttle very slowly in order to detect any abnormalities in the TPS voltage reading.
7. If the sensor voltage is not as specified, replace the sensor.

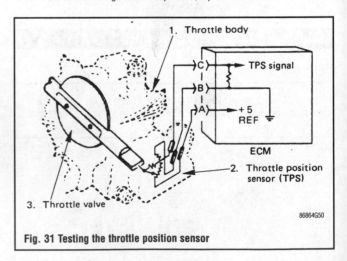

Fig. 31 Testing the throttle position sensor

REMOVAL & INSTALLATION

▶ **See Figure 32**

1. Disconnect the negative battery cable and remove the air cleaner and gasket.

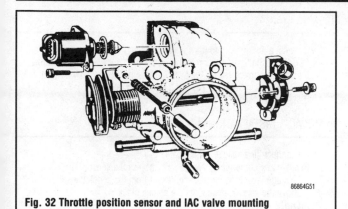

Fig. 32 Throttle position sensor and IAC valve mounting

2. Disengage the electrical connector.
3. Unfasten the two TPS attaching screw assemblies.
4. Remove the TPS from the throttle body assembly.
5. Remove the TPS seal.

To install:

6. Install the TPS seal over the throttle shaft.
7. With the throttle valve closed, install the TPS on the throttle shaft. Rotate it counterclockwise, to align the mounting holes.
8. Install the two TPS attaching screw assemblies.
9. Engage the electrical connector.
10. Install the air cleaner and gasket.
11. Connect the negative battery cable.

Idle Air Control (IAC) Valve

OPERATION

The engine idle speed is controlled by the ECM through the Idle Air Control (IAC) valve mounted on the throttle body. The ECM sends voltage pulses to the IAC motor causing the IAC motor shaft and pintle to move in or out a given distance (number of steps) for each pulse, (called counts).

This movement controls air flow around the throttle plate, which in turn, controls engine idle speed, either cold or hot. IAC valve pintle position counts can be seen using a scan tool. Zero counts corresponds to a fully closed passage, while 140 or more counts (depending on the application) corresponds to full flow.

TESTING

1. Disengage the IAC electrical connector.
2. Using an ohmmeter, measure the resistance between the IAC terminals. Make a note of the results.
3. Verify that the resistance between one set of IAC terminals is 20–80 ohms, and that the resistance between the other terminals is infinite. If not, the IAC may be faulty.
4. Also, with a small mirror, inspect IAC air inlet passage and pintle for debris. Clean as necessary, as this can cause IAC malfunction.

REMOVAL & INSTALLATION

♦ See Figure 32

1. Disconnect the negative battery cable.
2. Disengage the electrical connection.
3. Remove the IAC valve. On thread-mounted units, use 1¼ in. (32mm) wrench and on flange-mounted units, remove the screw assemblies.
4. Remove the IAC valve gasket or O-ring and discard it.

To install:

5. Clean the old gasket material from the surface of the throttle body assembly on the thread mounted valve. On the flange-mounted valve clean the surface to ensure proper O-ring sealing
6. Install the valve with a new gasket or O-ring. Tighten the thread mounted assembly 13 ft. lbs. (18 Nm) and tighten the flange mounted attaching screws to 28 inch. lbs. (3 Nm).

7. Engage the electrical connector to the IAC valve.
8. Connect the negative battery cable.

Manifold Absolute Pressure (MAP) Sensor

OPERATION

The Manifold Absolute Pressure (MAP) sensor measures the changes in intake manifold pressure, which result from the engine load and speed changes, and converts this to a voltage output.

A closed throttle on engine coastdown will produce a low MAP output, while a wide-open throttle will produce a high output. This high output is produced because the pressure inside the manifold is the same as outside the manifold, so 100 percent of the outside air pressure is measured.

The MAP sensor reading is the opposite of what you would measure on a vacuum gauge. When manifold pressure is high, vacuum is low. The MAP sensor is also used to measure barometric pressure under certain conditions, which allows the ECM to automatically adjust for different altitudes.

The ECM sends a 5 volt reference signal to the MAP sensor. As the manifold pressure changes, the electrical resistance of the sensor also changes. By monitoring the sensor output voltage, the ECM knows the manifold pressure. A higher pressure, low vacuum (high voltage) requires more fuel, while a lower pressure, higher vacuum (low voltage) requires less fuel.

The ECM uses the MAP sensor to control fuel delivery and ignition timing.

TESTING

Sensor

♦ See Figures 33 and 34

1. Backprobe with a high impedance voltmeter at MAP sensor terminals **A** and **C** on 2.8L, 3.1L and 3.2L engines. On other engines, backprobe between terminals **1** and **3**.
2. With the key **ON** and engine off, the voltmeter reading should be approximately 5.0 volts.

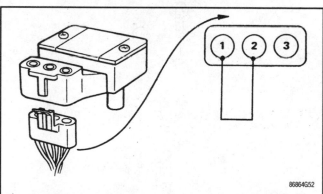

Fig. 33 MAP sensor terminal identification—except 2.8L, 3.1L and 3.2L engines

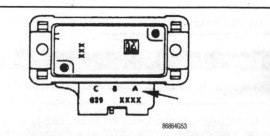

Fig. 34 Terminal identification is stamped on the MAP sensor—except 2.8L, 3.1L and 3.2L engines

3. If the voltage is not as specified, either the wiring to the MAP sensor or the ECM may be faulty. Correct any wiring or ECM faults before continuing test.

4. Backprobe with the high impedance voltmeter at MAP sensor terminals **B** and **A** on 2.8L, 3.1L and 3.2L engines. On other engines, backprobe between terminals **1** and **2**.

5. Verify that the sensor voltage is approximately 0.5 volts with the engine not running (at sea level).

6. Record MAP sensor voltage with the key **ON** and engine off.

7. Start the vehicle.

8. Verify that the sensor voltage is greater than 1.5 volts (above the recorded reading) at idle.

9. Verify that the sensor voltage increases to approximately 4.5 volts (above the recorded reading) at Wide Open Throttle (WOT).

10. If the sensor voltage is as specified, the sensor is functioning properly.

11. If the sensor voltage is not as specified, check the sensor and the sensor vacuum source for a leak or a restriction. If no leaks or restrictions are found, the sensor may be defective and should be replaced.

Vacuum Switching Valve

→This component is only used on the 2.3L carbureted engine.

1. Unplug the connector from the valve.

2. Using an ohmmeter, check the resistance between the terminals. It should be between 30–40 ohms. If not, replace the valve.

REMOVAL & INSTALLATION

▶ **See Figure 35**

1. Disconnect the negative battery cable.

2. Tag and disconnect the vacuum hose(s).

3. Disengage the electrical connector.

4. Release the locktabs or unfasten the bolts and remove the sensor/valve.

5. Installation is the reverse of removal.

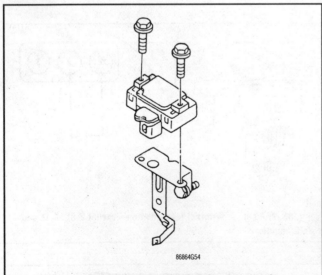

Fig. 35 Common MAP sensor mounting found on Isuzu trucks

Knock Sensor

OPERATION

Located in the engine block, the knock sensor retards ignition timing during a spark knock condition to allow the ECM to maintain maximum timing advance under most conditions.

TESTING

1. Connect a timing light to the vehicle and start the engine.

2. Check that the timing is correct before testing knock sensor operation.

3. If timing is correct, tap on the front of the engine block with a metal object while observing the timing to see if the timing retards.

4. If the timing does not retard the knock sensor may be defective.

REMOVAL & INSTALLATION

1. Disconnect the negative battery cable.

2. Remove any components necessary to access the sensor.

3. Disengage the wiring harness connector from the knock sensor.

4. Remove the knock sensor from the engine block.

To install:

5. Apply a water base caulk to the knock sensor threads and install the sensor in the engine block.

✳✳ WARNING

Do not use silicon tape to coat the knock sensor threads as this will insulate the sensor from the engine block.

6. Engage the wiring harness connector.

7. Install any components removed to access the sensor.

8. Connect the negative battery cable.

Crankshaft Position Sensor

OPERATION

The Crankshaft Position Sensor (CKP) provides a signal through the ignition module which the ECM uses as a reference to calculate rpm and crankshaft position.

TESTING

1996 2.6L Engines

1. Backprobe with a high impedance voltmeter between terminals **2** (red wire) and **1** (white wire) of the crankshaft position sensor.

2. Have an assistant crank the engine.

3. Observe the voltage display while the engine is being cranked. It should be approximately 2.5 volts.

4. Replace the sensor if necessary.

1996 3.2L Engines

1. Backprobe with a high impedance voltmeter between the yellow wire and the black/blue wire of the crankshaft position sensor.

2. Have an assistant crank the engine.

3. Observe the voltage display while the engine is being cranked. It should be approximately 2.5 volts.

4. Replace the sensor if necessary.

REMOVAL & INSTALLATION

1996 2.6L and 3.2L Engines

▶ **See Figure 36**

1. Disconnect the negative battery cable.

2. Unplug the electrical connector from the sensor.

3. Remove the bolt securing the sensor to the engine block, then remove the sensor.

To install:

4. Lubricate a new O-ring with engine oil, and install the O-ring on the sensor.

5. Install the sensor in the engine block. Tighten to 78 inch lbs. (9 Nm).

6. Engage the electrical connection and the negative battery cable.

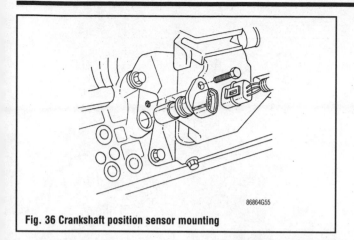

Fig. 36 Crankshaft position sensor mounting

Camshaft Position Sensor (CMP)

OPERATION

The ECM uses the camshaft signal to determine the position of the No. 1 cylinder piston during its power stroke. The signal is used by the ECM to calculate fuel injection mode of operation.

If the cam signal is lost while the engine is running, the fuel injection system will shift to a calculated fuel injected mode based on the last fuel injection pulse, and the engine will continue to run.

TESTING

1996 2.6L Engine

1. Backprobe with a high impedance voltmeter between terminals **A** (white/purple wire) and **B** (white wire) of the camshaft position sensor.
2. Have an assistant crank the engine.
3. Observe the voltage display while the engine is being cranked. It should toggle between 0–4 volts.
4. Replace the sensor if necessary.

1996 3.2L Engine

1. Backprobe with a high impedance voltmeter between the blue wire and black/blue wire of the camshaft position sensor.
2. Have an assistant crank the engine.
3. Observe the voltage display while the engine is being cranked. It should toggle between 0–4 volts.
4. Replace the sensor if necessary.

REMOVAL & INSTALLATION

1996 2.6L Engine

If the camshaft position sensor is found to be defective in this engine, the entire distributor assembly must be replaced.

1996 3.2L Engine

♦ See Figure 37

1. Disconnect the negative battery cable.
2. Unplug the electrical connector from the sensor.
3. Remove the bolt securing the sensor to the timing cover, then remove the sensor.

To install:

4. Lubricate a new O-ring with engine oil, and install the O-ring on the sensor.
5. Install the sensor in the engine block. Tighten to 78 inch lbs. (9 Nm).
6. Engage the electrical connection and the negative battery cable.

Vehicle Speed Sensor (VSS)

OPERATION

The Vehicle Speed Sensor (VSS) is mounted behind the speedometer in the instrument cluster or on the transmission/speedometer drive gear. It provides electrical pulses to the ECM from the speedometer head. The pulses indicate the road speed. The ECM uses this information to operate the IAC, canister purge, and TCC.

Some vehicles use a sensor located in the transmission. The vehicle speed sensor is made up of a coil mounted on the transmission and a tooth rotor mounted to the output shaft of the transmission. As each tooth nears the coil, the coil produces an AC voltage pulse. As the vehicle speed increases the number of voltage pulses per second increases.

TESTING

Except Transmission Mounted Sensor

♦ See Figures 38 and 39

✳✳ WARNING

If equipped with an air bag system, disarm the system before removing the cluster. Refer to Section 6 for more Information.

1. Remove the instrument cluster assembly.
2. Connect the leads of an ohmmeter across terminals **1** and **2** at the rear face of the cluster.
3. Turn the inner shaft slowly and check that the ohmmeter indicates continuity and an open circuit condition alternately.
4. Replace the speedometer assembly if necessary.

Transmission Mounted Sensor

1. To test the VSS, backprobe the VSS terminals with a high impedance voltmeter (set at the AC voltage scale).
2. Safely raise and support the entire vehicle using jackstands. Make absolutely sure the vehicle is stable.
3. Start the vehicle and place it in gear.
4. Verify that the VSS voltage increases as the drive shaft speed increases.
5. If the VSS voltage is not as specified the VSS may be faulty.

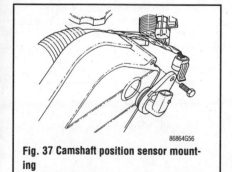

Fig. 37 Camshaft position sensor mounting

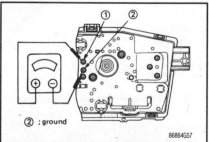

Fig. 38 VSS terminal identification on LS models

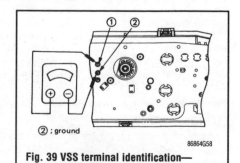

Fig. 39 VSS terminal identification— except LS models

REMOVAL & INSTALLATION

Except Transmission Mounted Sensor

On these models, the speedometer must be replaced if the sensor is found to be faulty. Refer to Section 6 for procedures.

Transmission Mounted Sensor

▶ **See Figure 40**

1. Disconnect the negative battery cable.
2. Disengage the electrical connection.
3. Unfasten the sensor retainers.
4. Remove the sensor and gasket or O-ring.

To install:

5. Install the sensor with a new gasket or O-ring.
6. Fasten the sensor retainers.
7. Engage the electrical connections.
8. Connect the negative battery cable.

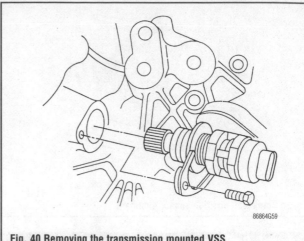

86864G59

Fig. 40 Removing the transmission mounted VSS

TROUBLE CODES

General Information

Since the control module is programmed to recognize the presence and value of electrical inputs, it will also note the lack of a signal or a radical change in values. It will, for example, react to the loss of signal from the vehicle speed sensor or note that engine coolant temperature has risen beyond acceptable (programmed) limits. Once a fault is recognized, a numeric code is assigned and held in memory. The dashboard warning lamp: CHECK ENGINE or SERVICE ENGINE SOON (SES), will illuminate to advise the operator that the system has detected a fault. This lamp is also known as the Malfunction Indicator Lamp (MIL).

More than one code may be stored. Keep in mind not every engine uses every code. Additionally, the same code may carry different meanings relative to each engine or engine family.

In the event of an computer control module failure, the system will default to a pre-programmed set of values. These are compromise values which allow the engine to operate, although possibly at reduced efficiency. This is variously known as the default, limp-in or back-up mode. Driveability is almost always affected when the ECM enters this mode.

SCAN TOOLS

On most models, the stored codes may be read with only the use of a small jumper wire, however the use of a hand-held scan tool such as the TECH-1® or equivalent is recommended. On 1996 models, an OBD-II compliant scan tool must be used. There are many manufacturers of these tools; a purchaser must be certain that the tool is proper for the intended use. If you own a scan type tool, it probably came with comprehensive instructions on proper use. Be sure to follow the instructions that came with your unit if they differ from what is given here; this is a general guide with useful information included.

The scan tool allows any stored codes to be read from the ECM or PCM memory. The tool also allows the operator to view the data being sent to the computer control module while the engine is running. This ability has obvious diagnostic advantages; the use of the scan tool is frequently required for component testing. The scan tool makes collecting information easier; the data must be correctly interpreted by an operator familiar with the system.

An example of the usefulness of the scan tool may be seen in the case of a temperature sensor which has changed its electrical characteristics. The ECM is reacting to an apparently warmer engine (causing a driveability problem), but the sensor's voltage has not changed enough to set a fault code. Connecting the scan tool, the voltage signal being sent to the ECM may be viewed; comparison to normal values or a known good vehicle reveals the problem quickly.

ELECTRICAL TOOLS

The most commonly required electrical diagnostic tool is the digital multimeter, allowing voltage, ohmage (resistance) and amperage to be read by one instrument. The multimeter must be a high-impedance unit, with 10 megohms

of impedance in the voltmeter. This type of meter will not place an additional load on the circuit it is testing; this is extremely important in low voltage circuits. The multimeter must be of high quality in all respects. It should be handled carefully and protected from impact or damage. Replace batteries frequently in the unit.

Diagnosis and Testing

Diagnosis of a driveability and/or emissions problems requires attention to detail and following the diagnostic procedures in the correct order. Resist the temptation to perform any repairs before performing the preliminary diagnostic steps. In many cases this will shorten diagnostic time and often cure the problem without electronic testing.

The proper troubleshooting procedure for these vehicles is as follows:

VISUAL/PHYSICAL INSPECTION

This is possibly the most critical step of diagnosis and should be performed immediately after retrieving any codes. A detailed examination of connectors, wiring and vacuum hoses can often lead to a repair without further diagnosis. Performance of this step relies on the skill of the technician performing it; a careful inspector will check the undersides of hoses as well as the integrity of hard-to-reach hoses blocked by the air cleaner or other component. Wiring should be checked carefully for any sign of strain, burning, crimping, or terminal pull-out from a connector. Checking connectors at components or in harnesses is required; usually, pushing them together will reveal a loose fit.

INTERMITTENTS

If a fault occurs intermittently, such as a loose connector pin breaking contact as the vehicle hits a bump, the ECM will note the fault as it occurs and energize the dash warning lamp. If the problem self-corrects, as with the terminal pin again making contact, the dash lamp will extinguish after 10 seconds but a code will remain stored in the computer control module's memory.

When an unexpected code appears during diagnostics, it may have been set during an intermittent failure that self-corrected; the codes are still useful in diagnosis and should not be discounted.

CIRCUIT/COMPONENT REPAIR

The fault codes and the scan tool data will lead to diagnosis and checking of a particular circuit. It is important to note that the fault code indicates a fault or loss of signal in an ECM-controlled system, not necessarily in the specific component.

Refer to the appropriate Diagnostic Code chart to determine the codes meaning. The component may then be tested following the appropriate component test procedures found in this section. If the component is OK, check the wiring for shorts or opens. Further diagnoses should be left to an experienced drive-ability technician.

If a code indicates the ECM to be faulty and the ECM is replaced, but does not correct the problem, one of the following may be the reason:

• There is a problem with the ECM terminal connections: The terminals may have to be removed from the connector in order to check them properly.

• The ECM or PROM is not correct for the application: The incorrect ECM or PROM may cause a malfunction and may or may not set a code.

• The problem is intermittent: This means that the problem is not present at the time the system is being checked. In this case, make a careful physical inspection of all portions of the system involved.

• Shorted solenoid, relay coil or harness: Solenoids and relays are turned on and off by the ECM using internal electronic switches called drivers. Each driver is part of a group of four called Quad-Drivers. A shorted solenoid, relay coil or harness may cause an ECM to fail, and a replacement ECM to fail when it is installed. Use a short tester, J34696, BT 8405, or equivalent, as a fast, accurate means of checking for a short circuit.

• The Programmable Read Only Memory (PROM) may be faulty: Although the PROM rarely fails, it operates as part of the ECM. Therefore, it could be the cause of the problem. Substitute a known good PROM.

• The replacement ECM may be faulty: After the ECM is replaced, the system should be rechecked for proper operation. If the diagnostic code again indicates the ECM is the problem, substitute a known good ECM. Although this is a very rare condition, it could happen.

Reading Codes

♦ **See Figures 41 and 42**

EXCEPT 1996 MODELS

Listings of the trouble for the various engine control system covered in this manual are located in this section. Remember that a code only points to the faulty circuit NOT necessarily to a faulty component. Loose, damaged or corroded connections may contribute to a fault code on a circuit when the sensor or component is operating properly. Be sure that the components are faulty before replacing them, especially the expensive ones.

The Assembly Line Diagnostic Link (ALDL) connector or Data Link Connector (DLC) may be located under the dash and sometimes covered with a plastic cover labeled DIAGNOSTIC CONNECTOR.

1. The diagnostic trouble codes can be read as follows:

   a. On models with the 12 cavity ALDL, ground test terminal **B**. The terminal is most easily grounded by connecting it to terminal **A** (internal ECM ground). This is the terminal to the right of terminal **B** on the top row of the ALDL connector.

   b. On models with a 3 cavity DLC, connect the two outside terminals (terminals **1** and **2**) together.

   c. Other models are equipped with white and black diagnostic terminals located under the instrument panel next to the left pick panel. Connect them together.

2. Once the terminals have been connected, the ignition switch must be moved to the **ON** position with the engine not running.

3. The Service Engine Soon or Check Engine light should be flashing. If it isn't, turn the ignition **OFF** and remove the jumper wire. Turn the ignition **ON**

and confirm that light is now on. If it is not, replace the bulb and try again. If the bulb still will not light, or if it does not flash with the test terminal grounded, the system should be diagnosed by an experienced driveability technician. If the light is OK, proceed as follows.

4. The code(s) stored in memory may be read through counting the flashes of the dashboard warning lamp. The dash warning lamp should begin to flash Code 12. The code will display as one flash, a pause and two flashes. Code 12 is not a fault code. It is used as a system acknowledgment or handshake code; its presence indicates that the ECM can communicate as requested. Code 12 is used to begin every diagnostic sequence. Some vehicles also use Code 12 after all diagnostic codes have been sent.

5. After Code 12 has been transmitted 3 times, the fault codes, if any, will each be transmitted 3 times. The codes are stored and transmitted in numeric order from lowest to highest.

➡ **The order of codes in the memory does not indicate the order of occurrence.**

6. If there are no codes stored, but a driveability or emissions problem is evident, the system should be diagnosed by an experienced driveability technician.

7. If one or more codes are stored, record them. Refer to the applicable Diagnostic Code chart in this section.

8. Switch the ignition **OFF** when finished with code retrieval or scan tool readings.

➡ **After making repairs, clear the trouble codes and operate the vehicle to see if it will reset, indicating further problems.**

1996 MODELS

♦ **See Figure 43**

On 1996 models, an OBD-II compliant scan tool must be used to retrieve the trouble codes. Follow the tool manufacturer's instructions to connect the tool and retrieve the codes.

Clearing Codes

Stored fault codes may be erased from memory at any time by removing power from the ECM for at least 30 seconds. It may be necessary to clear stored codes during diagnosis to check for a recurrence, but the codes should be written down for reference (they may still be required for troubleshooting). Whenever a repair is complete, the codes must be erased and the vehicle test driven to confirm correct operation.

✷✷ WARNING

The ignition switch must be OFF any time power is disconnected or restored to the ECM. Severe damage may result if this precaution is not observed.

Depending on the particular vehicle, power to the ECM may be disconnected by removing the ECM fuse in the fusebox, disconnecting the in-line fuse holder near the positive battery terminal or disconnecting the ECM power lead at the battery terminal. Disconnecting the negative battery cable will clear codes, but this will also clear other memory data such as radio presets.

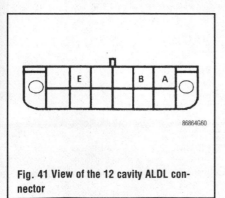

Fig. 41 View of the 12 cavity ALDL connector

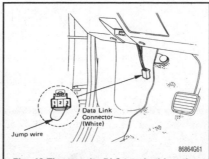

Fig. 42 Three cavity DLC terminal location and identification

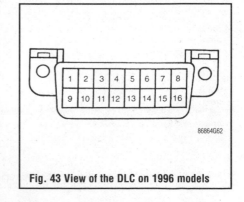

Fig. 43 View of the DLC on 1996 models

TROUBLE CODE 12	No ignition reference pulses to the ECM. This code is not stored in memory and will only flash while the fault is present.
TROUBLE CODE 13	Oxygen sensor circuit — The engine must run up 1 minute at part throttle, under road load, before this code will set. This code does not set when the coolant temperature is below 70°C and/or the time since engine start has exceeded 2 minutes.
TROUBLE CODE 14	Shorted coolant sensor circuit — The engine must run up to 2 minutes before this code will set.
TROUBLE CODE 15	Open coolant sensor circuit — The engine must run up to 5 minutes before this code will set.
TROUBLE CODE 21	Idle switch circuit open or WOT switch circuit shorted — The engine must run up to 10 seconds at following two conditions concurrently before this code will set. Idle switch output is in a low voltage state. WOT switch output is in a high voltage state.
TROUBLE CODE 22	Fuel cut solenoid circuit open or grounded — The engine must run under the decelerating condition over 2000 engine rpm before this code will set.
TROUBLE CODE 23	Mixture control solenoid circuit open or grounded.
TROUBLE CODE 25	Air switching solenoid circuit open or grounded.
TROUBLE CODE 31	No ignition reference pulses to the ECM to 10 seconds at part throttle, under road load. This code will store in memory.
TROUBLE CODE 44	Lean oxygen sensor indication — The engine must run up to 2 minutes at part throttle, under road load, before this code will set. This code does not set when the coolant temperature is below 70°C and/or the air temperature in air cleaner is below 0°C.
TROUBLE CODE 45	Rich System indication — The engine must run up to 2 minutes at part throttle, under road load, before this code will set. This code does not set when the engine exceeds 2500 rpm and/or the coolant temperature is below 70°C and/or the barometric pressure is below 575 mmHg (above 2500m altitude).
TROUBLE CODE 51	Shorted fuel cut solenoid circuit and/or faulty ECM.
TROUBLE CODE 52	Faulty ECM — Problem of RAM in ECM.
TROUBLE CODE 53	Shorted air switching solenoid and/or faulty ECM.
TROUBLE CODE 54	Shorted vacuum control solenoid and/or faulty ECM.
TROUBLE CODE 55	Faulty ECM — Problem of A/D converter in ECM.

86864GA3

Fig. 44 Diagnostic trouble codes—1.8L and 2.0L engines

DTC 12 No ignition reference pulses to the ECM. This DTC is not stored in memory and will only flash while the fault is present. This DTC is displayed before the engine is started.

DTC 13 Oxygen sensor (O2S) circuit — The engine must run 1 minute at part throttle, under road load, before this DTC will set. This DTC does not set when the engine coolant temperature is below 70°C (158°F) and/or the time since engine start has exceeded 2 minutes.

DTC 14 Shorted engine coolant temperature (ECT) sensor circuit — The engine must run 2 minutes before this DTC will set.

DTC 15 Open engine coolant temperature (ECT) sensor circuit — The engine must run 5 minutes before this DTC will set.

DTC 21 Idle switch and manifold absolute pressure (MAP) sensor failure.

(1) * Vehicle speed is 0 km/h and engine speed is between 200 and 1000 rpm.
  * MAP sensor output is more than 500 mmHg abs as input signal, for 5 seconds.

(2) * Idle switch is "OFF"
  * MAP sensor output is less than 100 mmHg abs as input signal, for 5 seconds.

(3) * MAP sensor output is between 400 and 450 mmHg abs as input signal, and engine speed is more than 1500 rpm.
  * Idle switch is "ON" for more than 5 seconds.
  If either condition (1), (2), (3) exists, this DTC will set.

DTC 22 Fuel cut solenoid circuit open or grounded — The engine must run under the decelerating condition over 2000 engine rpm before this DTC will set.

DTC 23 Duty solenoid circuit open or grounded.

DTC 25 Air management valve circuit open or grounded.

DTC 26 Evaporative emission (EVAP) canister V.S.V. circuit open or grounded.

DTC 27 Constant high voltage from evaporative emission (EVAP) canister V.S.V. to ECM.

DTC 31 No ignition reference pulses to the ECM after 10 seconds at part throttle, under load. This DTC will store in memory.

DTC 32 Exhaust gas recirculation (EGR) system failure and sensor circuit failure.

DTC 34 Exhaust gas recirculation (EGR) temperature sensor circuit failure.

DTC 35 Constant high voltage from manifold absolute pressure (MAP) sensor V.S.V. to ECM.

DTC 36 Manifold absolute pressure (MAP) sensor V.S.V. circuit open or grounded.

86864GA4

Fig. 45 Diagnostic trouble codes—2.3L carbureted engines

DTC 44 Fuel metering faulty lean signal
(1) Engine coolant temperature is more than 158°F (70°C).
(2) Engine throttle is partially open.
(3) Engine speed is less than 2500 rpm.
(4) More than 5 seconds after fuel cut recovering.
The timer of this DTC will start to count when all (1) — (4) conditions exist. Then ECM judges to set DTC 44, to use the timer information, except when condition A or condition B exists:
Condition A "BAROMETRIC MAP" is under 596 mmHg abs.
Condition B DTC 13 or 21 is stored in memory, or the engine coolant temperature is more than 302°F (150°C).

DTC 45 Fuel metering faulty rich signal
(1) Engine coolant temperature is more than 158°F (70°C).
(2) Engine throttle is partially open.
(3) Engine speed is less than 2500 rpm.
(4) Vehicle speed is between 20 and 80 km/h (12-50 mph).
(5) More than 30 seconds after starting EVAP canister purge.
The timer of this DTC will start to count when all (1) — (5) conditions exist.
This DTC does not set when the high altitude condition (Above 2500 m or 8000 feet) is judged by ECM.
(MAP sensor output voltage is less than 596 mmHg abs as the input signal of atmospheric pressure.)
Then ECM judges to set DTC 45, to use the timer information except when condition A or condition B exists:
Condition A "BAROMETRIC MAP" is under 596 mmHg abs.
Condition B DTC 13 or 21 is stored in memory, or the engine coolant temperature is more than 302°F (150°C).

DTC 51 Shorted fuel cut solenoid circuit and/or faulty ECM.

DTC 52 Faulty ECM — Problem is RAM in ECM.

DTC 53 Shorted air management valve and/or faulty ECM.

DTC 54 Shorted vacuum control solenoid and/or faulty ECM.

DTC 55 Faulty ECM — Problem is A/D converter in ECM.

AIR : Secondary AIR injection system
ECM : Engine Control Module
WOT : Wide Open Throttle
V.S.V. : Vacuum Switching Valve

86864GA5

Fig. 46 Diagnostic trouble codes—2.3L carbureted engines (continued)

DIAGNOSED ITEM		DIAGNOSED CONTENT		DTC NO.	DTC MEMORY	FAIL-SAFE FUNCTION OF MICRO-COMPUTER	ENGINE CONDITION	VEHICLE CONDITION
		FAULT MODE	MICRO-COMPUTER INPUT					
Engine is not started		—	Engine speed less than 200 rpm	12	No	None	Normal	Normal
Heated oxygen sensor system		Harness open. Sensor deterioration	Intermediate voltage	13	Yes	Fuel is not compensated by HO2S signal	Exhaust emission is worsened	No noticeable abnormal operation
Fuel metering system		Incorrect signal (Lean)	Lean signal (Low voltage)	44	Yes			
		Incorrect signal (Rich)	Rich signal (High voltage)	45	Yes			
Engine coolant temperature sensor system		Shorted with ground	Insufficient signal	14	Yes	Engine coolant temperature is assumed to be 85°C (185°F)	· The engine does not operate normally when temperature is low and signal is insufficient, or when temperature is high and signal is excessive. Or the engine cannot be started. · The engine does not operate smoothly when temperature is low after the fail-safe function is actuated.	
		Harness open	Excessive signal	15	Yes			
WOT switch system	Both idle contact and full contact	Both idle contact and full make contact simultaneously	Both contacts make simultaneously	21	Yes	Both signals are assumed to be OFF.	Coasting Fuel-cut is not made, after the fail-safe function is actuated, and lean fuel is resulted when the throttle valve is fully opened.	Fuel consumption rate is worsened after the fail-safe function is actuated. Fuel tends to be lean when the throttle valve is fully opened.
	Idle contact	Continuously make contact	Signal is sent continuously Not diagnosed when the mass air flow sensor system is defective	43	Yes	Assumed to be OFF.	· Fuel cut range appears during running before fail-safe function is actuated. · Coasting Fuel-cut is not made, after the fail-safe function is actuated.	· The vehicle does not run smoothly. · Fuel consumption rate is worsened after the fail-safe function is actuated.
	Full contact	Continuously make contact	Signal is sent continuously	65	Yes	Assumed to be OFF.	· Air-fuel ratio is high when partially loaded. · Fuel tends to be lean when the throttle valve is fully opened after the fail-safe function is actuated.	· Fuel consumption rate and exhaust are worsened. The spark plugs are carboned or the engine stalls depending on the condition. · Fuel tends to be lean when the throttle valve is fully opened after the fail-safe function is actuated.

86864GA6

Fig. 47 Diagnostic trouble codes—2.3L and 1988–95 2.6L fuel injected engines

DIAGNOSED ITEM	DIAGNOSED CONTENT		DTC NO.	DTC MEMORY	FAIL-SAFE FUNCTION OF MICRO-COMPUTER	ENGINE CONDITION	VEHICLE CONDITION
	FAULT MODE	MICRO-COMPUTER INPUT					
Vacuum switching valve system for EVAP canister purge	· Open circuit harness connector VSV or inside of ECM	—	26	Yes	None	Air/Fuel ratio tends to be rich under the idle or partial conditions before warmed up	Fuel consumption rate is worsened when engine is cold.
	· Ground shorted harness connector VSV or inside of ECM	—				Air/Fuel ratio tends to be lean at hot restart	The engine can not be restarted smoothly when engine coolant temp. is very high.
	· Driver transister in ECM open	—	27	Yes			
Vacuum switching valve system for fuel pressure control	· Open circuit harness connector VSV or inside of ECM	—	25	Yes	None	Air/Fuel ratio tends to be rich under the idle or partial conditions before warmed up	Fuel consumption rate is worsened when engine is cold.
	· Ground shorted harness connector VSV or inside of ECM	—				Air/Fuel ratio tends to be lean at hot restart	The engine can not be restarted smoothly when engine coolant temp. is very high.
	· Driver transister in ECM open	—	53	Yes			
Fuel injector system	· Open circuit harness connector injector, dropping resister, or inside of ECM	—	33	Yes	None	Air/Fuel ratio tends to be rich under the idle or partial conditions before warmed up	Fuel consumption rate is worsened when engine is cold.
	· Ground shorted harness connector injector, dropping register, or inside of ECM	—				Air/Fuel ratio tends to be lean at hot restart	The engine can not be restarted smoothly when engine coolant temp. is very high.
	· Driver transister in ECM open	—	64	Yes			
EGR temperature sensor system	Mulfunction	—	32	Yes	None	Exhaust is worsened	No noticeable abnormal operation
	Sensor or harness NG	—	34	Yes	None	Normal	No abnormality is felt.

86864GA7

Fig. 48 Diagnostic trouble codes—2.3L and 1988–95 2.6L fuel injected engines (continued)

DIAGNOSED ITEM	DIAGNOSED CONTENT		DTC NO.	DTC MEMORY	FAIL-SAFE FUNCTION OF MICRO-COMPUTER	ENGINE CONDITION	VEHICLE CONDITION
	FAULT MODE	MICRO-COMPUTER INPUT					
Starter signal system	Harness open or ground shorted	Signal is not input	22	Yes	None	Normal	No abnormality is felt.
Crankshaft position sensor system	· Harness open · Faulty signal	· No sensor signal is input. · Idling speed is lower than the actual speed.	41	Yes	None	· The engine stalls. The engine cannot be started. · Ignition timing may be changed.	· Stalls or cannot be started. · The driveability is affected.
Mass air flow sensor system	Harness open, shorting with ground, or broken hot wire.	Insufficient signal	61	Yes	Injection pulse is changed over at throttle valve position.	· The engine stalls depending on the condition. · The engine may be slightly unstable after the fail-safe function is actuated.	· The engine stalls depending on the condition. · The accelerator response is worsened after the fail-safe function is actuated. The engine may not operate smoothly.
	Broken cold wire.	Excessive signal	62	Yes			
Vehicle speed sensor system	· Harness open or ground shorted. · Car speed sensor broken.	No signal is input (Not diagnosed with the air flow sensor system is defective)	63	Yes	None	The fuel cut operates even when running under a low speed.	Does not run smoothly and shakes.
Micro-computer unit (ECM)	Abnormal LSI (1)	—	51	Yes	· Injection pulse is changed over at throttle valve position · Fixed ignition timing.	· In the worst case, the engine stalls, or the engine does not operate smoothly at a certain time. · The engine does not stall but it does not satisfy the specification.	· In the worst case, the engine stalls, or the engine does not operate smoothly at a certain time. · The exhaust and running performance deviate from the specification.
	Abnormal LSI (2)	—	52	Yes			
Power transistor system for ignition	Output terminal shorted with ground.	—	23	Yes	None	· The engine stalls. · Cannot be started.	· The engine stalls. · Cannot be started.
	Harness open.	—	35	Yes			
	Defective transistor or grounding system.	—	54	Yes			

86864GA8

Fig. 49 Diagnostic trouble codes—2.3L and 1988–95 2.6L fuel injected engines (continued)

Code 13 Oxygen Sensor Circuit (Open Circuit)
Code 14 Coolant Temperature Sensor Circuit (High Temperature Indicated)
Code 15 Coolant Temperature Sensor Circuit (Low Temperature Indicated)
Code 21 Throttle Position Sensor (TPS) Circuit (Signal Voltage High)
Code 22 Throttle Position Sensor (TPS) Circuit (Signal voltage Low)
Code 24 Vehicle Speed Sensor (VSS) Circuit
Code 32 EGR System Failure
Code 33 Manifold Absolute Pressure (MAP) Sensor Circuit (Signal Voltage High-Low Vacuum)
Code 34 Manifold Absolute Pressure (MAP) Sensor Circuit (Signal Voltage Low-High Vacuum)
Code 42 Electronic Spark Timing (EST) Circuit
Code 43 Electronic Spark Control (ESC) Circuit
Code 44 Oxygen (O_2) Sensor Circuit (Lean Exhaust Indicated)
Code 45 Oxygen (O_2) Sensor Circuit (Rich Exhaust Indicated)
Code 54 Fuel Pump Circuit (Low Voltage)
Code 51 Prom Error (Faulty or Incorrect CAL-PAK)
Code 52 CAL-PAK Error (Faulty or Incorrect CAL-PAK)
Code 55 ECM Error

86864GA9

Fig. 50 Diagnostic trouble codes—2.8L, 3.1L and 3.2L engines

DTC	Description
P0106	Manifold Absolute Pressure (MAP) System Performance
P0107	Manifold Absolute Pressure (MAP) Sensor Circuit – Low Voltage
P0108	Manifold Absolute Pressure (MAP) Sensor Circuit – High Voltage
P0112	Intake Air Temperature (IAT) Sensor Circuit – Low Voltage
P0113	Intake Air Temperature (IAT) Sensor Circuit – High Voltage
P0117	Engine Coolant Temperature (ECT) Sensor Circuit – Low Voltage
P0118	Engine Coolant Temperature (ECT) Sensor Circuit – High Voltage
P0121	Throttle Position (TP) System Performance
P0122	Throttle Position (TP) Sensor Circuit – Low Voltage
P0123	Throttle Position (TP) Sensor Circuit – High Voltage
P0125	ECT Excessive Time to Closed Loop Fuel Control
P0131	Bank 1 Heated Oxygen Sensor (HO2S) 1 Circuit – Low Voltage
P0132	Bank 1 Heated Oxygen Sensor (HO2S) 1 Circuit – High Voltage
P0133	Bank 1 Heated Oxygen Sensor (HO2S) 1 Circuit – Slow Response
P0134	Bank 1 Heated Oxygen Sensor (HO2S) 1 Circuit – Insufficient Activity
P0135	Bank 1 Heated Oxygen Sensor (HO2S) 1 – Heater Circuit
P0137	Bank 1 Heated Oxygen Sensor (HO2S) 2 Circuit – Low Voltage
P0138	Bank 1 Heated Oxygen Sensor (HO2S) 2 Circuit – High Voltage
P0140	Bank 1 Heated Oxygen Sensor (HO2S) 2 Circuit – Insufficient Activity
P0141	Bank 1 Heated Oxygen Sensor (HO2S) 2 – Heater Circuit
P0171	Bank 1 Fuel Trim System Too Lean
P0172	Bank 1 Fuel Trim System Too Rich
P0201	Injector 1 Control Circuit
P0202	Injector 2 Control Circuit
P0203	Injector 3 Control Circuit
P0204	Injector 4 Control Circuit
P0300	Engine Misfire Detected
P0336	Crankshaft Position (CKP) Sensor Circuit 58X Reference Signal
P0337	Crankshaft Position (CKP) Sensor Circuit Low Frequency
P0341	Camshaft Position (CMP) Sensor Circuit Performance
P0342	Camshaft Position (CMP) Sensor Circuit Low
P0351	Ignition Control Circuit
P0401	Exhaust Gas Recirculation (EGR) Flow Insufficient
P0420	Bank 1 Three-Way Catalyst (TWC) System Low Efficiency
P0441	Evaporative Emission Control System – No Flow During Purge

86864GB3

Fig. 51 Diagnostic trouble codes—1996 2.6L engines

DTC	Description
P0502	Vehicle Speed Sensor Circuit – Low Input
P0506	Idle Air Control System – Low RPM
P0507	Idle Air Control System – High RPM
P0562	System Voltage Low
P0563	System Voltage High
P0601	Powertrain Control Module (PCM) Memory
P1106	Manifold Absolute Pressure (MAP) Sensor Circuit – Intermittent High Voltage
P1107	Manifold Absolute Pressure (MAP) Sensor Circuit – Intermittent Low Voltage
P1111	Intake Air Temperature (IAT) Sensor Circuit – Intermittent High Voltage
P1112	Intake Air Temperature (IAT) Sensor Circuit – Intermittent Low Voltage
P1114	Engine Coolant Temperature (ECT) Sensor Circuit – Intermittent Low Voltage
P1115	Engine Coolant Temperature (ECT) Sensor Circuit – Intermittent High Voltage
P1121	Throttle Position (TP) Sensor Circuit – Intermittent High Voltage
P1122	Throttle Position (TP) Sensor Circuit – Intermittent Low Voltage
P1133	Bank 1 Heated Oxygen Sensor (HO2S) 1 Circuit – Insufficient Switching
P1134	Bank 1 Heated Oxygen Sensor (HO2S) 1 Circuit – Transition Time Ratio
P1171	Fuel System Lean During Acceleration
P1390	G Sensor Circuit – Intermittent Low Voltage
P1391	G Sensor Circuit – Performance
P1392	G Sensor Circuit – Low Voltage
P1393	G Sensor Circuit – High Voltage
P1394	G Sensor Circuit – Intermittent High Voltage
P1406	Exhaust Gas Recirculation (EGR) Valve – Pintle Position Circuit
P1441	Evaporative Emission System – Flow During Non-Purge
P1442	EVAP Vacuum Switch – High Voltage During Ignition ON
P1640	Driver 1 Input High Voltage

86864GB4

Fig. 52 Diagnostic trouble codes—1996 2.6L engines (continued)

DTC	Description
P0101	Mass Air Flow (MAF) System Performance
P0102	Mass Air Flow (MAF) Circuit – Low Frequency
P0103	Mass Air Flow (MAF) Circuit – High Frequency
P0106	Manifold Absolute Pressure (MAP) System Performance Problem
P0107	Manifold Absolute Pressure (MAP) Circuit – Low Voltage
P0108	Manifold Absolute Pressure (MAP) Circuit – High Voltage
P0112	Intake Air Temperature (IAT) Circuit – Low Voltage
P0113	Intake Air Temperature (IAT) Circuit – High Voltage
P0117	Engine Coolant Temperature (ECT) Circuit – Low Voltage
P0118	Engine Coolant Temperature (ECT) Circuit – High Voltage
P0121	Throttle Position (TP) Performance
P0122	Throttle Position (TP) Sensor Circuit – Low Voltage
P0123	Throttle Position (TP) Sensor Circuit – High Voltage
P0125	Insufficient Coolant Temperature For Closed Loop Fuel Control
P0131	Bank 1 Heated Oxygen Sensor (HO2S) 1 Circuit – Low Voltage
P0132	Bank 1 Heated Oxygen Sensor (HO2S) 1 Circuit – High Voltage
P0133	Bank 1 Heated Oxygen Sensor (HO2S) 1 Circuit – Slow Response
P0134	Bank 1 Heated Oxygen Sensor (HO2S) 1 Circuit – Insufficient Activity
P0135	Bank 1 Heated Oxygen Sensor (HO2S) 1 – Heater Circuit Malfunction
P0137	Bank 1 Heated Oxygen Sensor (HO2S) 2 Circuit – Low Voltage
P0138	Bank 1 Heated Oxygen Sensor (HO2S) 2 Circuit – High Voltage
P0140	Bank 1 Heated Oxygen Sensor (HO2S) 2 Circuit – Insufficient Activity
P0141	Bank 1 Heated Oxygen Sensor (HO2S) 2 – Heater Circuit
P0143	Bank 1 Heated Oxygen Sensor (HO2S) 3 Low Voltage (Manual Transmission Only)
P0144	Bank 1 Heated Oxygen Sensor (HO2S) 3 High Voltage (Manual Transmission Only)
P0146	Bank 1 Heated Oxygen Sensor (HO2S) 3 Insufficient Activity (Manual Transmission Only)
P0147	Bank 1 Heated Oxygen Sensor (HO2S) 3 Heater (Manual Transmission Only)
P0151	Bank 2 Heated Oxygen Sensor (HO2S) 1 Circuit – Low Voltage
P0152	Bank 2 Heated Oxygen Sensor (HO2S) 1 Circuit – High Voltage
P0153	Bank 2 Heated Oxygen Sensor (HO2S) 1 Circuit – Slow Response
P0154	Bank 2 Heated Oxygen Sensor (HO2S) 1 Circuit – Insufficient Activity Detected
P0155	Bank 2 Heated Oxygen Sensor (HO2S) 1 – Heater Circuit
P0157	Bank 2 Heated Oxygen Sensor (HO2S) 2 Circuit – Low Voltage (Automatic Transmission Only)
P0158	Bank 2 Heated Oxygen Sensor (HO2S) 2 Circuit – High Voltage (Automatic Transmission Only)

86864GB5

Fig. 53 Diagnostic trouble codes—1996 3.2L engines

DTC	Description
P0160	Bank 2 Heated Oxygen Sensor (HO2S) 2 Circuit – Insufficient Activity Detected (Automatic Transmission Only)
P0161	Bank 2 Heated Oxygen Sensor (HO2S) 2 Circuit – Heater Circuit Malfunction (Automatic Transmission Only)
P0171	Bank 1 System Too Lean
P0172	Bank 1 System Too Rich
P0174	Bank 2 System Too Lean
P0175	Bank 2 System Too Rich
P0201	Injector 1 Control Circuit Fault
P0202	Injector 2 Control Circuit Fault
P0203	Injector 3 Control Circuit Fault
P0204	Injector 4 Control Circuit Fault
P0205	Injector 5 Control Circuit Fault
P0206	Injector 6 Control Circuit Fault
P0218	Transmission Overtemperature Condition (Automatic Transmission Only)
P0300	Engine Misfire Detected
P0301	Cylinder 1 Misfire Detected
P0302	Cylinder 2 Misfire Detected
P0303	Cylinder 3 Misfire Detected
P0304	Cylinder 4 Misfire Detected
P0305	Cylinder 5 Misfire Detected
P0306	Cylinder 6 Misfire Detected
P0325	Knock Sensor (KS) Circuit Malfunction
P0327	Knock Sensor (KS) Circuit
P0336	Crankshaft Position (CKP) Sensor Circuit 58X Reference Signal
P0337	Crankshaft Position (CKP) Sensor Circuit Low Frequency
P0341	Camshaft Position (CMP) Sensor Circuit Performance
P0342	Camshaft Position (CMP) Sensor Low Frequency
P0351	Ignition Coil 1 Circuit
P0352	Ignition Coil 2 Circuit
P0353	Ignition Coil 3 Circuit
P0354	Ignition Coil 4 Circuit
P0355	Ignition Coil 5 Circuit
P0356	Ignition Coil 6 Circuit
P0401	Exhaust Gas Recirculation (EGR) Flow Insufficient
P0420	Bank 1 Three-Way Catalyst (TWC) System Low Efficiency
P0430	Bank 2 Three-Way Catalyst (TWC) System Low Efficiency Threshold (Automatic Transmission Only)
P0440	EVAP System
P0442	EVAP System Small Leak Detected
P0446	EVAP Canister Vent Blocked
P0461	Fuel Level Sensor Circuit Performance
P0462	Fuel Level Sensor Circuit – Low Voltage

86864GB6

Fig. 54 Diagnostic trouble codes—1996 3.2L engines (continued)

DTC	Description
P1154	Bank 2 Heated Oxygen Sensor (HO2S) 1 Circuit – Transition HO2S Time Ratio
P1171	Fuel Supply System Lean During Acceleration
P1300	Rough Road Sensor (G-sensor) Circuit – Intermittent Low Voltage
P1391	Rough Road Sensor (G-sensor) Circuit – Performance
P1392	Rough Road Sensor (G-sensor) Circuit – Low Voltage
P1393	Rough Road Sensor (G-sensor) Circuit – High Voltage
P1394	Rough Road Sensor (G-sensor) Circuit – Intermittent High Voltage
P1406	Exhaust Gas Recirculation (EGR) System – Pintle Position Circuit
P1441	Evaporative Emission Control System – Continuous Open Purge Flow
P1508	Idle Air Control System Counts Low RPM
P1509	Idle Air Control System Counts High RPM
P1618	Special Peripheral Interface (SPI) PCM Interprocessor Error (Automatic Transmission Only)
P1640	Output Drivers Module (ODM) "A" Fault

86864GB7

Fig. 55 Diagnostic trouble codes—1996 3.2L engines (continued)

COMPONENT LOCATIONS

The following illustrations contain information to help you locate various components of the electronic engine and emission control systems. The photographs also show how these trucks have evolved over the years from central fuel supply systems such as the feedback carburetor or throttle body injection unit to multi-port fuel injection systems which have become a standard to much of the industry.

ELECTRONIC ENGINE CONTROLS AND EMISSION ITEMS - 2.8L ENGINE SHOWN

1. EVAP canister
2. TCA vacuum motor
3. MAP sensor
4. Throttle body (under air cleaner)
5. EGR solenoid
6. Engine harness connectors
7. Secondary air control solenoid

ELECTRONIC ENGINE CONTROLS AND EMISSION ITEMS - 1996 3.2L ENGINE SHOWN

1. Camshaft position sensor
2. Mass air flow sensor
3. Intake air temperature sensor
4. Linear EGR valve
5. Idle air control valve
6. EVAP canister purge valve
7. Ignition control module
8. MAP sensor

VACUUM DIAGRAMS

Following are vacuum diagrams for most of the engine and emissions package combinations covered by this manual. Because vacuum circuits will vary based on various engine and vehicle options, always refer first to the vehicle emission control information label, if present. Should the label be missing, or should vehicle be equipped with a different engine from the vehicle's original equipment, refer to the diagrams below for the same or similar configuration.

If you wish to obtain a replacement emissions label, most manufacturers make the labels available for purchase. The labels can usually be ordered from a local dealer.

Diesel Engines

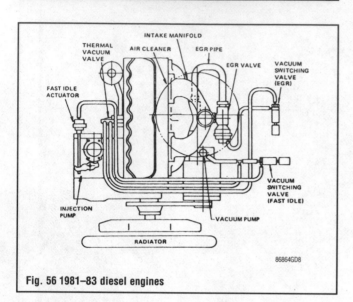

Fig. 56 1981–83 diesel engines

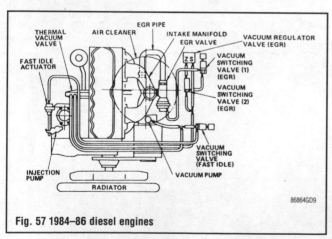

Fig. 57 1984–86 diesel engines

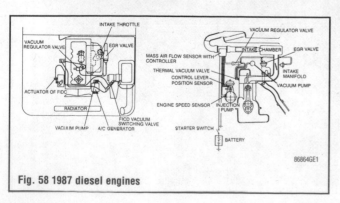

Fig. 58 1987 diesel engines

Gasoline Engines

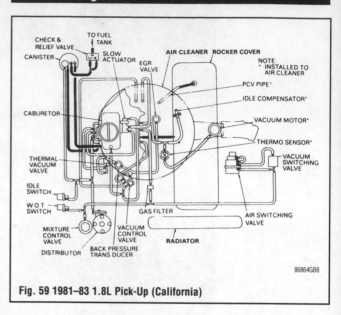

Fig. 59 1981–83 1.8L Pick-Up (California)

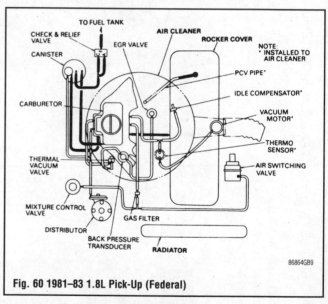

Fig. 60 1981–83 1.8L Pick-Up (Federal)

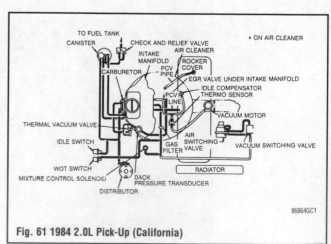

Fig. 61 1984 2.0L Pick-Up (California)

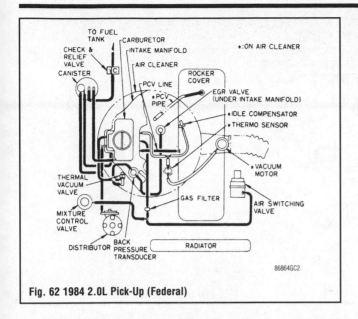

Fig. 62 1984 2.0L Pick-Up (Federal)

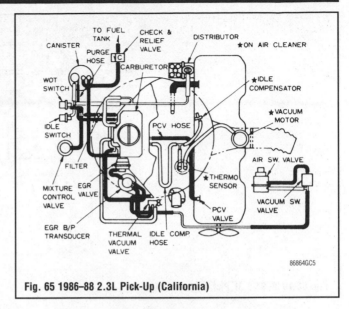

Fig. 65 1986–88 2.3L Pick-Up (California)

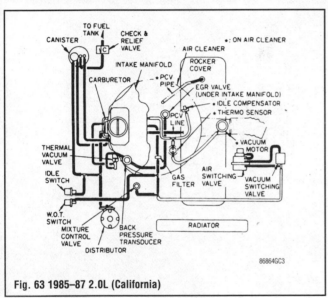

Fig. 63 1985–87 2.0L (California)

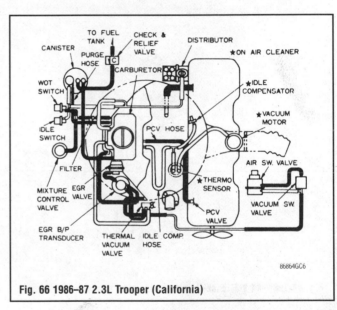

Fig. 66 1986–87 2.3L Trooper (California)

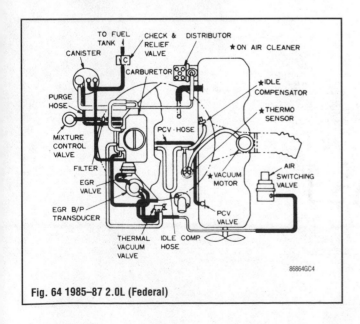

Fig. 64 1985–87 2.0L (Federal)

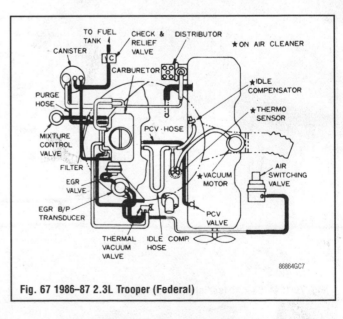

Fig. 67 1986–87 2.3L Trooper (Federal)

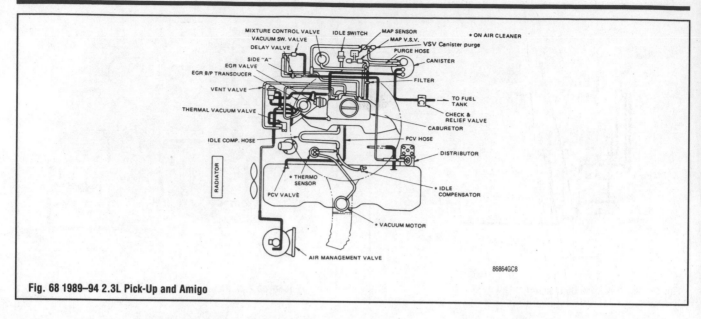

Fig. 68 1989–94 2.3L Pick-Up and Amigo

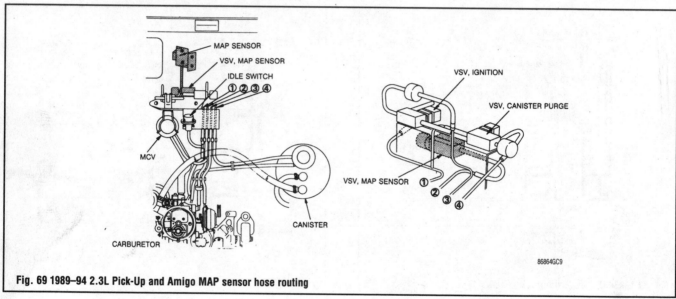

Fig. 69 1989–94 2.3L Pick-Up and Amigo MAP sensor hose routing

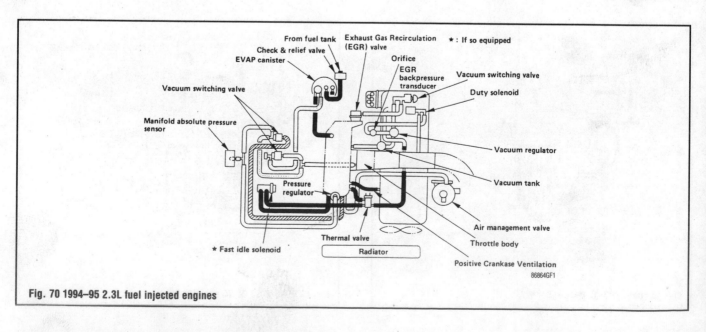

Fig. 70 1994–95 2.3L fuel injected engines

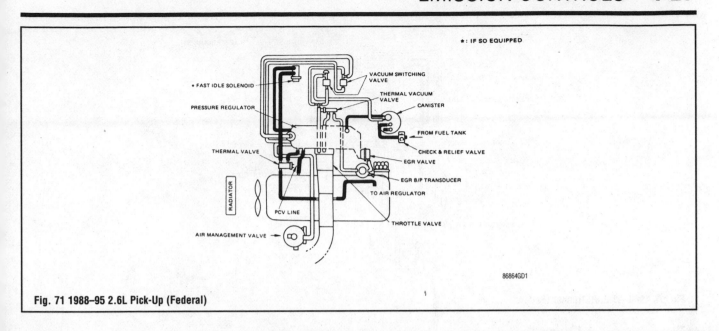

Fig. 71 1988–95 2.6L Pick-Up (Federal)

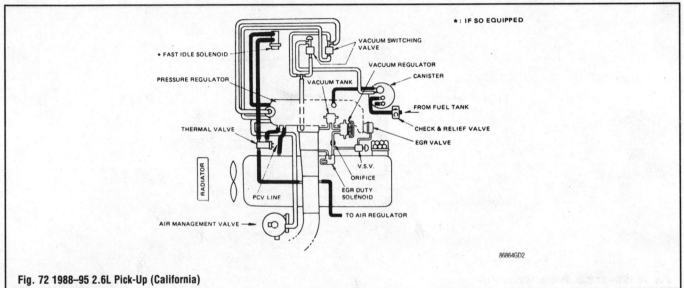

Fig. 72 1988–95 2.6L Pick-Up (California)

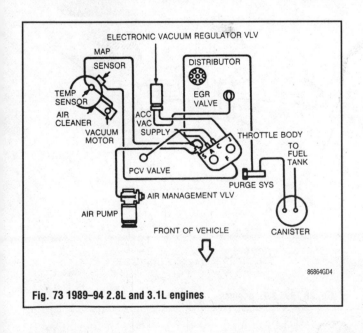

Fig. 73 1989–94 2.8L and 3.1L engines

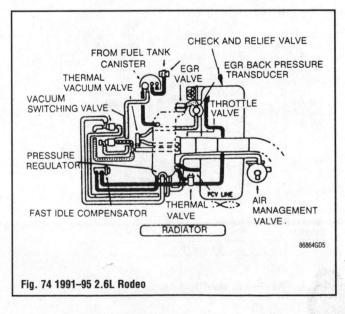

Fig. 74 1991–95 2.6L Rodeo

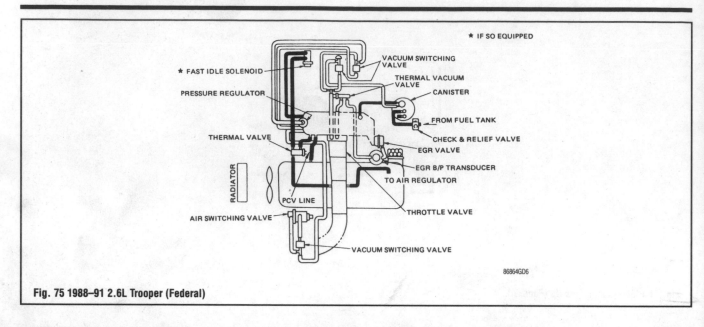

Fig. 75 1988–91 2.6L Trooper (Federal)

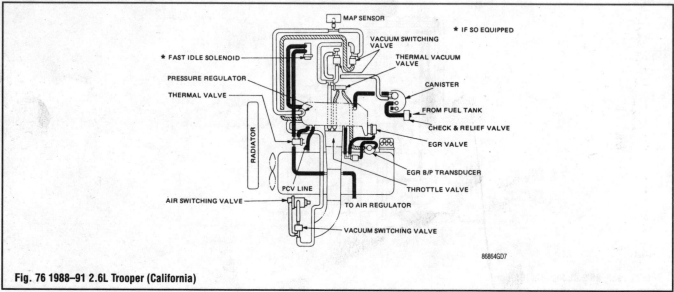

Fig. 76 1988–91 2.6L Trooper (California)

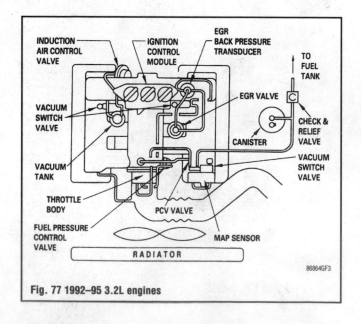

Fig. 77 1992–95 3.2L engines

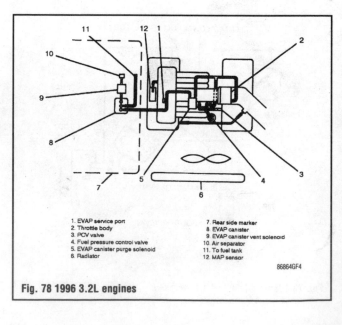

1. EVAP service port
2. Throttle body
3. PCV valve
4. Fuel pressure control valve
5. EVAP canister purge solenoid
6. Radiator
7. Rear side marker
8. EVAP canister
9. EVAP canister vent solenoid
10. Air separator
11. To fuel tank
12. MAP sensor

Fig. 78 1996 3.2L engines

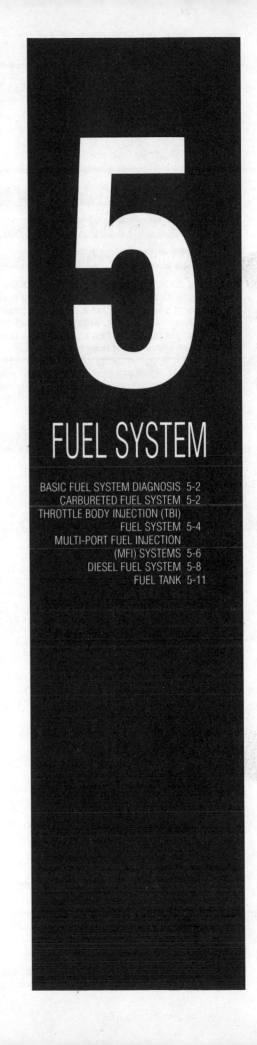

5

FUEL SYSTEM

BASIC FUEL SYSTEM DIAGNOSIS

When there is a problem starting or driving a vehicle, two of the most important checks involve the ignition and the fuel systems. The questions most mechanics attempt to answer first, "is there spark?" and "is there fuel?" will often lead to solving most basic problems. For ignition system diagnosis and testing, please refer to the information on engine electrical components and ignition systems found in Section 2 of this manual. If the ignition system checks out (there is spark), then you must determine if the fuel system is operating properly (is there fuel?).

CARBURETED FUEL SYSTEM

Relieving Fuel System Pressure

✷✷ WARNING

Disconnect the negative battery cable. Keep a Class B dry chemical fire extinguisher available. Always relieve the fuel pressure before disconnecting a fuel line. Wrap a shop cloth around a fuel line when disconnecting the line. Always use new O-rings. Do not replace the fuel pipes with fuel hoses. Always use a back-up wrench when opening or closing a fuel line.

1. Release the fuel vapor pressure in the fuel tank by removing the fuel tank cap and reinstalling it.
2. Cover the fuel line with an absorbent shop cloth and loosen the connection slowly to release the fuel pressure gradually.

Mechanical Fuel Pump

REMOVAL & INSTALLATION

G180Z and G200Z Engines

The fuel pump is located beside the distributor at the right, front side of the engine.
1. Relieve the fuel pressure.
2. Disconnect the negative battery cable.
3. Mark the distributor rotor and housing location before removing the distributor. Remove the distributor cap, with the wires attached, and the distributor assembly.
4. Disconnect and plug the fuel lines from the fuel pump.
5. Remove the engine hanger.
6. Remove the fuel pump-to-engine bolts and remove the pump assembly.
To install:
7. Installation is the reverse of removal.

4ZD1 Engine

♦ See Figure 1

The fuel pump is located at the right side of the engine, directly under the intake manifold.
1. Relieve the fuel pressure.
2. Disconnect the negative battery cable.

3. Remove the air cleaner assembly.
4. Remove the intake manifold assembly.
5. Disconnect and plug the fuel lines at the fuel pump.
6. Remove the fuel pump-to-engine bolts and the pump assembly.
To install:
7. Remove the cylinder head cover.
8. Rotate the engine to position the No. 4 piston at TDC of its compression stroke.
9. Lift the fuel pump pushrod toward the camshaft and hold it in the raised position.
10. Using a new gasket, install the fuel pump on the engine; tighten the bolts to 15–25 ft. lbs. (20–34 Nm).
11. Connect the fuel hoses to the fuel pump.
12. Using a new gasket, install the intake manifold.
13. Install the air cleaner assembly.
14. Connect the negative battery cable.
15. Start the engine and check for fuel leaks.

TESTING

♦ See Figure 2

1. Remove the fuel pump from the vehicle.
2. Check the outside of the pump for cracks, leakage and other damage; replace if necessary.
3. Check for excessive wear between the rocker arm and camshaft contact surfaces.
4. Check the inlet valve by moving the rocker arm to the pump side and hold it in this position. Shut both the return and outlet pipes with your fingers. When the rocker arm has returned to its original position, there should show a marked increase in the amount of play. If there is no increase, replace the pump.
5. Check the outlet valve by closing the inlet pipe. The rocker arm must not move when the pipe is closed. Do not use excessive force.
6. Check the diaphragm. The rocker arm must not move when the inlet, outlet and return pipes are shut; if so, replace the pump.

Carburetors

ADJUSTMENTS

Fast Idle

The automatic choke fast idle is adjusted by the opening angle of the throttle valve on the carburetor.

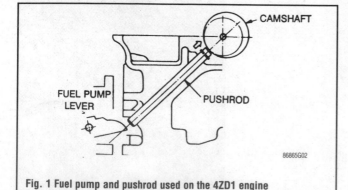

Fig. 1 Fuel pump and pushrod used on the 4ZD1 engine

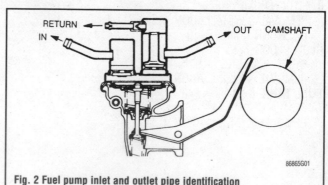

Fig. 2 Fuel pump inlet and outlet pipe identification

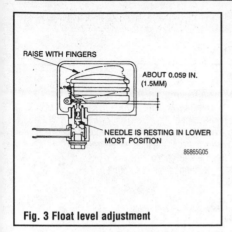

Fig. 3 Float level adjustment

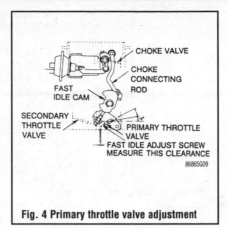

Fig. 4 Primary throttle valve adjustment

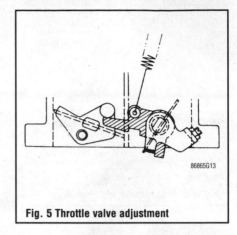

Fig. 5 Throttle valve adjustment

1. Disconnect and plug the vacuum line to the distributor, idle compensator and EGR valve.
2. Adjust the throttle valve opening at the first step of the fast idle cam to 16° for manual transmissions or 18° for automatics.
3. Start the engine. The fast idle should be approximately 3200 rpm after the engine is warm.
4. Shut the engine off. Attach the vacuum lines disconnected earlier.

Float Level

▶ See Figure 3

1. Remove the carburetor and float cover.
2. The fuel level is normal if it is within the mark on the window glass of the float chamber when the engine is stationary.
3. If the level is outside the line, make necessary adjustments by bending the float seat. The needle valve should have an effective stroke of about 0.059 in. (1.5mm). Check this measurement between the valve stem and the float seat.

➡ **Do not bend the needle valve rod when installing the float.**

4. Install the float cover and carburetor.

Primary Throttle Valve

EXCEPT 4ZD1 ENGINE

▶ See Figure 4

The primary throttle valve is opened by means of the fast idle adjusting screw to an angle of 16° when the choke valve is completely closed. The primary throttle valve opening angle may be checked as follows:
1. Close the choke valve completely and measure the clearance between the center of the throttle valve and the wall of the throttle valve chamber. Standard clearance is 0.051–0.059 in. (1.3–1.5mm).
2. Adjust the throttle valve opening angle with the fast idle adjusting screw.

➡ **Be sure to turn the throttle stop screw all the way in before measuring the clearance.**

4ZD1 ENGINE

▶ See Figure 5

1. Slowly open the primary throttle valve until the kick lever tang contacts the return plate.
2. Measure the clearance between the choke valve and the choke valve chamber wall.
3. If the clearance measured is not 0.27–0.33 in. (7.0–8.5mm), bend the kick lever tang to adjust.

Kick Lever

▶ See Figure 6

1. Turn out the throttle valve adjusting screw to completely close the primary side of the throttle valve.

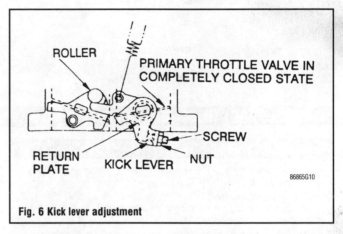

Fig. 6 Kick lever adjustment

2. Loosen the locknut on the kick lever screw and turn the screw until it is in contact with the return plate.
3. Tighten the locknut.

Choke Valve Opening

4ZD1 ENGINES

▶ See Figure 7

1. Move the fast idle screw tip against the 2nd step of the fast idle cam.
2. Measure the clearance between the choke valve and the choke valve chamber wall.
3. If the clearance measured is not 0.031–0.051 in. (0.8–1.3mm), bend the counter lever tang to adjust.

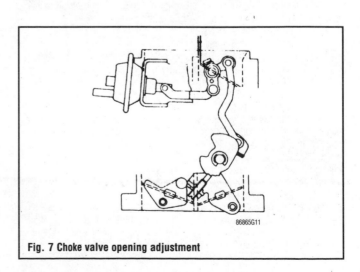

Fig. 7 Choke valve opening adjustment

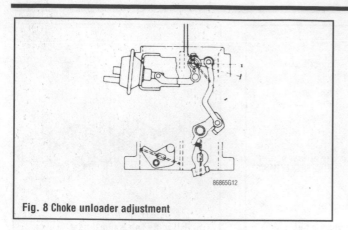

Fig. 8 Choke unloader adjustment

Unloader

4ZD1 ENGINE

▶ **See Figure 8**

1. Open the primary valve fully.
2. Measure the clearance between the choke valve and the choke valve chamber wall.

3. If the clearance measured is not 0.098–0.129 in. (2.5–3.3mm), bend the adjusting lever tang to adjust.

REMOVAL & INSTALLATION

1. Disconnect the negative (–) battery cable.
2. Disconnect the PCV and AIR hoses.
3. Remove the air cleaner assembly with the vacuum hose and air duct.
4. Remove the throttle return spring.
5. Label and disconnect the emission control vacuum hoses.
6. Disconnect the lead wire connectors and accelerator cable.
7. Release the fuel pressure and disconnect the fuel pipes.
8. Remove the carburetor retaining nuts and carburetor.
9. Remove the old gasket.

To install:

10. Install the carburetor, new gaskets and retaining nuts.
11. Connect the fuel pipes.
12. Fasten the lead wire connectors and accelerator cable.
13. Connect the emission control vacuum hoses.
14. Install the throttle return spring.
15. Install the air cleaner assembly with the vacuum hose and air duct.
16. Connect the PCV and AIR hoses.
17. Connect the negative (–) battery cable, start the engine and check for leaks.

THROTTLE BODY INJECTION (TBI) FUEL SYSTEM

General Information

The Throttle Body Injection (TBI) system is a fuel metering system in which the amount of fuel delivered by the throttle body injectors is determined by an electronic signal supplied by the Electronic Control Module (ECM). The ECM monitors various engine and vehicle conditions to calculate the fuel delivery time (pulse width) of the injectors. The fuel pulse may be modified by the ECM to account for special operating conditions, such as cranking, cold starting, altitude, acceleration, and deceleration.

The ECM controls the exhaust emissions by modifying fuel delivery to achieve, as near as possible, an air/fuel ratio of 14.7:1. The injector on-time is determined by various inputs to the ECM. By increasing the injector pulse, more fuel is delivered, enriching the air/fuel ratio. Decreasing the injector pulse leans the air/fuel ratio.

Pulses are sent to the injectors in 2 different modes: synchronized and non-synchronized. In synchronized mode operation, the injectors are pulsed alternately. In non-synchronized mode operation, the injectors are pulsed once every 12.5 milliseconds or 6.25 milliseconds depending, on calibration. This pulse time is totally independent of distributor reference pulses. Non-synchronized mode results only under the following conditions:

- The fuel pulse width is too small to be delivered accurately by the injectors (approximately 1.5 milliseconds).
- During the delivery of prime pulses (prime pulses charge the intake manifold with fuel during or just prior to engine starting).
- During acceleration enrichment.
- During deceleration leanout.

The basic TBI unit is made up of 2 major casting assemblies: (1) a throttle body with a valve to control airflow and (2) a fuel body assembly with an integral pressure regulator and fuel injectors to supply the required fuel. An electronically operated device to control the idle speed, and a device to provide information regarding throttle valve position, are included as part of the TBI unit.

Each fuel injector is a solenoid-operated device controlled by the ECM. The incoming fuel is directed to the lower end of the injector assembly, which has a fine screen filter surrounding the injector inlet. The ECM actuates the solenoid, which lifts a normally closed ball valve off a seat. The fuel under pressure is injected in a conical spray pattern at the walls of the throttle body bore, above the throttle valve. The excess fuel passes through a pressure regulator before being returned to the vehicle's fuel tank.

The pressure regulator is a diaphragm-operated relief valve with injector pressure on one side and air cleaner pressure on the other. The function of the regulator is to maintain a constant pressure drop across the injectors throughout the operating load and speed range of the engine.

The throttle body portion of the TBI unit may contain ports located at, above or below the throttle valve. These ports generate the vacuum signals for the EGR valve, MAP sensor, and the canister purge system.

The Throttle Position Sensor (TPS) is a variable resistor used to convert the degree of throttle plate opening into an electrical signal for the ECM. The ECM uses this signal as a reference point of throttle valve position. In addition, an Idle Air Control (IAC) assembly, mounted in the throttle body, is used to control idle speeds. A cone-shaped valve in the IAC assembly is located in an air passage in the throttle body that leads from the point beneath the air cleaner to below the throttle valve. The ECM monitors idle speeds and, depending on engine load, moves the IAC cone in the air passage to increase, or decrease air bypassing the throttle valve to the intake manifold for control of idle speeds.

Relieving Fuel System Pressure

✲✲ WARNING

Disconnect the negative battery cable. Keep a Class B dry chemical fire extinguisher available. Always relieve the fuel pressure before disconnecting a fuel line. Wrap a shop cloth around a fuel line when disconnecting the line. Always use new O-rings. Do not replace the fuel pipes with fuel hoses. Always use a back-up wrench when opening or closing a fuel line.

1. Allow the engine to cool. Then, remove the fuel pump fuse from the fuse block or disconnect the fuel pump relay.
2. Crank the engine; it will start and run until the fuel supply remaining in the fuel lines is exhausted. When the engine stops, engage the starter again for 3 seconds to assure dissipation of any remaining pressure.
3. With the ignition **OFF**, reinstall the fuel pump fuse or connect the fuel pump relay.

Electric Fuel Pump

TESTING

▶ **See Figure 9**

1. Relieve the fuel pressure.
2. Disconnect the fuel line near the engine and install a fuel pressure gauge T-connector in the line.

3. Connect the fuel pressure gauge to the T-connector.

4. Start the engine and check the fuel pressure; it should be 9–13 psi (62–90 kPa) at the fuel pressure line after the fuel filter.

REMOVAL & INSTALLATION

✳✳ CAUTION

Fuel is under high pressure. If the following steps are not followed, fuel could spray out and result in a fire hazard or possible injury.

➡ **The fuel pump is mounted inside the fuel tank.**

1. Relieve the fuel pressure, then disconnect the negative battery cable.

2. Raise and support the vehicle safely. Drain the fuel tank. Remove the undercover screws and undercover, if so equipped.

3. Remove all gas line hose connections and the fuel pump ground wire.

4. Remove the filler neck hose and clamp.

5. Remove the breather hose and clamp.

6. Disconnect the fuel tank hose to evaporator pipe. Place a suitable floor jack with a piece of wood on it under the fuel tank.

7. Remove the fuel tank mounting bolts and lower the tank from the vehicle. At this point remove hose from pump to fuel filter.

8. Remove the fuel pump bracket plate and fuel pump as an assembly.

9. Remove the pump bracket, rubber cushion and fuel pump filter.

To install:

10. Install the pump to the bracket and rubber cushion. Install the fuel pump filter.

11. Install the fuel pump bracket plate and fuel pump as an assembly.

12. Raise the tank and connect the hoses. Fasten the tank straps.

13. Connect the fuel tank hose to the evaporator pipe.

14. Install the breather hose and clamp.

15. Connect the fuel pump ground wire. Install the undercover and screws.

16. Lower the vehicle safely. Refill the fuel tank and check for leaks.

17. Connect the negative battery cable, then start the engine and check operation.

Throttle Body

REMOVAL & INSTALLATION

◗ **See Figure 10**

1. Disconnect the negative (–) battery cable.

2. Relieve the fuel pressure and remove the air cleaner.

3. Disconnect the throttle body electrical connectors.

4. Disconnect the throttle cable, transmission cable and cruise control cable.

5. Remove the cable support brackets.

6. Label and disconnect the vacuum hoses.

7. Using a back-up wrench, disconnect the fuel pressure and return lines.

8. Remove the throttle body unit attaching bolts, then the unit and gasket.

9. Place a shop towel in the intake manifold openings to prevent dirt from entering the engine.

To install:

10. Clean the gasket mating surfaces.

11. Install the new gasket, throttle body unit and bolts. Tighten the bolts to 18 ft. lbs. (25 Nm).

12. Install the fuel lines with new O-ring gaskets. Tighten the lines to 20 ft. lbs. (27 Nm).

13. Connect the vacuum hoses.

14. Install the cable support bracket.

15. Install the throttle, transmission and cruise control cables.

16. Connect all electrical wiring. Make sure the connectors are fully seated and latched.

17. Install the air cleaner and connect the battery cable.

18. Reset the IAC pintle by depressing the accelerator pedal slightly, then start the engine and run for three seconds, turn the ignition **OFF** for ten seconds, restart the engine and check for proper idle.

Fuel Injectors

REMOVAL & INSTALLATION

◗ **See Figure 11**

The engine is equipped with 2 fuel injectors; both are located in the throttle body.

1. Relieve the fuel pressure.

2. Disconnect the negative battery cable.

3. Remove the air cleaner.

4. At the injector electrical connectors, squeeze the 2 tabs together and pull them straight upward.

5. Remove the fuel meter cover and leave the cover gasket in place.

6. Using a small prybar, carefully pry the injectors upward until they are free of the throttle body.

7. Remove the small O-ring from the nozzle end of the injector. Carefully rotate the injector's fuel filter back-and-forth to remove it from the base of the injector.

8. Discard the fuel meter cover gasket.

9. Remove the large O-ring and back-up washer from the top of the counterbore of the fuel meter body injector cavity.

To install:

10. Lubricate the O-rings with automatic transmission fluid and push the injectors into the cavities.

11. Install the new fuel meter cover gasket and cover.

12. Install the electrical connectors to the injectors.

13. Install the air cleaner and connect the negative battery cable.

Fig. 9 A fuel pressure gauge can be a valuable diagnostic tool

TCCS4P04

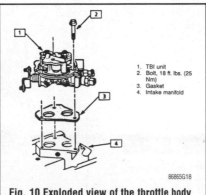

1. TBI unit
2. Bolt, 18 ft. lbs. (25 Nm)
3. Gasket
4. Intake manifold

86865G18

Fig. 10 Exploded view of the throttle body mounting

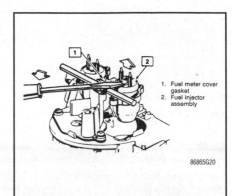

1. Fuel meter cover gasket
2. Fuel injector assembly

86865G20

Fig. 11 Carefully remove the injectors to avoid damaging the throttle body

MULTI-PORT FUEL INJECTION (MFI) SYSTEMS

General Information

The Multi-port Fuel Injection (MFI) system is a fuel metering system where the amount of fuel delivered by the injectors is determined by an electronic signal supplied by the Electronic Control Module (ECM). The ECM monitors various engine and vehicle conditions to calculate the fuel delivery time (pulse width) of the injectors. The fuel pulse may be modified by the ECM to account for special operating conditions, such as cranking, cold starting, altitude, acceleration, and deceleration.

The ECM controls the exhaust emissions by modifying fuel delivery to achieve, as near as possible, an air/fuel ratio of 14.7:1. The injector on-time is determined by various inputs to the ECM. By increasing the injector pulse, more fuel is delivered, enriching the air/fuel ratio. Decreasing the injector pulse leans the air/fuel ratio.

Each fuel injector (one per cylinder) is a solenoid-operated device controlled by the ECM. The incoming fuel is directed to the lower end of the injector assembly which has a fine screen filter surrounding the injector inlet. The ECM actuates the solenoid, which lifts a normally closed pintle off a seat. The fuel, under pressure, is injected in a conical spray pattern just above the intake valve. The excess fuel passes through a pressure regulator before being returned to the vehicle's fuel tank.

The pressure regulator is a diaphragm-operated relief valve. The function of the regulator is to maintain a constant pressure drop across the injector throughout the operating load and speed range of the engine.

Relieving Fuel System Pressure

PROCEDURE

> **✳✳ WARNING**
>
> **Disconnect the negative battery cable. Keep a Class B dry chemical fire extinguisher available. Always relieve the fuel pressure before disconnecting a fuel line. Wrap a shop cloth around a fuel line when disconnecting the line. Always use new O-rings. Do not replace the fuel pipes with fuel hoses. Always use a back-up wrench when opening or closing a fuel line.**

1. Allow the engine to cool. Then, remove the fuel pump fuse from the fuse block or disconnect the fuel pump relay.
2. Crank the engine; it will start and run until the fuel supply remaining in the fuel lines is exhausted. When the engine stops, engage the starter again for 3 seconds to assure dissipation of any remaining pressure.
3. With the ignition **OFF**, reinstall the fuel pump fuse or connect the fuel pump relay.

Electric Fuel Pump

TESTING

1. Relieve the fuel pressure.
2. Disconnect the fuel line near the engine and install a fuel pressure gauge T-connector in the line.
3. Connect the fuel pressure gauge to the T-connector.
4. Start the engine and check the fuel pressure. Compare the pressure readings to the figures listed in the Tune-up Specifications chart in Section 1.

REMOVAL & INSTALLATION

> **✳✳ CAUTION**
>
> **Fuel is under high pressure; if the following steps are not followed the fuel could spray out and result in a fire hazard or possible injury.**

1. Relieve the fuel pressure then disconnect the negative battery cable.
2. Raise and support the vehicle safely. Drain the fuel tank. Remove the undercover screws and undercover, if so equipped.
3. Unfasten all gas line hose connections and the fuel pump ground wire.
4. Remove the filler neck hose and clamp.
5. Remove the breather hose and clamp.
6. Disconnect the fuel tank hose-to-evaporator pipe. Place a suitable floor jack with a piece of wood on it under the fuel tank.
7. Remove the fuel tank mounting bolts and lower the tank from the vehicle. Disconnect the hose from the pump to the fuel filter.
8. Remove the fuel pump bracket plate and fuel pump as an assembly.
9. Remove the pump bracket, rubber cushion and fuel pump filter.

To install:
10. Install the pump to the bracket and rubber cushion. Install the fuel pump filter.
11. Install the fuel pump bracket plate and fuel pump as an assembly.
12. Raise the tank and connect the hoses. Fasten the tank straps.
13. Connect the fuel tank hose-to-evaporator pipe.
14. Install the breather hose and clamp.
15. Connect the fuel pump ground wire. Install the undercover and screws, if equipped.
16. Lower the vehicle safely. Refill the fuel tank and check for leaks.
17. Connect the negative battery cable and check operation.

Throttle Body

REMOVAL & INSTALLATION

▶ **See Figure 12**

1. Disconnect the negative (−) battery cable.
2. Remove the air intake duct.
3. Drain the engine coolant below the level of the throttle body assembly.
4. Disconnect the accelerator cable, vacuum and coolant hoses.
5. Unplug the electrical connections.
6. Remove the throttle body attaching bolts and throttle body assembly.

To install:
7. Clean the gasket mating surfaces with a scraper and solvent.
8. Position a new gasket, then install the throttle body attaching bolts and throttle body assembly.
9. Connect the accelerator cable, vacuum and coolant hoses.
10. Engage the electrical connections.
11. Refill the engine coolant.
12. Install the air intake duct.
13. Connect the negative (−) battery cable and check for leaks.

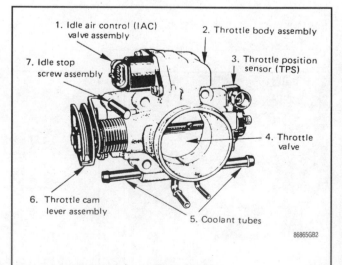

1. Idle air control (IAC) valve assembly
2. Throttle body assembly
3. Throttle position sensor (TPS)
4. Throttle valve
5. Coolant tubes
6. Throttle cam lever assembly
7. Idle stop screw assembly

86865GB2

Fig. 12 Throttle body and related components

Fuel Injectors

REMOVAL & INSTALLATION

Except 3.2L Engine

▶ See Figure 13

1. Relieve the fuel pressure.
2. Disconnect the negative battery cable.
3. Remove the air intake duct.
4. Remove the throttle body for extra working room.
5. Label and disconnect the harnesses from the fuel injectors.
6. Disconnect the fuel lines from the fuel rail.

❊❊ CAUTION

Do not allow fuel spray or fuel vapors to come in contact with a spark or open flame. Keep a dry chemical fire extinguisher nearby. Never store fuel in an open container due to risk of fire or explosion.

7. Clean up any fuel that spilled on the engine or intake manifold.
8. Remove the fuel rail and injectors from the intake manifold as an assembly.
9. Separate the fuel injectors from the fuel rail.

To install:

10. Lubricate new O-rings with clean engine oil and install them onto the fuel injectors.
11. Install the fuel injectors onto the fuel rail.
12. Lubricate the fuel injector O-rings with clean engine oil and install them, along with the fuel rail, onto the intake manifold.
13. Install the fuel rail mounting bolts and tighten them to 14 ft. lbs. (19 Nm).
14. Connect the fuel lines to the fuel rail using new sealing washers.
15. Connect the harnesses to the injectors.
16. Install the throttle body with a new gasket, and tighten the mounting bolts to 14 ft. lbs. (19 Nm).
17. Install the air intake duct.
18. Connect the negative battery cable.
19. Turn the ignition to the **ON** position to pressurize the fuel system. Then, check the injectors and fuel line fittings for leaks.
20. After warming the engine up to normal operating temperature, check the operation of the throttle cable and adjust it if necessary.

3.2L Engine

▶ See Figures 13 and 14

1. Relieve the fuel system pressure.
2. Disconnect the negative battery cable and reinstall the fuel pump fuse or relay.

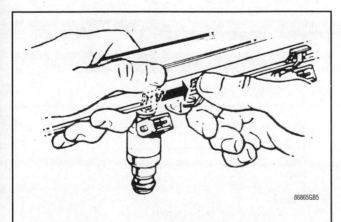

86865GB5

Fig. 13 Remove the clip retaining the injector to the fuel rail

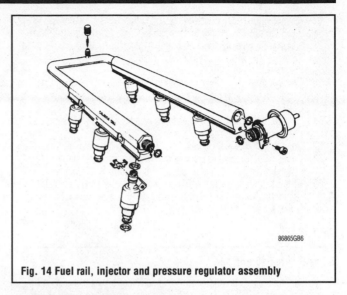

86865GB6

Fig. 14 Fuel rail, injector and pressure regulator assembly

3. Remove the air cleaner assembly.
4. Disconnect the accelerator pedal cable from the throttle body and bracket.
5. Disconnect the charcoal canister hose from the vacuum pipe.
6. Disconnect the air vacuum hose and booster hose from the common chamber.
7. Disconnect the harnesses from the MAP sensor, charcoal canister vacuum switching valve, exhaust gas recirculation valve and intake air temperature sensor. Disconnect the engine ground cable.
8. Disconnect the spark plug wires from the valve covers.
9. Remove the ignition module assembly with the spark plug wires attached.
10. Disconnect the vacuum hoses from the throttle body.
11. Remove the throttle body mounting bolts. Then, remove the throttle body.
12. Disconnect the PCV hose, fuel pressure control valve vacuum hose, evaporative emission canister purge hose and EGR valve assembly from the common chamber.
13. Remove the common chamber from the intake manifold (six bolts, two nuts and three brackets).
14. Disconnect the fuel feed and return hoses from the fuel rail. Unbolt the fuel rail brackets from the cylinder head cover.
15. Disconnect the thermo sensor.
16. Remove the fuel rail mounting bolts. Lift the fuel rail up with the injectors still attached. Remove the fuel rail and injector assembly from the vehicle.
17. Slide the retainer clip sideways to remove each fuel injector from the fuel rail.
18. Clean up any fuel that has spilled.

To install:

➡**Always use new O-rings when assembling the fuel injectors and installing the fuel rail assembly to the intake manifold. Always use new sealing washers when reconnecting fuel lines.**

19. Lubricate new O-rings with engine oil and install them on the fuel injectors.
20. Install the fuel injectors onto the fuel rail and secure with the retaining clips.
21. Install the fuel rail to the intake manifold. Make sure the injectors are securely seated into the manifold ports.
22. Connect the harnesses to the fuel injectors and the thermo sensor.
23. Connect the fuel return and feed hoses to the fuel rail.
24. Install the common chamber. Tighten the bolts and nuts in a crisscross pattern to 17 ft. lbs. (23 Nm).

➡**Replace any gaskets between the throttle body, common chamber, and intake manifold to prevent the possibility of leaks.**

25. Install the EGR assembly. Tighten the bolts to 78 inch lbs. (9 Nm).
26. Connect the charcoal canister purge hose, fuel pressure regulator vacuum hoses and PCV hose to the common chamber.

27. Install the throttle body assembly and connect the vacuum hoses to the throttle body. Tighten the throttle body mounting bolts to 16 ft. lbs. (22 Nm).

28. Install the ignition module assembly. Tighten the mounting bolts to 16 ft. lbs. (22 Nm).

29. Reconnect the spark plug wires.

30. Connect the MAP sensor, charcoal canister vacuum switching valve, exhaust gas recirculation valve, intake air temperature sensor and engine ground cable.

31. Connect the air vacuum and vacuum booster hoses to the common chamber.

32. Connect the charcoal canister vacuum hose to the vacuum pipe.

33. Connect the accelerator cable to the throttle body and bracket.

34. Install the air cleaner and reconnect the negative battery cable.

35. Turn the ignition key to the **ON** position for two seconds, then **OFF**. Turn the ignition **ON** again to pressurize the fuel system and check for leaks where the fuel system was disconnected.

TESTING

▶ **See Figures 15 and 16**

1. With the engine running, listen to the injector noise with a stethoscope. Normal operation is indicated when a regular click, which varies with engine speed, is heard. If a regular click is not heard, the injector is probably malfunctioning.

2. To check if the injector is receiving its pulse signal, use a noid light. Simply unplug the connector and install the light, then crank the engine. If the light pulses, the injector is receiving its signal from the ECM.

3. The injector may also be checked with a fuel injector tester. This tool

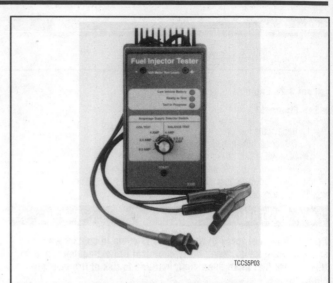

Fig. 16 Fuel injector testers can be purchased or sometimes rented

substitutes the signal from the ECM to pulse the injector. Follow the tool manufacturer's instructions to test the injector.

Fuel Pressure Regulator

REMOVAL & INSTALLATION

1. Properly relieve the fuel system pressure and disconnect the negative battery cable.

2. Disconnect the vacuum hose from the regulator.

3. Disconnect the fuel hoses or pipes from the regulator. If a pipe is used, use a back-up and flare nut wrench to avoid twisting the tube.

4. If applicable, remove any retaining hardware securing the regulator, then remove the regulator from the vehicle.

To install:

5. If the old pressure regulator is being installed, check the filter screen (if equipped) for contamination and replace, if necessary.

6. Lubricate new O-rings with clean engine oil, then install them on the pressure regulator.

7. Place the pressure regulator in position. If applicable, coat the regulator attaching screw threads with Loctite®262 or an equivalent threadlocking compound. Install and tighten the attaching hardware until snug.

8. Connect the vacuum hose to the regulator.

9. Connect the fuel pipes or hoses to the pressure regulator. If hoses are used, use new clamps.

10. Connect the negative battery cable, then pressurize the fuel system by cycling the ignition (without attempting to start the engine) and check for leaks.

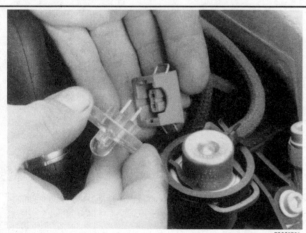

Fig. 15 A noid light can be attached to the fuel injector harness in order to test for injector pulse

DIESEL FUEL SYSTEM

Injection Lines

REMOVAL & INSTALLATION

1. Disconnect the negative battery cable.

2. Use a back-up and flare nut wrench to remove the pump-to-injector nozzle lines. These lines may be damaged if the proper wrenches are not used. Wrap a shop rag around the fitting, then slowly turn the wrench to allow any residual fuel pressure to be relieved.

3. Remove the injection line.

To install:

4. Position the line in place, then thread the fitting on by hand.

5. Using a back-up and flare nut wrench, tighten the fittings until snug.

6. Connect the negative battery cable.

Injectors

REMOVAL & INSTALLATION

1. Remove the fuel pressure line(s) and return line(s) from the fuel injector(s).

2. Remove the fuel injector(s) from the engine.

3. Remove the O-rings from the fuel injector(s).

To install:

4. Using new O-rings, lubricate them in diesel fuel and install them onto the fuel injector(s).

5. Install the fuel injector(s) into the engine.

6. Using new O-rings, install the fuel pressure line(s) and return line(s) to the fuel injector(s).

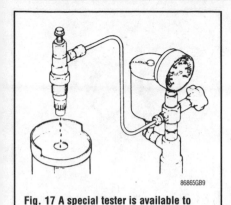

Fig. 17 A special tester is available to check opening pressure and spray patterns

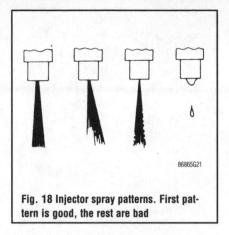

Fig. 18 Injector spray patterns. First pattern is good, the rest are bad

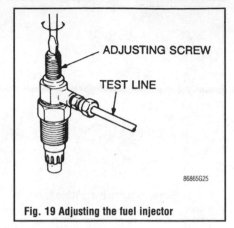

Fig. 19 Adjusting the fuel injector

TESTING

▶ See Figures 17 and 18

❈❈ CAUTION

When using the injector tester, test fluid will spray out of the injector nozzle at high pressure, which can easily puncture the skin or eyes. Since a defective injector may spray in any direction, make sure that hands and eyes are away from the injector outlet and that protective clothing and safety glasses are used.

1. Remove the injector and install injector tester J-28829 or equivalent. Measure the injector pressure. Pressure should be:
   - C223 engine—1493 psi (105 kg/cm)
   - C223-T engine—1920 psi (135 kg/cm)
2. Using injector tester J-28829 or equivalent, maintain a pressure of 284 psi (20 kg/cm). If there is no leakage, the injector is satisfactory.
3. Observe the spray pattern coming from the outlet. It should be a fine uniform spray. If not, clean or replace the injector.

DISASSEMBLY & ASSEMBLY

▶ See Figure 19

1. Remove the injector from the vehicle.
2. Place the injector in a vise, clamping the hexagonal portion in the vise. Loosen the retaining nut and remove it.
3. Remove the eye bolt, gasket, cap nut and gasket.
4. Remove the adjusting screw, nozzle spring and pushrod.
5. Remove the inlet connector, gasket and retaining nut.
6. Remove the setting screw and nozzle from the holding body.

To install:
7. Install the nozzle and setting screw.
8. Install the inlet connector, gasket and retaining nut.
9. Install the adjusting screw, nozzle spring and pushrod.
10. Using the injector holder and injector tester, adjust the opening pressure by setting the pressure adjusting screw until the desired pressure is obtained.
11. Install the cap nut and tighten to 22–29 inch lbs. (3–4 Nm).
12. Assemble the injector and tighten the retaining nut to 65 ft. lbs. (88 Nm).

CLEANING

▶ See Figure 20

Remove the carbon from the outside of the nozzle body with a soft brush. Clean the internal portion of the body with rod J-28826-2 or equivalent. Clean the nozzle seat of the body with cleaning tool J-28826 or equivalent. Clean the injection hole of the body with rod J-28826-4 or equivalent.

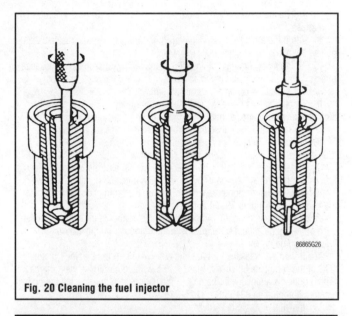

Fig. 20 Cleaning the fuel injector

Injection Pump

REMOVAL & INSTALLATION

1. Disconnect the negative battery cable.
2. Remove the timing belt cover.
3. Remove the fuel lines.
4. Using a prybar, remove the tension spring from the timing belt tensioner.

➡ **When removing the tension spring, avoid using excessive force, or the spring may become distorted.**

5. Remove the tensioner pulley bolt and the pulley.
6. Remove the timing belt and discard it.
7. Using a 6mm x 1.25 pitch bolt, install the threaded portion into the threaded hole in the timing pulley housing through the hole in the pulley. This prevents the pulley from turning.
8. Remove the injection pump pulley-to-shaft bolts.
9. Using a wheel puller, connect it to the injection pump pulley and press it from the shaft.
10. Remove the injection pump bracket-to-timing pulley housing bolts, the rear injection pump-to-bracket bolts and the injection pump.

To install:
11. Install the injection pump. Tighten the injection pump-to-timing pulley housing bolts and leave the rear pump-to-bracket bolts semi-tight.
12. Install the injection pump pulley by aligning it with the key groove and tighten the bolt to 42–52 ft. lbs. (57–70 Nm).

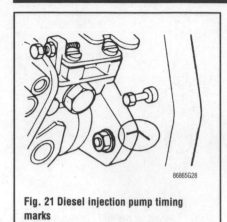

Fig. 21 Diesel injection pump timing marks

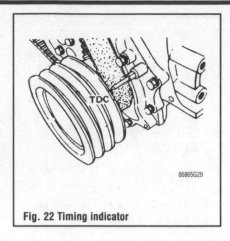

Fig. 22 Timing indicator

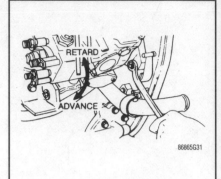

Fig. 23 Turning the injection pump in its mount will advance or retard the timing

13. Rotate the crankshaft to bring the No. 1 piston to TDC of the compression stroke.

14. Align the timing marks on the injection pump pulley with the camshaft pulley; the marks must be facing each other.

15. Using a new timing belt, install it in the following sequence: crankshaft pulley, camshaft pulley and the injection pump pulley; the slack must be between the injection pump and camshaft pulleys.

16. Install the tension center and the tension pulley so the end of the tension center is fitted against both pins on the timing pulley housing.

17. Hand-tighten the nut so the tension pulley can be rotated freely.

18. Install the tension spring and tighten the pulley nut to 22–36 ft. lbs. (29–48 Nm).

19. Rotate the crankshaft 2 full turns clockwise to seat the belt and further turn the crankshaft 90° beyond TDC to settle the injection pump.

20. Loosen the tension pulley nut to take up the timing belt slack. Tighten the tension pulley nut to 79–94 ft. lbs. (108–130 Nm).

21. Install the injection pump pulley flange; the hole in the outer circumference of the flange should be aligned with the triangular timing mark on the injection pump pulley.

22. Rotate the crankshaft 2 full turns clockwise to bring the No. 1 piston to TDC of the compression stroke. Make sure the triangular timing mark on the timing pulley is aligned with the hole in the flange, then measure the timing belt tension; it should be 33–55 lbs. (147–246 N).

23. Install the timing belt cover.

24. Connect the negative battery cable.

INJECTION TIMING

▶ **See Figures 21, 22 and 23**

1. Check to see if the notched lines on the injection pump and mounting plate are aligned.

2. Bring the No. 1 piston to Top Dead Center (TDC) on the compression stroke by turning the crankshaft. The correct notch must be used for alignment, as the damper pulley is provided with a total of seven notches.

3. Remove the front upper timing belt cover, then check the timing belt for proper tension and alignment of the timing marks.

4. Remove the cam cover and rear plug, then check that the fixing plate (J–29761 or equivalent) fits smoothly into the slit at the rear end of the camshaft. Remove the fixing plate.

5. Disconnect the injection pipe from the injection pump and remove the distributor head screw and gasket, then install a static timing gauge. Set the lift about 0.039 in. (1mm) from the plunger.

6. Bring the No. 1 piston to a point 45–60° before TDC by turning the crankshaft, then calibrate the dial indicator to zero.

➡ **The damper is provided with notched lines. The four lines at one side are for static timing and should be used for service purposes. The three lines are for dynamic timing and used only at the factory.**

7. Turn the crankshaft until the line 12° on the damper is brought into alignment with the pointer, then take a reading of the dial indicator. It should be 0.019 in. (0.5mm).

8. If the reading on the dial indicator deviates from the specified range, hold the crankshaft to the injection pump setting listed in the Diesel Tune-up Specifications chart in Section 1. Loosen the two nuts on the injection pump flange.

9. Move the pump to a point where the dial indicator gives a reading of 0.019 in. (0.5mm). Tighten the flange nuts.

Glow Plugs

SYSTEM TESTING

▶ **See Figures 24, 25 and 26**

1. To test the dropping resistor, check for continuity across the terminals as described in the illustration. If no continuity exists, replace the unit.

2. To test the thermo switch, first remove the switch. Submerge the end of the switch in water and raise the temperature gradually. The switch should be off at 126–140°F (53–60°C) or lower. The switch should be on at 134–145°F (57–63°C) or higher. If not, replace the switch.

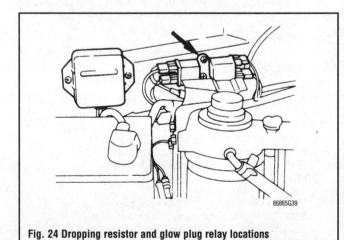

Fig. 24 Dropping resistor and glow plug relay locations

REMOVAL & INSTALLATION

▶ **See Figure 27**

The glow plugs are located under the injection nozzles, and are threaded into the cylinder head.

1. Disconnect the negative (–) battery cable.

2. Disconnect the glow plug and unscrew it from the engine.

To install:

3. Lubricate with anti-seize compound before installing the plug.

4. Install and tighten the plug to 65 ft. lbs. (88 Nm).

5. Reconnect the plug wiring.

6. Connect the battery cable and check operation.

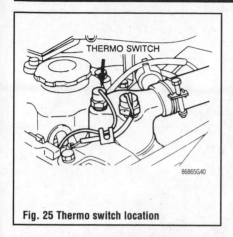

Fig. 25 Thermo switch location

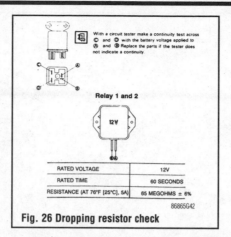

Fig. 26 Dropping resistor check

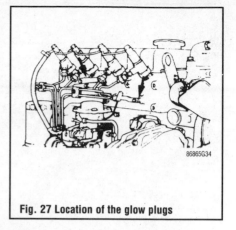

Fig. 27 Location of the glow plugs

FUEL TANK

Tank Assembly

REMOVAL & INSTALLATION

Pick-Up and Amigo

♦ **See Figure 28**

1. Disconnect the negative (–) battery cable. Release the fuel system pressure.
2. Drain the fuel tank using an approved pump.
3. Disconnect the feed, return and evaporative hoses.
4. Disconnect all vapor and fuel hoses.
5. Remove the fuel tank band (long bed only).
6. Disconnect the filler neck.
7. Place a floor jack under the tank.
8. Remove the retainers, then lower the tank far enough to disconnect any hoses or wires not already disconnected. Remove the tank.
   To install:
9. Raise the tank far enough to connect any hoses or wires. Install the tank retainers.

10. Connect the filler neck.
11. Install the fuel tank band (long bed only).
12. Connect all vapor and fuel hoses.
13. Connect the feed, return and evaporative hoses.
14. Refill the fuel tank and check for leaks.
15. Connect the negative (–) battery cable.

Trooper

♦ **See Figure 29**

1. Disconnect the negative (–) battery cable. Release the fuel system pressure.
2. Drain the tank using an approved pump. Remove the fuel tank undercover.
3. Disconnect the feed, return and evaporative hoses.
4. Detach all harness connectors.
5. Disconnect the filler neck.
6. Position a floor jack under the tank, then remove the retainers and lower the tank far enough to disconnect any wiring or hoses. Remove the tank.
   To install:
7. Position a floor jack under the tank, and raise it far enough to connect any wiring or hoses. Install the retainers.

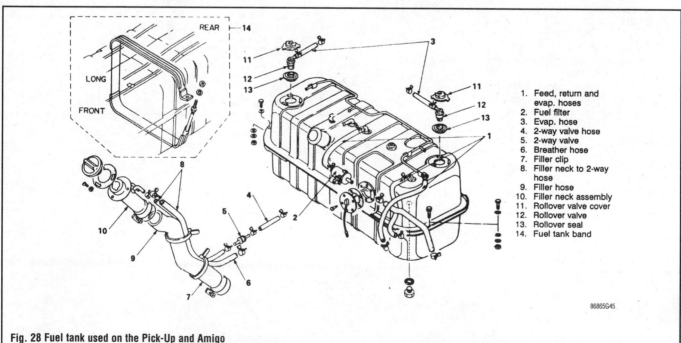

1. Feed, return and evap. hoses
2. Fuel filter
3. Evap. hose
4. 2-way valve hose
5. 2-way valve
6. Breather hose
7. Filler clip
8. Filler neck to 2-way hose
9. Filler hose
10. Filler neck assembly
11. Rollover valve cover
12. Rollover valve
13. Rollover seal
14. Fuel tank band

Fig. 28 Fuel tank used on the Pick-Up and Amigo

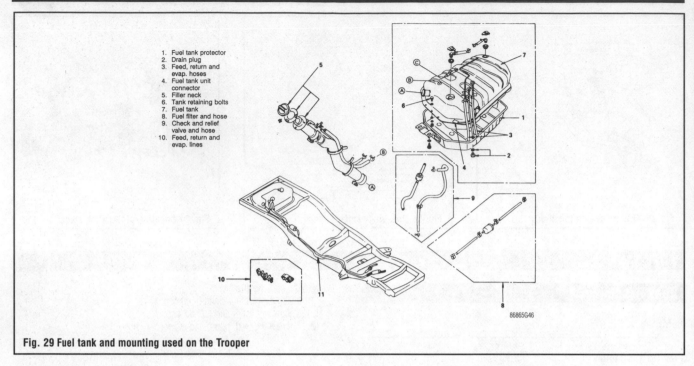

1. Fuel tank protector
2. Drain plug
3. Feed, return and
   evap. hoses
4. Fuel tank unit
   connector
5. Filler neck
6. Tank retaining bolts
7. Fuel tank
8. Fuel filter and hose
9. Check and relief
   valve and hose
10. Feed, return and
    evap. lines

86865G46

Fig. 29 Fuel tank and mounting used on the Trooper

8. Connect the filler neck.
9. Fasten all harness connectors.
10. Connect the feed, return and evap. hoses.
11. Refill the tank. Install the fuel tank undercover.
12. Connect the negative (–) battery cable and check for leaks.

Rodeo

▶ **See Figure 30**

1. Disconnect the negative (–) battery cable. Release the fuel system pressure.
2. Drain the tank using an approved pump.
3. Disconnect the tank harness connectors.
4. Remove the undercover.
5. Disconnect the evaporative, filler, breather, feed and return hoses.
6. Position a floor jack under the tank and remove the tank retainers.
7. Lower the tank, and remove the fuel pump, if needed.

To install:

8. If applicable, install the fuel pump.
9. Raise the tank and install the tank retainer.
10. Connect the evaporative, filler, breather, feed and return hoses.
11. Install the undercover.
12. Fasten the tank harness connectors.
13. Refill the tank and check for leaks.
14. Connect the negative (–) battery cable.

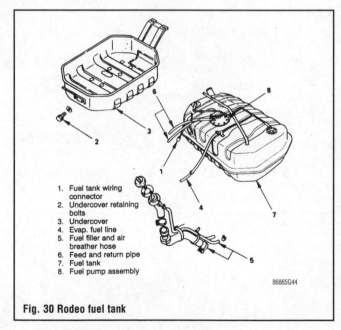

1. Fuel tank wiring
   connector
2. Undercover retaining
   bolts
3. Undercover
4. Evap. fuel line
5. Fuel filler and air
   breather hose
6. Feed and return pipe
7. Fuel tank
8. Fuel pump assembly

86865G44

Fig. 30 Rodeo fuel tank

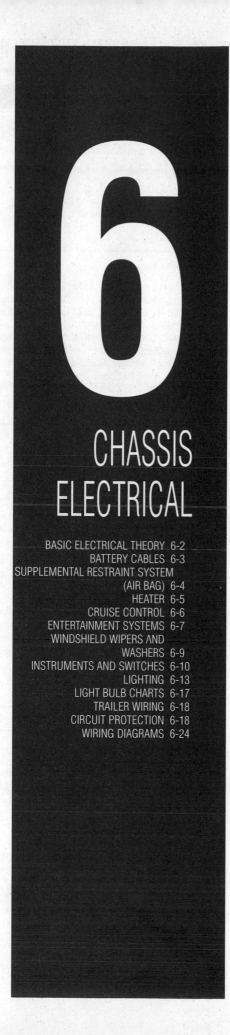

6

CHASSIS
ELECTRICAL

BASIC ELECTRICAL THEORY

Understanding Electricity

For any electrical system to operate, there must be a complete circuit. This simply means that the power flow from the battery must make a full circle. When an electrical component is operating, power flows from the battery to the components, passes through the component (load) causing it to function, and returns to the battery through the ground path of the circuit. This ground may be either another wire or a metal part of the vehicle (depending upon how the component is designed).

BASIC CIRCUITS

♦ See Figures 1 and 2

Perhaps the easiest way to visualize a circuit is to think of connecting a light bulb (with two wires attached to it) to the battery. If one of the two wires was attached to the negative post of the battery and the other wire to the positive post (+), the circuit would be complete and the light bulb would illuminate. Electricity could follow a path from the battery to the bulb and back to the battery. It's not hard to see that with longer wires on our light bulb, it could be mounted anywhere on the vehicle. Further, one wire could be fitted with a switch so that the light could be turned on and off. Various other items could be added to our primitive circuit to make the light flash, become brighter or dimmer under certain conditions, or advise the user that it's burned out.

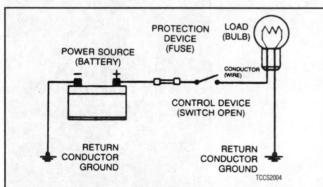

Fig. 1 Here is an example of a simple automotive circuit. When the switch is closed, power from the positive battery terminal flows through the fuse, then to the switch and to the load (light bulb). The light illuminates and the circuit is completed through the return conductor and the vehicle ground. If the light did not work, the tests could be made with a voltmeter or test light at the battery, fuse, switch or bulb socket

Fig. 2 Damaged insulation can allow wires to break (causing an open circuit) or touch (causing a short)

Ground

Some automotive components are grounded through their mounting points. The electrical current runs through the chassis of the vehicle and returns to the battery through the ground cable; if you look, you'll see that the battery ground cable connects between the battery and the body of the vehicle.

Load

Every complete circuit must include a "load" (something to use the electricity coming from the source). If you were to connect a wire between the two terminals of the battery (DON'T do this, but take out word for it) without the light bulb, the battery would attempt to deliver its entire power supply from one pole to another almost instantly. This is a short circuit. The electricity is taking a short cut to get to ground and is not being used by any load in the circuit. This sudden and uncontrolled electrical flow can cause great damage to other components in the circuit and can develop a tremendous amount of heat. A short in an automotive wiring harness can develop sufficient heat to melt the insulation on all the surrounding wires and reduce a multiple wire cable to one sad lump of plastic and copper. Two common causes of shorts are broken insulation (thereby exposing the wire to contact with surrounding metal surfaces or other wires) or a failed switch (the pins inside the switch come out of place and touch each other).

Switches and Relays

Some electrical components which require a large amount of current to operate also have a relay in their circuit. Since these circuits carry a large amount of current (amperage or amps), the thickness of the wire in the circuit (wire gauge) is also greater. If this large wire were connected from the load to the control switch on the dash, the switch would have to carry the high amperage load and the dash would be twice as large to accommodate wiring harnesses as thick as your wrist. To prevent these problems, a relay is used. The large wires in the circuit are connected from the battery to one side of the relay and from the opposite side of the relay to the load. The relay is normally open, preventing current from passing through the circuit. An additional, smaller wire is connected from the relay to the control switch for the circuit. When the control switch is turned on, it grounds the smaller wire to the relay and completes its circuit. The main switch inside the relay closes, sending power to the component without routing the main power through the inside of the vehicle. Some common circuits which may use relays are the horn, headlights, starter and rear window defogger systems.

Protective Devices

It is possible for larger surges of current to pass through the electrical system of your vehicle. If this surge of current were to reach the load in the circuit, it could burn it out or severely damage it. To prevent this, fuses, circuit breakers and/or fusible links are connected into the supply wires of the electrical system. These items are nothing more than a built-in weak spot in the system. It's much easier to go to a known location (the fuse box) to see why a circuit is inoperative than to dissect 15 feet of wiring under the dashboard, looking for what happened.

When an electrical current of excessive power passes through the fuse, the fuse blows (the conductor melts) and breaks the circuit, preventing the passage of current and protecting the components.

A circuit breaker is basically a self repairing fuse. It will open the circuit in the same fashion as a fuse, but when either the short is removed or the surge subsides, the circuit breaker resets itself and does not need replacement.

A fuse link (fusible link or main link) is a wire that acts as a fuse. One of these is normally connected between the starter relay and the main wiring harness under the hood. Since the starter is usually the highest electrical draw on the vehicle, an internal short during starting could direct about 130 amps into the wrong places. Consider the damage potential of introducing this current into a system whose wiring is rated at 15 amps and you'll understand the need for protection. Since this link is very early in the electrical path, it's the first place to look if nothing on the vehicle works, but the battery seems to be charged and is properly connected.

TROUBLESHOOTING

♦ See Figures 3, 4 and 5

Electrical problems generally fall into one of three areas:
- The component that is not functioning is not receiving current.
- The component is receiving power but is not using it or is using it incorrectly (component failure).
- The component is improperly grounded.

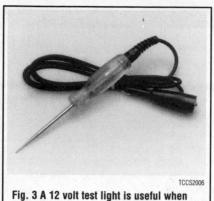

Fig. 3 A 12 volt test light is useful when checking parts of a circuit for power

TCCS2006

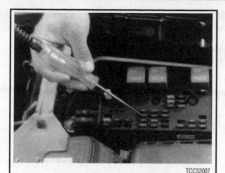

Fig. 4 Here, someone is checking a circuit by making sure there is power to the component's fuse

TCCS2007

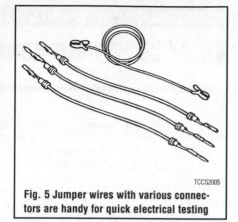

Fig. 5 Jumper wires with various connectors are handy for quick electrical testing

TCCS2005

The circuit can be can be checked with a test light and a jumper wire. The test light is a device that looks like a pointed screwdriver with a wire on one end and a bulb in its handle. A jumper wire is simply a piece of wire with alligator clips or special terminals on each end. If a component is not working, you must follow a systematic plan to determine which of the three causes is the villain.

1. Turn **ON** the switch that controls the item not working.

➡**Some items only work when the ignition switch is turned ON.**

2. Disconnect the power supply wire from the component.
3. Attach the ground wire of a test light or a voltmeter to a good metal ground.
4. Touch the end probe of the test light (or the positive lead of the voltmeter) to the power wire; if there is current in the wire, the light in the test light will come on (or the voltmeter will indicate the amount of voltage). You have now established that current is getting to the component.
5. Turn the ignition or dash switch **OFF** and reconnect the wire to the component.

If there was no power, then the problem is between the battery and the component. This includes all the switches, fuses, relays and the battery itself. The next place to look is the fuse box; check carefully either by eye or by using the test light across the fuse clips. The easiest way to check is to simply replace the fuse. If the fuse is blown, and upon replacement, immediately blows again, there is a short between the fuse and the component. This is generally (not always) a sign of an internal short in the component. Disconnect the power wire at the component again and replace the fuse; if the fuse holds, the component is the problem.

※※ WARNING

DO NOT test a component by running a jumper wire from the battery UNLESS you are certain that it operates on 12 volts. Many electronic components are designed to operate with less voltage and connecting them to 12 volts could destroy them. Jumper wires are best used to bypass a portion of the circuit (such as a stretch of wire or a switch) that DOES NOT contain a resistor and is suspected to be bad.

If all the fuses are good and the component is not receiving power, find the switch for the circuit. Bypass the switch with the jumper wire. This is done by connecting one end of the jumper to the power wire coming into the switch and the other end to the wire leaving the switch. If the component comes to life, the switch has failed.

※※ WARNING

Never substitute the jumper for the component. The circuit needs the electrical load of the component. If you bypass it, you will cause a short circuit.

Checking the ground for any circuit can mean tracing wires to the body, cleaning connections or tightening mounting bolts for the component itself. If the jumper wire can be connected to the case of the component or the ground connector, you can ground the other end to a piece of clean, solid metal on the vehicle. Again, if the component starts working, you've found the problem.

A systematic search through the fuse, connectors, switches and the component itself will almost always yield an answer. Loose and/or corroded connectors, particularly in ground circuits, are becoming a larger problem in modern vehicles. The computers and on-board electronic (solid state) systems are highly sensitive to improper grounds and will change their function drastically if one occurs.

Remember that for any electrical circuit to work, ALL the connections must be clean and tight.

➡**For more information on Understanding and Troubleshooting Electrical Systems, please refer to Section 6 of this manual.**

BATTERY CABLES

Before removing the old battery or cables, take note of the location of the positive and negative terminals. The battery and cables must be installed correctly to avoid the positive terminal or cable from contacting any part of the vehicle. Careless installation can destroy the battery and cause damage to on-board computers. Follow all service precautions when disconnecting, connecting or charging the battery. Most important is to NEVER disconnect or charge the battery with the ignition switch ON.

Disconnecting the Cables

First make certain the ignition switch is in the off position. This will avoid the electrical an surge from being created in components like the ignition coil, air conditioner clutch, solenoids and relays. This electrical surge can cause damage to engine control computers, radios and other electrical components. As long as the ignition switch is off, damage can't occur.

Next, always disconnect the negative or ground cable first. Since the negative cable is connected to the vehicle body, if your wrench touches the vehicle no spark or voltage surge will occur. You should isolate the negative cable. If you have an air bag you MUST isolate the negative cable. Simply wrap the metal part of the battery cable with electrical tape. A section of an old bicycle inter tube can be cut and used the cover the terminals. After the negative cable is isolated, disconnect the positive cable. If you have an air bag system, you should isolate the positive cable too.

Always clean the terminals and terminal ends before re-connecting to the battery. Attach the connectors exactly as they were before. Start with the positive cable. Do not over tighten the cables, you only want a good electrical connection. Install the negative cable last, make certain that the ignition switch is off and the lights and accessories turned off too. Finish the job by applying corrosion preventative (or petroleum jelly) to the cables, terminals and hold down bolts.

SUPPLEMENTAL RESTRAINT SYSTEM (AIR BAG)

General Information

The air bag system used on many vehicles is referred to as the Supplemental Restraint System (SRS). The air bag is designed to deploy when the vehicle is involved in a front end collision of sufficient force, up to 30 degrees off center line of the vehicle.

This system has an energy reserve, which can store a large enough electrical charge to deploy the air bag for 15 seconds (on the Rodeo) or 2 minutes (on the Trooper) after the battery has been disconnected or damaged. This system must be disabled if any service is to be performed on the SRS system or steering wheel assembly.

The vehicle may be equipped with a driver side and a passenger side air bag. When a frontal crash occurs of sufficient force, the bag(s) are deployed from both the center of the steering wheel and from above the instrument panel compartment on the passenger's side.

This system has self-diagnostic ability. If any problem is found by the computer the air bag system is disabled and the instrument panel light is turned on. There is no danger of accidental air bag deployment if this light is on, but the air bag system will not work during a collision. The vehicle should be taken to a professional service center if the light remains on.

SYSTEM OPERATION

The air bag system contains a Sensing and Diagnostic Module (SDM), deployment loop and an air bag module. The function of the deployment loop is to supply current through the air bag module in the steering wheel or dash panel, which will cause air bag deployment during a severe accident. The SDM supplies this power, even if the battery has been damaged. The SDM is the heart of the air bag system, it is the computer that performs all the function necessary to deploy the air bag.

SERVICE PRECAUTIONS

✳✳ CAUTION

To avoid personal injury when servicing the SRS system or components in the immediate area, do not use electrical test equipment such as battery or A.C. powered voltmeter, ohmmeter, etc. or any type of tester other than specified. Do not use a non-powered probe tester. Instructions must be followed in detail to avoid deployment.

- Never disconnect any electrical connection with the ignition switch **ON** unless instructed to do so in a test.
- Always wear a grounded wrist static strap when servicing any control module or component labeled with a Electrostatic Discharge (ESD) sensitive device symbol.
- Avoid touching module connector pins.
- Leave new components and modules in the shipping package until ready to install them.
- Always touch a vehicle ground after sliding across a vehicle seat or walking across vinyl or carpeted floors to avoid static charge damage.
- The DERM can maintain sufficient voltage to cause a deployment for up to 2 minutes (on some models), even if the battery is disconnected.
- Sensor mounting and wiring must never be modified.

- Never strike or jar a sensor, or deployment could occur.
- Never power up the SRS system when any sensor, SDM or other component is not rigidly attached to the vehicle.
- Always carry an inflator module with the trim cover away from your body.
- Always place an inflator module on the workbench with the trim cover up, away from loose objects.
- The inflator module is to be stored and shipped under DOT E–8236 flammable solid regulations.
- The inflator module must be deployed before it is discarded.
- After deployment the air bag surface may contain sodium hydroxide dust. Always wear gloves and safety glasses when handling the assembly. Wash hands with mild soap and water afterwards.
- Absolutely no wire connector, or terminal repair is to be attempted on the sensors, air bag modules or SRS coil assembly
- Never use a battery or A.C. powered test light or tester on the SRS system or deployment could occur.
- Never use an ohmmeter on the SRS system, or deployment could occur.
- Never bake dry paint on vehicle or allow to exceed temperatures over 300°F, without disabling the SIR system and removing the inflator module.
- Sensors and air bags are not interchangeable between models or years.
- Never allow welding cables to lay on, near or across any vehicle electrical wiring.
- Avoid extension cords for power tools or droplights to lay on, near or across any vehicle electrical wiring.

DISARMING THE SYSTEM

Simply disconnecting and isolating the battery cable will disarm the system. If you need to remove the air bag module or work around the air bag you should also disconnect the deployment loop wiring as follows:
1. Read all service precautions.
2. Turn the wheels straight ahead.
3. Turn the ignition switch **OFF**.
4. Disconnect and isolate the negative battery cable.
5. Remove the SRS fuses.
6. Remove the lower knee bolster.
7. Disconnect the yellow 3-way connector from the base of the steering column.
8. Disconnect the yellow 2-way connector from behind the glove box.

ARMING THE SYSTEM

If the battery was disconnected, the system will automatically re-arm and perform a self-diagnostics when the battery is connected. Make certain no one is in the vehicle while connecting the battery cables.

If the modules were disconnected perform the following:
1. Read all service precautions.
2. Turn the ignition switch **OFF**.
3. Connect the yellow 2-way connector from behind the glove box.
4. Connect the yellow 3-way connector from the base of the steering column.
5. Install the lower knee bolster.
6. Replace the SRS fuses.
7. Connect the battery cable.

HEATER

Blower Motor

REMOVAL & INSTALLATION

♦ **See Figures 6 and 7**

The blower motor is located under the instrument panel next to the right side kick panel.
1. Disconnect the negative battery cable.
2. Remove the instrument panel trim panel, if so equipped.
3. Disconnect the blower motor wiring.
4. Remove the retaining screws and motor assembly.
5. Remove the cage retaining clip and cage from the motor.
To install:
6. Install the cage onto the motor and install the clip.
7. Install the motor, retaining screws and wiring connector.
8. Connect the battery cable and check operation.

Auxiliary Heater Blower Motor

REMOVAL & INSTALLATION

Trooper

1. Disconnect the negative battery cable.
2. Drain the coolant into a suitable container.

✺✺ CAUTION

When draining the coolant, keep in mind that cats and dogs are attracted by the ethylene glycol antifreeze, and are quite likely to drink any that is left in an uncovered container or in puddles on the ground. This will prove fatal in sufficient quantity. Always drain the coolant into a sealable container. Coolant should be reused unless it is contaminated or several years old.

3. Remove the rear seat.
4. Disconnect the coolant hoses at the heater assembly.
5. Remove the mounting bolts and disengage the electrical connector.
6. Remove the heater unit.
7. Disassemble the heater unit to remove the blower motor.
8. Remove the housing retaining screws and clips.
9. Carefully disassemble the housing being careful not to damage the assembly. Remove the blower motor and cage assembly.
To install:
10. If the seals are damaged, install new seals before assembly.

11. Install the blower motor and cage assembly. Assemble the housing.
12. Install the housing and reconnect the coolant hoses.
13. Refill the engine with coolant, connect the battery cable and check for leaks.

Heater Core

REMOVAL & INSTALLATION

♦ **See Figure 8**

1. Disconnect the negative battery cable.
2. Drain the engine coolant into a suitable container.

✺✺ CAUTION

When draining engine coolant, keep in mind that cats and dogs are attracted to ethylene glycol antifreeze and could drink any that is left in an uncovered container or in puddles on the ground. This will prove fatal in sufficient quantity. Always drain coolant into a sealable container. Coolant should be reused unless it is contaminated or is several years old.

3. Disconnect the heater hoses. Be careful not to damage the core by pulling on the hose to remove. Cut the hoses if they will not come off easily.
4. Remove the instrument panel.
5. Disconnect the resistor assembly.
6. If possible, disconnect and move the duct (non air conditioning) or the evaporator housing (air conditioning) to the right to gain clearance for the heater unit. If equipped with air conditioning, do not disconnect air conditioning system until absolutely necessary. Refer to Section 1 for discharging, evacuating and recharging the system.
7. Remove the instrument panel stay and heater unit.
8. Disassemble the heater unit by removing the duct, mode control case, core assembly and heater core.
To install:
9. Assemble the heater unit by installing the duct, mode control case, core assembly and heater core.
10. Install the heater unit and instrument panel stay.
11. Connect the duct (non air conditioning) or the evaporator housing (air conditioning) to the heater unit. Evacuate and recharge the air conditioning system if the system was discharged to remove the evaporator assembly.
12. Connect the resistor assembly.
13. Install the instrument panel as outlined in this section.
14. Connect the heater hoses. Be careful not to damage the core by pulling on the hose.

Fig. 6 Removing the heater blower retaining screw under the dash panel—1991 Trooper shown

Fig. 7 Removing the heater blower assembly—1991 Trooper shown

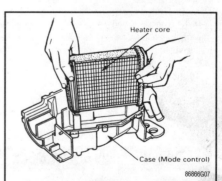

Fig. 8 When installing the new heater core take great care not to bend or damage the fins or tubing

15. Refill the engine coolant into a suitable container.
16. Connect the negative battery cable and check for leaks.

Heater Water Control Valve

REMOVAL & INSTALLATION

On early models the heater control valve was part of the heater core inlet. To replace the control valve, remove the heater core as outlined in this section. Remove the control valve from the heater core, being careful not to damage the core. Use new gaskets when installing new valves.

The remainder of the vehicles are not equipped with heater water control valves. They use heater unit doors to regulate the amount of heat entering the vehicle.

CRUISE CONTROL

The cruise control is a speed control system which maintains a desired vehicle speed under normal driving conditions. The main components of the cruise control system are the mode control switches, controller, actuator unit, speed sensor, vacuum supply and electrical release switches.

The circuit may consists most or all of the following: the starter switch, cruise control main switch, cruise control switch, cruise control unit, pump and actuator, brake pedal switch, clutch switch, A/T mode switch and vehicle speed sensor (usually incorporated into the speedometer).

Control Switches

The circuit may consists of several switches. The combination switch is the most common switch. The combination switch may include turn signals, windshield wipers, cruise control, high beam lamps functions, dependent on vehicle options. Other switches in the circuit may include; cruise control main switch, cruise control switch usually in the combination switch, brake pedal switch and clutch switch. Refer to one of these switches as necessary.

Main Control Switch

The main control switch may be included in the combination switch. Many vehicles have a single toggle switch in the interment panel that turns the power on and off to the cruise control system. This is called the cruise control main switch. The following procedure may need to be altered, depending on the vehicle and interior options.
1. Disconnect the negative battery cable.
2. Remove the instrument panel trim, if necessary remove the instrument panel.
3. The switch is usually released by pushing the lock from the back side of the cluster assembly.
4. On models like the Trooper, where the just the instrument panel trim may need to be removed, you can release the lock by inserting a very thin screwdriver between the panel and switch bezel. Then released by pushing the lock back and remove the switch from the cluster assembly.
5. Disconnect the wiring connector.
To install:
6. Connect the wiring connector.
7. Snap the switch back into the instrument panel.
8. Install any instrument panel trim that was removed.
9. Connect the negative battery cable.

Combination Switch

REMOVAL & INSTALLATION

The combination switch assembly is a multiple function switch mounted on the steering column and including such functions turn signal, cruise control and headlight and/or wiper operation, depending on the year and model. For more

Air Conditioning Components

REMOVAL & INSTALLATION

Repair or service of air conditioning components is not covered by this manual, because of the risk of personal injury or death, and because of the legal ramifications of servicing these components without the proper EPA certification and experience. Cost, personal injury or death, environmental damage, and legal considerations (such as the fact that it is a federal crime to vent refrigerant into the atmosphere), dictate that the A/C components on your vehicle should be serviced only by a Motor Vehicle Air Conditioning (MVAC) trained, and EPA certified automotive technician.

➡ **If your vehicle's A/C system uses R-12 refrigerant and is in need of recharging, the A/C system can be converted over to R-134a refrigerant (less environmentally harmful and expensive). Refer to Section 1 for additional information on R-12 to R-134a conversions, and for additional considerations dealing with your vehicle's A/C system.**

details, please refer to the Turn Signal (Combination) Switch assembly procedures found in Section 8 of this manual.

Pump and Actuator Assembly

REMOVAL & INSTALLATION

♦ **See Figures 9, 10 and 11**

1. Disconnect the negative battery cable.
2. Disconnect the pump electrical connector.
3. Disconnect the pump vacuum hose.

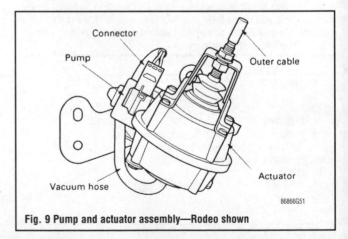

Fig. 9 Pump and actuator assembly—Rodeo shown

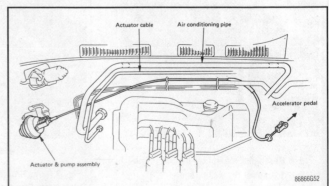

Fig. 10 Care must be taken not be bend or kink the actuator cable—Rodeo shown

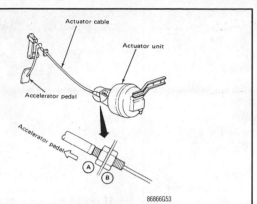

Fig. 11 Adjustment of the actuator cable must be checked to safe operation

86866G53

4. Remove the pump.
5. Disconnect the inner cables of the actuator from the accelerator pedal.
6. Remove the outer cable clips.
7. Remove the actuator.
To install:
8. Reassemble pump and actuator.

✳ CAUTION

Cruise control cables that aren't adjusted properly can cause dangerously high idle conditions.

9. Secure the accelerator pedal at the fully returned position (throttle valves fully closed).
10. Loosen inside nut (A) and outside nut (B).
11. With the outer cable pulled to toward the accelerator pedal so the cable has no play, tighten the inside nut (A) until it just hits the bracket.
12. Tighten the outside nut (B) to lock into position.

ENTERTAINMENT SYSTEMS

Radio

REMOVAL & INSTALLATION

Early Model Pick-Up

1. Disconnect the negative battery cable.
2. Remove the radio knobs by pulling off.
3. Remove the jam nuts, washers and face panel.
4. Remove the instrument cluster panel and radio retaining screws.
5. Remove the radio and disconnect the harness connector.
To install:
6. Connect the harness connector, install the radio and screws.
7. Install the instrument cluster panel.
8. Install the jam nuts, washers and face panel.
9. Install the radio knobs by pushing on.
10. Connect the negative battery cable and check operation.

Late Model Pick-Up And Amigo

✳ CAUTION

If equipped with an air bag, the system must be properly disarmed before any work takes place near the bag or wiring. For details, please refer to the information on the Supplemental Restraint System in this section.

1. Disconnect the negative battery cable.
2. Remove the front console and disconnect the harness connector and feeder cable, if so equipped.

3. Remove the radio retaining screws and radio assembly.
4. Remove the radio bracket and bolts.
To install:
5. Install the radio bracket and bolts.
6. Install the radio retaining screws and radio assembly.
7. Install the front console and connect the harness connector and feeder cable, if so equipped.
8. Connect the negative battery cable and check operation.

Trooper And Rodeo

▶ See Figures 12 thru 17

✳ CAUTION

If equipped with an air bag, the system must be properly disarmed before any work takes place near the bag or wiring. For details, please refer to the information on the Supplemental Restraint System in this section.

1. Disconnect the negative battery cable.
2. Remove the radio knobs, nuts and washers.
3. Remove the case, radio and screws.
4. Disconnect the wiring harness and remove the radio retaining screws.
5. Remove the brackets from the radio chassis.
To install:
6. Install the brackets to the radio chassis.
7. Connect the wiring harness and install the radio retaining screws.
8. Install the case, radio and screws.
9. Install the radio washers, nuts and knobs.
10. Connect the negative battery cable.

Fig. 12 Remove the trim screws (on some models it may be necessary to remove the center console)

86866P04

Fig. 13 Remove the trim to access the radio

86866P05

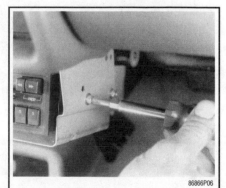

Fig. 14 Remove the radio retaining screws from each side

86866P06

Fig. 15 Carefully slide the radio out of the bracket, taking care not the pull on the wiring and connectors

Fig. 16 Pull the antenna cable from the radio by the plug, NOT by the wire

Fig. 17 Disconnect the power and speaker connectors

Speakers

REMOVAL & INSTALLATION

▶ See Figures 18, 19 and 20

Instrument Panel Mounted

1. Disconnect the negative battery cable
2. Remove the front speaker grille screws, then lift and remove the grille.

➡On most models the grille screws retain the speaker as well. But, always check to make sure no additional fasteners are hidden under the grilles.

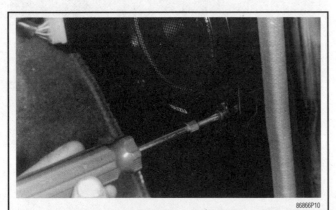

Fig. 18 Removing the speaker grille screws on Trooper

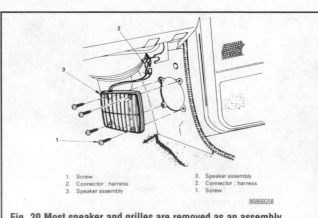

Fig. 19 Gently unplug the connector. Be careful, as the speaker can be easily damaged

3. If equipped, remove the speaker-to-instrument panel screws.
4. Lift the speaker and disengage the electrical connection(s), then remove the speaker from the vehicle.
5. Installation is the reverse of the removal. Make sure the speaker wiring is properly connected before attempting to test the radio.

Under Dash Mounted

1. Disconnect the negative battery cable
2. Remove the front speaker grille screws, then lift and remove the grille.

➡On most models the grille screws retain the speaker as well. But, always check to make sure no additional fasteners are hidden under the grilles.

3. If equipped, remove the speaker-to-body panel screws,
4. Lift the speaker and disengage the electrical connection(s), then remove the speaker from the vehicle.
5. Installation is the reverse of the removal. Make sure the speaker wiring is properly connected before attempting to test the radio.

Door Mounted

Some later model trucks (or early model trucks with aftermarket sound systems) may be equipped with door mounted radio speakers. Access to factory mounted speakers on late model vehicles usually requires removal of inner door trim panel. Aftermarket speakers may be mounted in a variety of ways, but will often not require trim panel removal. In order to save time, be sure removal of the panel is necessary before starting. If the grille fasteners are accessible with the trim panel installed, then panel removal may not be necessary.

1. Disconnect the negative battery cable
2. For late model vehicles, remove the door trim panel. On early model vehicles, check for any accessible fasteners on the speaker grille. If the grille can be removed, do that first to see if the speaker may be removed without removing the trim panel.

Fig. 20 Most speaker and grilles are removed as an assembly

3. Drill out the heads of the old speaker retaining rivets. Again, aftermarket systems may not contain rivets. If equipped with screws, unthread and remove them.

4. Pull the speaker from the door and disengage the electrical connectors, then remove the speaker from the vehicle.

5. Installation is the reverse of removal. If the speaker was retained with rivets, use new ones to fasten it to the door.

WINDSHIELD WIPERS AND WASHERS

Windshield Wiper Blade and Arm

REMOVAL & INSTALLATION

♦ **See Figures 21 and 22**

If the wiper assembly has a press type release tab at the center, simply depress the tab and remove the blade. If the blade has no release tab, use a screwdriver to depress the spring at the center. This will release the assembly. To install the assembly, position the blade over the pin at the tip of the arm and press until the spring retainer engages the groove in the pin.

To remove the element, either depress the release button or squeeze the spring type retainer clip at the outer end together, and slide the blade element out. Just slide the new element in until it latches.

Two design arms may be found. One design simply requires the removal of a nut and washer to remove the arm. Removal of the other design wiper arms requires the use of a special tool, G.M. J-8966 or its equivalent. Versions of this tool are generally available in auto parts stores.

1. Remove the nut and washer or insert the tool under the wiper arm and lever the arm off the shaft.

➡**Raising the hood on some models may facilitate easier wiper arm removal.**

Rear

1. Disconnect the negative battery cable
2. Remove the necessary trim panel for access to the speaker.
3. Disengage the necessary wiring.
4. Remove the speaker retaining nuts.
5. Remove the speaker from the vehicle.
6. Installation is the reverse of removal.

2. Disconnect the washer hose from the arm (if so equipped). Remove the arm.

To install:
3. Be sure that the motor is in the park position before installing the arms.
4. Gently press the arms onto the shafts.
5. Install the nut and washer if equipped.
6. Check for proper operation of wiper and washer.

Rear Windshield Wiper Blade and Arm

REMOVAL & INSTALLATION

♦ **See Figure 23**

If the wiper assembly has a press-type release tab at the center, simply depress the tab and remove the blade. If the blade has no release tab, use a screwdriver to depress the spring at the center. This will release the assembly. To install the assembly, position the blade over the pin at the tip of the arm and press until the spring retainer engages the groove in the pin.

To remove the element, either depress the release button or squeeze the spring type retainer clip at the outer end together, and slide the blade element out. Just slide the new element in until it latches.

1. Remove the nut and washer.

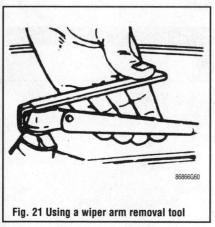

Fig. 21 Using a wiper arm removal tool

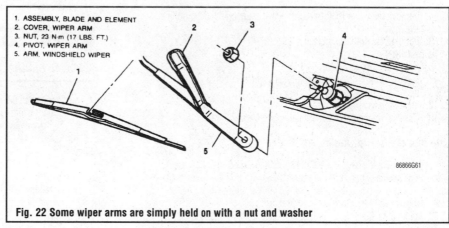

1. ASSEMBLY, BLADE AND ELEMENT
2. COVER, WIPER ARM
3. NUT, 23 N·m (17 LBS. FT.)
4. PIVOT, WIPER ARM
5. ARM, WINDSHIELD WIPER

Fig. 22 Some wiper arms are simply held on with a nut and washer

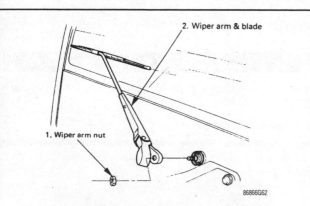

1. Wiper arm nut
2. Wiper arm & blade

Fig. 23 Rear wiper arm is held on with a nut and washer—Trooper

To install:
2. Be sure that the motor is in the park position before installing the arms.
3. Gently press the arms onto the shafts.
4. Install the nut and washer.
5. Check for proper operation of wiper and washer.

Windshield Wiper Motor and Linkage

REMOVAL & INSTALLATION

♦ **See Figures 24, 25, 26 and 27**

Early Model Pick-Up

1. Disconnect the negative battery cable.
2. Remove the wiper blade and arm.
3. Remove the seal and nut.

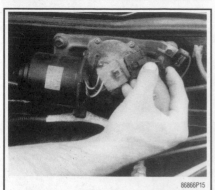

Fig. 24 Disconnecting the wiper motor electrical connectors

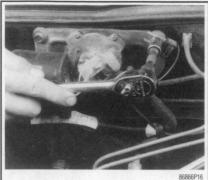

Fig. 25 Removing the wiper motor mounting bolts

Fig. 26 Gently lift the motor assembly back to gain access to the linkage

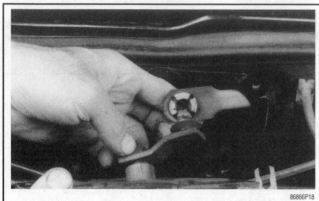

Fig. 27 Disconnecting the linkage from the wiper motor arm

4. Remove the wiper motor assembly by removing retaining bolts and remove the motor link nut.

5. Remove the link assembly.

To install:

6. Install the link assembly.

7. Install the wiper motor assembly and retaining bolts.

8. Install the seal and nut.

9. Install the wiper blade and arm.

10. Connect the negative battery cable and check operation.

Late Model Pick-Up, Amigo and Rodeo

1. Disconnect the negative battery cable and wiper motor connector.

2. Remove the wiper motor bracket screws and pull the motor out of the cowl far enough to disconnect the motor from the linkage at the ball joint.

3. Remove the wiper arm cap, nut and arm.

4. Remove the cowl vent cover and linkage from the access hole.

To install:

5. Install the linkage and cowl vent cover.

6. Install the wiper arm cap, nut and arm.

7. Connect the motor to the linkage at the ball joint, install the motor and retaining screws.

8. Connect the negative battery cable and wiper motor connector.

Trooper

1. Disconnect the negative battery cable.

2. Remove the wiper arm assembly from the linkage.

3. Remove the link pivot nut.

4. Remove the center and left work hole covers.

5. Disconnect the motor wiring.

6. Remove the wiper motor assembly with the link assembly intact.

To install:

7. Install the wiper motor assembly with the link assembly intact.

8. Connect the motor wiring.

9. Install the center and left work hole covers.

10. Install the link pivot nut.

11. Install the wiper arm assembly to the linkage.

12. Connect the negative battery cable and check operation.

Rear Window Wiper Motor

REMOVAL & INSTALLATION

1. Disconnect the negative battery cable.

2. Open the liftgate or hatchback. Remove the trim panel.

3. Remove the wiper arm assembly.

4. Remove the motor shaft nut, motor retaining bolts and disconnect wiring connectors.

5. Remove the motor from the access panel.

To install:

6. Install the motor into the access panel.

7. Install the motor shaft nut, motor retaining bolts and disconnect wiring connectors.

8. Install the wiper arm assembly.

9. Install the trim panel.

10. Connect the negative battery cable and check operation.

INSTRUMENTS AND SWITCHES

Instrument Cluster

REMOVAL & INSTALLATION

There are two basic designs used for instrumentation and switches on Isuzu trucks. Early models had the lighting and wiper control switches in a instrument cluster pack. Later models placed all switch control is the combination switch stalks coming from the steering column. The combination switch function combine turn signals, headlights, wiper, cruise control and other options in the combination switch. If your vehicle is equipped with the combination switch design in a control stalk coming from the steering column, refer to "Combination Switch" for all applicable switches.

Instrument Cluster Design

1. Disconnect the negative battery cable.

2. Move the tilt steering wheel to the full down position, if s o equipped.

3. Loosen the cluster screws and remove the cluster far enough to disconnect the lighting switch connector.

4. Disconnect the wiper and washer connector from the switch.

5. Remove the cluster from the hood, if needed.

To install:
6. Install the cluster to the hood, if removed.
7. Connect the wiper and washer connector to the switch.
8. Install the cluster and connect the lighting switch connector.
9. Connect the negative battery cable and check operation.

Combination Switch Design

♦ **See Figures 28, 29 and 30**

Some late model vehicles incorporate all functions in the combination switch. On early models that just include cruise control in the combination switch, take care to disconnect the wiper, and light control switches when removing the cluster.

❊❊ CAUTION

If equipped with an air bag, the system must be properly disarmed before any work takes place near the bag or wiring. For details, please refer to the information on the Supplemental Restraint System in this section.

1. Disconnect the negative battery cable.
2. Move the tilt steering wheel to the full down position, if so equipped. It may be necessary to remove the steering wheel.
3. On most models it is necessary to remove the steering column cowl.
4. On some models it may be necessary to remove the center console and lower dash trim to gain access to mounting screws.
5. Loosen the cluster screws and remove the cluster far enough to disconnect the lighting switch connector.

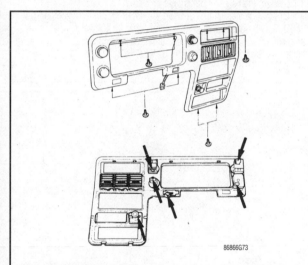

Fig. 28 Remove the mounting screws and disconnect the control switches from the instrument panel assembly—1994 Trooper shown

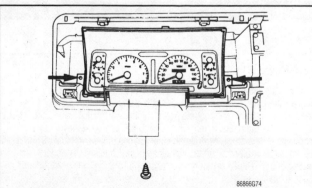

Fig. 29 Removing the instrument speedometer assembly—1994 Trooper shown

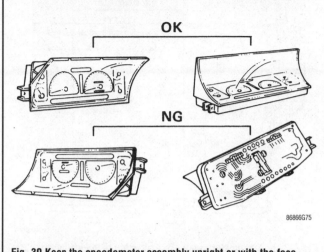

Fig. 30 Keep the speedometer assembly upright or with the face side up. Make certain to sit on a clean dry surface

6. Disconnect the hazard, lighting, cigar lighter and wiper and washer connector from the switch, if equipped.
7. Remove the cluster from the instrument hood, as needed.
To install:
8. Install the cluster to the hood, if removed.
9. Connect the wiper and washer connector to the switch.
10. Install the cluster and connect electrical connectors.
11. Install the steering cowl, center console and lower dash trim as necessary.
12. Connect the negative battery cable and check operation.

Gauges

REMOVAL & INSTALLATION

♦ **See Figures 31 and 32**

1. Disconnect the negative battery cable.
2. Remove the instrument cluster from the vehicle as outlined in this section.
3. Remove the housing retaining screws or release the cluster cover snaps. Be careful not to damage the cluster cover during removal.
4. Remove the gauge assembly from the cluster housing.
To install:
5. Install the gauge assembly into the cluster housing.
6. Install the cluster cover to the housing and tighten retaining screws, if so equipped.
7. Install the cluster assembly into the vehicle as outlined in this section.
8. Connect the battery cable and check operation.

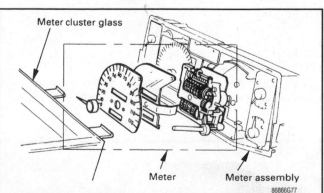

Fig. 31 Remove the speedometer and vehicle speed sensor assembly—1994 Trooper shown

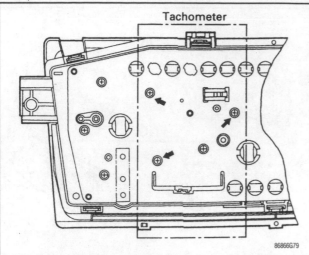

Fig. 32 The tachometer assembly is attached to the instrument cluster by several screws—1994 Trooper shown

Console

REMOVAL & INSTALLATION

▶ **See Figure 33**

1. Disconnect the negative battery cable.
2. Remove the climate control lever knob.
3. Remove the ashtray, front console panel and console side panel.
4. Remove the shift knob or indicator cover.
5. Remove the console pad and floor panel.
6. Remove the knee pad and glove box.
7. Remove the control lever assembly and radio.
8. Remove the control unit behind the climate control assembly.
9. Remove the front console bracket.

To install:

10. Install the front console bracket.
11. Install the control unit behind the climate control assembly.
12. Install the control lever assembly and radio.
13. Install the knee pad and glove box.
14. Install the console pad and floor panel.
15. Install the shift knob or indicator cover.
16. Install the ashtray, front console panel and console side panel.
17. Install the climate control lever knob.
18. Connect the negative battery cable and check operation.

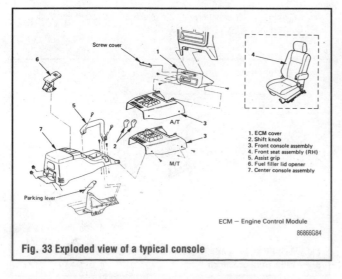

Fig. 33 Exploded view of a typical console

Windshield Wiper Switch

REMOVAL & INSTALLATION

There are two basic designs used for instrumentation and switches on Isuzu trucks. Early models had the lighting and wiper control switches in a instrument cluster pack. Later models placed all switch control is the combination switch stalks coming from the steering column. The combination switch function combine turn signals, headlights, wiper, cruise control and other options in the combination switch. If you vehicle is equipped with the combination switch design in a control stalk coming from the steering column, refer to "Combination Switch" for all applicable switches.

1. Disconnect the negative battery cable.
2. Remove the steering wheel as outlined in Section 8 of this manual.
3. Remove the steering column shroud and disengage the multi-switch connector.
4. Remove the multi-switch assembly from the steering column.
5. Install the switch, column shroud and steering wheel.
6. Connect the battery cable and check operation.

Rear Window Wiper Switch

REMOVAL & INSTALLATION

▶ **See Figure 34**

1. Disconnect the negative battery cable.
2. Carefully slide a small prybar under the lower lip of the switch and pry outward. Be careful not to damage the switch or the instrument panel.
3. Remove the switch and disengage the electrical connector.
4. Install the switch and connect the battery cable.

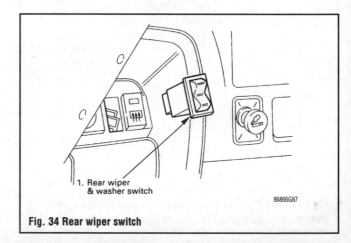

1. Rear wiper & washer switch

Fig. 34 Rear wiper switch

Headlight Switch

REMOVAL & INSTALLATION

▶ **See Figure 35**

Most early models had the lighting and wiper control switches in a instrument cluster pack. Early Trooper and P'up had a knob design headlight switch. Later models placed light controls in the combination switch stalks coming from the steering column. The combination switch function combine turn signals, headlights, wiper, cruise control and other options in the combination switch. If you vehicle is equipped with the combination switch design in a control stalk coming from the steering column, refer to "Combination Switch" for all applicable switches.

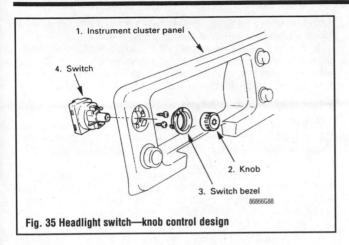

Fig. 35 Headlight switch—knob control design

1. Instrument cluster panel
4. Switch
2. Knob
3. Switch bezel
86866G88

Knob Design

1. Disconnect the negative battery cable.
2. Using a small screwdriver, loosen the knob set screw and remove the switch knob.
3. Remove the retaining nut, being careful not to damage the instrument panel.

LIGHTING

Headlights

REMOVAL & INSTALLATION

Non-Aerodynamic

▶ **See Figure 36**

1. Disconnect the negative battery cable.
2. Remove the front grille and/or headlight bezel.
3. Remove the headlight bulb retaining rim, headlight and disconnect the wiring.
4. Before installing, spray some silicone grease into the bulb socket.
5. Connect the wiring and install the bulb.
6. Install the retaining rim and grille.
7. **Adjustment:** turn the adjusting screw (A) for vertical adjustment. Turn the screw (B) for horizontal adjustment.

4. Remove the switch and disconnect the wiring.
To install:
5. Install the switch and connect the wiring.
6. Install the retaining nut and knob.
7. Connect the battery cable and check operation.

Instrument Cluster Design

1. Disconnect the negative battery cable.
2. Remove the instrument cluster as outlined in this section.
3. Loosen the switch screws and remove the switch.
4. Install the switch and tighten screws.
5. Install the cluster and connect the negative battery cable.

Combination Switch

REMOVAL & INSTALLATION

The combination switch assembly is a multiple function switch mounted on the steering column and including such functions turn signal, cruise control and headlight and/or wiper operation, depending on the year and model. For more details, please refer to the Turn Signal (Combination) Switch assembly procedures found in Section 8 of this manual.

Aerodynamic

▶ **See Figures 37 and 38**

1. Disconnect the negative battery cable.
2. Open the hood and disconnect the headlight bulb electrical connector.
3. There are two possible designs. For the first design, turn the bulb to remove it from the housing, for the second unscrew the retaining cap and remove the bulb.

✷✷ WARNING

Do not touch the glass portion of the halogen bulb. Any contamination on the bulb may cause the bulb to burst when turned ON. If the bulb is contaminated, clean the glass portion with rubbing alcohol.

4. Hold the bulb by the plastic portion only. Install the bulb and connect the wiring harness. Make sure the sealing ring is in place.

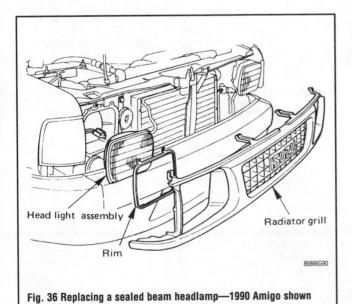

Head light assembly
Rim
Radiator grill
86866G90

Fig. 36 Replacing a sealed beam headlamp—1990 Amigo shown

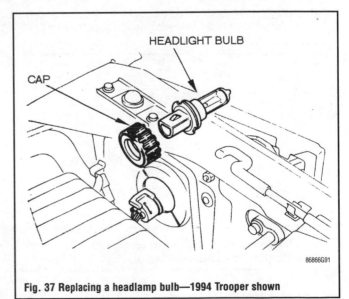

HEADLIGHT BULB
CAP
86866G91

Fig. 37 Replacing a headlamp bulb—1994 Trooper shown

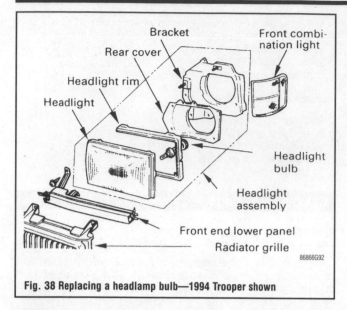

Fig. 38 Replacing a headlamp bulb—1994 Trooper shown

AIMING

▶ **See Figure 39**

The headlights must be properly aimed to provide the best, safest road illumination. The lights should be checked for proper aim and adjusted as necessary. Certain state and local authorities have requirements for headlight aiming; these should be checked before adjustment is made.

Headlight adjustment may be temporarily made using a wall, as described below, or on the rear of another vehicle. When adjusted, the lights should not glare in oncoming car or truck windshields, nor should they illuminate the passenger compartment of vehicles driving in front of you. These adjustments are rough and should always be fine-tuned by a repair shop which is equipped with headlight aiming tools. Improper adjustments may be both dangerous and illegal.

For most vehicles, horizontal and vertical aiming of each sealed beam unit is provided by two adjusting screws which move the retaining ring and adjusting plate against the tension of a coil spring. There is no adjustment for focus; this is done during headlight manufacturing.

➡**Because the composite headlight assembly is bolted into position, no adjustment should be necessary . Some applications have an adjuster plate or may be retained used adjusting screws. If so, follow this procedure when adjusting the lights, BUT always have the adjustment checked by a reputable shop.**

Before removing the headlight bulb or disturbing the headlamp in any way, note the current settings in order to make adjusting the headlights upon

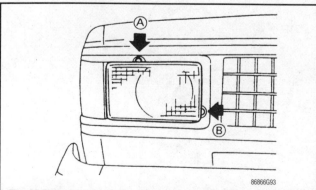

Fig. 39 There are two aiming screws for each headlamp (A for vertical and B for horizontal adjustment)

reassemble easier. If the high or low beam setting of the old lamp still works, this can be done using the wall of a garage or a building:

1. Park the truck on a level surface, with the fuel tank no more than ½ full and with the vehicle empty of all extra cargo (unless normally carried). The vehicle should be facing a wall which is no less the 6 feet high and 12 feet wide. The front of the vehicle should be about 25 feet (8m) from the wall.

➡**Tires should be properly inflated.**

2. If this is be performed outdoors, it is advisable to wait until dusk in order to properly see the headlight beams on the wall. If done in a garage, darken the area around the wall as much as possible by closing shades or hanging cloth over the windows.

3. Turn the headlights **ON** and mark the wall at the center of each light's low beam, then switch on the brights and mark the center of each light's high beam. A short length of masking tape which is visible from the front of the truck may be used. Although marking all 4 positions is advisable, marking 1 position from each light should be sufficient.

4. If neither beam on 1 side of the vehicle is working, park another like-sized truck in the exact spot where the truck was and mark the beams using the same side light on that truck. Then switch the trucks so the Isuzu is back in the original spot. The truck must be parked no closer to or farther away from the wall than the second vehicle.

5. Perform the necessary repairs, but make sure the truck is not moved or is returned to the exact spot from which the lights were marked. Turn the headlights **ON** and adjust the beams to match the marks on the wall.

6. Have the headlight adjustment checked as soon as possible by a reputable repair shop.

Signal and Marker Lights

There are two basic designs of lens. The most common lens is held in with screws that are visible from the outside. Use the following procedure to remove that type lens and replace the bulb. The other design lens may be retained from the back of the lens or with clips. That bulb is usually service from the back side of the lamp, by simply turning the socket ¼ turn. First check for access to the rear of the lens assembly before removing the lens, it may save you time.

REMOVAL & INSTALLATION

Front Turn Signal and Parking

▶ **See Figures 40 thru 46**

1. Make sure the lamps are turned OFF.
2. Remove the lens retaining screws.
3. Pull the assembly out of the bumper or fender.
4. Remove the bulb by pushing in slightly and turn bulb ¼ turn.

To install:

5. Spray a small amount of silicone or other lubricant in the socket to keep the new bulb from sticking next time.
6. Install the bulb and check for proper operation before you install the socket or lens.
7. Install the socket and lens.

Side Marker Lights

▶ **See Figures 40 thru 46**

1. Make sure the lamps are turned OFF.
2. Check to see if you can access the bulb from the back. It not, remove the lens retaining screws, lens assembly and bulb.
3. Turn bulb socket ¼ turn to remove.
4. Most marker lamp bulbs are a size 194. This bulb is simply pushed into the socket. Pull out to remove.

To install:

5. Spray a small amount of silicone or other lubricant in the socket to keep the new bulb from sticking next time.
6. Install the bulb and check for proper operation before you install the socket or lens.
7. Install the socket and lens.

Fig. 40 Most bulbs are replaced by removing the lens

Fig. 41 The light sockets are attached to the back of the lens. Gently twist the socket and remove

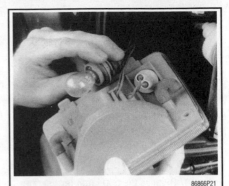

Fig. 42 Turn the light sockets slightly to detached for the lens

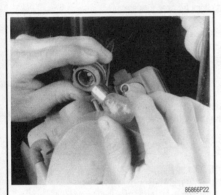

Fig. 43 Gently press in and turn to remove the turn signal and parking lamp bulb

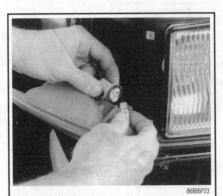

Fig. 44 Side marker bulbs are usually the 194 press-in type

Fig. 45 Check the bulb operation before putting everything back together

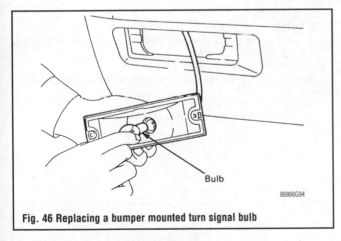

Bulb

Fig. 46 Replacing a bumper mounted turn signal bulb

Rear Turn Signal, Brake and Parking Lights

▶ See Figures 47, 48, 49 and 50

1. Make sure the lamps are turned OFF.
2. Remove the lens retaining screws, lens and bulb. You may need to open the back door or tailgate to gain access to all of the screws.
3. Turn bulb socket ¼ turn to remove it from the lens.
4. Remove the bulb by pushing in slightly and turn bulb ¼ turn.

To install:

5. Spray a small amount of silicone or other lubricant in the socket to keep the new bulb from sticking next time.
6. Install the bulb and check for proper operation before you install the socket or lens.
7. Install the socket and lens.

Center High-Mount Stop Lamp

There are two basic designs of lens. The most common lens is held in with screws that are visible from the outside. These are serviced the same as side mark lamps. The other design is held by the dome lamp inside the cab of the vehicle. Use the following procedure to remove that type lens and replace the bulb.

1. Disconnect the negative battery cable.
2. Make sure the lamps are turned OFF.
3. Remove the dome lamp lens retaining screws, lens and bulb.
4. Remove the dome lamp connectors, by squeezing and sliding out of the assembly.
5. Remove the screws attaching the high-mount stop lamp to the dome lamp.
6. Remove the bulb.

To install:

7. Spray a small amount of silicone or other lubricant in the socket to keep the new bulb from sticking next time.
8. Connect the negative battery cable.
9. Install the bulb and check for proper operation before you install the socket or lens.
10. Disconnect the negative battery cable.
11. Install the screws attaching the high-mount stop lamp to the dome lamp.
12. Reassemble and install the screws the dome lamp.
13. Install the socket and lens.
14. Connect the negative battery cable.

Fig. 47 Remove the rear lamp lens screws (some models have screws hidden behind the tailgate)

Fig. 48 Remove the rear lens

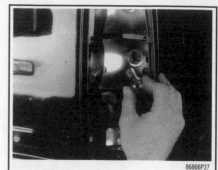

Fig. 49 The turn signal and brake lamp are removed by pushing in slightly and turning the bulb

Fig. 50 The marker lamps are usually a small push-in bulb

Dome Light

▶ See Figures 51 and 52

There are two basic designs of lens. The most common lens is held in with screws that are visible from the outside. Use the following procedure to remove that type lens and replace the bulb. The other design is remove by gentle squeezing the plastic lens cover.

1. Disconnect the negative battery cable.
2. Make sure the lamps are turned OFF.
3. Remove the dome lamp lens retaining screws and lens.
4. Gently remove the dome lamp bulb.

To install:

5. Spray a small amount of silicone or other lubricant in the socket to keep the new bulb from sticking next time.
6. Connect the negative battery cable.

7. Install the bulb and check for proper operation before you install the socket or lens.
8. Disconnect the negative battery cable.
9. Install the socket and lens.
10. Connect the negative battery cable.

Cargo Lamps

There are two basic designs of lens. The most common lens is held in with screws that are visible from the outside. These are serviced the same as side mark lamps. The other design is held by the dome lamp inside the cab of the vehicle. Use the following procedure to remove that type lens and replace the bulb.

1. Disconnect the negative battery cable.
2. Make sure the lamps are turned OFF.
3. Remove the dome lamp lens retaining screws, lens and bulb.
4. Remove the dome lamp connectors, by squeezing and sliding out of the assembly.
5. Remove the screws attaching the cargo lamp to the dome lamp.
6. Remove the bulb.

To install:

7. Spray a small amount of silicone or other lubricant in the socket to keep the new bulb from sticking next time.
8. Connect the negative battery cable.
9. Install the bulb and check for proper operation before you install the socket or lens.
10. Disconnect the negative battery cable.
11. Install the screws attaching the cargo lamp to the dome lamp.
12. Reassemble and install the screws the dome lamp.
13. Install the socket and lens.
14. Connect the negative battery cable.

Fig. 51 Most dome light lenses snap into place. To remove, gently depress the retaining tabs and pull

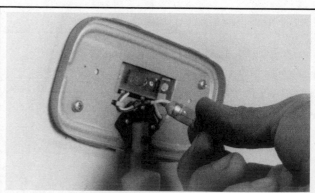

Fig. 52 Replacing the dome lamp bulb

License Plate Lamps

1. Make sure the lamps are turned OFF.
2. Most lamps lens are held in with screws. Remove the lens retaining screws, lens and bulb. On the some step bumpers, you may need to remove the bumper pads and bumper bolts. Then rotate the bumper slightly to gain access to the bulb.

3. Remove the bulb.
To install:
4. Spray a small amount of silicone or other lubricant in the socket to keep the new bulb from sticking next time.
5. Install the bulb and check for proper operation before you install the socket or lens.
6. Install the socket and lens. Reassemble the bumper as needed.

LIGHT BULB CHARTS

▶ See Figures 53, 54, 55 and 56

Application	Bulb No.	Quantity	Rating Candlepower
Front Lights			
Headlight—Halogen	9004	2	65/45 W
Turn Signal	1073	2	23W
Parking Light	67	2	8W
Sidemarker	194	2	3.8W
Rear Lights			
Back-up	1073	2	23W
License	—	1	5W
Tail, Stop	1034	2	23/8W
Sidemarker	194	2	3.8W
Turn Signal	1073	2	23W
Interior Illumination			
A/C—Heater Cont.	74	1	0.7W
Dome Light	—	1	10W
Instrument Cluster	158/74	4/3	2/0.7W
Luggage compartment	—	1	10W

86866GR0

Fig. 53 Light bulb chart for 1991 and earlier Troopers

Application	Bulb No.	Quantity	Rating Wattage/ Amperage
Front Lights			
Headlight—Halogen	9004	2	65/45 W
Turn Signal and Parking Light	1157	2	27/8 W
Sidemarker	194	2	3.8 W
Cornering Light	1156	2	27 W
Fog Light	—	2	55 W
Rear Lights			
Back-up	1156	2	27 W
License	—	1	5 W
Tail, Stop and Sidemarker	1157	2	8/27 W
Turn Signal	1156	2	27 W
Interior Illumination			
A/C Bezel	74	2	150 mA
Dome Light	—	1	10 W
Map Light	—	2	5 W
Luggage Compartment Light	—	1	8 W
Courtesy Light	194	4	3.8 W
Glove Box	—	1	1.2 W
Ashtray	74	1	1.4 W
Meter	194	4	3.4 W
A/T Shift Indicator	74	1	1.4 W
A/T Driving Mode Switch	—	2	50 mA
Main Cruse Control Switch	—	1	50 mA
Power Window Control Switch			
Front, Driver	—	3	0.84 W
Front, Passenger	—	1	1.4 W
Rear, LH	—	1	1.4 W
Rear, RH	—	1	1.4 W

86866GA9

Fig. 54 Light bulb chart for 1992 and later Troopers

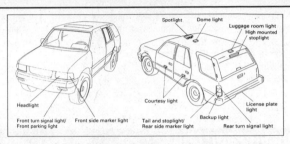

Light Name	Bulb No.	Rated power CP	Number of Bulbs	Color	Remarks
Headlight	9004	65W/45W	2	White	
Front turn signal light/ Front parking light	1034	32/3	2	Amber	
Front side marker light	194	2	2	Amber	
Rear turn signal light	1156	32	2	Amber	
Tail and stoplight Rear side marker light	1157	32/3	2	Red	
Backup light	1156	32	2	White	
License plate light	—	5W	1	White	
High mounted stoplight	—	5W	4	Red	
Dome light	—	8W	1	White	
Luggage room light	—	10W	1	White	
Spotlight	—	5W	2	White	
Courtesy light	—	5W	4	White	
Indicator/Warning light					
Air conditioning switch	—	0.84W	1		
Rear defogger switch	—	0.84W	1		
Mirror defogger switch	—	0.84W	1		
Hatch gate opener switch	—	0.84W	1		
Check trans	74	1.4W	1		
A/T oil temp	74	1.4W	1		
Cruise set	—	0.84W	1		
Cruise main	—	0.84W	1		
Power drive	—	0.84W	1		
Winter driver	—	0.84W	1		

86866GB5

Fig. 55 Light bulb chart—Rodeo

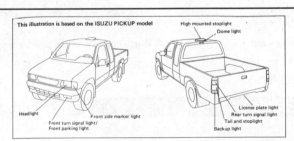

Light Name	Bulb No.	Rated power V-cp	Number of Bulbs	Color	Remarks
Headlight-Halogen	H6054	12-65/35W	2	White	
Front turn signal light/ Front parking light	1034	12-32/3	2	Amber	
Front side marker light	194	12-2	2	Amber	
Rear turn signal light	1156	12-32	2	Amber	
Tail and stoplit	1157	12-32/3	2	Red	
Backup light	1156	12-32	2	White	
High mounted stoplight	—	12-5	4 (ISUZU PICKUP model) 52 (AMIGO model)	Red	LED (AMIGO model)
License plate light	—	12-5W	2 (ISUZU PICKUP model) 1 (AMIGO model)	White	
Indicator and warning light					
Seat belt reminder	74	12-1.4	1		
Charging system	74	12-1.4	1		
Checkengine	74	12-1.4	1		
Turn signal	158	12-3.4	2		
High beam	74	12-1.4	1		
Lowfuel	74	12-1.4	1		
Oil pressure	74	12-1.4	1		
Brake system	74	12-1.4	1		
4WD indicator	74	12-1.4	1		4WD model only
Rear wheel anti-lock	74	12-1.4	1		
Overdrive off	74	12-3.4/1.4	1		A/Tmodel only
Instrument cluster light	158/74	12-3.4/12-1.4	3/6 or 2/6		
A/C-Heater control light	74	12-1.4	1		
Dome light	—	12-10W	1	White	

86866GB6

Fig. 56 Light bulb chart—Amigo and Pick-up

TRAILER WIRING

Wiring the vehicle for towing is fairly easy. There are a number of good wiring kits available and these should be used, rather than trying to design your own.

All trailers will need brake lights and turn signals as well as tail lights and side marker lights. Most areas require extra marker lights for over-wide trailers. Also, most areas have recently required back-up lights for trailers, and most trailer manufacturers have been building trailers with back-up lights for several years.

Additionally, some Class I, most Class II and just about all Class III trailers will have electric brakes. Add to this number an accessories wire, to operate trailer internal equipment or to charge the trailer's battery, and you can have as many as seven wires in the harness.

Determine the equipment on your trailer and buy the wiring kit necessary. The kit will contain all the wires needed, plus a plug adapter set which includes the female plug, mounted on the bumper or hitch, and the male plug, wired into, or plugged into the trailer harness.

When installing the kit, follow the manufacturer's instructions. The color coding of the wires is usually standard throughout the industry. One point to note: some domestic vehicles, and most imported vehicles, have separate turn signals. On most domestic vehicles, the brake lights and rear turn signals operate with the same bulb. For those vehicles without separate turn signals, you can purchase an isolation unit so that the brake lights won't blink whenever the turn signals are operated, or, you can go to your local electronics supply house and buy four diodes to wire in series with the brake and turn signal bulbs. Diodes will isolate the brake and turn signals. The choice is yours. The isolation units are simple and quick to install, but far more expensive than the diodes. The diodes, however, require more work to install properly, since they require the cutting of each bulb's wire and soldering in place of the diode.

One, final point, the best kits are those with a spring loaded cover on the vehicle mounted socket. This cover prevents dirt and moisture from corroding the terminals. Never let the vehicle socket hang loosely; always mount it securely to the bumper or hitch.

CIRCUIT PROTECTION

Fuses

▶ **See Figures 57, 58 and 59**

The fuse box on most models is located on the lower left-hand side of the instrument panel or under the instrument panel near the steering column. There is usually a relay box with additional fuses located near the battery or on fenderwell.

Each fuse block uses miniature fuses which are designed for increased circuit protection and greater reliability. The compact fuse is a blade terminal design which allows fingertip removal and replacement.

Although the fuses are interchangeable, the amperage values are molded in bold, color coded (on blade fuses) or stamped (glass fuses, easy to read numbers on the fuse body. Use only fuses of equal replacement valve.

A blown fuse can easily be checked by visual inspection or by continuity testing.

REPLACEMENT

1. Pull the fuse from the fuse block.
2. Inspect the fuse element (through the clear plastic body) to the blade terminal for defects.

➡**When replacing the fuse, DO NOT use one of a higher amperage.**

3. Once repairs are completed, install a replacement fuse of the same amperage.

Fusible Links

In addition to circuit breakers and fuses, the wiring harness incorporates fusible links to protect the wiring. Links are used rather than a fuse, in wiring circuits that are not normally fused, such as the ignition circuit. Isuzu fusible links are color coded and load circuits to match the color coding of the circuits they protect. Each link is four gauges smaller than the cable it protects, and is marked on the insulation with the gauge size because the insulation makes it appear heavier than it really is. The engine compartment wiring harness has several fusible links. The same size wire with a special hypalon insulation must be used when replacing a fusible link.

On early models the links are located in the at the starter solenoid or near the main battery terminal. Later models have a fuse link compartment on the fenderwell under the hood. Many later models use MAX fuses instead of the old style fusible links. A MAX fuse is really a fusible link in a cartridge which looks like a fuse (but with a very high ampere rating). The MAX fuses are usually found near the battery or main relay case.

REPLACEMENT

▶ **See Figures 60 thru 65**

Removable Type Fusible Links

Plug in fusible link or MAX fuses simply plug into the fuse link box or the relay center. Some models may use short fusible links with spade connectors on each end. The spade connector type simply unplug also. Care must be taken on the wire design to replace them with the same ampere rating fuse link or fire could result.

Wire Type Fusible Links

1. Determine which circuit is damaged, its location and the cause of the open fuse link. If the damaged fuse link is one of three fed by a common No. 10 or 12 gauge feed wire, determine the specific affected circuit.

Fig. 57 Replacing a spade fuse. Never replace a fuse with a higher number

Fig. 58 The fuses, fusible links and relays are usually identified on the cover or the fuse block itself

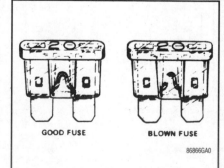

GOOD FUSE   BLOWN FUSE

86866GA0

Fig. 59 Visual examination will reveal a blown fuse

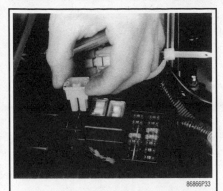

Fig. 60 MAX fusible links are a plug-in design circuit protector like fuses

Fig. 61 Replaceable fusible links are a plug-in design

Fig. 62 Replacing a plug-in design fusible link

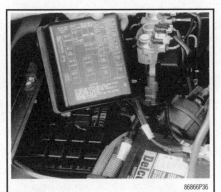

Fig. 63 The main relay box and fusible links are usually mounted near the battery

Fig. 64 Relays also help protect circuits. Relays simply plug into the relay box

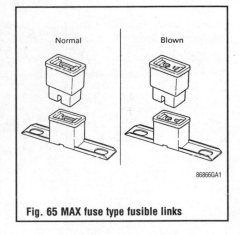

Fig. 65 MAX fuse type fusible links

2. Disconnect the negative battery cable.

3. Cut the damaged fuse link from the wiring harness and discard it. If the fuse link is one of three circuits fed by a single feed wire, cut it out of the harness at each splice end and discard it.

4. Identify and procure the proper fuse link and butt connectors for attaching the fuse link to the harness.

5. To repair any fuse link in a 3-link group with one feed:

 a. After cutting the open link out of the harness, cut each of the remaining undamaged fuse links close to the feed wire weld.

 b. Strip approximately ½ in. (13mm) of insulation from the detached ends of the two good fuse links, Then insert two wire ends into one end of a butt connector and carefully push one stripped end of the replacement fuse link into the same end of the butt connector and crimp all three firmly together.

➠**Care must be taken when fitting the three fuse links into the butt connector as the internal diameter is a snug fit for three wires. Make sure to use a proper crimping tool. Pliers, side cutter, etc. will not apply the proper crimp to retain the wires and withstand a pull test.**

 c. After crimping the butt connector to the three fuse links, cut the weld portion from the feed wire and strip approximately ½ in. (13mm) of insulation from the cut end. Insert the stripped end into the open end of the butt connector and crimp very firmly.

 d. To attach the remaining end of the replacement fuse link, strip approximately ½ in. (13mm) of insulation from the wire end of the circuit from which the blown fuse link was removed, and firmly crimp a butt connector or equivalent to the stripped wire. Then, insert the end of the replacement link into the other end of the butt connector and crimp firmly.

 e. Using rosin core solder with a consistency of 60 percent tin and 40 percent lead, solder the connectors and the wires at the repairs and insulate with electrical tape.

6. To replace any fuse link on a single circuit in a harness, cut out the damaged portion, strip approximately ½ in. (13mm) of insulation from the two wire

ends and attach the appropriate replacement fuse link to the stripped wire ends with two proper size butt connectors. Solder the connectors and wires and insulate with tape.

7. To repair any fuse link which has an eyelet terminal on one end such as the charging circuit, cut off the open fuse link behind the weld, strip approximately ½ in. (13mm) of insulation from the cut end and attach the appropriate new eyelet fuse link to the cut stripped wire with an appropriate size butt connector. Solder the connectors and wires at the repair and insulate with tape.

8. Connect the negative battery cable to the battery and test the system for proper operation.

➠**Do not mistake a resistor wire for a fuse link. The resistor wire is generally longer and has print stating, "Resistor-don't cut or splice".**

When attaching a single No. 16, 17, 18 or 20 gauge fuse link to a heavy gauge wire, always double the stripped wire end of the fuse link before inserting and crimping it into the butt connector for positive wire retention.

Circuit Breakers

One device used to protect electrical components from burning out due to excessive current is a circuit breaker. Circuit breakers open and close the flow path for the electricity rapidly in order to protect the circuit if current is excessive. A circuit breaker is used on components which are more likely to draw excessive current such as a breaker often found in the light switch that protects the headlight circuit. The circuit breakers allow the component to work for a short time before they trip. This allows for power windows to go up a small amount be for the breaker trips. The headlamps may flash on and off and the circuit breaker heats and cools. This function may allow a vehicle to make it back to the repair shop. Some circuit breakers are built into the various components. Most circuit breakers are located under the instrument panel and in the fuse and relay box in the engine compartment.

Many circuit breaker has a reset button on the top. If pushing the reset button doesn't recover the circuit, repair the short and replace the breaker.

Flashers

The turn signal and hazard flasher is located under the instrument panel next to the steering column on or in the fuse box.

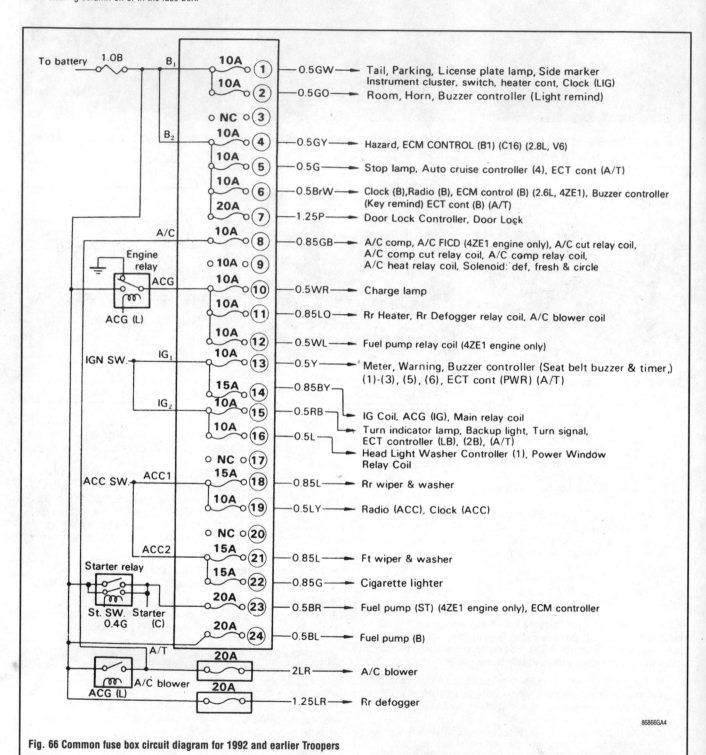

Fig. 66 Common fuse box circuit diagram for 1992 and earlier Troopers

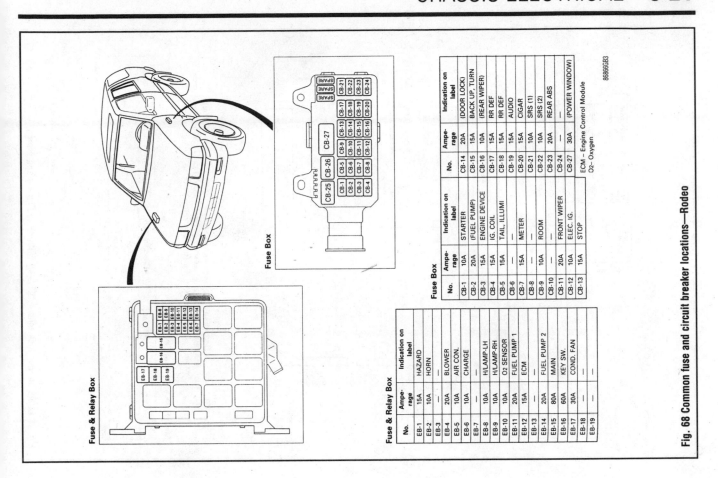

Fuse & Relay Box

No.	Amperage	Indication on label
EB-1	15A	HAZARD
EB-2	10A	HORN
EB-3	–	–
EB-4	20A	BLOWER
EB-5	10A	AIR CON.
EB-6	10A	CHARGE
EB-7	–	–
EB-8	10A	H/LAMP-LH
EB-9	10A	H/LAMP-RH
EB-10	10A	O2 SENSOR
EB-11	20A	FUEL PUMP 1
EB-12	15A	ECM
EB-13	–	–
EB-14	20A	FUEL PUMP 2
EB-15	80A	MAIN
EB-16	60A	KEY SW.
EB-17	30A	COND. FAN
EB-18	–	–
EB-19	–	–

Fuse Box

No.	Amperage	Indication on label	No.	Amperage	Indication on label
CB-1	10A	STARTER	CB-14	20A	(DOOR LOCK)
CB-2	20A	(FUEL PUMP)	CB-15	20A	BACK UP. TURN
CB-3	15A	ENGINE DEVICE	CB-16	10A	(REAR WIPER)
CB-4	15A	IG. COIL	CB-17	15A	RR DEF
CB-5	15A	TAIL, ILLUMI	CB-18	15A	RR DEF
CB-6	–	–	CB-19	15A	AUDIO
CB-7	15A	METER	CB-20	15A	CIGAR
CB-8	–	–	CB-21	10A	SRS (1)
CB-9	10A	ROOM	CB-22	10A	SRS (2)
CB-10	–	–	CB-23	20A	REAR ABS
CB-11	20A	FRONT WIPER	CB-24	–	–
CB-12	10A	ELEC. IG.	CB-27	30A	(POWER WINDOW)
CB-13	15A	STOP			

ECM – Engine Control Module
O2– Oxygen

Fig. 68 Common fuse and circuit breaker locations—Rodeo

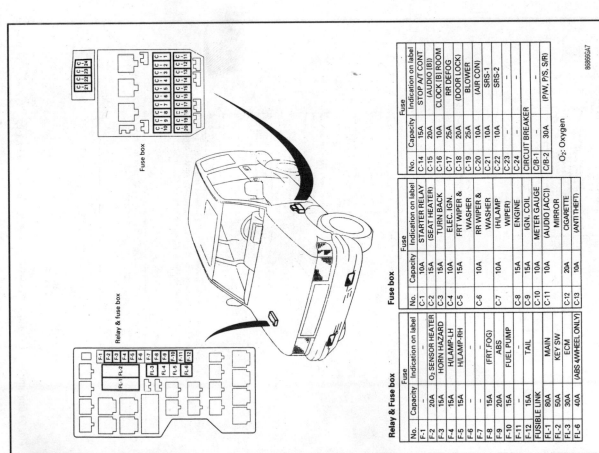

Relay & Fuse box

No.	Capacity	Indication on label
F-1	20A	O2 SENSOR HEATER
F-2	15A	HORN HAZARD
F-3	15A	H/LAMP-LH
F-4	15A	H/LAMP-RH
F-5	15A	
F-6	–	
F-7	15A	(FRT.FOG)
F-8	20A	ABS
F-9	15A	FUEL PUMP
F-10		
F-11	15A	TAIL
F-12		
FUSIBLE LINK		
FL-1	80A	MAIN
FL-2	50A	KEY SW
FL-3	30A	ECM
FL-6	40A	(ABS 4WHEEL ONLY)

Fuse box

No.	Capacity	Indication on label	No.	Capacity	Indication on label
C-1	10A	STARTER RELAY	C-14	15A	STOP A/T CONT
C-2	15A	(SEAT HEATER)	C-15	20A	(AUDIO (B))
C-3	15A	TURN BACK	C-16	10A	CLOCK (B) ROOM
C-4	10A	ELEC. IGN.	C-17	25A	RR DEFOG
C-5	15A	FRT WIPER & WASHER	C-18	15A	(DOOR LOCK)
C-6	10A	RR WIPER & WASHER	C-19	25A	BLOWER
C-7	10A	(H/LAMP WIPER)	C-20	10A	(AIR CON)
C-8	15A	ENGINE	C-21	15A	SRS-1
C-9	15A	IGN. COIL	C-22	10A	SRS-2
C-10	10A	METER GAUGE	C-23	–	
C-11	10A	(AUDIO (ACC))	C-24	–	
C-12	20A	CIGARETTE	CIRCUIT BREAKER		
C-13	10A	(ANTITHEFT)	C/B-1	–	(PW, P/S, S/R)
			C/B-2	30A	

O2: Oxygen

Fig. 67 Common fuses, fusible links and circuit breakers for 1993 and later Troopers

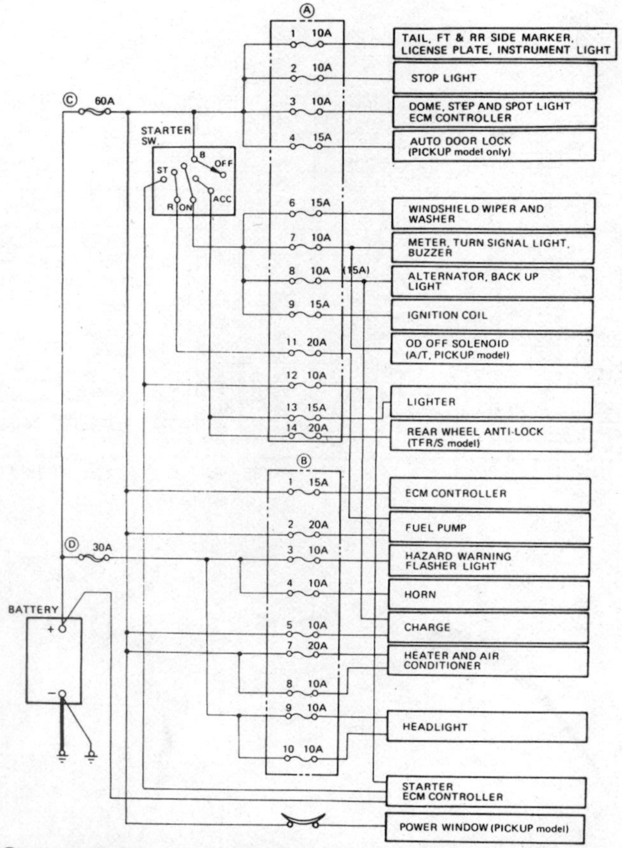

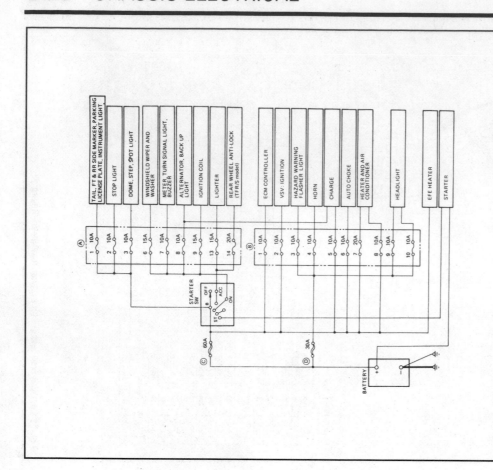

Note:
Ⓐ Fuse box (Installed at the lower left-hand side of the instrument panel).
Ⓑ Fuse and relay box (Installed at the right-hand side of the engine compartment).
Ⓒ, Ⓓ. Main fuse (Installed in the fuse and relay box).

Main Fuse Specifications

Type	Rating	Case Color	Maximum Circuit Current (Amps)
Connector	30A	Pink	15
Bolt	60A	Yellow	30

Fig. 70 Common fuse locations—1987–90 carbureted Pick-up and Amigo

Note:
Ⓐ Fuse box (Installed at the lower left-hand side of the instrument panel).
Ⓑ Fuse and relay box (Installed at the right-hand side of the engine compartment).
Ⓒ, Ⓓ. Main fuse (Installed in the fuse and relay box).

Main Fuse Specifications

Type	Rating	Case Color	Maximum Circuit Current (Amps)
Connector	30A	Pink	15
Bolt	60A	Yellow	30

Fig. 69 Common fuse locations—1987–90 fuel injected Amigo and Pick-up

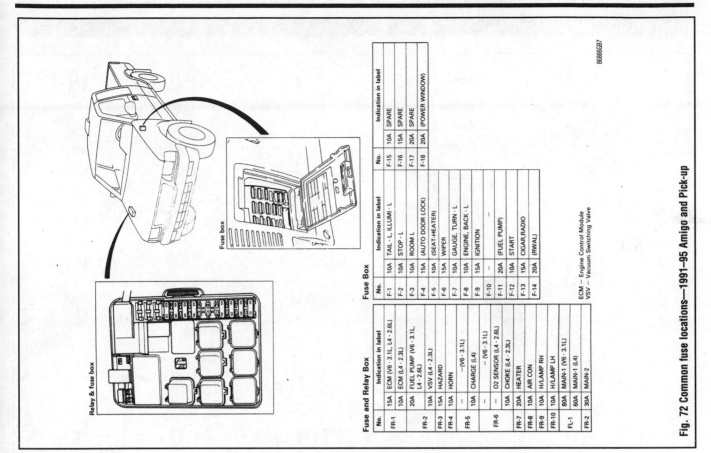

Fuse and Relay Box

No.		Indication in label
FR-1	15A	ECM (V6 · 3.1L, L4 · 2.6L)
	10A	ECM (L4 · 2.3L)
FR-2	20A	FUEL PUMP (V6 · 3.1L, L4 · 2.6L)
	10A	VSV (L4 · 2.3L)
FR-3	15A	HAZARD
FR-4	10A	HORN
FR-5	—	(V6 · 3.1L)
	10A	CHARGE (L4)
FR-6	—	(V6 · 3.1L)
	10A	O2 SENSOR (L4 · 2.6L)
	10A	CHOKE (L4 · 2.3L)
FR-7	20A	HEATER
FR-8	10A	AIR CON
FR-9	10A	H/LAMP RH
FR-10	10A	H/LAMP LH
FL-1	80A	MAIN-1 (V6 · 3.1L)
	60A	MAIN-1 (L4)
FR-2	30A	MAIN-2

Fuse Box

No.		Indication in label
F-1	10A	TAIL · L, ILLUMI · L
F-2	10A	STOP · L
F-3	10A	ROOM L
F-4	15A	(AUTO DOOR LOCK)
F-5	10A	(SEAT·HEATER)
F-6	15A	WIPER
F-7	10A	GAUGE, TURN · L
F-8	10A	ENGINE, BACK · L
F-9	15A	IGNITION
F-10	—	—
F-11	20A	(FUEL PUMP)
F-12	10A	START
F-13	15A	CIGAR,RADIO
F-14	20A	(RWAL)
F-15	10A	SPARE
F-16	15A	SPARE
F-17	20A	SPARE
F-18	20A	(POWER WINDOW)

ECM — Engine Control Module
VSV — Vacuum Switching Valve

86066GB7

Fig. 72 Common fuse locations—1991–95 Amigo and Pick-up

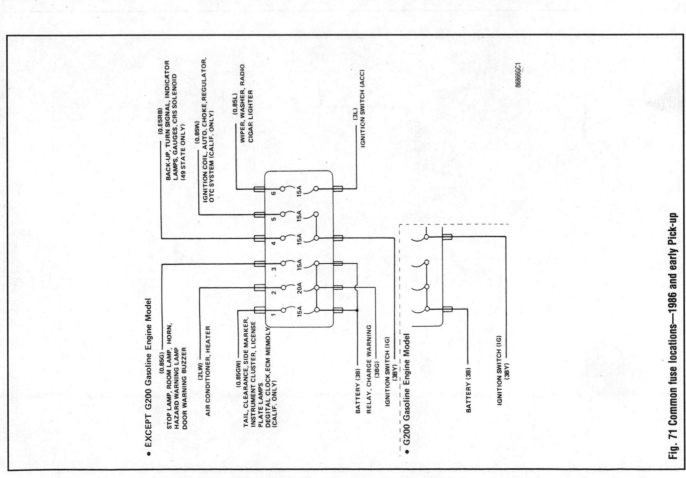

86066GC1

Fig. 71 Common fuse locations—1986 and early Pick-up

WIRING DIAGRAMS

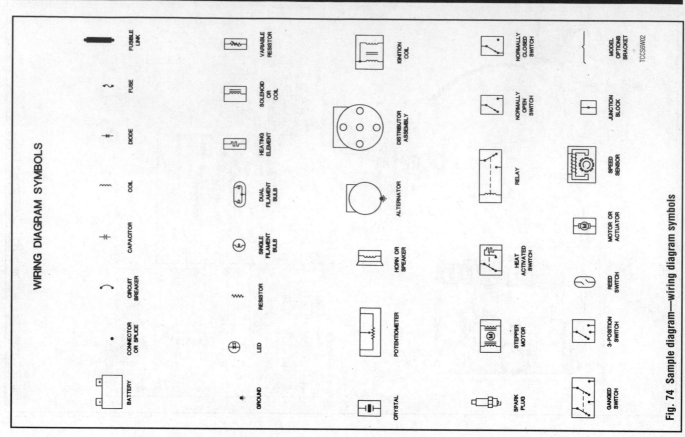

Fig. 74 Sample diagram—wiring diagram symbols

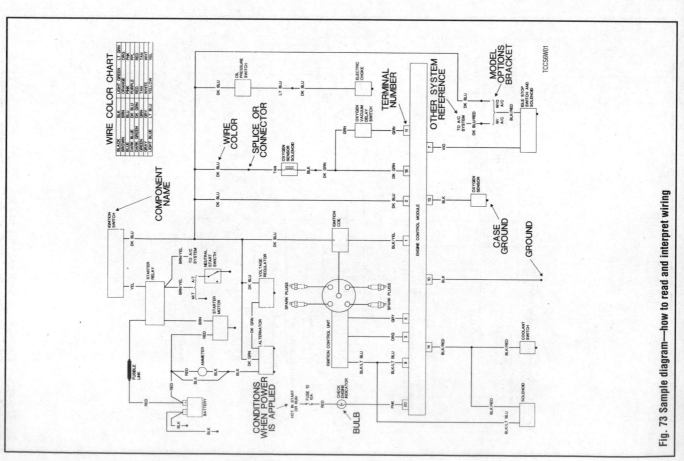

Fig. 73 Sample diagram—how to read and interpret wiring

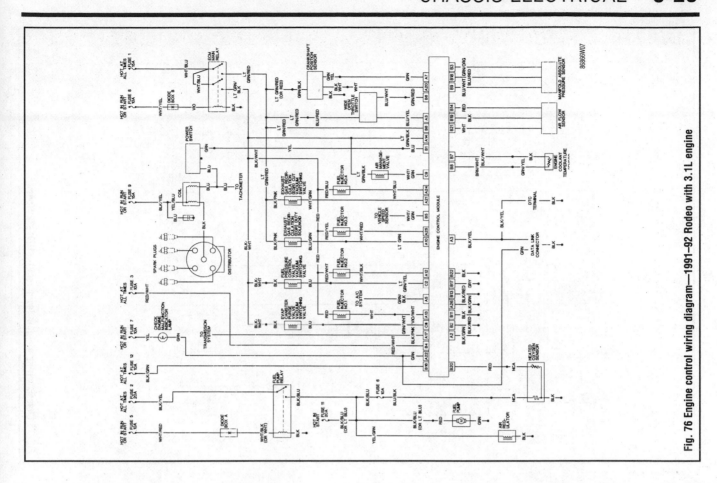

Fig. 76 Engine control wiring diagram—1991–92 Rodeo with 3.1L engine

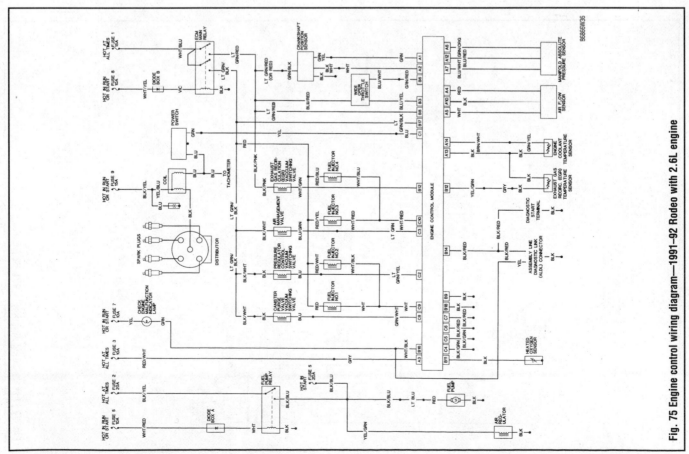

Fig. 75 Engine control wiring diagram—1991–92 Rodeo with 2.6L engine

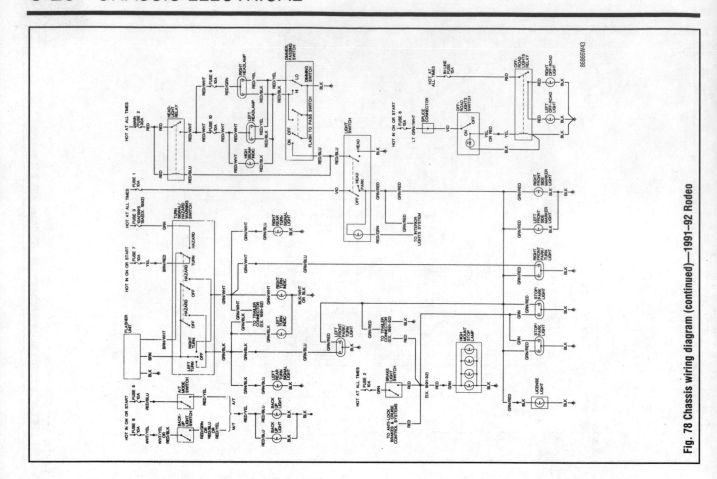

Fig. 78 Chassis wiring diagram (continued)—1991-92 Rodeo

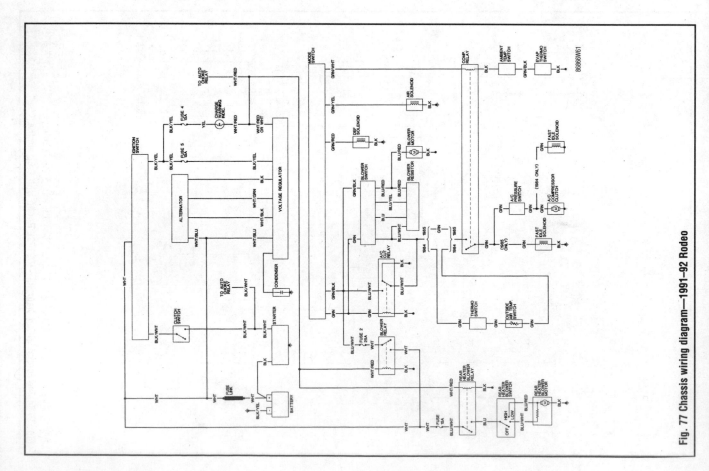

Fig. 77 Chassis wiring diagram—1991-92 Rodeo

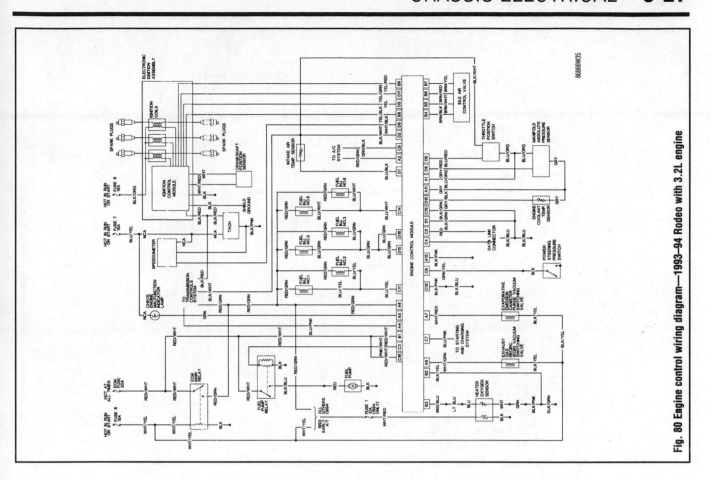

Fig. 80 Engine control wiring diagram—1993–94 Rodeo with 3.2L engine

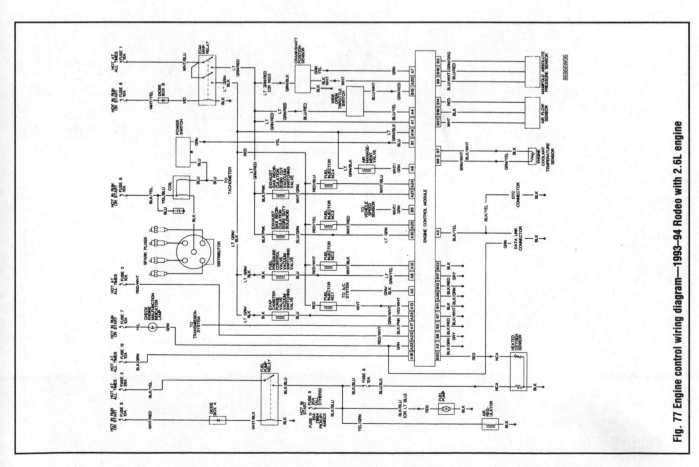

Fig. 77 Engine control wiring diagram—1993–94 Rodeo with 2.6L engine

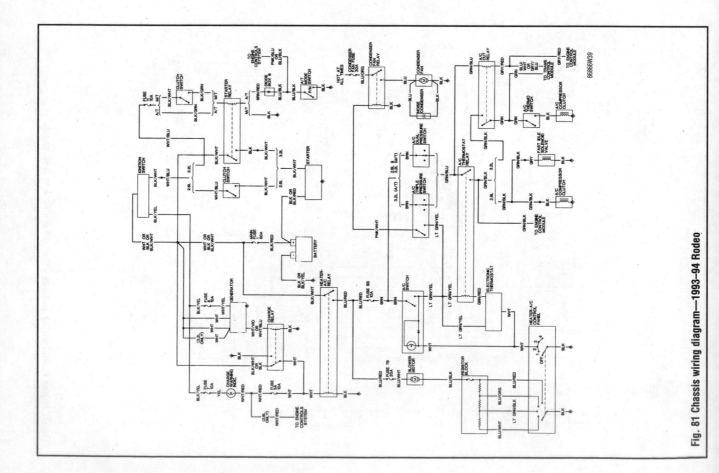

Fig. 82 Chassis wiring diagram (continued)—1993–94 Rodeo

Fig. 81 Chassis wiring diagram—1993–94 Rodeo

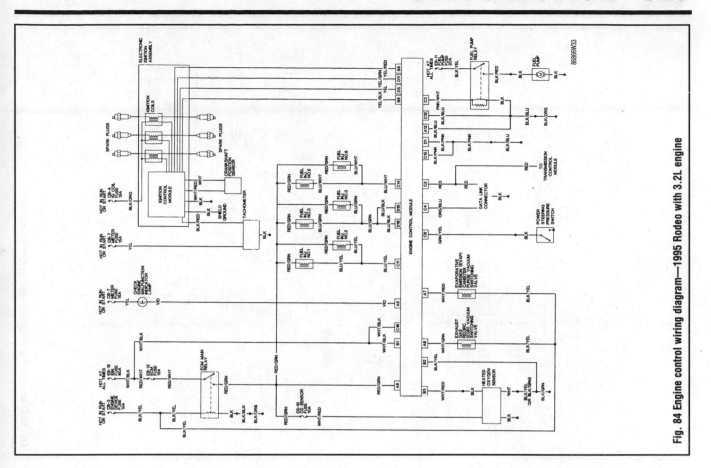

Fig. 84 Engine control wiring diagram—1995 Rodeo with 3.2L engine

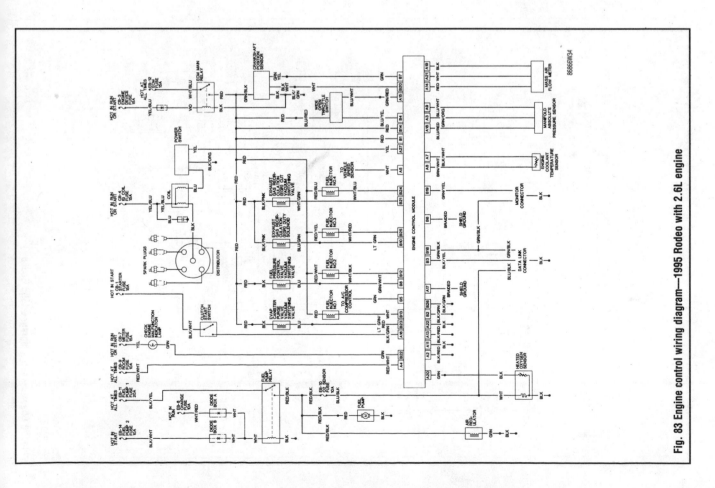

Fig. 83 Engine control wiring diagram—1995 Rodeo with 2.6L engine

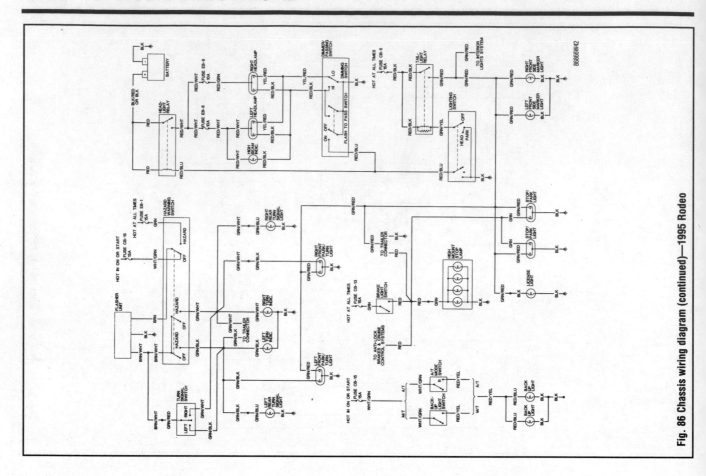

Fig. 86 Chassis wiring diagram (continued)—1995 Rodeo

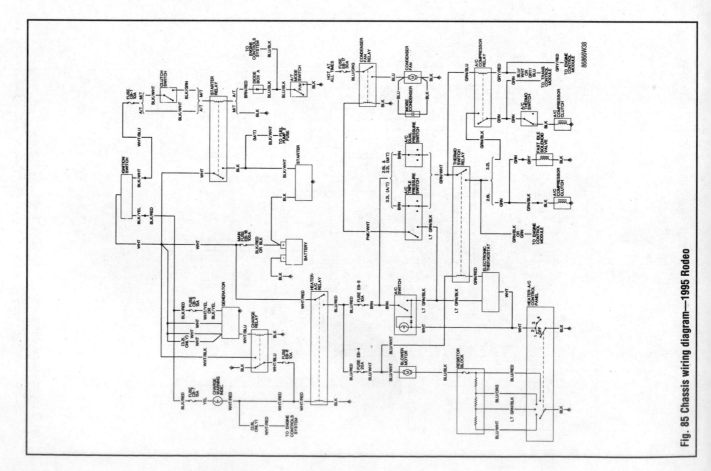

Fig. 85 Chassis wiring diagram—1995 Rodeo

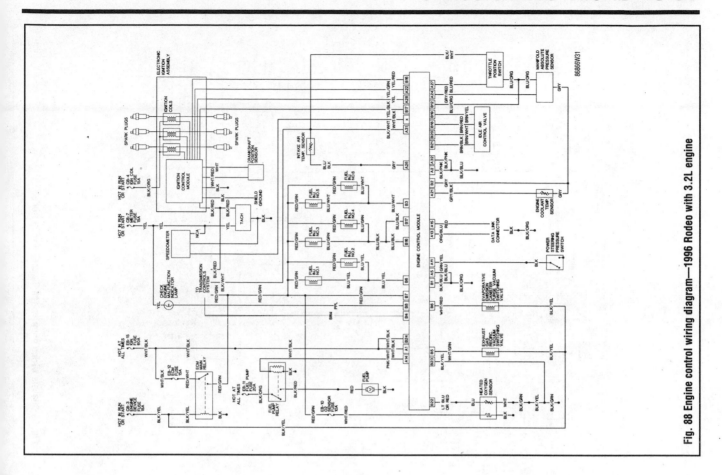

Fig. 88 Engine control wiring diagram—1996 Rodeo with 3.2L engine

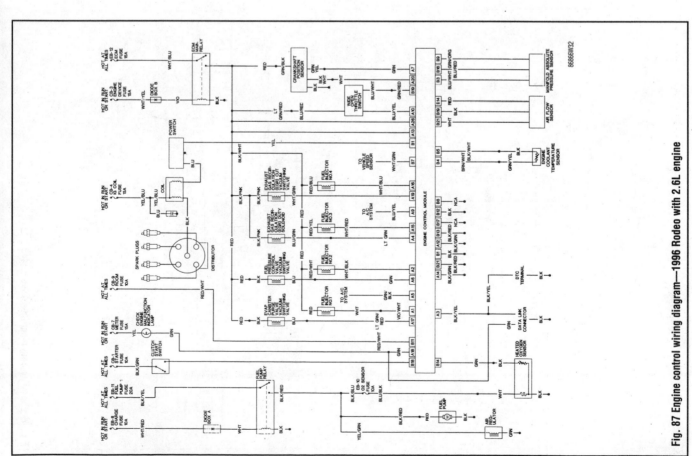

Fig. 87 Engine control wiring diagram—1996 Rodeo with 2.6L engine

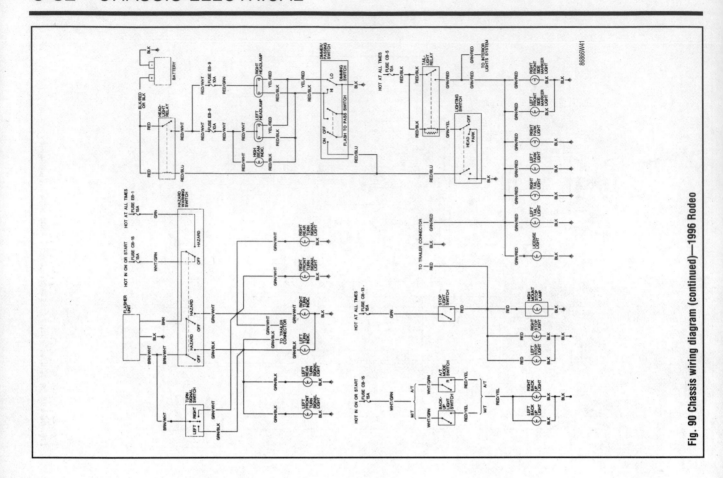

Fig. 90 Chassis wiring diagram (continued)—1996 Rodeo

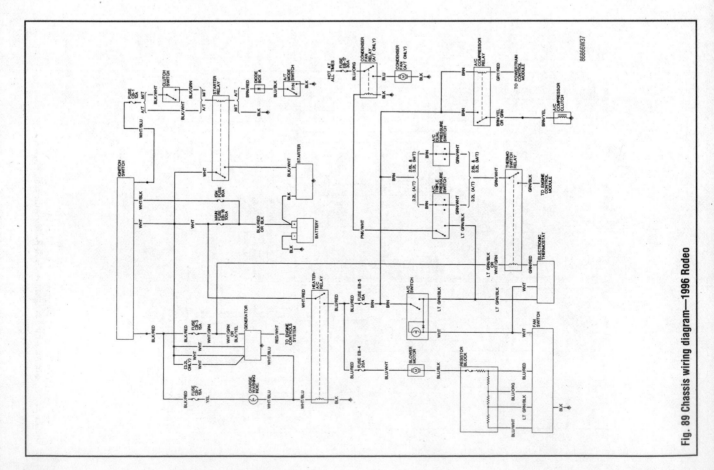

Fig. 89 Chassis wiring diagram—1996 Rodeo

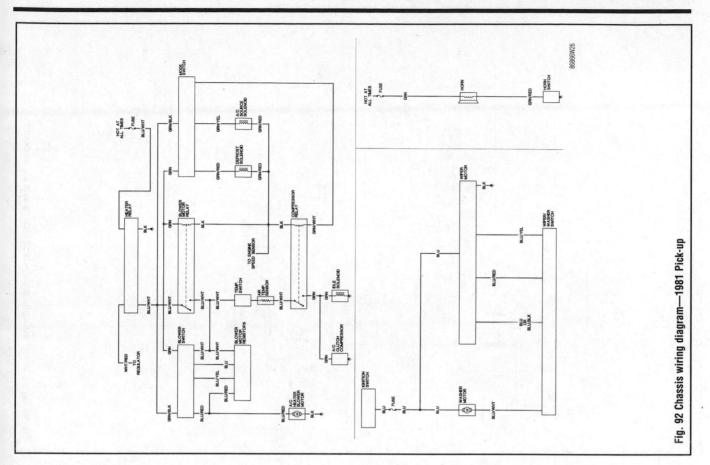

Fig. 92 Chassis wiring diagram—1981 Pick-up

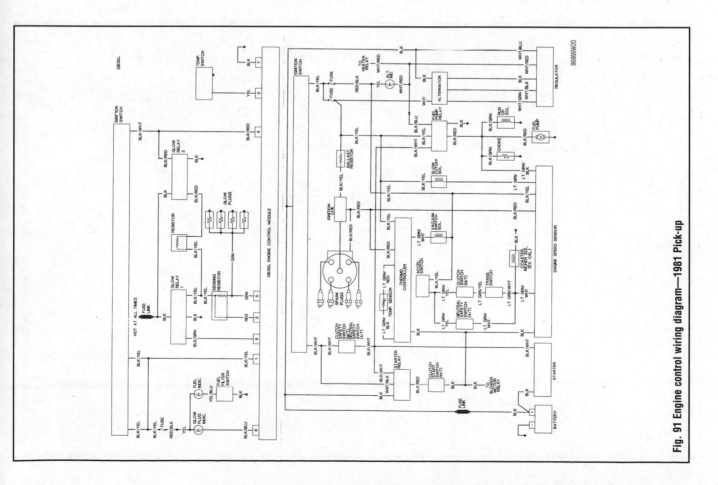

Fig. 91 Engine control wiring diagram—1981 Pick-up

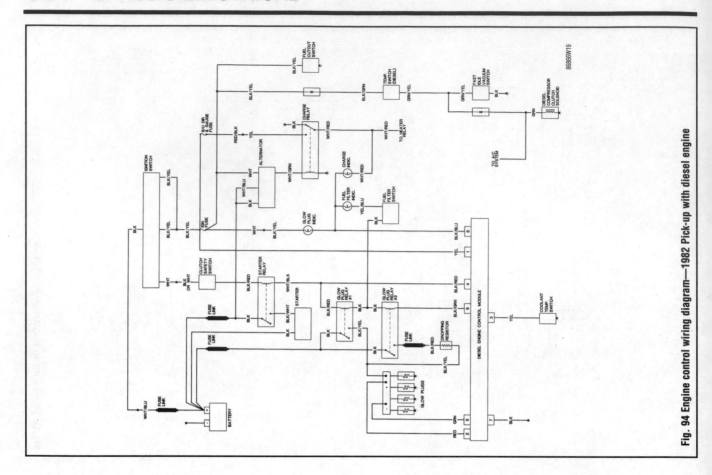

Fig. 94 Engine control wiring diagram—1982 Pick-up with diesel engine

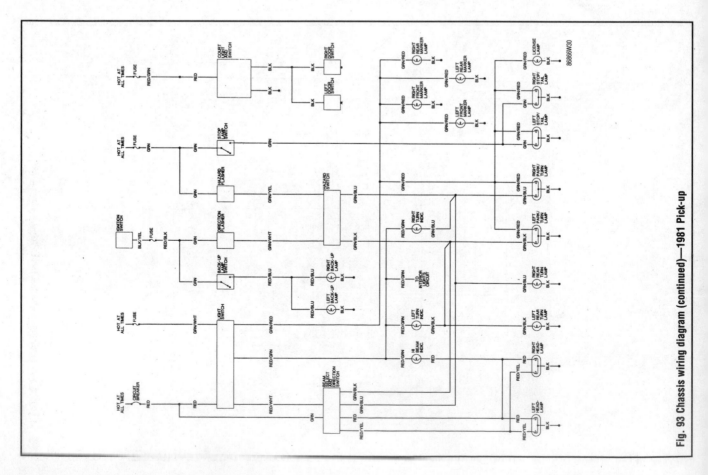

Fig. 93 Chassis wiring diagram (continued)—1981 Pick-up

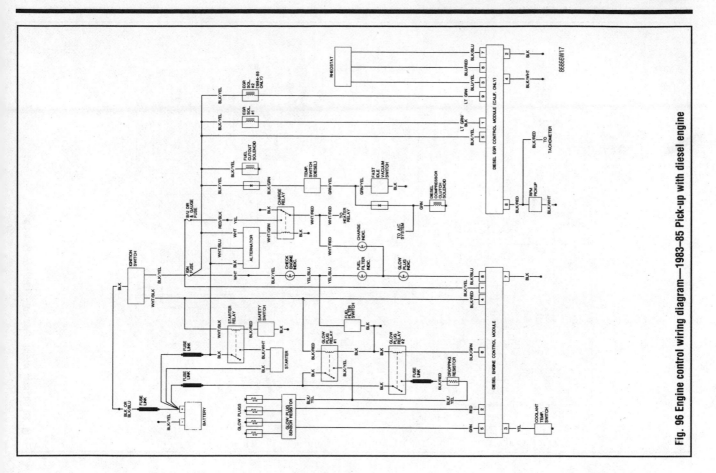

Fig. 96 Engine control wiring diagram—1983–85 Pick-up with diesel engine

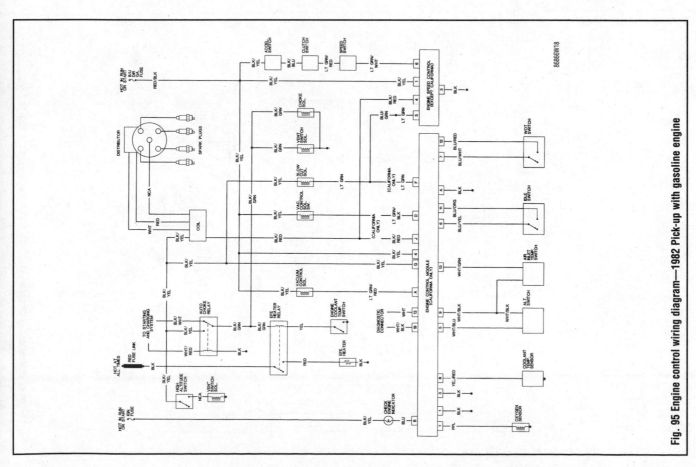

Fig. 95 Engine control wiring diagram—1982 Pick-up with gasoline engine

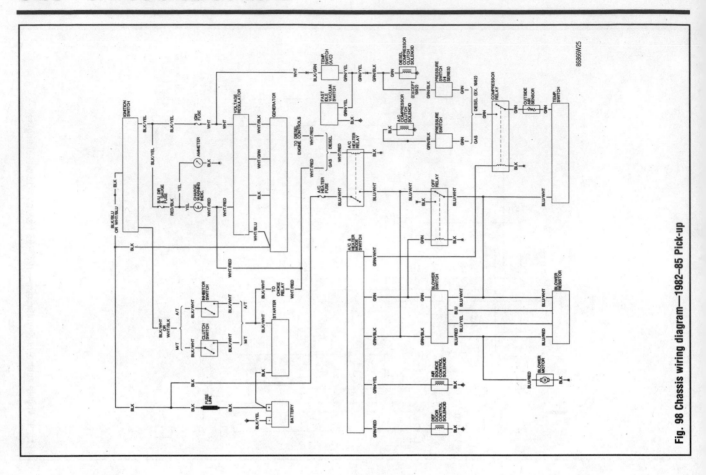

Fig. 98 Chassis wiring diagram—1982–85 Pick-up

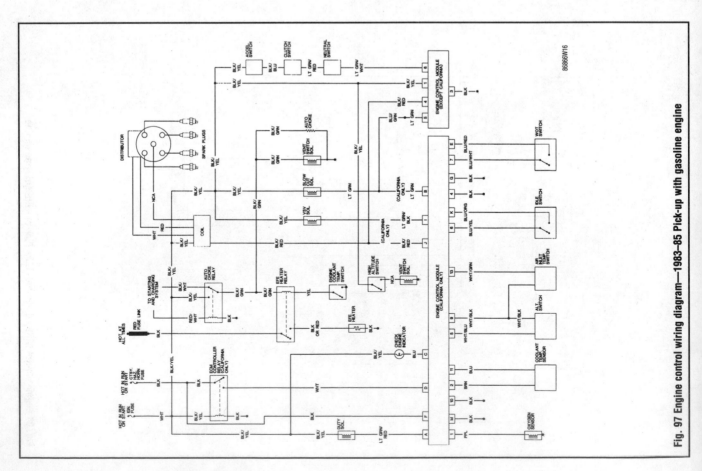

Fig. 97 Engine control wiring diagram—1983–85 Pick-up with gasoline engine

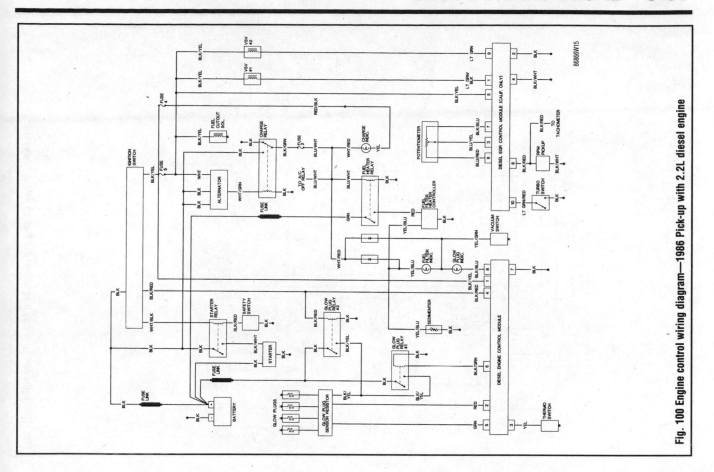

Fig. 100 Engine control wiring diagram—1986 Pick-up with 2.2L diesel engine

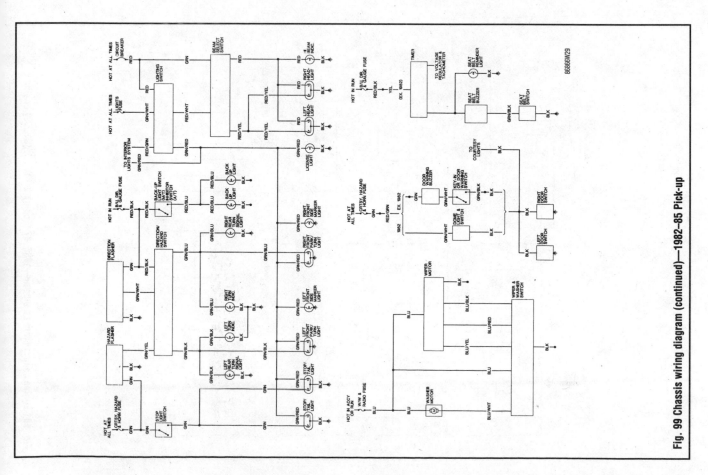

Fig. 99 Chassis wiring diagram (continued)—1982-85 Pick-up

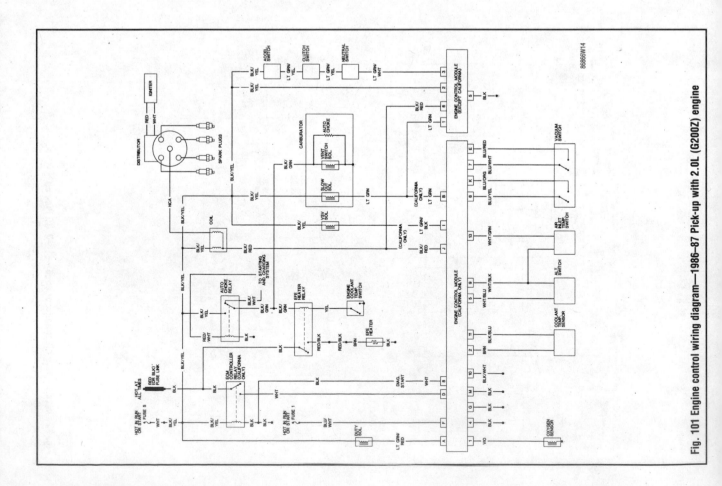

Fig. 102 Engine control wiring diagram—1987 Pick-up with 2.2L diesel engine

Fig. 101 Engine control wiring diagram—1986–87 Pick-up with 2.0L (G200Z) engine

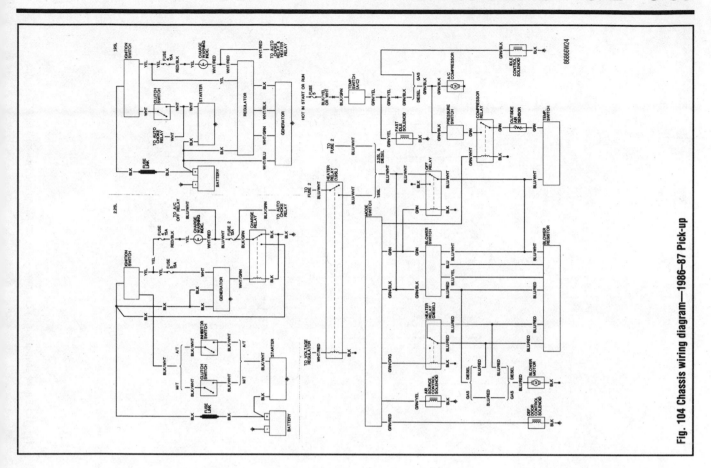

Fig. 104 Chassis wiring diagram—1986–87 Pick-up

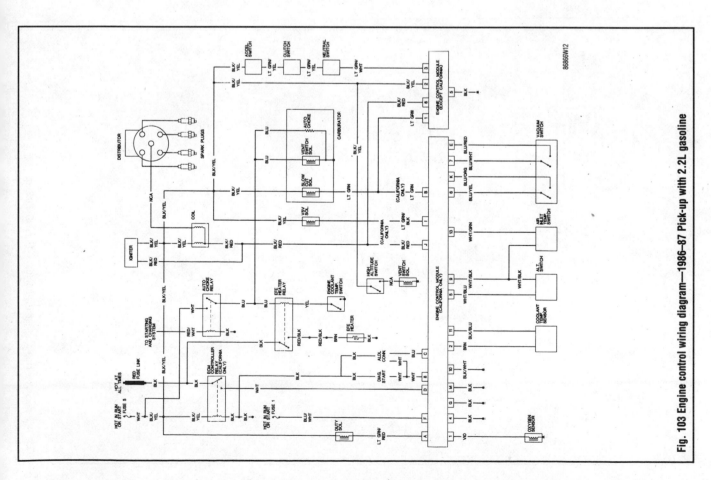

Fig. 103 Engine control wiring diagram—1986–87 Pick-up with 2.2L gasoline

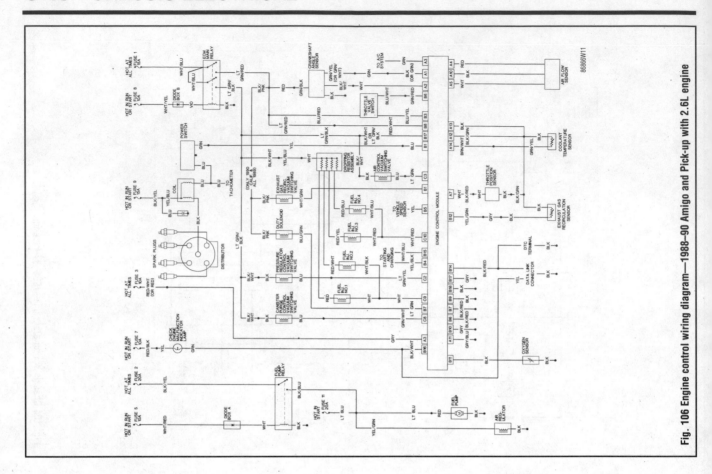

Fig. 106 Engine control wiring diagram—1988-90 Amigo and Pick-up with 2.6L engine

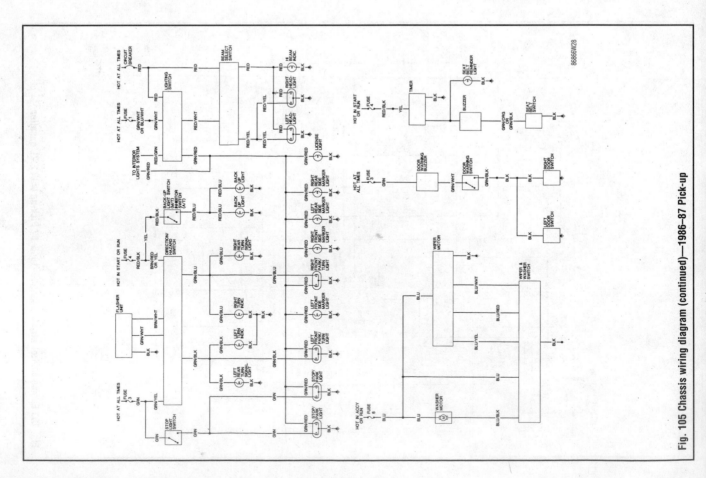

Fig. 105 Chassis wiring diagram (continued)—1986-87 Pick-up

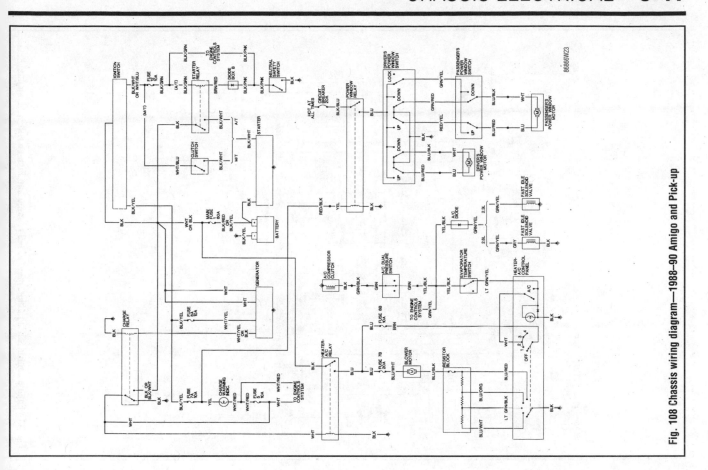

Fig. 108 Chassis wiring diagram—1988-90 Amigo and Pick-up

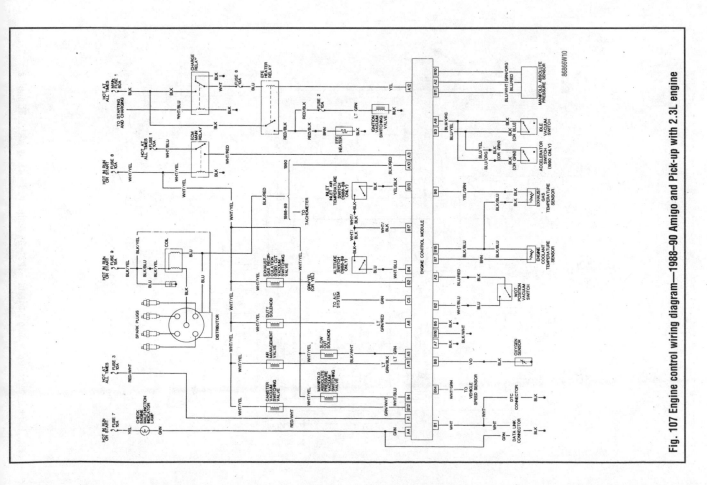

Fig. 107 Engine control wiring diagram—1988-90 Amigo and Pick-up with 2.3L engine

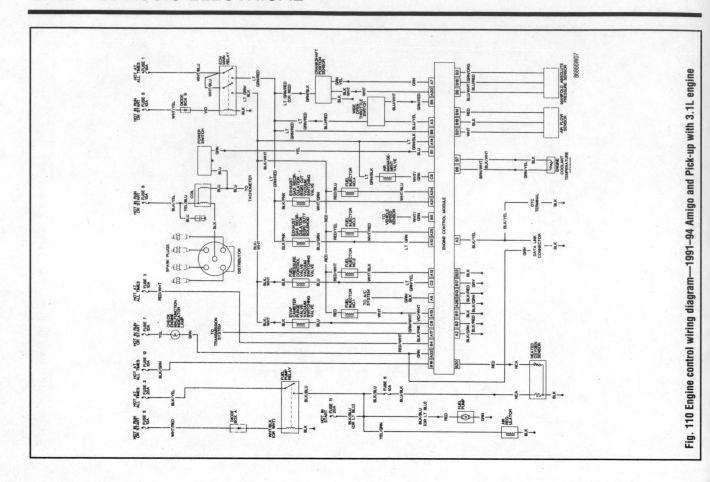

Fig. 110 Engine control wiring diagram—1991–94 Amigo and Pick-up with 3.1L engine

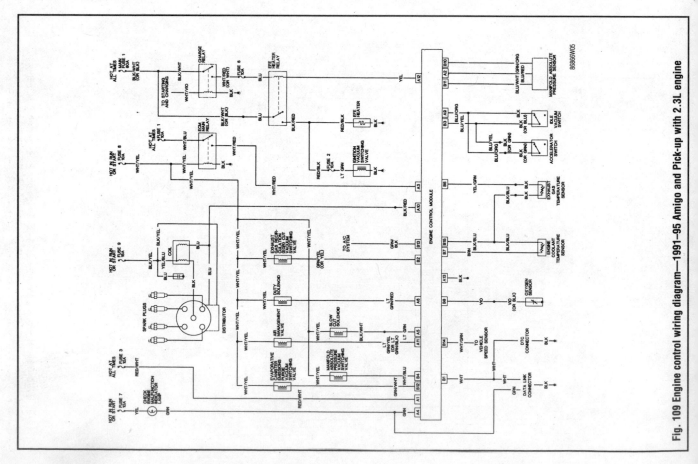

Fig. 109 Engine control wiring diagram—1991–95 Amigo and Pick-up with 2.3L engine

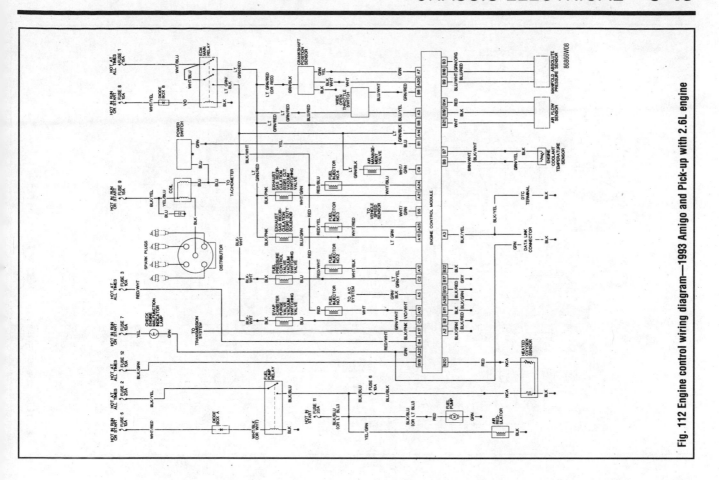

Fig. 112 Engine control wiring diagram—1993 Amigo and Pick-up with 2.6L engine

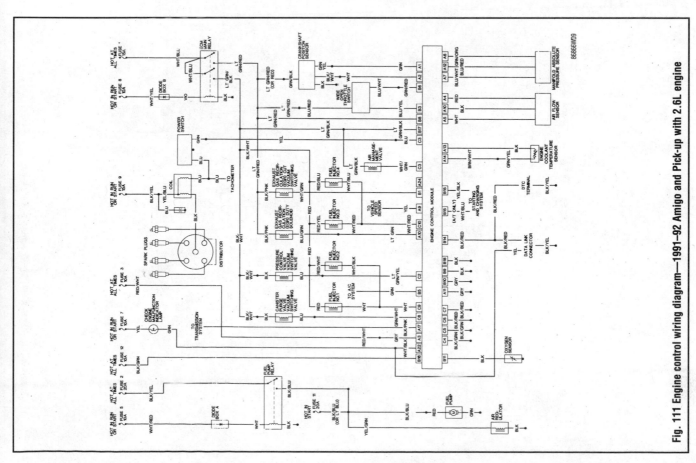

Fig. 111 Engine control wiring diagram—1991–92 Amigo and Pick-up with 2.6L engine

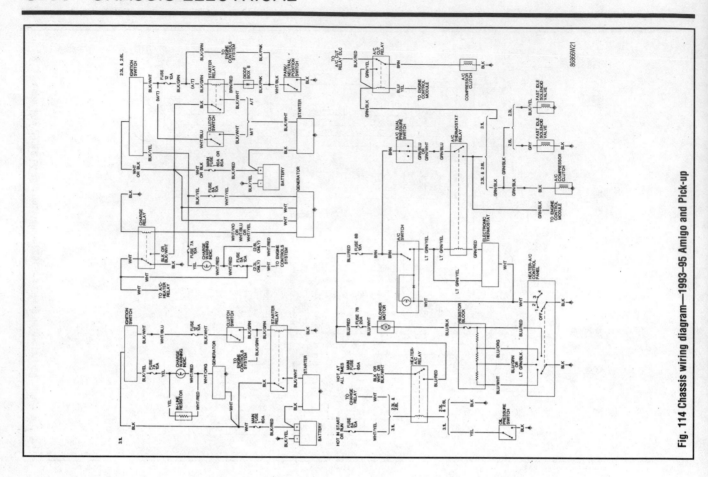

Fig. 114 Chassis wiring diagram—1993-95 Amigo and Pick-up

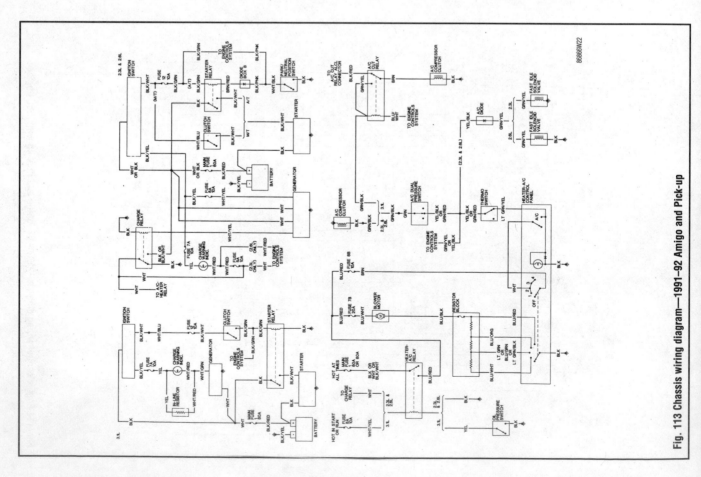

Fig. 113 Chassis wiring diagram—1991-92 Amigo and Pick-up

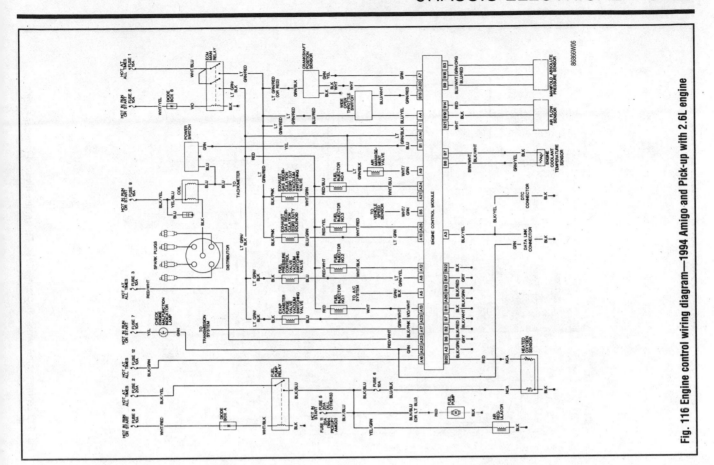

Fig. 116 Engine control wiring diagram—1994 Amigo and Pick-up with 2.6L engine

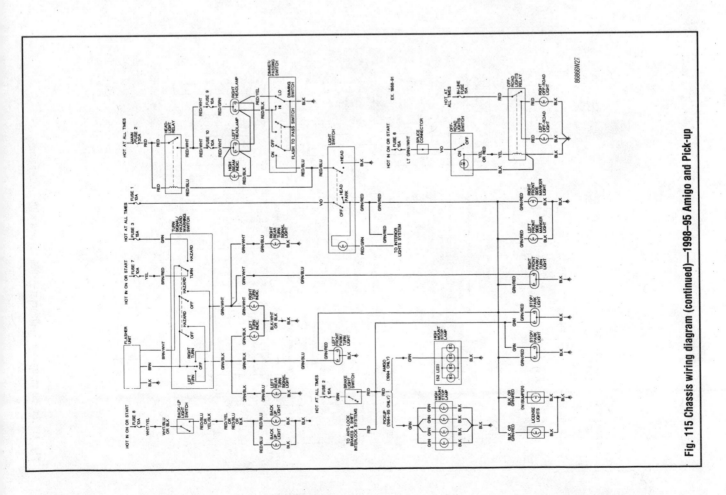

Fig. 115 Chassis wiring diagram (continued)—1998–95 Amigo and Pick-up

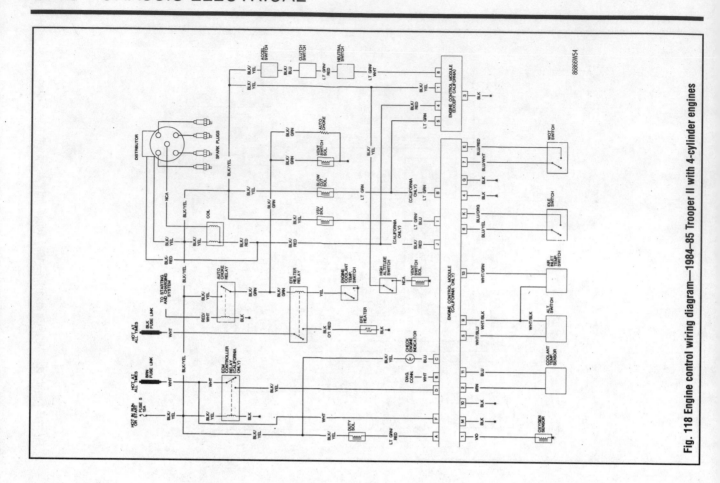

Fig. 118 Engine control wiring diagram—1984–85 Trooper II with 4-cylinder engines

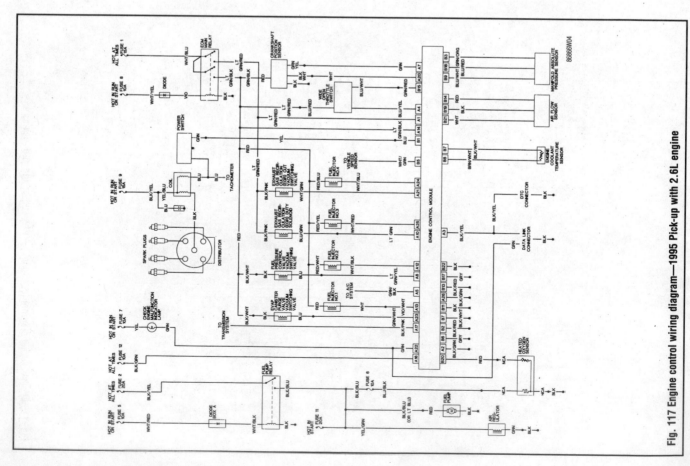

Fig. 117 Engine control wiring diagram—1995 Pick-up with 2.6L engine

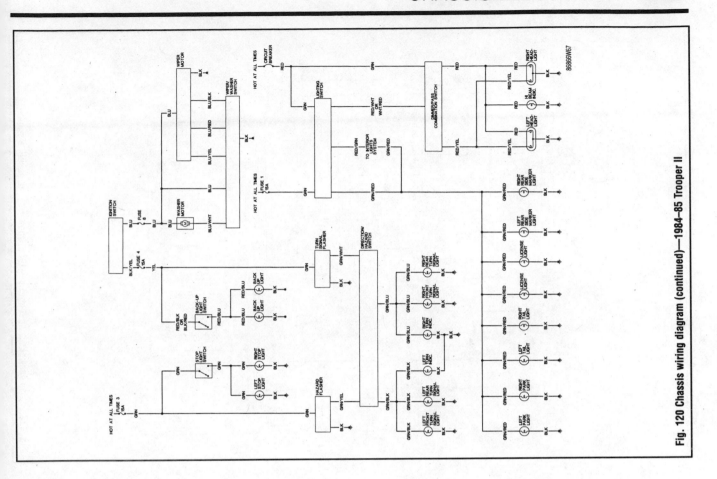

Fig. 120 Chassis wiring diagram (continued)—1984–85 Trooper II

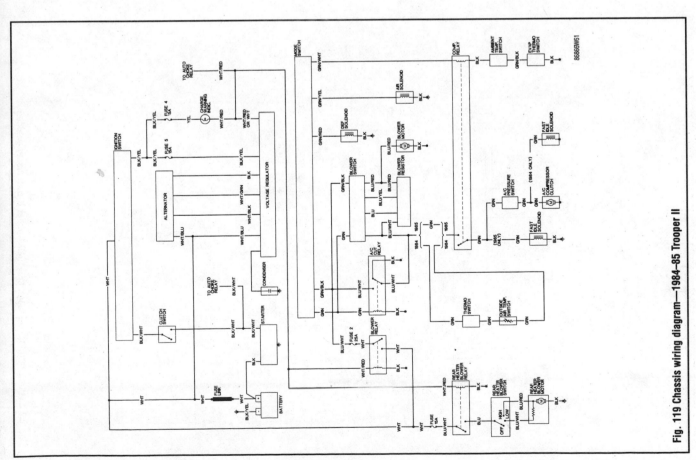

Fig. 119 Chassis wiring diagram—1984–85 Trooper II

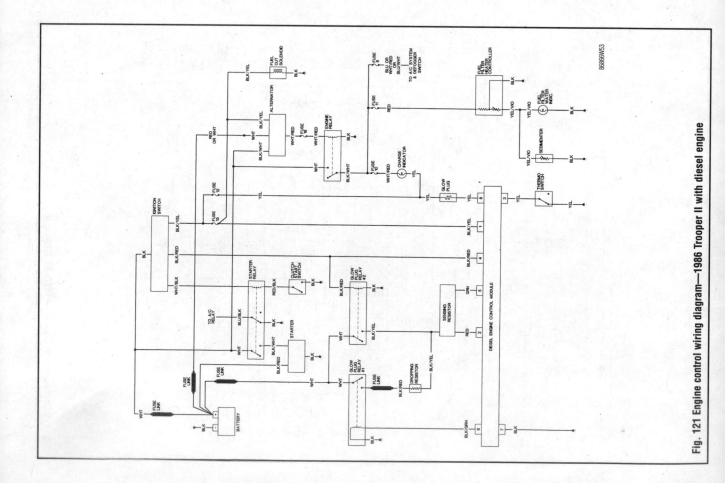

Fig. 122 Engine control wiring diagram—1986 Trooper II with gasoline engine

Fig. 121 Engine control wiring diagram—1986 Trooper II with diesel engine

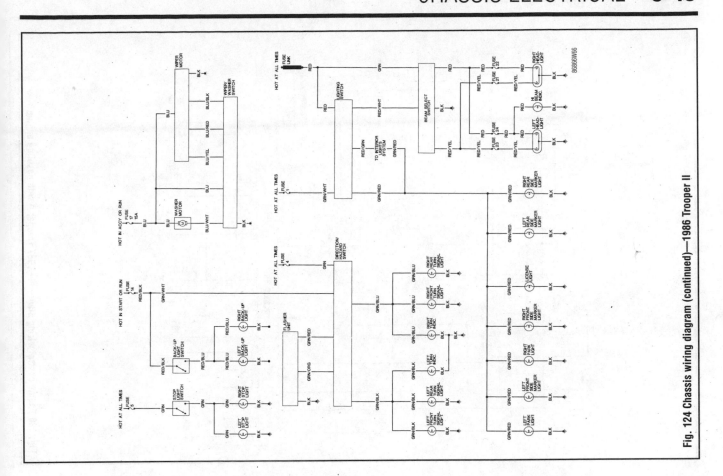

Fig. 124 Chassis wiring diagram (continued)—1986 Trooper II

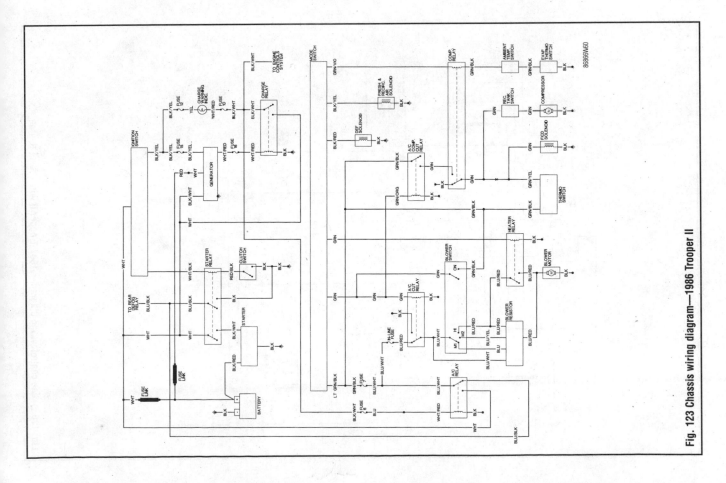

Fig. 123 Chassis wiring diagram—1986 Trooper II

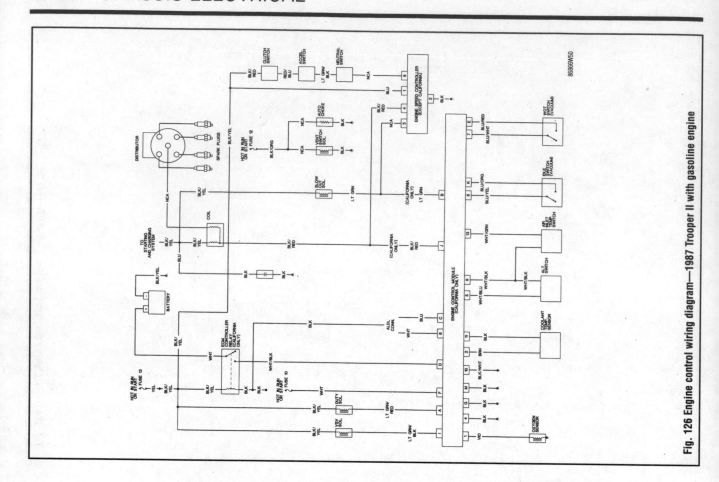

Fig. 126 Engine control wiring diagram—1987 Trooper II with gasoline engine

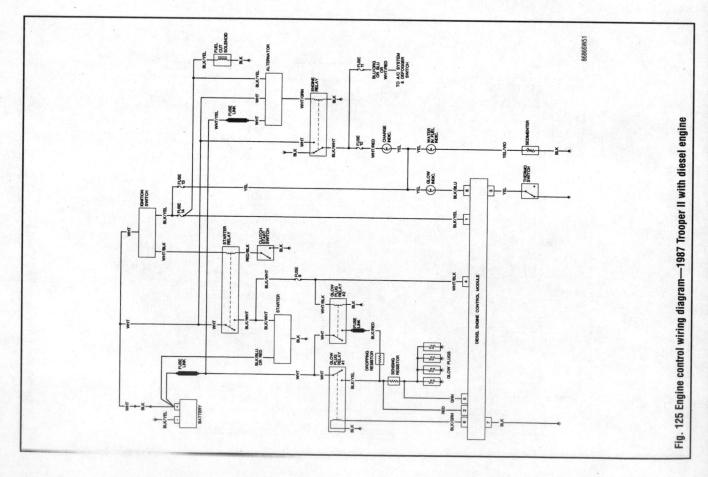

Fig. 125 Engine control wiring diagram—1987 Trooper II with diesel engine

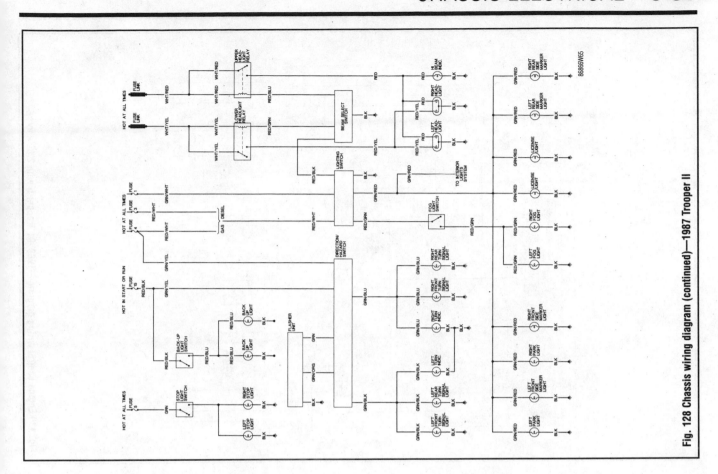

Fig. 128 Chassis wiring diagram (continued)—1987 Trooper II

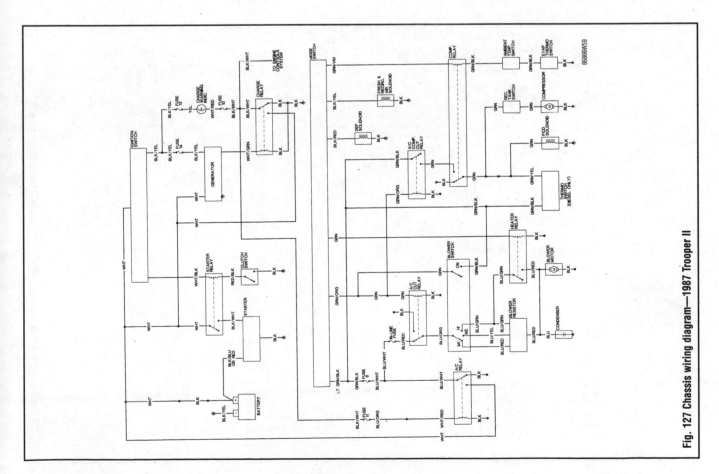

Fig. 127 Chassis wiring diagram—1987 Trooper II

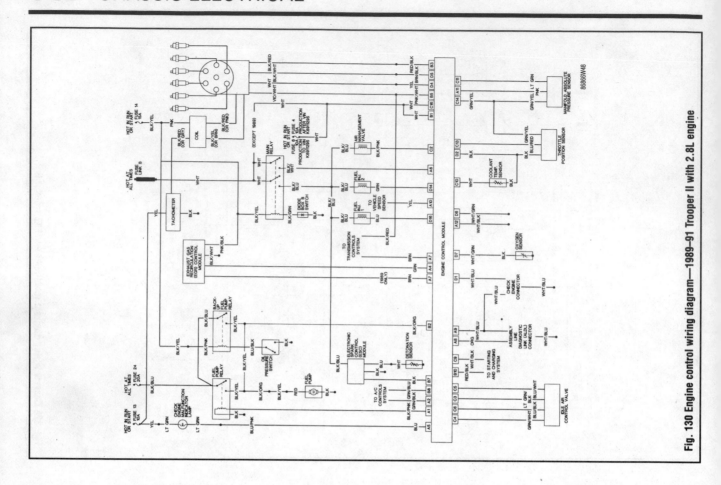

Fig. 130 Engine control wiring diagram—1989–91 Trooper II with 2.8L engine

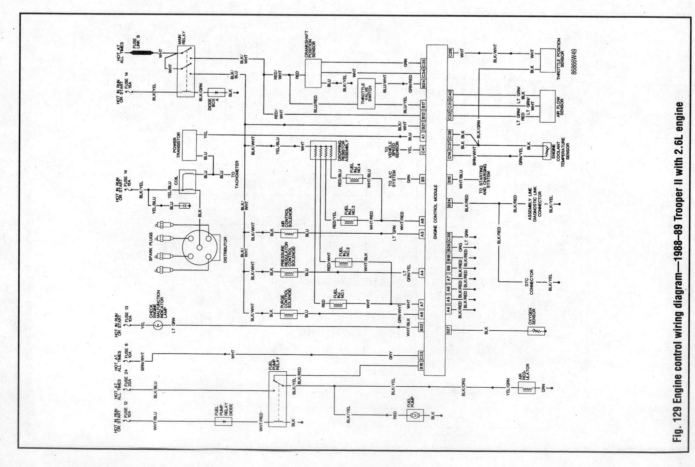

Fig. 129 Engine control wiring diagram—1988–89 Trooper II with 2.6L engine

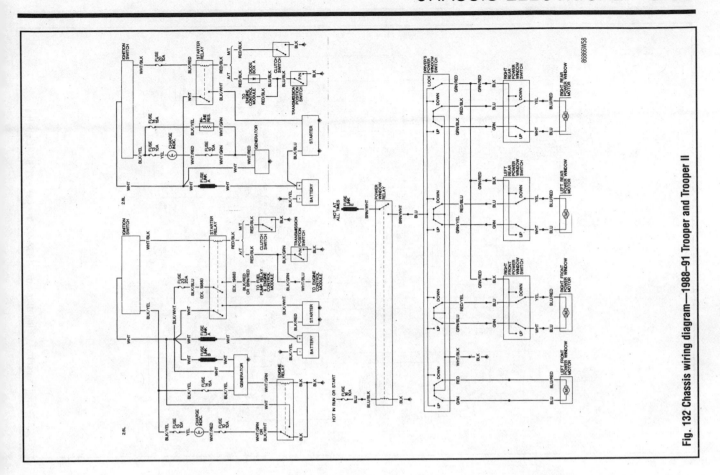

Fig. 132 Chassis wiring diagram—1988-91 Trooper and Trooper II

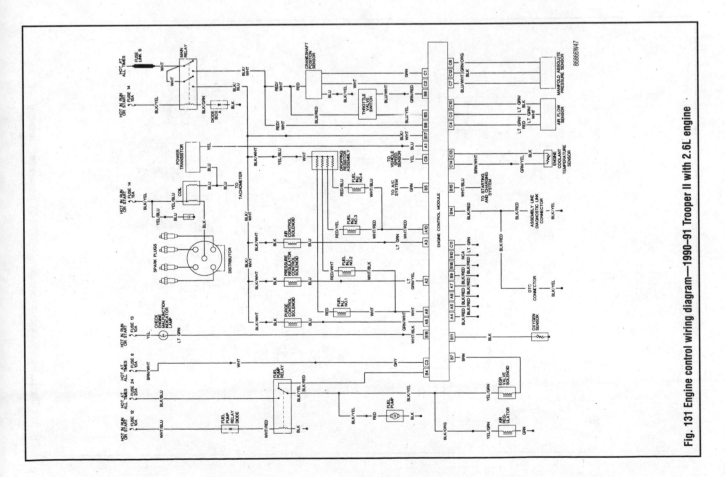

Fig. 131 Engine control wiring diagram—1990-91 Trooper II with 2.6L engine

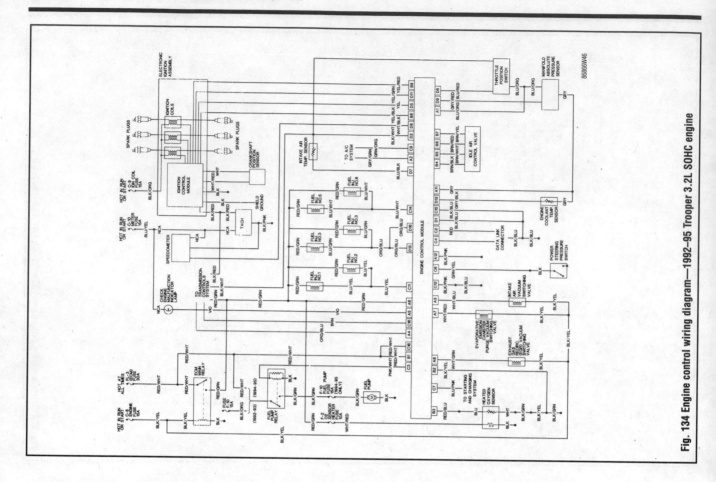

Fig. 134 Engine control wiring diagram—1992-95 Trooper 3.2L SOHC engine

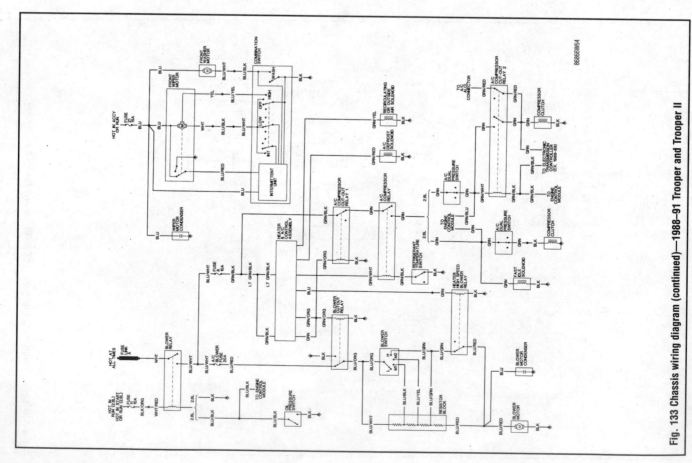

Fig. 133 Chassis wiring diagram (continued)—1988-91 Trooper and Trooper II

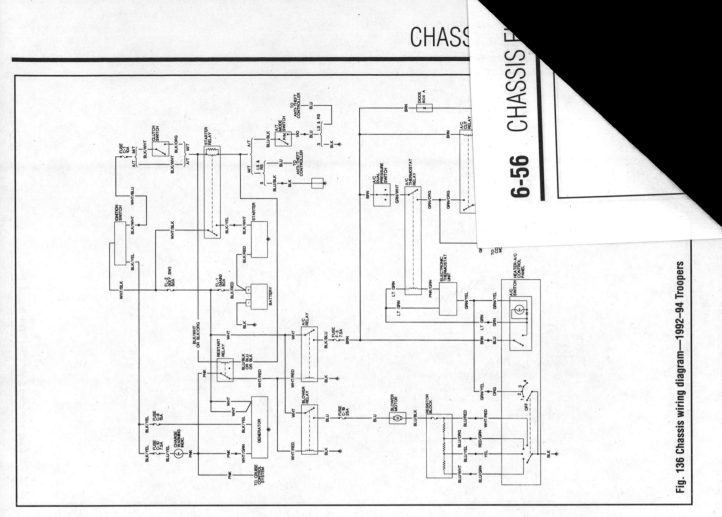

Fig. 136 Chassis wiring diagram—1992–94 Troopers

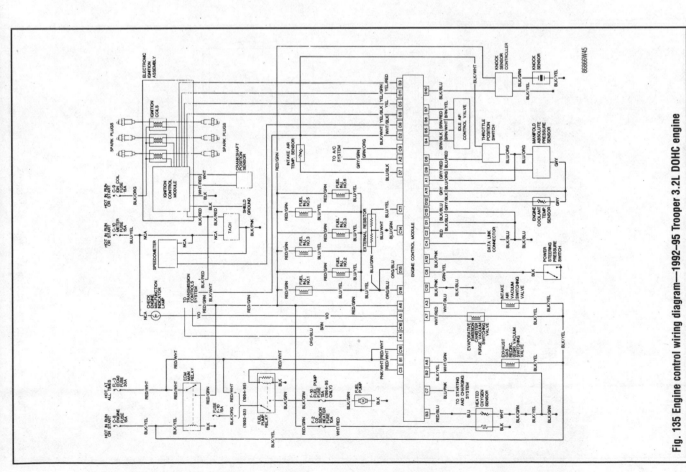

Fig. 135 Engine control wiring diagram—1992–95 Trooper 3.2L DOHC engine

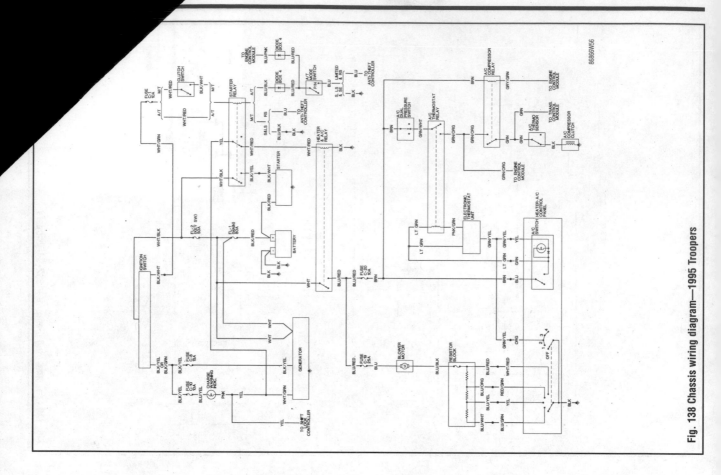

86866W56

Fig. 138 Chassis wiring diagram—1995 Troopers

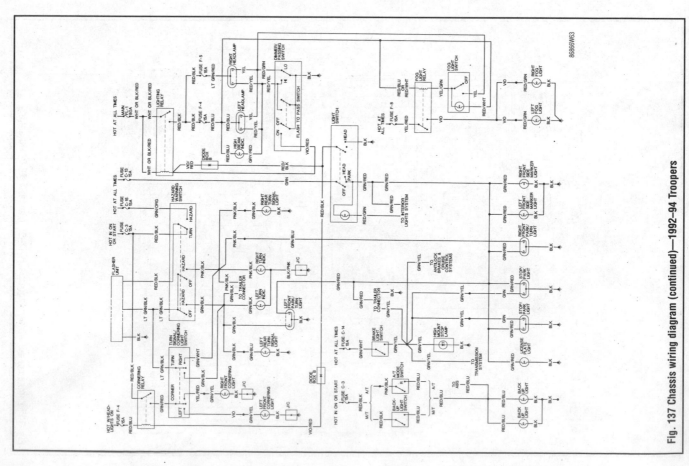

86866W63

Fig. 137 Chassis wiring diagram (continued)—1992-94 Troopers

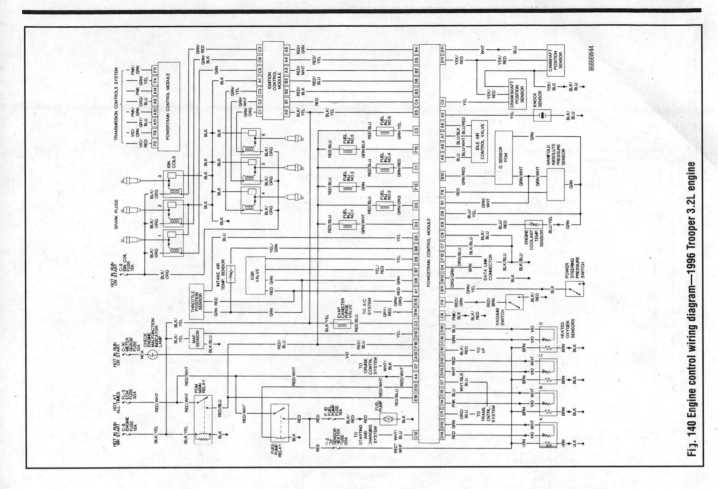

Fig. 140 Engine control wiring diagram—1996 Trooper 3.2L engine

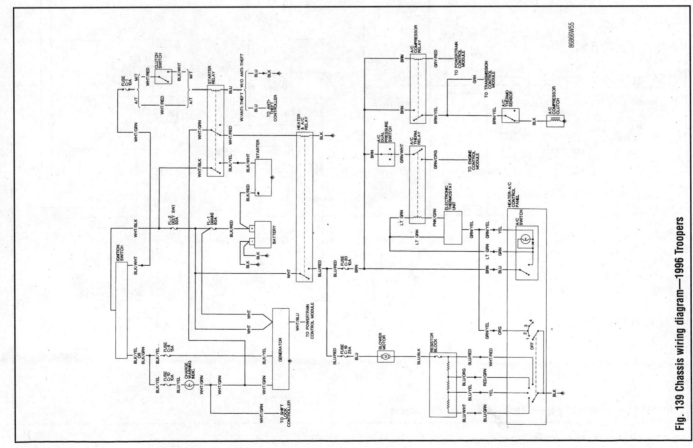

Fig. 139 Chassis wiring diagram—1996 Troopers

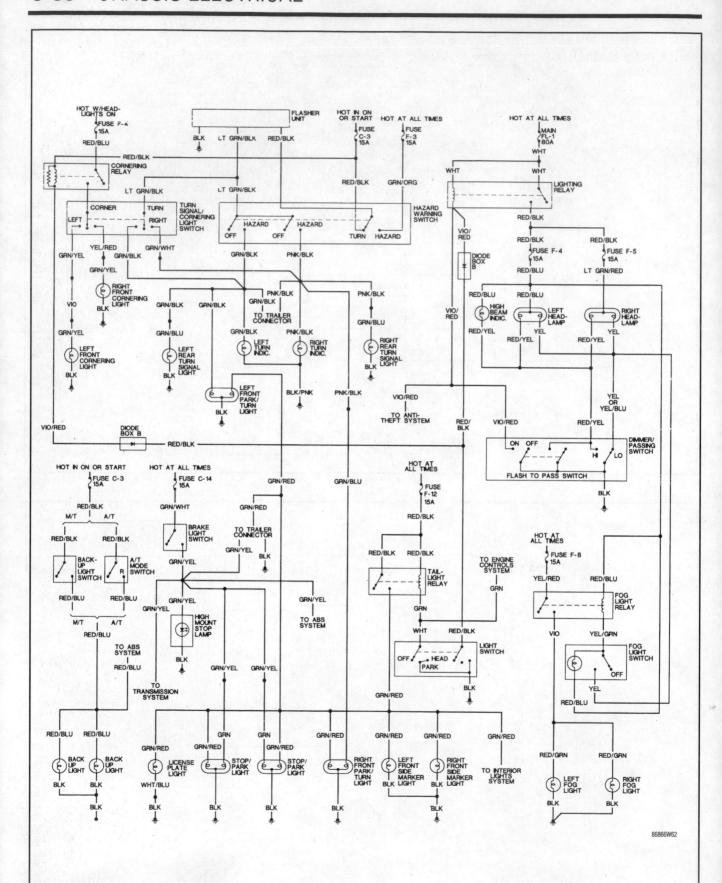

Fig. 141 Chassis wiring diagram (continued)—1995–96 Troopers

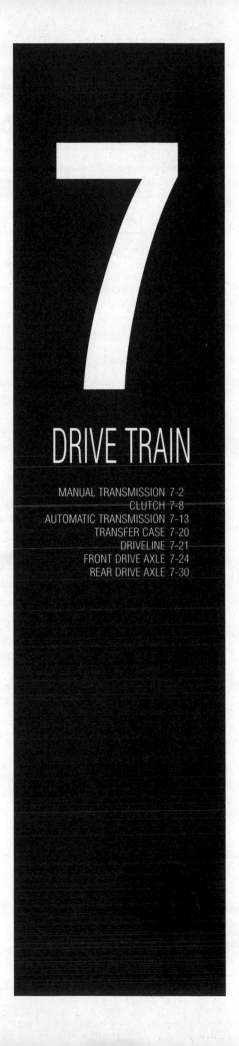

7

DRIVE TRAIN

MANUAL TRANSMISSION

Identification

The transmission identification number is stamped onto the left-hand side of the transmission body. For more details, refer to Section 1.

Adjustments

LINKAGE & SHIFTER

All of the manual transmissions in the Isuzu trucks and Sport Utility vehicles are designed with the shifter level mounted directly to the top of the transmission case. The linkage or shifter handle is non-adjustable. If problems with shifting arise, inspect the clutch or have the internal mechanisms of the transmission inspected by a reputable transmission technician.

CLUTCH SWITCH

MSG-Type Transmission

The clutch switch used on the MSG-type transmissions cannot be adjusted. If the clutch switch is not functioning normally, first adjust the clutch pedal height and free-play, as described later in this section. If, after adjusting the clutch pedal, the clutch switch still does not function correctly, perform the clutch switch test in the clutch switch adjustment procedure.

MUA-Type and T5R Transmissions

To adjust the clutch switch, please refer to the clutch pedal height and free-play procedure later in this section. The clutch pedal free-play and height and the clutch switch adjustment should all be performed together as 1 procedure. If you want to test the clutch switch for a defect, refer to the clutch switch adjustment procedure.

Back-Up Light Switch

REMOVAL & INSTALLATION

♦ See Figure 1

➡**The back-up light switch is mounted on the right-hand side of the transmission housing body, just below the gear shift lever housing. This is a simple ON/OFF type switch.**

1. Disconnect the negative battery cable.
2. Raise and safely support the vehicle on jackstands.

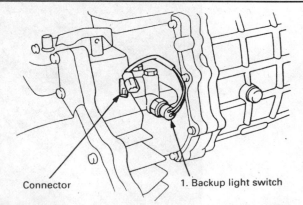

Connector 1. Backup light switch

86867G05

Fig. 1 The back-up lamp switch is located on the right-hand side of the transmission, just below the gear shift lever housing—all manual transmissions

3. Detach the back-up switch connector from the vehicle wiring harness.
4. Using either a wrench or a "crow's foot" socket and ratchet wrench, remove the switch from the transmission body. Draining the transmission is not necessary, since the switch is mounted above the fluid level; a little fluid may dribble out of the hole however.
5. If the switch is going to be reinstalled, remove the used O-ring from it.
To install:
6. If reinstalling the old back-up switch, install a new O-ring (the new switches should come with a new O-ring already installed.
7. Apply liquid gasket to the threaded portion of the switch, then slowly thread the switch into the transmission housing by hand. Tighten it first finger-tight, then to 15 ft. lbs. (20 Nm).
8. The balance of the installation is the reverse of removal.

Extension Housing Seal

REMOVAL & INSTALLATION

Except 1991–96 4WD Rodeo and Trooper

♦ See Figure 2

➡**Although draining the transmission is not necessary for this procedure, it would be a good time for a routine fluid change.**

1. Raise and safely support the vehicle on jackstands.
2. If so desired, drain the transmission fluid.
3. Matchmark the rear driveshaft flange to the rear differential flange for reassembly.
4. Remove the 4 driveshaft retaining bolts from the rear differential.
5. If equipped, remove the center bearing retainer bolts.
6. Lower the rear of the driveshaft assembly down from the differential and pull the rear driveshaft front yoke gently free of the transmission extension housing. Remove the driveshaft assembly completely from the vehicle.
7. If equipped, remove the extension housing dust shield from the transmission.
8. Using an oil seal puller (usually a specially designed J-shaped prytool), remove the rear housing oil seal.
To install:
9. Install a new oil seal using an installer tool, such as J-29769 for the MUA-type or J-38763 for the T5R transmissions, or the equivalent. Make certain that the oil seal is seated completely and flush in the rear extension housing bore.
10. Lubricate the inside lip of the fluid oil seal with fresh, clean engine oil.
11. Position the driveshaft assembly under the vehicle, then lift the front end of the driveshaft up and slide it carefully into the rear extension housing of the transmission.
12. If applicable, lift the center bearing up and install the retaining bolts finger-tight. Position the rear driveshaft flange against the differential flange so the matchmarks align and install the attaching bolts and nuts finger-tight. Make sure the driveshaft-to-differential bolts are installed from the backside of the differential flange (the threaded portion of the bolt should be toward the front of the vehicle).
13. If equipped, tighten the center bearing bolts to 45 ft. lbs. (60 Nm).
14. Tighten the driveshaft-to-differential flange bolts and nuts to 46 ft. lbs. (63 Nm).
15. If necessary, install the transmission drain plug and fill the transmission until the fluid just starts to dribble out of the filler hole (make sure the dribble is not a by-product of a sloppy transmission filling technique—spillage while filling). Install the filler plug.
16. Lower the vehicle.

1991–96 4WD Rodeo and Trooper

♦ See Figures 3 and 4

These vehicles are equipped with a transmission-to-driveshaft flange; rather than sliding the driveshaft yoke into the rear extension housing, the driveshaft bolts to the transmission flange.

Fig. 2 The extension housing oil seal is pressed into the extension housing tail—except 1991–96 4WD Rodeo and Trooper models

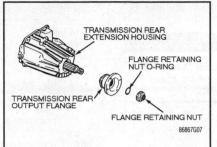

Fig. 3 Unlike the other transmissions, the 4WD versions of the MUA-5C and T5R transmissions utilize a transmission flange equipped with a sealing O-ring

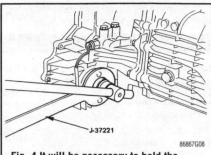

Fig. 4 It will be necessary to hold the flange steady with special tool J-37221, or equivalent, to remove the flange retaining nut

➡Although draining the transmission is not necessary for this procedure, it would be a good time for a routine fluid change.

1. Raise and safely support the vehicle on jackstands.
2. If so desired, drain the transmission fluid.
3. Matchmark the rear driveshaft flange to the rear differential flange and the front driveshaft flange to the rear transmission flange for reassembly.
4. Remove the 4 driveshaft retaining bolts from the rear differential.
5. If equipped, remove the center bearing retainer bolts.
6. Remove the 4 driveshaft retaining bolts from the transmission rear flange.
7. Lower the rear of the driveshaft assembly out of the vehicle.
8. Use a rear flange holder, such as J-37221, to hold the rear flange steady while loosening the flange retaining nut.
9. Remove the flange retaining nut and the old O-ring. Discard the O-ring.

To install:

10. Install a new O-ring onto the transmission rear flange and install the flange nut.
11. Use the flange holding tool to hold the flange stationary while tightening the flange nut to 123 ft. lbs. (167 Nm).
12. Position the driveshaft assembly under the vehicle, then lift the front end of the driveshaft up and hold it against the transmission flange so the matchmarks align. Install the driveshaft-to-transmission flange bolts and nuts finger-tight.
13. If applicable, lift the center bearing up and install the retaining bolts finger-tight. Position the rear driveshaft flange against the differential flange so the matchmarks align and install the attaching bolts and nuts finger-tight. Make sure the driveshaft-to-differential bolts are installed from the backside of the differential flange (the threaded portion of the bolt should be toward the front of the vehicle).
14. If equipped, tighten the center bearing bolts to 45 ft. lbs. (60 Nm).
15. Tighten the driveshaft-to-differential flange and driveshaft-to-transmission flange bolts and nuts to 46 ft. lbs. (63 Nm).
16. If necessary, install the transmission drain plug and fill the transmission until the fluid just starts to dribble out of the filler hole (make sure the dribble is not a by-product of a sloppy transmission filling technique—spillage while filling). Install the filler plug.
17. Lower the vehicle.

Transmission

REMOVAL & INSTALLATION

MSG-Type Transmissions

1981–88 PICK-UP AND TROOPER MODELS

♦ **See Figures 5, 6 and 7**

➡This procedure covers all 1981–88 Pick-Ups and Trooper models equipped with MSG-type transmissions.

1. Disconnect the negative battery cable.
2. Block the rear wheels from rolling and apply the parking brake, then raise and safely support the vehicle on jackstands.
3. Position a drain pan large enough to hold a minimum of 5–6 qts. (4.7–5.7L) under the transmission drain plug. Clean the dirt from around the drain and filler plugs, then remove the filler plug first. Remove the drain plug and allow the transmission to drain completely into the catch pan. Once the transmission is completely drained, install the filler and rain plugs hand-tight.
4. Remove the transmission gear shift lever and, if equipped, the transfer case gear shift lever. For more information, refer to the shift handle removal and installation procedures earlier in this section.
5. Remove the starter motor from the engine.
6. Detach the speedometer cable from the transmission by loosening the speedometer cable retaining ring and pulling the cable end out of the transmission. Be careful when pulling the cable out of the transmission, the speedometer gear may be damaged.
7. Matchmark the front, if applicable, and rear driveshafts to the differential flanges. Remove the front and rear driveshafts. For more details, refer to the driveshaft removal and installation procedures located later in this section.
8. Disconnect the clutch cable from the clutch lever. For more information, refer to the clutch linkage removal and installation procedures later in this section.
9. Remove the flywheel stone guard.
10. Remove the transfer case from the transmission, as described later in this section.

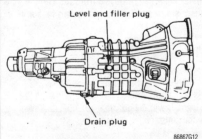

Fig. 5 Before removing the transmission, remove the filler plug and drain the transmission fluid into a catch pan

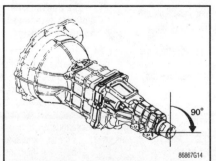

Fig. 6 To ease removal, rotate the transmission axially 90 degrees as shown

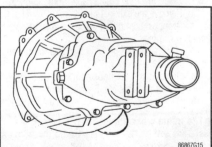

Fig. 7 When installing the transmission, turn the transmission on its right side as when the transmission was removed

11. Remove the transmission frame member mounting bolts, then lower the frame member off the vehicle. Move it aside.

※※ WARNING

Support the rear of the engine while the transmission is removed from the vehicle, otherwise the engine will shift and can cause damage to the engine mounts and other components.

12. Using an engine hoist, or similar supporting tool, support the rear of the engine from falling. Once the transmission is removed, the rear of the engine will have no support and will definitely fall.

13. Support the transmission with a transmission jack, or similar hydraulic floor jack, and remove the rear mount bolts and nuts.

14. Remove the transmission mounting bolts. Rotate the transmission assembly axially (around an axis which runs from the front of the vehicle to the back) 90 degrees clockwise to ease removal.

15. Slowly lower the transmission assembly out of the vehicle with the transmission jack.

To install:

16. Position the transmission at the rear of the engine with the transmission jack and with the transfer case side facing down. Slide the input shaft into the clutch disc hub and rotate the transmission 90 degrees counterclockwise along the same axis as when removed. Install the mounting bolts to 34 ft. lbs. (46 Nm).

17. Install the frame-to-rear housing mount bolts and tighten until secure.

18. Install the transfer case to the transmission by aligning the grooves in the shift arms and shift sleeves, while held in the **2H** position. Tighten the transfer case-to-transmission retaining bolts to 34 ft. lbs. (46 Nm).

19. Install the flywheel stone guard and clutch cable.

20. Install the driveshafts, making certain that the matchmarks on the differential flanges and driveshaft flanges align. If applicable, tighten the center bearing bolts to 46 ft. lbs. (65 Nm). Tighten the driveshaft-to-differential bolts to 22 ft. lbs. (30 Nm).

21. Install the speedometer cable, starter motor, shift levers and boots.

22. If not already done, install the drain plug. Remove the filler plug and refill the transmission with 30W SAE engine oil. Install the fill plug and tighten the fill plug and drain plug to 25 ft. lbs. (34 Nm).

23. Lower the vehicle and remove the wheel blocks.

24. Connect the negative battery cable.

1989–95 AMIGO AND PICK-UP MODELS

1. Disconnect the negative and positive battery cables.
2. Remove the battery.
3. Support the hood as far open as possible. If you choose to remove the hood, first matchmark the hood hinge plates with a felt-tipped marker.
4. Remove the console and shift boot. Unbolt the shift lever from the transmission case and remove it. Cover the quadrant box hole to prevent contaminants from entering the transmission.
5. Raise and support the vehicle safely.
6. Drain the transmission oil. Install the drain plug with a new washer.
7. If equipped with a two-piece driveshaft, remove the center bearing retainer bolts.
8. Matchmark the driveshaft to transmission and differential flanges. Remove the driveshaft.
9. Remove the starter.
10. Disconnect the speedometer cable.
11. Disconnect the clutch cable from the release fork.
12. Remove the exhaust pipe bracket from the transmission case. Disconnect the front exhaust pipe from the exhaust manifold and disconnect the second exhaust pipe.
13. Use a lifting chain or jack to support the engine. Support the transmission with a jack.
14. Remove the rear housing mount from the transmission. Remove the mount bracket from the No. 3 crossmember.
15. Remove the quadrant box from the transmission.

➡**The frame crossmember may interfere with transmission removal. An assistant will be helpful for shifting the transmission back and away from the engine.**

16. Position a jack under the transmission and remove the transmission case bolts. Move the transmission as far to the rear of the vehicle as possible to

clear the mainshaft. Then, lower the clutch housing end of the transmission toward the jack and lower the transmission from the vehicle.

To install:

17. Using a transmission jack, position the transmission-to-engine and tighten the retaining bolts to 28 ft. lbs. (37 Nm). Install the quadrant box.

18. Install the mount bracket and tighten the bolt to 27 ft. lbs. (37 Nm).

19. Install the frame-to-rear housing mount bolts at the No. 3 crossmember. Tighten the rear mount nut to 62 ft. lbs. (83 Nm).

20. Tighten the engine mount nuts to 30 ft. lbs. (40 Nm).

21. The balance of the installation is the reverse of removal.

MUA-Type Transmissions

1988–95 2WD AMIGO AND PICK-UP

1. Disconnect the negative and positive battery cables.
2. Remove the battery.
3. Support the hood as far open as possible. If you choose to remove the hood, first matchmark the hood hinge plates with a felt-tipped marker.
4. Remove the console and shift boot. Unbolt the shift lever from the transmission case and remove it. Cover the quadrant box hole to prevent contaminants from entering the transmission.
5. Raise and support the vehicle safely.
6. Drain the transmission oil. Install the drain plug with a new washer.
7. If equipped with a two-piece driveshaft, remove the center bearing retainer bolts.
8. Matchmark the driveshaft flanges to the differential and transmission flanges. Remove the driveshaft.
9. Remove the starter.
10. Disconnect the speedometer cable.
11. Unbolt the slave cylinder from the side of the transmission case. Don't disconnect the hydraulic line.
12. Remove the exhaust pipe bracket from the transmission case. Disconnect the front exhaust pipe from the exhaust manifold and the second exhaust pipe.
13. Support the engine with a lifting chain or jack. Support the transmission with a jack.
14. Remove the rear housing mount from the transmission. Remove the mount bracket from the third crossmember.
15. Remove the quadrant box from the transmission.

➡**The frame crossmember may interfere with transmission removal. An assistant will be helpful for shifting the transmission back and away from the engine.**

16. Position a jack under the transmission and remove the engine-to-transmission bolts. Move the transmission as far to the rear of the vehicle as possible, and then lower the clutch housing end of the transmission toward the jack.

To install:

17. Using a transmission jack, position the transmission-to-engine and tighten the retaining bolts to 28 ft. lbs. (37 Nm). Install the quadrant box.

18. Install the mount bracket and tighten the bolt to 27 ft. lbs. (37 Nm).

19. Install the frame-to-rear housing mount bolts at the No. 3 crossmember, and tighten to 62 ft. lbs. (83 Nm).

20. Tighten the engine mount nuts to 30 ft. lbs. (40 Nm).

21. The balance of the installation is the reverse of removal.

1988–95 4WD AMIGO AND PICK-UP

➡**The transmission and transfer case are removed from the vehicle as a unit. Once removed, the transmission and transfer case can be separated for servicing.**

1. Disconnect the negative and positive battery cables.
2. Remove the battery.
3. Support the hood as far open as possible. If you choose to remove the hood, first matchmark the hood hinge plates with a felt-tipped marker.
4. Remove the console and shift boots. Unbolt the shift levers from the transmission case and remove them. Cover the quadrant box hole to prevent contaminants from entering the transmission.
5. Raise and support the vehicle safely.
6. Drain the transmission oil. Install the drain plug with a new washer.
7. Remove the transfer case skid plates.
8. Disconnect the speedometer cable.

9. Remove the starter motor and the clutch slave cylinder. Don't disconnect the hydraulic lines.

10. Mark the driveshafts to the differential flanges and remove the front and rear driveshafts.

11. Remove the exhaust pipe bracket from the transmission case. Disconnect the front exhaust pipe from the exhaust manifold and the second exhaust pipe.

12. Support the engine with a lifting chain or jack.

13. Remove the crossmember and transmission mount.

14. Support the transmission with a jack.

15. Remove the transmission-to-engine bolts.

➡️**The frame crossmember may interfere with transmission removal. An assistant will be helpful for shifting the transmission back and away from the engine.**

16. Move the transmission toward the rear of the vehicle. Then, slowly lower it from the vehicle using the jack.

To install:

17. Raise the transmission into position.

18. With an assistant, install the transmission to the engine. Make sure the input shaft is splined properly into the clutch disc. Tighten the mounting bolts to 28 ft. lbs. (37 Nm).

19. Install the crossmember and tighten the mounting bolts to 27 ft. lbs. (37 Nm).

20. Install the transmission mount and tighten the nut to 62 ft. lbs. (83 Nm).

21. The balance of the installation is the reverse of removal.

1988–91 TROOPER

➡️**The transfer case is an integral part of the transmission housing. Although the 2 cases can be separated, the transfer case should be removed with the transmission.**

1. Disconnect the negative battery cable. Drain the transmission and transfer case oil.

2. Remove the transfer case undercover, starter motor, speedometer cable and gear shift levers.

3. Remove the front exhaust pipes (2.8L V6 only).

4. Mark the driveshafts to the flanges and remove the front and rear driveshafts.

5. Leave the clutch slave cylinder fluid hose connected and remove the cylinder from the transmission and support it out of the way.

6. Raise the transmission slightly with a jack and remove the crossmember and transmission mount. Support the engine with an adjustable stand.

7. Remove the transmission mounting bolts.

8. With an assistant, remove the transmission/transfer case as an assembly.

To install:

9. With an assistant, raise the transmission to the rear of the engine and install the transmission mounting bolts. Make sure the input shaft splines align properly with the clutch disc.

10. Install the clutch slave cylinder and crossmember.

11. Install the front exhaust pipe on vehicles equipped with 2.8L engine.

12. Install the front and rear driveshafts in the marked locations.

13. Install the speedometer cable, starter motor and gear shift lever.

14. Refill the transmission and transfer case with the specified amount of SAE 30 oil.

15. Install the undercover and connect the negative battery cable.

1992–96 TROOPER

♦ **See Figures 8 thru 14**

➡️**The transfer case is an integral part of the transmission housing. Although the 2 cases can be separated, the transfer case should be removed with the transmission.**

1. Shift the transmission into **N**. Shift the transfer case into **2H** and drive the vehicle forward and backward a few feet/meters to make sure the front axle is not engaged.

2. Use a felt–tipped marker to matchmark the hood to the hood hinges. Remove the hood.

3. Disconnect the negative battery cable.

4. Remove the shift knobs and the console and shift boots.

5. Remove the shift lever and the transfer case shift lever, by unbolting their mounting plates from the transmission case.

6. Raise and safely support the vehicle.

7. Drain the transmission fluid.

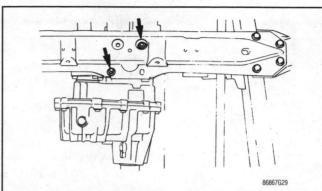

Fig. 8 Locations of the 2 rear transfer case-to-vehicle frame attaching bolts

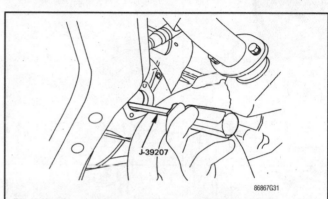

Fig. 9 Use the special tool J-39207, or equivalent, to disconnect the clutch release bearing from the clutch pressure plate

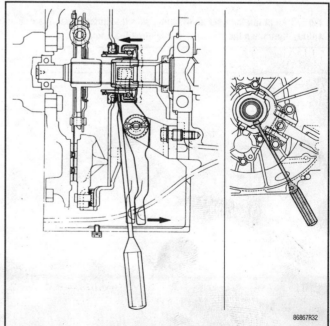

Fig. 10 Insert J-39207, between the wedge collar and the release bearing, then . . .

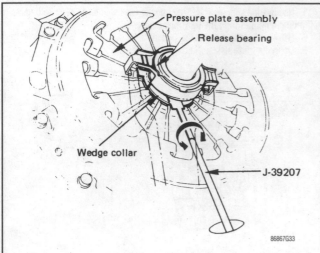

Fig. 11 . . . twist the tool to separate the release bearing from the pressure plate

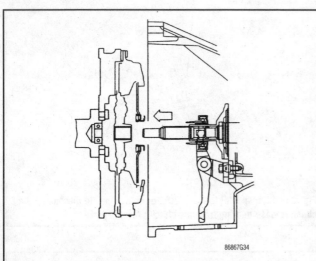

Fig. 12 Align the top gear shaft spline with the clutch driven plate spline, then push the transmission against the engine

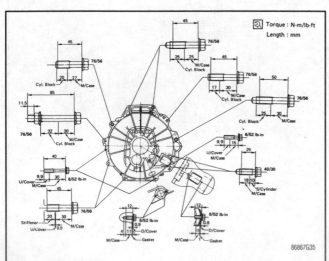

Fig. 13 When installing the transmission-to-engine bolts, make sure they are installed in their proper locations

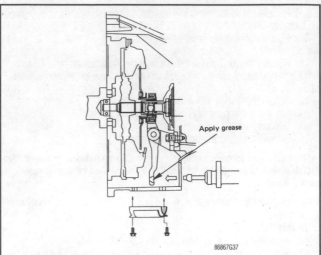

Fig. 14 Apply grease to the top hole portion of the shift fork, then install the slave cylinder

8. Remove the exhaust and transfer case skid plates.

9. Label and disconnect the oxygen sensor connectors from the transmission harness.

10. Remove the catalytic converter, left front, and center exhaust pipes.

11. Remove the harness heat protector.

12. Remove the slave cylinder heat protector. Unbolt and remove the slave cylinder. Don't disconnect the hydraulic line.

13. Remove the slave cylinder dust covers.

14. Matchmark the driveshafts at the their flanges. Unbolt and remove the driveshafts.

15. Label and disconnect the reverse light switch, 4WD indicator switch, and 1–2 and 3–4 indicator switch harness connectors.

16. Disconnect the speed sensor harness connector.

17. Remove the 2 harness clamps from the transmission case.

18. Using a transmission jack, raise the transmission slightly. Remove the 2 rear transmission mounting nuts.

19. Remove the center crossmember (8 bolts).

20. Attach a chain hoist to the engine lifting brackets, but don't raise the engine yet.

21. Remove the front crossmember.

➡**Make sure the engine assembly is properly supported when removing the front crossmember.**

22. Remove the 3 flywheel inspection cover bolts.

23. Use the clutch release bearing remover J–39207, or an equivalent, pry tool to release the bearing from the pressure plate. Push the release fork toward the rear of the vehicle. Insert the tool between the release bearing and the pressure plate collar. Move the lever toward the rear to pry.

24. Raise the engine slightly with a chain hoist and remove the bolts and nuts securing the transmission to the engine.

25. Carefully pull the transmission rearward. Lower the transmission from the vehicle.

To install:

➡**Make sure the transmission dowel pins are installed in the correct position. If the dowels are in the wrong hole, the transmission case may crack.**

26. Apply a thin coating of molybdenum grease to the spline of the input shaft, slowly raise the transmission into position with the rear of the engine. Align the splines of the input shaft with the grooves of the clutch disc hub and install the transmission to the engine.

➡**It may be helpful the put the transmission in gear and rotate the driveshaft flange so the input shaft will turn and engage the grooves in the clutch disc hub.**

27. Install the transmission case bolts. Tighten the upper 6 bolts to 56 ft. lbs. (76 Nm). Tighten the 2 remaining large bolts to 56 ft. lbs. (76 Nm). Tighten the remaining 3 bolts to 5.2 inch lbs. (6 Nm).

28. Push the release bearing fork rearward with a force of 13–18 lbs. (59–78 N) to engage the release bearing with the pressure plate. A click sound will be heard when the bearing engages the pressure plate properly.
29. Install the flywheel inspection cover.
30. Install the front crossmember and the front driveshaft. Tighten the crossmember bolts to 58 ft. lbs. (78 Nm). Tighten the driveshaft flange bolts to 46 ft. lbs. (60 Nm).
31. Install the rear crossmember and mount. Tighten the crossmember mounting bolts to 37 ft. lbs. (50 Nm) and the transmission mounting nuts to 30 ft. lbs. (41 Nm).
32. Remove the transmission jack and the engine hoist.
33. The balance of the installation is the reverse of removal.

1991 RODEO

1. Disconnect the negative battery cable.
2. Remove the engine hood and cooling fan. Place the fan on the fan guide.
3. Place the shift lever in Neutral, pull up the shift lever grommet and dust cover. Remove the gear shift lever. Cover the opening with a rag to prevent dirt from entering the transmission.
4. Remove the suspension crossmember.
5. Remove the starter motor assembly.
6. Remove the clutch slave cylinder from the transmission. Be careful not to allow the cylinder piston from falling out of the bore.
7. Remove the rear driveshaft.
8. Disconnect the exhaust pipe from the manifold and catalytic converter and remove the pipe.
9. Disconnect all electrical connectors and speedometer cable from the transmission.
10. Remove the flywheel dust cover.
11. Attach an engine lifting cable to the engine hanger and take the engine weight off the crossmember. Remove the center crossmember.
12. Install a transmission jack under the transmission and remove the retaining nuts and bolts. Remove the assembly from the vehicle.

To install:

13. Install a transmission jack under the transmission and install the transmission into the vehicle. Install the retaining nuts and bolts.
14. Install the center crossmember. Lower the engine onto the crossmember. Install the retaining nuts and bolts.
15. Install the flywheel dust cover.
16. Connect all electrical connectors and speedometer cable to the transmission.
17. Connect the exhaust pipe to the manifold and catalytic converter.
18. Install the rear driveshaft.
19. Install the clutch slave cylinder to the transmission. Be careful not to allow the cylinder piston from falling out of the bore.
20. Install the starter motor assembly.
21. Install the suspension crossmember.
22. Install the gear shift lever.
23. Install the engine hood and cooling fan.
24. Connect the negative battery cable and check operation.

1992–96 RODEO

➡The transfer case is an integral part of the transmission housing. Although the 2 cases can be separated, the transfer case should be removed with the transmission.

1. Shift the transmission into **N**. Shift the transfer case into **2H** and drive the vehicle forward and backward a few feet/meters to make sure the front axle is not engaged.
2. Use a felt–tipped marker to matchmark the hood to the hood hinges. Remove the hood.
3. Disconnect the negative battery cable.
4. Remove the shift knobs and the console and shift boots.
5. Remove the shift lever and the transfer case shift lever (if equipped), by unbolting their mounting plates from the transmission case.
6. Raise and safely support the vehicle.
7. Drain the oil from the transmission and transfer case.

8. Remove the exhaust and transfer case skid plates.
9. Disconnect the oxygen sensor connector from the transmission harness.
10. Unbolt the exhaust flanges. Separate and remove the catalytic converter, left front, and center exhaust pipes.
11. Remove the harness heat protector.
12. Remove the slave cylinder heat protector. Unbolt and remove the slave cylinder. Don't disconnect the hydraulic line.
13. Remove the slave cylinder dust covers.
14. Matchmark the driveshafts at the flanges and remove them.
15. Disconnect the reverse light switch, 4WD indicator switch, 1–2 and 3–4 indicator switch harness connectors.
16. Disconnect the speed sensor harness connector.
17. Remove the 2 harness clamps from the transmission case.
18. Attach a chain hoist to the engine.
19. Using a transmission jack, raise the transmission slightly. Remove the 2 rear transmission mounting nuts.
20. Remove the center crossmember (8 bolts).
21. On 4WD vehicles, remove the front crossmember and the front driveshaft.

➡**Make sure the engine assembly is properly supported when removing the front crossmember.**

22. Remove the 3 flywheel inspection cover bolts.
23. Use clutch release bearing remover J–39207 or an equivalent pry tool to release the bearing from the pressure plate. Push the release fork toward the rear of the vehicle. Insert the tool between the release bearing and the pressure plate collar. Move the lever to the rear to pry.
24. Raise the engine slightly with a chain hoist and remove the bolts and nuts securing the transmission to the engine.
25. Carefully pull the transmission rearward. Lower the transmission from the vehicle.

To install:

26. Apply a thin coating of molybdenum grease to the splines of the input shaft, and then slowly raise the transmission into position against the rear of the engine. Align the splines of the input shaft with the grooves of the clutch disc hub and install the transmission to the engine.

➡**It may be helpful the put the transmission in gear and rotate the driveshaft flange so the input shaft will turn and engage the grooves in the clutch disc hub.**

27. Install the transmission case bolts. Tighten the upper 6 bolts to 56 ft. lbs. (76 Nm). Tighten the 2 remaining large bolts to 56 ft. lbs. (76 Nm). Tighten the remaining 3 bolts to 4.4 ft. lbs. (6 Nm).
28. Push the release bearing fork rearward with a force of 13–18 lbs. (59–78 N) to engage the release bearing with the pressure plate. A click sound will be heard when the bearing engages the pressure plate properly.
29. Install the flywheel inspection cover.
30. On 4WD vehicles, install the front crossmember and the front driveshaft. Tighten the crossmember bolts to 58 ft. lbs. (78 Nm). Tighten the driveshaft flange bolts to 46 ft. lbs. (60 Nm).
31. Install the center crossmember and transmission mount. Tighten the center crossmember mounting bolts to 37 ft. lbs. (50 Nm) and the transmission mounting nuts to 30 ft. lbs. (41 Nm).
32. Remove the transmission jack and the engine hoist.
33. The balance of the installation is the reverse of removal.

Borg-Warner T5R Transmission

RODEO MODELS

➡**The transfer case is an integral part of the transmission housing. Although the 2 cases can be separated, the transfer case should be removed with the transmission.**

1. Disconnect the negative battery cable.
2. Shift the transmission into Neutral. Remove the gearshift and transfer case shift knobs.
3. Remove the 4 console screws and lift the console and shift boot over the shift levers.

4. Unbolt and remove the shift lever and its cover plate from the transmission case. If equipped, remove the transfer case shift lever.

5. Raise and safely support the vehicle.

6. Drain the transmission oil.

7. Disconnect and remove the starter.

8. Unbolt the slave cylinder from the transmission case. Don't disconnect the hydraulic line.

9. Matchmark the driveshaft U–joints to the transmission and differential flanges.

10. If the vehicle is equipped with 4WD; matchmark the front driveshaft U–joints to the differential and transfer case.

➡**On 4WD vehicles, the transfer case skid plates and front exhaust pipe must be removed before removing the front driveshaft.**

11. Remove the driveshaft and the center bearing.

12. Disconnect the front exhaust pipe from the manifold and the catalytic converter. It is not necessary to remove the exhaust pipe from the chassis.

13. Disconnect the reverse and neutral switch connectors from the transmission.

14. Disconnect the speedometer cable or speed sensor connector from the transmission.

15. Remove the flywheel inspection cover.

16. Support the transmission with a transmission jack.

17. Raise the transmission slightly so the jack supports its weight.

18. Support the rear of the engine with a jack or chain hoist.

19. Unbolt and remove the center crossmember and the transmission mount.

20. With the engine and transmission supported, remove the bolts securing the transmission case to the engine.

21. Pull the transmission away from the engine so the mainshaft clears the pressure plate. Remove the transmission from the vehicle.

To install:

22. Apply a thin coating of molybdenum grease to the splines of the mainshaft and raise the transmission to the rear of the engine. Align the shaft splines with the clutch driven plate splines. Push the transmission toward the engine to engage the splines of the mainshaft with the grooves in the clutch disc hub. Install the mounting bolts and nuts.

23. Tighten the 10mm transmission case bolts and nuts to 28–30 ft. lbs. (37–40 Nm). Tighten the 6mm bolts to 4.4 ft. lbs. (6 Nm).

24. Install the center crossmember to the frame. Then, install the transmission mount. Tighten the crossmember bolts to 56 ft. lbs. (76 Nm) and the mount nuts to 30 ft. lbs. (41 Nm).

25. Remove the transmission jack and engine lifting equipment.

26. The balance of the installation is the reverse of removal.

CLUTCH

✳✳ CAUTION

The clutch driven disc may contain asbestos, which has been determined to be a cancer causing agent. Never clean the clutch surfaces with compressed air! Avoid inhaling any dust from any clutch surface! When cleaning clutch surfaces, use a commercially available brake cleaning fluid.

Adjustments

LINKAGE

➡**The hydraulic clutch system found on later model Isuzu trucks and Sport Utility vehicles is self-adjusting and does not require period servicing.**

Clutch Cable

◆ **See Figure 15**

1. Open the hood and from inside the engine compartment, pull the outer clutch cable toward the front of the truck.

2. While holding the clutch cable in this position, turn the adjusting nut inward until the rubber lip on the washer damper is pushed against the firewall.

3. From inside the vehicle, depress and release the clutch pedal 3 times.

4. From the engine compartment, while once again pulling the outer cable forward, fully tighten the adjusting nut until the rubber lip is pressed against the firewall and loosen the adjusting nut until there is 0.20 in. (5mm) between the rubber washer damper and the adjusting nut.

5. Release the outer cable and tighten the locknut to secure the adjusting nut.

PEDAL HEIGHT & FREE-PLAY

Hydraulic Clutch Control System

◆ **See Figure 16**

RODEO AND TROOPER MODELS—WITH CLUTCH SWITCH

◆ **See Figure 17**

1. Disconnect the negative battery cable.

2. Remove the instrument panel lower cover, the driver knee bolster panel assembly and the vent duct.

3. Detach the clutch switch connector from the clutch switch.

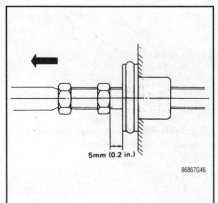

Fig. 15 Adjust the outer cable until there is 0.20 in. (5mm) clearance between the adjusting nut and the rubber washer—the arrow points toward the front of the vehicle

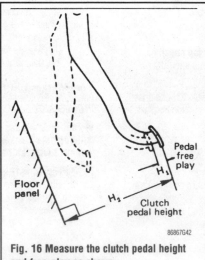

Fig. 16 Measure the clutch pedal height and free-play as shown

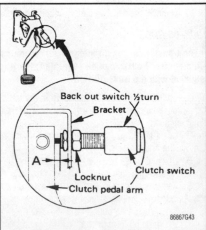

Fig. 17 The clutch switch clearance measurement should be measured at A—1996 Rodeo models

4. Loosen the clutch switch locknut, then turn the switch out until there is a gap between the switch plunger and the clutch pedal.

5. Loosen the clutch master cylinder pushrod locknut. Turn the pushrod by hand to set the clutch pedal height (H_2) to within specification, as follows:
- 1991–93 Rodeo with I4 engine—6.73–7.13 in. (171–181mm)
- 1991–92 Rodeo with V6 engine—7.6–8.0 in. (192–202mm)
- 1993–96 Rodeo with V6 engine—7.64–8.03 in. (194–204mm)
- 1994–96 Rodeo with I4 engine—7.28–7.68 in. (18.5–19.5cm)
- 1988 Trooper II—6.4–6.8 in. (163.5–173.5mm)
- 1989–90 Trooper/Trooper II—9.15–9.55 in. (232.5–242.5mm)
- 1991–96 Trooper—8.602–8.996 in. (218.5–228.5mm)

6. Tighten the pushrod locknut.

7. For 1990–96 models, turn the clutch switch until the switch bolt just touches the clutch pedal arm.

8. For 1989 models, turn the clutch switch until the switch plunger is fully retracted against the clutch pedal arm.

9. For 1990–96 models, adjust the clutch switch by backing it out ½ turn, then measure the clearance (A) between the clutch pedal arm and the clutch switch bolt end. The clutch switch bolt and clutch pedal clearance should be 0.020–0.059 in. (0.5–1.5mm).

10. For 1989 models, back the switch out ½ turn.

11. Tighten the clutch switch locknut.

12. Attach the clutch switch connector.

13. After adjusting the pedal height, push the clutch pedal by hand to ensure the clutch pedal free-play (H_1) is within specifications. The clutch pedal free-play should be 0.20–0.59 in. (5–15mm).

RODEO AND TROOPER MODELS—WITHOUT CLUTCH SWITCH

♦ See Figure 18

1. Disconnect the negative battery cable.

2. Remove the instrument panel lower cover, the driver knee bolster panel assembly and the vent duct.

3. Loosen the clutch pedal adjusting bolt so there is enough gap between the clutch pedal and the adjusting bolt to allow pushrod adjustment.

4. Loosen the clutch master cylinder pushrod locknut. Turn the pushrod by hand to set the clutch pedal height (H_2) to within specification, as follows:
- 1991–93 Rodeo with I4 engine—6.73–7.13 in. (171–181mm)
- 1991–92 Rodeo with V6 engine—7.6–8.0 in. (192–202mm)
- 1993–96 Rodeo with V6 engine—7.64–8.03 in. (194–204mm)
- 1994–96 Rodeo with I4 engine—7.28–7.68 in. (18.5–19.5cm)
- 1988 Trooper II—6.4–6.8 in. (163.5–173.5mm)
- 1989–90 Trooper/Trooper II—9.15–9.55 in. (232.5–242.5mm)
- 1991–96 Trooper—8.602–8.996 in. (218.5–228.5mm)

5. Tighten the pushrod locknut.

6. Turn the adjusting bolt until it just touches the clutch pedal arm.

7. For 1990–96 models, adjust the clutch pedal adjusting bolt by backing it out ½ turn, and measure the clearance between the clutch pedal arm and the clutch pedal adjusting bolt. The clearance should be 0.20–0.59 in. (0.5–1.5mm).

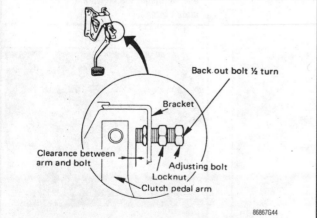

Fig. 18 For vehicles without a clutch switch, the adjusting bolt-to-clutch pedal arm should be 0.020–0.059 in. (0.5–1.5mm)

8. Tighten the adjusting bolt locknut.

9. After adjusting the pedal height, push the clutch pedal by hand to ensure the clutch pedal free-play (H_1) is within specifications. The clutch pedal free-play should be 0.20–0.59 in. (5–15mm).

PICK-UP AND AMIGO MODELS

♦ See Figures 16 and 19

1. Loosen the clutch pedal adjusting bolt (3) or clutch switch.

2. Loosen the clutch master cylinder pushrod locknut (2).

3. Turn the pushrod by hand to set the clutch pedal height (H_2) to within specifications. The height specifications are as follows:
- 1992–95 models with 2.6L engine—6.73–7.13 in. (171–181mm)
- 1992–95 models with 3.1L or 2.3L engine—7.28–7.68 in. (185–195mm)
- 1990–91 models—6.73–7.13 in. (171–181mm)
- 1988–89 models—7.28–7.68 in. (185–195mm)

4. Tighten the pushrod locknut (2).

5. Turn the adjusting bolt, or clutch switch until it just touches the clutch pedal arm, then back it out ½ turn on 1992–95 models or to 0.020–0.039 in. (0.5–1.0mm) for 1988–91 models (distance L).

6. There should be clearance between the arm and the end of the bolt.

➡ Clutch pedal free-play and pedal stroke are self-adjusting and do not require manual adjustment.

Cable Clutch Control System

♦ See Figure 16

1. Loosen the clutch pedal adjusting bolt.

2. Turn the adjusting bolt by hand to set the clutch pedal height (H_2) to within specification. The pedal height specification is as follows:
- 1992–95 Pick-Up and Amigo with 2.6L engine—6.7–7.1 in. (171–181mm)
- 1992–95 Pick-Up and Amigo with 3.1L or 2.3L engine—7.3–7.7 in. (185–195mm)
- 1988–91 Pick-Up and Amigo—7.3–7.7 in. (185–195mm)
- 1985–87 Pick-Up—8.12–8.51 in. (206–216mm)
- 1981–84 Pick-Up—6.5–6.8 in. (164–174mm)
- 1987 Trooper II—9.1–9.5 in. (231–241mm)
- 1985–86 Trooper II—8.12–8.51 in. (206–216mm)

3. After setting the clutch pedal height, adjust the clutch cable linkage. For more details, refer to the clutch linkage adjustment procedure earlier in this section.

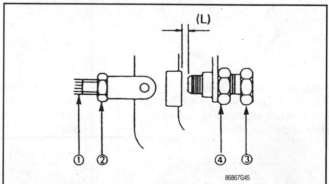

Fig. 19 The adjusting bolt and master cylinder pushrod—(1) master cylinder pushrod, (2) pushrod locknut, (3) adjusting bolt, (4) adjusting bolt locknut and (L) gap between adjusting bolt and clutch pedal arm

Driven Disc and Pressure Plate

REMOVAL & INSTALLATION

♦ See Figures 20 thru 30

1. Remove the transmission from the vehicle. For more information, refer to the procedures earlier in this section.

2. Mark the clutch assembly position on the flywheel with paint or by a similar method.

3. Install a clutch aligning tool (or drive plate aligner), or equivalent, and remove the pressure plate retaining bolts in a crisscross fashion.

4. Remove the pressure plate assembly from the flywheel.

5. Remove the driven disc from the flywheel.

❊❊ WARNING

Do not allow oil or grease to come in contact with the working face of the clutch driven plate.

6. Inspect all parts for wear or deep scoring. Replace any parts that show excessive wear.

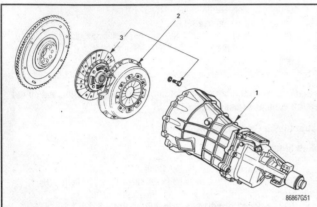

Fig. 20 Exploded view of a common clutch assembly drive disc and pressure plate

To install:

➡️ Due to clutch friction, the engine flywheel becomes scored. Putting a new clutch with an old flywheel can cause chatter and premature clutch plate wear. It is good insurance to remove the flywheel and have it resurfaced at a qualified machine shop. You have spent a lot of time removing the clutch assembly and you do not want to do it twice.

7. Clean the flywheel surface, the facing surface, and the pressure plate surfaces.

8. Use the clutch aligning tool to install the driven plate assembly onto the flywheel.

9. Align the pressure plate assembly with the flywheel knock pin.

10. Install the pressure plate assembly against the flywheel, then tighten the clutch cover bolts a little at a time in the sequence shown in the illustration. Tighten the pressure plate assembly bolts to 13 ft. lbs. (18 ft. lbs.).

11. Remove the clutch aligning tool from the rear of the engine.

12. Install the transmission, as previously described in this section.

Clutch Master Cylinder

REMOVAL & INSTALLATION

◆ See Figure 31

❊❊ WARNING

The hydraulic clutch system utilizes DOT 3 brake fluid, which will eat through the vehicle's paint. Clean up any spills immediately.

1. Disconnect the negative battery cable.

2. From inside the vehicle, disconnect the master cylinder pushrod from the clutch pedal.

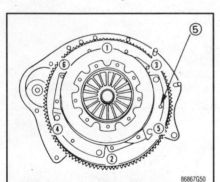

Fig. 21 For pressure plate assemblies with 6 mounting bolts, loosen and tighten the bolts in this sequence—(5) is the aligning pin on the flywheel

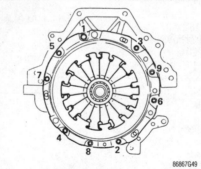

Fig. 22 For pressure plate assemblies with 9 mounting bolts, make certain to loosen and tighten the bolts in the sequence shown

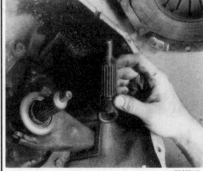

Fig. 23 View of the clutch alignment arbor, used to install the clutch and pressure plate assembly

Fig. 24 Removing the clutch and pressure plate bolts

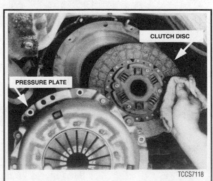

Fig. 25 Removing the clutch and pressure plate

Fig. 26 Check across the flywheel surface, it should be flat

✳✳ WARNING

After disconnecting the fluid lines from the clutch component, immediately plug the line. The brake fluid in the system will absorb moisture, which will decrease the system's effectiveness.

3. Using a flare nut wrench, remove the fluid line from the master cylinder. Immediately plug the clutch fluid line to prevent contamination of the clutch hydraulic system.

4. Remove the cylinder retaining bolts from the firewall and remove the cylinder.

To install:

5. Install the master cylinder to the firewall. Tighten the mounting bolts to 12 ft. lbs. (16 Nm).

6. Using a flare nut wrench, install the fluid line to the master cylinder. Make certain not to crossthread the flare fitting in the master cylinder. Start the fitting into the master cylinder first by hand, then tighten the fitting with the flare nut wrench.

7. From inside the vehicle, connect the master cylinder pushrod to the clutch pedal.

8. Connect the negative battery cable.

9. Bleed the clutch hydraulic system.

Damper Cylinder

REMOVAL & INSTALLATION

▶ See Figure 31

Some newer models equipped with V6 engines utilize a damper cylinder to prevent the shift fork from snapping back into place if the clutch pedal is released suddenly. It acts as a sort of brake fluid filled shock absorber for the clutch system.

1. To ascertain whether your particular vehicle is equipped with a damper cylinder, trace the clutch master cylinder fluid lines until they are threaded into a component. If this component is mounted on the transmission and is only equipped with 1 fluid line, it is the slave cylinder and your vehicle is not equipped with damper cylinder. If, however, the next component down the clutch lines from the master cylinder is mounted to a frame rail or the lower section of the firewall and is attached to 2 or 3 fluid lines, it is the damper cylinder. If equipped with 3 fluid lines, 1 of the fluid lines should lead to the damper cylinder bleeder valve.

2. Using a flare nut wrench, disconnect and plug all 3 fluid lines from the cylinder.

3. Remove the damper cylinder mounting bracket bolts and remove the cylinder from the vehicle.

To install:

4. Position the damper cylinder in place, install the mounting bolts and tighten until secure.

5. Attach all 3 fluid lines to the damper cylinder. Thread the flare fitting of the fluid lines in carefully by hand to avoid crossthreading them. Once adequately started, use the flare nut wrench to tighten the fittings.

6. Bleed the clutch system.

Clutch Slave Cylinder

REMOVAL & INSTALLATION

▶ See Figure 32

✳✳ WARNING

The hydraulic clutch system utilizes DOT 3 brake fluid, which will eat through the vehicle's paint. Clean up any spills immediately.

Fig. 27 Checking the pressure plate for excessive wear

Fig. 28 Install a clutch alignment arbor, to align the clutch assembly during installation

Fig. 29 Clutch plate installed with the arbor in place

Fig. 30 Be sure to use an torque wrench to tighten all bolts

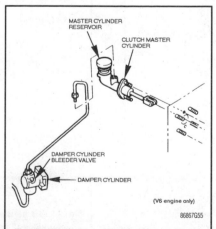

Fig. 31 View of a common master cylinder and a damper cylinder (V6 engines only)

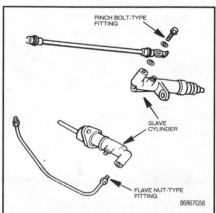

Fig. 32 The slave cylinder fluid line fittings will be either of the flare nut fitting type (left) or the pinch bolt type (right)

1. Disconnect the negative battery cable.

✳✳ WARNING

After disconnecting the fluid lines from the clutch component, immediately plug the line. The brake fluid in the system will absorb moisture, which will decrease the system's effectiveness.

2. Using a flare nut wrench (for systems equipped with flare fittings) or a socket and ratchet wrench (for systems equipped with pinch bolt fittings), remove the fluid line from the slave cylinder. Immediately plug the clutch hydraulic fluid line to prevent excessive clutch fluid leakage or system contamination.

3. Remove the cylinder retaining bolts from the clutch housing and carefully pull the slave cylinder from the transmission housing. Make certain that the slave cylinder separates from the shift fork.

To install:

4. Install the cylinder, making sure the slave cylinder pushrod is correctly seated against the shift fork, and retaining bolts to the transmission housing. Tighten the slave cylinder bolts until secure.

5. Using a flare nut wrench, install the fluid line to the slave cylinder. Some fluid lines utilize a pinch bolt instead of a conventional brake line fitting. Tighten the fitting/pinch bolt until secure.

6. Connect the cylinder pushrod to the clutch release fork.

7. Bleed the clutch hydraulic system.

HYDRAULIC SYSTEM BLEEDING

Models Without a Damper Cylinder

▶ **See Figure 33**

1. Remove the clutch master cylinder reservoir cap.

2. Fill the reservoir with fresh, clean DOT 3 brake fluid to the top, then reinstall the cap.

3. Apply the parking brake and block the rear wheels. Raise and safely support the front of the vehicle with jackstands.

4. Install a vinyl tube to the bleeder screw and insert the other end of the tube into a transparent container.

5. Have an assistant pump the clutch pedal repeatedly, then hold it depressed.

6. From under the vehicle, remove the rubber cap from the bleeder valve, open the slave cylinder bleeder screw to release the clutch fluid with bubbles into the container, then tighten the bleeder screw immediately.

7. Have the assistant release the clutch pedal slowly. If the clutch pedal is released while the bleeder screw is open, air will be sucked into the clutch system, necessitating even more bleeding.

8. Inspect the clutch master cylinder level; pour more brake fluid into the reservoir if the level falls below the full mark.

➡ **Never allow the clutch master cylinder to run dry.**

9. Repeat Steps 5 through 8 until the fluid released out through the bleeder screw is free of bubbles. This may take several times of releasing the clutch fluid, especially if a large quantity of fluid leaked out of the fluid lines during servicing.

10. Lower the vehicle and remove the rear wheel blocks.

Models With a Damper Cylinder

▶ **See Figures 33 and 34**

A damper cylinder is used on some of the newer vehicles equipped with V6 engines. It is bled in the same manner as the slave cylinder. The damper cylinder keeps the clutch shift fork from snapping back into place too quick when the clutch pedal is released rapidly.

1. Open the hood.

2. Remove the clutch master cylinder reservoir cap.

3. Fill the reservoir with fresh, clean DOT 3 brake fluid to the top, then reinstall the cap.

4. Remove the rubber cap from the damper cylinder bleeder valve. Install a vinyl tube to the bleeder screw on the damper cylinder and insert the other end of the tube into a transparent container.

5. Have an assistant pump the clutch pedal repeatedly, then hold it depressed.

6. Open the damper cylinder bleeder screw to release the clutch fluid with bubbles into the container, then tighten the bleeder screw immediately.

7. Have the assistant release the clutch pedal slowly. If the clutch pedal is released while the bleeder screw is open, air will be sucked into the clutch system, necessitating even more bleeding.

8. Inspect the clutch master cylinder level; pour more brake fluid into the reservoir if the level falls below the full mark.

➡ **Never allow the clutch master cylinder to run dry.**

9. Repeat Steps 5 through 8 until the fluid released out through the bleeder screw is free of bubbles. This may take several times of releasing the clutch fluid, especially if a large quantity of fluid leaked out of the fluid lines during servicing.

10. Install the rubber cap onto the damper cylinder bleeder valve.

11. Apply the parking brake and block the rear wheels. Raise and safely support the front of the vehicle with jackstands.

12. Install the vinyl tube onto the slave cylinder bleeder screw and insert the other end of the tube into a transparent container.

13. Repeat Steps 5 through 9 for the slave cylinder.

14. Install the rubber cap on the slave cylinder bleeder valve.

15. Lower the vehicle, remove the rear wheel blocks and close the hood.

16. Test drive the vehicle to ensure that the clutch system is working properly.

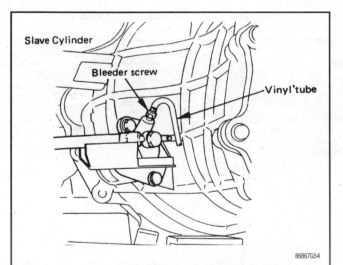

Fig. 33 The bleeder valve location on a common slave cylinder—the exact location may vary slightly from model to model

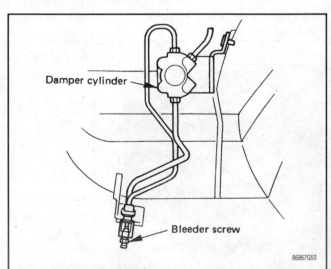

Fig. 34 This particular damper cylinder is equipped with a remote bleeder valve (3 fluid lines)

AUTOMATIC TRANSMISSION

Identification

There are generally 3 automatic transmissions available in the 1981–96 Isuzu trucks and Sport Utility vehicles. The first transmission, or actually family of transmissions, is the AW03 type. There were four AW03 transmissions available: the AW03–55, the AW03–70, the AW03–75 and the AW03–72L (lock-up torque converter). All of the AW03 transmissions were only available in the Pick-Up and Amigo models. The AW03–55 and AW03–70 were available from 1981 through 1987. The AW03–75 was only available in 1986–87. The AW03–72L took over the AW03 line of transmissions in 1988 and continued being the only AW03 transmission through 1995.

The second transmission available was the AW30–80LE transmission. This particular transmission was available in the Pick-Up during 1988–89. The AW30–80LE was also available in the 1988–91 Trooper/Trooper II models.

The last transmission available in the Isuzu line of trucks and Sport Utility vehicles was, and still is, the Turbo Hydra-Matic 4L30-E transmission. This transmission was, and is, available in the Rodeo models and the 1992–96 Trooper models.

Fluid Pan

REMOVAL & INSTALLATION

For the removal and installation of the transmission fluid pan, refer to Section 1 under the Fluids and Lubricants portion.

FILTER SERVICE

For the transmission fluid filter servicing procedures, please refer to Section 1.

Adjustments

THROTTLE LINKAGE

1981–87 Models

WITH GASOLINE ENGINES

▶ See Figures 35 and 36

1. Open the hood and remove the air cleaner housing.
2. Loosen the throttle valve control cable adjusting nuts.
3. Check that the carburetor throttle adjusting screw is in contact with the stopper for normal idling.

➡**If the adjusting screw is not resting on the stopper, the fast idle mechanism is working and setting of the adjusting screw should be performed to obtain normal idling.**

4. To obtain normal idling, perform the following procedure:
   a. Disconnect the battery ground cable.
   b. Remove the air cleaner cover, if not already done.

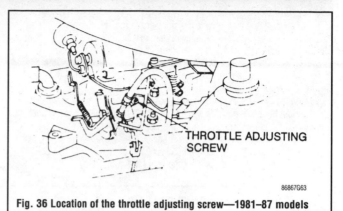

Fig. 36 Location of the throttle adjusting screw—1981–87 models with gasoline engines

   c. Fully depress and release the accelerator pedal to place the choke in the wide open position; do not depress the pedal again.
   d. Check that the throttle adjusting screw is in contact with the stopper.
   e. Install the air cleaner housing.
   f. Connect the battery cable.
5. Remove the rubber boot from the outer cable and turn the adjusting nuts to bring the outer cable setting to within 0.032–0.059 in. (0.8–1.5mm). Once this clearance is achieved, tighten the adjusting nuts. The proper clearance should be measured between the outer cable end and the inner cable stopper.
6. After adjusting the throttle cable, check that the inner cable stroke is 1.30–1.36 in. (32.9–33.9mm) from the closed position of the throttle valve to the wide open position.
7. Install the rubber boot onto the outer cable.

WITH DIESEL ENGINES

▶ See Figure 37

➡**Normal idling position can not be obtained with the air conditioner operating and the engine coolant temperature higher than 59°F (15°C).**

1. Loosen the throttle valve control cable adjusting nuts.
2. Have an assistant fully depress the accelerator pedal to place the injection pump lever in contact with the maximum speed adjusting screw, then hold the lever in that position.
3. If the injection pump lever is not in contact with the adjusting screw, adjust the accelerator linkage.
4. Turn the outer cable adjusting nuts to adjust the outer cable setting to 0.032–0.059 in. (0.8–1.5mm) and tighten the adjusting nuts; the setting is the distance between the upper face of the rubber boot, on the end of the outer cable, and the inner cable stopper.
5. After adjusting, check that the inner cable stroke, from the normal idling position to the maximum speed position is 1.30–1.36 in. (32.9–33.9mm).

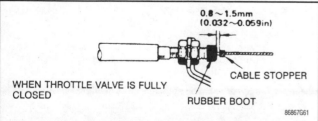

Fig. 35 Adjust the throttle valve cable so there is 0.032–0.059 in. (0.8–1.5mm) clearance between the rubber boot and the cable stopper—1981–87 models with gasoline engines

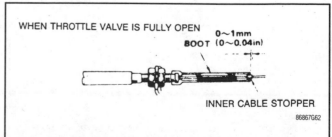

Fig. 37 The throttle cable free-play should be between 0–0.04 in. (0–1mm)—Diesel engines

1988–90 Models

▶ See Figure 38

1. Open the hood and remove the air cleaner housing.
2. Have an assistant depress the accelerator pedal all the way to the floor. Check that the throttle valve in the carburetor opens fully.
3. If the throttle valve does not open fully, adjust the accelerator link.
4. Have your assistant fully depress the accelerator pedal and hold it there during the adjustment procedure.
5. Loosen the adjustment nuts on the carburetor end of the throttle cable.
6. Adjust the cable housing so the distance between the end of the boot and stopper on the cable is the 0.03–0.06 in. (0.8–1.5mm).
7. Tighten the adjusting nuts until snug.
8. Reinspect the throttle cable adjustment.
9. Install the air cleaner housing, then shut the hood.

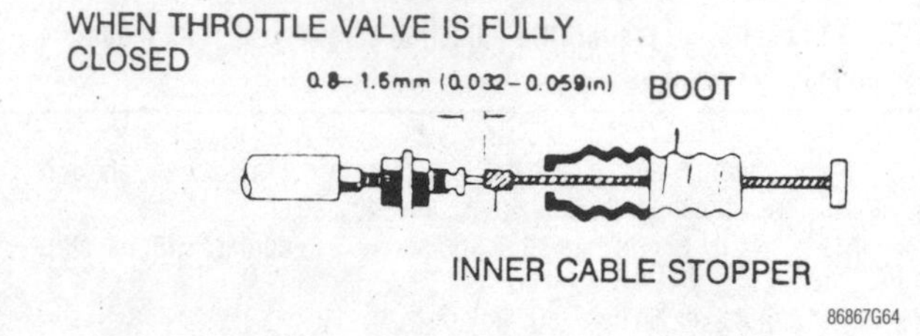

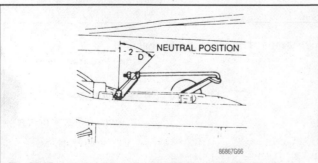

Fig. 38 Adjust the throttle cable so there is 0.032–0.059 in. (0.8–1.5mm) between the inner cable stopper and the tip of the cable housing—1988–90 models

1991–96 Models

The 1991–96 models utilize a Powertrain Control Module (PCM), which controls the idle speed and mixture settings automatically. There is no transmission-controlled throttle linkage on these vehicles and the PCM requires no adjustment.

SHIFT LINKAGE

Shift Control Cable

1981–87 PICK-UP MODELS

▶ See Figure 39

1. Remove the trim panel from around the automatic shifter assembly.
2. Raise the vehicle and safely support the vehicle on jackstands.
3. From under the vehicle, loosen the control rod locknuts so the trunnion will slide on the control rod.
4. Turn the manual shaft on the transmission fully clockwise (viewed from the left side of the transmission), then back it off to the 3rd stop, which should be the **N** position.
5. While holding the shaft in this position, have an assistant in the vehicle move the gear shift lever to the **N** position.
6. Push the shift shaft, with the shift control lower lever rearward to remove play, then tighten the adjusting nuts.

Fig. 39 After rotating the manual shaft fully clockwise, turn it counterclockwise to the 3rd position—1981–87 models

7. Lower the vehicle and install all trim panels removed.
8. Road test the vehicle and check for proper operation of the transmission in all ranges.

1988–95 PICK-UP, 1988–91 TROOPER AND 1992–94 AMIGO MODELS

▶ See Figure 40

1. Apply the parking brake and block the rear wheels.
2. If necessary for access under the vehicle, raise and safely support the front of the vehicle with jackstands.
3. Loosen the nut on the shift linkage (the nut holds the shift rod to the gear shift lower lever).
4. On the transmission, push the shift lever fully rearward (counterclockwise). The shift lever is mounted to the right-hand side of the transmission; do not mistake this for the gear shift selector lever, which is mounted in the vehicle's passenger compartment.
5. Push the shift lever, in the clockwise direction, 2 notches, which should position the lever in the **N** position.
6. Have an assistant move the gear shift selector lever in the passenger's compartment to the **N** position. The assistant should press the selector lever, while remaining in the **N** range, slightly toward the **R** range. With the selector lever held in this position, tighten the shift linkage nut until snug. Do not tighten it so much that it pulls the transmission shift lever out of the **N** position.
7. Lower the vehicle and remove the rear wheel blocks.
8. Make sure the transmission shift linkage functions correctly.

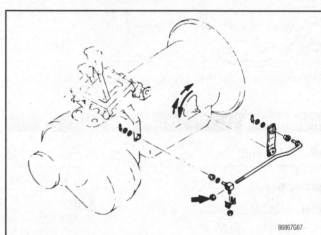

Fig. 40 The nut on the end of the shift linkage rod is the one which should be loosened when adjusting the shift linkage

Select Lever and Control Rod

1992–96 TROOPER AND RODEO MODELS

▶ See Figure 41

1. Disconnect the negative battery cable.
2. Remove the interior trim panels from around the shift selector lever in the passenger's compartment.
3. If necessary for access to the underside of the vehicle, apply the parking brake, block the rear wheels, raise and safely support the front of the vehicle on jackstands.
4. Set the select lever in the **N** position.
5. Push the select lever forward and secure it (using a rubber band or piece of string) so the pin on the lever comes into contact with the wall of the detent plate.
6. Turn nut (1) by hand until it comes into contact with the boss (3).

➡Clean the rod threads, but do not apply oil to the threads.

7. While holding nut (1) with a wrench or similar tool, tighten nut (2) to 20 ft. lbs. (27 Nm).
8. Install the clip (4) and tighten the nut (5) to 61 inch lbs. (7 Nm).
9. After adjustment, operate the select lever on a trial basis to make sure of its smooth operation and no abnormal indication in each transmission position.

10. Lower the vehicle and remove the rear wheel blocks, if necessary.
11. Install any interior trim panels removed earlier.
12. Connect the negative battery cable.

Shift Lock Cable

1992–96 TROOPER AND RODEO MODELS

♦ See Figure 42

1. Place the ignition switch in the **LOCK** position and the transmission gear selector lever in the **P** position.
2. Remove the shift lever trim piece.
3. Adjust the cable screw cap on the select lever side to provide a gap (slack of cable) of 0.059–0.098 in. (1.5–2.5mm) between the rod on the steering lock side and the stopper. Adjust the cap as follows:
   a. Hand turn the nut (A) until it comes in contact with the bracket while pulling the screw cap in the direction of the arrow (as in illustration) to prevent slack in the inner cable.
   b. Loosen the nut (A) 2 revolutions to provide 0.078 in. (2mm) slack for 1992–95 models or 0.20 in. (5mm) slack for 1996 models to the inner cable.
   c. Lock the inner cable by tightening the nut (B) to 33 inch lbs. (3.7 Nm) while holding nut (A) in place with a wrench.

➡ Clean the cable threads, but do not apply oil to the threaded portions.

4. Check the operation of the shift lever and make certain it meets the following criteria:
   a. The select lever should not be able to move out of the **P** position with the ignition switch in the **LOCK** position.
   b. The select lever should be able to move out of the **P** position when the ignition switch is in the **ON** position only when the brake pedal is depressed.
   c. The ignition switch should be able to be turned to the **LOCK** position only when the select lever is in the **P** position (the key can be pulled out).
5. If the vehicle failed Steps 4a and 4c, readjust the shift lock cable. If the vehicle failed Step 4b, readjust the connector wiring and the brake pedal switch.
6. Install the shift lever trim piece.

Neutral Safety Switch

➡ In all Isuzu trucks and Sport Utility vehicles, the automatic transmission neutral safety or start inhibitor switch also incorporates the functions of the back-up light switch.

REMOVAL & INSTALLATION

1981–87 Models

➡ The inhibitor switch is a part of the shift control lever assembly; partial disassembly of the shift control lever is necessary for replacement of this switch. The back-up light switch is an integral part of the inhibitor switch.

1. Disconnect the negative battery cable.
2. Remove the shift control lever from the vehicle, as described later in this section.
3. Place the shift control lever assembly on a clean work table. Remove the shift lever knob setscrew.

➡ The threaded portion of the setscrew is nylon coated to prevent loosening. Discard the old setscrew and purchase a new one for reassembly.

4. Remove the knob from the lever.
5. Remove the 4 screws holding the indicator upper cover onto the lever assembly, then remove the upper cover, the slider and the lower cover (with indicator light) from the shift lever bracket.
6. Remove the 2 screws holding the inhibitor switch, then remove the switch from the shift lever bracket.

To install:

7. Insert the projected portion of the inhibitor switch into the slot in the shift lever and attach these parts to the shift lever bracket, leaving the setscrews semi-tight.

➡ These setscrews are to be fully tightened after the adjustment procedure. For more information, refer to the neutral safety switch adjustment procedure later in this section.

8. Apply a small amount of grease to the projected portion of the inhibitor switch. Do not grease the points within the switch case, otherwise poor contact will be the result.
9. Install the indicator light on the lower cover, then attach the lower cover, the slider and the upper cover onto the shift lever bracket. Tighten the setscrews only finger-tight.
10. Place the shift lever into each transmission gear position. Adjust the position of the upper cover so the red colored mark on the slider aligns with the window in the indicator plate.
11. Install the knob onto the shift lever handle, then tighten the new knob setscrew until snug.
12. Check that the free-play of the push button is within 0.028–0.048 in. (0.71–1.22mm) when the shift lever is in the **P** or **N** position. If the amount of free-play deviates from the range specified, adjust the shift lever linkage, as described earlier in this section.
13. Check that the shift lever operates smoothly in all ranges without binding.
14. Install the shift lever assembly into the vehicle.
15. Connect the negative battery cable.

1988–96 Models

♦ See Figures 43 and 44

➡ The neutral safety switch for the late model transmissions is mounted onto the transmission at the shift lever. The back-up switch is incorporated into this assembly.

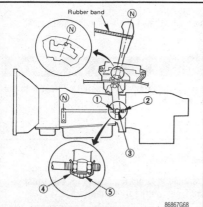

Fig. 41 Identification of the select lever and control rod components—make sure to hold the select lever so the pin contacts the detent plate wall (upper inset)

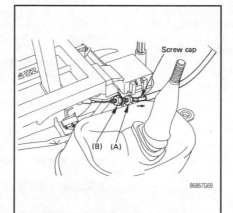

Fig. 42 The shift lock cable is adjusted on the select lever end of the cable—removal of the interior select lever trim panels is necessary for access

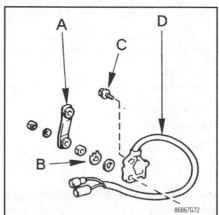

Fig. 43 Neutral safety switch and related components—(A) control shaft lever, (B) lockwasher, (C) mounting bolts and nut, and (D) neutral safety switch

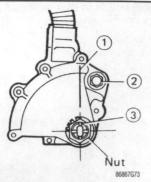

Fig. 44 To adjust the neutral safety switch, align the neutral standard line (1) and the switch groove (3), then tighten the adjusting bolt (2)

1. Disconnect the negative (-) battery cable.
2. Apply the parking brake and block the rear wheels, then set the transmission select lever in the passenger's compartment to the **N** position.
3. If necessary for access to the underside of the vehicle, apply the parking brake, block the rear wheels, raise and safely support the front of the vehicle on jackstands.
4. Disconnect the shift linkage from the transmission control shaft lever (A), as described later in this section.
5. Unstake the lockwasher (B) and remove it from the neutral safety switch (D).
6. Remove the neutral safety switch mounting nut and bolts (C), then pull the switch from the transmission shaft.
7. Remove the lockwasher and grommet from the transmission control shaft.

To install:
8. Position a new bushing and lockwasher onto the transmission control shaft.
9. Using the control shaft lever, turn the manual lever of the neutral safety switch counterclockwise as far as it will go, then turn it clockwise 2 notches. The switch should now be in Neutral.
10. Insert the neutral safety switch onto the manual valve shaft and temporarily tighten the adjusting bolt.
11. Install the lockwasher and tighten the nut to 5 ft. lbs. (6.8 Nm).
12. Align the neutral standard line (1) and the switch groove (3), then tighten the adjusting bolt (2) to 9 ft. lbs. (12 Nm).
13. Bend the at least 2 of the tabs on the lockwasher.
14. Install the control shaft lever onto the switch, then tighten the attaching nut to 12 ft. lbs. (16 Nm).
15. Attach the shift linkage to the control shaft lever, as described later in this section.
16. Lower the vehicle, if necessary.
17. Set the transmission select lever to the **P** position, then remove the rear wheel blocks.
18. Connect the negative battery cable.
19. Check that the engine will not start in any position except for **P** or **N**.

ADJUSTMENT

1981–87 Models

▶ See Figure 45

Adjust the setting of the inhibitor switch if the engine can be started with the shift lever set in any position other than **N** or **P**, when the shift linkage is adjusted, or when the shift lever assembly is disassembled (this includes removal of the inhibitor switch itself).
1. Remove the interior trim panels from around the transmission shift lever assembly.
2. Loosen the 2 screws holding the inhibitor switch to the shift lever bracket, then adjust the setting position of the switch so the center of the moving piece of the switch aligns with the neutral position indicator line on the steel case when the shift lever is set in the **N** position.

SHIFT LEVER POSITION	COLOR OF CABLE					
	BW	BW	RL	RL	Lg	Lg
P	○—	—○				
R			○—	—○		
N	○—	—○				
D,2,1					○—	—○

BW . . . . STARTING CIRCUIT
RL . . . . REVERSE CIRCUIT
Lg . . . . CRS CIRCUIT (Only for california)

Fig. 45 After adjusting the inhibitor switch, make certain that continuity of the switch is as shown

3. Tighten the 2 inhibitor mounting screws until snug.
4. When the adjustment operation is complete, check the continuity of the inhibitor switch as follows:
• With the shift lever in the **P** or **N** position, continuity should exist only between the **BW** circuit terminals
• With the shift lever in the **R** position, continuity should exist only between the **RL** circuit terminals
• With the shift lever in the **D**, **2** or **1** position, continuity should exist between the **Lg** circuit terminals only
5. If the switch does not function as specified, readjust the switch. If, after readjusting the switch, it still does not function as specified, a new inhibitor switch should be installed.
6. Install any trim panels removed earlier.

1988–91 Models

▶ See Figure 46

If the engine will start with the shift selector in any range other than **P** or **N**, adjustment is required.
1. Disconnect the negative battery cable.
2. Apply the parking brake and block the rear wheels, then set the transmission select lever in the **N** position.
3. If necessary for access to the underside of the vehicle, raise and safely support the front of the vehicle on jackstands.
4. Loosen the neutral safety switch bolt.
5. Align the groove and the neutral basic line by turning the switch.
6. Hold the switch in position, then tighten the adjusting bolt to 9 ft. lbs. (12 Nm).
7. Lower the vehicle.
8. Set the transmission select lever in the **P** position and remove the rear wheel blocks.
9. Connect the negative battery cable.
10. Make sure the engine can only be started when the transmission select lever is in the **P** or **N** positions.

Extension Housing Seal

➡This procedure is for replacing the extension housing oil seal with the transmission installed in the vehicle.

REMOVAL & INSTALLATION

Models Without a Rear Transmission Flange

➡Although draining the transmission is not necessary for this procedure, it would be a good time for a routine fluid change.

1. Raise and safely support the vehicle on jackstands.
2. If so desired, drain the transmission fluid. For more information regarding automatic transmission fluid draining and fluid pan procedures, please refer to Section 1 of this manual.

3. Matchmark the rear driveshaft flange to the rear differential flange for reassembly.

4. Remove the 4 driveshaft retaining bolts from the rear differential.

5. If equipped, remove the center bearing retainer bolts.

6. Lower the rear of the driveshaft assembly down from the differential and pull the rear driveshaft front yoke gently free of the transmission extension housing. Remove the driveshaft assembly completely from the vehicle.

7. If equipped, remove the extension housing dust shield from the transmission.

8. Using an oil seal puller (usually a specially designed J-shaped prytool), remove the rear housing oil seal.

To install:

9. Install a new oil seal using an installer tool (such as J-37239 for the AW30–80LE transmission) which is the correct size to drive the new seal into the extension housing, or the equivalent. Start the new oil seal into the extension housing, position the installation tool against it and gently tap the new oil seal into the transmission with a mallet. Make certain that the oil seal is seated completely and flush in the rear extension housing bore.

10. Lubricate the inside lip of the fluid oil seal with fresh, clean transmission fluid.

11. Position the driveshaft assembly under the vehicle, then lift the front end of the driveshaft up and slide it carefully into the rear extension housing of the transmission.

12. If applicable, lift the center bearing up and install the retaining bolts finger-tight. Position the rear driveshaft flange against the differential flange so the matchmarks align and install the attaching bolts and nuts finger-tight. Make sure the driveshaft-to-differential bolts are installed from the backside of the differential flange (the threaded portion of the bolt should be toward the front of the vehicle).

13. If equipped, tighten the center bearing bolts to 45 ft. lbs. (60 Nm).

14. Tighten the driveshaft-to-differential flange bolts and nuts to 46 ft. lbs. (63 Nm).

15. If necessary, install a new transmission fluid filter and the fluid pan. For more details, refer to Section 1.

16. Lower the vehicle.

17. Start the engine and test drive the transmission. After driving the vehicle, look for transmission fluid leaks from the rear oil seal.

Models With a Rear Transmission Flange

These vehicles are equipped with a transmission-to-driveshaft flange; rather than sliding the driveshaft yoke into the rear extension housing, the driveshaft bolts to the transmission flange.

➡**Although draining the transmission is not necessary for this procedure, it would be a good time for a routine fluid change.**

1. Raise and safely support the vehicle on jackstands.

2. If desired, drain the transmission fluid. For more information on automatic transmission fluid and filter service refer to Section 1.

3. Matchmark the rear driveshaft flange to the rear differential flange and the front driveshaft flange to the rear transmission flange for reassembly.

4. Remove the 4 driveshaft retaining bolts from the rear differential.

5. If equipped, remove the center bearing retainer bolts.

6. Remove the 4 driveshaft retaining bolts from the transmission rear flange.

7. Lower the rear of the driveshaft assembly out of the vehicle.

8. Use a rear flange holding tool to hold the rear flange steady while loosening the flange retaining nut.

9. Remove the flange retaining nut and the old O-ring. Discard the O-ring.

10. Using an oil seal removal tool, pry the old oil seal out of the extension housing.

To install:

11. Apply a film of clean engine oil to the inner lip of the oil seal, then install it into the transmission extension housing with an oil seal installation tool.

12. Install a new O-ring onto the transmission rear flange and install the flange nut.

13. Use the flange holding tool to hold the flange stationary while tightening the flange nut to 76 ft. lbs. (103 Nm).

14. Position the driveshaft assembly under the vehicle, then lift the front end of the driveshaft up and hold it against the transmission flange so the matchmarks align. Install the driveshaft-to-transmission flange bolts and nuts finger-tight.

15. If applicable, lift the center bearing up and install the retaining bolts finger-tight. Position the rear driveshaft flange against the differential flange so the matchmarks align and install the attaching bolts and nuts finger-tight. Make sure the driveshaft-to-differential bolts are installed from the backside of the differential flange (the threaded portion of the bolt should be toward the front of the vehicle).

16. If equipped, tighten the center bearing bolts to 45 ft. lbs. (60 Nm).

17. Tighten the driveshaft-to-differential flange and driveshaft-to-transmission flange bolts and nuts to 46 ft. lbs. (63 Nm).

18. If necessary, install a new transmission fluid filter and the fluid pan. For more details, refer to Section 1.

19. Lower the vehicle.

20. Start the engine and test drive the transmission. After driving the vehicle, look for transmission fluid leaks from the rear oil seal.

Transmission Assembly

REMOVAL & INSTALLATION

AW03–55 and AW03–75 Transmissions

1981–87 PICK-UP MODELS

◆ **See Figures 47 and 48**

1. Disconnect the negative battery cable. Raise and safely support the vehicle on jackstands.

2. Remove the transmission dipstick assembly.

3. Drain the transmission fluid.

4. Disconnect and plug the oil cooler lines from the transmission.

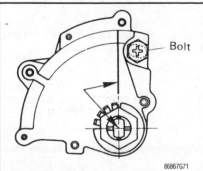

Fig. 46 To adjust the neutral safety switch, loosen the bolt and turn the switch until the groove and neutral basic line are aligned

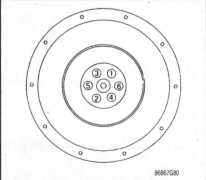

Fig. 47 When installing the flexplate mounting bolts, make certain to tighten the bolts in a crisscross pattern, as shown

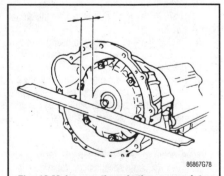

Fig. 48 Make sure there is the appropriate amount of clearance between the converter housing and the front face of the converter

5. Remove the torque converter cover. Matchmark the torque converter at the flywheel, and remove the torque converter bolts from the flywheel; rotate the torque converter to expose the bolts.

6. Remove the exhaust pipe nuts from the exhaust manifold, and separate the pipe from the manifold.

7. Disconnect the shift lever control rod from the transmission shift lever.

8. Disconnect the neutral safety switch and transmission wiring from the transmission.

9. Support the engine assembly.

10. Remove the starter motor and disconnect the speedometer cable from the transmission.

11. Matchmark and remove the driveshaft.

12. Remove the transmission-to-crossmember bolts.

13. Lift the engine/transmission slightly with a hydraulic floor jack and remove the transmission frame bracket from the crossmember. Remove the rear mount from the crossmember. Remove the exhaust pipe bracket from the transmission.

14. Support the transmission with a transmission floor jack.

15. Remove the bell housing-to-engine bolts and the transmission from the vehicle.

➡**Be careful that the torque converter does not drop from the transmission.**

To install:

16. Raise the transmission on a jack and install the bell housing bolts to the engine. Tighten the bolts to 29 ft. lbs. (39 Nm).

➡**Make sure the torque converter is fully seated in the transmission. If the transmission does not mount flush to the engine block during installation, check the torque converter. Do not use the bolts to pull the transmission flush to the engine block or damage may occur.**

17. Install the torque converter-to-flywheel bolts. Tighten the bolts to 14 ft. lbs. (19 Nm). Install the flywheel cover.

18. Support the transmission with a hydraulic floor jack.

19. Lift the engine/transmission slightly and install the transmission frame bracket to the crossmember. Install the rear mount to the crossmember.

20. Install the exhaust pipe bracket to the transmission.

21. Install the driveshaft.

22. Install the transmission-to-crossmember bolts.

23. Install the starter motor and connect the speedometer to the transmission.

24. Remove the engine and transmission support floor jacks.

25. The balance of the installation is the reverse of removal.

AW30–80LE Transmission

1988–89 PICK-UP AND 1988–91 TROOPER MODELS

➡**The transfer case is an integral part of the transmission housing. Although the 2 cases can be separated, the transfer case should be removed with the transmission.**

1. Disconnect the negative battery cable.

2. Raise and safely support the vehicle on jackstands.

3. Remove the undercover, if equipped.

4. Drain the transmission fluid from the oil pan. For more information, refer to Section 1.

5. Loosen the throttle cable adjusting nuts and disconnect the throttle cable from the bracket. Remove the transmission dipstick.

6. Disengage the wiring connectors at the neutral safety switch.

7. Unbolt the starter motor and place it aside in a safe location. Support the starter so it does not strain the electrical connections.

8. Remove the front driveshaft, as described later in this section.

9. Remove the 1-piece rear driveshaft at the flanges, as described in this section.

10. Disconnect the shift cable at the transmission and transfer case, if equipped.

11. Disconnect the speedometer cable from the transmission.

12. Disconnect the oil cooler lines and position the cooler bypass line close to the transmission case to prevent damage during transmission removal.

13. Remove the engine rear dust cover.

14. Remove the torque converter attaching bolts. The bolts can be removed through the starter hole.

15. Remove the front exhaust pipe from the exhaust manifold.

16. Place a transmission jack under the transmission and raise it slightly.

17. Remove the nuts connecting the rear mount to the transmission.

18. Remove the nuts and bolts connecting the rear mount to the crossmember, then remove the mount.

19. Remove the transmission mounting bolts.

20. Move the transmission back and carefully lower the transmission out of the vehicle. Do not let the torque converter fall out of the transmission.

To install:

➡**Installation of the transmission will require an assistant.**

21. Make sure the torque converter if fully seated in the transmission. The correct distance from the converter to the mounting surface is 1.02 in. (31mm).

22. Raise the rear of the transmission and move it into position on the crossmember.

23. Move the transmission forward and engage it with the engine.

➡**If the transmission does not seat flush against the engine block before the bolts are installed, check to see that the torque converter is seated properly in the transmission, do not use the bolts to draw the transmission against the engine block.**

24. Install the transmission mounting bolts and tighten them to 47 ft. lbs. (64 Nm).

25. Install the rear mount to the crossmember.

26. Install the rear mount-to-transmission nuts.

27. Install the bolts attaching the flexplate to the torque converter through the starter hole and tighten them to 22 ft. lbs. (30 Nm).

28. The balance of the installation is the reverse of removal.

AW03–72L Transmission

1988–95 PICK-UP AND 1992–94 AMIGO MODELS

1. Disconnect the negative battery cable. Raise and safely support the vehicle on jackstands.

2. Drain the transmission fluid from the oil pan. For more details on fluid and filter servicing, refer to Section 1.

3. Detach the throttle cable at the engine end and remove the transmission dipstick.

4. Unbolt the starter motor and position it aside in a safe location. Support the starter so it does not strain the electrical connections.

5. If equipped with a 1-piece driveshaft, remove the driveshaft flange nuts at the pinion, lower the driveshaft and pull it from the transmission.

6. If equipped with a 2-piece driveshaft, perform the following procedures:

   a. Remove the rear driveshaft flange nuts at the pinion.

   b. Remove the rear driveshaft flange bolts from the front driveshaft flange. Remove the rear driveshaft.

   c. Remove the center bearing bolts from the chassis, move the front driveshaft rearward and from the transmission.

7. Disconnect the shift control rod at the shifter end.

8. Disconnect the speedometer cable from the transmission.

9. Disconnect the oil cooler lines and position the cooler bypass line close to the transmission case to prevent damage during transmission removal.

10. Remove the torque converter bolts from the flexplate through the starter hole.

11. Place a transmission jack under the transmission and raise it slightly.

12. Remove the rear mount nuts from the transmission.

13. Remove the rear mount nuts and bolts from the crossmember. Remove the mount.

14. Remove the transmission-to-engine bolts.

15. Move the transmission back and lower the transmission out of the vehicle.

To install:

➡**Installation of the transmission will require an assistant.**

16. Raise the transmission into position.

17. Raise the rear of the transmission and move it into position on the crossmember.

18. Move the transmission forward and engage it with the engine.

19. Install the engine-to-transmission bolts and tighten them to 47 ft. lbs. (64 Nm).

➡**Make sure the torque converter is seated properly. The transmission should mount flush to the engine block; if the transmission does not mount flush, check the torque converter. Do not use the mounting bolts to pull the transmission flush to the engine or torque converter damage may occur.**

20. Install the mount and the rear mount nuts and bolts to the crossmember.

21. Install the rear mount nuts to the transmission. Tighten them to 30 ft. lbs. (41 Nm).

22. Install the torque converter bolts to the flexplate through the starter hole, and tighten them to 22 ft. lbs. (30 Nm).

23. The balance of the installation is the reverse of removal.

THM4L30-E Transmission

1990–91 TROOPER MODELS

➡**The transfer case is an integral part of the transmission housing. Although the 2 cases can be separated, the transfer case should be removed with the transmission.**

1. Disconnect the negative battery cable.

2. Remove the center and rear console from inside of the passenger's compartment.

3. Remove the transfer case control lever.

4. Raise and safely support the vehicle on jackstands.

5. Disconnect the shift control rod from the transmission, as described earlier in this section.

6. Remove the 2 piece undercover for access to the crankshaft balancer for turning the crankshaft as needed.

7. Disconnect the center bearing bracket and remove the rear driveshaft. Remove the front driveshaft. For more information, refer to the driveshaft procedures later in this section.

8. Disconnect the parking brake cable at the equalizer.

9. Disconnect the speedometer cable at the transfer case.

10. Remove the left front exhaust pipe.

11. Disconnect and plug the fluid cooling lines from the transmission.

12. Remove the starter motor, as described in Section 2.

13. Disengage the harness connector from the inhibitor switch.

14. Detach the 5 electrical connectors from the transmission.

15. Remove the breather hose from the top of the transmission.

16. Remove the flexplate inspection cover.

17. Remove the 3 bolts securing the torque converter to the flexplate. Use a socket on the crankshaft center bolt to rotate or hold the crankshaft as needed.

18. Remove the transmission undercovers, lift up the transmission slightly with a hydraulic transmission floor jack and remove the 3rd crossmember with the rear engine mount.

19. Remove the exhaust pipe and catalytic converter, as described in Section 3.

20. Remove the dipstick and tube with the bracket.

21. Remove the transmission mounting bolts, pull the transmission slightly rearward and carefully lower the transmission from the vehicle. Be careful not to drop the torque converter out of the transmission.

➡**Support the rear of the engine with an engine hoist or an hydraulic floor jack while the transmission and/or transfer case is removed.**

To install:

22. Make sure the torque converter is fully seated in the front pump and slowly raise the transmission into position until the front is flush with the rear of the engine. Install the transmission mounting bolts and tighten them to 29 ft. lbs. (39 Nm).

➡If the transmission does not seat flush against the engine block before the bolts are installed, check to see that the torque converter is seated properly in the transmission, do not use the bolts to draw the transmission to the engine block.

23. Install the dipstick tube with the bracket.

24. Install the exhaust pipe and catalytic converter, as described in Section 3.

25. Install the 3rd crossmember and rear mount. Tighten the crossmember bolts to 37 ft. lbs. (50 Nm) and the mount nuts to 30 ft. lbs. (41 Nm).

26. Remove the transmission jack and engine support.

27. The balance of the installation is the reverse of removal.

1992–96 TROOPER AND 1991–96 RODEO MODELS

▸ **See Figures 49, 50 and 51**

➡**The transfer case is an integral part of the transmission housing. Although the 2 cases can be separated, the transfer case should be removed with the transmission.**

1. Use a felt–tipped marker to matchmark the hood to the hood hinges. Remove the hood.

2. Disconnect the negative battery cable.

3. Shift the transmission into the **N** position, and the transfer case into the **2H** position.

4. Remove the air cleaner assembly.

5. Remove the transfer case shift knob. Remove the 4 transmission cover console retaining screws.

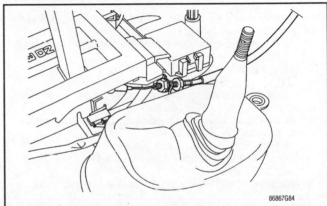

86867G84

Fig. 49 Detach the selector lever end of the shift lock cable from the lever assembly by loosening the adjusting nuts and sliding the end out of the bracket

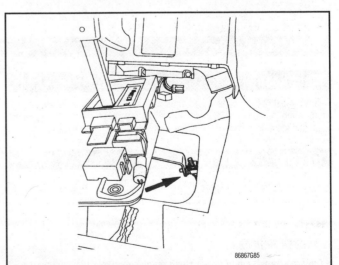

86867G85

Fig. 50 Disconnect the shift control rod from the selector lever lower lever arm

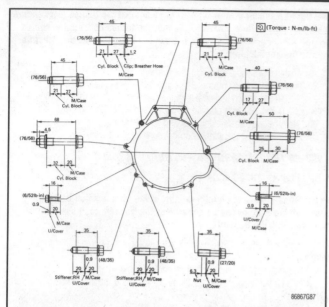

Fig. 51 Make certain to tighten the transmission-to-engine mounting bolts to the proper amount of torque—the torque measurements are shown in parentheses

6. Remove the center console assembly and disengage the console switch wiring connectors.

7. Disconnect the shift lock cable and the shift control rod from the selector lever assembly.

8. Unbolt and remove the transfer case control lever.

9. Raise and safely support the vehicle on jackstands.

10. Remove the transmission and transfer case skid plates.

11. Remove the exhaust pipe protectors.

12. Drain the transmission fluid. For more information servicing the transmission fluid pan and filter, refer to Section 1.

13. Label and detach the oxygen sensor connectors.

14. Remove the catalytic converter, center exhaust pipe and front exhaust pipe, as described in Section 3.

15. Matchmark the front and rear driveshafts to the differential and transfer case flanges.

16. Unbolt and remove the front and rear driveshafts, as described later in this section.

17. Disconnect the oil cooler lines from the transmission. Plug the lines to prevent fluid loss and contamination.

18. Remove the brackets securing the oil cooler lines to the engine stiffener.

19. Remove the front suspension crossmember.

20. Remove the dipstick and tube. Disconnect the breather hoses from the tube.

21. Remove the 5 engine stiffener bracket bolts and the stiffener bracket.

22. Remove the heat protector.

23. Disengage the transmission harness connectors and the mode switch harness connector from the engine harness.

24. Disconnect the harness clamp from the clamp bracket.

25. Disconnect the ground cable from the engine.

26. Remove the starter motor, as described in Section 2.

27. Remove the flexplate inspection cover.

28. Remove the 3 bolts securing the flexplate to the torque converter. Turn the crankshaft to gain access to all 3 bolts.

➡ **Remove the radiator upper fan shroud and the cooling fan to access the crankshaft center bolt to turn the crankshaft.**

29. Place a suitable transmission jack under the transmission and transfer case unit for support.

30. Raise the transmission slightly and remove the 8 bolts securing the rear mount and the transmission crossmember.

➡ **Make sure the engine and transmission assembly is properly supported before removing the rear mount and third crossmember.**

31. Raise the engine slightly with an engine hoist and remove the transmission-to-engine bolts.

32. Separate the transmission from the engine and lower the transmission from the vehicle.

To install:

➡ **Use new self–locking nuts when reconnecting the exhaust system. Replace any color–coded self–locking bolts when installing the frame crossmembers.**

33. Install the transfer case onto the transmission case, if the 2 cases were separated.

34. Install a new O–ring on the front pump shaft.

➡ **Make sure the transmission dowel pins are installed in the correct position. If the dowels are in the wrong hole, the transmission case may crack.**

35. Make sure the torque converter is fully seated in the front pump and slowly raise the front of the transmission into position until it is flush with the rear of the engine. Install the transmission-to-engine bolts and tighten the upper 6 mounting bolts to 56 ft. lbs. (76 Nm) and the lower 3 mounting bolts to 35 ft. lbs. (48 Nm). Tighten the remaining 2 bolts to 52 inch lbs. (6 Nm).

36. Install the third crossmember. Tighten the bolts to 37 ft. lbs. (50 Nm).

37. Install the rear mount and lower the engine from the hoist. Tighten the rear mount nuts to 30 ft. lbs. (41 Nm).

38. Remove the transmission jack and the engine hoist.

39. The balance of the installation is the reverse of removal.

TRANSFER CASE

Identification

Since most of the transfer cases on Isuzu trucks and Sport Utility vehicles are integral with the transmissions with which they are mated, refer to the manual or automatic identification portions of this section for transfer case identification.

Transfer Case Assembly

REMOVAL & INSTALLATION

1981–87 Models

TRANSFER SIDE CASE

➡ **Only the transfer side case can be removed without dismantling the entire transmission.**

1. Disconnect the negative battery cable.

2. Place the shift lever in the **2H** position.

3. Remove the boot and the shift lever from the transfer case from inside the vehicle.

4. Raise and safely support the vehicle.

5. Drain the transmission and the transfer case.

6. Matchmark the driveshafts to the flanges and remove the driveshafts.

7. Position a jack under the transfer case and remove the transfer case mounting bolts.

8. Pull the transfer case away from the transmission and remove the transfer case.

To install:

9. Clean the sealing surfaces on the transmission and the transfer case. Align the shift forks and the sleeve in the **2H** position, using a new gasket, install the transfer case to the transmission. Tighten the mounting bolts to 27 ft. lbs. (37 Nm).

10. Align the matchmarks and install the driveshafts.

11. Refill the transmission and the transfer case with 5W–30 engine oil.
12. Lower the vehicle to the floor.
13. Install the shift lever and the boot.
14. Connect the negative battery cable.

1988–96 Models

EXCEPT 1995–96 TROOPER AND RODEO MODELS WITH AUTOMATIC TRANSMISSIONS

The transfer case is an integral part of the transmission housing. Although the 2 cases can be separated, the transfer case should be removed with the transmission.

1995–96 TROOPER AND RODEO MODELS WITH AUTOMATIC TRANSMISSIONS

♦ **See Figure 52**

1. Shift the transfer case into the **2H** position. Drive the vehicle forward and backward for a few feet/meters to make sure the front axle and hubs are disengaged. Shift the transmission to the **N** position.
2. Disconnect the negative battery cable.
3. Remove the center console.
4. Remove the shift knob and boot from the transfer case shift lever. Unbolt the shift lever from the transfer case.
5. Disconnect the shift lock cable from the transmission shift lever.
6. Raise and safely support the vehicle.
7. Remove the transmission and transfer case skid plates.
8. Disconnect the oxygen sensor from the front exhaust pipe.
9. Unbolt the front exhaust pipe from the exhaust manifolds and the catalytic converter. Remove the exhaust pipe and converter assembly.
10. Matchmark the front and rear driveshafts to the differential and transfer case flanges.
11. Unbolt and remove the front driveshaft.
12. Unbolt the rear driveshaft from the rear differential and transfer case flanges.
13. Unbolt the center bearing and remove the rear driveshaft.
14. Drain the transfer case oil.
15. Disconnect the transmission shift linkage from the shift lever rod.
16. Disconnect the 2 wiring harnesses from the transfer case.
17. Support the transfer case with a transmission jack.

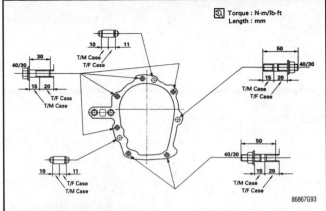

Fig. 52 When installing the transfer case, make sure to install the bolts in their proper locations—1995–96 Trooper and Rodeo models with 4WD automatic transmissions

18. Remove the transfer case–to–transmission bolts.
19. Separate the transfer case from the transmission output shaft. Lower the transfer case from the vehicle.

To install:

➡**Use new self–locking nuts when installing the exhaust pipe and converter.**

20. Apply a thin coating of molybdenum grease to transfer case input shaft splines.
21. Raise the transfer case to the level of the transmission and align the output and input shaft splines.
22. Install the transfer case–to–transmission case bolts, and tighten them to 34 ft. lbs. (46 Nm).
23. Remove the transmission jack.
24. Fill the transfer case with fresh engine oil.
25. The balance of the installation is the reverse of removal.

DRIVELINE

Front Driveshaft and U-Joints

REMOVAL & INSTALLATION

♦ **See Figure 53**

Except 1995–96 Trooper and Rodeo

1. Apply the parking brake and block the rear wheels.
2. Raise and safely support the front of the vehicle on jackstands.
3. Matchmark the driveshaft flange-to-transfer case flange and the driveshaft-to-differential pinion flange for reassembly.
4. Matchmark the front and rear parts of the driveshaft so they can be reassembled in the same position.
5. Remove the front driveshaft's splined yoke flange-to-transfer case bolts and separate the front driveshaft from the transfer case. Do not allow the splined flange to fall away from the transfer case; lower the driveshaft carefully.
6. Remove the driveshaft flange-to-differential pinion flange bolts and separate the driveshaft from the front differential.

To install:

7. Align the matchmarks and install the driveshaft to the differential unit and the transfer case.
8. Install the driveshaft flange-to-differential pinion flange bolts. Tighten the bolts to 46 ft. lbs. (63 Nm).
9. Connect the driveshaft flange to the transfer case yoke and install the front driveshaft's splined yoke flange-to-transfer case bolts. Tighten the bolts to 46 ft. lbs. (63 Nm).
10. Lower the vehicle and remove the rear wheel blocks.

1995–96 Trooper and Rodeo

1. Shift the transmission into **N**, and the transfer case into **2H**. Make sure the front axle and hubs are disengaged.
2. Apply the parking brake and block the rear wheels.
3. Raise and safely support the front of the vehicle on jackstands.

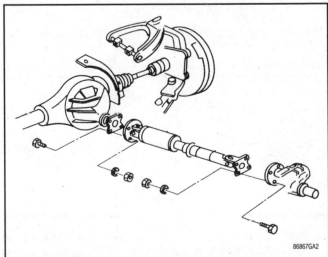

Fig. 53 Exploded view of a common front driveshaft and mounting fasteners

4. Remove the transmission and transfer case skid plates.

5. Matchmark the driveshaft flanges to the transfer case flange and differential pinion flange.

6. Matchmark the front and rear parts of the driveshaft so they can be reassembled in the same position, if the sliding yoke is going to be separated from the rear part of the driveshaft.

7. Remove the bolts attaching the front driveshaft flange to the transfer case flange and separate the front driveshaft from the transfer case.

8. Remove the bolts attaching the driveshaft flange to the differential pinion flange and separate the driveshaft from the front differential.

9. Remove the driveshaft from the vehicle.

10. Clean the flange mounting surfaces to remove any rust or dirt.

To install:

11. Align the matchmarks and install the driveshaft.

12. Install the bolts attaching the driveshaft flange to the differential pinion flange. Tighten the bolts to 46 ft. lbs. (63 Nm).

13. Connect the driveshaft flange to the transfer case flange and install the attaching bolts. Tighten the bolts to 46 ft. lbs. (63 Nm).

14. Repaint the exposed portions of the flanges so they do not rust.

15. Install the transfer case and transmission skid plates and tighten their bolts to 27 ft. lbs. (37 Nm).

16. Lower the vehicle and remove the rear wheel blocks.

U-JOINT REPLACEMENT

▶ **See Figures 54, 55 and 56**

1. Raise and support the vehicle safely. Remove the driveshaft.

2. If the front yoke is to be disassembled, matchmark the driveshaft and sliding splined yoke so driveline balance is preserved upon reassembly. Remove the snaprings that retain the bearing caps on the U-joint.

3. Select 2 press components, with one being small enough to pass through the yoke holes for the bearing caps and the other being large enough to receive the bearing cap.

4. Use a vise or a press and position the small and large press components on either side of the U-joint. Press in on the smaller press component so it presses the opposite bearing cap out of the yoke and into the larger press component. If the cap does not come all of the way out, grasp it with a pair of pliers and work it out.

5. Reverse the position of the press components so the smaller press component presses on the U-joint spider (cross-shaped center piece). Press the opposite bearing cap out of the yoke.

6. Repeat the procedure on the other bearings.

7. If equipped, remove the old seals from the bearing caps. Discard the old seals.

8. Remove the U-joint cross piece from the U-joint retaining bracket.

To install:

9. Grease the bearing caps and needles thoroughly with a molybdenum-disulfide grease or a multipurpose type grease NLG1 No. 2, if they are not pregreased. Install a new oil seal into each bearing cap so its outer surface is flush with the bearing cap surface.

10. Start a new bearing cap into a side of the yoke, then position the spider in the yoke.

➡Some U-joints have a grease fitting that must be installed in the joint before assembly. When installing the fitting, make sure once the driveshaft is installed in the vehicle that the fitting is accessible to be greased at a later date.

11. Select 2 press components small enough to pass through the yoke holes. Put the press components against the cross and the cap and press the bearing cap ¼ in. (6mm) below the surface of the yoke. If there is a sudden increase in the force needed to press the cap into place, or if the cross starts to bind, the bearings are cocked. They must be removed and restarted in the yoke. Failure to do so will cause premature bearing failure.

12. Install a new snapring.

13. Start the new bearing into the opposite side. Place a press component on it and press in until the opposite bearing contacts the snapring.

14. Install a new snapring. It may be necessary to grind the facing surface of the snapring slightly to permit easier installation.

15. Install the other bearings in the same manner.

16. Check the joint for free movement. If binding exists, smack the yoke ears with a brass or plastic faced hammer to seat the bearing needles. If binding still exists, disassemble the joint and check to see if the needles are in place. Do not strike the bearings unless the shaft is supported firmly. Do not install the driveshaft until free movement exists at all joints.

17. Install the driveshafts into the vehicle.

18. Lower the vehicle.

19. Test drive the vehicle and check for driveline vibrations.

Rear Driveshaft and U-Joint

GENERAL DESCRIPTION

Torque is transmitted from the transmission to the rear axle through the driveshaft and Universal joint (U-joint) assemblies.

All driveshafts are the balanced tubular type. A splined slip-joint is provided in some drivelines.

The driveshaft is designed and built with the yoke lugs (ears) in line with each other. This design produces the smoothest running shaft possible, called phasing.

Vibration can be caused by an out-of-phase driveshaft. The propeller shaft will absorb vibrations from speeding up and slowing down each time the U-joint revolves. This vibration would be the same as a person snapping a rope and watching the "wave" reaction flow to the end of the rope. A driveshaft working in phase would be similar to 2 people snapping the same rope at the same time, and watching the "waves" meet and cancel each other out. In comparison, this would be the same as the U-joints on the driveshaft. A total cancellation of vibration produces a smooth flow of power in the driveline. It is very important to apply a reference mark (matchmark) to the driveshaft before removal, to assure installation alignment.

Center bearings support the driveline when 2 propeller shafts are used. The center bearing is a ball-type bearing mounted in a rubber cushion that is attached to a crossmember. The bearing is pre-lubricated and sealed by the manufacturer.

A Universal joint (U-joint) consists of 2 Y-shaped yokes connected by a crossmember called a spider. The spider is shaped like a cross.

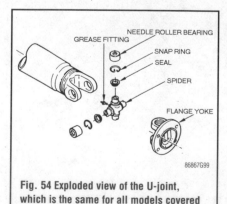

Fig. 54 Exploded view of the U-joint, which is the same for all models covered by this manual

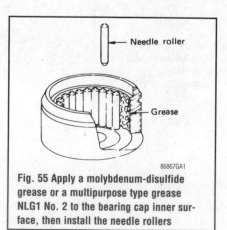

Fig. 55 Apply a molybdenum-disulfide grease or a multipurpose type grease NLG1 No. 2 to the bearing cap inner surface, then install the needle rollers

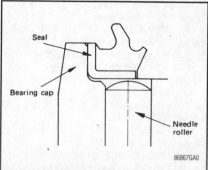

Fig. 56 Install the oil seal so its outer lip is flush with the outer edge of the bearing cap

Universal joints are designed to handle the effects of various loads and front or rear axle wind-up during acceleration. Within the designed angle variations, the U-joint will operate efficiently and safely. When the design angle is changed or exceeded the operational life of the joint may decrease. The bearings used in U-joints are of the needle roller type. The needle rollers are held in place on the trunnions by round bearing cups. The bearing cups are held in the yokes by snaprings.

REMOVAL & INSTALLATION

Except 1995–96 Trooper and Rodeo

2WD MODELS

1. Raise and support the vehicle safely on jackstands.
2. Matchmark the driveshaft to the transmission yoke flange and the rear differential yoke flange.
3. Remove the driveshaft retaining bolts and remove the driveshaft.
To install:
4. Position the driveshaft against the flanges so the matchmarks align, then install the retaining bolts to 26 ft. lbs. (35 Nm) for vehicles with 2.3L engines, or to 46 ft. lbs. (63 Nm) for all other models.
5. Lower the vehicle.

4WD MODELS

▶ See Figure 57

1. Raise and safely support the vehicle on jackstands.
2. Matchmark the driveshaft flange-to-rear differential pinion flange.
3. If equipped with a one-piece driveshaft, remove the driveshaft flange-to-pinion nuts, lower the rear end of the driveshaft and pull it out of the transmission.
4. If equipped with a two-piece driveshaft, perform the following procedure:
   a. Remove the rear driveshaft flange-to-rear differential pinion flange nuts.
   b. Remove the rear driveshaft flange-to-front driveshaft flange bolts, then remove the rear driveshaft section from the vehicle.
   c. Remove the center bearing-to-chassis bolts, then move the front driveshaft section rearward to disengage it from the transmission.
To install:
5. If equipped with a two-piece driveshaft, install it into the vehicle as follows:
   a. Carefully slide the front driveshaft yoke into the transmission extension housing. Lift the rear of the front driveshaft section up against the underside of the vehicle, then install the center bearing-to-chassis bolts. Tighten the center bearing bolts to 45 ft. lbs. (61 Nm).

   b. Position the rear driveshaft front flange against the front driveshaft rear flange, then install the rear driveshaft flange-to-front driveshaft flange bolts. Tighten the flange bolts to 16 ft. lbs. (21 Nm).
   c. Install the rear driveshaft flange-to-rear differential pinion nuts and bolts. Tighten them to 46 ft. lbs. (63 Nm).
6. If equipped with a one-piece driveshaft, insert the driveshaft yoke into the transmission extension housing, then install the driveshaft flange-to-rear differential pinion flange nuts and bolts to 46 ft. lbs. (63 Nm).
7. Lower the vehicle.

1995–96 Trooper and Rodeo

1. Shift the transmission into **N**, and the transfer case into **2H**. Make sure the front axle and hubs are disengaged.
2. Raise and safely support the vehicle on jackstands.
3. Matchmark the driveshaft flanges to the transmission flange and differential pinion flange.
4. Matchmark the front and rear parts of the driveshaft so they can be reassembled in the same position if the sliding yoke is to be separated from the rear part of the driveshaft.
5. Remove the bolts attaching the driveshaft flange to transmission flange and separate the driveshaft from the transmission.
6. Remove the bolts attaching the driveshaft flange to the rear differential pinion flange and separate the driveshaft from the rear differential.
7. Remove the driveshaft from the vehicle.
8. Clean the flange mounting surfaces to remove any rust or dirt.
To install:
9. Align the matchmarks and install the driveshaft.
10. Install the bolts attaching the driveshaft flange to the differential pinion flange. Tighten the bolts to 46 ft. lbs. (63 Nm).
11. Connect the driveshaft flange to the transmission flange and install the attaching bolts. Tighten the bolts to 46 ft. lbs. (63 Nm).
12. Repaint the exposed portions of the flanges so they do not rust.
13. Lower the vehicle.

U-JOINT REPLACEMENT

For the rear driveshaft U-joint replacement procedures, refer to the U-joint procedure found under front driveshaft earlier in this section.

Center Bearing

REMOVAL & INSTALLATION

▶ See Figure 58

1. Raise and safely support the vehicle on jackstands.
2. Remove the driveshaft assembly from the vehicle, as described earlier in this section.
3. Remove the locknut, then pull the flange off the driveshaft with a gear puller.

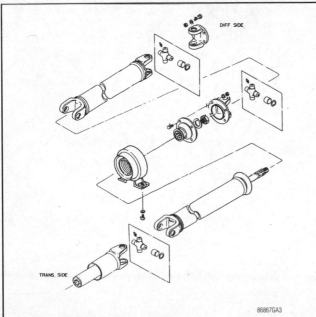

Fig. 57 Exploded view of the 2-piece rear driveshaft assembly and center bearing unit—4WD models

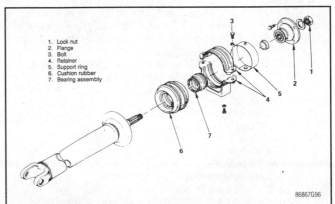

1. Lock nut
2. Flange
3. Bolt
4. Retainer
5. Support ring
6. Cushion rubber
7. Bearing assembly

Fig. 58 Exploded view of the center bearing assembly on 4-wheel drive vehicles (except 1995–96 Trooper)

4. Remove retainer bolt and retainer.
5. Remove the supporting ring and cushion rubber.
6. Remove the bearing assembly using a gear puller.

To install:

7. Repack the bearing with multipurpose type grease. Install it into the cushion rubber.

FRONT DRIVE AXLE

Identification

For the identification of the front drive axle, refer to Section 1.

Halfshaft, Bearing and Seal

REMOVAL & INSTALLATION

Halfshaft Without the DOJ Case

➡If the DOJ case does not require servicing, as is the case with outer CV-joint servicing or inner CV-joint overhaul, use this procedure. The halfshaft, with the exception of the DOJ case, can be removed without removing the entire front axle assembly.

1. If equipped with 4-wheel drive, shift the transfer case shift lever into **2H**. Drive the vehicle a few feet forward and reverse to verify that the front axle is disengaged.
2. Set the front wheels and steering wheel in the straight–ahead position. Lock the steering column in this position, and remove the key.
3. Apply the parking brake and block the rear wheels.
4. Raise and safely support the front of the vehicle on jackstands.
5. Remove the front wheels and underside skid plate.
6. Remove the front brake calipers and caliper mounting brackets. Do not disconnect the brake line. Hang the brake calipers from a wire, do not allow the calipers to hang from the brake hoses. For more information, refer to Section 9.
7. Remove the locking hub assembly and rotors on both sides, as described earlier in this section.
8. If equipped with ABS, unbolt the front wheel sensor brackets from the steering knuckles. Move the sensors out of the work area. They do not need to be disconnected.
9. Use a ball joint separator tool to disconnect the upper and lower ball joints and tie rod ends, and then remove the steering knuckles.
10. If necessary for added clearance, matchmark and disconnect the pitman arm and idler arm. Remove the steering linkage as an assembly.
11. Remove the inner CV-joint boot clamp, then slide the boot away from the joint. To remove the clamp, it may be necessary to pry the hooked end of the clamp up with a small prytool.
12. Remove the circlip from the DOJ case, then pull the halfshaft away from the DOJ case.
13. Remove the halfshaft from the vehicle.

To install:

14. If the halfshaft was not overhauled, clean the DOJ joint of all dirt and grease, then fill the inner boot and DOJ with 5.25 oz. (150g) new grease. Install the halfshaft into the DOJ case and install the circular clip into the groove so the open ends are positioned away from the ball groove.
15. Slide the boot onto the DOJ case, insert a tool under the boot lip to allow the pressure to equalize and tighten the new boot clamps. The boot should be installed so the edge of the smaller end is 6.5 in. (16.5cm) from the opposite edge of the DOJ case.
16. Install the steering knuckles and assemble any suspension components that were disconnected or removed.
17. Install the rotor and hub assemblies, as described earlier in this section.
18. Install the caliper mounting brackets and the brake calipers. For more information, refer to Section 9.
19. If necessary, install the steering linkage assembly.
20. If equipped, reconnect the ABS front wheel sensors.
21. Install the radiator skid plate. Tighten the bolts to 58 ft. lbs. (78 Nm).
22. Install the transfer case skid plates and tighten their bolts to 27 ft. lbs. (37 Nm).

8. Install the cushion rubber and support ring onto the driveshaft.
9. Install the retainer and retainer bolt.
10. Slide the flange onto the driveshaft and draw it into place by tightening the locknut to 90 ft. lbs. (122 Nm).
11. Install the driveshaft, as described earlier in this section.
12. Lower the vehicle.

23. Install the front wheels.
24. Lower the vehicle, remove the rear wheel blocks and adjust the ride height.
25. If the steering linkage was removed, have the front wheel alignment checked by a reputable automotive technician.
26. If necessary, bleed the brake system.
27. Verify that the front axle and hubs engage and disengage properly.
28. Road test the vehicle.

Entire Halfshaft Assembly, Bearing and Seal

➡If the entire halfshaft (including the DOJ case) must be removed from the vehicle, the entire front axle assembly should be removed from the vehicle for ease of disassembly, since the mounting brackets for the axle assembly are also the halfshaft-to-differential mounting brackets. These brackets must be unfastened to remove the inner DOJ case from the assembly.

1981–87 PICK-UP AND 1985–87 TROOPER MODELS

▶ See Figure 59

1. Apply the parking brake and block the rear wheels.
2. Raise and safely support the front of the vehicle on jackstands.
3. Remove the front wheels and underside skid plate.
4. Remove the front brake calipers and caliper mounting brackets. Do not disconnect the brake line. Hang the brake calipers from a wire, do not allow the calipers to hang from the brake hoses. For more information, refer to Section 9.
5. Remove the locking hub assembly and rotors on both sides, as described earlier in this section.
6. Remove the front differential housing and axles as an assembly. Refer to the axle assembly removal and installation procedure later in this section.

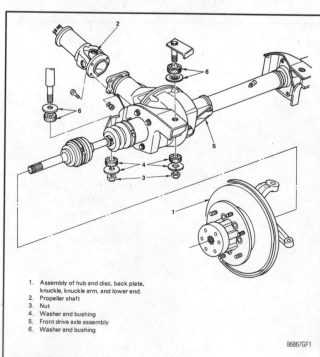

1. Assembly of hub and disc, back plate, knuckle, knuckle arm, and lower end.
2. Propeller shaft
3. Nut
4. Washer and bushing
5. Front drive axle assembly
6. Washer and bushing

86867GF1

Fig. 59 Front axle assembly on all 1981–95 models

7. Drain the differential case and remove the 4 bolts attaching the axle mounting brackets to the case and to the axle tube flange.

8. Pull the shaft and mounting assemblies from the case on both sides.

9. Remove the outer snapring and remove the front axle shaft bearing.

10. Remove the inner snapring, the O-ring, and the front axle shaft seal.

11. Remove the halfshaft from the axle mounting bracket.

To install:

12. Install the halfshaft into the axle mounting bracket.

13. Install a new grease seal and O-ring.

14. Install the inner snapring, the front axle shaft bearing, and the outer snapring.

➡**Before installing the axle shaft bearing, lightly lubricate the bearing with differential lube.**

15. Connect the axle mounting bracket and halfshaft assembly to the differential. Tighten the axle mounting bracket bolts to 40–47 ft. lbs. (54–64 Nm) for 1981–87 Pick-Up models, or to 61 ft. lbs. (83 Nm) for 1985–91 Trooper models.

16. Install the differential and axle assembly into the vehicle.

17. Install the rotors and locking hub assemblies on both sides.

18. Install the front disc brake calipers and caliper mounting brackets.

19. Install the front wheels and skid plate.

20. Lower the vehicle and adjust ride height.

21. Refill the differential with the proper lubricant. For more information regarding filling the front drive axle, refer to Section 1. If necessary, bleed the brake system.

22. Road test the vehicle and verify proper operation.

1988–95 TROOPER AND PICK-UP, 1989–94 AMIGO AND 1991–95 RODEO MODELS

▶ **See Figure 59**

➡**The right axle shaft is an integral part of the right halfshaft assembly. Removal of the left axle shaft involves disassembling the shift-on-the-fly four-wheel drive gearbox. The inboard joints of both halfshafts fit through the axle mounting brackets, which are bolted to the axle housing, therefore the axle housing should be removed from the vehicle for ease of disassembly.**

1. Shift the transfer case shift lever into **2H**. Drive the vehicle a few feet forward and reverse to verify that the front axle is disengaged.

2. Set the front wheels and steering wheel in the straight–ahead position. Lock the steering column in this position, and remove the key.

3. Apply the parking brake and block the rear wheels.

4. Raise and safely support the front of the vehicle on jackstands.

5. Remove the front wheels.

6. Remove the radiator skid plate.

7. Remove the transfer case skid plates.

8. Drain the oil from the differential.

9. Unbolt the calipers from their brackets. Support the calipers out of the way on wire hangers. Don't disconnect the brake hoses. For more information, refer to Section 9.

10. Remove the caliper mounting bracket from the steering knuckle.

11. Remove the automatic hub and brake rotor assemblies. Note the positions of the hub snaprings, shims, and lockwashers for reassembly.

12. If equipped with ABS, unbolt the front wheel sensor brackets from the steering knuckles. Move the sensors out of the work area. They do not need to be disconnected.

13. Use a ball joint separator tool to disconnect the upper and lower ball joints and tie rod ends, and then remove the steering knuckles.

14. Matchmark and disconnect the pitman arm and idler arm. Remove the steering linkage as an assembly.

15. Unbolt and remove the suspension crossmember from its brackets at the lower control arms.

16. Matchmark the front driveshaft flanges to the differential and transfer case flanges. Unbolt and remove the front driveshaft.

17. Support the front axle assembly with a floor jack and safety stands.

18. Remove the 4 bolts which secure the right halfshaft axle mounting bracket to the differential. Do not unbolt the left halfshaft from the axle.

19. Remove the mounting bracket bolts which secure the right and left axle mounting brackets to the vehicle's frame.

20. Separate the right halfshaft and axle mounting bracket assembly from the differential and allow it to rest on the lower control arm. If only the right halfshaft needs servicing, stop the axle removal procedure at this point. Remove the right halfshaft from the vehicle along with the axle assembly mounting bracket. Skip to Step 22 for further right halfshaft disassembly.

✳ WARNING

Be careful not to damage the CV–joints, boots, or splined shafts when removing the axle.

21. Follow these steps to remove the axle assembly:

   a. Verify that the axle assembly is securely supported by the floor jack. Remove the safety stands.

   b. First, slide the axle to the left to release the splined stub axle of the right halfshaft, if still installed.

   c. Next, lower the axle slightly and slide it to the right so the left halfshaft clears the left lower control arm.

   d. Finally, completely lower the axle from the vehicle.

22. Remove the right halfshaft from the vehicle. Follow these steps to remove the right axle shaft seal and bearing:

   a. Remove the snapring from the splined shaft.

   b. Remove the shaft bearing. Use a puller if necessary, but don't damage the shaft or splines.

   c. Remove the inner snapring.

   d. Remove the axle mounting bracket and oil seal from the right halfshaft.

23. With the axle out of the vehicle, unbolt the left halfshaft from the axle case. Remove the halfshaft together with the left axle mounting bracket.

24. Follow these steps to remove the left axle shaft seal and bearing:

   a. Remove the snapring from the splined shaft.

   b. Remove the shaft bearing. Use a puller if necessary, but do not damage the shaft or splines.

   c. Remove the inner snapring.

   d. Remove the axle mounting bracket and oil seal from the left halfshaft.

To install:

➡**Use new self–locking nuts and color–coded bolts when assembling the axle assembly mounts and suspension components. Suspension fasteners should be tightened to their final torque specifications when the vehicle is on the ground.**

25. Visually inspect the axle shafts for wear and damage.

26. Lightly lubricate the bearing and grease seal with differential oil before installation.

27. Assemble the left and right halfshaft and axle mounting bracket assemblies

   a. Install the axle mounting bracket onto the halfshaft.

   b. Lubricate and install a new oil seal.

   c. Install a new inner snapring.

   d. Install a new bearing.

   e. Install a new outer snapring.

28. Place the right halfshaft and axle mounting bracket assembly into position, and rest it on the right lower control arm. If only the right halfshaft was removed, skip Step 28.

29. Position the axle and left halfshaft assembly on a floor jack. Raise the axle into position.

30. Fit the right halfshaft and axle mounting bracket assembly into the differential. Make sure the splined stub axle shaft is fully seated. Be careful not to distort the oil seal when connecting the right mounting bracket to the differential.

31. Install the mounting brackets and halfshafts to the axle housing. Tighten the mounting bolts to the following specifications:

   • 1995½ Rodeo with air bags—85 ft. lbs. (116 Nm)
   • 1988–95 Amigo, Rodeo, and Pick-Up—61 ft. lbs. (82 Nm)
   • 1995 Trooper—85 ft. lbs. (116 Nm)
   • 1988–94 Trooper—61 ft. lbs. (82 Nm)

32. Raise the axle assembly into its final position and support it with safety stands.

33. Install the mounting bracket bolts, nuts, and spacers. The washer fits under the bolt and the spacer is used with the nut. Tighten the mounting nuts and bolts:

   • 1988–96 Amigo and Pick-Up—112 ft. lbs. (152 Nm)
   • 1988–95 Trooper and Rodeo—112 ft. lbs. (152 Nm)

34. Install the steering knuckles and assemble any suspension components that were disconnected or removed.
35. Install the brake backing plates and the rotor and hub assemblies.
36. Install the caliper mounting brackets and the brake calipers.
37. Check the lubricant level in the differential and add oil if needed.
38. Verify that all axle assembly mounting components have been installed.
39. Align the front driveshaft matchmarks. Install the driveshaft flange bolts and tighten them to 46 ft. lbs. (63 Nm).
40. Install the suspension crossmember and tighten the bolts to 58 ft. lbs. (78 Nm).
41. Install the steering linkage assembly.
42. If equipped, reconnect the ABS front wheel sensors.
43. Install the radiator skid plate. Tighten the bolts to 58 ft. lbs. (78 Nm).
44. Install the transfer case skid plates and tighten their bolts to 27 ft. lbs. (37 Nm).
45. Install the front wheels.
46. Lower the vehicle, remove the rear wheel blocks and adjust the ride height.
47. Check and adjust the front wheel alignment.
48. Tighten the suspension bushing fasteners to their final torque specifications. Refer to Section 8 for these specifications.

49. If necessary, bleed the brake system.
50. Verify that the front axle and hubs engage and disengage properly.
51. Road test the vehicle.

1996 MODELS

♦ **See Figures 60, 61, 62, 63 and 64**

➡**The procedure for the 1996 Trooper and Rodeo models is very similar to the earlier procedure, however since the 1996 models utilize a shift-on-the-fly system, certain steps will vary greatly.**

➡**The right axle shaft is an integral part of the right halfshaft assembly. Removal of the left axle shaft involves disassembling the shift–on–the–fly four–wheel drive gearbox. The inboard joints of both halfshafts fit through the axle mounting brackets, which are bolted to the axle housing, thereby requiring the removal of the axle assembly as a unit.**

1. Shift the transfer case shift lever into **2H**. Drive the vehicle a few feet forward and reverse to verify that the front axle is disengaged.
2. Set the front wheels and steering wheel in the straight–ahead position. Lock the steering column in this position, and remove the key.

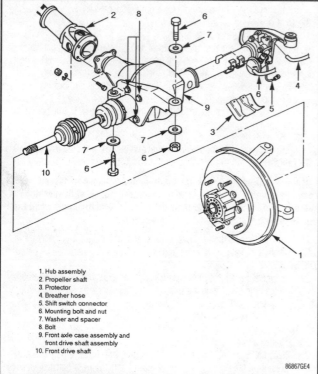

1. Hub assembly
2. Propeller shaft
3. Protector
4. Breather hose
5. Shift switch connector
6. Mounting bolt and nut
7. Washer and spacer
8. Bolt
9. Front axle case assembly and front drive shaft assembly
10. Front drive shaft

86867GE4

Fig. 60 Exploded view of the front axle and mounting fasteners— 1996 Trooper and Rodeo models

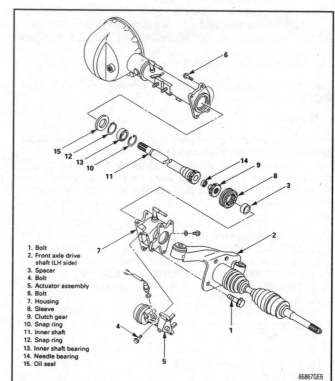

1. Bolt
2. Front axle drive shaft (LH side)
3. Spacer
4. Bolt
5. Actuator assembly
6. Bolt
7. Housing
8. Sleeve
9. Clutch gear
10. Snap ring
11. Inner shaft
12. Snap ring
13. Inner shaft bearing
14. Needle bearing
15. Oil seal

86867GE6

Fig. 61 Exploded view of the left-hand halfshaft, axle shaft and Shift-on-the-fly housing

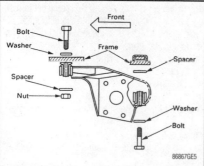

86867GE5

Fig. 62 Make sure to install the front axle mounting bracket bolts in the proper direction

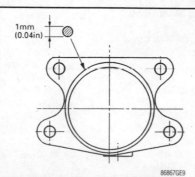

86867GE9

Fig. 63 Apply a bead of liquid gasket to the contact surface of the front axle case, then install the Shift-on-the-fly housing

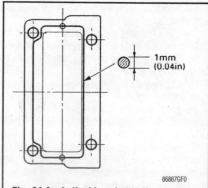

86867GF0

Fig. 64 Apply liquid gasket to the contact surface on the actuator, as shown

3. Apply the parking brake and block the rear wheels.

4. Raise and safely support the front of the vehicle on jackstands.

5. Remove the front wheels.

6. Remove the radiator skid plate.

7. Remove the transfer case skid plates.

8. Drain the oil from the differential.

9. Unbolt the calipers from their brackets. Support the calipers out of the way on wire hangers. Don't disconnect the brake hoses. For more information, refer to Section 9.

10. Remove the caliper mounting brackets from the steering knuckle.

11. Remove the automatic hub and brake rotor assemblies. Note the positions of the hub snaprings, shims, and lockwashers for reassembly.

12. If equipped with four-wheel ABS, unbolt the front wheel sensor brackets from the steering knuckles. Move the sensors out of the work area. They don't need to be disconnected.

13. Remove the shift-on-the-fly four-wheel drive actuator:

   a. Remove the skid plate from the shift-on-the-fly gear housing.

   b. Label and disconnect the Vacuum Switching Valve (VSV) hoses and 2P connector from the gear housing.

   c. Unbolt the VSV assembly from the left axle tube and remove it so it will not be damaged. Do not disconnect the 2 vacuum hoses from the body of the VSV.

14. Use a ball joint separator tool to disconnect the upper and lower ball joints and tie rod ends, and then remove the steering knuckles.

15. Matchmark and disconnect the pitman arm and idler arm. Remove the steering linkage as an assembly.

16. Unbolt and remove the suspension crossmember from its brackets at the lower control arms.

17. Matchmark the front driveshaft flanges to the differential flange and transfer case flange. Unbolt and remove the front driveshaft.

18. Support the front axle assembly with a floor jack and safety stands.

19. Remove the 4 bolts which secure the right halfshaft axle mounting bracket to the differential. Do not unbolt the left halfshaft from the axle.

20. Remove the mounting bracket bolts which secure the right and left axle mounting brackets to the vehicle's frame.

21. Separate the right halfshaft and axle mounting bracket assembly from the differential and allow it to rest on the lower control arm. If only the right halfshaft needs servicing, remove it from the vehicle and skip to Step 23.

✳✳ WARNING

Be careful not to damage the CV-joints, boots, or splined shafts when removing the axle.

22. Follow these steps to remove the axle assembly:

   a. Verify that the axle assembly is securely supported by the floor jack. Remove the safety stands.

   b. First, slide the axle to the left to release the splined stub axle of the right halfshaft.

   c. Next, lower the axle slightly and slide it to the right so the left halfshaft clears the left lower control arm.

   d. Finally, completely lower the axle from the vehicle.

23. Remove the right halfshaft from the vehicle. Follow these steps to remove the right axle shaft seal and bearing:

   a. Remove the snapring from the splined shaft.

   b. Remove the shaft bearing. Use a puller if necessary, but don't damage the shaft or splines.

   c. Remove the inner snapring.

   d. Remove the axle mounting bracket and oil seal from the right halfshaft.

24. Drain the lubricant from the shift-on-the-fly gearbox.

25. With the axle out of the vehicle, unbolt the left halfshaft from the axle case. Remove the halfshaft together with the left axle mounting bracket.

26. Loosen the shift-on-the-fly actuator mounting bolts in a crisscross pattern. Remove the actuator assembly from the gearbox.

27. Unbolt the shift-on-the-fly actuator gearbox from the axle tube flange.

28. Slowly pull the gearbox straight off the axle tube. Be careful not to loose the sleeve and clutch gear if they fall out of the gearbox.

29. Remove the outer snapring from the left axle shaft. Draw the axle shaft out of the axle tube.

30. Remove the left axle shaft oil seal from the axle tube. Be careful not to damage the sealing surface.

31. Inspect the axle shaft, bearing, and clutch gear components for any damage:

   a. Inspect the axle shaft splines for damage, and replace as necessary. Use a dial gauge and center blocks to inspect the shaft run-out. If run-out exceeds 0.02 in. (0.5mm), replace the shaft. Don't try to heat the axle shaft to correct excess run-out.

   b. Insert the clutch gear into the axle shaft and inspect the motion and play of the inner bearing and needle bearing. If either bearing exhibits smoothness or play, they should be replaced.

   c. Check the clutch sleeve for wear. First, coat the clutch gear with gear oil, and then slide the clutch sleeve back and forth over the gear to simulate operation. If the sleeve and gear exhibit smoothness or play, they must be replaced.

   d. Check the clutch sleeve groove width. Groove width should not exceed 0.28 in. (7.1mm).

   e. Check the external diameter of the narrowest part of the clutch gear. The diameter shouldn't exceed 1.456 in. (36.98mm).

32. Remove the inner snapring from the axle shaft bearing.

33. Remove the inner shaft bearing:

   a. Install tool No. J-37452, or an equivalent bearing remover onto the axle shaft.

   b. Place the axle shaft and the bearing remover into a press.

   c. Press the bearing from the axle shaft. Don't damage the axle shaft.

34. Remove the needle bearing from the axle shaft clutch gear:

   a. Support the axle shaft in a padded vise.

   b. Install tool No. J-26941 into the bearing. Install tool No. J-2619-01, or an equivalent slide hammer onto the bearing removal tool.

   c. Work the slide hammer to gradually remove the needle bearing from the axle shaft.

To install:

➡**Use new self-locking nuts and color-coded bolts when assembling the axle assembly mounts and suspension components. Suspension fasteners should be tightened to their final torque specifications when the vehicle is on the ground.**

35. Clean and dry all axle and shift-on-the-fly gearbox sealing surfaces.

36. Thoroughly lubricate a new axle shaft seal with clean gear oil. Use tool No. J-41693, or an equivalent seal driver to install it into the axle tube.

37. Use tool No. J-41694, or an equivalent bearing driver to install a new needle bearing.

38. Install a new inner snapring.

39. Use tool No. J-4169, or an equivalent press base to press a new bearing onto the axle shaft.

40. Install the axle shaft into the axle tube. Don't damage the new oil seal. Install a new outer snapring.

41. Lubricate the clutch gear and clutch sleeve with SAE 75W-90 GL-5 gear oil and install them.

42. Apply a 1mm-wide bead of liquid gasket to the axle tube sealing surface. Install the shift-on-the-fly gearbox onto the axle tube before the sealant cures.

43. Tighten the shift-on-the-fly gearbox bolts to 85 ft. lbs. (116 Nm) in a two-step crisscross pattern.

44. Install the shift position switch onto the actuator and tighten it to 29 ft. lbs. (39 Nm).

45. Install the actuator assembly:

   a. Apply a 1mm-wide bead of liquid gasket to the actuator sealing surface. Don't allow the sealant to cure before installation.

   b. Align the shift fork arms with the groove of the clutch sleeve and install the actuator.

   c. Tighten the actuator mounting bolts to 10 ft. lbs. (13 Nm) in a crisscross sequence.

46. Install the spacer onto the left front halfshaft.

47. Install the halfshaft and axle mounting bracket assembly onto the axle. Tighten the bolts to 85 ft. lbs. (116 Nm) in a crisscross sequence.

48. After the sealant has fully cured, refill the shift-on-the-fly gearbox with SAE 75W-90 GL-5 gear oil.

49. Assemble the right halfshaft and axle mounting bracket assembly, as follows:

    a. Install the axle mounting bracket onto the halfshaft.

    b. Lubricate and install a new oil seal.

    c. Install a new inner snapring.

    d. Install a new bearing.

    e. Install a new outer snapring.

50. Place the right halfshaft and axle mounting bracket assembly into position, and rest it on the right lower control arm.

51. Position the axle and left halfshaft assembly on a floor jack. Raise the axle into position.

52. Fit the right halfshaft and axle mounting bracket assembly into the differential. Make sure the splined stub axle shaft is fully seated. Be careful not to distort the oil seal when connecting the right mounting bracket to the differential.

53. Tighten the right halfshaft and axle mounting bracket assembly mounting bolts to 85 ft. lbs. (116 Nm) in a crisscross sequence.

54. Raise the axle assembly into its final position and support it with safety stands.

55. Install the mounting bracket bolts, nuts, and spacers. The washer fits under the bolt and the spacer is used with the nut. Tighten the mounting nuts and bolts to 112 ft. lbs. (152 Nm).

56. Install the steering knuckles and assemble any suspension components that were disconnected or removed.

57. Install the brake backing plates and the rotor and hub assemblies.

58. Install the caliper mounting brackets and the brake calipers.

59. Install the VSV onto the axle tube. Reconnect the vacuum hoses and the 2P connector. Then, install the VSV skid plate.

60. Refill the differential with gear oil. Check the oil level in the gear case. Use new crush washers and tighten both drain plugs to 58 ft. lbs. (78 Nm).

61. Verify that all axle assembly mounting components have been installed.

62. Align the front driveshaft matchmarks. Install the driveshaft flange bolts and tighten them to 46 ft. lbs. (63 Nm).

63. Install the suspension crossmember and tighten the bolts to 58 ft. lbs. (78 Nm).

64. Install the steering linkage assembly.

65. If equipped, reconnect the ABS front wheel sensors.

66. Install the radiator skid plate. Tighten the bolts to 58 ft. lbs. (78 Nm).

67. Install the transfer case skid plates and tighten their bolts to 27 ft. lbs. (37 Nm).

68. If necessary, bleed the brake system.

69. Install the front wheels.

70. Lower the vehicle and remove the rear wheel blocks.

71. Tighten the suspension bushing fasteners to their final torque specifications.

72. Verify that the front axle and hubs engage and disengage properly.

73. If equipped with shift–on–the–fly four–wheel drive, make sure the VSV and actuator function correctly.

74. Check and adjust the front wheel alignment and ride height.

75. Road test the vehicle.

CV-JOINT OVERHAUL

♦ See Figures 65 thru 71

The Isuzu trucks and Sport Utility vehicles use a Double Offset Joint (DOJ) for the inner CV-joint and a Birfield Joint (BJ) for the outer CV-joint. The BJ is not serviceable and must be replaced as an assembly.

1. Remove the halfshaft from the vehicle, as described earlier in this section.

2. Clean the assembly of all grease and dirt.

3. Remove the inner CV-joint boot clamp, then slide the boot away from the joint. To remove the clamp, it may be necessary to pry the hooked end of the clamp up with a small prytool.

4. Remove the circlip from the DOJ case, then pull the case and inner shaft off the inner joint (ball guide, ball retainer and ball assembly).

5. Carefully pry the balls out of the ball guide with a prytool.

6. Using snapring pliers, remove the ball retainer snapring. Slide the ball retainer and ball guide from the splined shaft.

7. Remove the smaller inner boot clamp, then slide the inner boot off the shaft.

8. Remove the 2 outer CV-joint boot clamps, then slide the outer boot off the shaft.

9. The Birfield joint is not serviceable; replace the entire BJ assembly, if defective.

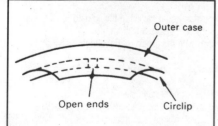

Fig. 65 To separate the halfshaft from the DOJ case, remove the DOJ case retaining circlip

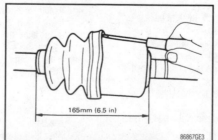

Fig. 66 Remove the ball retainer snapring, then slide the ball retainer and ball guide off the shaft

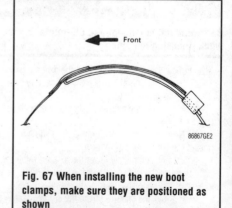

Fig. 67 When installing the new boot clamps, make sure they are positioned as shown

Fig. 68 Install the DOJ case-to-DOJ assembly circlip so the ends are positioned away from the ball groove (as shown)

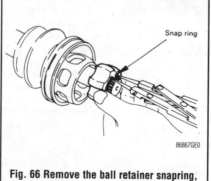

Fig. 69 Position the boot on the DOJ case and shaft as shown, then allow excess pressure out of the boot

Fig. 70 Removing the outer band from the CV-boot

10. Clean all grease and dirt from the CV-joint components. Inspect the DOJ case, balls, ball guide, and ball retainer for wear, damage, corrosion or any other abnormal condition. Replace the components, if necessary.

To assemble:

11. With the Birfield joint shafts bent at a 40 degree angle, turn one of the shafts and make sure it turns smoothly and normally.

12. Place tape on the splines to prevent damage to the joint boots.

13. Coat the inner BJ shaft with a thin film of grease to help installation of the boots, then slide the outer boot and clamps onto the inner shaft. Make sure the boot is installed so the big end faces toward the BJ.

14. Fill the outer CV-joint boot with 5.25 oz. (150g) of new CV-joint grease, then install new clamps to hold the boot to the joint. Make sure the boot is free of distortion after installing the boot clamps.

15. Slide the inner joint boot and vibration damper, if so equipped, onto the shaft. Make sure the big end of the inner boot faces toward the inner end of the halfshaft.

16. Install the ball retainer, guide and snapring onto the shaft. Install the ball retainer with the smaller diameter side toward the Birfield joint end of the shaft.

17. Align the track on the ball retainer with the windows in the ball guide, then install the 6 DOJ balls.

18. Fill the inner boot and DOJ with 5.25 oz. (150g) new grease, then install the DOJ case over the ball guide and retainer. Install the circular clip into the groove so the open ends are positioned away from the ball groove.

19. Slide the boot over the DOJ and onto the DOJ case, insert a tool under the boot lip to allow the pressure to equalize and tighten the new clamps. Make sure the boot is installed so the edge of the smaller end is 6.5 in. (16.5cm) from the opposite edge of the DOJ case (refer to the illustration).

20. Install the shaft into the vehicle, as described earlier in this section.

Pinion Seal

REMOVAL & INSTALLATION

♦ **See Figures 72 and 73**

1981–94 Models

1. Apply the parking brake and block the rear wheels.

2. Raise and safely support the front of the vehicle on jackstands. If necessary, remove the skid plate.

3. Matchmark and remove the driveshaft, as described earlier in this section.

4. Using a torque meter, check the turning torque of the pinion before proceeding. This is the torque that must be reached during installation of the pinion nut.

5. Using a pinion flange holding tool, remove the pinion nut and washer.

6. Remove the pinion flange (driveshaft yoke) from the pinion gear.

7. Remove the dust cover, if equipped.

8. Pry the pinion seal out of the differential carrier.

9. Clean and inspect the sealing surface of the carrier.

To install:

10. Apply oil to the lip of the seal.

11. Using a seal driver tool, drive the new seal into the carrier until the flange on the seal is flush with the carrier.

12. If applicable, install the dust shield.

13. Install the pinion flange (driveshaft yoke).

14. With the seal installed, the pinion bearing preload must be set. Tighten the pinion nut while holding the flange, until the turning torque is the same as before removal of the nut.

15. Align the matchmarks and install the driveshaft.

16. Check the level of the differential lubricant when finished.

17. Lower the vehicle and remove the rear wheel blocks.

1995–96 Models

1. Apply the parking brake and block the rear wheels.

2. Safely raise and support the front of the vehicle on jackstands.

3. Matchmark the front driveshaft, then remove the bolts attaching the driveshaft to the front axle flange.

4. Remove the driveshaft from the pinion flange and support it out of the way

5. Note the number of threads of the pinion gear that protrude from the flange nut, this will help to obtain the proper pinion bearing preload during installation. Remove the flange nut. Use a flange holding wrench (J-8614–01 for Pick-Up models, J-37221 for Trooper models, J-8614–01 for Rodeo models, or equivalent) when removing the flange nut.

6. Place a suitable container under the differential to catch any gear oil.

7. Remove the flange and dust cover from the front differential.

8. Remove the pinion oil seal from the differential.

To install:

9. Lubricate the new oil seal with axle lubricant.

10. Install the new oil seal with a seal installer (J-24250 or equivalent).

11. Install the dust cover and the flange.

12. Lubricate the pinion threads, then install a new flange nut. Tighten the flange nut to 66–101 ft. lbs. (89–137 Nm) for a used pinion bearing, or to 130–203 ft. lbs. (177–275 Nm) for a new bearing. Do not overtighten the flange nut.

13. Measure the pinion bearing preload with a torque meter, the starting torque should be 3.9 inch lbs. (0.44 Nm), or if a new pinion bearing was installed, the torque should be 7.8 inch lbs. (0.88 Nm).

14. Stake the flange nut at 2 locations and recheck the bearing preload (readjust the preload if necessary).

15. Install the front driveshaft, tighten the driveshaft nut and bolts to 46 ft. lbs. (63 Nm).

16. Check the level of lubricant in the front axle and add, if necessary.

17. Lower the vehicle and remove the rear wheel blocks.

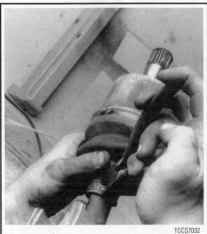

TCCS7032

Fig. 71 Removing the inner band from the CV-boot

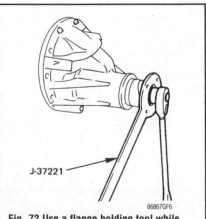

J-37221

86867GF6

Fig. 72 Use a flange holding tool while loosening and tightening the flange nut— Tool J-37221 is specifically for Trooper models, other models similar

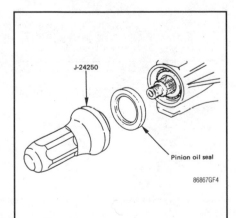

J-24250

Pinion oil seal

86867GF4

Fig. 73 Install a new pinion seal by driving it into place with the Tool J-24250 (or equivalent) and a hammer

REAR DRIVE AXLE

Identification

For axle identification, refer to Section 1.

Axle Shaft, Bearing and Seal

REMOVAL & INSTALLATION

Pick-Up, Amigo, 1991–94 Rodeo and 1985–94 Trooper Models

BANJO TYPE—WITH REAR DISC BRAKES

♦ See Figures 74 and 75

1. Block the front wheels.
2. Raise and safely support the rear of the vehicle on jackstands.
3. Remove the rear wheel assembly and rear brake components. For more information on removing the brake components, refer to Section 9.
4. Remove the 4 axle retaining nuts and lockwashers.
5. Pull the axle shaft assembly out of the axle housing.
6. Remove the snapring and bearing cup from the axle shaft.
7. Grind the retainer ring down until thin enough to be broken with a chisel and hammer; do not grind the axle shaft. Break the retainer ring with a hammer and chisel.
8. Break the bearing cage with a hammer and chisel and remove the bearing cage and rollers.
9. Remove the oil seal, retainer and the parking brake assembly from the axle.
10. Remove the inner race from the axle shaft using a press and a bearing splitter.

To install:

11. Install the parking brake assembly and the oil seal, in the proper direction, into the bearing holder. Install the bearing holder onto the axle assembly.
12. Press the bearing onto the axle shaft using a steel pipe 25.5 in. (64.77cm) long, 2 in. (50.8mm) O.D and 1.625 in. (41.27mm) I.D.

→Install the bearing with the cup toward the inboard side.

13. Install the retainer ring using a press. If equipped with a bearing retainer bolt, tighten the bolt to 275 ft. lbs. (372 Nm).
14. Install the snapring.
15. Slide the axle shaft into the axle tube. Make sure the splines on the axle shaft properly engage the grooves in the differential unit.
16. Install the lockwashers and nuts. Tighten the nuts to 55 ft. lbs. (75 Nm), or to 76 ft. lbs. (103 Nm) for 1992–95 Pick-Up models.
17. Install the rear brake components, as described in Section 9.
18. Install the wheel and tire assemblies, lower the vehicle and remove the front wheel blocks.

BANJO TYPE—WITH REAR DRUM BRAKES

1. Block the front wheels.
2. Raise and safely support the rear of the vehicle on jackstands.
3. Remove the rear wheels and brake components.

4. Remove the 4 axle retaining bolts.
5. Using a slide hammer, pull the axle out of the housing.
6. Support the axle shaft and remove the bearing retainer locknut.
7. Remove the retainer, bearing and seal from the axle shaft.
8. Using a seal driver tool, remove the seal from the bearing holder.

To install:

9. Install a new seal in the bearing holder with the seal driver tool. Install the bearing holder.
10. Position the bearing and lockwasher. Tighten the bearing retaining nut to 188–195 ft. lbs. (250–275 Nm).
11. If your vehicle had shims between the bearing holder and the axle case at disassembly (1992–95 Pick-Up and Amigo models), perform the following procedure:

   a. Install the axle assembly into the axle housing, making sure the end splines of the axle shaft engage the grooves in the differential unit correctly, with a 0.079 in. (2mm) thick spacer between the bearing holder and the axle case flange.

   b. Install the axle shaft assembly on the opposite side and push it in until it fits against the differential thrust block.

   c. Measure the clearance between the bearing holder and the axle case flange and determine the thickness of the shim to be installed by the following formula: Measured clearance + 0.012 in. (0.3mm) = thickness of shim to be installed on the second axle shaft. Shims are available in the following thicknesses: 0.039 in. (1mm), 0.026 in. (0.5mm), 0.005 in. (0.13mm), 0.003 in. (0.076mm), 0.002 in. (0.05mm).

12. If the vehicle did not utilize shims, install the axle shaft into the housing, making sure the splines on the end of the axle shaft properly engage the grooves in the differential unit.
13. Tighten the 4 axle retaining bolts to 50–58 ft. lbs. (68–81 Nm).
14. Install the rear brake components. Adjust the rear brakes if necessary. Refer to Section 9 for more information regarding rear brake procedures.
15. Install the rear wheels.
16. Check the level of the axle lubricant and add fluid, if necessary. For more details, refer to Section 1.
17. Lower the vehicle and remove the front wheel blocks.

SALISBURY (SAGINAW) REAR AXLE

♦ See Figures 76, 77, 78 and 79

1. Block the front wheels.
2. Raise and safely support the front of the vehicle on jackstands.
3. Remove the rear wheels and brake drums.
4. Drain the rear axle lubricant into a catch pan by removing the rear axle housing cover. For more information, refer to Section 1.
5. Remove the pinion shaft lockbolt and the pinion shaft.

→Do not turn the driveshaft or rotate the ring gear with the pinion shaft removed or the spider gears will not be properly aligned and may fall out.

6. From the wheel mounting flange, push the axle shaft slightly inward and remove the **C** lockclip from the innermost end of the axle shaft.
7. Pull the axle shaft out of the axle housing.

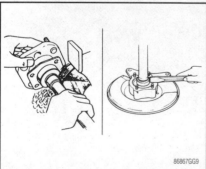

86867GG9

Fig. 74 To remove the retainer, first grind the retainer until it is thin, then break it in ½ with a hammer and chisel

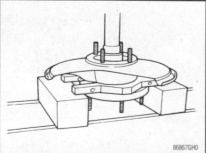

86867GH0

Fig. 75 Support the bearing holder with Bearing Remover Tool J-33949, or an equivalent sized pair of wooden blocks, and drive the axle out

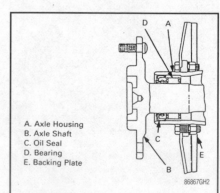

A. Axle Housing
B. Axle Shaft
C. Oil Seal
D. Bearing
E. Backing Plate

86867GH2

Fig. 76 Cross-section of the axle shaft bearings and seal

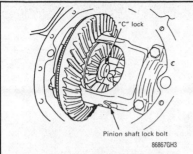

Fig. 77 After removing the pinion shaft lockbolt and pinion shaft, push the axle in toward the differential and remove the C lockclip

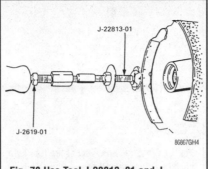

Fig. 78 Use Tool J–22813–01 and J–2619–01, or their equivalents, to pull the old axle shaft bearing out of the axle tube

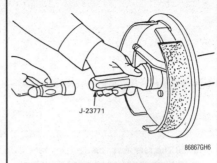

Fig. 79 Use Tool J–23771, or equivalent, and a hammer to tap a new oil seal into the axle tube bore

8. Pry the oil seal out of the axle housing with an oil seal removing tool.

9. Use tool No. J–22813–01, or a similar slide hammer with a hook, to remove the axle bearing from the end of the axle tube.

To install:

10. Use a bearing driver, or properly–sized large socket, to drive the new bearing into the axle shaft housing. Make sure it is installed until it is completely flush against the bearing stop In the axle tube.

11. Use an oil seal installer, or properly-sized large socket, to install the new oil seal into the axle housing.

12. Carefully slide the axle shaft into the axle housing, taking care not to damage the oil seal. The axle may have to be rotated a little to properly engage the splines in the differential side gear.

13. Push the axle shaft in until the **C** lockclip groove is accessible, then install the **C** lockclip.

14. Pull the axle shaft out to seat the **C** lockclip against the stop. Install the pinion shaft and pinion shaft lockbolt. Tighten the lockbolt to 25 ft. lbs. (34 Nm).

15. Install the differential cover using a new gasket. Tighten the cover bolts to 20 ft. lbs. (27 Nm).

16. Fill the differential with the proper amount of lubricant. For more information, refer to Section 1.

17. Install the rear brake drums and rear wheels.

18. Lower the vehicle and remove the front wheel blocks.

1995–96 Trooper Models

1. Block the front wheels.

2. Raise and safely support the front of the vehicle on jackstands.

3. Remove the rear wheels.

4. Remove the brake caliper and caliper brackets. Support the calipers up and out of the way with wire. Do not disconnect the brake hoses.

5. Remove the rear brake rotors. If equipped with ABS, unbolt the wheel sensor wire brackets from the axle tubes. Be careful not to damage the wheel sensors.

6. Disconnect the parking brake cable from the parking brake shoe assembly. Unbolt the brake cable bracket from the backing plate. Remove the parking brake shoe assembly. For more information, refer to Section 9.

7. Matchmark the bearing case to the axle tube flange. Mark the hubs so the axle shafts will not be confused.

8. Remove the bearing case mounting nuts from the axle tube flanges.

9. Remove the axle shafts from the axle.

10. Remove the snapring from the bearing case retainer.

11. Mount the axle shaft and bearing assembly into the special press holder, tool No. J–39211 or equivalent. Place the axle shaft assembly and the special holder into a hydraulic press.

12. Press the retainer from the axle shaft.

13. Remove the axle shaft bearing, bearing case, and brake rotor backing plate from the axle shaft.

14. Inspect the axle shaft and its splines for signs of wear, scoring, or other damage. Replace the retainer if it is damaged in the press.

To install:

15. Use tool No. J–39379 or a suitably–sized seal installer to install a new shaft seal into the bearing case.

16. Assemble the brake backing plate and bearing case onto the axle shaft.

17. Install a new bearing onto the axle shaft. Place the retainer into position on the axle shaft.

18. Mount the axle shaft and bearing assembly into the special press base, tool No. J–39212. Place the axle shaft assembly and the special base into a hydraulic press.

19. Press the retainer onto the axle shaft. Do not exert more pressing force than is necessary to fit the retainer and bearing assembly together.

20. Install a new snapring onto the bearing case retainer.

21. Install the axle shaft assembly into the axle tube. Make sure the splines engage into the differential carrier. Use the matchmarks as reference points.

22. Install the bearing case nuts with new lockwashers. Tighten the nuts to 54 ft. lbs. (74 Nm).

23. Install the parking brake shoes. Reconnect the parking brake cable to the shoes and install its backing plate bracket mounting bolts.

24. Install the ABS wheel sensor wire brackets onto the axle tubes.

25. Install the rear brake rotors.

26. Install the brake caliper brackets and calipers. Tighten the bracket bolts on 1995 models to 109 ft. lbs. (148 Nm), or to 76 ft. lbs. (103 Nm) for 1996 models. Tighten the caliper bolts to 32 ft. lbs. (44 Nm).

27. Install the rear wheels.

28. Bleed the brakes, if necessary.

29. Check the differential oil level and refill as necessary. For more details, refer to Section 1.

30. Road test the vehicle and check for abnormal bearing and gear noises.

1995–96 Rodeo Models

➡The Dana rear drive axle on the 1995–96 Rodeo models is easy to distinguish from the Saginaw rear drive axle as follows: the Dana rear differential cover is asymmetrical and angular, whereas the Saginaw rear cover is symmetrical and oval-shaped.

SALISBURY TYPE (DANA)

▶ See Figures 80 thru 85

1. Block the front wheels.

2. Raise and safely support the front of the vehicle on jackstands.

3. Remove the rear wheels.

4. If equipped with disc brakes, remove the rear brake caliper and support bracket. Use wire hooks to support the calipers.

5. If equipped with drum brakes, remove the brake drums and shoe assemblies.

6. Place a container under the axle flange to catch any dripping gear oil.

7. Remove the 4 axle retaining nuts and lockwashers.

8. Remove the axle shaft assembly from the axle housing.

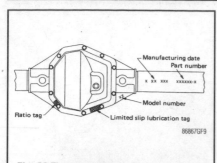

Fig. 80 The rear cover on the Dana rear axle is angular and asymmetrical, unlike the Saginaw rear axle

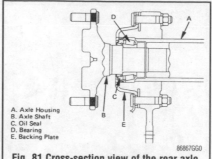

A. Axle Housing
B. Axle Shaft
C. Oil Seal
D. Bearing
E. Backing Plate

Fig. 81 Cross-section view of the rear axle shaft bearings and oil seal—Dana Salisbury Type rear axle with disc brakes

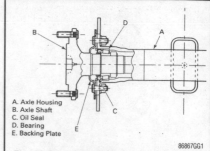

A. Axle Housing
B. Axle Shaft
C. Oil Seal
D. Bearing
E. Backing Plate

Fig. 82 Cross-section view of the rear axle shaft bearings and oil seal—Dana Salisbury Type rear axle with drum brakes

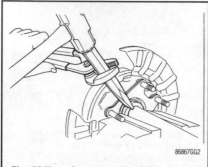

Fig. 83 Use a hammer and chisel to break the old retainer ring off the axle shaft

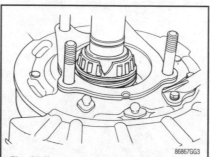

Fig. 84 Use the hammer and chisel to also break the bearing cage so it can be removed from the axle shaft as well

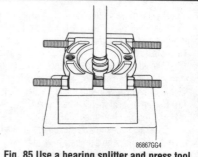

Fig. 85 Use a bearing splitter and press tool (OTC-1126 or equivalent) to remove the old inner bearing race from the axle shaft

9. Remove the snapring and bearing cup from the axle shaft.

10. Break the retainer ring with a hammer and chisel.

11. Break the bearing cage with a hammer and chisel and remove the bearing cage and roller.

12. Remove the oil seal and retainer. Then, remove the parking brake assembly and brake backing plate from the axle.

13. Use a press and a bearing splitter to remove the inner race from the axle shaft.

To install:

14. Install the parking brake assembly and brake backing plate. Then, install the retainer plate.

15. Install the oil seal into the bearing holder. Install the bearing holder onto the axle assembly. The cup side of the

bearing faces the inboard side of the axle shaft.

16. Press the bearing assembly on the axle shaft.

17. Install the retainer ring using a press.

18. Install the snapring.

19. Place the axle assembly into the axle housing, making sure the splines on the end of the axle shafts engage the grooves in the differential unit properly, then install the lockwashers and retaining nuts. Tighten the retaining nuts to 55 ft. lbs. (75 Nm).

20. Install the rear brake components.

21. Refill the differential with the proper type of gear oil. For more details, refer to Section 1.

22. Install the rear wheels, lower the vehicle and remove the front wheel blocks.

SALISBURY TYPE (SAGINAW)

1. Block the front wheels.

2. Raise and safely support the front of the vehicle on jackstands.

3. Remove the rear wheels and brake drums.

4. Drain the rear axle lubricant into a catch pan by removing the rear axle housing cover. For more information, refer to Section 1.

5. Remove the pinion shaft lockbolt and the pinion shaft.

➡**Do not turn the driveshaft or rotate the ring gear with the pinion shaft removed or the spider gears will not be properly aligned and may fall out.**

6. From the wheel mounting flange, push the axle shaft slightly inward and remove the **C** lockclip from the innermost end of the axle shaft.

7. Pull the axle shaft out of the axle housing.

8. Pry the oil seal out of the axle housing with an oil seal removing tool.

9. Use tool No. J–22813–01, or a similar slide hammer with a hook, to remove the axle bearing from the end of the axle tube.

To install:

10. Use a bearing driver, or properly–sized large socket, to drive the new bearing into the axle shaft housing. Make sure it is installed until it is completely flush against the bearing stop in the axle tube.

11. Use an oil seal installer, or properly-sized large socket, to install the new oil seal into the axle housing.

12. Carefully slide the axle shaft into the axle housing, taking care not to damage the oil seal. The axle may have to be rotated a little to properly engage the splines in the differential side gear.

13. Push the axle shaft in until the **C** lockclip groove is accessible, then install the **C** lockclip.

14. Pull the axle shaft out to seat the **C** lockclip against the stop. Install the pinion shaft and pinion shaft lockbolt. Tighten the lockbolt to 25 ft. lbs. (34 Nm).

15. Install the differential cover using a new gasket. Tighten the cover bolts to 20 ft. lbs. (27 Nm).

16. Fill the differential with the proper amount of lubricant. For more information, refer to Section 1.

17. Install the rear brake drums and rear wheels.

18. Lower the vehicle and remove the front wheel blocks.

Pinion Seal

REMOVAL & INSTALLATION

Pick-Up, Amigo and Trooper Models

BANJO TYPE

1. Safely raise and support the vehicle.
2. Matchmark the driveshaft, then remove the bolts attaching the driveshaft to the rear axle flange.
3. Remove the driveshaft from the pinion flange and support out of the way.
4. Check the preload with an inch–pound torque wrench.
5. Remove the flange nut. Use a flange holding wrench (Tool J–8614–01 for 1995 Pick-Ups, Tool J-37221 for 1995–96 Troopers), or equivalent, when removing the flange nut.
6. Place a suitable container under the differential to catch any gear oil.
7. Remove the pinion flange.
8. Remove the pinion oil seal from the differential.
9. Remove the oil seal slinger.
10. Remove the pinion bearing using a outer bearing remover (Tool J–39602 or equivalent).
11. Remove and discard the collapsible spacer from the differential.

To install:

12. Inspect the pinion flange for tool marks, nicks, or damage such as a groove worn by the seal. Replace the flange if necessary. Inspect the carrier bore for burrs that may cause leaks around the outside of the seal.
13. Install a new collapsible spacer onto the pinion.
14. Install the outer bearing onto the pinion. Do not drive the bearing into position; it will be installed when the flange nut is tightened.
15. Install the oil seal slinger.
16. Lubricate the new oil seal with axle lubricant.
17. Install the new oil seal with a seal installer (Tool J–23911 for 1995 Pick-Ups, J-37263 for 1995–96 Troopers, or equivalent).
18. Install the pinion flange to the pinion, by tapping it lightly with a soft faced hammer, until a few threads show through the pinion flange.
19. Install the pinion washer and nut. Tighten the pinion nut to the following torque values:
   - Trooper—180–216 ft. lbs. (245–294 Nm)
   - Pick-Up and Amigo with drum brakes—130–202 ft. lbs. (177–275 Nm) for new bearings, 65–101 ft. lbs. (88–137 Nm) for used bearings
   - Pick-Up and Amigo with disc brakes—181–217 ft. lbs. (245–294 Nm) for new bearings, 90–109 ft. lbs. (123–147 Nm)

Rotate the pinion while tightening the nut to seat the bearings.

20. Check the preload torque (the amount of force necessary to turn the pinion flange). Use an inch–pound torque wrench to check the preload, make sure the pinion preload is equal to or slightly over the reading recorded during removal.
21. Stake the flange nut at 2 points, to keep the flange nut from loosening.
22. Connect the driveshaft to the flange and install the nuts and bolts. Tighten the nuts and bolts to 46 ft. lbs. (63 Nm).

23. Check the level of lubricant in the rear axle and add as necessary.
24. Lower the vehicle.

SALISBURY TYPE (SAGINAW)

1. Block the front wheels.
2. Safely raise and support the front of the vehicle on jackstands.
3. Matchmark the driveshaft flanges and remove the bolts from the rear driveshaft flange.
4. Remove the driveshaft from the pinion flange and support out of the way.
5. Matchmark the pinion flange, pinion shaft and the nut to obtain the proper bearing preload during installation. Remove the flange nut and washer. Use a flange–holding wrench (Tool J–8614–01 or equivalent) when removing the flange nut.
6. Place a drain pan under the differential to catch any gear oil.
7. Remove the pinion flange by using the special Tools J-8614–1, J-8614–2 and J-8614–3, or their equivalents.
8. Remove the pinion oil seal from the differential.

To install:

9. Inspect the pinion flange for tool marks, nicks, or damage such as a groove worn by the seal. Replace the flange if necessary. Inspect the carrier bore for burrs that may cause leaks around the outside of the seal.
10. Lubricate the new oil seal with axle lubricant.
11. Install the new oil seal with a seal installer (Tool J–23911 or equivalent).
12. Apply a small amount of sealant to the spline of the pinion flange. Install the pinion flange to the pinion, by tapping it lightly with a soft–faced hammer, until a few threads show through the pinion flange.
13. Install the washer and nut to the pinion, hold the flange in place and tighten the nut. Tighten the nut $\frac{1}{16}$ in. (1.59 mm) beyond the alignment marks.
14. Connect the driveshaft to the flange and install the nuts and bolts. Tighten the nuts and bolts to 46 ft. lbs. (63 Nm).
15. Refill the rear axle with lubricant. For more information, refer to Section 1.
16. Lower the vehicle and remove the front wheel blocks.

Rodeo Models

SALISBURY TYPE (DANA)

▶ **See Figures 86, 87 and 88**

➡ **The Dana rear drive axle on the 1995–96 Rodeo models is easy to distinguish from the Saginaw rear drive axle as follows: the Dana rear differential cover is asymmetrical and angular, whereas the Saginaw rear cover is symmetrical and oval-shaped.**

1. Block the front wheels.
2. Safely raise and support the front of the vehicle on jackstands.
3. Matchmark the driveshaft flanges. Remove the bolts from the rear driveshaft flange.
4. Separate the driveshaft from the pinion flange and support it out of the way.
5. Check and record the amount of torque required to turn the pinion shaft (preload) with an inch pound torque wrench. This figure will represent the preload of the pinion bearing and seal.

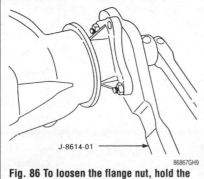

Fig. 86 To loosen the flange nut, hold the flange stable with Tool J-8614–01, or equivalent

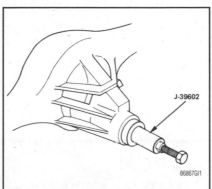

Fig. 87 Remove the pinion oil seal with Special Tool J-39602, or equivalent

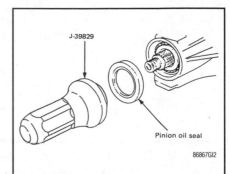

Fig. 88 Use the oil seal installer tool J-39829, or equivalent, to drive the new oil seal into the differential case

6. Remove the flange nut. Use a flange–holding wrench (part No. J–8614–01 or equivalent) when removing the flange nut.

7. Place a drain pan under the differential to catch any gear oil.

8. Pull the flange from the pinion shaft.

9. Remove the pinion oil seal from the differential with a small prytool. Make sure not to scratch, gouge or otherwise damage the inside bore of the differential case.

10. Remove the oil seal slinger, if equipped.

11. Remove the pinion bearing using a outer bearing remover (Tool J–39602 or equivalent).

12. Remove and discard the collapsible spacer from the differential.

To install:

13. Inspect the pinion flange for tool marks, nicks, or damage such as a groove worn by the seal. Replace the flange if any such damage is evident. Inspect the carrier bore for burrs that may cause leaks around the outside of the seal.

14. Install a new collapsible spacer onto the pinion.

15. Install the outer bearing onto the pinion. Do not drive the bearing into position; it will be correctly positioned when the flange nut is tightened.

16. Install the oil seal slinger.

17. Lubricate the new oil seal with axle lubricant, then install the new oil seal with a seal installer (part No. J–39829, or equivalent).

18. Fit the pinion flange to the pinion. Then, install it by tapping lightly with a soft–faced hammer until a few threads show through the pinion flange.

19. Install the pinion washer and nut. Tighten the pinion nut until the end–play starts to disappear. Rotate the pinion while tightening the nut to evenly seat the bearings.

20. Once there is no end-play in the pinion, check the preload torque. Use an inch–pound torque wrench to check the preload, make sure the pinion preload is equal to or slightly greater than the reading recorded during removal.

21. Connect the driveshaft to the pinion flange and install the nuts and bolts. Tighten the nuts and bolts to 46 ft. lbs. (63 Nm).

22. Refill the rear axle with lubricant.

23. Lower the vehicle and remove the front wheel blocks.

SALISBURY TYPE (SAGINAW)

1. Block the front wheels.

2. Safely raise and support the front of the vehicle on jackstands.

3. Matchmark the driveshaft flanges and remove the bolts from the rear driveshaft flange.

4. Remove the driveshaft from the pinion flange and support out of the way.

5. Matchmark the pinion flange, pinion shaft and the nut to obtain the proper bearing preload during installation. Remove the flange nut and washer. Use a flange–holding wrench (Tool J–8614–01 or equivalent) when removing the flange nut.

6. Place a drain pan under the differential to catch any gear oil.

7. Remove the pinion flange.

8. Remove the pinion oil seal from the differential.

To install:

9. Inspect the pinion flange for tool marks, nicks, or damage such as a groove worn by the seal. Replace the flange if necessary. Inspect the carrier bore for burrs that may cause leaks around the outside of the seal.

10. Lubricate the new oil seal with axle lubricant.

11. Install the new oil seal with a seal installer (Tool J–23911 or equivalent).

12. Apply a small amount of sealant to the spline of the pinion flange. Install the pinion flange to the pinion, by tapping it lightly with a soft–faced hammer, until a few threads show through the pinion flange.

13. Install the washer and nut to the pinion, hold the flange in place and tighten the nut. Tighten the nut 1/16 in. (1.59 mm) beyond the alignment marks.

14. Connect the driveshaft to the flange and install the nuts and bolts. Tighten the nuts and bolts to 46 ft. lbs. (63 Nm).

15. Refill the rear axle with lubricant. For more information, refer to Section 1.

16. Lower the vehicle and remove the front wheel blocks.

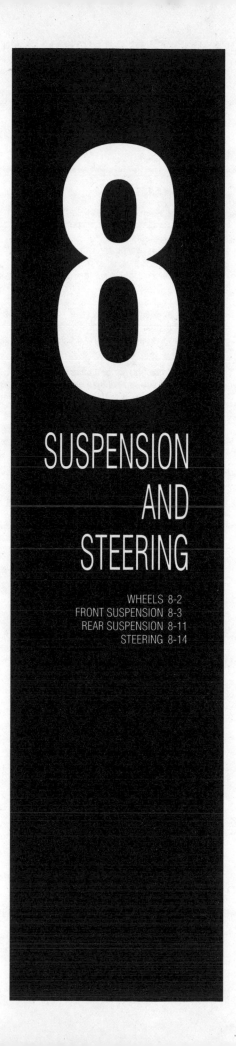

8

SUSPENSION
AND
STEERING

WHEELS

Wheel Assembly

REMOVAL & INSTALLATION

▶ **See Figures 1, 2 and 3**

1. Park the vehicle on a level surface.
2. Remove the jack, tire iron and, if necessary, the spare tire from their storage compartments.
3. Check the owner's manual or refer to Section 1 of this manual for the jacking points on your vehicle. Then, place the jack in the proper position.
4. If equipped with lug nut trim caps, remove them by either unscrewing or pulling them off the lug nuts, as appropriate. Consult the owner's manual, if necessary.
5. If equipped with a wheel cover or hub cap, insert the tapered end of the tire iron in the groove and pry off the cover.
6. Apply the parking brake and block the diagonally opposite wheel with a wheel chock or two.

➡**Wheel chocks may be purchased at your local auto parts store, or a block of wood cut into wedges may be used. If possible, keep one or two of the chocks in your tire storage compartment, in case any of the tires has to be removed on the side of the road.**

7. If equipped with an automatic transmission/transaxle, place the selector lever in **P** or Park; with a manual transmission/transaxle, place the shifter in Reverse.
8. With the tires still on the ground, use the tire iron/wrench to break the lug nuts loose.

➡**If a nut is stuck, never use heat to loosen it or damage to the wheel and bearings may occur. If the nuts are seized, one or two heavy hammer blows directly on the end of the bolt usually loosens the rust. Be careful, as continued pounding will likely damage the brake drum or rotor.**

9. Using the jack, raise the vehicle until the tire is clear of the ground. Support the vehicle safely using jackstands.

10. Remove the lug nuts, then remove the tire and wheel assembly.

To install:

11. Make sure the wheel and hub mating surfaces, as well as the wheel lug studs, are clean and free of all foreign material. Always remove rust from the wheel mounting surface and the brake rotor or drum. Failure to do so may cause the lug nuts to loosen in service.
12. Install the tire and wheel assembly and hand-tighten the lug nuts.
13. Using the tire wrench, tighten all the lug nuts, in a crisscross pattern, until they are snug.
14. Raise the vehicle and withdraw the jackstand, then lower the vehicle.
15. Using a torque wrench, tighten the lug nuts in a crisscross pattern to 58–87 ft. lbs. (75–113 Nm). Check your owner's manual or refer to Section 1 of this manual for the proper tightening sequence.

✳✳ WARNING

Do not overtighten the lug nuts, as this may cause the wheel studs to stretch or the brake disc (rotor) to warp.

16. If so equipped, install the wheel cover or hub cap. Make sure the valve stem protrudes through the proper opening before tapping the wheel cover into position.
17. If equipped, install the lug nut trim caps by pushing them or screwing them on, as applicable.
18. Remove the jack from under the vehicle, and place the jack and tire iron/wrench in their storage compartments. Remove the wheel chock(s).
19. If you have removed a flat or damaged tire, place it in the storage compartment of the vehicle and take it to your local repair station to have it fixed or replaced as soon as possible.

INSPECTION

Inspect the tires for lacerations, puncture marks, nails and other sharp objects. Repair or replace as necessary. Also check the tires for treadwear and air pressure as outlined in Section 1 of this manual.

Check the wheel assemblies for dents, cracks, rust and metal fatigue. Repair or replace as necessary.

TCCA8P00

Fig. 1 Place the jack at the proper lifting point on your vehicle

TCCA8P01

Fig. 2 Before jacking the vehicle, block the diagonally opposite wheel with one or, preferably, two chocks

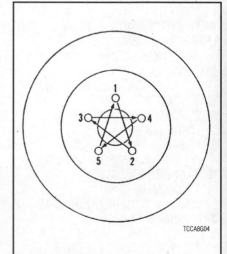

TCCA8G04

Fig. 3 Typical wheel lug tightening sequence

FRONT SUSPENSION

♦ See Figures 4 and 5

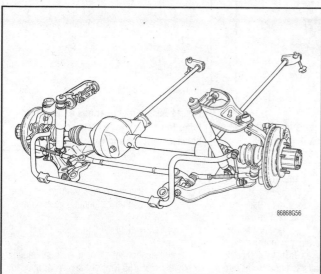

Fig. 4 Diagram of front suspension—4WD Rodeo shown

Fig. 5 Underside view of front suspension assembly—Trooper shown

Torsion Bar

REMOVAL & INSTALLATION

♦ See Figures 6 thru 11

1. Raise and safely support the vehicle on jackstands.
2. Remove the cotter pin from the control arm.
3. Scribe alignment marks, then remove the adjusting bolt from the height control arm.
4. Scribe alignment marks and remove the height control arm from the torsion bar and the third crossmember.
5. Mark the location and withdraw the torsion bar from the lower control arm.
6. Inspect all components for excessive wear or damage and replace as needed.

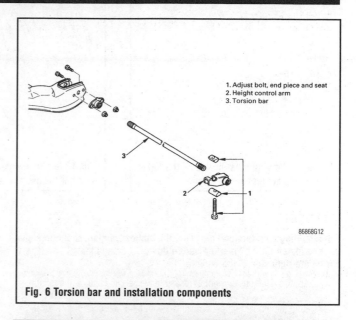

1. Adjust bolt, end piece and seat
2. Height control arm
3. Torsion bar

Fig. 6 Torsion bar and installation components

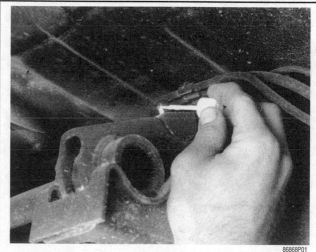

Fig. 7 Paint scribe marks on the adjustment bolt and end plate

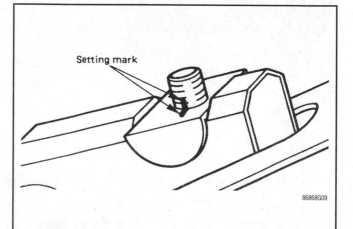

Setting mark

Fig. 8 Make sure the scribe marks accurately show the alignment between the adjustment bolt and end plate

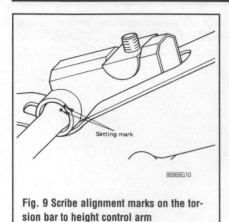

Fig. 9 Scribe alignment marks on the torsion bar to height control arm

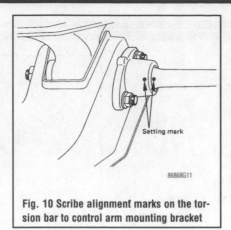

Fig. 10 Scribe alignment marks on the torsion bar to control arm mounting bracket

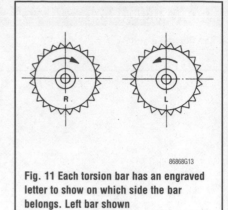

Fig. 11 Each torsion bar has an engraved letter to show on which side the bar belongs. Left bar shown

To install:

➡**If installing both torsion bars, note the embossed mark on the torsion bar and install the "L" marked bar on the left side and the "R" marked bar on the right side of the vehicle.**

7. Apply a generous amount of grease to the serrated ends of the torsion bar.

8. Hold the rubber bumpers in contact with the lower control arm. Raise the vehicle if needed, to accomplish this.

9. Insert the front end of the torsion bar into the control arm.

10. Install the height control arm in position so the end is reaching the adjusting bolt. Lubricate with grease the part of the height control arm that fits into the chassis.

11. Install a new cotter pin in the control arm.

12. Turn the adjusting bolt to the location marked before removal.

13. Lower the vehicle and check the vehicle trim height.

Shock Absorbers

REMOVAL & INSTALLATION

2 Wheel Drive Models

♦ **See Figure 12**

1. Raise and support the front of the vehicle safely with jackstands.

2. Remove the wheel and tire assembly for added access.

3. Using an open end wrench, hold the shock absorber upper stem from turning, then remove the upper stem retaining nut, the washer and rubber grommet.

4. Remove the shock absorber-to-lower control arm through-bolt or retaining bolts and remover the shock absorber assembly from the bottom of the control arm.

5. Inspect and test the shock absorber; replace it, if necessary.

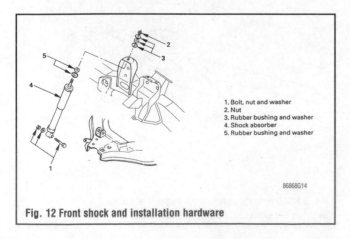

1. Bolt, nut and washer
2. Nut
3. Rubber bushing and washer
4. Shock absorber
5. Rubber bushing and washer

Fig. 12 Front shock and installation hardware

To install:

6. Fully extend the shock absorber stem, then push it up through the upper control arm so that the upper stem passes through the mounting hole in the upper control arm frame bracket.

7. Install the upper shock absorber nut and tighten to 14 ft. lbs. (18 Nm). Be careful not to crush the rubber bushing.

8. Install the shock absorber-to-lower control arm through-bolt or retaining bolts and tighten the through-bolt to 45 ft. lbs. (58 Nm) or the retainer bolts to 22 ft. lbs. (30 Nm).

9. Remove the jackstands and carefully lower the vehicle.

4 Wheel Drive Models

♦ **See Figures 13, 14, 15, 16 and 17**

1. Raise and support the front of the vehicle safely on jackstands.

2. Remove the wheel and tire assembly for added access.

3. Remove the shock absorber-to-lower control arm through-bolt or retainer nuts and bolts, then compress the shock absorber.

4. Using an open end wrench, hold the shock absorber upper stem from turning, remove the upper shock absorber-to-frame nut.

5. Inspect and test the shock absorber; replace it, if necessary.

To install:

6. Position the shock absorber in the control arm mounting bracket, or align the holes in the shock with the holes in the control arm.

7. Install the upper nut, then the lower through-bolt or retaining bolts.

8. Tighten the upper nut to 14 ft. lbs. (18 Nm) and the lower control arm through-bolt to 45 ft. lbs. (58 Nm), or the retainer bolts to 22 ft. lbs. (30 Nm).

9. Install the tire and wheel assembly, then remove the jackstands and carefully lower the vehicle.

Fig. 13 While securing the shock piston rod, loosen the upper retainer nut

Fig. 14 Remove the retainer nut from the shock . . .

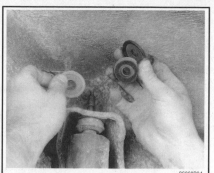

Fig. 15 . . . then remove the washer, rubber bushing and washer from the upper shock mount

Fig. 16 Loosen and remove the lower shock retainer nut and bolt

Fig. 17 Compress the shock, then remove it from the lower and upper shock mount

TESTING

Visually inspect the shock absorber. If there is evidence of leakage and the shock absorber is covered with oil, the shock is most likely defective and should be replaced.

If there is no sign of excessive leakage (a small amount of weeping is normal), bounce the truck at one corner by pressing down on the bumper and releasing it. When you have the truck bouncing as much as you can, release the bumper. The truck should stop bouncing after the first rebound. If the bouncing continues past the center point of the bounce more than once, the shock absorbers are worn and should be replaced.

Upper Ball Joint

INSPECTION

➡Before performing any ball joint inspection, make sure that the wheel bearings are adjusted correctly and that the control arm bushings are in good condition.

1. Make sure the vehicle is parked on a level surface.
2. Raise and support the front of the vehicle safely with jackstands. Place the jackstand under each lower control arm as close as possible to the lower ball joint. Make sure that the vehicle is stable and the control arm bumpers, if equipped, are not contacting the frame.
3. Wipe the ball joints clean and check the seals for cuts or tears. If a seal is cut or torn, the ball joint MUST be replaced.
4. Check the ball joints for horizontal deflection (looseness):
   a. Position a dial indicator against the lowest outboard point on the rim.
   b. Grasp the tire (top and bottom), then pull outward on the top and push inward on the bottom; record the reading on the dial indicator.
   c. Grasp the tire (top and bottom), then pull outward on the bottom and push inward on the top; record the reading on the dial indicator.

d. The difference in the dial indicator reading is the horizontal deflection of both joints. If the reading exceeds 0.125 in. (3.2mm), the lower ball joint should be checked for wear in order to determine what component(s) must be replaced.
   e. With the vehicle still supported by jackstands, place a dial indicator against the spindle in order to measure vertical movement.

✽✽ WARNING

DO NOT pry between the lower control arm and the drive axle seal or damage to the seal may result.

f. Pry between the lower control arm and the outer bearing race while reading the dial indicator. This reading will show vertical deflection (looseness).
   g. The lower ball joint is not a pre-loaded joint and may show some looseness, but it should be replaced if movement exceeds 0.125 in. (3.2mm).
   h. If necessary, disconnect the upper ball joint from the steering knuckle.
   i. Check for any looseness or if the stud can be twisted by hand. If so, the joint should be replaced.

REMOVAL & INSTALLATION

◗ See Figure 18

1. Raise and support the front of the vehicle safely on jackstands.
2. Remove the tire and wheel assembly.
3. Remove the brake caliper and support it from the vehicle using a coat hanger or wire. Make sure the brake line is not stretched or damaged.

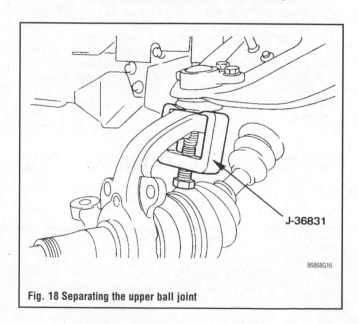

Fig. 18 Separating the upper ball joint

4. Remove the lower shock absorber through-bolt, then remove the shock from the lower mount. If equipped with front torsion bars, release the tension from the bar, then remove the torsion bar and place aside.

5. Remove the cotter pin and retaining nut from the upper ball joint.

6. Position a suitable ball joint separator tool between the upper joint stud and the steering knuckle. Use the tool to separate the upper ball joint from the steering knuckle. Pull the control arm free of the steering knuckle after removal.

➡ **After separating the steering knuckle from the upper ball joint, be sure to support the steering knuckle/hub assembly to prevent damaging the brake hose.**

7. Remove the retainer nuts, bolts and washers securing the ball joint to the upper control arm.

8. Clean and inspect the steering knuckle hole. Replace the steering knuckle if the hole is out of round.

To install:

9. Position the joint in the upper control arm, then install the joint retaining nuts and bolts. Position the bolts threaded upward from under the control arm. Tighten the ball joint retainers to 19 ft. lbs. (25 Nm).

10. Remove the support from the steering knuckle, then install the ball joint to the knuckle. Make sure the joint is seated properly, then install the stud nut and tighten to 75 ft. lbs. (97 Nm) for vehicles through 1986 or to 98 ft. lbs. (127 Nm) for 1987–96 vehicles. Install a new cotter pin.

➡ **When installing the cotter pin, never loosen the castle nut to expose the cotter pin hole.**

11. Reposition and secure the brake caliper.
12. Install the tire and wheel assembly.
13. Remove the jackstands and carefully lower the vehicle.
14. Check and adjust the front end alignment, as necessary.

Lower Ball Joint

INSPECTION

➡ **Before performing any ball joint inspection, make sure that the wheel bearings are adjusted correctly and that the control arm bushings are in good condition.**

1. Make sure the vehicle is parked on a level surface.
2. Raise and support the front of the vehicle safely with jackstands. Place the jackstand under each lower control arm as close as possible to the lower ball joint. Make sure that the vehicle is stable and the control arm bumpers, if equipped are not contacting the frame.
3. Wipe the ball joints clean and check the seals for cuts or tears. If a seal is cut or torn, then ball joint MUST be replaced.
4. Check the ball joints for horizontal deflection (looseness):

a. Position a dial indicator against the lowest outboard point on the rim.

b. Grasp the tire (top and bottom), then pull outward on the top and push inward on the bottom; record the reading on the dial indicator.

c. Grasp the tire (top and bottom), then pull outward on the bottom and push inward on the top; record the reading on the dial indicator.

d. The difference in the dial indicator reading is the horizontal deflection of both joints. If the reading exceeds 0.125 in. (3.2mm), the lower ball joint should be checked for wear in order to determine what component(s) must be replaced.

e. With the vehicle still supported by jackstands, place a dial indicator against the spindle in order to measure vertical movement.

❊❊ WARNING

DO NOT pry between the lower control arm and the drive axle seal or damage to the seal may result.

f. Pry between the lower control arm and the outer bearing race while reading the dial indicator. This reading will show vertical deflection (looseness).

g. The lower ball joint is not a pre-loaded joint and may show some looseness, but it should be replaced if movement exceeds 0.125 in. (3.2mm).

h. If necessary, disconnect the upper ball joint from the steering knuckle.

i. Check for any looseness or if the stud can be twisted by hand. If so, the joint should be replaced.

REMOVAL & INSTALLATION

▸ **See Figure 19**

1. Raise and safely support the vehicle.
2. Remove the wheel and tire assembly.
3. Release the torsion bar tension, if needed.
4. Remove the cotter pin and castellated nut which retains the ball joint to the steering knuckle.
5. Remove the lower ball joint-to-lower control arm nuts and bolts.
6. Remove the ball joint.

To install:

7. Position the ball joint on the lower control arm and secure in place with new nuts and bolts tightened to 45–56 ft. lbs. (61–76 Nm) for 2WD models, or to 68–83 ft. lbs. (93–113 Nm) for 4WD models.

8. Install the ball joint stud on to the steering knuckle and secure with the castellated nut and tighten to 101–116 ft. lbs. (137–157 Nm) for 2WD models, or 87–111 ft. lbs. (117–137 Nm) for 4WD models. Tighten additionally enough to align the cotter pin hole with a castellation on the nut. Install a new cotter pin.

9. Lubricate the lower ball joint through the grease fitting.
10. Install and adjust the torsion bar tension.
11. Install the wheel assembly and lower the vehicle.
12. Check and adjust the front end alignment, as necessary.

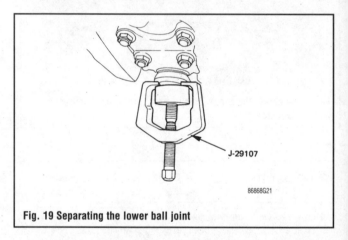

Fig. 19 Separating the lower ball joint

Stabilizer Bar

REMOVAL & INSTALLATION

▸ **See Figure 20**

1. Raise and support the vehicle safely on jackstands.
2. Remove the stabilizer bar link nuts, bolts and insulators securing it to the control arm.
3. Remove the nut, washer and bracket retaining the stabilizer bar rod to the body.
4. Remove the stabilizer bar from the vehicle.
5. Inspect the rubber insulator for signs of wear and replace if needed.

To install:

6. Install new rubber insulators, if needed. Coat the contact surfaces with a light coating of grease.

7. Position the stabilizer bar to the vehicle.

8. Install the bracket, nut and washer retaining the stabilizer bar rod to the body. Tighten the bracket nuts to 16 ft. lbs. (22 Nm).

9. Install the link nuts, bolts and insulators retaining it to the control arm.

10. Install the front wheels and lower the vehicle.

11. With the vehicle on the ground, tighten the stabilizer bar link nuts to 37 ft. lbs. (50 Nm).

12. Check and adjust the front end alignment, as necessary.

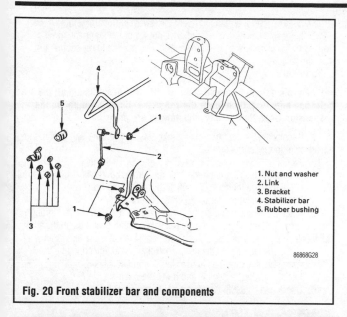

Fig. 20 Front stabilizer bar and components

1. Nut and washer
2. Link
3. Bracket
4. Stabilizer bar
5. Rubber bushing

86868G28

Strut Rod

REMOVAL & INSTALLATION

♦ **See Figure 21**

1. Raise the vehicle and support safely on jackstands. Remove the front wheel and tires.
2. Remove the stabilizer bar, if equipped.
3. Remove the strut rod-to control arm retainer bolts.
4. Remove the strut rod locknuts and washers from the front of the vehicle.
5. Remove the strut rod, by sliding it out of the front mount.
6. Remove the rubber cushions and strut rod.
7. Inspect the rubber cushions and replace if needed,

To install:

8. Apply a light coat of grease to the rubber cushions and install the cushions and strut rod.
9. Install the strut rod-to-body nut and washers.
10. Install the strut rod-to-control arm bolts. Tighten the bolts to 80 ft. lbs. (108 Nm).
11. Install the stabilizer bar, if so equipped.
12. Install the wheels and tires, then lower the vehicle.
13. Check and adjust the front end alignment, as necessary.

Upper Control Arms

REMOVAL & INSTALLATION

1. Raise and support the front of the vehicle safely by placing jackstands securely under the lower control arms. Because the vehicle's weight is used to relieve tension on the upper control arm, the floor stands must be positioned between the seats and the lower control arm ball joints for maximum leverage.

�֎ CAUTION

Make sure the jackstands are firmly positioned and cannot move, or personal injury could result.

2. Remove the tire and wheel assembly.
3. Remove the brake caliper and support it from the vehicle with wire. Make sure the brake line is not stretched or damaged and that the caliper's weight is not supported by the line.
4. Remove the cotter pin and retaining nut from the upper ball joint.
5. Position J-23742 or an equivalent ball joint separator tool between the upper joint stud and the control arm. Use the tool to separate the upper ball joint from the steering knuckle. Pull the steering knuckle free of the ball joint after removal.

➡**After separating the steering knuckle from the upper ball joint, be sure to support the steering knuckle/hub assembly to prevent damaging the brake hose.**

6. Remove the upper control arm-to-frame nuts and bolts, then lift and remove the upper control arm from the vehicle.

➡**If equipped with shims between the pivot shaft and vehicle body, tape the shims together and identify them to assure that they are re-installed in the same place.**

7. Clean and inspect the steering knuckle hole. Replace the steering knuckle if any out of roundness is noted.
8. Remove the pivot shaft if needed.

To install

9. If removed, position the pivot shaft to the control arm and install. Loosely install the bushing retaining nuts and washers.
10. Loosely install the control arm to the frame using the bolts and nuts. Position the shims between the control arm and vehicle body, if equipped, then tighten the retainers to 45 ft. lbs. (60 Nm) for 1981–86 models, or to 65 ft. lbs. (88 Nm) for 1987–96 vehicles.
11. Install the ball joint to the steering knuckle. Make sure the joint is seated, then install the stud nut and tighten to specification. Install a new cotter pin.

➡**When installing the cotter pin, never loosen the castle nut to expose the cotter pin hole.**

12. Reposition and secure the brake caliper.
13. Install the tire and wheel assembly.
14. Remove the jackstands and carefully lower the vehicle.
15. If the control arm bushings were replaced on 1981–86 vehicles, tighten the pivot shaft nuts to 65 ft. lbs. (88 Nm).
16. Check and adjust the front end alignment, as necessary.

BUSHING REPLACEMENT

♦ **See Figures 22 and 23**

1. Remove the control arm from the vehicle.
2. Mount the control arm in a soft jawed vise. Remove the pivot shaft nuts, washers and shaft.

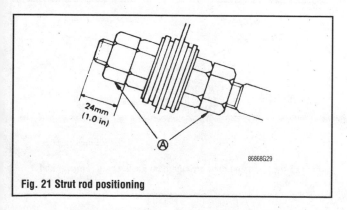

Fig. 21 Strut rod positioning

24mm
(1.0 in)

Ⓐ

86868G29

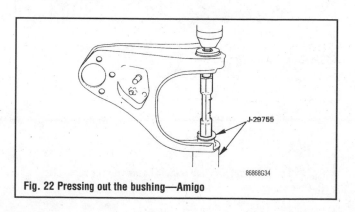

Fig. 22 Pressing out the bushing—Amigo

J-29755

86868G34

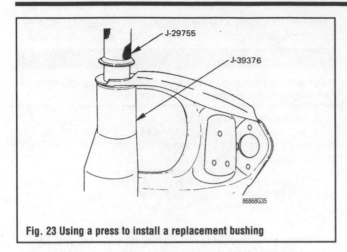

Fig. 23 Using a press to install a replacement bushing

3. Use either a press or a control arm bushing fixture (C-clamp like tool) along with a slotted washer and a piece of pipe (slightly larger than the bushing) and press out the old bushing.

4. Clean the inside bushing contact surfaces of rust and old rubber.

To install

5. Apply a light coating of grease to both the replacement busing and bushing contact surfaces on the control arm.

6. Position a pivot shaft to the control arm and install the bushing using the press tool. A bushing install clamp can also be used to compress the bushing into the control arm.

7. Install the pivot shaft.

8. Loosely install the bushing retaining nuts and washers.

9. Install the control arm on the vehicle. Tighten the pivot shaft retainer nuts to 80 ft. lbs. (108 Nm).

Lower Control Arm

REMOVAL & INSTALLATION

▶ **See Figure 24**

1. Raise and safely support the vehicle on jackstands.

2. Remove the wheel and tire assembly.

3. Remove the strut bar from the control arm and front of the vehicle, if equipped.

4. Disconnect the stabilizer bar from the lower control arm, if equipped.

5. Remove the torsion bar.

6. Disconnect the shock absorber from the lower control arm.

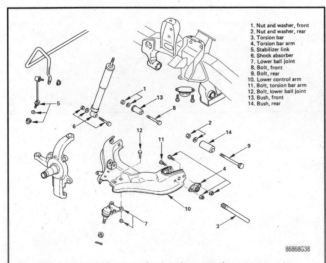

Fig. 24 Lower control arm and related suspension components—Trooper shown

1. Nut and washer, front
2. Nut and washer, rear
3. Torsion bar
4. Torsion bar arm
5. Stabilizer link
6. Shock absorber
7. Lower ball joint
8. Bolt, front
9. Bolt, rear
10. Lower control arm
11. Bolt, torsion bar arm
12. Bolt, lower ball joint
13. Bush, front
14. Bush, rear

7. Remove the lower ball joint from the lower control arm joint.

8. Remove the retaining nut and drive out the bolt holding the lower control arm to the chassis with a soft metal drift. Remove the lower control arm from the vehicle.

To install:

➡ **When reinstalling front end components, it is best to snug all the bolts and nuts first, then lower the car so that there is weight on the suspension when final torque adjustments are made.**

9. If replacing the control arm assembly, install the lower ball joint to the replacement lower control arm.

10. Mount the lower control arm to the frame. Drive the retainer bolt into position carefully. Use care not to damage the serrated portions. Tighten the nut on the end of the pivot bolt to 145–196 ft. lbs. (188–255 Nm).

11. Install the stabilizer bar to the lower control arm.

12. Place the washers and bushings on the strut rod and install it through the frame bracket. Install the second set of washers and bushings on the strut rod together with the lockwashers and nut. Leave the nut loose temporarily.

13. Install the strut rod to the lower control arm and tighten the bolts.

14. Assemble the lower ball joint to the steering knuckle.

15. Install the wheel assembly and lower the vehicle.

16. Check and adjust the front end alignment, as necessary.

BUSHING REPLACEMENT

▶ **See Figure 25**

1. Remove the control arm from the vehicle.

2. Mount the control arm in a soft jawed vise. Remove the pivot shaft nuts and washers.

3. Use a control arm bushing fixture (C-clamp like tool) along with a slotted washer and a piece of pipe (slightly larger than the bushing) and press out the old bushing. A large nut and bolt can also be used to remove and install lower control arm bushings.

4. Clean the inside bushing contact surfaces of rust and old rubber.

To install

5. Apply a light coating of grease to both the replacement busing and bushing contact surfaces on the control arm.

6. Position a pivot shaft to the control arm and install the bushing using the fixture tool, washer and a length of pipe with the same outer diameter as the bushing. Tighten the tool until the bushing is properly seated. Loosely install the bushing retaining nuts and washers.

7. Install the control arm on the vehicle.

Knuckle and Spindle

REMOVAL & INSTALLATION

2-Wheel Drive Models

1. Raise the vehicle and support safely with jackstands. Remove the front wheel.

2. Place a hydraulic jack under the lower control arm and raise to release the and shock pressure.

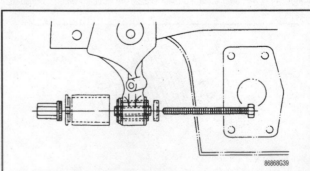

Fig. 25 Nut, bolt and pipe arrangement for bushing removal and installation

3. Remove the upper and lower ball joint cotter pins and loosen the nuts until they are flush with the top of the stud.

4. Using a tie rod end removing tool, disconnect the tie rod end from the knuckle.

5. Remove the brake caliper and hang with a piece of wire. Never let a caliper hang by the flexible hose. Refer to Section 9 for further details on caliper removal and installation.

6. Remove the brake rotor and backing plate as outlined in Section 9.

7. Disconnect the upper and lower ball joints. Refer to the procedure in this section.

8. Remove the knuckle/spindle assembly by lifting the steering knuckle from the lower control arm.

9. Clean and inspect the steering knuckle and spindle for signs of wear or damage; if necessary, replace the steering knuckle. If any out-of-roundness is found in the tapered knuckle hole.

To install:

10. Position the steering knuckle onto the lower ball joint stud, then lift the upper control arm to insert the upper ball joint stud into the steering knuckle. Loosely install both ball joint stud nuts to secure the components in position. Be careful not to damage the ball joint boots.

11. Tighten the ball joint nuts to specification and install new cotter pins.

12. Install the brake rotor and backing plate as outlined in Section 9.

13. Install the brake caliper as outlined in Section 9.

14. Install the tie rod end and tighten the nuts to specification. Install a new cotter pin.

15. Install the front wheels and lower the vehicle. Have the front alignment checked by a qualified technician.

4-Wheel Drive

1. Raise the vehicle and support safely with jackstands. Remove the front wheel and tire assemblies.

2. Remove the brake caliper, rotor and backing plate as outlined in Section 9.

3. Place a hydraulic jack under the lower control arm and raise to release shock or torsion bar pressure.

4. Remove the upper and lower ball joint cotter pins and loosen the nuts until they are flush with the top of the stud.

5. Using a tie rod end removing tool, disconnect the tie rod end from the knuckle.

6. Disconnect the upper and lower ball joints.

7. Remove the knuckle/spindle assembly. Be careful not to damage the ball joint boots.

To install:

8. Install the knuckle/spindle assembly. Be careful not to damage the ball joint boots.

9. Connect the upper and lower ball joints as outlined in this Section. Tighten the nuts to specification. Install new cotter pins.

10. Install the brake rotor and backing plate as outlined in Section 9.

11. Install the brake caliper as outlined in Section 9.

12. Install the tie rod end and tighten the nuts to specification. Install a new cotter pin.

13. Install the front wheels and lower the vehicle. Have the front alignment checked by a qualified technician.

Front Wheel Bearings

✴✴ CAUTION

Some brake pads may contain asbestos, which has been determined to be a cancer causing agent. Never clean the brake surfaces with compressed air! Avoid inhaling any dust from any brake surface! When cleaning brake surfaces, use a commercially available brake cleaning fluid.

ADJUSTMENT

2-Wheel Drive Models

1. Raise the car and support safely on jackstands.

2. Remove the hub dust cover and spindle cotter pin. Loosen the nut.

3. While spinning the wheel, snug the nut down to seat the bearings. Do not exert more than 12 ft. lbs. 16 Nm) of force on the nut.

4. Back the nut off ¼ turn or until it is just loose. Line up the cotter pin hole in the spindle with the hole in the nut.

➡**Do not loosen the nut more than ½ turn.**

5. Insert a new cotter pin. End-play should be between 0.001–0.005 in. (0.03–0.13mm). If end-play exceeds this tolerance, the wheel bearings should be replaced.

4-Wheel Drive Models

The front wheel bearing on 4WD models is not adjustable or serviceable. If excessive noise is produced by the wheel bearing, the assembly must be replaced.

REMOVAL & INSTALLATION

2-Wheel Drive Models

◗ See Figures 26, 27 and 28

1. Raise support the vehicle on jackstands.

2. Remove the front wheel and tire assembly.

3. Remove the brake caliper and support it with wire. Do not allow the caliper to hang from the flexible hose.

4. Remove the dust cap, cotter pin, castle nut, thrust washer and outside wheel bearing. Pull the disc/hub assembly from the steering knuckle and place on a clean work surface.

5. Pry out the inner seal using a suitable seal remover, then remove the inner bearing. If necessary, use a hammer and a brass drift to drive the bearing race from the hub.

6. Clean all parts in kerosene or equivalent, DO NOT use gasoline. After cleaning, check the parts for excessive wear and replace any damaged parts.

Fig. 26 Removing the inner bearing seal

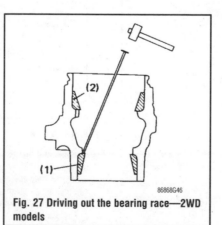

Fig. 27 Driving out the bearing race—2WD models

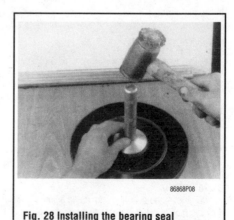

Fig. 28 Installing the bearing seal

To install:

7. Pack the wheel bearing and race with grease.

8. Install the bearing races into the hub, using a hammer and an installation tool or a brass drift. Drive the races in until they seat against the shoulder of the hub.

9. Install the inner bearing in the hub. Install a new grease seal using a seal installation tool. Be careful not to damage the seal.

10. Install the disc/hub assembly onto the steering knuckle. Install the outer bearing, thrust washer and castle nut. Tighten the nut until the wheel does not turn freely.

11. Back off the nut until the wheel turns freely and install the cotter pin. Install the dust cap, caliper and wheel. Lower the vehicle.

4-Wheel Drive Models

▶ See Figures 29 and 30

1. Raise and safely support the vehicle on jackstands. Remove the wheel and tire assembly.

2. Remove the brake caliper and support it on a wire. Remove the rotor and dust shield.

3. Remove the axle shaft from the hub.

4. Remove the tie rod end-to-steering knuckle nut and separate the tie rod from the steering knuckle.

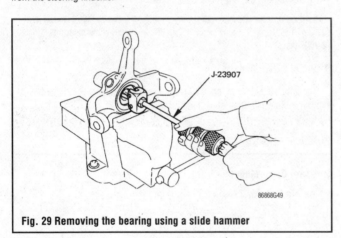

Fig. 29 Removing the bearing using a slide hammer

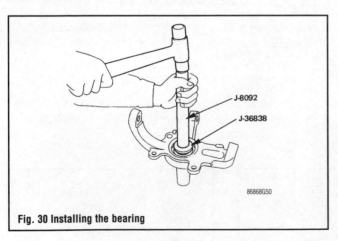

Fig. 30 Installing the bearing

5. Support the lower control arm and separate the steering knuckle from the lower ball joint.

6. Separate the steering knuckle from the upper ball joint.

7. Remove the steering knuckle from the vehicle and place on a clean work surface.

8. Remove the bearing seal and bearing, then the races using a hammer and a brass drift.

To install:

9. Install the bearing races using a suitable race installer and a press. If a bearing race installer is not available. Grind about 0.010–0.020 in.

(0.25–0.50mm) off of the outer portion of the old race and use that to drive the new race into position. Be careful not to damage the new race. Bearing damage will result.

10. Install the steering knuckle to the upper, then lower ball joints. Attach the retainer nuts

11. Torque the ball joint nuts to 75 ft. lbs. (97 Nm). Install new cotter pins.

12. Install the tie rod end-to-steering knuckle nut.

13. Install the axle shaft to the hub. Tighten the retainer bolts to 9 ft. lbs. (12 Nm).

14. Install the dust cover, rotor and brake caliper as outlined in Section 9.

15. Install the front wheel and lower the vehicle.

Wheel Alignment

If the tires are worn unevenly, if the vehicle is not stable on the highway or if the handling seems uneven in spirited driving, the wheel alignment should be checked. If an alignment problem is suspected, first check for improper tire inflation and other possible causes. These can be worn suspension or steering components, accident damage or even unmatched tires. If any worn or damaged components are found, they must be replaced before the wheels can be properly aligned. Wheel alignment requires very expensive equipment and involves minute adjustments which must be accurate; it should only be performed by a trained technician. Take your vehicle to a properly equipped shop.

Following is a description of the alignment angles which are adjustable on most vehicles and how they affect vehicle handling. Although these angles can apply to both the front and rear wheels, usually only the front suspension is adjustable.

CASTER

▶ See Figure 31

Looking at a vehicle from the side, caster angle describes the steering axis rather than a wheel angle. The steering knuckle is attached to a control arm or strut at the top and a control arm at the bottom. The wheel pivots around the line between these points to steer the vehicle. When the upper point is tilted back, this is described as positive caster. Having a positive caster tends to make the wheels self-centering, increasing directional stability. Excessive positive caster makes the wheels hard to steer, while an uneven caster will cause a pull to one side. Overloading the vehicle or sagging rear springs will affect caster, as will raising the rear of the vehicle. If the rear of the vehicle is lower than normal, the caster becomes more positive.

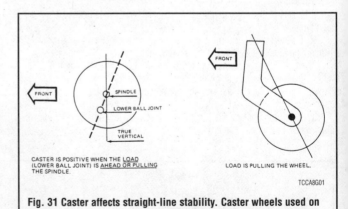

Fig. 31 Caster affects straight-line stability. Caster wheels used on shopping carts, for example, employ positive caster

CAMBER

▶ See Figure 32

Looking from the front of the vehicle, camber is the inward or outward tilt of the top of wheels. When the tops of the wheels are tilted in, this is negative camber; if they are tilted out, it is positive. In a turn, a slight amount of negative camber helps maximize contact of the tire with the road. However, too much negative camber compromises straight-line stability, increases bump steer and torque steer.

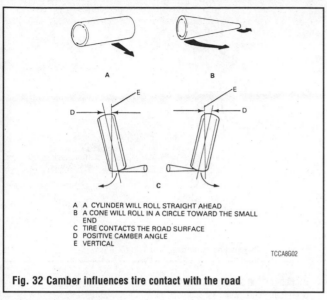

A A CYLINDER WILL ROLL STRAIGHT AHEAD
B A CONE WILL ROLL IN A CIRCLE TOWARD THE SMALL
   END
C TIRE CONTACTS THE ROAD SURFACE
D POSITIVE CAMBER ANGLE
E VERTICAL

TCCA8G02

Fig. 32 Camber influences tire contact with the road

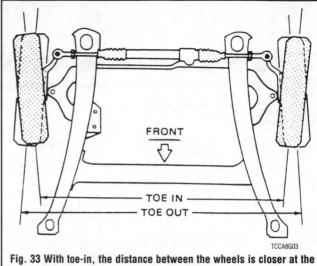

TCCA8G03

Fig. 33 With toe-in, the distance between the wheels is closer at the front than at the rear

TOE

▶ See Figure 33

Looking down at the wheels from above the vehicle, toe angle is the distance between the front of the wheels, relative to the distance between the back of the wheels. If the wheels are closer at the front, they are said to be toed-in or to have negative toe. A small amount of negative toe enhances directional stability and provides a smoother ride on the highway.

REAR SUSPENSION

Leaf Springs

REMOVAL & INSTALLATION

▶ See Figures 34, 35 and 36

1. Raise and support the rear frame of the vehicle safely using jackstands. Support the rear axle with the second set of jackstands.

➡When supporting the rear of the vehicle, support the axle and the body separately in order to relieve the load on the rear spring.

2. Remove the tire and wheel assembly.
3. Remove the shock absorber.
4. Remove the parking brake cable clips.
5. Remove the spare tire, if mounted under the vehicle.
6. Remove the nuts from the U-bolts holding the springs to the axle housing.
7. Support the rear axle housing with jackstands and remove the front and rear shackle pin nuts.
8. Drive out the rear shackle pin using a hammer and drift.

9. Lower the rear end of the leaf spring assembly to the floor.
10. Drive out the front shackle pin and remove the leaf spring assembly rearward.
11. Remove the shackle pin from the rear spring bracket and remove the shackle.
12. Check the leaf springs for worn or broken leaves. Replace any leaves found to be cracked, fatigued or seriously worn.
13. Check the shackles for bending and the pins for wear.
14. Check the U-bolts for distortion or other damage.

To install:
15. Install the shackle to the rearward spring eye using the bolt, washers and nut, but do not fully tighten at this time.
16. Position the spring assembly to the vehicle.
17. Align the front end of the leaf spring assembly with the front bracket and install the shackle pin.
18. Loosely install the shackle pin nuts and install the U-bolts. Tighten the U-bolt nuts to 40 ft. lbs. (54 Nm).
19. Clip the parking brake cable to the bracket.
20. Remove the axle housing support and lower the vehicle so the weight is on the leaf springs.

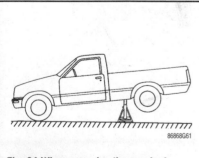

86868G61

Fig. 34 When removing the rear leaf spring, support the vehicle at the frame before the front leaf spring connection point

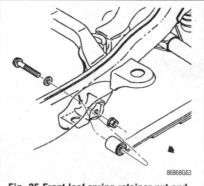

86868G63

Fig. 35 Front leaf spring retainer nut and bolt

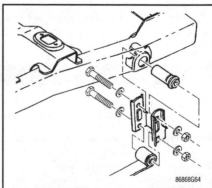

86868G64

Fig. 36 Shackle-to-frame installation hardware

21. Tighten the shackle pin nuts to 130 ft. lbs. (176 Nm).
22. Install the shock absorber.
23. Remove the jackstands and carefully lower the vehicle.

Coil Spring

REMOVAL & INSTALLATION

▶ **See Figure 37**

1. Raise and safely support the rear of the vehicle on jackstands. Position the jackstands on the frame before the rear axle.
2. Disconnect the parking brake cable bracket retainer bolt from the trailing arm.
3. Disconnect and remove the rear stabilizer bar and end links.
4. Support the rear axle assembly and remove the shock absorbers. Refer to the rear shock absorber procedure in this section for removal and installation steps.
5. Slowly lower the rear axle and remove the coil spring and insulator.
6. Inspect the insulator, and replace any insulators that are worn through.

To install:

7. Position the insulator on the top and of the coil spring.
8. Position the bottom end of the coil spring to the coil spring seat on the rear axle. Make sure the spring is seated flat on the mount.
9. Raise the rear axle and position the insulator and spring in the frame mount.
10. Install the shock to the vehicle frame and rear axle assembly. Install the shock retainer nut and hand-tighten. Tighten the nut to specification with the vehicle on the ground.
11. Install the stabilizer bar and end links.
12. Attach the parking brake cable bracket retainer bolt.
13. Lower the vehicle, and tighten the shock retainer nuts.

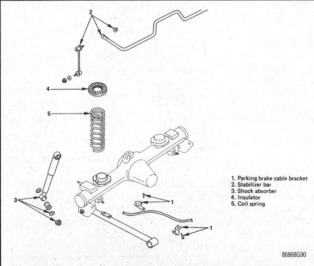

Fig. 37 Exploded view of coil spring and related components—Trooper

1. Parking brake cable bracket
2. Stabilizer bar
3. Shock absorber
4. Insulator
5. Coil spring

86868G90

Shock Absorbers

REMOVAL & INSTALLATION

▶ **See Figure 38**

1. Raise and safely support the vehicle.
2. Remove the wheel and tire assembly, for additional access.
3. Remove the shock absorber-to-lower mount nut, washers and bushings.
4. On all models remove the shock absorber-to-chassis nut, washers and bushings.

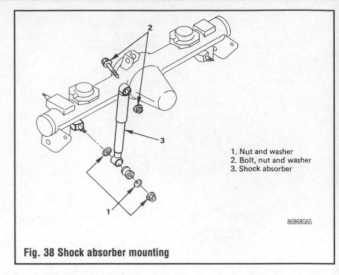

1. Nut and washer
2. Bolt, nut and washer
3. Shock absorber

86868G65

Fig. 38 Shock absorber mounting

5. Remove the shock absorber.
6. If reinstalling the original shock, check the rubber bushings on the shock and replace if torn or excessively worn.

To install:

7. Install the shock absorber to the upper mount and secure in place with the nut and washer.
8. Attach the shock to the lower mount and secure in place with the nut and washer.
9. Tighten the shock absorber-to-chassis nut to 20–22 ft. lbs. (26–29 Nm) for Rodeo and Trooper, 28–39 ft. lbs. (36–51 Nm) for Amigo and Pick-up models.
10. Tighten the shock absorber-to-lower mount nut to 29–32 ft. lbs. (38–42 Nm) for all models.
11. Install the wheel and tire assembly, then lower the vehicle.

TESTING

Refer to Shock TESTING found earlier in this Section under Front Shocks.

Sway Bar

REMOVAL & INSTALLATION

▶ **See Figure 39**

1. Raise the vehicle and support safely with jackstands.
2. Disconnect the outer sway bar attaching link nuts and/or bolts.

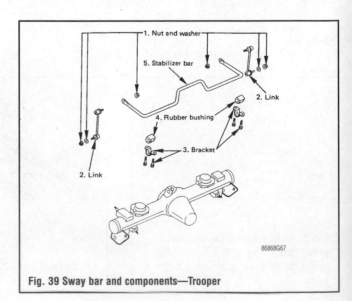

1. Nut and washer
5. Stabilizer bar
2. Link
4. Rubber bushing
3. Bracket
2. Link

86868G67

Fig. 39 Sway bar and components—Trooper

3. Remove the sway bar-to-body retaining bolts securing the clamps and sway bar assembly to the vehicle.

4. Inspect the sway bar bushings and retainer brackets for signs of wear or damage, and replace parts as needed.

To install:

5. Install the bushing and bracket on the sway bar if removed. Position the sway bar to the vehicle and secure in place with the bracket retainer bolts. Tighten the bolts to 22 ft. lbs. (29 Nm).

6. Attach the sway bar link nuts and bolts and tighten.

7. Install the wheel and tire assembly, if removed.

8. Lower the vehicle.

Rear Wheel Bearings

ADJUSTMENT

Drum Brakes

1. Raise the vehicle and support it with jackstands.

2. Remove the hub dust cover and spindle cotter pin. Loosen the nut.

3. While spinning the wheel, snug the nut down to seat the bearings. Do not exert over 12 ft. lbs. (16 Nm) of force on the nut.

4. Back the nut off ¼ turn or until it is just loose. Line up the cotter pin hole in the spindle with the hole in the nut.

➡**Do not loosen the nut more than ½ turn.**

5. Insert a new cotter pin. End-play should be between 0.001–0.005 in. (0.03–0.13mm). If play exceeds this amount, the wheel bearings should be replaced.

Disc Brakes

Rear disc brake equipped bearings are not adjustable or serviceable. If excessive bearing noise is produced, the bearing and holder must be replaced.

REMOVAL & INSTALLATION

Drum Brakes

✳✳ CAUTION

Some brake shoes may contain asbestos, which has been determined to be a cancer causing agent. Never clean the brake surfaces with compressed air! Avoid inhaling any dust from any brake surface! When cleaning brake surfaces, use a commercially available brake cleaning fluid.

1. Raise the car and support it with jackstands. Remove the wheel.

2. Remove the dust cap, cotter pin, castle nut, thrust washer and outside wheel bearing. Pull the drum assembly from the spindle. Place the drum on a clean work surface.

3. Using a suitable seal puller, pry out the inner seal. With the seal removed, lift out the inner bearing. Remove the inner races. It may be necessary to use a hammer and a brass drift to drive the bearing races from the hub.

4. Clean all parts in kerosene or equivalent, DO NOT use gasoline. After cleaning, dry the parts with compressed air and check parts for excessive wear and replace damaged parts. Do NOT allow the bearings to spin while blowing dry.

To install:

5. Apply a coating of grease to the inside of the hub. Install the bearing races into hub, using a hammer and a brass drift. Drive the races in until they seat against the shoulder of the hub.

6. Pack the bearings with grease and install the inner bearing in the hub. Install a new grease seal, being careful not to damage the seal.

7. Install the drum assembly onto the spindle. Install the outer bearing, thrust washer and castle nut. Tighten the nut until the wheel does not turn freely.

8. Back off the nut until the wheel turns freely and install the cotter pin. Install the dust cap.

9. Install the wheel and lower the vehicle.

Disc Brakes

▶ **See Figures 40, 41 and 42**

1. Raise and support the vehicle safely on jackstands.

2. Remove the wheel and tire assembly.

3. Disconnect the parking brake cable from the caliper or if equipped the brake shoe.

4. Remove the caliper and suspend it with wire. The flexible hose does not need to be disconnected.

5. Remove the caliper bracket, followed by the brake rotor.

6. If equipped with Duo-Servo type brakes, remove the brake shoes.

7. Loosen and remove the bearing holder retainer nuts at the back side of the assembly.

8. With all the nuts removed, slide the axle shaft and bearing holder out.

9. Remove the snapring from the axle shaft and remove the axle shaft from the bearing housing.

10. Remove the bearing seal from the housing. Press out the bearing and discard.

To install:

11. Apply grease around the outside of the bearing assembly, and press into the bearing housing.

12. Install a new seal to the bearing housing.

13. Install the axle shaft into the bearing housing, and secure in place with the snapring.

14. Install the axle shaft and bearing housing to the rear axle, and secure in place with the retainer nuts and bolts. Tighten the nuts to 54 ft. lbs. (74 Nm).

15. If equipped with Duo-Servo brakes, install the brake shoes to the backing plate. Refer to Section 9 for installation steps.

16. Install the brake rotor and caliper.

17. Install the parking brake cable to the brake assembly.

18. Install the wheel and tire assembly, then lower the vehicle.

Fig. 40 Remove the bearing holder retainer nuts

Fig. 41 Remove the axle shaft and bearing holder

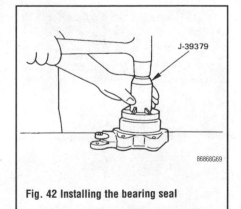

Fig. 42 Installing the bearing seal

STEERING

♦ See Figure 43

✳✳ CAUTION

Some vehicles are equipped with an air bag system, also known as the Supplemental Inflatable Restraint (SIR) or Supplemental Restraint System (SRS). The system must be disabled before performing service on or around system components, steering column, instrument panel components, wiring and sensors. Failure to follow safety and disabling procedures could result in accidental air bag deployment, possible personal injury and unnecessary system repairs.

Fig. 43 If equipped with an Air Bag, read all caution labels before working on the steering system

Steering Wheel

REMOVAL & INSTALLATION

Without Air Bag

♦ See Figures 44 thru 49

1. Set the steering wheel in the straight ahead position, so that the front wheels are pointing forward.
2. Disconnect the negative battery cable.
3. On models with the 2-spoke wheel, remove the two screws retaining the horn shroud and disconnect the horn contact.
4. On models with the 3-spoke wheel, remove the medallion cover from the center of the wheel by prying lightly around the edge with a small screwdriver.
5. On models with padded horn shrouds, use a suitable prybar to unsnap the shroud from the retaining clip.
6. Disconnect the horn lead.
7. Remove the steering wheel retainer nut.
8. Scribe an alignment mark on the steering wheel and steering shaft for reassembly.
9. Using a suitable steering wheel puller, remove the steering wheel from the steering shaft.

➡ Do not strike the steering column or use air tools to loosen the steering wheel nut. The impact may damage the steering column's energy-absorbing properties.

To install:

10. Align the matchmarks on the steering column and wheel, and install the steering wheel on the shaft. Tighten the steering wheel nut to 22–29 ft. lbs. (30–39 Nm).

Fig. 44 Remove the center steering wheel center pad retainer screws from the back side of the wheel

Fig. 45 Lift off the center pad to access the steering wheel retainer nut

Fig. 46 Loosen and remove the retainer nut from the wheel

Fig. 47 Scribe and alignment mark on the steering wheel shaft and steering wheel

Fig. 48 Install a suitable steering wheel puller and loosen the wheel to steering shaft connection

Fig. 49 Lift the steering wheel off the shaft

11. Reconnect the horn lead and install the horn pad.
12. Connect the negative battery cable.
13. Check the steering wheel spoke angle and test the operation of the horn.

With Air Bag

▶ **See Figures 50 and 51**

✳✳ CAUTION

The Air Bag system must be disabled before the steering wheel and steering column are removed. Failure to disable the system may result in system repairs and possible personal injury. Do not damage, cut, or attempt to alter the yellow Air Bag wiring harness.

1. Turn the steering wheel so that the vehicle's front wheels are pointing straight ahead.
2. Turn the ignition switch to the **LOCK** position. Remove the key.
3. Disconnect the negative battery cable, followed by the positive battery cable.
4. Properly disarm the Air Bag system.
5. Use a Torx® driver to remove the driver's Air Bag module retaining screws from the back of the steering wheel.
6. Carefully lift the driver's Air Bag module straight out of the steering wheel. Disconnect the yellow 2–way connector from the Air Bag
7. Remove the Air Bag module from the vehicle and place it face–up on a clean bench away from your work area.

✳✳ CAUTION

Always carry a live Air Bag with its trim cover and cushion pointed away from your body. When placing a live Air Bag on a bench or other surface, always point the trim cover up, away from the surface. Following these precautions will lessen the chance of personal injury if the Air Bag accidentally deploys.

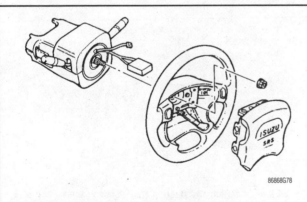

Fig. 50 SRS equipped steering wheel and components

Fig. 51 Air bag retainer nuts

8. Disconnect the horn leads.
9. Make alignment marks on the steering wheel and steering column shaft.
10. Loosen and remove the steering wheel nut. Use tool No. J–29752 or an equivalent steering wheel puller to remove the steering wheel.

✳✳ WARNING

The steering wheel puller bolts may damage the Air Bag cable reel if they are threaded too deeply into the steering wheel.

To install:
11. Check the alignment of the Air Bag cable reel.
  a. Turn the cable reel clockwise to the fully locked position. Do not turn the cable reel past the point at which you begin to feel resistance to its rotation.
  b. Turn the cable reel about three turns in the opposite direction until the pointer on the cable reel is aligned with the neutral mark.
12. Align the steering wheel matchmarks. Install the steering wheel and tighten the retainer nut to 25 ft. lbs. (34 Nm). Connect the horn leads.
13. Carefully connect the yellow 2–way connector to the Air Bag module. Install the Air Bag onto the steering wheel. Install the Torx® bolts while supporting the Air Bag module with your hand. Tighten each bolt to 6 ft. lbs. (8 Nm).
14. Properly arm the Air Bag system.
15. Connect the positive and negative battery cables.
16. Turn the ignition to the **ON** position, but don't start the engine. The AIR BAG warning light should turn on and flash on and off for seven seconds, and then turn off. This light sequence indicates that the Air Bag system is functioning normally. If the AIR BAG light doesn't come on, or stays on longer than seven seconds, the system must be diagnosed.
17. Check the operation of the horn buttons.

Turn Signal (Combination) Switch

REMOVAL & INSTALLATION

Without Air Bag

▶ **See Figure 52**

1. Disconnect the negative battery cable.
2. Remove the steering wheel. Refer to the procedure in this section.

➡**Do not strike the steering column or use air tools to loosen the steering wheel nut. The impact may damage the steering column's energy-absorbing properties.**

3. Remove the steering column upper and lower covers. Remove the horn contact ring.
4. Remove the turn signal canceling sleeve.
5. Disconnect the harnesses from the combination switch.
6. Remove the combination switch-to-steering column screws. Then, remove the switch.

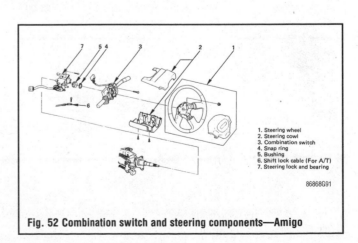

1. Steering wheel
2. Steering cowl
3. Combination switch
4. Snap ring
5. Bushing
6. Shift lock cable (For A/T)
7. Steering lock and bearing

Fig. 52 Combination switch and steering components—Amigo

➡On vehicles equipped with cruise control, the cruise control switch is an integral part of the combination switch.

To install:

7. Install the combination switch to the steering column and secure it with the retainer screws.

8. Connect the combination switch harness.

9. Install the steering column upper and lower covers.

10. Install the contact ring.

11. Install the steering wheel and horn pad.

12. Connect the negative battery cable.

13. Check both the combination switch and horn functions before driving the vehicle.

With Air Bag

▶ **See Figure 53**

➡1995 models are available with and without dual Air Bags. Air Bags were added as standard equipment during the middle of the year's production run. Air Bag equipped vehicles may be referred to as 1995½ models in parts and service listings.

※ CAUTION

The Air Bag system must be disabled before the steering wheel and combination switch are removed. Failure to disable the system may result in repairs and possible personal injury. Do not damage, cut, or attempt to alter the yellow Air Bag wiring harness.

➡On vehicles with Air Bags, the headlight and wiper switches are integral parts of the combination switch and Air Bag cable reel assembly.

1. Disconnect the negative then positive battery cables.

2. Disarm the Air Bag system.

3. Remove the steering wheel.

4. Remove the lower dashboard cover and disconnect the dimmer switch.

5. Remove the upper and lower steering column covers. Be careful with the wiring harness that runs through the lower cover; it contains the Air Bag wiring.

6. Unscrew and remove the combination switch and Air Bag cable reel assembly.

➡The combination switch and cable reel assembly cannot be disassembled. They are serviced and replaced as one complete assembly.

To install:

7. Install the combination switch and cable reel assembly onto the steering column shaft.

8. Reconnect the switch wiring harnesses.

9. Install the lower steering column cover, making sure that the Air Bag wiring is routed correctly and not pinched. Install the upper steering column cover.

10. Reconnect the dimmer switch and install the dashboard lower cover.

11. Check the alignment of the Air Bag cable reel.

a. Turn the cable reel clockwise to its fully locked position. Don't turn the cable reel past the point at which you begin to feel resistance to its rotation.

b. Turn the cable reel about three turns in the opposite direction until the pointer on the cable reel is aligned with the neutral mark.

12. Install the steering wheel and tighten the nut to 25 ft. lbs. (34 Nm).

13. Reconnect the positive and negative battery cables.

14. Turn the ignition to the **ON** position, but don't start the engine. The AIR BAG warning light should turn on and flash on and off for seven seconds, and then turn off. This light sequence indicates that the Air Bag system is functioning normally. If the AIR BAG light doesn't come on, or stays on longer than seven seconds, the system must be diagnosed.

15. Check the operation of the combination switch and horn controls.

Ignition Switch

REMOVAL & INSTALLATION

▶ **See Figures 54 and 55**

※ CAUTION

The Air Bag system must be disabled before the steering wheel and ignition switch are removed. Failure to disable the system may result in system repairs and possible personal injury. Do not damage, cut, or attempt to alter the yellow Air Bag wiring harness.

1. Turn the steering wheel so that the vehicle's front wheels are pointing straight ahead.

2. Turn the ignition switch to the **LOCK** position. Remove the key.

3. Disconnect the negative and positive battery cables.

4. If equipped, properly disarm the Air Bag system.

5. Remove the steering wheel.

6. Remove the lower dashboard cover and disconnect the dimmer switch.

7. Remove the upper and lower steering column covers. Be careful with the wiring harness that runs through the lower cover; it may contain the Air Bag wiring.

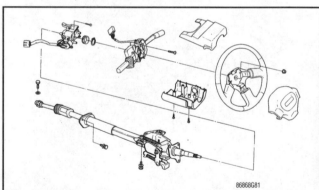

Fig. 54 Ignition switch and steering column components—non-SRS equipped models

86868G81

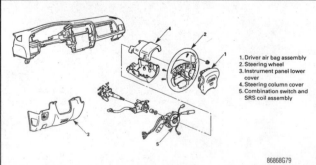

Fig. 53 Air bag equipped combination switch and steering wheel components

86868G79

1. Driver air bag assembly
2. Steering wheel
3. Instrument panel lower cover
4. Steering column cover
5. Combination switch and SRS coil assembly

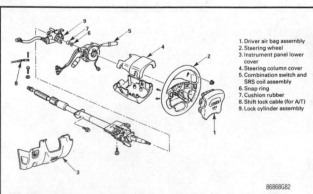

Fig. 55 Ignition switch and steering column components—SRS equipped models

86868G82

1. Driver air bag assembly
2. Steering wheel
3. Instrument panel lower cover
4. Steering column cover
5. Combination switch and SRS coil assembly
6. Snap ring
7. Cushion rubber
8. Shift lock cable (for A/T)
9. Lock cylinder assembly

8. Unscrew and remove the combination switch and Air Bag cable reel assembly, if equipped. The switch and cable reel assembly cannot be disassembled.

9. If equipped with an automatic transmission, disconnect the shift lock cable from the ignition lock cylinder.

10. Unscrew the switch from the ignition lock body and disconnect the harness from the fuse box.

To install:

11. Reconnect the ignition switch to the lock cylinder. Connect the wiring harness.

12. Connect the A/T shift lock cable to the ignition switch using a new lock pin.

13. Install the combination switch and cable reel assembly. Reconnect the switch harnesses.

14. Install the lower steering column cover, making sure that the Air Bag wiring, if equipped, is routed correctly and not pinched. Install the upper steering column cover.

15. Reconnect the dimmer switch and install the dashboard lower cover.

16. Check the alignment of the Air Bag cable reel, if equipped.

17. Install the steering wheel.

18. If equipped, properly arm the Air Bag system.

19. Reconnect the positive and negative battery cables.

20. Turn the ignition to the **ON** position, but don't start the engine. If equipped, the AIR BAG warning light should turn on and flash on and off for seven seconds, and then turn off. This indicator light sequence indicates that the Air Bag system is functioning normally. If the AIR BAG light doesn't come on, or stays on longer than seven seconds, the system must be diagnosed.

21. Check the operation of the ignition switch and combination switch controls.

Ignition Lock Cylinder

REMOVAL & INSTALLATION

✲✲ CAUTION

The Air Bag system must be disabled before the steering wheel and ignition switch are removed. Failure to disable the system may result in system repairs and possible personal injury. Do not damage, cut, or attempt to alter the yellow Air Bag wiring harness.

1. Turn the steering wheel so that the vehicle's front wheels are pointing straight ahead.

2. Turn the ignition switch to the **LOCK** position. Remove the key.

3. Disconnect the negative, then positive battery cables.

4. If equipped, disarm the Air Bag system. Matchmark and remove the steering wheel.

5. Remove the lower dashboard cover and disconnect the dimmer switch, if installed in this panel.

6. Remove the upper and lower steering column covers. Be careful with the wiring harness that runs through the lower cover; it may contain the Air Bag wiring.

7. Unscrew and remove the combination switch and Air Bag cable reel assembly, if equipped. The switch and cable reel assembly cannot be disassembled.

8. If equipped with an automatic transmission, disconnect the shift lock cable from the ignition lock cylinder.

9. Unscrew the ignition switch from the lock body and disconnect the wiring harness from the fuse box.

10. Unbolt the ignition lock cylinder from the steering column. Remove the snapring and the bushing to remove the lock cylinder from the steering column.

To install:

11. Install the lock cylinder to the steering column. Install and evenly tighten the bolts. Install a new bushing and snapring.

12. Reconnect the starter switch to the lock cylinder. Connect the wiring.

13. Connect the A/T shift lock cable to the ignition switch using a new lock pin.

14. Install the combination switch and cable reel assembly. Reconnect the switch harnesses.

15. Install the lower steering column cover, making sure that the Air Bag wiring, if equipped, is routed correctly and not pinched. Install the upper steering column cover.

16. Reconnect the dimmer switch, if removed, and install the dashboard lower cover.

17. Check the alignment of the Air Bag cable reel, if equipped;

   a. Turn the cable reel clockwise to the fully locked position. Don't turn the cable reel past the point at which you begin to feel resistance to rotation.

   b. Turn the cable reel about three turns in the opposite direction until the pointer on the cable reel is alignment with the neutral mark.

18. Install the steering.

19. Reconnect the battery cables, starting with the positive cable, then the negative.

20. Turn the ignition to the **ON** position, but don't start the engine. The AIR BAG warning light should turn on and flash on and off for seven seconds, and then turn off. This indicator light sequence indicates that the Air Bag system is functioning normally. If the AIR BAG light doesn't come on, or stays on longer than seven seconds, the system must be diagnosed.

21. Check the operation of the ignition switch and combination switch controls.

Steering Linkage

REMOVAL & INSTALLATION

Pitman Arm

♦ **See Figures 56, 57 and 58**

1. Raise and support the front of the vehicle safely on jackstands.

2. If necessary, remove the air snorkel for access to the intermediate shaft.

3. Matchmark the upper and lower intermediate shaft joints, then remove the retainers and remove the intermediate shaft.

4. Disconnect the oil cooler pipes at the crossmember, if equipped.

5. If equipped, remove the splash shield.

6. Remove the nut from the ball stud at the relay rod-to-Pitman arm connection.

7. Using a suitable universal steering linkage puller, such as J-24319-01 or equivalent, separate the relay rod from the Pitman arm. Pull down on the relay rod and separate the stud.

8. For vehicles where access to the Pitman arm/nut is restricted, remove the 2 lower steering gear bolts (leaving on the top bolt which should be loos-

Fig. 56 Remove the Pitman arm to steering linkage cotter pin

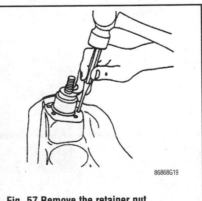

Fig. 57 Remove the retainer nut

Fig. 58 Use a suitable tie rod puller to loosen the Pitman arm-to-steering linkage connection

ened), then pivot the steering gear for Pitman arm clearance. Support the gear using a block of wood.

➡ **On 1994 vehicles, it may not be possible to pivot the gear for access to the Pitman shaft. If necessary, unbolt and remove the gear from the vehicle. For details, please refer to the gear procedures found later in this section.**

9. Remove the Pitman arm-to-Pitman shaft nut, then matchmark the relationship of the arm to the shaft to assure proper alignment during assembly.

10. Using a Pitman arm remover such as J-6632 or equivalent, separate the Pitman arm from the Pitman shaft and remove it from the vehicle.

➡ **When separating the Pitman arm from the shaft, DO NOT use a hammer or apply heat to the arm.**

To install:

➡ **If the Pitman arm is being replaced, transfer the alignment mark to the new component.**

11. Install the Pitman arm while aligning the arm-to-Pitman shaft matchmark. Use a steering linkage installer such as J-29193 (12mm), J-29194 (14mm) or equivalent (as applicable) to properly seat the arm on the shaft, and tighten to 40 ft. lbs. (54 Nm) to seat the taper.

12. Remove the installer tool, then install the Pitman shaft nut and tighten to 185 ft. lbs. (250 Nm).

13. Install the lower retaining bolts. Tighten all of the retaining bolts to 55 ft. lbs. (75 Nm).

14. Connect the Pitman arm to the relay rod (make sure that the seal is on the stud). Use a steering linkage installer such as J-29193 (12mm), J-29194 (14mm) or equivalent, and tighten to 40 ft. lbs. (54 Nm) to seat the taper.

15. After seating, remove the tool, install lockwashers and nuts, then tighten to 60 ft. lbs. (82 Nm).

➡ **If a prevailing torque nut was used, (no spring washer), then a new nut must be used.**

16. Install the splash shield, oil cooler pipes, intermediate shaft and air duct, as applicable.

17. Remove the jackstands and carefully lower the vehicle.

18. Check and adjust toe, as necessary.

Idler Arm

1. Raise and support the vehicle with jackstands. Place the jackstands under the frame so the wheels are free to turn.

➡ **Jerking the right wheel assembly back and forth is not an acceptable testing procedure; there is no control on the amount of force being applied to the idler arm. Before suspecting idler arm shimmying complaints, check the wheels for imbalance, run-out, force variation and/or road surface irregularities.**

2. To inspect for a defective idler arm:
   a. Position the wheels in the straight ahead position.
   b. Position a spring scale near the relay rod end of the idler arm, then exert 25 ft. lbs. (110 Nm) of force upward and then downward. Measure the distance between the upward and downward directions that the idler arm moves. The allowable deflection is 1/8 in. (3.18mm) for each direction for a total difference of 1/4 in. (6.35mm); if the idler arm deflection is beyond the allowable limits, replace it.

3. Remove the idler arm-to-frame bolts/nuts.

4. Remove the nut from the idler arm-to-relay rod ball joint.

5. Use a suitable steering linkage puller such as J-24319-01 or equivalent to separate the relay rod from the idler arm.

6. Remove the idler arm assembly from the vehicle.

To install:

7. Install the idler arm, then tighten the arm assembly-to-frame bolts to 60 ft. lbs. (82 Nm).

8. Connect the relay rod to the idler arm. Use a steering linkage installer such as J-29193 (12mm), J-29194 (14mm) or equivalent (as applicable) to seat the relay rod-to-idler arm ball joint stud. Tighten the tool to 40 ft. lbs. (54 Nm), then remove the tool.

9. Install the idler arm-to-relay rod stud nut and tighten to 35 ft. lbs. (47 Nm) for 2WD vehicles or 60 ft. lbs. (81 Nm) for 4WD vehicles.

10. Remove the jackstands and carefully lower the vehicle.

11. Check and/or adjust the toe, as necessary.

Intermediate Rod

1. Raise and safely support the vehicle on jackstands.

2. Remove the cotter pin from the ball studs connecting the tie rods-to-intermediate rod and the steering damper. Remove the castellated nuts. Using a ball joint separator tool or equivalent, separate the components.

3. Remove the nut and lockwasher on the ball stud connecting the intermediate rod to the idler arm. Using a ball joint separator tool or equivalent, separate the intermediate rod from the idler arm.

4. Remove the intermediate rod with the tie rods attached.

5. If the tie rod is in need of replacement, paint alignment marks on the rod, then disconnect the intermediate rod from the tie rod.

To install:

6. If removed, install the tie rod to the intermediate rod.

7. Make sure the threads on all the components are clean and smooth.

8. Install the intermediate rod-to the idler arm and secure with the nut. Tighten the nut to 50 ft. lbs. (65 Nm).

9. Install the rod on to the Pitman arm. Tighten the nut to 44 ft. lbs. (57 Nm). Tighten the nut just enough to insert a new cotter pin.

10. Install the intermediate rod to steering damper end. Tighten the nut to 87 ft. lbs. (113 Nm), then advance the nut just enough to insert a new cotter pin.

11. Install the tie rods and tighten the nut to 44 ft. lbs. (57 Nm), then advance the nut just enough to insert a new cotter pin.

12. Install the wheels and lower the vehicle.

Outer Tie Rod

▶ **See Figures 59, 60, 61, 62 and 63**

➡ **DO NOT attempt to separate the tie rod-to-steering knuckle joint by driving a wedge type tool between the joint and knuckle or seal damage could result.**

1. Raise the vehicle and support safely on jackstands. Remove the front wheel assemblies.

2. Remove the cotter pin and castle nut from the tie rod end. Using a tie rod removal tool, separate the tie rod from the steering knuckle.

➡ **Tie rod adjustment components tend to rust in service. If the torque required to remove the nut from the bolt exceeds 62 inch lbs. (9 Nm), the nuts should be replaced. Also, the components should be lubricated with a penetrating oil, then the clamps should be rotated until the move freely. Pay attention to the clamp positioning before loosening or removing them.**

3. Remove the tie rod end as follows:
   a. Measure the installed length of the tie rod end(s) for installation purposes.
   b. Loosen the adjuster tube clamp bolt(s).
   c. Unscrew the tie rod end from the adjuster tube; count the number of turns necessary to remove the tie rod end. This can be used to help preserve the toe adjustment during installation.

To install:

4. If one or both of the tie rod ends were removed:
   a. Clean, inspect and lubricate the adjuster tube threads.
   b. Thread the tie rod end into the adjuster tube using the same number of turns necessary to remove it. Once installed, measure the length of the tie rod end, as done during removal to help assure toe adjustment.

Fig. 59 Remove the cotter pin from the stud ball

Fig. 60 Loosen and remove the tie rod retainer nut

Fig. 61 Use a suitable tie rod puller to loosen the tie rod from the steering knuckle

Fig. 62 Remove the tie rod from the knuckle

Fig. 63 Unscrew the tie rod end. Count the number of turns for installation

c. Position the clamp bolts between the adjuster tube dimples (located at each end) and in the proper location. Tighten the adjuster tube clamp bolt 14 ft. lbs. (19 Nm). Tighten the locknut to 25 ft. lbs. (34 Nm).

5. Position the tie rod ends to the steering knuckle and/or the relay rod. Use a steering linkage installer such as J-29193 (12mm), J-29194 (14mm) or equivalent (as applicable), install the correct one onto the ball stud and tighten it to 40 ft. lbs. (54 Nm) to seat the taper(s).

6. Once the ends are properly seated, remove the tool and install the retaining nut(s).

7. Tighten the inner and/or outer tie rod end retaining nuts to 35 ft. lbs. (47 Nm).

8. Install a new cotter pin to the castle nut(s), as applicable.

9. Check and adjust the toe, as necessary.

10. Remove the jackstands and carefully lower the vehicle, then check the steering linkage for proper operation.

11. Have the front end aligned by a qualified technician.

Manual Steering Gear

REMOVAL & INSTALLATION

1. Disconnect the negative battery cable.

2. Raise and safely support the front of the vehicle on jackstands. Turn the wheels so they are facing in the straight ahead position.

3. If equipped, remove the retainers and the shield from the base of the intermediate shaft.

4. Matchmark the intermediate shaft-to-steering gear connection in order to assure proper installation.

5. Remove the intermediate shaft-to-steering gear pinch

To install:

6. If necessary, align and install the Pitman shaft to the gear.

7. Position the steering gear to the frame and secure with the retaining bolts.

8. Install the gear retaining bolts and tighten to 55–60 ft. lbs. (75–81 Nm).

➡When installing the steering gear, be sure that the intermediate shaft bottoms on the worm shaft, so that the pinch bolt passes through the undercut on the worm shaft. Check and/or adjust the alignment of the Pitman arm-to-Pitman shaft.

9. Align and install the intermediate shaft coupling using the pinch bolt. Tighten the bolt to 30 ft. lbs. (41 Nm).

10. If not done already, align and install the Pitman arm to the shaft. Refer to the procedure in this section for details.

11. If applicable, install the coupling shield over the intermediate shaft-to-gear coupling.

12. Remove the jackstands and carefully lower the vehicle.

13. Connect the negative battery cable.

ADJUSTMENTS

Steering gear adjustments are made only as corrections and NOT as periodic adjustments. Before adjusting the gear, check the remainder of the steering linkage and front suspension for wear or damage and repair/replace components, as necessary. Adjustment takes place in 2 major steps. First the worm bearing preload adjustment is made using the adjuster plug, then the overcenter preload is adjusted using the adjuster screw/bolt and jam nut.

1. Position the front wheels in a straight ahead position.

2. Loosen the locknut on the adjusting screw of the steering gear unit.

3. Turn the adjusting screw clockwise to decrease the free-play or counterclockwise to increase it.

4. When the steering wheel free-play is between 0.39–1.17 in. (10–30mm), tighten the locknut to 15–22 ft. lbs. (20–29 Nm).

Power Steering Gear

The recirculating ball type power steering gear used on these vehicles is basically the same as the manual steering gear, except that it uses a hydraulic assist on the rack piston.

The power steering gear control valve directs the power steering fluid to either side of the rack piston, which rides up and down the worm shaft. The steering rack converts the hydraulic pressure into mechanical force. Should the vehicle loose the hydraulic pressure, it can still be controlled mechanically.

REMOVAL & INSTALLATION

♦ See Figure 64

1. Raise and safely support the front of the vehicle on jackstands.

2. Place a suitable drain pan under the power steering gear.

3. Tag and disconnect the feed and return hoses from the steering gear. Immediately cap or plug the openings to prevent system contamination or excessive fluid loss.

➡Be sure to plug the pressure hoses and the openings of the power steering pump to keep dirt out of the system.

4. If equipped, remove the intermediate shaft lower coupling shield.

5. Remove the intermediate shaft-to-steering gear bolt. Matchmark the

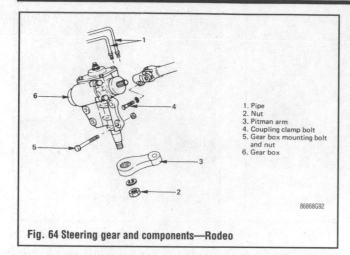

Fig. 64 Steering gear and components—Rodeo

1. Pipe
2. Nut
3. Pitman arm
4. Coupling clamp bolt
5. Gear box mounting bolt and nut
6. Gear box

86868G92

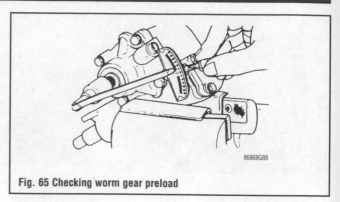

Fig. 65 Checking worm gear preload

86868G88

intermediate shaft-to-power steering gear and separate the shaft from the gear.

6. Matchmark and remove the Pitman arm from the gear Pitman shaft.

7. Remove the power steering gear-to-frame bolts and washers, then carefully remove the steering gear from the vehicle.

To install:

8. Position the steering gear to the vehicle and secure the retainer bolts finger-tight. If necessary, align and install the Pitman arm to the shaft at this time.

9. Tighten the power steering gear-to-frame bolts to 55 ft. lbs. (75 Nm).

10. Align and install the intermediate shaft to the power steering, then secure using the pinch bolt.

11. If equipped, install the shield over the intermediate shaft lower coupling.

12. Remove the caps, then connect the feed and return hoses to the power steering gear. Refill the pump reservoir.

13. Remove the jackstands and carefully lower the vehicle.

14. Properly bleed the power steering system.

15. Road test the vehicle.

ADJUSTMENTS

Steering gear adjustments are made only as corrections and NOT as periodic adjustments. Before adjusting the gear, check the remainder of the steering linkage and front suspension for wear or damage and repair/replace components, as necessary.

➡To perform adjustments to the power steering gear, it is recommended to remove the power steering gear from the vehicle and place it in a soft-jawed vise. Before any adjustments are performed, check and repair any problems relating to hydraulic pressures and performance.

Worm Bearing Preload

▶ See Figure 65

1. Remove the gear from the truck and mount in a vise.
2. Remove the adjuster plug locknut at the gear's end.
3. Use an adjustable spanner wrench to turn the adjuster plug inward, until it firmly bottoms in the housing with a torque of 20 ft. lbs. (27 Nm).
4. Use a scribing tool to place a matchmark next to the one of the spanner wrench holes in the adjuster plug.
5. Measure ½ in. (13mm) counterclockwise from the scribed mark (on the housing) and place another mark.
6. Use the spanner to turn the adjuster plug (counterclockwise) until the hole in the adjuster plug aligns with the 2nd scribed mark.
7. While holding the adjuster plug in alignment, install and tighten the adjuster plug locknut.

Overcenter Preload

1. Adjust the worm bearing preload.
2. Rotate the stub shaft from stop-to-stop and count the number of turns necessary.
3. Starting from one stop, turn the stub shaft back ½ the number of turns (to the center of the gear).

➡With the stub gear centered, the flat on top of the shaft should face upward and be parallel with the side cover; the master spline on the Pitman shaft should be in line with the adjuster screw.

4. Loosen the Pitman shaft adjuster screw locknut, then turn the adjuster screw counterclockwise until it is fully extended. Turn the screw clockwise one full turn.

5. Place a 0–50 inch lbs. (0–6 Nm) torque wrench vertically on the stub shaft, then rotate it 45° (to each side) and record the highest drag measured near or on the center.

6. Turn the adjuster screw inward until the stub shaft torque is 6–10 inch lbs. (0.6–1.2 Nm) more than the initial reading.

7. Tighten the adjuster screw jam nut to 20 ft. lbs. (27 Nm) while holding the adjuster screw from turning. Double check for the proper measurement to assure the screw was not turned while tightening the nut.

8. Install the power steering gear into the vehicle.

Power Steering Pump

REMOVAL & INSTALLATION

1. Position a drain pan under the power steering pump.
2. Tag and disconnect the hoses from the pump.
3. Remove the drive belt from the pulley.
4. Install a suitable puller tool onto the power steering pump pulley, and remove the pulley.
5. Remove the power steering pump-to-bracket bolts and, if installed, the rear brace, then remove the pump.

To install:

6. Position the pump to the vehicle and secure using the retaining bolts and, if equipped, the rear brace.

7. Use a pulley installer to press the drive pulley onto the power steering pump. Check that the pulley is flush within 0.010 in. (0.25mm) of the shaft end.

8. Install the drive belt and adjust the tension (as applicable).

➡Be sure to secure any hoses which may get in the way or rub other components.

9. Connect the feed and return hoses to the pump.
10. Properly refill and bleed the power steering system.
11. Test drive the vehicle.

SYSTEM BLEEDING

1. Fill the steering reservoir to the proper Cold level.
2. Run the engine until it reaches normal operating temperature.
3. Turn the engine **OFF** and check the fluid level. If necessary, fill the reservoir to the proper level.
4. Run the engine and turn the steering wheel from lock-to-lock (both directions) 3–4 times; don't hold the wheel at a lock position for more than 5 seconds or fluid temperature will rise.
5. Return the steering wheel to center, turn the engine **OFF** and allow the fluid to sit for 5 minutes before adding.
6. If necessary, repeat the bleeding procedure until the air bubbles are removed from the system.
7. Fill the system to the proper level when finished.

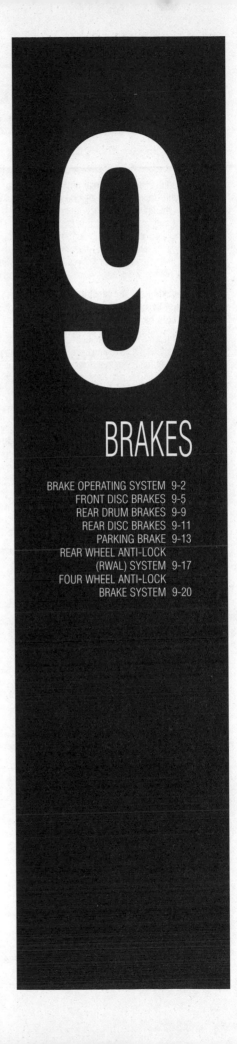

9

BRAKES

BRAKE OPERATING SYSTEM

Adjustments

REAR DRUM BRAKES

Normal adjustments of the rear drum brakes are automatic and are made during the reverse applications of the brakes. The following procedure should be used only if the linings have been replaced.

1. Raise and support the rear of the vehicle safely on jackstands.
2. Using a punch and a hammer on the rear of the backing plates, knock out the lanced metal areas near the star wheel assemblies on each plate. The metal areas may already have been removed and covered with rubber adjustment plugs, if so remove the plugs by grasping and pulling out with a pair of pliers.

➡ **After knocking out the lanced metal areas from the backing plate, the wheels must be removed and all of the metal pieces discarded, then the wheels should be reinstalled for adjustment.**

3. Insert a suitable brake adjustment tool such as J-4735 or equivalent, into the breaking plate slots and engage the lowest possible tooth on the star wheel. Move the end of the brake tool downward to move the star wheel upward and expand the adjusting screw. Repeat this operation until the wheels can just be turned by hand. This is a position immediately before the brakes lock.

➡ **The brake drag should be equal at both wheels.**

4. Back off the adjusting screws 24 notches (clicks). By the time you have backed off the adjustment 12 clicks, the brakes should have no drag. If a heavy drag is still present, the parking brake cable is likely in need of adjustment.
5. Make sure both sides of the brakes are properly adjusted. When backing off the brakes on the other side, the adjusting lever must be backed off the same number of turns to prevent side-to-side brake pull.
6. After the brakes are adjusted, install a rubber cover into each of the backing plate slots. To complete the brake adjustment operation, make several stops while backing the vehicle to fully equalize the adjustment.

➡ **Pump the brake pedal to seat the brake shoes before moving the vehicle.**

7. Road test the vehicle.

BRAKE PEDAL TRAVEL

▶ **See Figure 1**

The brake pedal travel is the distance the pedal moves toward the floor from the fully released position.

1. Start the engine and allow it to reach normal operating temperature. Measure brake pedal height (L_2) between the floor of the vehicle and the top of the pedal after the engine is revved several times. Ensure pedal is fully returned by the pedal return spring. Pedal height should be between 6.85–7.24 in. (174–184mm).
2. Depress the pedal with approximately 110 lbs. (50 kg) of weight and measure the pedal height (L_3) between the floor of the vehicle and the top of the

pedal after the engine is revved several times. Pedal height should be between 3.7 in (95mm).

3. Turn **OFF** the engine. Depress the brake pedal several times. Measure the pedal free-play (L). If the measured free-play is not within the specification of 0.23–0.39 in. (6–10mm), adjust brake pedal as follows:
   a. Disconnect the stop light switch connector.
   b. Loosen the stop light switch locknut and back the switch away from brake pedal.
   c. Loosen the locknut on the pushrod and adjust the brake pedal to the specified height.
   d. Tighten the locknut to 15 ft. lbs. (19 Nm).
   e. Adjust the stop light switch (A) to specification, tighten nut and install connector.

Brake Light Switch

REMOVAL & INSTALLATION

1. Disconnect the negative battery cable.
2. Locate the stop light switch on the brake pedal support.
3. Unfasten the connector from the stop light switch.
4. Remove the locknut and the stop light switch.

To install:

5. Install the switch on brake pedal support and adjust to specification.
6. Tighten the locknut to 14 ft. lbs.
7. Fasten the stop light switch and connect the negative battery cable.
8. Check the operation of the switch.

ADJUSTMENT

▶ **See Figure 2**

Adjust the stop light switch to the specified clearance of 0.02–0.04 in. (0.5–1.0mm) between the switch housing and brake pedal by rotating the switch housing assembly. When the specified clearance is reached, tighten the switch locknut.

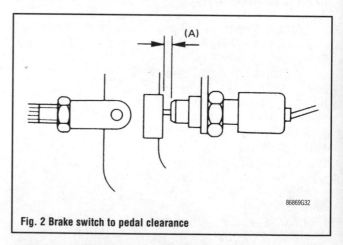

Fig. 2 Brake switch to pedal clearance

Master Cylinder

REMOVAL & INSTALLATION

▶ **See Figures 3, 4, 5 and 6**

❄❄ WARNING

Clean, high quality brake fluid is essential to the safe and proper operation of the brake system. You should always buy the highest quality brake fluid that is available. If the brake fluid becomes contaminated, drain and flush the system, then refill the master cylin-

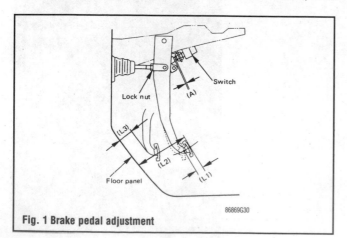

Fig. 1 Brake pedal adjustment

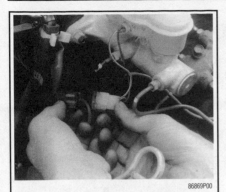

Fig. 3 Disconnect the level indicator harness at the master cylinder

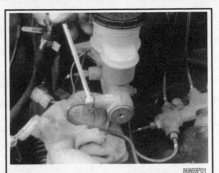

Fig. 4 Use a suitable flare-end or box wrench to disconnect the bake lines from the master cylinder

Fig. 5 Remove the retainer nuts securing the master cylinder to the booster

Fig. 6 Lift the master cylinder off the booster studs

der with new fluid. Never reuse any brake fluid. Any brake fluid that is removed from the system should be discarded.

1. Apply the parking brake and block the drive wheels.
2. Disconnect the negative battery cable.
3. Using a turkey baster or other suitable device, remove as much brake fluid from the reservoir as possible.

➡Brake fluid is highly corrosive to paint. Take care not to spill brake fluid on any painted surface of the vehicle.

4. Disconnect the reservoir fluid level indicator harness at the master cylinder, if equipped.
5. Tag and remove all brake lines from the master cylinder using a suitable flare or box-end wrench. Plug the lines to prevent system contamination or excessive fluid loss.
6. Remove the retainer nuts securing the master cylinder in place.
7. Remove the master cylinder by pulling straight out.
8. Remove the reservoir from the top of the master cylinder if needed. Grasp the reservoir and gently rock it back and forth as you pull it out.

To install:

9. In order to ease installation, bench bleed the master cylinder before installation:

    a. Plug the master cylinder outlet ports. This can be done using rubber or plastic plugs or, more effectively, using a single length of brake line with appropriately sized flares/flare nuts on each end.

    b. Mount the cylinder in a soft-jawed vise with the front end tilted slightly downward.

    c. Fill the reservoir with clean brake fluid, then use a tool with a smooth rounded end (such as a wooden dowel or pencil eraser) to stroke the primary piston about 1 in. (25mm) several times. As air is bled from the cylinder, the primary piston will no longer travel the full distance.

    d. Reposition the master cylinder in the vise with the front end tilted slightly up, then continue stroking the primary piston to further bleed air.

    e. Reposition the master cylinder so it is level, then loosen the plugs one

at a time and push the piston into the bore, forcing air from the cylinder. DO NOT allow the piston to return with the plugs loosened or air will be drawn back into the master cylinder.

    f. Make sure the plugs are tightly sealed, then check and refill the reservoir.

10. Install the reservoir to the master cylinder, if removed. Apply a coating of brake fluid to the reservoir seals, then press the reservoir in place.

11. Attach the master cylinder to the mounting stud in the engine compartment. Before installing the retainer nuts, make sure the master cylinder is properly seated, and the brake pedal pushrod is position correctly in the master cylinder. Install the retainer nuts and hand-tighten.

12. Tighten the master cylinder retainer nuts to 113 inch lbs. (13 Nm).

13. Install the brake lines to the master cylinder. Tighten the line fittings to 105 inch lbs. (12 Nm).

14. Connect the negative battery cable.

15. Bleed and refill the entire brake system.

Combination Valve

⬧ See Figure 7

REMOVAL & INSTALLATION

✳✳ WARNING

Clean, high quality brake fluid is essential to the safe and proper operation of the brake system. You should always buy the highest quality brake fluid that is available. If the brake fluid becomes contaminated, drain and flush the system, then refill the master cylinder with new fluid. Never reuse any brake fluid. Any brake fluid that is removed from the system should be discarded.

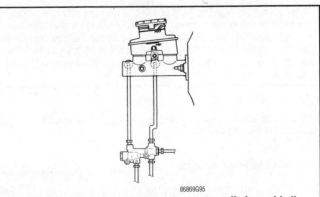

Fig. 7 Combination valve in between the master cylinder and individual brakes

Combination valves on Isuzu vehicles are mounted in two locations: (1) on the master cylinder, inline with the rear brake lines and (2) on the frame rail below the master cylinder.

Without ABS

1. Disconnect the negative battery cable.
2. Unfasten the harness attached to the bracket on top of the valve, if equipped.
3. Tag and disconnect the brake lines at the combination valve. Immediately plug the lines to prevent system contamination or excessive fluid loss.
4. Remove the proportioning valve retainer bolts, then remove the valve.

To install:

5. Position the combination valve in place and secure with the retainer bolts. If the valve is equipped with a warning sensor harness, the bracket for the harness must be installed between the valve assembly and the bolt head. Tighten the bolts to 51 inch lbs. (6 Nm).
6. Connect the warning sensor harness.
7. Install the brake lines to the combination valve. Tighten the brake lines to 12 ft. lbs. (16 Nm).
8. Connect the negative battery cable.
9. Bleed the brake system.

With ABS

1. Disconnect the negative battery cable.
2. Disconnect the hydraulic lines from the combination valve one at a time. Immediately plug all openings to prevent system contamination or excessive fluid loss.
3. Disengage the electrical connector from the combination valve pressure switch.
4. Disengage the RWAL pressure valve connector.
5. Remove the master cylinder/combination valve-to-bracket retaining nuts, then remove the valve from the vehicle.
6. Remove the RWAL pressure valve.

➡**The combination valve is not repairable and must be replaced as a complete assembly.**

To install:

7. Install the RWAL pressure valve.
8. Install the combination valve and bracket assembly, then install and tighten the master cylinder/valve bracket retaining nuts.
9. Engage the RWAL pressure valve connector.
10. Engage the pressure switch electrical connector.
11. Remove the caps (one at a time) and connect the brake lines to the combination valve, then tighten the fittings to 12 ft. lbs. (16 Nm).
12. Connect the negative battery cable.
13. Check and refill the master cylinder reservoir, then properly bleed the hydraulic brake system.

Brake System Bleeding

♦ See Figures 8 and 9

☼☼☼ WARNING

Clean, high quality brake fluid is essential to the safe and proper operation of the brake system. You should always buy the highest quality brake fluid that is available. If the brake fluid becomes contaminated, drain and flush the system, then refill the master cylinder with new fluid. Never reuse any brake fluid. Any brake fluid that is removed from the system should be discarded.

1. Set the parking brake and start the engine.

➡**The vacuum booster will be damaged if the bleeding operation is performed with the engine OFF.**

2. Remove the master cylinder reservoir cap and fill the reservoir with brake fluid. Keep the reservoir at least half full during the bleeding operation.
3. If the master cylinder is replaced or overhauled, first bleed the air from the master cylinder and then from each caliper or wheel cylinder. Bleed the master cylinder as follows:
    a. Disconnect the left front wheel brake line from the master cylinder.
    b. Have an assistant depress the brake pedal slowly once and hold it depressed.

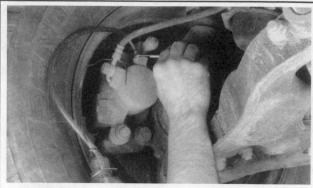

Fig. 8 Bleeding a front brake caliper

Fig. 9 Bleeding a rear brake caliper

    c. Seal the delivery port of the master cylinder where the line was disconnected with a finger, then release the brake pedal slowly.
    d. Release the finger from the delivery port when the brake pedal returns completely.
    e. Reconnect the brake line to the master cylinder.
    f. Have an assistant depress the brake pedal slowly once and hold it depressed.
    g. Loosen the left front wheel brake line at the master cylinder.
    h. Retighten the brake line, then release the brake pedal slowly.
    i. Repeat Steps g–i, until no air comes out from the port when the brake line is loosened.
    j. Bleed the air from the right front wheel brake line connection by repeating Steps a–l, but this time disconnect/loosen the right front wheel brake line.
4. Bleed the air from each wheel in the following order: left front caliper, right rear caliper or wheel cylinder, right front caliper, left rear caliper or wheel cylinder. Bleed the air as follows:
    a. Place the proper size flare or box-end wrench over the bleeder screw.
    b. Cover the bleeder screw with a transparent tube and submerge the free end of the tube in a transparent container containing brake fluid.
    c. Have an assistant pump the brake pedal 3 times, then hold it depressed.
    d. Remove the air along with the brake fluid by loosening the bleeder screw.
    e. Retighten the bleeder screw, then release the brake pedal slowly.
    f. Repeat Steps c–e until the air is completely removed. It may be necessary to repeat the bleeding procedure 10 or more times for front wheels and 15 or more times for rear wheels.
    g. After the bleeding operation is completed on each individual wheel, check the level of brake fluid in the reservoir and replenish up to the **MAX** level, if necessary.
    h. Go to the next wheel in sequence after each wheel is bled.
5. Depress the brake pedal to check if sponginess is felt after the air has been removed from all wheel cylinders and calipers. If the pedal feels spongy, the entire bleeding procedure must be repeated.
6. Install the master cylinder reservoir cap.

FRONT DISC BRAKES

✱✱ CAUTION

Brake pads may contain asbestos, which has been determined to be a cancer causing agent. Never clean the brake surfaces with compressed air! Avoid inhaling any dust from any brake surface! When cleaning brake surfaces, use a commercially available brake cleaning fluid.

Brake Pads

INSPECTION

▶ **See Figures 10 and 11**

Brake pads should be inspected once a year or at 6,000 miles (9,600 km) intervals, whichever occurs first. Check both ends of the outboard pad, looking in at each end of the caliper; then check the lining thickness of the inboard pad, looking down through the inspection hole. On riveted pads, the lining should be more than 1/32 in. (0.8mm) thick above the rivet (so that the lining is thicker than the metal backing in most cases) in order to prevent the rivet from scoring the rotor. On bonded brake pads, a minimum lining thickness of 1/32 in. (0.8mm) above the backing plate should be used to determine necessary replacement intervals. Keep in mind that any applicable state inspection standards that are more stringent take precedence. All four front pads MUST be replaced as a set if one shows excessive wear.

➡All models should be equipped with a wear indicator that makes a noise when the linings have worn to a degree where replacement is necessary. The spring clip is an integral part of the inboard pad and lining. When the brake pad reaches a certain degree of wear, the clip will contact the rotor and produce a warning noise.

REMOVAL & INSTALLATION

▶ **See Figures 12 thru 17**

1. Use a turkey baster or other suitable device to remove half of the volume of brake fluid from the master cylinder. Discard of the brake fluid properly. Do not reuse old brake fluid.
2. Raise and safely support the vehicle on jackstands.
3. Remove the wheel and tire assemblies.
4. Install a C-clamp on the caliper with the solid frame side of the clamp against the back of the caliper and the driving screw end against the metal part (center backing plate) of the outboard pad.
5. Tighten the clamp until the caliper moves sufficiently to bottom the piston in the bore, then remove the clamp.
6. Remove the lower caliper mounting bolt from the back of the caliper.
7. Swing the caliper up and support using a coat hanger or length of wire.
8. Remove the inboard and outboard pads from the caliper or bracket.
9. Remove any brake pads retainer clips from the brake pad or caliper bracket.
10. Remove the bolt ear sleeves and rubber bushings for cleaning, inspection and lubrication.

To install:

11. Check the inside of the caliper for leakage and the condition of the piston dust boot. If necessary, remove the caliper and overhaul or replace it.
12. Lubricate the sleeves and bushings using a suitable silicone lubricant, then attach them to the caliper.
13. Make sure the piston is fully seated in the caliper providing clearance for the new brake pads. If the piston is not compressed, install the old inboard pad and use the C-clamp on the pad and back on the caliper to bottom the piston. BE CAREFUL not to pinch and damage the piston boot.
14. Attach the retainer clips to the brake pads.

86869P09

Fig. 10 Use a tape measure to check the pad thickness

86869P10

Fig. 11 Remove the pads and check for deep grooves, indicating needed rotor service

86869P11

Fig. 12 Use a C-clamp to compress the caliper piston

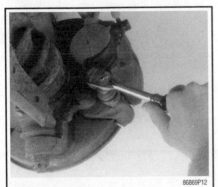

86869P12

Fig. 13 Loosen the lower caliper retainer bolt

86869P13

Fig. 14 Slide the caliper retainer bolt out

86869P14

Fig. 15 Lift the caliper up and remove the pad

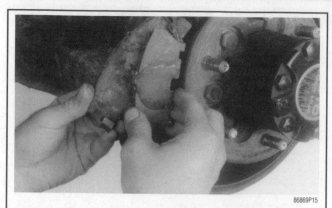

Fig. 16 Remove the plate from the back of the pad, if equipped

➡**Make sure that the wear sensor is facing in the proper direction. On most vehicles it should face toward the rear of the caliper.**

15. On all other models, install the inboard and outboard pads on the caliper bracket.

16. Place the caliper over the rotor, lining up the hole in the caliper ears with the holes in the mounting bracket. Make sure that the brake hose is not twisted or distorted.

17. Carefully insert the mounting bolt through the bracket and caliper (bushing and sleeves), then tighten to 22–25 ft. lbs. (28–32 Nm).

18. Pump the brake pedal a several times to seat the linings against the rotors.

19. Install the wheels, then remove the jackstands and carefully lower the vehicle.

20. Check and refill the master cylinder reservoirs with clean brake fluid.

✳✳ CAUTION

DO NOT attempt to move the vehicle until a firm brake pedal is obtained.

21. Pump the brake pedal to make sure that it is firm. If necessary, bleed the brakes.

Brake Caliper

REMOVAL & INSTALLATION

▶ **See Figures 18 and 19**

✳✳ CAUTION

Brake shoes may contain asbestos, which has been determined to be a cancer causing agent. Never clean the brake surfaces with compressed air! Avoid inhaling any dust from any brake surface! When cleaning brake surfaces, use a commercially available brake cleaning fluid.

1. Use a turkey baster or other suitable device to remove the brake fluid from the master cylinder reservoir. Discard of the brake fluid properly. Do not reuse old brake fluid.

2. Raise and safely support the vehicle on jackstands.

3. Remove the wheel and tire assemblies.

4. If the brake pads are being replaced (and the caliper is NOT being overhauled), install a C-clamp on the caliper with the solid frame side of the clamp rests against the back of the caliper and the driving screw end rests against the metal part (center backing plate) of the outboard pad. Tighten the clamp until the caliper moves sufficiently to bottom the piston in the bore, then remove the clamp.

5. Remove the caliper mounting bolts from the back of the caliper. If the caliper is not being completely removed from the vehicle, detach it from the mounting bracket and support it using a coat hanger or length of wire. DO NOT allow the hose to be stretched, twisted, kinked or otherwise damaged.

6. If the caliper is being completely removed from the vehicle, place a drip pan below the caliper and disconnect the flexible brake hose-to-caliper banjo-bolt. Discard the pressure fitting washers, then remove the brake caliper from the vehicle and place it on a clean work surface.

7. To inspect the caliper assembly, perform the following procedures:

    a. Check the inside of the caliper assembly for pitting or scoring. If heavy scoring or pitting is present, caliper replacement is recommended.

    b. Check the mounting bolts and sleeves for signs of corrosion; if necessary, replace the bolts.

➡**If the mounting bolts have signs of corrosion, DO NOT attempt to polish away the corrosion. Instead the bolts must be replaced to assure proper caliper sliding and prevent the possibility of brake drag or locking.**

To install:

8. Lubricate and position the caliper bushings and sleeves. Apply silicone lube to the mounting bolts.

9. With both pads installed, place the caliper over the disc, lining up the hole in the caliper ears with the holes in the mounting bracket.

10. If the caliper was completely removed, install the flexible hose to the caliper and secure using the banjo bolt and new washers. Make sure that the brake hose is not twisted or kinked, then tighten the bolt to 24–27 ft. lbs. (31–35 Nm).

11. Carefully insert the mounting bolts through the bracket and caliper (bushing and sleeves), then tighten to 22–25 ft. lbs. (28–32 Nm).

12. Pump the brake pedal a few times to seat the linings against the rotors.

13. Install the wheels, then remove the jackstands and carefully lower the vehicle.

14. Check and refill the master cylinder reservoirs with brake fluid.

15. Properly bleed the hydraulic brake system.

OVERHAUL

▶ **See Figures 20, 21, 22, 23 and 24**

1. Remove the brake caliper from the vehicle and place on a clean work surface.

Fig. 17 If caliper separation is needed, support the caliper so the brake hose is not distorted

Fig. 18 Loosen and remove the brake hose-to-caliper retainer bolt—Trooper

Fig. 19 After removing the caliper retainer bolts, remove the caliper from the vehicle

2. Remove the inlet fitting from the brake caliper and drain all brake fluid.

3. Place a clean shop towel or a piece of wood in the caliper opening. Use a small amount of compressed air and force the piston from the bore.

❊❊ CAUTION

DO NOT apply too much air pressure to the caliper bore. The piston may jump out, causing damage to the piston and/or the operator. Be ABSOLUTELY SURE to keep your fingers away from the piston while air is being applied.

4. Remove and discard the piston boot and seal. Be careful not to scratch the bore while removing the pieces. Use of a metal tool is NOT recommended.

5. Inspect the piston and the caliper bore for damage or corrosion. Replace the caliper and/or the piston if necessary.

6. Remove the bleeder screw and rubber cap if equipped.

7. Clean all of the parts with non-mineral based solvent and blow dry with compressed air. All rubber parts should be replaced.

8. Inspect the guide pins for corrosion, replace if necessary. When installing the guide pins, coat them with a silicone lubricant.

To assemble:

9. Lubricate the piston, caliper and seal with clean brake fluid.

10. Install the seal into the caliper bore making sure it is not twisted in the bore groove.

11. Install the boot onto the piston, then position the piston into the caliper bore.

12. Bottom the piston into the bore using your hand and a piece of wood to compress the piston. Secure the boot to the housing using J-26267 or an equivalent piston seal installer tool.

13. Install the bleeder valve and tighten to 6–7 ft. lbs. (8–9 Nm).

14. Install the caliper to the vehicle and properly bleed the hydraulic brake system.

Brake Disc (Rotor)

INSPECTION

▶ **See Figures 25 and 26**

Check the disc brake rotor for scoring, cracks or other damage. If rotor run-out is checked, this should be measured while the rotor is installed. Use a dial gauge to check rotor run-out.

1. Raise and support the front of the vehicle safely using jackstands.

2. Remove the front wheels.

3. Visually inspect the rotor for cracks, excessive scoring or other damage.

Fig. 20 With a piece of wood in the caliper, use low pressure compressed air to push the piston out

86869P20

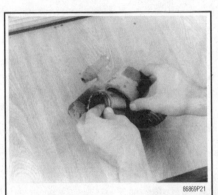

Fig. 21 Remove the piece of wood and piston from the caliper

86869P21

Fig. 22 If equipped, remove the dust boot retainer ring

86869P22

Fig. 23 Remove the dust boot

86869P23

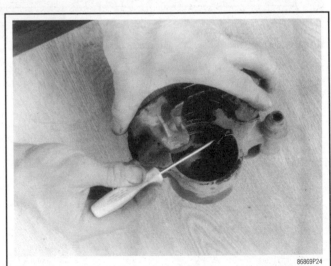

Fig. 24 Use a suitable pick tool to remove the ring seal from inside the caliper bore

86869P24

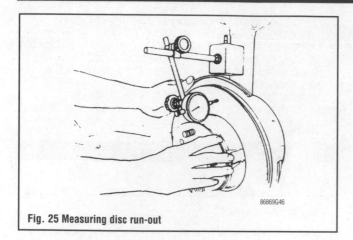

Fig. 25 Measuring disc run-out

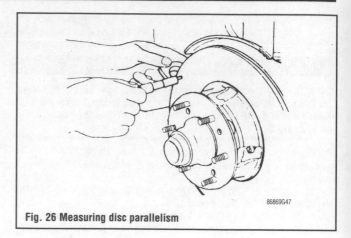

Fig. 26 Measuring disc parallelism

A light scoring of the surface which does not exceed 0.06 in. (1.5mm) in depth is normal and should not be considered detrimental to brake operation.

➡Before attempting to check rotor run-out on all vehicles, the bearings must be in good condition and exhibit no excessive play.

4. Check the disc for excessive run-out using a dial indicator:
   a. Position and secure a dial indicator so that the button contacts the disc about 1 in. (25mm) from the outer edge. Set the dial indicator to zero.
   b. Rotate the disc one complete revolution. The lateral run-out reading should not exceed 0.005 in. (0.13mm) on 1981–92 models On 1993–96 models, the lateral run-out reading should not exceed or 0.003 in. (0.08mm). If the reading is excessive, recondition or replace the disc.
5. Check the disc minimum thickness and the disc parallelism (thickness variation):
   a. Use a micrometer to check the disc thickness at 4 locations around the disc. Make sure the measuring point is at the same distance from the edge at all locations.
   b. The thickness should be greater than the minimum specification (which is normally cast onto the disc) and should not vary more than 0.0005 in. (0.013mm). If the variations are excessive, recondition or replace the disc. A disc which is smaller than the discard dimension MUST be replaced for safety.

REMOVAL & INSTALLATION

2WD Models

♦ See Figure 27

1. Raise and support the front of the vehicle safely on jackstands.
2. Remove the wheel and tire assembly.
3. Remove the brake caliper mounting bolts and carefully remove the caliper (along with the brake pads) from the rotor. Do not disconnect the brake line. Secure the caliper out of the way with the flexible line still connected.

➡Once the hub/rotor is removed from the vehicle the wheel bearings may be cleaned and repacked or the bearings and races may be replaced. For more information, please refer to the wheel bearing procedures in Section 1 of this manual.

4. Carefully pry out the grease cap, then remove the cotter pin, spindle nut, and washer. Remove the hub/rotor, being careful not to drop the outer wheel bearings. As the hub/rotor is pulled forward, the outer wheel bearings will often fall forward.
5. Once the hub/rotor is removed, secure the assembly in a soft-jawed vise. Remove the retainer bolts securing the rotor and hub together. Inspect the hub and replace if needed.
   To install:
6. With the rotor secured in a vise, attach the wheel hub to the rotor using the retainer bolts. Tighten the bolts to 47–58 ft. lbs. (61–75 Nm).
7. Carefully install the wheel hub/rotor over the spindle.
8. Using your hands, firmly press the outer bearing into the hub.
9. Loosely install the spindle washer and nut, but do not install the cotter pin or dust cap at this time.

10. Install the brake caliper.
11. Install the tire and wheel assembly.
12. Properly adjust the wheel bearings:
    a. Spin the wheel forward by hand and tighten the nut to 22 ft. lbs. (29 Nm) in order to fully seat the bearings and remove any burrs from the threads.
    b. Back off the nut until it is just loose, then finger-tighten the nut.
    c. Loosen the nut ¼-½ turn until either hole in the spindle lines up with a slot in the nut, then install a new cotter pin. This may appear to be too loose, but it is the correct adjustment.
13. Install the dust cap.
14. Install the wheel/hub cover, then remove the supports and carefully lower the vehicle.

4WD Models

♦ See Figures 28, 29, 30, 31 and 32

1. Place the Transfer shift in the **2H** position.
2. Raise and support the front of the vehicle safely on jackstands.
3. Remove the wheel and tire assembly.
4. Loosen the hub to rotor retainer bolts.
5. Remove the brake caliper mounting bolts and carefully remove the caliper (along with the brake pads) from the rotor. Do not disconnect the brake line. Secure the caliper out of the way with the flexible line still connected.

➡Once the hub/rotor is removed from the vehicle the wheel bearings may be cleaned and repacked or the bearings and races may be replaced. For more information, please refer to the wheel bearing procedures in Section 1 of this manual.

6. Remove the hub nut using hub wrench J-29020-A or equivalent.
7. Remove the hub cap assembly retainer bolts. Remove the spindle nut, washers, and other components. Remove the hub/rotor, being careful not to drop the outer wheel bearings. As the hub/rotor is pulled forward, the outer wheel bearings will often fall forward.
8. Once the hub/rotor is removed, remove the retainer bolts securing the rotor and hub together. Inspect the hub and replace if needed.
   To install:
9. With the rotor secured in a vise, attach the wheel hub to the rotor using the retainer bolts. Tighten the bolts to 47–58 ft. lbs. (61–75 Nm). Apply 2.12 oz. (60 gm) of grease to the hub before installing.
10. Carefully install the wheel hub/rotor over the spindle.
11. Install the bearings washers and other components. Position the lock washer so the hub cap assembly bolt holes line up properly.
12. Install the spindle washer and nut and secure using hub wrench J-29020-A or equivalent. Preload the bearing to 3.31 lbs. (1.5 kg).
13. Install the inner cam and any shims. Install the hub cap assembly and secure in place with retainer bolts. Tighten grade M8 bolts to 17–22 ft. lbs. (22–29 Nm), tighten grade M10 bolts to 40–47 ft. lbs. (52–61 Nm).
14. Install the brake caliper.
15. Install the tire and wheel assembly.
16. Remove the supports and carefully lower the vehicle.

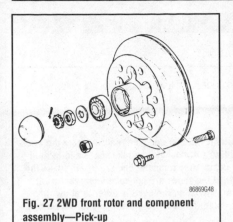

Fig. 27 2WD front rotor and component assembly—Pick-up

Fig. 28 With the rotor installed on the vehicle, loosen the hub-to-rotor retainer bolts

Fig. 29 Loosen and remove the hub retainer bolts—automatic hub shown, manual hub removal is similar

Fig. 30 With the outer bearing and clutch components removed, lift off the rotor/hub assembly

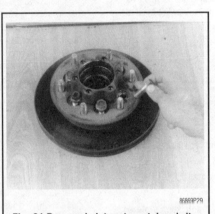

Fig. 31 Remove hub to rotor retainer bolts

Fig. 32 With the retainer bolts removed, separate the hub assembly from the rotor

REAR DRUM BRAKES

♦ See Figure 33

✳✳ CAUTION

Brake shoes may contain asbestos, which has been determined to be a cancer causing agent. Never clean the brake surfaces with compressed air! Avoid inhaling any dust from any brake surface! When cleaning brake surfaces, use a commercially available brake cleaning fluid.

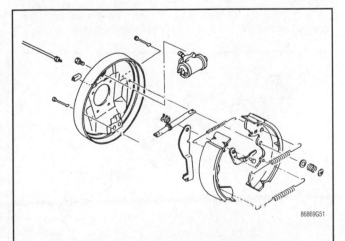

Fig. 33 Rear drum brake assembly—drum not shown—Pick-up

Brake Drums

REMOVAL & INSTALLATION

1. Raise and support the rear of the vehicle safely on jackstands.
2. Remove the rear tire and wheel assemblies.
3. Matchmark the drum to the hub or hub studs for installation purposes.
4. Remove the brake drum retainer screw.
5. Pull the brake drum from the hub studs. It may by necessary to gently tap the rear edges of the drum using a soft-faced mallet to start it off the studs.
6. If the drum will not come off past the shoes, it will be necessary to retract the brake shoe adjusting screw. Remove the access hole cover from the backing plate and turn the adjuster to retract the linings away from the drum.

To install:

7. If removed, install a rubber adjustment hole cover before installing the drum.
8. Install the drum aligning the match marks made during removal.
9. Install the brake drum retainer screw.
10. Install the rear tire and wheel assemblies.
11. Remove the jackstands and carefully lower the vehicle.

INSPECTION

Clean all grease, brake fluid, and other contaminants from the brake drum using a suitable brake cleaner. Visually check the drum for scoring, cracks, or other damage and replace, if necessary.

Check the drum inner diameter using a brake shoe clearance gauge. There are 2 important specifications when discussing rear drum diameters. The refinish diameter is the maximum diameter to which the drum may be machined.

This diameter allows room for drum wear after it has been machined and returned to service. The discard diameter is the point at which the drum becomes unsafe to use and must be discarded. NEVER refinish a drum to the discard diameter. If after refinishing the drum the diameter is within 0.030 in. (0.76mm) of the discard diameter, the drum MUST be replaced.

Brake Shoes

INSPECTION

Remove the drum and inspect the lining thickness of both brake shoes. The rear brake shoes should be replaced if the lining is less than 0.039 in. (1mm) thick above the rivet (so that the lining is thicker than the metal shoe backing in most cases) in order to prevent the rivet from scoring the drum. On bonded shoes the same specification should be used and the thickness of the bonded lining should be 0.039 in. (1mm) thick above the metal shoe backing plate. As with all brake service, keep in mind that local regulations take precedence over these specifications. Always check with your local authorities to be sure you are in compliance with local laws.

➡**Brake shoes should always be replaced in sets.**

REMOVAL & INSTALLATION

1. Raise and support the rear of the vehicle safely on jackstands.
2. Remove the rear wheel and tire assemblies.
3. Matchmark and remove the brake drums.

➡**Always work on one side at a time. This will allow for visual comparison if you run into removal or installation problems.**

4. Remove the shoe return springs and actuator link, then remove the shoe guide from the stud at the top of the backing plate.

➡**Special brake spring tools are available from most auto supply stores, which will ease the removal and installation of the return and hold-down springs.**

5. Remove the shoe hold-down springs and pins.
6. Remove the actuator lever, pivot and return spring.
7. Remove the parking brake strut and strut spring, then remove the parking brake lever from the shoe (it may be easier to wait until the shoe is being removed to separate the lever).
8. Remove the brake shoes as well as the adjuster screw and spring assembly.
9. Clean and inspect all of the brake parts. Replace parts as needed.
10. Check the wheel cylinders for seal condition and leaking.
11. Inspect the axle seal for leakage and replace, if necessary.
   To install:
12. Inspect the replacement shoes for nicks or burrs, lightly lubricate the backing plate contact points, the brake cable, the levers and adjusting screws with a white lithium brake grease. Do not get any grease on the braking surface, or stopping performance will be effected.
13. Install the star wheel in between the two brake shoes. The star wheel should be nearest to the secondary shoe when correctly installed.
14. Install the adjusting screw assembly and spring to both shoes, then position the shoes to the backing plate.
15. Install the parking brake lever to the secondary shoe.
16. Install the strut spring to the parking brake strut, then position the strut.
17. Install the actuator lever, lever pivot and the link. Install the lever return spring.
18. Install the shoe hold-down pins and springs.
19. Install the shoe guide over the stud at the top of the backing plate.
20. Install the return springs.
21. Lightly sandpaper the shoes to make sure they are clean, then align and install the drum.
22. Install the rear tire and wheel assemblies.
23. Adjust the brakes as described in this section.
24. Remove the jackstands and carefully lower the vehicle, then road test the vehicle.

Wheel Cylinder

REMOVAL & INSTALLATION

1. Raise and support the rear of the vehicle safely on jackstands.
2. Remove the tire and wheel assembly.
3. Matchmark and remove the brake drum to access the wheel cylinder assembly.

➡**In most cases, the wheel cylinders may be removed from the backing plate without completely removing the brake shoes and related components, however completely removing the shoes will make the operation MUCH easier. If the shoes are not completely removed, some of the upper springs must be removed in order to allow the shoes to spread and provide the necessary clearance for wheel cylinder removal.**

4. Remove the brake shoes or disconnect them sufficiently for adequate wheel cylinder clearance.
5. Clean away all dirt and foreign material from around wheel cylinder. It is important that dirt be kept away from the brake line when the cylinder is disconnected.
6. Disconnect the inlet tube line from the back of the wheel cylinder. Immediately plug or cap the line to prevent system contamination or excessive fluid loss.
7. Loosen and remove the bolts from the rear of the backing plate, then remove the wheel cylinder assembly.
   To install:
8. Position the wheel cylinder, then install the retaining bolts and tighten to 115 inch lbs. (13 Nm).
9. Remove the cap or plug, then connect and secure the hydraulic inlet line. Tighten the fitting to 16 ft. lbs. (22 Nm).
10. Install the brake shoes and remaining brake components.
11. Align and install the brake drum, then install the tire and wheel assembly.
12. Adjust the brake shoes and bleed the brake system. Refer to the drum adjustment and bleeding procedures in this section.
13. Remove the jackstands and carefully lower the vehicle.

OVERHAUL

♦ **See Figure 34**

Wheel cylinder overhaul kits are available for most wheel cylinders, but often at little or no savings as compared to a reconditioned wheel cylinder. It often makes sense with these components to substitute a new or reconditioned part instead of attempting to overhaul.

If no replacement is available, or you would prefer to overhaul your wheel cylinders, the following procedure may be used. When rebuilding and installing wheel cylinders, avoid getting any contaminants into the system. Always install clean, new, high-quality brake fluid. If dirty or improper fluid has been used, it will be necessary to drain the entire system, flush the system with proper brake fluid, replace all rubber components, refill, and bleed the system.

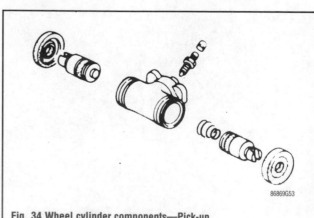

Fig. 34 Wheel cylinder components—Pick-up

86869G53

1. Remove the wheel cylinder from the vehicle and place on a clean work surface.

2. First remove and discard the old rubber boots from either side of the cylinder.

3. Withdraw the pistons from the cylinder. Piston cylinders are equipped with seals and a spring assembly, all located behind the pistons in the cylinder bore.

4. Remove the remaining inner components seals and spring assembly. Compressed air may be useful in removing these components if needed. If no compressed air is available, be VERY careful not to score the wheel cylinder bore when removing parts from it. Discard all components for which replacements were supplied in the rebuild kit.

5. Wash the cylinder and metal parts in denatured alcohol or clean brake fluid.

✳✳ CAUTION

Never use a mineral-based solvent such as gasoline, kerosene, or paint thinner for cleaning purposes. These solvents will swell rubber components and quickly deteriorate them.

6. Allow the parts to air dry or use compressed air. Do not use rags for cleaning since lint will remain in the cylinder bore.

7. Inspect the piston and replace it if it shows scratches.

8. Lubricate the cylinder bore and seals using clean brake fluid.

9. Position the spring assembly.

10. Install the inner seals then the pistons.

11. Insert the new boots into the counterbores by hand. Do not lubricate the boots.

12. Install the wheel cylinder to the vehicle.

REAR DISC BRAKES

✳✳ CAUTION

Brake pads may contain asbestos, which has been determined to be a cancer causing agent. Never clean the brake surfaces with compressed air! Avoid inhaling any dust from any brake surface! When cleaning brake surfaces, use a commercially available brake cleaning fluid.

Brake Pads

INSPECTION

Brake pads should be inspected once a year or at 6,000 miles (9,600 km) intervals, whichever occurs first. Check both ends of the outboard pad, looking in at each end of the caliper; then check the lining thickness of the inboard pad, looking down through the inspection hole. On riveted pads, the lining should be more than 1/32 in. (0.8mm) thick above the rivet (so that the lining is thicker than the metal backing in most cases) in order to prevent the rivet from scoring the rotor. On bonded brake pads, a minimum lining thickness of 1/32 in. (0.8mm) above the backing plate should be used to determine necessary replacement intervals. Keep in mind that any applicable state inspection standards that are more stringent take precedence. All four front pads MUST be replaced as a set if one shows excessive wear.

REMOVAL & INSTALLATION

♦ **See Figures 35 thru 40**

1. Use a turkey baster or other suitable device to remove half of the volume of brake fluid from the master cylinder. Discard the brake fluid properly. Do not reuse old brake fluid.

2. Raise and safely support the vehicle on jackstands.

3. Remove the wheel and tire assemblies.

4. Install a C-clamp on the caliper with the solid frame side of the clamp against the back of the caliper and the driving screw end against the metal part (center backing plate) of the outboard pad.

5. Tighten the clamp until the piston moves inward slightly. Unlike front calipers where the piston can be compressed in until it bottoms out in the piston bore, the rear caliper piston is attached to a screw that most be rotated inward.

6. Remove the caliper mounting bolts from the back of the caliper.

7. Remove the caliper from the mounting bracket and support from the suspension using a coat hanger or length of wire. DO NOT allow the brake line to support the caliper's weight.

8. Remove the inboard and outboard pads from the caliper or bracket.

9. Remove any brake pads retainer clips and shims from the brake pad or caliper bracket.

10. Remove the bolt ear sleeves and rubber bushings for cleaning, inspection and lubrication.

11. Using a pair of needlenose pliers, rotate the piston clockwise until the piston bottoms out in the caliper bore.

To install:

12. Check the inside of the caliper for leakage and the condition of the piston dust boot. If necessary, remove the caliper and overhaul or replace it.

13. Lubricate the sleeves and bushings using a suitable silicone lubricant, then attach them to the caliper.

14. Attach the retainer clips and shims to the brake pads. Install the inboard and outboard pads on the caliper bracket.

15. Place the caliper over the rotor, lining up the hole in the caliper ears with the holes in the mounting bracket. Make sure that the brake hose is not twisted or kinked.

16. Carefully insert the mounting bolts through the bracket and caliper (bushing and sleeves), then tighten to 32 ft. lbs. (44 Nm).

17. Pump the brake pedal a several times to seat the linings against the rotors.

18. Install the wheels, then remove the jackstands and carefully lower the vehicle.

19. Check and refill the master cylinder reservoirs with clean brake fluid.

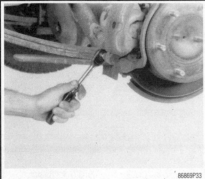

Fig. 35 Loosen and remove the caliper retainer bolts

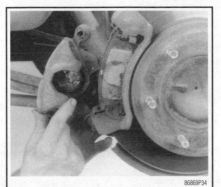

Fig. 36 Lift the caliper off the pads and rotor assembly

Fig. 37 Remove the brake pads—outer pad shown

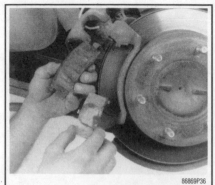

Fig. 38 Remove the plate from the back of the brake pad

Fig. 39 Remove and inspect all hardware including the upper and lower retainer clips

Fig. 40 Use a pair of needlenose pliers, and rotate the piston clockwise to reposition the piston in the bore

⁂ CAUTION

DO NOT attempt to move the vehicle until a firm brake pedal is obtained.

20. Pump the brake pedal to make sure that it is firm. If necessary, bleed the brakes.

Brake Caliper

REMOVAL & INSTALLATION

⁂ CAUTION

Brake shoes may contain asbestos, which has been determined to be a cancer causing agent. Never clean the brake surfaces with compressed air! Avoid inhaling any dust from any brake surface! When cleaning brake surfaces, use a commercially available brake cleaning fluid.

1. Use a turkey baster or other suitable device to remove the brake fluid from the master cylinder reservoir. Discard of the brake fluid properly. Do not reuse old brake fluid.
2. Raise and safely support the vehicle on jackstands.
3. Remove the wheel and tire assemblies.
4. Install a C-clamp on the caliper with the solid frame side of the clamp rests against the back of the caliper and the driving screw end rests against the metal part (center backing plate) of the outboard pad. Tighten the clamp until the caliper moves sufficiently to allow the brake pads to move, then remove the clamp.
5. Remove the parking brake cable from the caliper assembly. Refer to the procedure in this section.
6. Remove the caliper mounting bolts from the back of the caliper. If the caliper is not being completely removed from the vehicle, detach it from the mounting bracket and support it using a coat hanger or length of wire. DO NOT allow the hose to be stretched, twisted, kinked or otherwise damaged.
7. If the caliper is being completely removed from the vehicle, place a drip pan below the caliper and disconnect the flexible brake hose-to-caliper banjo-bolt. Discard the pressure fitting washers, then remove the brake caliper from the vehicle and place it on a clean work surface.
8. To inspect the caliper assembly, perform the following procedures:
   a. Check the inside of the caliper assembly for pitting or scoring. If heavy scoring or pitting is present, caliper replacement is recommended.
   b. Check the mounting bolts and sleeves for signs of corrosion; if necessary, replace the bolts.

➡If the mounting bolts have signs of corrosion, DO NOT attempt to polish away the corrosion. Instead the bolts must be replaced to assure proper caliper sliding and prevent the possibility of brake drag or locking.

To install:
9. Lubricate and position the caliper bushings and sleeves. Apply silicone lube to the mounting bolts.
10. With both pads installed, place the caliper over the disc, lining up the hole in the caliper ears with the holes in the mounting bracket.
11. If the caliper was completely removed, install the flexible hose to the caliper and secure using the banjo bolt and new washers. Make sure that the brake hose is not twisted or kinked, then tighten the bolt to 26 ft. lbs. (35 Nm).
12. Carefully insert the mounting bolts through the bracket and caliper (bushing and sleeves), then tighten to 32 ft. lbs. (44 Nm).
13. Attach the parking brake cable to the caliper.
14. Pump the brake pedal a few times to seat the linings against the rotors.
15. Install the wheels, then remove the jackstands and carefully lower the vehicle.
16. Check and refill the master cylinder reservoirs with brake fluid.
17. Properly bleed the hydraulic brake system.

OVERHAUL

See front disc brake caliper overhaul earlier in this Section.

Brake Disc (Rotor)

INSPECTION

Check the disc brake rotor for scoring, cracks or other damage. If rotor run-out is checked, this should be measured while the rotor is installed. Use a dial gauge to check rotor run-out.
1. Raise and support the rear of the vehicle safely using jackstands.
2. Remove the rear wheels.
3. Visually inspect the rotor for cracks, excessive scoring or other damage. A light scoring of the surface is normal and should not be considered detrimental to brake operation.

➡Before attempting to check rotor run-out on all vehicles, the bearings must be in good condition and exhibit no excessive play.

4. Check the disc for excessive run-out using a dial indicator:
   a. Position and secure a dial indicator so that the button contacts the disc about 1 in. (25mm) from the outer edge. Set the dial indicator to zero.
   b. Rotate the disc one complete revolution. The lateral run-out reading should not exceed 0.005 in. (0.13mm). If the reading is excessive, recondition or replace the disc.
5. Check the disc minimum thickness and the disc parallelism (thickness variation):
   a. Use a micrometer to check the disc thickness at 4 locations around the disc. Make sure the measuring point is at the same distance from the edge at all locations.
   b. The thickness should be greater than the minimum specification (which is normally cast onto the disc) and should not vary more than 0.0005 in. (0.013mm). If the variations are excessive, recondition or replace the

disc. A disc which is smaller than the discard dimension MUST be replaced for safety.

REMOVAL & INSTALLATION

▶ **See Figures 41, 42 and 43**

➡ **When removing the rotor, make sure the hand brake is not engaged.**

1. Raise and support the rear of the vehicle safely on jackstands.
2. Remove the wheel and tire assembly.
3. Disconnect the parking brake cable from the caliper. Refer to the procedure in this section.
4. Remove the brake caliper mounting bolts and carefully remove the caliper (along with the brake pads) from the rotor. Do not disconnect the brake line. Secure the caliper out of the way with the flexible line still connected.

5. Remove the caliper bracket retainer bolts from the rear of the brake assembly.
6. Slide the rotor off the wheel studs. If the rotor will not come off easily, use a soft-faced hammer and tap around the rotor. If the rotor will still not come off, remove the rubber cap from the rear of the brake assembly, and loosen the hand brake adjuster star wheel for the brake shoes.

To install:

7. Slide the rotor over the wheel studs and secure in place.
8. Install the caliper bracket, and tighten the retainer bolts to 37 ft. lbs. (50 Nm).
9. Install the brake pads and caliper.
10. Attach the parking brake cable to the caliper assembly.
11. If equipped with Duo-Servo type rear brakes, adjust the brake shoes, then install the rubber cap at the rear of the brake assembly.
12. Install the tire and wheel assembly.
13. Remove the supports and carefully lower the vehicle.

Fig. 41 Use a suitable socket or wrench to remove the caliper bracket retainer bolts

Fig. 42 Spray a liquid rust penetrant on the hub assembly to loosen the hub-to-rotor connection

Fig. 43 With the caliper removed and supported, remove the rotor from the hub axle

PARKING BRAKE

Parking Brake Cable

REMOVAL & INSTALLATION

Pull Handle Type

▶ **See Figures 44, 45 and 46**

This type parking brake is identified by a pull handle to the lower right of the steering wheel. To engage this brake, the handle must be pulled toward the driver. To release the brake, turn the handle toward the passenger and push in.

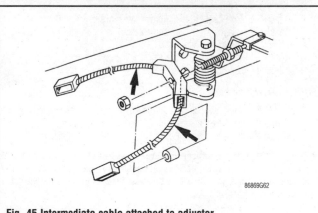
Fig. 45 Intermediate cable attached to adjuster

FRONT

▶ **See Figure 44**

➡ **The parking brake equalizer nut threads will often rust in service, making adjustment or removal difficult. If necessary, spray a penetrating lubricant on the nut and equalizer threads, then allow time for the lubricant to work.**

1. Set the parking brake pedal to the fully released position. Loosen the parking brake cable adjuster nut enough to slacken the cable tension on the front brake cable.
2. Remove the plastic trim panel below the steering column.
3. Release the front cable from the brake handle by rotating the cable and detaching it from the tab at the rear of the assembly.
4. Unfasten the cable from the intermediate bracket.

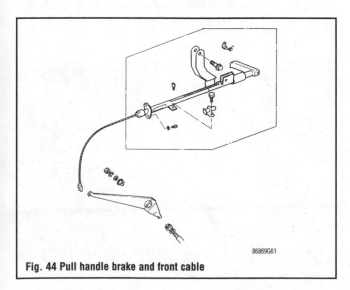
Fig. 44 Pull handle brake and front cable

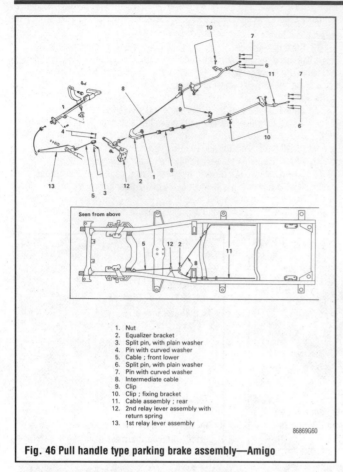

1. Nut
2. Equalizer bracket
3. Split pin, with plain washer
4. Pin with curved washer
5. Cable ; front lower
6. Split pin, with plain washer
7. Pin with curved washer
8. Intermediate cable
9. Clip
10. Clip ; fixing bracket
11. Cable assembly ; rear
12. 2nd relay lever assembly with return spring
13. 1st relay lever assembly

86869G60

Fig. 46 Pull handle type parking brake assembly—Amigo

To install:
5. Apply a small amount of lithium grease to both ends of the brake cable.
6. Attach the brake cable to the intermediate bracket.
7. Attach the brake cable to the handle assembly by inserting the cable and rotating the cable into the handle.
8. Install the trim panel below the steering column.
9. Adjust the parking brake.

FRONT LOWER

This cable is located between the intermediate bracket and relay lever assembly.
1. Block the rear wheels.
2. Raise and support the front of the vehicle safely using jackstands.

➥The parking brake equalizer nut threads will often rust in service making adjustment or removal difficult. If necessary, spray a penetrating lubricant on the nut and equalizer threads, then allow time for the lubricant to work.

3. Set the parking brake pedal to the fully released position. Loosen the parking brake cable adjuster nut enough to slacken the cable tension on the front brake cable.
4. Remove the cotter pin followed by the pin and washer attaching the front lower cable to the relay lever.
5. Detach the front lower cable from the intermediate bracket.
To install:
6. Apply a small amount of lithium grease to both ends of the brake cable.
7. Attach the brake cable to the intermediate bracket.
8. Attach the brake cable to the relay lever by inserting the pin and washer and securing in place with a new cotter pin.
9. Adjust the parking brake.
10. Remove the jackstands and carefully lower the vehicle.

INTERMEDIATE

♦ **See Figure 45**

This cable attaches the equalizer bracket to both rear brake cable assemblies.
1. Block the front wheels.
2. Raise and support the rear of the vehicle safely using jackstands.

➥The parking brake equalizer nut threads will often rust in service making adjustment or removal difficult. If necessary, spray a penetrating lubricant on the nut and equalizer threads, then allow time for the lubricant to work.

3. Set the parking brake pedal to the fully released position.
4. Loosen and remove the parking brake cable adjuster nut and equalizer bracket.
5. Remove the cotter pin followed by the pin and washer attaching the intermediate cable to each of the rear cables.
6. Remove the cable from the vehicle.
To install:
7. Apply a small amount of lithium grease to both ends of the brake cable and the equalizer bracket.
8. Attach the brake cable to the equalizer bracket.
9. Attach the brake cable ends to the rear cables by inserting the pin and washer, and securing in place with a new cotter pin.
10. Adjust the equalizer bracket and cable using the adjuster nut.
11. Remove the jackstands and carefully lower the vehicle.

REAR

♦ **See Figures 47 thru 52**

These cables, one at each rear wheel, attaches the brake shoes to the intermediate cable.
1. Block the front wheels.
2. Raise and support the rear of the vehicle safely using jackstands. Remove the rear wheel and tire assemblies.
3. Set the parking brake pedal to the fully released position.

➥The parking brake equalizer nut threads will often rust in service, making adjustment or removal difficult. If necessary, spray a penetrating lubricant on the nut and equalizer threads, then allow time for the lubricant to work.

86869P45

Fig. 47 If equipped with rear disc brakes, remove the cotter pin from the caliper cable retainer pin

86869P46

Fig. 48 Remove the washer from the retainer pin, and place aside

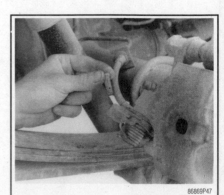

86869P47

Fig. 49 Remove the cable retainer pin from the caliper

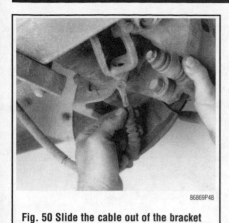

Fig. 50 Slide the cable out of the bracket

Fig. 51 Remove the cable retainer bracket retainer bolts

Fig. 52 Remove the retainer bracket to ease removal

4. Loosen the parking brake cable adjuster nut at the equalizer bracket to slacken the intermediate cable.

5. If rear disc brake equipped, remove the cotter pin, followed by the pin and washer attaching the intermediate cable to the rear cable.

6. If drum brake equipped, remove the drum to access the cable end.

7. Detach the cable end from the brake shoe cable retainer hook. The brakes shoes may have to be removed to access the retainer hook and cable on some models.

8. Slide the cable end out the rear of the brake backing plate.

9. Remove the retainer nut securing the rear cable bracket to the vehicle underbody. Remove the retainer clip securing the front of the cable assembly to the vehicle.

10. Remove the cable from the vehicle.

To install:

11. Apply a small amount of lithium grease to both ends of the brake cable.

12. Slide the end of the cable through the hole at the rear of the brake backing plate.

13. If equipped with drum brakes, attach the brake cable to the brake shoe retainer hook. If the shoes were removed, install them to the backing plate, along with the springs and other components removed earlier.

14. Install the brake drum assembly.

15. If equipped with rear disc brakes, attach the cable to the caliper using the pin, washer and cotter pin.

16. Attach the brake cable end to the intermediate cable by inserting the pin and washer, and securing in place with a new cotter pin.

17. Attach the cable to the vehicle underbody using the retainer bolts to secure the brackets in place. Tighten the bolts to 10 ft. lbs. (13 Nm). Attach the retainer clip to secure the front of the cable.

18. Adjust the brake shoes, if equipped.

19. Adjust the parking brake using the adjuster nut.

20. Install the wheel and tire assembly.

21. Remove the jackstands and carefully lower the vehicle.

Center Console Type

▶ **See Figures 53 and 54**

The console parking brake, most easily identified by the center console mounted control handle, uses a ratcheting type locking device to secure a lever in a desired position.

FRONT

▶ **See Figure 53**

1. Disconnect the negative battery cable.

2. Remove the center console assembly. Refer to the procedure in Section 10 for removal and installation details.

3. With the lever handle in the released position, loosen and remove the adjuster nut. Slide the end of the cable through the bracket at the base of the handle.

4. Lift the carpet behind the lever handle and unfasten the front cable from the rear cable floor connector.

5. Remove the cable from the vehicle.

6. Remove the cable from the bracket at the back of the cable.

To install:

7. Attach the cable to the rear bracket.

8. Apply a small amount of lithium grease to the cable end bracket where it contacts the rear cables.

9. Attach the cable bracket to the floor connector and rear brake cables.

10. Slide the cable under the carpet and lever handle, then through the bracket hole at the base of the handle. Secure in place with the adjuster nut.

11. Adjust the brake cable.

12. Position the carpet in place, and connect the negative battery cable.

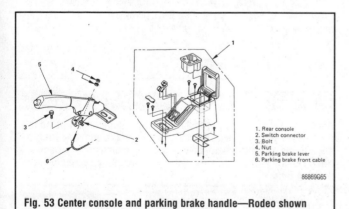

1. Rear console
2. Switch connector
3. Bolt
4. Nut
5. Parking brake lever
6. Parking brake front cable

Fig. 53 Center console and parking brake handle—Rodeo shown (other center console types similar)

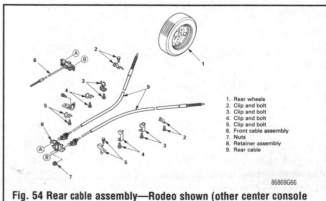

1. Rear wheels
2. Clip and bolt
3. Clip and bolt
4. Clip and bolt
5. Clip and bolt
6. Front cable assembly
7. Nuts
8. Retainer assembly
9. Rear cable

Fig. 54 Rear cable assembly—Rodeo shown (other center console types similar)

REAR

♦ See Figures 54 and 55

1. Block the front wheels.
2. Raise and support the rear of the vehicle safely using jackstands. Remove the wheel and tire assemblies.
3. Matchmark the rear drum/disc assembly, then remove the drum/disc to access the rear cable attachment point.
4. Remove the cable from the brake shoe retainer clip. In some cases, the entire brake shoe will have to be removed to detach the cable. Refer to the necessary procedures in this section.
5. Slide the cable out through the rear of the backing plate.
6. Remove the bolts securing the cable brackets to the vehicle.
7. Remove the cable from the vehicle.

To install:

8. Apply a light coating of lithium grease to both ends of the cable.
9. Slide the brake cable through the hole in the bottom of the vehicle underbody. Make sure the rubber sealing ring is seated properly.
10. Slide the cable through the brake backing plate and engage the cable end to the brake shoe. If necessary, install the brake shoes followed by the drum/disc assembly.
11. Adjust the brake shoes.
12. Attach the brake cable to the vehicle using the retainer brackets and bolts. Tighten the bolts to 10 ft. lbs. (13 Nm).
13. Attach the cable end to the floor connector and front cable. Make sure that the tab on the bracket engage correctly.
14. Adjust the brake cable.
15. Install the wheel and tire assembly.
16. Remove the jackstands and carefully lower the vehicle.

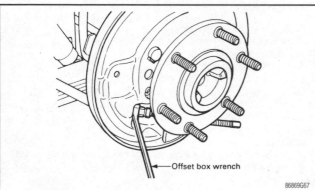

Fig. 55 Remove the cable assembly from the brake using a suitable wrench to remove the retainer nut

ADJUSTMENT

Pull Handle Type

♦ See Figure 56

The brake cables should be adjusted any time one of the cables has been disconnected or replaced.

➡Before adjusting the parking brakes, check the condition of the brake shoes and components; replace any necessary parts.

1. Block the front wheels.
2. Raise and support the rear of the vehicle safely on jackstands.
3. Fully release the parking brake pedal.

➡The parking brake equalizer threads will often rust in service making adjustment or removal difficult. Spray a penetrating lubricant on the nut and equalizer threads, then allow time for the lubricant to work before loosening or removing.

4. Under the left-center of the vehicle, loosen the adjuster nut on the cable equalizer assembly.
5. Tighten the equalizer nut until the rear wheels cannot be turned forward by hand without excessive force.

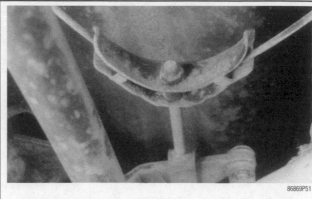

Fig. 56 Pull handle adjuster—Trooper

6. Loosen the equalizer nut until there is moderate drag when the rear wheels are rotated forward.
7. Engage the parking brake handle three or four times. If properly adjusted, the traveling range between released and engaged will be between 12–14 notches. If not within this range, adjust the nut further.
8. Remove the jackstands and carefully lower the vehicle.

Center Console Type

To adjust the parking brake tension, the cable adjuster nuts at the base of the center console lever must be tightened or loosened.

➡Before adjusting the parking brakes, check the condition of the brake shoes and components; replace any necessary parts.

1. Block the front wheels.
2. Raise and support the rear of the vehicle safely using jackstands.
3. Locate the parking brake cable adjuster nut at the base of the lever assembly. If additional working space is needed, the center console can be removed. Refer to the procedure in Section 10.
4. Set the parking brake pedal to the fully released position.
5. Grasp the end of the cable and rotate the adjuster nut until all cable slack disappears.
6. Engage the parking brake handle three or four times. If properly adjusted, the traveling range between released and engaged will be between 6–8 notches. If not within this range, adjust the nut further.
7. If removed, install the center console.
8. Remove the jackstands and carefully lower the vehicle.

Brake Shoes

♦ See Figure 57

The only models equipped with separate parking brake shoes are those models equipped with rear disc brakes (Duo-Servo Brake or DSB system). On these models, the parking brake shoes are installed inside the brake "disc hat" housing.

REMOVAL & INSTALLATION

✳✳ CAUTION

Brake shoes may contain asbestos, which has been determined to be a cancer causing agent. Never clean the brake surfaces with compressed air! Avoid inhaling any dust from any brake surface! When cleaning brake surfaces, use a commercially available brake cleaning fluid.

1. Raise and support the rear of the vehicle safely on jackstands.
2. Remove the rear wheel and tire assemblies.
3. Matchmark and remove the brake discs.

➡Always work on one side at a time. This will allow for visual comparison if you run into removal or installation problems.

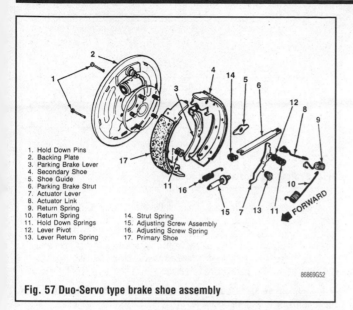

1. Hold Down Pins
2. Backing Plate
3. Parking Brake Lever
4. Secondary Shoe
5. Shoe Guide
6. Parking Brake Strut
7. Actuator Lever
8. Actuator Link
9. Return Spring
10. Return Spring
11. Hold Down Springs
12. Lever Pivot
13. Lever Return Spring
14. Strut Spring
15. Adjusting Screw Assembly
16. Adjusting Screw Spring
17. Primary Shoe

86869G52

Fig. 57 Duo-Servo type brake shoe assembly

4. Remove the shoe return springs and actuator link, then remove the shoe guide from the stud at the top of the backing plate.

➡**Special brake spring tools are available from most auto supply stores, which will ease the removal and installation of the return and hold-down springs.**

5. Remove the shoe hold-down springs and pins.
6. Remove the actuator lever, pivot and return spring.
7. Remove the brake strut and strut spring, then remove the brake lever from the shoe (it may be easier to wait until the shoe is being removed to separate the lever).
8. Remove the brake shoes along with the adjuster screw and spring assembly.
9. Clean and inspect all of the brake parts. Replace parts as needed
10. Inspect the axle seal for leakage and replace, if necessary.

To install:

11. Inspect the shoes for nicks or burrs, and correct as necessary. Lightly lubricate the backing plate contact points, brake cable, levers and adjusting screws with a white lithium brake grease. Do not get any grease on the braking surface, or stopping performance will be affected.
12. Install the adjusting screw assembly and spring to both shoes, then position the shoes to the backing plate.
13. Install the parking brake lever to the secondary shoe.
14. Install the strut spring to the parking brake strut, then position the strut.

15. Install the actuator lever, lever pivot and the link. Install the lever return spring.
16. Install the shoe hold-down pins and springs.
17. Install the shoe guide over the stud at the top of the backing plate.
18. Install the return springs.
19. Lightly sandpaper the shoes to make sure they are clean, then align and install the disc.
20. Install the rear tire and wheel assemblies.
21. Adjust the brakes as described in this section.
22. Remove the jackstands and carefully lower the vehicle, then road test the vehicle.

ADJUSTMENT

1. Raise and support the rear of the vehicle safely on jackstands.
2. Using a punch and a hammer on the rear of the backing plates, knock out the lanced metal areas near the star wheel assemblies on each plate. The metal areas may already have been removed and covered with rubber adjustment plugs; if so, remove the plugs by grasping and pulling out with a pair of pliers.

➡**After knocking out the lanced metal areas from the backing plate, the wheels must be removed and all of the metal pieces discarded, then the wheels should be reinstalled for adjustment.**

3. Insert a suitable brake adjustment tool such as J-4735 or equivalent, into the backing plate slots and engage the lowest possible tooth on the star wheel. Move the end of the brake tool downward to move the star wheel upward and expand the adjusting screw. Repeat this operation until the wheels can barely be turned by hand. This is a position immediately before the brakes lock.

➡**The brake drag should be equal at both wheels.**

4. Back off the adjusting screws 20–24 notches (clicks). By the time you have backed off the adjustment 12 clicks, the brakes should have no drag. If a heavy drag is still present, the parking brake cable is likely in need of adjustment.
5. Make sure both sides of the brakes are properly adjusted. When backing off the brakes on the other side, the adjusting lever must be backed off the same number of turns to prevent side-to-side brake pull.
6. After the brakes are adjusted, install a rubber cover into each of the backing plate slots.
7. Remove the jackstands, and lower the vehicle.

➡**Pump the brake pedal to seat the brake shoes before moving the vehicle.**

8. Before driving, make several stops while backing the vehicle, to fully equalize the adjustment.
9. Road test the vehicle.

REAR WHEEL ANTI-LOCK (RWAL) SYSTEM

General Information

◆ **See Figure 58**

The Rear Wheel Anti-Lock (RWAL) system was introduced in 1989 on a limited number of Rodeo models. The system is particularly useful because of the wide loading variations the vehicle may experience. Preventing rear wheel lock-up often makes the difference in controlling the vehicle during hard or sudden stops.

Found on both 2WD and 4WD vehicles, the RWAL system is designed to regulate rear hydraulic brake line pressure, preventing rear wheel lock-up during hard braking. On most 4WD vehicles, the system is deactivated when operating in four wheel drive. In this case, the braking system acts as a normal hydraulic system. Pressure regulation is managed by the control valve, located under the master cylinder. The control valve is capable of holding, increasing or decreasing brake line pressure based on electrical commands from the Electronic Brake Control Module (EBCM), originally known as the RWAL Electronic Control Unit (ECU).

The control valve holds pressure when the control module energizes the isolation solenoid. This isolates the rear hydraulic circuit and prevents fluid from entering or leaving, therefore holding constant at a given pressure. Pressure is

decreased when the module keeps the isolation solenoid energized and then energizes a dump solenoid, which allows fluid from the rear hydraulic circuit to enter an accumulator, thereby reducing pressure and preventing wheel lock-up. Pressure may be increased (though never over the driver's input) when both the isolation and dump solenoids are de-energized, allowing the rear hydraulic circuit to function normally from full master cylinder pressure.

The RWAL ECU/EBCM is a separate and dedicated microcomputer mounted next to the master cylinder; it is not to be confused with the engine management computers also found in these vehicles. The ECU/EBCM receives signals from the speed sensor. The speed sensor sends its signals to the Vehicle Speed Sensor (VSS) buffer (previously known as the Digital Ratio Adapter Controller or DRAC), usually found within the instrument cluster. The buffer translates the sensor signal into a form usable by the computer module. The brake control module reads this signal and commands the control valve to function.

The RWAL system is connected to the BRAKE warning lamp on the instrument cluster. A RWAL self-check and a bulb test are performed every time the ignition switch is turned to **ON**. The BRAKE warning lamp should illuminate for about 2 seconds and then go off. Problems within the RWAL system will be indicated by the BRAKE warning lamp remaining illuminated after this initial test period.

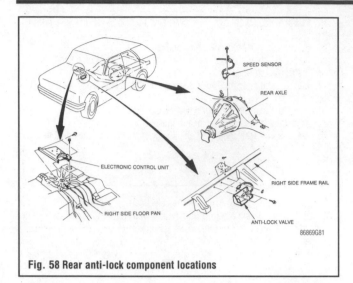

Fig. 58 Rear anti-lock component locations

If a fault is detected within the system, the control module will assign a diagnostic fault code and store the code in memory. The code may be read to aid in diagnosis, much in the same way codes are used in the engine emission control systems used by these vehicles.

SYSTEM PRECAUTIONS

• Certain components within the RWAL system are not intended to be serviced or repaired. Only those components with removal & Installation procedures should be serviced. DO NOT ATTEMPT to disassemble or overhaul RWAL system components.

• Do not use rubber hoses or other parts not specifically specified for the RWAL system. When using repair kits, replace all parts included in the kit. Partial or incorrect repair may lead to functional problems.

• Lubricate rubber parts with clean, fresh brake fluid to ease assembly. Do not use lubricated shop air to clean parts; damage to rubber components may result.

• Use only brake fluid from an unopened container. Use of suspect or contaminated brake fluid can reduce system performance and/or durability.

• A clean repair area is essential. Perform repairs after components have been thoroughly cleaned; use only denatured alcohol to clean components. Do not allow components to come into contact with any substance containing mineral oil; this includes used shop rags.

• The RWAL ECU/EBCM is a microprocessor similar to other computer units in the vehicle. Insure that the ignition switch is **OFF** before removing or installing controller harnesses. Avoid static electricity discharge at or near the controller.

• Never disengage any electrical connection with the ignition switch **ON** unless instructed to do so in a test.

• Always wear a grounded wrist strap when servicing any control module or component labeled with a Electrostatic Discharge (ESD) symbol.

• Avoid touching module connector pins.

• Leave new components and modules in the shipping package until ready to install them.

• To avoid static discharge, always touch a vehicle ground after sliding across a vehicle seat or walking across carpeted or vinyl floors.

• Never allow welding cables to lie on, near or across any vehicle electrical wiring.

• Do not allow extension cords for power tools or droplights to lie on, near or across any vehicle electrical wiring.

Diagnostic Trouble Codes

READING CODES

▶ **See Figure 59**

The computer control module (ECU/EBCM) will assign a code to the first fault found in the system. If there is more than one fault, only the first recognized code will the stored and transmitted.

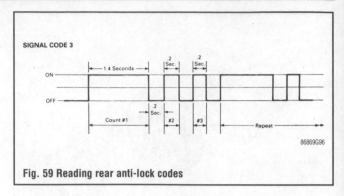

Fig. 59 Reading rear anti-lock codes

Trouble codes may be read either though the use of a Tech-1 or equivalent scan tool, or by connecting a jumper wire from pin H on the ALDL/DLC to pin A. If the jumper method is used, the fault code will be displayed through the flashing of the BRAKE warning lamp on the dash. The terminals must be connected for about 20 seconds before the display begins. The display will begin with 1 long flash followed by shorter ones—count the long flash as part of the display.

➡**Sometimes the first display sequence will be inaccurate or short; subsequent displays will be accurate.**

If using a hand scanner, note if a soft code is stored; only the last recognized code will be retained and displayed on the scanner. Soft fault Codes 6, 9 and 10 (1989–93 models) or soft Codes 2, 3, 4, 6, 7, 8, 9, and 10 (1994–96 models) can only be read with a scan tool. On some models, Codes 1, 11 and 12 will not read on the scan tool and must be read using the jumper wire method.

➡**Never ground terminal H of the ALDL to terminal A if the BRAKE warning lamp is not lit. Doing so will usually set a false code 9 and illuminate the BRAKE warning lamp. With the brake lamp on, the RWAL system will be disabled.**

CLEARING CODES

Stored trouble codes must be cleared with the ignition switch **OFF**. NEVER attempt to clear codes while the ignition switch is in the **ON** position or the computer module will likely be destroyed. Remove the ECMB fuse for at least 5 seconds, then reinstall the fuse.

Electronic Brake Control Module

REMOVAL & INSTALLATION

▶ **See Figure 60**

The Electronic Brake Control Module (EBCM), also known as the RWAL Electronic Control Unit (ECU), is a non-serviceable unit. It must be replaced when diagnosis indicates it is faulty. Because it is expensive and normally non-returnable, be absolutely sure the module is at fault before replacement.

1. Turn the ignition switch **OFF**. The switch MUST be **OFF** whenever you

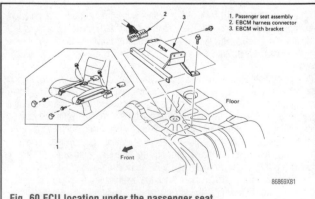

1. Passenger seat assembly
2. EBCM harness connector
3. EBCM with bracket

Fig. 60 ECU location under the passenger seat

are connecting/disconnecting power from the module. Failure to do this may destroy the computer.

2. Disengage the wiring harness connector(s) from the computer control module.

3. Grasp the module and remove it by pulling toward the front of the vehicle. If necessary, gently pry the tab at the rear of the module while pulling.

➡ **Do not touch the electrical connectors or pins; do not allow them to contact brake fluid. If contaminated with brake fluid, clean them with water followed by isopropyl alcohol.**

To install:

4. Install the computer module by aligning it, then carefully sliding it into the bracket until the tab locks into place.

5. Attach the wiring harness connector(s) to the module.

6. Turn the ignition **ON**, and verify proper system operation.

Anti-Lock Pressure Valve

REMOVAL & INSTALLATION

The Anti-Lock Pressure Valve (APV), also known as the isolation/dump or control valve assembly, is not serviceable. The entire component must be replaced as an assembly should a malfunction be found.

1. Turn the ignition switch **OFF**. The switch MUST be **OFF** whenever you are connecting/disconnecting power from the module (as will be done later in this procedure). Failure to do this may destroy the computer.

2. Tag and disconnect the brake line fittings at the valve, then immediately cap or plug all openings to prevent system contamination or excessive fluid loss. Remember to protect the surrounding paint work from damage by fluid spillage.

3. Disengage the bottom connector from the RWAL ECU/EBCM. At no time should you allow the APV to hang by the wiring.

➡ **Do not touch the electrical connectors or pins. Do not allow the connectors to contact brake fluid. If contaminated with brake fluid, clean with water followed by isopropyl alcohol.**

4. Remove the bolts holding the valve to the bracket.

5. Remove the valve from the vehicle.

To install:

6. Place the valve in position and install the retaining bolts. Tighten the bolts to 21 ft. lbs. (29 Nm).

7. Engage the electrical harness to the RWAL ECU/EBCM.

8. Remove the caps or plugs, then install the brake lines and tighten the fittings to 18 ft. lbs. (24 Nm).

9. Properly bleed the RWAL hydraulic brake system at all 4 wheels.

Speed Sensor

REMOVAL & INSTALLATION

▶ **See Figure 61**

The speed sensor is not serviceable and be must replaced if malfunctioning. The sensor is usually located in the left rear of the transmission case on 2WD vehicles and on the transfer case of 4WD vehicles.

The speed sensor may be tested with an ohmmeter; the correct resistance is normally 900–2000 ohms. To remove the speed sensor:

1. Disconnect the negative battery cable.

2. Raise and support the vehicle safely on jackstands.

3. Disengage the electrical harness from the speed sensor.

4. If equipped, remove the sensor retaining bolt.

5. Place a drip pan below the sensor to catch any spilled fluid. Remove the speed sensor.

➡ **If equipped with the 4L30-E automatic transmission, use J-38417 or an equivalent speed sensor remover/installer tool whenever the sensor is serviced.**

6. Remove the O-ring used to seal the sensor. Discard the O-ring.

To install:

7. Coat the new O-ring with a thin film of transmission fluid.

8. Install the O-ring and speed sensor.

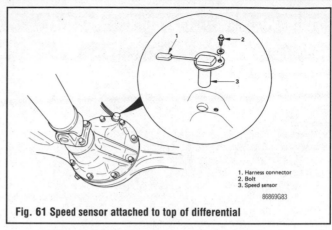

1. Harness connector
2. Bolt
3. Speed sensor

86869G83

Fig. 61 Speed sensor attached to top of differential

9. If a retaining bolt is used, tighten the bolt to 97 inch lbs. (11 Nm) in automatic transmissions or 107 inch lbs. (12 Nm) for manual transmissions.

10. If the sensor is a screw-in unit, tighten it to 32 ft. lbs. (43 Nm).

11. Engage the wire harness to the sensor.

12. Remove the jackstands and carefully lower the vehicle.

Bleeding

On RWAL systems for 1989–1992 vehicles, the brake system may be bled in the usual manner with no special procedures. On 1993–94 vehicles, a few steps (listed below) are added to the bleeding sequence in order to ease the procedure and assure that all air is removed from the system. If you have access to the additional tools required, you may use these extra steps on all RWAL vehicles to assure proper bleeding.

The use of a power bleeder is recommended, but the system may also be bled manually. If a power bleeder is used, it must be of the diaphragm type and provide isolation of the fluid from air and moisture.

Do not pump the pedal rapidly when bleeding; this can make the circuits very difficult to bleed. Instead, press the brake pedal slowly 1 time and hold it down while bleeding takes place. Tighten the bleeder screw, release the pedal and wait 15 seconds before repeating the sequence. Because of the length of the brake lines and other factors, it may take 10 or more repetitions of the sequence to bleed each line properly. When necessary to bleed all 4 wheels, the correct order is right rear, left rear, right front and left front.

The master cylinder is filled in the usual manner with no special procedures being necessary. Only DOT 3 or 4 brake fluid must be used. DO NOT use silicone or DOT 5 fluid. Do not use any fluid which contains a petroleum base; these fluids will cause swelling and distortion of the rubber parts within the system. Do not use old or contaminated brake fluid.

❋❋ CAUTION

Do not move the vehicle until a firm brake pedal is achieved. Failure to properly bleed the system may cause impaired braking and the possibility of injury and/or property damage.

On all 1993–94 RWAL vehicles, or earlier vehicles if desired, use the bleeding procedure found earlier in this section, with the following additions:

1. Make sure the ignition is in the **OFF** position to prevent setting a false trouble code.

2. After properly bleeding the master cylinder, install J-39177 or an equivalent combination valve depressor tool to the combination valve. This tool is used to hold the internal valve open allowing the entire system to be completely bled.

➡ **This tool is relatively inexpensive and should be available from various aftermarket companies.**

3. Recheck the master cylinder fluid level and add, as necessary.

4. Bleed the wheel cylinders as described in this section.

5. Attach the Tech-1 or an equivalent scan tool, then perform 3 RWAL function tests.

6. Re-bleed the rear wheel cylinders.

7. Check for a firm brake pedal, if necessary repeat the entire bleeding procedure.

8. Once finished, be sure to remove the combination valve depressor tool.

FOUR WHEEL ANTI-LOCK BRAKE SYSTEM

General Information

▶ See Figures 62 and 63

The four wheel anti-lock brake system first saw use on a limited number of 1991 models. The number of Izuzu vehicles equipped with ABS has grown with each year.

There are 3 slightly different systems used, depending upon the model and year of vehicle. The 4WD models are equipped with 4 wheel speed sensors (one located at each wheel) while the 2WD models use the Vehicle Speed Sensor (VSS) signal for the rear wheel speed. One system utilizes a separate EBCM, like the RWAL systems, while the other system utilizes a Vehicle Control Module (VCM). On the VCM equipped model, the computer control module (which is mounted in the engine compartment) controls both the ABS system and the engine emission control/fuel injection systems.

All versions of the 4 wheel anti-lock system are designed to reduce brake lock-up during severe brake application. The basic function of each system is similar to the RWAL system described earlier in this manual, the major difference simply being that the 4 wheel system monitors and controls wheel spin/lock-up on the front wheels as well as the rear.

Instead of the APV (control valve) used on RWAL systems, the 4WAL systems utilize a Brake Pressure Modulator Valve (BPMV), formerly known as the Electro-Hydraulic Control Unit (EHCU). The EHCU/BPMV is located near the master cylinder and controls the hydraulic pressure within the brake lines.

In a severe brake application, the EHCU/BPMV will, depending on the circumstance: allow pressure to increase within the system, maintain (isolate) the pressure within the system, or release existing pressure through the dump valves into the accumulators.

The EHCU/BPMV operates by receiving signals from the speed sensors, located at each wheel, and from the brake lamp switch. The speed sensors connect directly to the EHCU/BPMV through a multi-pin connector.

The system is connected to the ANTI-LOCK warning lamp on the dashboard. The warning lamp will illuminate for about 2 seconds every time the vehicle is started as a lamp check. The warning lamp will illuminate if the computer detects a problem within the anti-lock system during vehicle operation: If the warning light comes on when the vehicle is started and does not go out, or if the light comes on and remains on during vehicle operation, trouble has been detected by the computer module.

Fig. 63 Brake pressure modulator valve in engine compartment—Rodeo

Diagnostic Trouble Codes

READING CODES

▶ See Figures 64, 65, 66 and 67

Stored trouble codes may be transmitted through the flashing of the ANTI-LOCK dash warning lamp. The system may be placed in the diagnostic mode using a jumper wire, however, the use of the Tech-1 scan tool or equivalent is highly recommended. For all systems, the scan tool will allow performance of the specific system tests called for by the "trouble tree" for each code.

On vehicles where flash-diagnosis is possible, trouble code read out may be started using a jumper wire to connect Terminal H on the ALDL/DLC (diagnostic connector located under the instrument panel) to either a body ground or to terminal A (internal ground). The terminals must be connected for a few seconds before a code will transmit. Observe the ANTI-LOCK light on the dash and count the flashes in groups: for example, a group of 4 flashes, a pause and a group of 3 flashes indicates Code 43.

Remember that trouble codes cannot specify the exact cause of the problem, and may only relate which circuit is affected by the problem. Before replacing any component, be sure that it is the cause of the problem, especially when dealing with a control module fault. Control modules are quite expensive and are usually not returnable.

CLEARING CODES

Stored codes may be erased with the scan tool, if available, or by using a jumper wire:

1. If a hand-held scanner is available, use it to erase the computer module code memory.

2. On some VCM equipped models, a code cannot clear on the same ignition cycle it was set. Before attempting to clear the code using a scan tool, it may be necessary to cycle the ignition to the **OFF** position for at least 10 seconds, then back to **ON** again to start another cycle.

3. Except for VCM equipped models, codes may be cleared without a scan tool as follows:

    a. Turn the ignition switch **ON**, but do not start the engine.

    b. Use a jumper wire to ground ALDL/DLC terminal H to terminal A for 2 seconds.

    c. Remove the jumper wire for 1 second.

    d. Repeat the grounding for 2 more seconds.

    e. When the trouble codes are cleared, the ANTI-LOCK and BRAKE lamps should both illuminate and then extinguish.

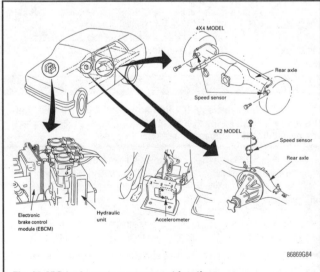

Fig. 62 ABS brake system component locations

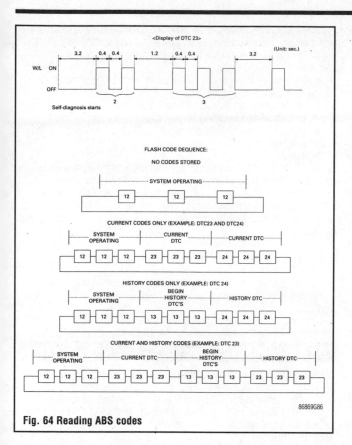

Fig. 64 Reading ABS codes

DIAGNOSTIC TROUBLE CODE	DESCRIPTION	
14	ABS ENABLE RELAY CONTACT CIRCUIT OPEN	5A4-34
15	ABS ENABLE RELAY CIRCUIT SHORTED TO BATTERY OR ALWAYS CLOSED	5A4-42
16	ABS ENABLE RELAY COIL CIRCUIT OPEN	5A4-44
17	ABS ENABLE RELAY COIL CIRCUIT SHORTED TO GROUND	5A4-46
18	ABS ENABLE RELAY COIL CIRCUIT SHORTED TO BATTERY	5A4-48
21	LEFT FRONT WHEEL SPEED=0	5A4-50
22	RIGHT FRONT WHEEL SPEED=0	5A4-56
23	LEFT REAR WHEEL SPEED=0 (4WD)	5A4-62
24	RIGHT REAR WHEEL SPEED=0 (4WD)	5A4-68
24	REAR WHEEL SPEED=0 (2WD)	5A4-74
25	LEFT FRONT EXCESSIVE WHEEL SPEED VARIATION	5A4-80
26	RIGHT FRONT EXCESSIVE WHEEL SPEED VARIATION	5A4-86
27	LEFT REAR EXCESSIVE WHEEL SPEED VARIATION (4WD)	5A4-92
28	RIGHT REAR EXCESSIVE WHEEL SPEED VARIATION (4WD)	5A4-98
28	REAR EXCESSIVE WHEEL SPEED VARIATION (2WD)	5A4-104
32	LEFT FRONT WHEEL SPEED SENSOR CIRCUIT OPEN OR SHORTED TO GROUND/BATTERY	5A4-110
33	RIGHT FRONT WHEEL SPEED SENSOR CIRCUIT OPEN OR SHORTED TO GROUND/BATTERY	5A4-116
34	LEFT REAR WHEEL SPEED SENSOR CIRCUIT OPEN OR SHORTED TO GROUND/BATTERY (4WD)	5A4-122
34	REAR WHEEL SPEED SENSOR CIRCUIT OPEN OR SHORTED TO GROUND/BATTERY (2WD)	5A4-128
35	RIGHT REAR WHEEL SPEED SENSOR CIRCUIT OPEN OR SHORTED TO GROUND/BATTERY (4WD)	5A4-134
36	LOW SYSTEM VOLTAGE	5A4-140
37	HIGH SYSTEM VOLTAGE	5A4-142
38	LEFT FRONT ESB WILL NOT HOLD MOTOR	5A4-144
41	RIGHT FRONT ESB WILL NOT HOLD MOTOR	5A4-146
42	REAR ESB WILL NOT HOLD MOTOR	5A4-148
44	LEFT FRONT CHANNEL WILL NOT MOVE	5A4-150
45	RIGHT FRONT CHANNEL WILL NOT MOVE	5A4-152
46	REAR CHANNEL WILL NOT MOVE	5A4-154
47	LEFT FRONT MOTOR FREE SPINS	5A4-156
48	RIGHT FRONT MOTOR FREE SPINS	5A4-160
51	REAR MOTOR FREE SPINS	5A4-164
55	EBCM MALFUNCTION	5A4-168
56	LEFT FRONT MOTOR CIRCUIT OPEN	5A4-170

Fig. 66 ABS diagnostic code chart

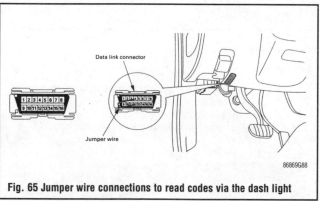

Fig. 65 Jumper wire connections to read codes via the dash light

DIAGNOSTIC TROUBLE CODE	DESCRIPTION	
57	LEFT FRONT MOTOR CIRCUIT SHORTED TO GROUND	5A4-172
58	LEFT FRONT MOTOR CIRCUIT SHORTED TO BATTERY	5A4-174
61	RIGHT FRONT MOTOR CIRCUIT OPEN	5A4-176
62	RIGHT FRONT MOTOR CIRCUIT SHORTED TO GROUND	5A4-178
63	RIGHT FRONT MOTOR CIRCUIT SHORTED TO BATTERY	5A4-180
64	REAR MOTOR CIRCUIT OPEN	5A4-182
65	REAR MOTOR CIRCUIT SHORTED TO GROUND	5A4-184
66	REAR MOTOR CIRCUIT SHORTED TO BATTERY	5A4-186
71	REAR SOLENOID CIRCUIT OPEN OR SHORTED TO GROUND	5A4-188
72	REAR SOLENOID CIRCUIT SHORTED TO BATTERY	5A4-190
76	LEFT FRONT SOLENOID CIRCUIT OPEN OR SHORTED TO GROUND	5A4-192
77	LEFT FRONT SOLENOID CIRCUIT SHORTED TO BATTERY	5A4-194
78	RIGHT FRONT SOLENOID CIRCUIT OPEN OR SHORTED TO GROUND	5A4-196
81	RIGHT FRONT SOLENOID CIRCUIT SHORTED TO BATTERY	5A4-198
82	CALIBRATION MALFUNCTION	5A4-200
91	OPEN BRAKE SWITCH DURING DECELERATION	5A4-202
92	OPEN BRAKE SWITCH WHEN ABS WAS REQUIRED	5A4-204
93	DTC 91 OR DTC 92 SET IN CURRENT OR PREVIOUS IGNITION CYCLE	5A4-206
94	BRAKE SWITCH CONTACTS ALWAYS CLOSED	5A4-208
95	BRAKE SWITCH CIRCUIT OPEN	5A4-210
96	FOUR-WHEEL-DRIVE SWITCH CIRCUIT OPEN OR SHORT TO BATTERY	5A4-212
97	ACCELEROMETER CIRCUIT SHORTED TO GROUND	5A4-216
98	ACCELEROMETER CIRCUIT OPEN OR SHORTED TO BATTERY	5A4-218

Fig. 67 ABS diagnostic code chart—continued

Brake Pressure Modulator Valve

The Brake Pressure Modulator Valve (BPMV) valve (formerly referred to as the Electro-Hydraulic Control Unit or EHCU) is mounted near or under the master cylinder and combination valve assemblies. The valve is not serviceable and must be replaced if malfunctioning. The valve is also the sight for the only additional attention required to properly bleed the 4WAL hydraulic system.

REMOVAL & INSTALLATION

♦ **See Figure 68**

The EHCU/BPMV is not serviceable and must never be disassembled or repaired. If tests indicate the unit is faulty, the entire assembly must be replaced.
1. Tag and disconnect the brake lines from the EHCU/BPMV. Immediately

cap or plug all openings to prevent system contamination or excessive fluid loss.
2. Tag and disengage the electrical connectors from the EHCU/BPMV.
3. Remove the retainers holding the EHCU/BPMV upper bracket to the lower bracket and vehicle. Remove the upper bracket and hydraulic unit as an assembly.
4. If necessary, once they are removed from the vehicle, separate the bracket from the EHCU/BPMV.

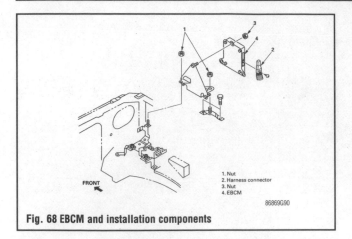

Fig. 68 EBCM and installation components

1. Nut
2. Harness connector
3. Nut
4. EBCM

86869G90

To install:

5. If removed, assemble the EHCU/BPMV to its bracket. Install the retainers and tighten to 84 inch lbs. (9 Nm). Be careful, as overtightening these bolts can cause excessive noise transfer during system operation.

6. Install the assembly into the vehicle, then tighten the retainers to 18–20 ft. lbs. (25–27 Nm).

7. Attach the electrical connectors. Make certain each is squarely seated and secure.

8. Remove the caps or plugs, then connect the brake lines to their original locations. Tighten the fittings to 16–21 ft. lbs. (25–29 Nm).

9. Properly bleed the hydraulic brake system, including the EHCU/BPMV valve.

Front Wheel Speed Sensors

On most 2WD and 4WD vehicles, the front wheel speed sensors are permanently mounted to the brake rotor splash shield, which must be replaced as an assembly should the sensor fail. On 2WD vehicles, the rotor must be removed for access.

The front wheel speed sensors operate with the help of sensor tone wheels. The tone wheels are metal rings equipped with teeth on their outer diameter. The AC voltage is produced as the teeth come within and leave alignment with the sensor. The tone wheels are attached to the rotor on 2WD vehicles and to the front hub and bearing assembly on 4WD vehicles.

A properly operating speed sensor should have a resistance value of 900–2000 ohms.

REMOVAL & INSTALLATION

♦ **See Figure 69**

1. Raise and support the front of the vehicle safely on jackstands.
2. Remove the tire and wheel assembly.
3. Remove the brake caliper from the mounting bracket and support using

a coat hanger or wire. Make sure the brake line is not stretched, kinked or otherwise damaged. The line should NEVER support the weight of the caliper.

4. For 2WD models, remove the hub and rotor assembly. Refer to the brake disc procedure in this section.

5. For 4WD vehicles, remove the brake disc. Refer to the procedure in this section, then remove the hub and bearing assembly.

6. Disengage the sensor wiring connector.

7. Disconnect the sensor wire from the clip(s) on the control arm.

8. Remove the splash shield retaining bolts, then remove the shield and sensor assembly.

To install:

9. Mount the sensor and splash shield assembly to the steering knuckle. Install the retaining bolts and tighten them to 11–19 ft. lbs. (15–26 Nm).

10. Connect the wiring to the clip(s) on the control arm. Check the wiring for correct routing. If removed, install and tighten the clip retaining bolt/nuts. The wiring on some vehicles/components may be marked at the appropriate clip mounting position; so look for a paint stripe on the sensor wire.

11. Engage the wiring connector.

12. On 4WD models, install the hub and bearing assembly.

13. Install the brake disc.

14. Remove the support, then reposition and secure the brake caliper.

15. Install the tire and wheel assembly. Adjust the wheel bearings on 2WD models.

16. Remove the jackstands and carefully lower the vehicle.

Rear Wheel Speed Sensors

Only 4WD models are equipped with separate rear wheel speed sensors. 2WD models do not utilize separate rear wheel speed sensors; instead their control modules utilize the VSS signal in order to determine the rate at which the rear wheels are spinning/approaching lock-up. In this way, the system monitors the rear wheel speed in the same fashion as the RWAL system described earlier in this section.

REMOVAL & INSTALLATION

Individual Wheel Type

♦ **See Figure 70**

1. Raise and support the rear of the vehicle safely on jackstands.
2. Remove the tire and wheel assembly.
3. Matchmark and remove the brake drum/disc.
4. Remove the primary brake shoe. Refer to the brake shoe procedure in this section.
5. Disengage the sensor wiring at the connector.
6. Remove the sensor wire from the rear axle clips.
7. Remove the 2 bolts holding the sensor to the brake backing plate, then remove the sensor by carefully working the wire through the hole in the backing plate.

To install:

8. Route the wire through the hole in the backing plate and fit the sensor into position.

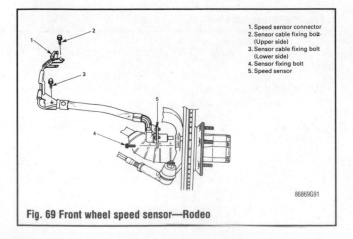

1. Speed sensor connector
2. Sensor cable fixing bolt (Upper side)
3. Sensor cable fixing bolt (Lower side)
4. Sensor fixing bolt
5. Speed sensor

86869G91

Fig. 69 Front wheel speed sensor—Rodeo

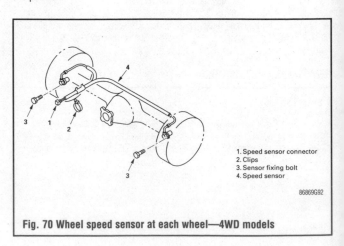

1. Speed sensor connector
2. Clips
3. Sensor fixing bolt
4. Speed sensor

86869G92

Fig. 70 Wheel speed sensor at each wheel—4WD models

9. Install the retaining bolts and tighten to 26 ft. lbs. (35 Nm).
10. Secure the sensor wire within the rear axle clips.
11. Engage the sensor wiring to the harness connector.
12. Install the primary brake shoe.
13. Align and install the brake drum/disc.
14. Install the tire and wheel assembly, then remove the jackstands and carefully lower the vehicle.

VSS Type

♦ **See Figure 71**

The speed sensor is not serviceable and must be replaced if malfunctioning. The sensor is usually located in the left rear of the transmission case.

The speed sensor may be tested with an ohmmeter. The correct resistance is normally 900–2000 ohms. To remove the speed sensor:
1. Raise and support the vehicle safely using jackstands.
2. Disengage the electrical connector from the speed sensor.
3. If equipped, remove the sensor retaining bolt.
4. Remove the speed sensor. Place a container below the sensor to catch fluid when the sensor is removed.

➡**If equipped with the 4L30-E automatic transmission, use J-38417 or an equivalent speed sensor remover/installer tool whenever the sensor is serviced.**

5. Remove and discard the O-ring used to seal the sensor. Discard the O-ring.

To install:
6. When installing, coat the new O-ring with a thin film of transmission fluid.
7. Install the O-ring and speed sensor.
8. If a retaining bolt is used, tighten the bolt to 97 inch lbs. (11 Nm) in automatic transmissions, or 107 inch lbs. (12 Nm) for manual transmissions.
9. Engage the wire harness to the sensor.
10. Remove the jackstands and carefully lower the vehicle.

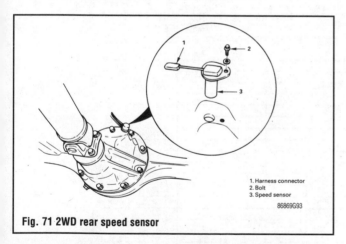

1. Harness connector
2. Bolt
3. Speed sensor

86869G93

Fig. 71 2WD rear speed sensor

Bleeding

The EHCU/BPMV is the one component which adds to the complexity of bleeding the 4WAL brake systems. For the most part, the system is bled in the same manner as non-ABS vehicles. Refer to the procedure earlier in this section for details. But because of the EHCU/BPMV's complex internal valve design, additional steps are necessary if the unit has been replaced or if it is suspected to contain air. These bleeding steps are NOT necessary if the only connection/fitting(s) opened were downstream of the unit. These steps may or may not be necessary after master cylinder replacement. If in doubt (or without the necessary special tools) thoroughly bleed the system and see if a firm brake pedal can be obtained; if not, the EHCU/BPMV must be bled as well.

As with the RWAL brake system, the use of a power bleeder is recommended, but the system may also be bled manually. If a power bleeder is used, it must be of the diaphragm type and provide isolation of the fluid from air and moisture.

Do not pump the pedal rapidly when bleeding; this can make the circuits very difficult to bleed. Instead, press the brake pedal slowly 1 time and hold it

down while bleeding takes place. Tighten the bleeder screw, release the pedal and wait 15 seconds before repeating the sequence. Because of the length of the brake lines and other factors, it may take 10 or more repetitions

of the sequence to bleed each line properly. When necessary to bleed all 4 wheels, the correct order is right rear, left rear, right front and left front.

> ☀☀☀ **CAUTION**

Do not move the vehicle until a firm brake pedal is achieved. Failure to properly bleed the system may cause impaired braking and the possibility of injury and/or property damage.

If the EHCU/BPMV requires bleeding, the following procedures may be used to free all trapped air from the component. The procedures differ because some models are equipped with external bleeders in addition to the internal bleeders. In either case, 3 combination valve depressor tools and a scan tool are required. The combination valve depressor tools are used to hold the internal passage (combination valve and EHCU/BPMV bleed accumulator) bleed stems open, allowing the entire system to be completely bled.

➡**The combination valve tools are relatively inexpensive and should be available from various aftermarket companies.**

The master cylinder reservoirs must be kept properly filled to prevent air from entering the system. No special filling procedures are required because of the anti-lock system.

When adding fluid, use only DOT 3 fluid. The use of DOT 5 or silicone fluids is prohibited. Use of improper or contaminated fluid may cause the fluid to boil or cause the rubber components in the system to deteriorate. Never use any fluid with a petroleum base or any fluid which has been exposed to water or moisture.

Finally, remember to always bleed the 4WAL brake system with the ignition **OFF** to prevent setting false trouble codes.

INTERNAL AND EXTERNAL BLEEDERS

♦ **See Figure 72**

These models are equipped with a pair of internal bleeder and a pair of external bleeder screws. These external bleeders look like normal brake bleeders and are found on top of the unit. Like any bleeder screw, they MUST remain closed when the unit is not pressurized.

The internal bleed valves on either side of the unit must be opened ¼–½ turn before bleeding begins. These valves open internal passages within the unit. The valve located on the left side (nearest the fender) is used for the rear brake section, while the valve on the right (nearest the engine) is used for the front brakes. Actual bleeding is performed at the two bleeders on the top of the EHCU module. The bleeders must not be opened when the system is not pressurized. The ignition switch must be **OFF** or false trouble codes may be set.
1. Make sure the ignition is in the **OFF** position to prevent setting false trouble codes.
2. Open the internal bleed valves ¼–½ turn each.
3. Install J–35856 or equivalent combination valve depressor tool on the left accumulator bleed stem of the EHCU. Install one tool on the right bleed stem and install the third tool on the combination valve (rear).

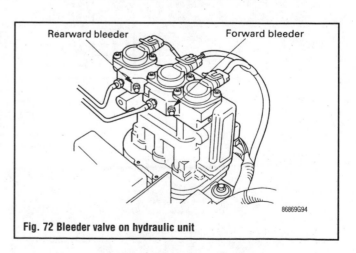

Rearward bleeder   Forward bleeder

86869G94

Fig. 72 Bleeder valve on hydraulic unit

4. Inspect the fluid level in the master cylinder. Add fluid if needed.

5. Have an assistant slowly depress the brake pedal and hold it down.

6. Open the left bleeder on top of the unit. Allow fluid to flow until no air is seen or until the brake pedal bottoms.

7. Close the left bleeder, then have your assistant release the pedal slowly and wait 15 seconds.

8. Repeat these steps, starting with depressing the brake pedal (including the 15 second pause), until no air is seen in the fluid.

9. Tighten the left internal bleed valve to 60 inch lbs. (7 Nm).

10. Bleed air from the right bleeder screw on top of the EHCU in the same manner as the left screw.

11. When bleeding of the right port is complete, tighten the right internal bleed valve to 60 inch lbs. (7 Nm).

12. Remove the 3 special combination valve tools.

13. Check the master cylinder fluid level, and refill if necessary.

14. Bleed the individual brake circuits at each wheel starting at the right rear. Refer to the hydraulic brake bleeding procedure located in this section.

15. Switch the ignition **ON** and use the hand-held scanner tool to perform function tests on the system.

16. Evaluate the brake pedal feel and repeat the bleeding procedure if needed.

17. Carefully test drive the vehicle at moderate speeds; check for proper pedal feel and brake operation. If any problem is noted in feel or function, repeat the entire bleeding procedure.

INTERNAL BLEEDERS ONLY

Because the EHCU/BPMV has no external bleeders, the unit can only be bled through the downstream bleeder screws (wheel cylinders/calipers). To accomplish this, the internal bleeder and the accumulator stems/combination valves must be opened to allow air/fluid to pass through the unit. The internal bleed valves on either side of the unit must be opened ¼–½ turn before bleeding begins. The ignition switch must be **OFF** or false trouble codes may be set.

1. Make sure the ignition is in the **OFF** position to prevent setting false trouble codes.

2. If necessary, bleed the master cylinder assembly as directed in the hydraulic brake bleeding procedure found earlier in this section. Check and add additional fluid, as needed.

3. Open the internal bleed valves ¼–½ turn each.

4. Install one J–39177 or equivalent combination valve depressor tool on the left accumulator bleed stem of the EHCU. Install one tool on the right accumulator bleed stem and install the third tool on the combination valve.

5. Properly bleed the wheel cylinders and calipers. Refer to the hydraulic brake bleeding procedure located in this section.

6. Remove the 3 special tools.

7. Check the master cylinder fluid level, and refill as needed.

8. Switch the ignition **ON** (engine not running) and use a scan tool to perform function tests on the system.

9. Repeat the wheel cylinder and caliper bleeding procedure to remove all air that was purged from the BPMV during the function tests.

10. Check for a firm brake pedal. If necessary, repeat the entire procedure.

11. Carefully test drive the vehicle at moderate speeds; check for proper pedal feel and brake operation. If any problem is noted in feel or function, repeat the entire bleeding procedure.

BRAKE SPECIFICATIONS
All measurements in inches unless noted

Year	Model		Master Cylinder Bore	Brake Disc Original Thickness	Brake Disc Minimum Thickness	Brake Disc Maximum Run-out	Brake Drum Diameter Original Inside Diameter	Brake Drum Diameter Max. Wear Limit	Brake Drum Diameter Maximum Machine Diameter	Minimum Lining Thickness Front	Minimum Lining Thickness Rear
1981–86	Pick-up		0.874	0.720	0.668 [1]	0.005	10.00	10.06	NA	0.067	0.039
	Trooper		1.000	0.886	0.811	0.005	10.00	10.06	NA	0.039	0.039
1987	Pick-up		0.874	0.720	0.668 [1]	0.005	10.00	10.06	NA	0.067	0.039
	Trooper		1.000	0.886	0.811	0.005	10.00	10.06	NA	0.039	0.039
1988–90	Amigo [2]	F	[3]	0.866	0.811	0.005	-	-	-	0.039	-
		R	-	0.472	0.417	0.005	10.00	10.06	NA	-	0.039
	Pick-up	F	[3]	0.866	0.811	0.005	-	-	-	0.039	-
		R	-	0.472	0.417	0.005	10.00	10.06	NA	-	0.039
	Trooper	F	1.000	0.866	0.811	0.005	-	-	-	0.039	-
		R	-	0.472	0.417	0.005	-	-	-	-	0.039
1991	Amigo	F	[3]	0.866	0.811	0.005	-	-	-	0.039	-
		R	-	0.472	0.417	0.005	10.00	10.06	NA	-	0.039
	Rodeo		1.000	0.866	0.811	0.005	10.00	10.06	NA	0.039	0.039
	Pick-up	F	[3]	0.866	0.811	0.005	-	-	-	0.039	-
		R	-	0.472	0.417	0.005	10.00	10.06	NA	-	0.039
	Trooper	F	1.000	0.866	0.811	0.005	-	-	-	0.039	-
		R	-	0.472	0.417	0.005	-	-	-	-	0.039
1992–95	Amigo [4]	F	1.000	1.026	0.970	0.003	-	-	-	0.039	-
		R	-	0.709	0.654 [5]	0.003	8.27 [6]	8.32 [6]	NA	-	0.039 [7]
	Pick-up	F	0.938	0.886	0.811	0.003	-	-	-	0.039	-
		R	-	0.472	0.417 [8]	0.003	10.01	10.06	10.06	-	0.039 [7]
	Rodeo [9]		1.000	0.866	0.811 [10]	0.003	10.00	10.06	10.06	0.039	0.039
	Rodeo [11]	F	1.000	1.024	0.969 [12]	0.003	-	-	-	0.039	-
		R	-	0.709	0.654 [5]	0.003	8.27 [6]	8.32 [6]	8.32 [6]	-	0.039 [7]
	Trooper	F	1.000	1.024	0.969 [12]	0.003	-	-	-	0.039	-
		R	-	0.709	0.654 [5]	0.003	8.27 [6]	8.32 [6]	8.32 [6]	-	0.039 [7]
1996	Rodeo [9]	F	1.000	1.020	0.983	0.003	-	-	-	0.039	-
		R	-			0.003	10.00	10.06	10.06	-	0.039
	Rodeo [11]	F	1.000	1.024	0.969 [12]	0.003	-	-	-	0.039	-
		R	-	0.710	0.654 [5]	0.003	8.27 [6]	8.32 [6]	8.32 [6]	-	0.039 [7]
	Trooper	F	1.000	1.024	0.969 [11]	0.003	-	-	-	0.039	-
		R	-	0.710	0.654 [5]	0.003	8.27 [6]	8.32 [6]	8.32 [6]	-	0.039 [7]

NA Not Available

1 1981–83 models: 0.453 in.; 1984–87 models: 0.668 in.
2 Amigo models were introduced in 1989
3 2.3L engine: 0.938 in.
    Except 2.3L engine: 1.000 in.
4 Only produced through 1994
5 Minimum machine diameter: 0.668 in.
6 Emergency brake drum surface

6 Emergency brake drum surface
7 Specification includes disc pads and parking brake shoes
8 Minimum machine diameter: 0.417 in.
9 2.6L engine
10 Minimum machine diameter: 0.826 in.
11 3.2L engine
12 Minimum machine diameter: 0.983 in.

86869CA1

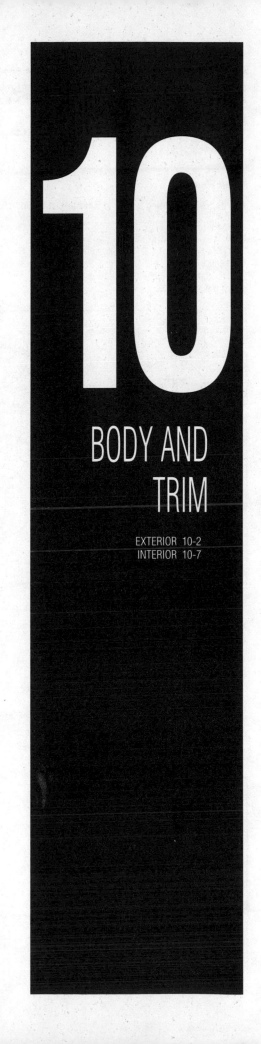

10

BODY AND TRIM

EXTERIOR

Doors

ADJUSTMENT

▶ **See Figure 1**

➡ **Whenever adjusting a door, always adjust in small increments.**

A door can be adjusted at either the hinge or the door striker, or in extreme conditions, both locations.

Before adjusting the striker, check and make sure the clearance between the door and vehicle body is the same around all sides of the door. If the clearance is the same, and further hinge adjustment does not properly align the door, then adjust the striker plate.

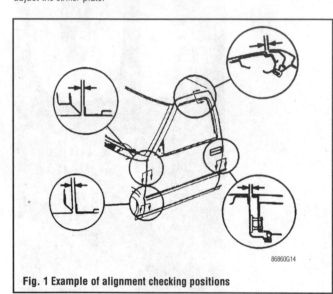

Fig. 1 Example of alignment checking positions

Hinge

1. Close the door and determine whether the door has to be moved up, down, in or out.

➡ **If the door is misaligned at one location more than another, then only one hinge should be adjusted.**

2. Loosen, but do not remove the hinge bolts; 2–3 turns should be enough the adjust the hinge.

   a. If the door needs to be moved out, once the bolts are loosened, carefully move the door outwards in small increments.

   b. If the door needs to be moved in, once the bolts are loosened, carefully press the door inwards in small increments.

   c. If the door needs to be moved to the left, once the bolts are loosened, carefully move the door left in small increments.

   d. If the door needs to be moved to the right, once the bolts are loosened, carefully move the door right in small increments.

3. After each adjustment, tighten the bolts and close the door. Check the alignment. Continue to adjust until correct.

4. When the door adjustment is correct, tighten each bolt to 18–25 ft. lbs. (23–32 Nm).

In some cases, shims will have to be placed between the hinge and vehicle pillar to correctly align the left and right clearances. In this case, install one shim at a time between the hinge and door, then adjust as outlined.

➡ **Be patient when adjusting the door; this procedure requires a great deal of trial and error to get it correct.**

Striker Plate

▶ **See Figures 2 and 3**

1. Scribe an alignment mark around the striker plate for reference during the adjustment procedure.

2. Loosen the mounting screws and carefully tap the striker plate with a plastic-faced hammer.

➡ **The striker should be parallel with the dovetail on the door latch mechanism.**

3. In the event engagement of striker with door latch does not take place, install 1 or more shims between the striker plate and the vehicle pillar.

4. When complete, tighten the striker screws to 10 ft. lbs. (13 Nm).

Hood

REMOVAL & INSTALLATION

▶ **See Figures 4 and 5**

1. Disconnect the negative battery cable.
2. Scribe an alignment mark showing the location of the hinges on the hood.
3. Disconnect under hood light harness, if equipped.
4. Remove the washer nozzle tubes, if routed through the hood.

✳✳ CAUTION

An assistant is needed to hold the hood in position during removal. Serious injury can result if the hood should close during removal.

5. While supporting the hood, remove the hood mounting bolts and lift hood from vehicle.

To install:

6. Position hood to the hinges and line up scribe line.
7. Install and tighten the mounting bolts with moderate torque. DO NOT tighten down all the way.

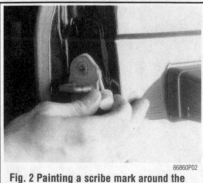

Fig. 2 Painting a scribe mark around the striker plate for reference during adjustment

Fig. 3 Loosen the striker plate retainer screws to adjust the plate

Fig. 4 Scribe an alignment mark around the hood hinge

8. Close the hood slowly to check the alignment. DO NOT slam the hood closed. In most cases hood adjustment will be necessary.

9. Adjust the hood clearances, if needed.

10. After the alignment is satisfactory, tighten the hood hinge bolts to 18–25 ft. lbs. (23–32 Nm).

11. Connect the negative battery cable.

ADJUSTMENT

➡**Whenever adjusting a body panel, always adjust in small increments.**

1. Close the hood and determine whether the panel has to be moved forward, backwards, in or out. Also check to see whether the hood is flush with the front fenders.

2. If adjustment is needed, loosen, but do not remove the hinge bolts; 2–3 turns should be enough to the adjust the hinge.

3. Once the bolts are loosened, adjust the hood to the desired position, then tighten the bolts. Do not tighten the bolts to specification until the adjustment procedure is complete.

4. When the hood adjustment is correct, tighten each bolt to 18–25 ft. lbs. (23–32 Nm).

In some cases, shims will have to be placed between the hinge and the panel to correctly align the left and right clearances. In this case, install 1 shim at a time between the hinge and hood and adjust as outlined.

➡**Be patient when adjusting a panel. This procedure requires a great deal of trail and error to get correct.**

Tailgate

ALIGNMENT

♦ **See Figure 6**

Align the tailgate so the gaps between all of the components are equal; it must be flush with the fenders. Center the tailgate in the opening between the fenders by adjusting the hinges and/or the striker bolts.

Fig. 5 Use a suitable sized wrench or socket to remove the hood hinge retainer bolts

86860P05

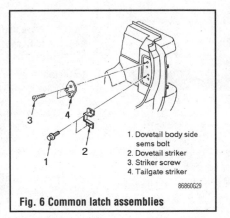

1. Dovetail body side sems bolt
2. Dovetail striker
3. Striker screw
4. Tailgate striker

86860G29

Fig. 6 Common latch assemblies

Grille

REMOVAL & INSTALLATION

✲✲ WARNING

On these models, the radiator grille is held in place with recessed plastic retainers which break easily. Use care when releasing these retainers.

Amigo, Rodeo and Pick-Up

♦ **See Figure 7**

1. Raise the hood and support it with the prop rod.

2. Remove the retainer screws from around each headlight and at the center of the grille, below the emblem.

3. Using a small prytool, press the tab on each of the grille retainer clips upward while pulling the grille away from the radiator support.

4. When all the tabs have been released, lift the grille up slightly and out to remove.

To install:

5. Engage the lower portion of the grille into the radiator support.

6. Carefully push the grille toward the radiator support, making sure the retainer clips align with their respective mounting hole. Once all the holes align, press the grille and retainer in until it clicks into position.

7. Install the retainer screws around the headlight and at the center of the grille.

Trooper

♦ **See Figures 8, 9 and 10**

1. Raise the hood and support it with the prop rod.

2. On 1981–94 models, remove the retainer screws from around each headlight.

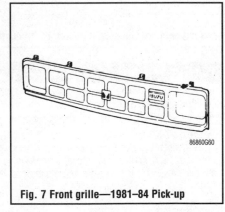

86860G60

Fig. 7 Front grille—1981–84 Pick-up

3. Remove the retainer screws from the corners and center of the grille.

4. Using a small prytool to press the tab on each of the grille retainer clips at the top of the grille upward while pulling the grille away from the radiator support.

5. When all the tabs have been released, lift the grille up slightly and out to remove.

To install:

6. Engage the lower portion of the grille into the radiator support.

7. Carefully push the grille toward the radiator support, making sure the retainer clips align with their respective mounting hole. Once all the holes align, press the grille and retainer in until it clicks into position.

8. Install the retainer screws from the corners and center of the grille.

9. On 1981–94 models, install the retainer screws around the headlight.

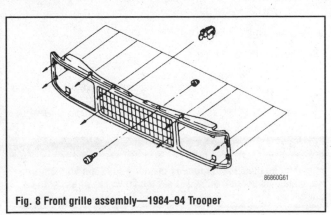

86860G61

Fig. 8 Front grille assembly—1984–94 Trooper

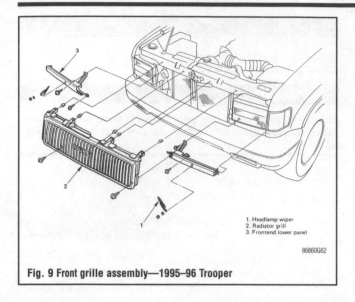

Fig. 9 Front grille assembly—1995–96 Trooper

1. Headlamp wiper
2. Radiator grill
3. Frontend lower panel

86860G62

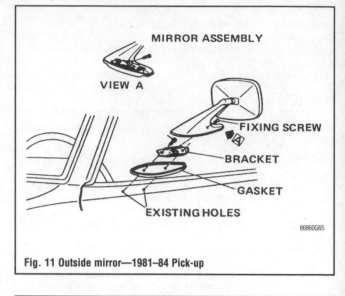

Fig. 11 Outside mirror—1981–84 Pick-up

86860G65

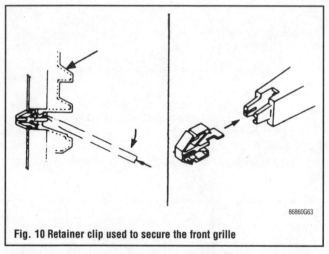

Fig. 10 Retainer clip used to secure the front grille

86860G63

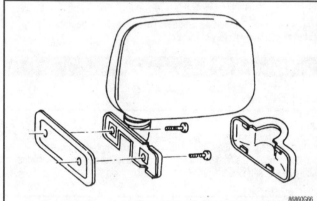

Fig. 12 Outside mirror mounted to door—1985–94 Pick-up; Amigo, Trooper and Rodeo

86860G66

Outside Mirrors

REMOVAL & INSTALLATION

There are 2 types of outside mirrors used on Isuzu vehicles. The first type has the mounting screws accessible from the outside of the vehicle. The second type of outside mirror has mounting screws accessible from the inside of the vehicle only. This design requires the removal of the inner door panel and trim.

Door Mounted

▶ See Figures 11 and 12

1. Disconnect the negative battery cable.
2. Remove the screw-on bezel around the interior panel mounted remote mirror control cable assembly, if equipped. Push the control knob through the mounting hole into the door.
3. Using a small prytool, remove the trim cover over the retainer screws at the base of the mirror.
4. While supporting the mirror with 1 hand, remove the retainer screws from the mirror and door. If equipped with a power mirror, pull the mirror away from the door and unfasten the wire harness fro the base of the mirror.
5. Remove the mirror and rubber gasket from between the door and mirror base.
6. Inspect the rubber gasket, and replace if torn or excessively cracked. Clean the mirror contact surface on the door. If any rust is present, remove and treat the effected area with a rust-proof type paint.

To install:

7. If equipped with power mirrors, attach the control harness to the base of the mirror.
8. If equipped with a cable driven mirror, feed the cable control assembly through the hole in the door, and position in the mounting hole in the interior panel. Secure in place using the retainer bezel. On some models, it may be necessary to remove the door panel in order to attach the control assembly to the door panel.
9. Position the mirror on the door with the rubber gasket between the mirror and door surface. Secure in place using the retainer screws. Tighten the screws to 4–6 ft. lbs. (5–8 Nm).
10. Install the trim panel over the retainer screws.
11. Connect the negative battery cable.

Window Mounted

▶ See Figures 13 and 14

1. Disconnect the negative battery cable.
2. Remove the interior door panel. Refer to the procedure in this section for removal and installation steps.
3. Remove the retainer screw from the trim panel at the front corner of the window covering the mirror retainer screws.

❉❉ WARNING

Be careful on models with remote mounted speakers on the mirror trim panel. Do not pull the panel out too far or the wires could be torn off.

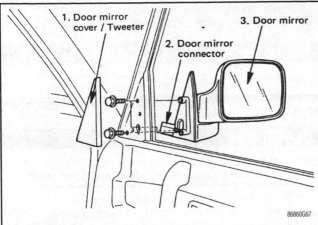

Fig. 13 Outside mirror mounted to window frame—Pick-up, Rodeo and Trooper

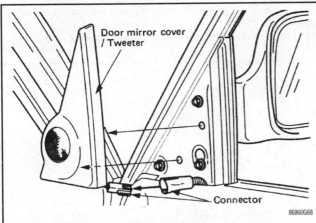

Fig. 14 Trim panel with remote speaker mounted over mirror retainer screws

4. If equipped with remote mounted speakers on the trim panel, remove the panel and disconnect the speaker wire harness from the back of the panel.

5. While supporting the mirror with 1 hand, remove the mirror retainer screws. Lower the mirror, and if equipped with power mirrors, disconnect the mirror control harness.

6. Remove the rubber gasket from between the door and mirror base.

7. Inspect the rubber gasket, and replace if torn or excessively cracked. Clean the mirror contact surface on the door. If any rust is present, remove and treat the effected area with a rust-proof type paint.

To install:

8. Attach the mirror control harness to the mirror.

9. Position the mirror on the door with the rubber gasket between the mirror and door surface. While holding the mirror in place with 1 hand, secure using the retainer screws. Tighten the screws to 4–6 ft. lbs. (5–8 Nm).

10. Install the trim panel over the mirror screws, securing in place with the retainer screw. If equipped with remote mounted speakers on the panel, connect the wire harness before installing the panel.

11. Install the interior door panel.

12. Connect the negative battery cable.

Antenna

REMOVAL & INSTALLATION

There are several types of antennae used on Isuzu vehicles. The first type is a single length mast type antenna mounted on the front fender. The second type is a power version of the fender-mount antenna. The last type is mounted in the windshield.

In the event a fender mount antenna becomes damaged or fails, either individual parts or the entire assembly can be replaced. In the case of the windshield mounted antenna, only the antenna cable can be replaced. If the antenna portion mounted in the windshield fails, the entire windshield most be replaced.

Fender Mounted

♦ **See Figure 15**

1. Disconnect the negative battery cable.

2. Remove the radio from the dash panel. Refer to the radio removal and installation procedure in Section 6 of this manual. With the radio removed from the dash panel, unfasten the antenna connection from the back of the radio.

3. Detach the antenna cable from under the dash panel retainer points until it is loose at the inner fender grommet.

※ WARNING

Never remove an antenna by pulling on the cable. Not only will this ruin the antenna cable, but it could also damage underdash wiring and components.

4. Remove the fender inner liner from above the wheel and tire assembly by removing the retainer screws. If additional access room is needed, raise and support the vehicle on jackstands.

5. Remove the rubber grommet from the inner fender, then remove the antenna cable.

6. Remove the antenna mast by unscrewing it from the antenna base.

7. Remove the antenna base retainer nut. Lower the antenna base out of the mounting hole.

8. Clean the antenna contact surface on the fender. If any rust is present, remove and treat the effected area with a rust-proof type paint.

To install:

9. Insert the antenna base through the mounting hole in the fender. Attach the plastic collar around the base and secure in place with the retainer nut.

10. Feed the antenna cable through the hole in the inner fender, and install the rubber grommet.

11. Install the antenna mast.

12. Install the fender inner liner, securing in place with the retainer screws.

13. From inside the vehicle, route the antenna cable through the dash panel, attaching it to the retainers, and out the radio opening in the center of the panel assembly. Connect the antenna to the back of the radio.

※ CAUTION

When routing the antenna cable, be careful to keep the cable away from the pedal assembly and any moving parts. Failure to do some could cause serious injury.

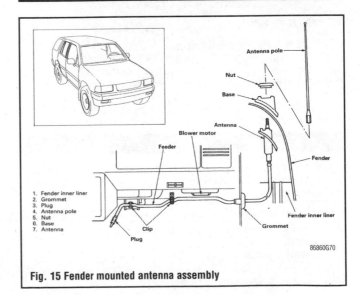

Fig. 15 Fender mounted antenna assembly

14. Install the radio to the dash panel.
15. Connect the negative battery cable. Test the radio for proper functioning.

Power Antenna

♦ See Figure 16

1. Disconnect the negative battery cable.
2. Remove the fender inner liner from above the wheel and tire assembly by removing the retainer screws. If additional access room is needed, raise and support the vehicle on jackstands.
3. Remove the rubber grommet from the inner fender. Detach the antenna cable and power harness connections.
4. Remove the antenna base retainer nut at the fender, and the bracket retainer screws inside the fender. Lower the antenna out of the mounting hole.
5. Clean the antenna contact surface on the fender. If any rust is present, remove and treat the effected area with a rust-proof type paint.

To install:

6. Insert the antenna through the mounting hole in the fender. Secure the bracket at the base of the antenna to the inner fender using the retainer screws. Attach the plastic collar around the base and secure in place with the retainer nut.
7. Connect the antenna cable and power harness to the plug in the inner fender.
8. Install the fender inner liner, securing in place with the retainer screws.
9. Connect the negative battery cable. Test the radio for proper functioning.

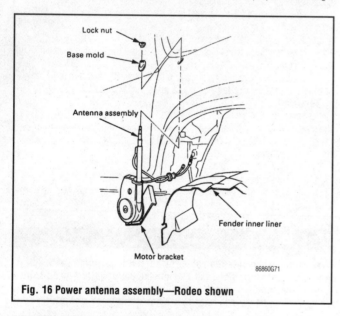

Fig. 16 Power antenna assembly—Rodeo shown

Windshield Mounted

1. Disconnect the negative battery cable.
2. Remove the radio from the dash panel. Refer to the radio removal and installation procedure in Section 6 of this manual. With the radio removed from the dash panel, unfasten the antenna connection from the back of the radio.
3. Detach the antenna cable from under the dash panel retainer points and at the connector at the base of the windshield.

✳✳ WARNING

Never remove an antenna by pulling on the cable. Not on it will this ruin the antenna cable, but it could also damage underdash wiring and components.

4. Remove the windshield from the vehicle. Refer to the windshield removal and installation procedure in this section for details.

To install:

5. Install the windshield.
6. Attach the antenna cable to the connector at the base of the windshield and the back of the radio.

7. Install the radio and dash components.
8. Connect the negative battery cable. Test the radio for proper functioning.

Pick-Up Truck Bed

REMOVAL & INSTALLATION

♦ See Figures 17 and 18

✳✳ CAUTION

Because of the weight of the bed, do not attempt this procedure without proper lifting equipment, or serious injury could result.

1. Disconnect the negative battery cable.
2. From under the vehicle, disconnect the clamps around the rubber hose connecting the fuel tank filler neck and fuel tank assembly. Disconnect the filler hose and evaporator hose from the filler neck assembly.
3. Attach suitable lifting wires to the rear body hooks, located in the corners of the bed assembly.
4. Remove the retainer bolts securing the bed to the frame assembly. Depending on the size of the bed, there are 1 or 2 retainer bolts in front of the rear wheel, and 2 bolts after the rear wheel on each side of the vehicle.
5. Raise the bed assembly up with a suitable lifting device.

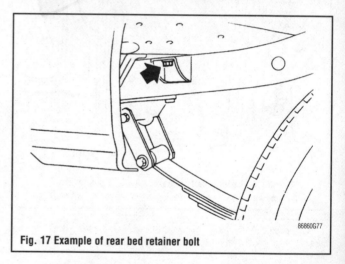

Fig. 17 Example of rear bed retainer bolt

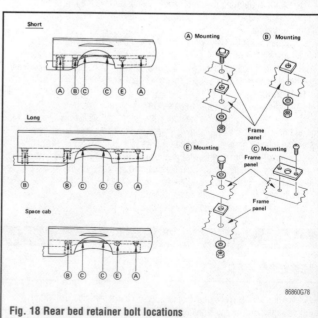

Fig. 18 Rear bed retainer bolt locations

6. Clean the bed contact surface on the frame. If any rust is present, remove and treat the effected area with a rust-proof type paint.

✳✳ WARNING

When lifting the rear bed assembly, take care not to dash the bed against the cab body.

INTERIOR

Instrument Panel

REMOVAL & INSTALLATION

1981–85 Pick-Up

◆ **See Figures 19, 20, 21 and 22**

1. Disconnect the negative battery cable.
2. Remove the knobs from the radio and ventilation controls.
3. Remove the radio from the dash assembly. Refer to Section 6 for radio removal and installation steps.
4. Remove the retainer screws from around the instrument cluster panel.
5. Lift the cluster panel off and remove the instrument cluster retainer screws. Lift the cluster assembly out slightly and disconnect the speedometer cable and gauge wire harnesses.

To install:

7. Slowly lower the cab on to the frame. Align the retainer holes on the frame with the corresponding hole in the bed.
8. Install the retainer bolts and hand-tighten. When all the retainer bolts are installed, tighten them each to 49–78 ft. lbs. (64–101 Nm).
9. Attach the fuel tank filler neck to the fuel tank and evaporator using the rubber hoses and clamps.
10. Connect the negative battery cable.

6. Remove the side ventilation retainer screws at the base of the assembly. Using a small prytool, carefully pry out the side ventilation ducts.
7. Unfasten the ventilation control assembly retainer screws. The assembly does not have to be disconnected.
8. Remove the dash retainer screws at the top and side of the panel assembly. Then remove the dash retainer panels from the bottom of the vehicle. Refer to the illustration for the exact location of the bolts.
9. With all the retainer bolts removed, slowly pull the dash assembly forward, then remove it from the vehicle.
10. If you wish to separate the top and bottom portion of the dash assembly, remove the retainer screws at the base of the instrument cluster housing, then carefully separate the halves.

To install:

11. If the dash assembly was separated, position the halves together and secure with retainer screws at the instrument cluster housing.
12. Position the dash assembly below the windshield, and carefully push toward the engine to engage the dash-to-firewall retainer clips. Once in place, install the dash retainer screws to the top, side and bottom of the assembly.
13. Position the ventilation control assembly flush with the dash panel, and secure in place with the retainer screws.
14. Install the side ventilation ducts and secure in place with the retainer screws.

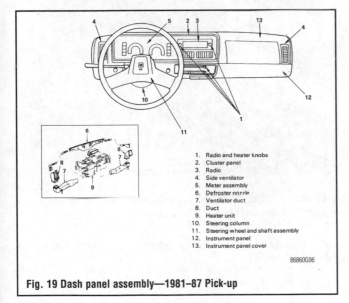

1. Radio and heater knobs
2. Cluster panel
3. Radio
4. Side ventilator
5. Meter assembly
6. Defroster nozzle
7. Ventilator duct
8. Duct
9. Heater unit
10. Steering column
11. Steering wheel and shaft assembly
12. Instrument panel
13. Instrument panel cover

86860G96

Fig. 19 Dash panel assembly—1981–87 Pick-up

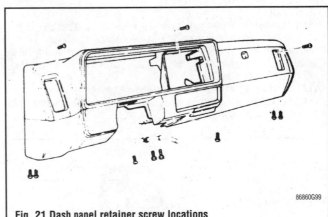

86860G99

Fig. 21 Dash panel retainer screw locations

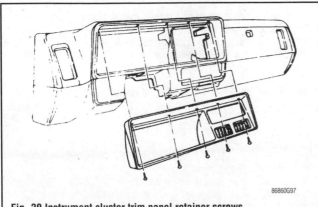

86860G97

Fig. 20 Instrument cluster trim panel retainer screws

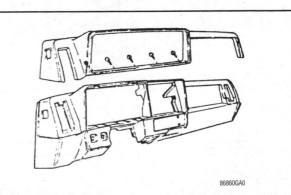

86860GA0

Fig. 22 To separate the dash panels, remove the indicated retainer screws

15. Attach the speedometer cable and gauge wire harness to the instrument cluster.

16. Position the instrument cluster to the dash panel and secure in place with the retainer screws.

17. Install the cluster panel and retainer screws.

18. Install the radio and components in the dash panel.

19. Install the ventilation and radio knobs.

20. Connect the negative battery cable. Test all switches, lights and gauges to make sure everything functions correctly.

1984–94 Trooper

♦ **See Figures 23, 24 and 25**

1. Disconnect the negative battery cable.

2. Remove the retainer screws from around the instrument cluster meter hood.

3. Lift the meter hood off and remove the instrument cluster retainer screws. Lift the cluster assembly out slightly and disconnect the speedometer cable and gauge wire harnesses.

4. Remove the parcel tray, or if equipped, combination gauge assembly from the center of the dash panel, by removing the Allen head bolts from the base of the tray/gauge panel. If equipped with gauges, lift the gauges out and unfasten the wire harnesses from the back of the panel.

5. Open the glove box and remove the retainer screws from around the rim of the assembly. When all the screws are removed, slide the glove box out and place aside.

6. Unfasten the ventilation control assembly retainer screws. The assembly does not have to be disconnected.

7. Remove the radio from below the dash assembly. Refer to Section 6 for radio removal and installation steps.

8. Using a small prytool, carefully pry out the side ventilation ducts.

9. Remove the 4 dash retainer bolts at the top of the panel assembly. Then remove the 4 dash retainer panels from the left and right side of the vehicle. Refer to the illustration for the exact location of the bolts.

10. With all the retainer bolts removed, slowly pull the dash assembly forward, then remove it from the vehicle.

To install:

11. Position the dash assembly below the windshield, and carefully push toward the engine to engage the dash-to-firewall retainer clips. Once in place, install the dash retainer bolts to the top and bottom of the assembly. Tighten the retainer bolts to 6–9 ft. lbs. (8–12 Nm).

12. Install the side ventilation ducts.

13. Install the radio and components below the dash panel.

14. Position the ventilation control assembly flush with the dash panel, and secure in place with the retainer screws.

Fig. 24 If equipped with dash mounted gauges, use an Allen wrench to remove the retainer screws . . .

Fig. 25 . . . then remove the gauge assembly and disconnect the gauge wire harnesses

15. Slide the glove box into the dash assembly, and secure in place with the retainer screws.

16. If equipped with combination gauges, attach the wire harnesses to the assembly. Install the combination gauge or parcel tray assembly to the dash panel, and secure in place with the Allen head retainer screws.

17. Attach the speedometer cable and gauge wire harness to the instrument cluster.

18. Position the instrument cluster to the dash panel and secure in place with the retainer screws.

19. Install the cluster meter hood and retainer screws.

20. Connect the negative battery cable. Test all switches, lights and gauges to make everything functions correctly.

1986–94 Pick-Up; 1990–94 Amigo and Rodeo

♦ **See Figures 26, 27 and 28**

1. Disconnect the negative battery cable.

2. If equipped with an Air Bag, disarm the Air Bag system. Remove the steering wheel. Refer to Section 8 for steering wheel removal and installation steps. Store the Air Bag face up.

3. Use a small prytool and remove the uppermost grille from the left and right sides of the dash panel. Use a suitable socket, remove the dash panel retainer nuts from within the recess.

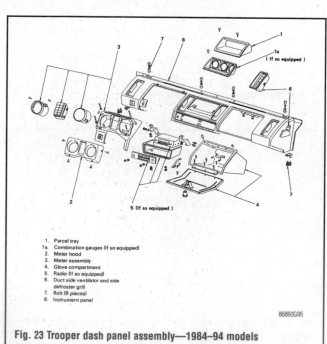

1. Parcel tray
1a. Combination gauges (if so equipped)
2. Meter hood
3. Meter assembly
4. Glove compartment
5. Radio (if so equipped)
6. Duct side ventilator and side
     defroster grill
7. Bolt (8 pieces)
8. Instrument panel

86860G95

Fig. 23 Trooper dash panel assembly—1984–94 models

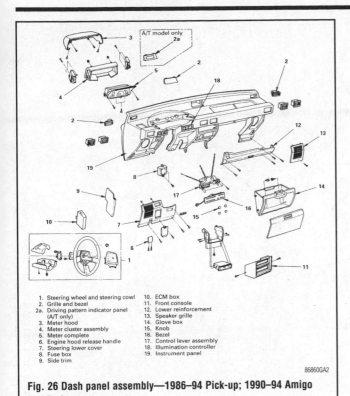

Fig. 26 Dash panel assembly—1986–94 Pick-up; 1990–94 Amigo and Rodeo

1. Steering wheel and steering cowl
2. Grille and bezel
2a. Driving pattern indicator panel (A/T only)
3. Meter hood
4. Meter cluster assembly
5. Meter complete
6. Engine hood release handle
7. Steering lower cover
8. Fuse box
9. Side trim
10. ECM box
11. Front console
12. Lower reinforcement
13. Speaker grille
14. Glove box
15. Knob
16. Bezel
17. Control lever assembly
18. Illumination controller
19. Instrument panel

86860GA2

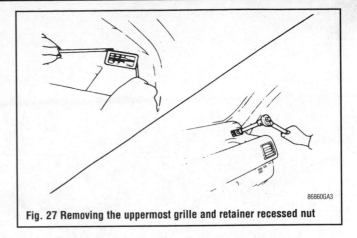

Fig. 27 Removing the uppermost grille and retainer recessed nut

86860GA3

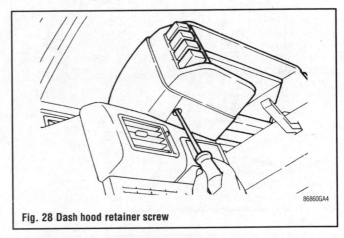

Fig. 28 Dash hood retainer screw

86860GA4

4. Remove the retainer screws from around the instrument cluster meter hood.

5. Lift the meter hood off and disconnect the speedometer cable and gauge wire harnesses.

6. Remove the engine hood release cable.

7. Remove the steering column under cover, fuse box retainer screws, lower reinforcement, speaker grille and speaker by removing the necessary retainer screws.

8. Open the glove box and depress the fixing pins. Lower the box and remove the retainer screws from around the rim of the assembly. When all the screws are removed, slide the glove box out and place aside.

9. Remove the ventilation control system knobs. Carefully pry off the trim plate, disconnecting the harness from the rear, and place aside. Unfasten the ventilation control assembly retainer screws. Push the control assembly toward the firewall, and tag and disconnect the cables attached.

10. Remove the dash retainer nuts and bolts at the top, side and bottom of the panel assembly.

11. With all the retainer bolts removed, slowly pull the dash assembly forward, then remove it from the vehicle.

To install:

12. Position the dash assembly below the windshield, and carefully push toward the engine to engage the dash-to-firewall retainer clips. Once in place, install the dash retainer nuts and bolts to the top, side and bottom of the assembly. Tighten the retainer nuts and bolts to 6–9 ft. lbs. (8–12 Nm).

13. Attach the ventilation cables to the control assembly. Position the ventilation control assembly flush with the dash panel, and secure in place with the retainer screws. Attach the trim panel and wire harness. Install the control knobs.

14. Slide the glove box into the dash assembly, and secure in place with the retainer screws. Depress the fixing pins and push the glove box into position.

15. Position and install using retainer screws the steering column under cover, fuse box, lower reinforcement, speaker grille and speaker.

16. Position the engine hood release cable handle, and install the retainer screws.

17. Attach the speedometer cable and gauge wire harness to the instrument cluster.

18. Position the instrument cluster to the dash panel and secure the meter hood with retainer screws.

19. Install the uppermost dash panel retainer nuts, and tighten to 13–15 ft. lbs. (17–19 Nm). When tight, install the grille over the hole.

20. Install the steering wheel. Arm the Air Bag system.

21. Connect the negative battery cable. Test all switches, lights and gauges to make everything functions correctly.

1995–96 Rodeo

♦ **See Figure 29**

1. Disconnect the negative battery cable.

2. Disarm the Air Bag system, if so equipped.

3. Remove the steering wheel. Refer to Section 8 for steering wheel removal and installation steps.

4. Remove the ashtray from the dash panel. Remove the retainer screw from the rear of the ashtray assembly. Remove the retainer screws from the top of the pocket above the ashtray. Slowly remove the lower cluster/ashtray assembly. When the assembly is out far enough, disconnect the wire harnesses attached to the rear of the panel.

5. Remove the glove box door retainer screws, then remove the glove box door.

6. Remove the glove box compartment retainer screws, then slide the compartment out of the dash panel. Detach the glove compartment interior light harness.

7. Working from inside the glove box opening, detach the passenger side Air Bag retainer nuts, then remove the Air bag assembly. Store the Air bag face up.

8. Remove the driver and passenger side lower dash trim panel retainer screws and bolts. Remove the trim panels and place aside. Remove the driver side lower reinforcement panel and retainer screws.

9. Remove the retainer screws from around the instrument cluster, radio, and center vents. Carefully remove the instrument panel trim panel. Detach the wire harnesses from the switches in the trim panel.

10. Remove the radio from the dash panel. Refer to the procedure in Section 6.

11. Remove the instrument cluster retainer screws. Pull the cluster assembly out enough to access the speedometer cable and cluster wire harnesses. Tag

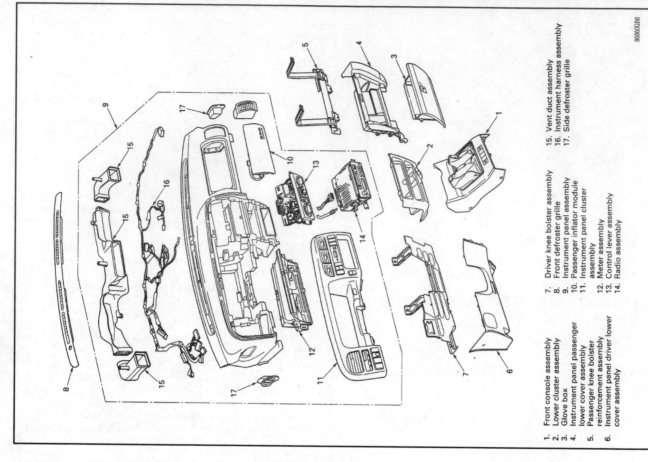

1. Front console assembly
2. Lower cluster assembly
3. Glove box
4. Instrument panel passenger lower cover assembly
5. Passenger knee bolster reinforcement assembly
6. Instrument panel driver lower cover assembly

7. Driver knee bolster assembly
8. Front defroster grille
9. Instrument panel assembly
10. Passenger inflator module
11. Instrument panel cluster assembly
12. Meter assembly
13. Control lever assembly
14. Radio assembly

15. Vent duct assembly
16. Instrument harness assembly
17. Side defroster grille

Fig. 30 Dash assembly and components—1995–96 Trooper

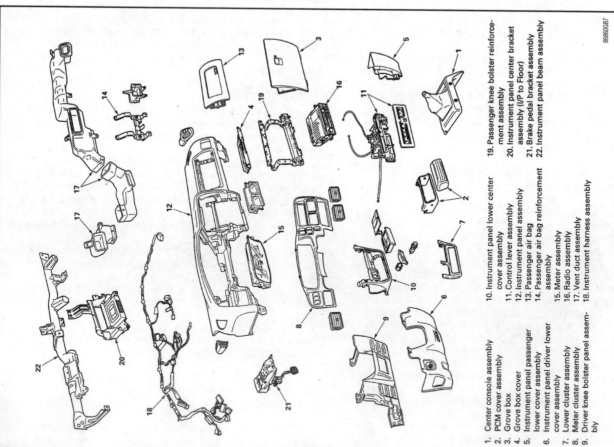

1. Center console assembly
2. PCM cover assembly
3. Grove box
4. Grove box cover
5. Instrument panel passenger lower cover assembly
6. Instrument panel driver lower cover assembly
7. Lower cluster assembly
8. Meter cluster assembly
9. Driver knee bolster panel assembly

10. Instrument panel lower center cover assembly
11. Control lever assembly
12. Instrument panel assembly
13. Passenger air bag
14. Passenger air bag reinforcement assembly
15. Meter assembly
16. Radio assembly
17. Vent duct assembly
18. Instrument harness assembly

19. Passenger knee bolster reinforcement assembly
20. Instrument panel center bracket assembly (I/P to Floor)
21. Brake pedal bracket assembly
22. Instrument panel beam assembly

Fig. 29 Dash assembly and components—1995–96 Rodeo

and disconnect the wire harnesses and speedometer cable. Remove the cluster assembly and place aside.

12.   Remove the heater/ventilation control assembly trim panel and dash light harness. Remove the heater/ventilation control panel retainer screws. Push the control panel into the dash panel assembly.

13.   Remove the attachment screws from the top, side and bottom of the dash panel. Carefully pull the dash panel forward, detaching it from the retainer clips under the windshield. Check to make sure no wire harnesses or heater/ventilation cables are caught in the assembly. Remove the dash panel from the vehicle, and place aside

To install:

14.   Install the dash panel to the vehicle, making sure the dash panel engages the retainer clips below the windshield. Before installing any retainer hardware, check and make sure no wires are caught in the assembly. Position the heater/ventilation control panel to the opening in the dash panel. Install the retainer screws to secure the control panel in place.

15.   Install the dash panel retainer screws at the top, side and bottom of the assembly. Tighten the retainer screws to 6–9 ft. lbs. (8–12 Nm).

16.   Install the heater/ventilation trim panel and dash light harness.

17.   Install the radio to the dash panel.

18.   Attach the instrument cluster wire harnesses and speedometer cable to the rear of the cluster assembly. Work the cluster into the dash panel, and secure with retainer screws.

19.   Attach the wire harnesses to the switches in the dash trim panel. Position the dash assembly trim panel to the dash and install the retainer screws around the instrument cluster, radio and center vents.

20.   Install the passenger side Air Bag, and secure in place with the retainer nuts.

21.   Connect the glove compartment interior light harness to the light. Insert the glove compartment into the dash opening, and install the retainer screws.

22.   Install the driver side lower reinforcement panel, and secure in place with the retainer screws. Tighten the screws to 6–9 ft. lbs. (8–12 Nm).

23.   Install the passenger and driver side lower trim panel. Secure the panels in place with the retainer screws.

24.   Position the glove compartment door to the dash panel and install the door retainer screws.

25.   Insert the lower cluster trim panel into the dash assembly and secure in place with retainer screws. Do not forget to install the retainer screw to the rear of the ashtray compartment.

26.   Install the steering wheel and center pad. If equipped with an Air Bag, connect the Air Bag.

27.   Connect the negative battery cable and arm the Air Bag system.

28.   Check and make sure all dash function work correctly. This include the radio, dash lights, heater/ventilation control and instrument cluster gauges and warning lights.

1995–96 Trooper

▶ **See Figures 30 and 31**

1.   Disconnect the negative battery cable.

2.   If equipped with an Air Bag, disarm the Air Bag system. Remove the steering wheel. Refer to Section 8 for steering wheel removal and installation steps. If equipped with an Air Bag, store the Air Bag face up.

3.   Remove the front center console assembly, by removing the manual transmission shift knob, if equipped, and the transfer knob, then the side retainer screws. Lift the console assembly off, and place aside.

4.   Remove the driver and passenger side lower trim panel retainer screws and panel assemblies.

5.   Remove the driver side reinforcement panel by removing the retainer screws.

6.   Pry off the grille assemblies from both sides of the dash panel, and remove the retainer screws from inside the grille opening.

7.   Remove the glove box door by unfastening the retainer screws. Remove the glove compartment retainer screws. Slide the compartment assembly out, and detach the glove box light harness.

8.   Working from inside the glove box opening, remove the passenger side Air bag retainer nuts, and remove the Air Bag assembly. Store the Air Bag face up.

9.   Remove the instrument trim panel retainer screws from around the instrument cluster, radio and center vents. Pull the vent forward, and detach the wire harness from the rear of the switches installed to the trim panel.

10.   Remove the retainer screws securing the ventilation control panel to the dash assembly. Pull the control panel forward, and unfasten the connectors.

11.   Remove the radio from the dash panel. Refer to Section 6 for removal and installation steps.

12.   Remove the retainer screws from around the instrument cluster. Pull the cluster forward and unfasten the speedometer cable and wire harnesses attached to the cluster assembly. Remove the instrument cluster and place aside.

13.   Remove the dash panel retainer nuts and bolts from top, bottom and middle of the dash assembly. Carefully pull the dash panel forward and out of the vehicle.

To install:

14.   Position the dash assembly below the windshield, and carefully push toward the engine to engage the dash-to-firewall retainer clips. Once in place, install the dash retainer nuts and bolts to the top, bottom and middle of the assembly. Tighten the retainer nuts and bolts to 6–9 ft. lbs. (8–12 Nm).

15.   Attach the wire harnesses and speedometer cable to rear of the instrument cluster. Work the instrument cluster into position, and secure in place with the retainer screws.

16.   Install the radio to the dash panel.

17.   Attach the wire harness to the ventilation control panel. Work the control panel into position in the dash, and secure with the retainer screws.

18.   Fasten the wire harnesses to the dash trim panel switches. Install the trim panel to the dash assembly, and install the retainer screws around the instrument cluster, radio and center vents.

19.   Install the passenger side Air Bag, and secure in place with the retainer nuts.

20.   Attach the glove box light harness to the glove compartment assembly. Slide the compartment into the dash assembly, and secure in place with retainer screws. Install the glove box door using retainer screws attached at the bottom of the door.

21.   Position the driver side reinforcement bracket to the dash assembly, and install the retainer screws. Tighten the screws to 6–9 ft. lbs. (8–12 Nm).

22.   Install the driver and passenger lower trim panels, and secure in place with retainer screws.

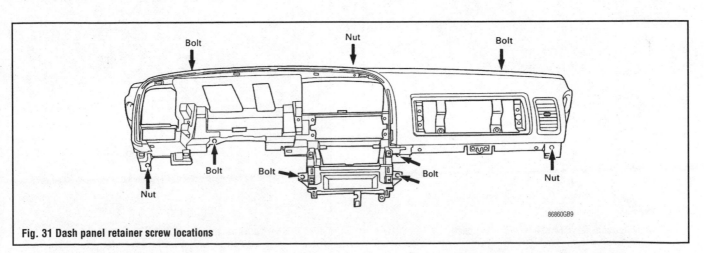

Fig. 31 Dash panel retainer screw locations

86860GB9

23. Position the front center console over the shifter assembly, and secure in place with retainer screws. Attach the transfer knob and shifter knob if equipped with a manual transmission.

24. Install the steering wheel. Arm the Air Bag system.

25. Connect the negative battery cable. Test all switches, lights and gauges to make sure everything functions correctly.

Center Console

REMOVAL & INSTALLATION

1991–96 Rodeo

▶ See Figure 32

1. Disconnect the negative battery cable.
2. To remove the front console assembly, proceed as follows:

   a. Remove the shift knob, if equipped with a manual transmission and the transfer knob.

   b. Remove the rear retainer screws from the left and right side of the assembly.

   c. Open the plastic caps at the front of the shift console, and remove the retainer screws from underneath.

   d. Lift the center console over the shifter and out.

3. To remove the rear console assembly, proceed as follows:

   a. Open the lid of the rear compartment, and if equipped, remove the cup holder. Remove the retainer screws at the base of the console assembly.

   b. If equipped, remove the power mirror switches in the center of the console and disconnect the harnesses.

   c. Use a small prytool to remove the plastic trim piece at the front of the console assembly. Remove the retainer screws from under the trim piece.

   d. Remove the console assembly from the vehicle.

To install:

4. To install the rear console assembly, proceed as follows:

   a. Position the console between the 2 front seats, aligning the mounting holes in the console with the holes in the floor or bracket.

   b. Install retainer screws to the front pocket and rear compartments of the console assembly to secure it in place. Install the plastic trim piece over the front screws.

   c. If equipped with power mirrors, connect the harnesses to the mirror switches and install them in the center of the console. If equipped with a cup holder, install it in the rear compartment.

5. To install the front console assembly, proceed as follows:

   a. Position the console assembly over the shifter assembly, and secure in place with retainer screws. Remember, the retainer screws with the plastic

caps covering the screw head should be install at the front of the console assembly.

   b. Install the shift and transfer knobs, if removed.

6. Connect the negative battery cable.

1995–96 Trooper

1. Disconnect the negative battery cable
2. Remove the shift knob, if equipped with a manual transmission, and the transfer knob.
3. Remove the retainer screws from the left and right sides of the front console.
4. Remove the right front seat assembly. Refer to the procedure in this section for removal and installation details.
5. Remove the retainer screws securing the assist grip to the rear console assembly.
6. Lift the fuel filler latch and disconnect the cable.
7. Remove the front console assembly.
8. Remove the retainer screws from the front of the rear console assembly.
9. Remove the rear cover at the back of the console, then unfasten the rear console retainer nuts.
10. Lift the rear console assembly up and out of the vehicle.

To install:

11. Position the rear console assembly in the vehicle. Align the studs in the console mounting holes, and secure in place with the retainer nuts. Install trim cover over the retainer nuts.
12. Install retainer screws to the front of the rear console assembly.
13. Attach the fuel filler lid cable to the latch assembly.
14. Position the assist grip to the rear console assembly, and secure in place with the retainer screws.
15. Install the front center console, and secure in place with retainer screws at the sides.
16. Install the right front seat assembly.
17. Install the shift knob, if equipped, and the transfer knob.
18. Connect the negative battery cable.

Door Panels

REMOVAL & INSTALLATION

▶ See Figures 33 thru 43

1. Disconnect the negative battery cable.
2. If equipped with an accessory switch panel, carefully pry the switch panel up and away from the door panel. Tag and disconnect the switches from the panel.

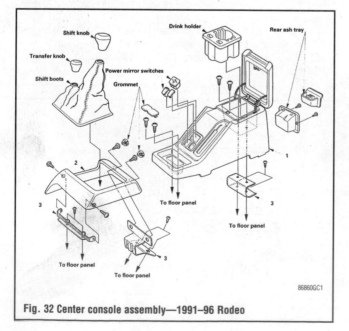

86860GC1

Fig. 32 Center console assembly—1991–96 Rodeo

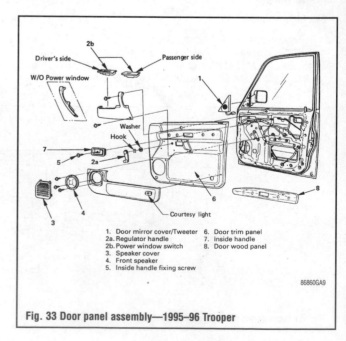

1. Door mirror cover/Tweeter
2a. Regulator handle
2b. Power window switch
3. Speaker cover
4. Front speaker
5. Inside handle fixing screw
6. Door trim panel
7. Inside handle
8. Door wood panel

86860GA9

Fig. 33 Door panel assembly—1995–96 Trooper

3. On 1981–86 models, remove armrest attaching screws.

4. On 1987–96 models, remove the retainer screws secure the pocket in the molded armrest on the door panel.

5. If equipped with crank type windows, remove window crank handle with the appropriate clip removal tool.

6. If equipped with manual remote mirrors, remove the control knob bezel.

7. Remove inside door handle cover attaching screw and trim plate.

8. If equipped with door mounted speakers, remove the speaker, and disconnect the speaker wires. For speaker removal and installation steps, refer to Section 6.

9. Remove all external screws securing the door panel. Insert an appropriate prytool between the door panel and door frame to remove the hidden clips securing the panel.

10. Holding door panel vertical lift straight up to release the upper clip.

11. Inspect all retaining clips and replace any broken or missing pieces.

Fig. 34 Remove the retainer screws from the bottom of the armrest—1986 Trooper shown

Fig. 35 With the screws removed from the armrest, detach the armrest from the door panel

Fig. 36 If equipped with an ashtray, remove the ashtray . . .

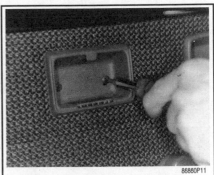

Fig. 37 . . . and remove the retainer screws securing the ashtray holder assembly

Fig. 38 Remove the ashtray holder from the panel and place aside

Fig. 39 Remove the door handle trim panel retainer screw

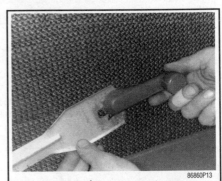

Fig. 40 Use a suitable window crank removal tool between the crank and door panel . . .

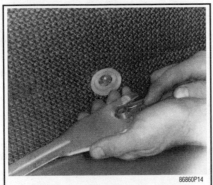

Fig. 41 . . . to separate the crank from the window regulator stud

Fig. 42 Insert the crank arm clip to the crank, and remove the washer, then place the pieces aside

Fig. 43 After removing the door panel, inspect the panel clip mounting holes for any clips which may have been left behind after panel removal

To install:

12. Position the door to the door and carefully press on the retainer clips to engage. If a clip will not engage, inspect the mounting hole behind the panel to make sure the clip is properly aligned. Install any panel-to-door retainer screws.

13. If equipped with crank windows, attach the washer and crank to the window regulator stud.

14. On 1981–86 models, attach the armrest to the door using the retainer screws.

15. On 1987–96 models, insert the armrest pocket and secure in place with retainer screws.

16. If equipped with door panel mounted speakers, attach the speaker wires to the speaker and secure the assembly to the door panel.

17. If equipped with remote cable mirrors, attach the control knob to the door panel with the retainer bezel.

18. If equipped with an ashtray, insert the holder assembly, and secure in place with retainer screws. Install the ashtray to the holder assembly.

19. Position the door handle trim panel around the door handle assembly, and secure in place with the retainer screw.

20. If equipped with accessory switch panel, attach the harnesses to the switches, and press the accessory plate into the door panel.

21. Connect the negative battery cable.

22. Check and make sure all panel components function correctly.

Door Locks

REMOVAL & INSTALLATION

♦ **See Figures 44, 45, 46, 47 and 48**

1. Disconnect the negative battery cable.

2. Remove door panel as described earlier in this section. Remove the plastic water seal carefully, it must be reused.

3. If equipped with a factory anti-theft system, tag and disconnect the wires attached to the back side of the door handle and lock cylinder.

4. Disconnect the inside handle rod clips. Disconnect and remove all lock control rods, noting their position for installation.

5. Remove the door lock assembly mounting screws from the outside of the door and remove the door lock assembly.

6. Remove the key cylinder by prying the retaining clip with an appropriate tool.

7. Remove the outside door handle by loosening the 2 outside handle mounting bolts from inside the door.

8. Remove the inside door handle by loosening the retaining screws. Some inside handles may be attached with rivets. In this case drill the rivets out with the appropriate size drill bit.

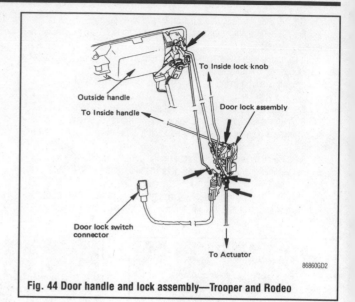

Fig. 44 Door handle and lock assembly—Trooper and Rodeo

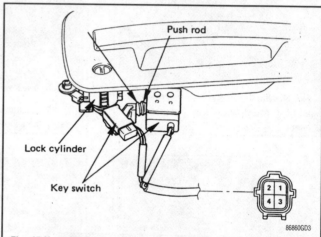

Fig. 45 If equipped with the factory anti-theft system, disconnect the key switch wires at the lock

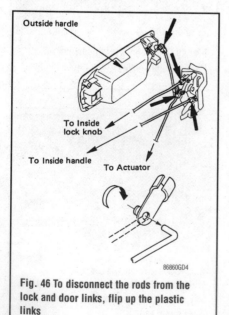

Fig. 46 To disconnect the rods from the lock and door links, flip up the plastic links

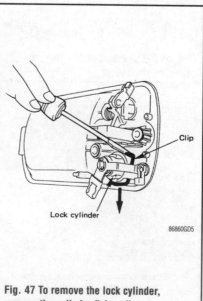

Fig. 47 To remove the lock cylinder, remove the cylinder fixing clip

Fig. 48 Lock cylinder—Amigo, Rodeo and Trooper (1981–95 Pick-Up similar)

9. If equipped with power door locks, disconnect the power door lock wiring harness, remove the attaching screws, then remove the assembly.

To install:

10. Lubricate all components prior to installation.

11. If the lock cylinder was removed, install the cylinder into the handle assembly, and secure with the retainer clip.

12. If equipped with power locks, connect the power door lock wiring harness. Install the assembly and attach the retainer screws.

13. Install the inside and/or outside door handle by install the retaining screws, or rivets.

14. Tighten the door lock assembly and outside door handle mounting screws to 48 inch lbs. (5 Nm).

15. Connect the inside handle rod clips to the control rods.

16. If equipped with a factory anti-theft system, connect the wires attached to the back side of the door handle and lock cylinder.

17. Install the door panel as described in this section.

18. Connect the negative battery cable.

19. Using the lock key, make sure the serviced lock(s) on the vehicle work correctly.

Door Glass and Regulator

REMOVAL & INSTALLATION

Pick-Up and Amigo

▶ **See Figures 49, 50, 51 and 52**

1. Disconnect the negative battery cable.
2. Remove the inside door panel and plastic weatherproof sheet.

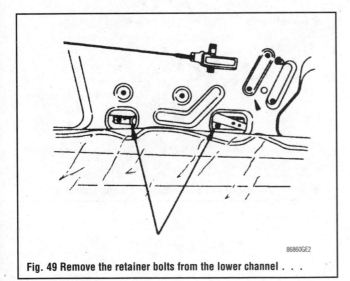

86860GE2

Fig. 49 Remove the retainer bolts from the lower channel . . .

3. Remove the inner and outer waist seals by prying with an appropriate prytool.

4. If equipped with vent windows, remove the vent assembly and glass.

5. Remove the screws attaching the bottom channel and regulator. Remove the glass by raising the glass out of the channel and tilting it out as necessary.

6. If equipped with power windows, disconnect the wire harness from the motor/regulator assembly.

7. Remove the regulator attaching screws and remove the regulator through the access hole in the rear of the door frame.

To install:

8. Install the regulator assembly through the rear section of the door. Install the regulator using the attaching screws.

9. If equipped with power windows, connect the wire harness for the motor/regulator assembly.

10. Install the window glass into the regulator assembly. Install the screws attaching the bottom channel and regulator, and insure that bottom channel is properly positioned.

11. Install the vent assembly and glass, if equipped.

12. Install waist seal with the cut away portion turned inward.

13. Install the inside door panel and plastic weatherproof sheet.

14. Connect the negative battery cable. Open the window, and make sure the window glass moves evenly.

Trooper and Rodeo

➡ **The procedure for removal and/or installation is the same for front and rear glass and regulators.**

1. Disconnect the negative battery cable.

2. Remove the door panel and weatherproof sheet. If equipped with power windows, disconnect wiring harness.

3. Remove the inner and outer waist seals by prying with an appropriate prytool.

4. If equipped with vent windows, remove the vent assembly and glass.

5. Remove the screws attaching the bottom channel and regulator. remove the glass by raising the glass out of the channel and tilting it out as necessary.

6. Remove the regulator attaching screws and remove the regulator through the access hole in the bottom of the door frame.

To install:

7. Install the regulator assembly through the bottom section of the door. Install the regulator using the attaching screws.

8. If equipped with power windows, connect the wire harness for the motor/regulator assembly.

9. Install the window glass into the regulator assembly. Install the screws attaching the bottom channel and regulator, and insure that bottom channel is properly positioned.

10. Install the vent assembly and glass, if equipped.

11. Install waist seal with the cut away portion turned inward.

12. Install the inside door panel and plastic weatherproof sheet.

13. Connect the negative battery cable. Open the window, and make sure the window glass moves evenly.

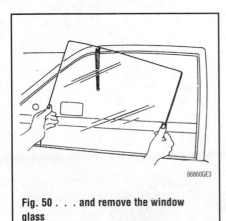

86860GE3

Fig. 50 . . . and remove the window glass

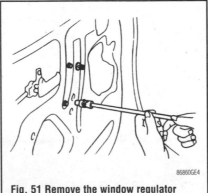

86860GE4

Fig. 51 Remove the window regulator retainer bolts

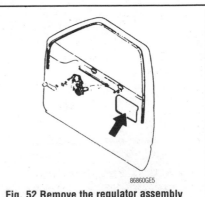

86860GE5

Fig. 52 Remove the regulator assembly from the rear opening in the door

Electric Window Motor

REMOVAL & INSTALLATION

The electric window motor assembly is and integral part of the window regulator. Because of this design, the motor cannot be separated, serviced or replace by itself.

If the window motor fails, refer to the regulator removal and installation procedure in this section for electric window motor/regulator removal and installation steps.

Inside Rear View Mirror

REMOVAL & INSTALLATION

♦ See Figures 53, 54 and 55

The rear view mirror on most Isuzu vehicles is attached to the center of the windshield brace in the interior. It is removed by simply unscrewing the attaching screw(s). On some models, the attaching screw(s) may be covered with plastic trim.

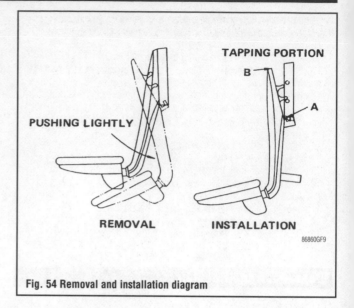

Fig. 54 Removal and installation diagram

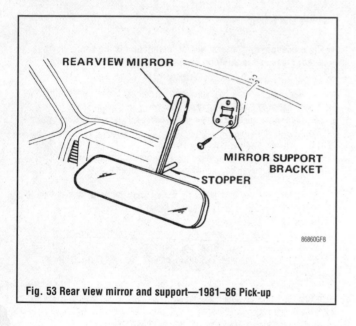

Fig. 53 Rear view mirror and support—1981–86 Pick-up

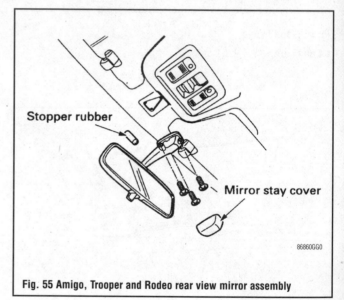

Fig. 55 Amigo, Trooper and Rodeo rear view mirror assembly

GLOSSARY

AIR/FUEL RATIO: The ratio of air-to-gasoline by weight in the fuel mixture drawn into the engine.

AIR INJECTION: One method of reducing harmful exhaust emissions by injecting air into each of the exhaust ports of an engine. The fresh air entering the hot exhaust manifold causes any remaining fuel to be burned before it can exit the tailpipe.

ALTERNATOR: A device used for converting mechanical energy into electrical energy.

AMMETER: An instrument, calibrated in amperes, used to measure the flow of an electrical current in a circuit. Ammeters are always connected in series with the circuit being tested.

AMPERE: The rate of flow of electrical current present when one volt of electrical pressure is applied against one ohm of electrical resistance.

ANALOG COMPUTER: Any microprocessor that uses similar (analogous) electrical signals to make its calculations.

ARMATURE: A laminated, soft iron core wrapped by a wire that converts electrical energy to mechanical energy as in a motor or relay. When rotated in a magnetic field, it changes mechanical energy into electrical energy as in a generator.

ATMOSPHERIC PRESSURE: The pressure on the Earth's surface caused by the weight of the air in the atmosphere. At sea level, this pressure is 14.7 psi at 32°F (101 kPa at 0°C).

ATOMIZATION: The breaking down of a liquid into a fine mist that can be suspended in air.

AXIAL PLAY: Movement parallel to a shaft or bearing bore.

BACKFIRE: The sudden combustion of gases in the intake or exhaust system that results in a loud explosion.

BACKLASH: The clearance or play between two parts, such as meshed gears.

BACKPRESSURE: Restrictions in the exhaust system that slow the exit of exhaust gases from the combustion chamber.

BAKELITE: A heat resistant, plastic insulator material commonly used in printed circuit boards and transistorized components.

BALL BEARING: A bearing made up of hardened inner and outer races between which hardened steel balls roll.

BALLAST RESISTOR: A resistor in the primary ignition circuit that lowers voltage after the engine is started to reduce wear on ignition components.

BEARING: A friction reducing, supportive device usually located between a stationary part and a moving part.

BIMETAL TEMPERATURE SENSOR: Any sensor or switch made of two dissimilar types of metal that bend when heated or cooled due to the different expansion rates of the alloys. These types of sensors usually function as an on/off switch.

BLOWBY: Combustion gases, composed of water vapor and unburned fuel, that leak past the piston rings into the crankcase during normal engine operation. These gases are removed by the PCV system to prevent the buildup of harmful acids in the crankcase.

BRAKE PAD: A brake shoe and lining assembly used with disc brakes.

BRAKE SHOE: The backing for the brake lining. The term is, however, usually applied to the assembly of the brake backing and lining.

BUSHING: A liner, usually removable, for a bearing; an anti-friction liner used in place of a bearing.

CALIPER: A hydraulically activated device in a disc brake system, which is mounted straddling the brake rotor (disc). The caliper contains at least one piston and two brake pads. Hydraulic pressure on the piston(s) forces the pads against the rotor.

CAMSHAFT: A shaft in the engine on which are the lobes (cams) which operate the valves. The camshaft is driven by the crankshaft, via a belt, chain or gears, at one half the crankshaft speed.

CAPACITOR: A device which stores an electrical charge.

CARBON MONOXIDE (CO): A colorless, odorless gas given off as a normal byproduct of combustion. It is poisonous and extremely dangerous in confined areas, building up slowly to toxic levels without warning if adequate ventilation is not available.

CARBURETOR: A device, usually mounted on the intake manifold of an engine, which mixes the air and fuel in the proper proportion to allow even combustion.

CATALYTIC CONVERTER: A device installed in the exhaust system, like a muffler, that converts harmful byproducts of combustion into carbon dioxide and water vapor by means of a heat-producing chemical reaction.

CENTRIFUGAL ADVANCE: A mechanical method of advancing the spark timing by using flyweights in the distributor that react to centrifugal force generated by the distributor shaft rotation.

CHECK VALVE: Any one-way valve installed to permit the flow of air, fuel or vacuum in one direction only.

CHOKE: A device, usually a moveable valve, placed in the intake path of a carburetor to restrict the flow of air.

CIRCUIT: Any unbroken path through which an electrical current can flow. Also used to describe fuel flow in some instances.

CIRCUIT BREAKER: A switch which protects an electrical circuit from overload by opening the circuit when the current flow exceeds a predetermined level. Some circuit breakers must be reset manually, while most reset automatically.

COIL (IGNITION): A transformer in the ignition circuit which steps up the voltage provided to the spark plugs.

COMBINATION MANIFOLD: An assembly which includes both the intake and exhaust manifolds in one casting.

COMBINATION VALVE: A device used in some fuel systems that routes fuel vapors to a charcoal storage canister instead of venting them into the atmosphere. The valve relieves fuel tank pressure and allows fresh air into the tank as the fuel level drops to prevent a vapor lock situation.

COMPRESSION RATIO: The comparison of the total volume of the cylinder and combustion chamber with the piston at BDC and the piston at TDC.

CONDENSER: 1. An electrical device which acts to store an electrical charge, preventing voltage surges. 2. A radiator-like device in the air conditioning system in which refrigerant gas condenses into a liquid, giving off heat.

CONDUCTOR: Any material through which an electrical current can be transmitted easily.

CONTINUITY: Continuous or complete circuit. Can be checked with an ohmmeter.

COUNTERSHAFT: An intermediate shaft which is rotated by a mainshaft and transmits, in turn, that rotation to a working part.

CRANKCASE: The lower part of an engine in which the crankshaft and related parts operate.

CRANKSHAFT: The main driving shaft of an engine which receives reciprocating motion from the pistons and converts it to rotary motion.

CYLINDER: In an engine, the round hole in the engine block in which the piston(s) ride.

CYLINDER BLOCK: The main structural member of an engine in which is found the cylinders, crankshaft and other principal parts.

CYLINDER HEAD: The detachable portion of the engine, usually fastened to the top of the cylinder block and containing all or most of the combustion chambers. On overhead valve engines, it contains the valves and their operating parts. On overhead cam engines, it contains the camshaft as well.

DEAD CENTER: The extreme top or bottom of the piston stroke.

DETONATION: An unwanted explosion of the air/fuel mixture in the combustion chamber caused by excess heat and compression, advanced timing, or an overly lean mixture. Also referred to as "ping".

DIAPHRAGM: A thin, flexible wall separating two cavities, such as in a vacuum advance unit.

DIESELING: A condition in which hot spots in the combustion chamber cause the engine to run on after the key is turned off.

DIFFERENTIAL: A geared assembly which allows the transmission of motion between drive axles, giving one axle the ability to turn faster than the other.

DIODE: An electrical device that will allow current to flow in one direction only.

DISC BRAKE: A hydraulic braking assembly consisting of a brake disc, or rotor, mounted on an axle, and a caliper assembly containing, usually two brake pads which are activated by hydraulic pressure. The pads are forced against the sides of the disc, creating friction which slows the vehicle.

DISTRIBUTOR: A mechanically driven device on an engine which is responsible for electrically firing the spark plug at a predetermined point of the piston stroke.

DOWEL PIN: A pin, inserted in mating holes in two different parts allowing those parts to maintain a fixed relationship.

DRUM BRAKE: A braking system which consists of two brake shoes and one or two wheel cylinders, mounted on a fixed backing plate, and a brake drum, mounted on an axle, which revolves around the assembly.

DWELL: The rate, measured in degrees of shaft rotation, at which an electrical circuit cycles on and off.

ELECTRONIC CONTROL UNIT (ECU): Ignition module, module, amplifier or igniter. See Module for definition.

ELECTRONIC IGNITION: A system in which the timing and firing of the spark plugs is controlled by an electronic control unit, usually called a module. These systems have no points or condenser.

END-PLAY: The measured amount of axial movement in a shaft.

ENGINE: A device that converts heat into mechanical energy.

EXHAUST MANIFOLD: A set of cast passages or pipes which conduct exhaust gases from the engine.

FEELER GAUGE: A blade, usually metal, or precisely predetermined thickness, used to measure the clearance between two parts.

FIRING ORDER: The order in which combustion occurs in the cylinders of an engine. Also the order in which spark is distributed to the plugs by the distributor.

FLOODING: The presence of too much fuel in the intake manifold and combustion chamber which prevents the air/fuel mixture from firing, thereby causing a no-start situation.

FLYWHEEL: A disc shaped part bolted to the rear end of the crankshaft. Around the outer perimeter is affixed the ring gear. The starter drive engages the ring gear, turning the flywheel, which rotates the crankshaft, imparting the initial starting motion to the engine.

FOOT POUND (ft. lbs. or sometimes, ft.lb.): The amount of energy or work needed to raise an item weighing one pound, a distance of one foot.

FUSE: A protective device in a circuit which prevents circuit overload by breaking the circuit when a specific amperage is present. The device is constructed around a strip or wire of a lower amperage rating than the circuit it is designed to protect. When an amperage higher than that stamped on the fuse is present in the circuit, the strip or wire melts, opening the circuit.

GEAR RATIO: The ratio between the number of teeth on meshing gears.

GENERATOR: A device which converts mechanical energy into electrical energy.

HEAT RANGE: The measure of a spark plug's ability to dissipate heat from its firing end. The higher the heat range, the hotter the plug fires.

HUB: The center part of a wheel or gear.

HYDROCARBON (HC): Any chemical compound made up of hydrogen and carbon. A major pollutant formed by the engine as a byproduct of combustion.

HYDROMETER: An instrument used to measure the specific gravity of a solution.

INCH POUND (inch lbs.; sometimes in.lb. or in. lbs.): One twelfth of a foot pound.

INDUCTION: A means of transferring electrical energy in the form of a magnetic field. Principle used in the ignition coil to increase voltage.

INJECTOR: A device which receives metered fuel under relatively low pressure and is activated to inject the fuel into the engine under relatively high pressure at a predetermined time.

INPUT SHAFT: The shaft to which torque is applied, usually carrying the driving gear or gears.

INTAKE MANIFOLD: A casting of passages or pipes used to conduct air or a fuel/air mixture to the cylinders.

JOURNAL: The bearing surface within which a shaft operates.

KEY: A small block usually fitted in a notch between a shaft and a hub to prevent slippage of the two parts.

MANIFOLD: A casting of passages or set of pipes which connect the cylinders to an inlet or outlet source.

MANIFOLD VACUUM: Low pressure in an engine intake manifold formed just below the throttle plates. Manifold vacuum is highest at idle and drops under acceleration.

MASTER CYLINDER: The primary fluid pressurizing device in a hydraulic system. In automotive use, It Is found In brake and hydraulic clutch systems and is pedal activated, either directly or, in a power brake system, through the power booster.

MODULE: Electronic control unit, amplifier or igniter of solid state or integrated design which controls the current flow in the ignition primary circuit based on input from the pick-up coil. When the module opens the primary circuit, high secondary voltage is induced in the coil.

NEEDLE BEARING: A bearing which consists of a number (usually a large number) of long, thin rollers.

OHM: (Ω) The unit used to measure the resistance of conductor-to-electrical flow. One ohm is the amount of resistance that limits current flow to one ampere in a circuit with one volt of pressure.

OHMMETER: An instrument used for measuring the resistance, in ohms, in an electrical circuit.

OUTPUT SHAFT: The shaft which transmits torque from a device, such as a transmission.

OVERDRIVE: A gear assembly which produces more shaft revolutions than that transmitted to it.

OVERHEAD CAMSHAFT (OHC): An engine configuration in which the camshaft is mounted on top of the cylinder head and operates the valve either directly or by means of rocker arms.

OVERHEAD VALVE (OHV): An engine configuration in which all of the valves are located in the cylinder head and the camshaft is located in the cylinder block. The camshaft operates the valves via lifters and pushrods.

OXIDES OF NITROGEN (NOx): Chemical compounds of nitrogen produced as a byproduct of combustion. They combine with hydrocarbons to produce smog.

OXYGEN SENSOR: Use with the feedback system to sense the presence of oxygen in the exhaust gas and signal the computer which can reference the voltage signal to an air/fuel ratio.

PINION: The smaller of two meshing gears.

PISTON RING: An open-ended ring with fits into a groove on the outer diameter of the piston. Its chief function is to form a seal between the piston and cylinder wall. Most automotive pistons have three rings: two for compression sealing; one for oil sealing.

PRELOAD: A predetermined load placed on a bearing during assembly or by adjustment.

PRIMARY CIRCUIT: the low voltage side of the ignition system which consists of the ignition switch, ballast resistor or resistance wire, bypass, coil, electronic control unit and pick-up coil as well as the connecting wires and harnesses.

PRESS FIT: The mating of two parts under pressure, due to the inner diameter of one being smaller than the outer diameter of the other, or vice versa; an interference fit.

RACE: The surface on the inner or outer ring of a bearing on which the balls, needles or rollers move.

REGULATOR: A device which maintains the amperage and/or voltage levels of a circuit at predetermined values.

RELAY: A switch which automatically opens and/or closes a circuit.

RESISTANCE: The opposition to the flow of current through a circuit or electrical device, and is measured in ohms. Resistance is equal to the voltage divided by the amperage.

RESISTOR: A device, usually made of wire, which offers a preset amount of resistance in an electrical circuit.

RING GEAR: The name given to a ring-shaped gear attached to a differential case, or affixed to a flywheel or as part of a planetary gear set.

ROLLER BEARING: A bearing made up of hardened inner and outer races between which hardened steel rollers move.

ROTOR: 1. The disc-shaped part of a disc brake assembly, upon which the brake pads bear; also called, brake disc. 2. The device mounted atop the distributor shaft, which passes current to the distributor cap tower contacts.

SECONDARY CIRCUIT: The high voltage side of the ignition system, usually above 20,000 volts. The secondary includes the ignition coil, coil wire, distributor cap and rotor, spark plug wires and spark plugs.

SENDING UNIT: A mechanical, electrical, hydraulic or electro-magnetic device which transmits information to a gauge.

SENSOR: Any device designed to measure engine operating conditions or ambient pressures and temperatures. Usually electronic in nature and designed to send a voltage signal to an on-board computer, some sensors may operate as a simple on/off switch or they may provide a variable voltage signal (like a potentiometer) as conditions or measured parameters change.

SHIM: Spacers of precise, predetermined thickness used between parts to establish a proper working relationship.

SLAVE CYLINDER: In automotive use, a device in the hydraulic clutch system which is activated by hydraulic force, disengaging the clutch.

SOLENOID: A coil used to produce a magnetic field, the effect of which is to produce work.

SPARK PLUG: A device screwed into the combustion chamber of a spark ignition engine. The basic construction is a conductive core inside of a ceramic insulator, mounted in an outer conductive base. An electrical charge from the spark plug wire travels along the conductive core and jumps a preset air gap to a grounding point or points at the end of the conductive base. The resultant spark ignites the fuel/air mixture in the combustion chamber.

SPLINES: Ridges machined or cast onto the outer diameter of a shaft or inner diameter of a bore to enable parts to mate without rotation.

TACHOMETER: A device used to measure the rotary speed of an engine, shaft, gear, etc., usually in rotations per minute.

THERMOSTAT: A valve, located in the cooling system of an engine, which is closed when cold and opens gradually in response to engine heating, controlling the temperature of the coolant and rate of coolant flow.

TOP DEAD CENTER (TDC): The point at which the piston reaches the top of its travel on the compression stroke.

TORQUE: The twisting force applied to an object.

TORQUE CONVERTER: A turbine used to transmit power from a driving member to a driven member via hydraulic action, providing changes in drive ratio and torque. In automotive use, it links the driveplate at the rear of the engine to the automatic transmission.

TRANSDUCER: A device used to change a force into an electrical signal.

TRANSISTOR: A semi-conductor component which can be actuated by a small voltage to perform an electrical switching function.

TUNE-UP: A regular maintenance function, usually associated with the replacement and adjustment of parts and components in the electrical and fuel systems of a vehicle for the purpose of attaining optimum performance.

TURBOCHARGER: An exhaust driven pump which compresses intake air and forces it into the combustion chambers at higher than atmospheric pressures. The increased air pressure allows more fuel to be burned and results in increased horsepower being produced.

VACUUM ADVANCE: A device which advances the ignition timing in response to increased engine vacuum.

VACUUM GAUGE: An instrument used to measure the presence of vacuum in a chamber.

VALVE: A device which control the pressure, direction of flow or rate of flow of a liquid or gas.

VALVE CLEARANCE: The measured gap between the end of the valve stem and the rocker arm, cam lobe or follower that activates the valve.

VISCOSITY: The rating of a liquid's internal resistance to flow.

VOLTMETER: An instrument used for measuring electrical force in units called volts. Voltmeters are always connected parallel with the circuit being tested.

WHEEL CYLINDER: Found in the automotive drum brake assembly, it is a device, actuated by hydraulic pressure, which, through internal pistons, pushes the brake shoes outward against the drums.

MASTER INDEX